RUSSIA AND THE SOVIET UNION

RUSSIA
and the
SOVIET UNION

A BIBLIOGRAPHIC GUIDE TO
WESTERN-LANGUAGE PUBLICATIONS

paul L. horecky
EDITOR

THE UNIVERSITY OF CHICAGO PRESS
CHICAGO & LONDON

This work was developed pursuant to a contract
between the United States Office of Education
and the American Council of Learned Societies,
and is published with permission of the United
States Office of Education.

International Standard Book Number: 0-226-35186-6
Library of Congress Catalog Card Number: 65-12041
THE UNIVERSITY OF CHICAGO PRESS, CHICAGO 60637
The University of Chicago Press, Ltd., London

KM
7-7-82

introduction

Over the centuries, Western travelers have been attracted, albeit spo-
radically, by the strangeness and separateness of Russia, and at times have
recorded their findings and impressions with insight and understanding.
From Baron Sigismund Herberstain, who visited Muscovy on diplomatic
missions in 1516 and 1526, to the Marquis de Custine, astute diarist and
commentator on life and manners in Russia in the 1830's, and to subsequent
perceptive observers of pre-Revolutionary Russia in the nineteenth and
twentieth centuries — among them Maurice Baring, Sir Bernard Pares,
Anatole Leroy-Beaulieu, and George Kennan — the Russian Empire has
found chroniclers whose travelogues and studies have remained classics to
this day. Others, such as Constance Garnett, have thrown open the treasures
of Russian literature to the Western world in English translations which
have thus far rarely been surpassed. Even before the First World War, a
small band of academic scholars who occupied chairs at leading universities
in this country and abroad helped to blaze a trail for the advance of Slavic
studies in the West, particularly in the realm of literature.

To the Western public at large, however, Russia remained terra incog-
nita until its metamorphosis into a Bolshevik colossus in the aftermath of
world war, revolution, and civil war. These events gave rise to a spate of
literature which prompted Leon Trotsky to comment plaintively in 1936
that "the bookstalls of all civilized countries are now loaded with books
about the Soviet Union. . . . The reader, however, would seek in vain on the
pages of this literature for a scientific appraisal of what is actually taking
place in the land of the October Revolution." One might add that in the
wake of the diplomatic recognition of the Soviet Union by the United States
and the entry of the USSR into the Second World War, growing numbers
of new books appeared, all too often characterized by exaggeration and
emotion rather than by sober scholarship.

It is only in the years since the Second World War that Western studies
and published research on Russia and the Soviet Union may be said to have

made their greatest strides on the journey from famine to feast. The scholarly investigation of the many facets which make up the mosaic of Russia, past and present, has become a specialized and well-established discipline, forming an integral part of the academic pursuits and programs of many colleges and universities, supported by an auxiliary apparatus of libraries, research institutes, training centers, and language laboratories. The government too has become a patron of research and publishing activities on the area. In addition, growing ranks of well-trained journalists and informed freelance writers have made original contributions to the advancement of knowledge in the field. It is not surprising that these developments should have unleashed a torrent of publications which often leaves even the specialist, not to speak of the informed general reader and student, overwhelmed and disoriented. Naturally, in a domain not only commanding acute public interest, but also holding out promise of success in the marketplace of publishing, mediocrity and repetitiousness have not been altogether absent.

Between 1956 and 1962, some 9,000 books and articles on Russian and Soviet affairs were published in scholarly journals in the United States alone, and to arrive at a worldwide aggregate one would have to multiply this figure many times. The need for a certain measure of bibliographical guidance to such a massive body of literature seems evident. Since an exhaustive registration would be of dubious utility, even in the unlikely event that it were practicable, the selective and annotative approach to bibliographical control suggests itself. These particular ground rules were applied previously to *Basic Russian Publications: An Annotated Bibliography on Russia and the Soviet Union*, to which the present work is a companion volume. Together, the two represent a rigorously pruned inventory of Russian and Western publications in the field of studies on Russia and the USSR. As area bibliographies they do not cover communism per se, but only its Soviet brand.

Specifically, this volume is a conspectus of those Western-language writings, chiefly in book form, which are considered to be particularly relevant to the study of the political, socio-economic, and intellectual life in the Russian Empire and in the Soviet Union. It is hoped that the serious reader, librarian, and perhaps even the expert seeking information on phases outside his area-subject specialization may find this guide to be of assistance. The pages of the bibliography show eloquently the evolving maturity of Western research on Russia and the Soviet Union. Indeed, these studies have shed light on many a subject which the ideological rigidity of the Soviet regime has caused to remain outside the bounds of permissible domestic investigation. Furthermore, this book may also have the useful, if negative, function of pointing up themes and subjects in Slavic studies which as yet have eluded full and adequate treatment.

The selective approach underlying this volume has, of course, its own pitfalls and imperfections. It is not a cure-all for the pressing needs of bibliographical control which arise from an increasingly unmanageable volume of publishing. A certain arbitrary quality attaches to book selection and appraisal, both of which involve value judgments which are necessarily subjective and fallible and which are sometimes bound to reflect, inadvertently, human idiosyncrasies and errors of interpretation. But it can be said with assurance that the group of experienced scholars who have joined in this collective effort have trained their sights on the goal of filtering, *sine ira et studio*, the vast mass of available material in order to arrive by gradual elimination at those selected titles which, in their personal view, are germane to the purpose and scope of the volume. No person who engages in such an endeavor can expect to remain immune from criticism, from some source or other, for having cast his net too far or too near, or for having used a mesh too coarse or too fine. As Mr. James T. Babb, Librarian of Yale University, remarked on his assignment to head the committee for the selection of the library for the White House: "The task of winnowing and deciding was one that would have fazed a King Solomon."

A few words should be said about the *modus operandi* by which this volume was prepared. In commissioning me to direct the effort, the sponsors gave me carte blanche to devise the scope, complexion, and form of the guide, and to assemble a team of contributors who were competent specialists in their fields. As soon as these tasks were accomplished, each contributor was invited to select and annotate a defined number of Western-language publications of intrinsic bearing on his section — principally in English and, as a rule, with stress on more recent imprint dates and developments. Simultaneously, the co-operation of contributing consultants for French and German publications was enlisted, so that subject contributors would have the benefit of checking their own selections of foreign-language titles against the wider range of those supplied by the consultants. The last word as to inclusion or omission of titles in any language lay with the contributors, who were also the final arbiters of the substance of the annotations. While I have endeavored to abstain from undue incursions into these spheres, I did deem it incumbent upon me to take such decisions — with the advice and consent of individual participants — as were thought to contribute to the emergence of *"unum e pluribus."*

In an undertaking which presents the vexatious challenge of compressing a quart of substance into a pint container, the allocation of space to individual fields of learning requires some explanation. Naturally, no hard and fast rules could be applied here, and some incidence of imbalance may therefore be unavoidable. The criteria observed were predicated on a variety of considerations, including the total reservoir of potential literature available on a given subject, the relative prominence and extent of representation of a discipline in university and college curricula, an estimation of readers' interests in certain branches of knowledge, and, last but not least, the contributor's judgment as to whether the number of entries assigned appeared sufficient. Subject to the practical need to condense a wide range of subjects into a single book-sized volume, I have sought, hopefully without bias toward any discipline, to make all feasible accommodation in the direction of an equitable distribution of coverage.

This work is a true exemplar of international and interdisciplinary scholarly collaboration in action, in which many distinguished specialists — a roster of whom appears elsewhere in this book — joined forces in response to my invitation. To have been associated with them in this venture has been a distinct privilege, and I acknowledge with profound gratitude the specialized expertise and spirited efforts which they so generously brought to this undertaking. Robert G. Carlton, the Assistant Editor, was singularly qualified for this task by dint of his combination of solid familiarity with Russian affairs and experience in bibliographical skills. Through his assiduous and devoted participation in all phases of the bibliographical operation, he has carried a material share of the burden of casting individual contributions into the mold of technical homogeneity and of helping to bring the work to a timely conclusion. He also prepared the Index. George Heard Hamilton was a most judicious reader of the section on the arts, and numerous constructive suggestions offered by him were of substantial benefit to the final version of that chapter. As the occasion arose, I consulted on specific problems with Robert V. Allen, Eleanor Buist, Murray Feshbach, Leon M. Herman, and Sergius Yakobson, and I am most grateful to have had the opportunity to draw upon their varied talents. To Mrs. Martha Rose I am indebted for her very intelligent execution of the exacting task of typing the manuscript. As always, my wife, Emily I. Horecky, gave fully of her considerable reviewing and administrative skills and bore patiently with my all too frequent absenteeism in connection with the preparation of this guide.

The present volume, as was its precursor, was sponsored by the Coordinating Committee for Slavic and East European Library Resources (COCOSEERS), under the chairmanship of Alexander Dallin. The American Council of Learned Societies, under its President, Frederick Burkhardt, and its Vice-President, Gordon B. Turner, generously consented to oversee the operational aspects of the project. I was most fortunate to enjoy their unstinting support and the privilege of complete freedom of action in directing this venture and in bringing it to fruition.

P. L. H.

Alexandria, Virginia. June 1964

scope
and
ORGANIZATION
of the GUIDE

SCOPE: This guide focuses on writings in the major Western languages, with emphasis on English-language publications; titles in non-Western languages are included only when they provide bibliographical access to publications within the scope of this work. The natural sciences and technology are not within the province of this book, although works on the socio-political, research, and organizational aspects of these disciplines are represented. While this bibliography is meant to embrace temporally the whole broad sweep of past and present, the accent is on more recent times and imprint dates, generally up to the beginning of 1964.

METHODOLOGICAL APPROACH: The presentation is according to broad fields of knowledge which are subdivided into more specialized categories as they relate to the area. Within these sections the materials are arranged alphabetically as a rule; when deviant forms of presentation are used — such as arrangement by chronological or by topical criteria — these are explicitly indicated in footnotes to the headings concerned.

ENTRIES: The bibliographical entries, which are kept as succinct and non-technical as possible, incorporate the elements deemed essential for an adequate identification of the title but exclude data of lesser importance. Except for a few instances when digressions were necessary, author entries are in keeping with the American Library Association's rules, which are widely followed by libraries in this country and are observed by the Library of Congress in its printed cards and catalogs. The Library of Congress transliteration system is used for Russian titles and names. If the latter have become part of the English vocabulary, they are given in their anglicized forms as listed in Webster's *Collegiate Dictionary* (6th ed.). For convenient book location through trade channels, different versions of authors' names as they appear on the title page or in other usage are sometimes given in parentheses after the author entry. Annotations comment descriptively or analytically on the publications listed and often point to additional or supplemental related readings. Occasionally, the reader will find the same title listed by more than one subject compiler in different contexts, and even with divergent evaluative remarks. Such multiple listings underscore effectively the relevance of one book to several subject categories and illustrate divergencies in book evaluation. The recurrence of a title in different locations is indicated in the title listings of the Index. In addition, cross-references connect principal entries within the bibliography. A detailed table of contents and a combined name-title-subject index are provided for convenient orientation.

SYMBOLS: An asterisk following an entry number indicates that the item is available in paperback according to the February 1964 edition of *Paperbound Books in Print*, which may be consulted in most libraries and bookstores. The student of Slavic affairs may consult with profit the *Checklist of Paperbound Books on Russia* (Albany, University of the State of New York, 1964), compiled by Sherman D. Spector.

participants

CONTRIBUTORS

ROBERT V. ALLEN, joint compiler, with Paul L. Horecky, of the section "General Reference Aids and Bibliographies," and principal compiler of the section "The Fine Arts," is Area Specialist (USSR), Slavic and Central European Division, Library of Congress. He was Assistant Editor of *Basic Russian Publications: an Annotated Bibliography on Russia and the Soviet Union* (Chicago: University of Chicago Press, 1962) and has contributed numerous articles and reviews to professional journals.

JOHN A. ARMSTRONG, compiler of the section "Politics and Government," is Professor of Political Science at the University of Wisconsin, where he has taught since 1954. He was Executive Secretary of the Russian Area Studies Program there from 1959 to 1963. He is the author of *The Politics of Totalitarianism: the Communist Party of the Soviet Union from 1934 to the Present* (New York: Random House, 1961); of *Ukrainian Nationalism* (2d ed., New York: Columbia University Press, 1963); and of *The Soviet Bureaucratic Elite: a Case Study of the Ukrainian Apparatus* (New York: Praeger, 1959); as well as of other books and of articles in professional journals.

JOHN P. BALYS, compiler of the section "Baltica," specializes in ethnology. He has taught at universities in Lithuania, Germany, and the United States, and is currently with the Slavic and Central European Division, Library of Congress. He is the author of *Lithuania and Lithuanians: A Selected Bibliography* (New York: Praeger, 1961) as well as of other books and articles on Baltic folklore, mythology, and bibliography.

ABRAHAM BRUMBERG, compiler of the section "Public Opinion, Propaganda, and Communications," is Editor of the bimonthly *Problems of Communism*. He was editor of *Russia under Khrushchev* (New York: Praeger, 1962), and his articles on Soviet affairs have appeared in numerous journals, including *Commentary*, the *New Leader*, the *New Republic*, and the *Reporter*.

ALEXANDER DALLIN, compiler of the section "Diplomacy and Foreign Relations," is Professor of International Relations at the Russian Institute, Columbia University. He has written *German Rule in Russia, 1941-1945* (London, New York: St. Martin's Press, 1957) and *The Soviet Union at the United*

Nations (New York: Praeger, 1962), and has edited *Soviet Conduct in World Affairs* (New York: Columbia University Press, 1960) and, more recently, *Diversity in International Communism* (New York: Columbia University Press, 1963).

JOSEPH DANKO is joint compiler, with Ivan L. Rudnytsky, of the section "Ukrainica." He is head of the Division of Slavic and East European Cataloguing at Yale University Library and has written on bibliographical topics.

MOSHE DECTER, compiler of the section on "Judaism," is Director of Jewish Minorities Research, specializing in research, publication, and consultation on the situation of Jews in the Soviet Union and Eastern Europe. He has published numerous studies and articles on Soviet Jewry. A working journalist for many years, he was formerly a political editor at the Voice of America and Managing Editor of the *New Leader* magazine. He was co-author, with James Rorty, of *McCarthy and the Communists* (Boston: Beacon Press, 1954), and author of *The Profile of Communism* (New York: Crowell-Collier, 1962).

NICHOLAS DE WITT, compiler of the section "Education and Research," is Associate Professor of Education at Indiana University, where he serves as Chairman of the Department of International and Comparative Education and as Director of the Non-Western Studies Project for the State of Indiana. His numerous writings include *Soviet Professional Manpower, Its Education, Training and Supply* (Washington: National Science Foundation, 1955) and *Education and Professional Employment in the USSR* (Washington: National Science Foundation, 1961).

DAVID DJAPARIDZE, who compiled the section "Literature Prior to the Nineteenth Century," is Directeur d'Études at the École des Hautes Études (Sorbonne) and Professor of Slavic Languages and Literatures at Princeton University. He prepared *Mediaeval Slavic Manuscripts* (Cambridge: Mediaeval Academy of America, 1957) and has written other bibliographical and literary studies.

The Very Reverend GEORGES FLOROVSKY, who compiled the section "Christianity," has served on the faculties of the Orthodox Theological Institute in Paris, St. Vladimir's Orthodox Theological Seminary (of which he was Dean), and Union Theological Seminary in New York City, and since 1957 has been Professor of Eastern Church History at Harvard Divinity School. He has been active in the Ecumenical movement. His works include *Puti russkago bogosloviia* (Paris: YMCA Press, 1937), *Vizantiiskie ottsy V-VIII vv.* (Paris: YMCA Press, 1933) and *Vostochnye ottsy IV-go vieka* (Paris: YMCA Press, 1931).

RAYMOND L. GARTHOFF compiled the section "Military Affairs." He is Special Assistant for Soviet Bloc Politico-Military Affairs, U. S. Department of State, and Professorial Lecturer in Soviet Affairs at George Washington University and at the School for Advanced International Affairs, Johns Hopkins University. He has written extensively on Soviet political and military affairs. His books include: *Soviet Strategy and the Nuclear Age* (rev. ed., New York: Praeger, 1962); *The Soviet Image of Future War* (Washington: Public Affairs Press, 1959); and *Soviet Military Doctrine* (Glencoe, Ill.: Free Press, 1953).

A. KENT GEIGER, compiler of the section "The Society," is Associate Professor of Sociology at Ohio State University. He is co-editor, with Alex Inkeles, of *Soviet Society* (Boston: Houghton Mifflin, 1961, and has written on Soviet affairs for professional journals.

CHAUNCY D. HARRIS, compiler of the section "The Land," is Professor of Geography at the University of Chicago. Specializing in Soviet economic and urban geography, he has edited translations from the Russian of S. S. Bal'zak's *Economic Geography of the USSR* (New York: Macmillan, 1949) and I. P. Gerasimov's *Soviet Geography; Accomplishments and Tasks* (New York: American Geographical Society, 1962), and is the author of numerous writings on Soviet geography. His bibliographical activities include the compilation of *An International List of Geographical Serials* (Department of Geography, University of Chicago, 1960).

JOHN N. HAZARD, compiler, with William B. Stern, of the section "Law," is Professor of Public Law at Columbia University and a member of the New York Bar. He attended the Moscow Juridical Institute from 1935 to 1937 as a Fellow of the Institute of Current World Affairs of New York. He is author of *Law and Social Change in the USSR* (London, Toronto: Carswell Co., 1953); *Settling Disputes in Soviet Society* (New York: Columbia University Press, 1960); *The Soviet System of Government* (3d rev. ed., Chicago: University of Chicago Press, 1964); *The Soviet Legal System* (Dobbs Ferry, N. Y.: Oceana Publications, 1962); and other works.

LEON M. HERMAN, compiler of the section "The Economy," is Senior Analyst in Soviet Economics of the Legislative Reference Service, Library of Congress, and Adjunct Professor, School of International Service, American University. He has written widely on Soviet economic matters for American economic and political publications, and has traveled to the USSR with official delegations.

PAUL L. HORECKY, Editor of this book and joint compiler, with Robert V. Allen, of the section "General Reference Aids and Bibliographies," is Assistant Chief, Slavic and Central European Division, Library of Congress. He was also the Editor of and a contributor to the companion volume, *Basic Russian Publications* (Chicago: University of Chicago Press, 1962). Other writings include: *Libraries and Bibliographic Centers in the Soviet Union* (Bloomington: Indiana University Publications, 1959); several bibliographical monographs on the USSR and Eastern Europe; and articles for the *Encyclopedia Americana* and professional journals.

GEORGE L. KLINE, compiler of the section "History of Thought and Culture," is Associate Professor of Philosophy and Russian at Bryn Mawr College. He is the translator of Vasilii V. Zenkovskii's *A History of Russian Philosophy* (London: Routledge and Kegan Paul; New York: Columbia University Press, 1953) and the author of *Spinoza in Soviet Philosophy* (London: Routledge and Kegan Paul; New York: Humanities Press, 1952), as well as the author of numerous articles on Russian philosophy and intellectual history.

BARBARA KRADER, compiler of the section "Folklore," is Slavic Bibliographer, Syracuse University Library, and a member of the Board of Russian Studies. She received her doctorate from Radcliffe, has served as editor for musicological journals, and has written articles on folklore, music, and East European cultural affairs.

LAWRENCE KRADER, compiler of the sections "Ethnology" and "The National Question," is Professor in the Department of Anthropology, Syracuse University, a member of the Board of Russian Studies, and Director of the Nomadism Program. His writings include *Population and Manpower of China; an Annotated Bibliography* (Washington, 1958); *Peoples of Central Asia*

(Bloomington: Indiana University Press, 1963); and *Social Organization of the Mongol-Turkic Pastoral Nomads* (The Hague: Mouton, 1963) as well as articles in professional journals.

FRANÇOIS DE LIENCOURT is compiler of the section "Theater." A staff member of the French Foreign Office, he served as a Counsellor at the Moscow Embassy from 1954 to 1957. He is Lecturer at the École Pratique des Hautes Études (Sorbonne), has written articles on the Soviet theater, and is author of the chapter "The Repertoire of the Fifties" in *Literature and Revolution in Soviet Russia* (London, New York: Oxford University Press, 1963).

HUGH McLEAN, compiler of the section "Literature, Nineteenth and Twentieth Centuries," is Professor of Russian Literature and Chairman of the Department of Slavic Languages and Literatures at the University of Chicago. Among his publications are articles on Gogol', Leskov, Maiakovskii, and Zoshchenko.

WRIGHT WATTS MILLER compiled the section "General and Descriptive Works." He spent two and one-half years in the USSR on six visits between 1934 and 1962, including eight months in Kuibyshev in 1943. He has been engaged in journalistic activities in London and Moscow for the British government. His writings include *Russians as People* (London: Phoenix House, 1960; New York: Dutton, 1961); *The Young Traveller in Russia* (London: Phoenix House; New York: Dent, 1958); *USSR-Reader's Guide* (Cambridge, England: Published for the National Book League by the University Press, 1961); and *The U.S.S.R.* (London: Oxford University Press, 1963).

JOHN ROBERT ANGUS MINCHINTON, compiler of the section "Cinema," is a historian of the film and has been engaged in various film activities in Great Britain. He has made English versions of numerous foreign films, is Chairman of the Society for Film History Research, a Programme Officer of the National Film Theatre, and a member of the General Selection Committee of the National Film Archive. He also specializes in the history of the postwar Polish cinema.

RICHARD PIPES, compiler of the section "History," is Professor of History at Harvard University and Associate Director of Harvard's Russian Research Center. His special interests are Russian political thought and institutions and the history of Russian nationality policy. Among his publications are: *The Formation of the Soviet Union* (Cambridge: Harvard University Press, 1954); *Karamzin's Memoir* (Cambridge: Harvard University Press, 1959); *The Russian Intelligentsia* (New York: Columbia University Press, 1961), of which he was editor; and *Social Democracy and the St. Petersburg Labor Movement, 1885-1897* (Cambridge: Harvard University Press, 1963).

MICHAEL ROOF, compiler of the section "Demography," is a specialist in demography in the Reference Department, Library of Congress. A graduate of George Washington University, he was associated for six years with the historian-demographer Eugene M. Kulischer, and did graduate work in demography under Frank Lorimer at American University. He has written articles and studies on the population and labor force of the Soviet Union.

IVAN L. RUDNYTSKY, who, with Joseph Danko, compiled the section "Ukrainica," is a graduate of the universities of Berlin and Prague, and of the Institute of International Studies in Geneva. He is an Associate Professor of History at La Salle College in Philadelphia, and writes on nineteenth-century Ukrainian intellectual history.

BORIS SCHWARZ, compiler of the section "Music," is Professor of Music at Queens College of the City University of New York. He did research in the Soviet Union as a Guggenheim Fellow in 1960 and as an exchange scholar with the Academy of Sciences in 1963, under the auspices of the American Council of Learned Societies. His articles on Russian music and musicology have appeared in *The Musical Quarterly*, *Saturday Review*, the *Listener*, etc. His book *Musical Thought in Soviet Russia* is near completion.

ROBERT M. SLUSSER, compiler of the section "The Police Power," is Associate Professor in the Department of History at Johns Hopkins University. He is co-editor of *The Soviet Secret Police* (New York: Praeger, 1957) and has published studies in the fields of Soviet foreign policy and disarmament, cultural affairs, and the history of the revolutionary movement.

WILLIAM B. STERN, joint compiler with John N. Hazard of the section "Law," is Foreign Law Librarian at the Los Angeles County Law Library. He is serving as President of the International Association of Law Libraries.

BORIS O. UNBEGAUN, who compiled the section "Language," is Professor of Comparative Slavic Philology at Oxford University. He wrote *inter alia*: *La langue russe au XVIe siècle* (Paris: Champion, 1935); *A Bibliographical Guide to the Russian Language* (Oxford: Clarendon Press, 1953); *Russian Grammar* (Oxford: Clarendon Press, 1957); and *Russian Versification* (2d ed., rev., Oxford: Clarendon Press, 1963).

GEOFFREY WHEELER, who compiled the section "Islam and Buddhism," has been Director of the Central Asian Research Centre, London, since 1953. He was formerly in the Indian Army and Political Service and has served in India, Iran, and the Arab Middle East. He is joint editor of the *Central Asian Review* and author of *Racial Problems in Soviet Muslim Asia* (London, New York: Oxford University Press, 1960).

CONSULTANTS

For French publications (order follows sequence of presentation in the Guide)

GENERAL AND DESCRIPTIVE WORKS
>   Alain Besançon, Research Associate at the Centre National de la Recherche Scientifique, Paris.

THE NATIONAL QUESTION AND ISLAM
>   Alexandre Bennigsen, Directeur d'Études at the École Pratique des Hautes Études, Paris.

LAW
>   René David, Professor at the Faculté de Droit de Paris, and Jacques Bellon, Maître de Requêtes à la Cour de Cassation, Paris.

HISTORY
>   Roger Portal, Professor at the Sorbonne, and François Xavier Coquin, Agrégé de l'Université, Pensionnaire à la Fondation Thiers, Paris.

POLITICS AND GOVERNMENT AND DIPLOMATIC HISTORY
>   M.ne. Hélène Carrère d'Encausse, Directeur de Recherche à la Fondation des Sciences Politiques, Paris.

MILITARY AFFAIRS

Mme. Michaud, Librarian at the Bibliothèque de Documentation Internationale Contemporaine, Paris.

ECONOMICS

Basile Kerblay and Henri Chambre, Directeurs d'Études à l'École Pratique des Hautes Études, Paris.

SOCIETY

Alain Besançon and Mme. Hélène Carrère d'Encausse.

LITERATURE

Pierre Pascal, Professor at the Sorbonne, Paris.

HISTORY OF THOUGHT AND PHILOSOPHY

Henri Chambre.

JUDAISM

Léon Poliakov, Chef de Travaux à l'École Pratique des Hautes Études, Paris.

For German Publications

Werner Markert, Professor at the University of Tübingen and Director of its Institut für Osteuropäische Geschichte und Landeskunde.

ASSISTANT EDITOR

ROBERT G. CARLTON is Area Librarian (USSR and East Europe), Slavic and Central European Division, Library of Congress, and a graduate of Columbia University's Russian Institute. He has participated in the preparation of various bibliographical aids on East Europe.

contents

I

GENERAL REFERENCE AIDS and BIBLIOGRAPHIES

by Paul L. Horecky and Robert V. Allen

A. BIBLIOGRAPHIES[1]

1. Of Bibliographies

1. Kirpicheva (Kirpičeva), Iraida K. Handbuch der russischen und sowjetischen Bibliographien. Leipzig, VEB Verlag für Buch- und Bibliothekswesen, 1962. 225 p. (Bibliothekswissenschaftliche Arbeiten aus der Sowjetunion und den Ländern der Volksdemokratien in deutscher Übersetzung, Reihe B, Band 5)

   A translation, supervised and edited by the author, of those portions of *Bibliografiia v pomoshch' nauchnoi rabote* (Bibliography in Aid of Study and Research; Leningrad, 1958, 480 p.) which deal with Russian and Soviet bibliographies. An informed guide to general and special bibliographies in the natural and social sciences.

2. New York. Public Library. *Slavonic Division*. A Bibliography of Slavonic Bibliography in English. New York, New York Public Library, 1947. 11 p.

   Of a total of 132 entries, 69 refer to bibliographies of materials

[1] Entries are listed in reverse chronological order by period treated.

about Russia and the Soviet Union, embracing topics in the natural sciences as well as in history, politics, and the arts. A subject index is provided. Reprinted from the *Bulletin of the New York Public Library* for April 1947.

2. Of Monographs

3. The American Bibliography of Russian and East European Studies. 1957– Bloomington, Ind. annual. (Indiana University Publications. Russian and East European Series)
See also entry no. 1534.

Since its inception, this work (originally titled *The American Bibliography of Slavic and East European Studies*) has covered publications for a given year, gradually expanding its coverage. The latest volume, issued in 1964 (for the year 1962), and containing 2,277 listings, "includes materials of scholarly interest published in English anywhere in the world outside the Soviet Union and the countries of East Europe." Entries are grouped by broad subject categories and, within these, by countries. Separate sections are devoted to the USSR. Index of authors and editors. So far published in seven volumes (volumes 9, 10, 18, 21, 26, 27, and 29 of the above series).

For a selective coverage of English-language materials, chiefly published in North America since 1941, *see* "Bibliography: Books and Articles on Russia in . . .," an annual feature which appeared from 1942 to 1959 (since 1949 in the July issue) in the *Russian Review* (*see* entry no. 39) and which listed noteworthy contributions published during the preceding year.

Publications on the Soviet Union issued in Western Europe in 1961 are listed in "Western Books on the USSR Published in 1961," *Soviet Studies*, v. 14, January 1963: 338-345. Included are books published in Britain and selected items appearing in France, West Germany, Belgium, and the Netherlands. Reprints, translations of Soviet literary works, and minor pamphlet literature are excluded. It is planned henceforth to include similar lists in each January issue.

A similar annual feature for publications on the USSR and Russia issued in France was inaugurated by "Bibliographie des travaux parus en France concernant la Russie et l'U.R.S.S. (année 1962)" in *Cahiers du monde russe et soviétique*, v. 4, no. 1-2, 1963: 150-195.

4. Maichel, Karol.   Guide to Russian Reference Books. v. 1– Edited by J. S. G. Simmons. Stanford, Calif., The Hoover Institution on War, Revolution, and Peace, 1962– (Hoover Institution Bibliographical Series)

This annotated guide to bibliographies and reference materials pertaining to the Soviet Union, in Russian and in West European languages, is to appear in six volumes containing some 3,500 items. Volume one lists 379 general bibliographies and reference books grouped into 21 categories; five additional volumes are planned to cover specific subject areas.

Tentativa de bibliografía razonada de la Rusia contemporánea (Mendoza, Argentina, Universidad Nacional de Cuyo, Biblioteca Central, 1961, 125 p.) by Alberto Falcionelli, though uneven in coverage and often lacking bibliographic accuracy, is useful for listing publications in the Romance languages, together with materials in other Western languages and in Russian.

5. Neiswender, Rosemary.   Guide to Russian Reference Books and Language Aids. New York, Special Libraries Association, 1962. 92 p. (Special Libraries Association Bibliography no. 4)

   A practical bibliography of more than 225 current Russian reference and linguistic works, with emphasis on grammars, readers, dictionaries, and research aids in Soviet science and technology. Critical annotations and prices are supplied. Appendixes include brief descriptions of Russian transliteration systems and a selective listing of retail sources for Russian publications. Author-title index.

   A selected list of references for young students of the area is offered in *Educational Materials Laboratory Report*, v. 5, June 26, 1963: 1-2, published by the U.S. Office of Education, International Studies and Services.

6.* Miller, Wright W.   USSR. Cambridge, England, published for the National Book League at the University Press, 1961. 32 p. (Reader's Guides, 4th Series, no. 6)

   A highly selective, annotated reading list of English-language books which the compiler, a seasoned student of the USSR, considers essential for an understanding of that country.

7. Mart'ianov, Nikolai N.   Books Available in English by Russians and on Russia, Published in the United States. 8th ed. New York, Martianoff, 1960. 65 p.

   An alphabetical listing of those English-language books in print which were published in the United States and pertain to Russia and the Soviet Union, or were written by authors of Russian origin. Prices are given.

8. Munich. Osteuropa-Institut.   Ost- und Südosteuropa im westlichen Schrifttum der Nachkriegzeit; ein bibliographischer Leitfaden für Dozenten und Hörer an Volkshochschulen. Munich, 1956. 113 p.

   An annotated bibliography intended for use by students and teachers in adult education courses. Over 50 pages list books about Russia, the Soviet Union, the Ukraine, the Baltic region, and Siberia, in addition to a general section and sections on the other Slavic peoples. Approximately 40 per cent of the books listed are in English, and 50 per cent in German, including translations from English.

9. Grierson, Philip.   Books on Soviet Russia, 1917-1942; a Bibliography and a Guide to Reading. London, Methuen, 1943. 354 p.

   A basic, detailed guide to research and reading on the Soviet Union for the period 1917-1942. Lists chiefly English-language books and pamphlets, irrespective of place of publication, together with some monographs in languages other than English, and a few articles. Meaningful annotations and interspersed bibliographical surveys provide valuable information. Organized in five main chapters. Four appendixes, including a list of Soviet literature in translation and an index of authors' names and principal subject headings.

This bibliography was carried to 1950 with a series of articles by Grierson which list books and pamphlets published in the United Kingdom and which appeared in *The Slavonic and East European Review* (January 1946: 123-147; April 1947: 508-517; May 1949: 556-562; April 1950: 486-492; June 1951: 550-557).

10. Mehnert, Klaus.   Die Sovet-Union, 1917-1932. Systematische, mit Kommentaren versehene Bibliographie der 1917-1932 in deutscher Sprache ausserhalb der Sovet-Union veröffentlichten 1900 wichtigsten Bücher und Aufsätze über den Bolschewismus und die Sovet-Union. Königsberg, Berlin, Ost-Europa-Verlag, 1933. 186 p.

   A basic bibliography of important German-language books and articles published between 1917 and 1932. Compiled with the co-operation of 36 subject specialists. Organized in 10 major chapters — each of which is subdivided into subject categories — covering all relevant aspects of Soviet life. Two of these chapters survey the pertinent English and French publications. Author index.

11. Viktorov-Toporov (Victoroff-Toporoff), Vladimir.   Rossica et Sovietica; bibliographie des ouvrages parus en français de 1917 à 1930 inclus rélatifs à la Russie et à l'U.R.S.S. Saint-Cloud, Éditions documentaires et bibliographiques, 1931. 130 p.

   A bibliographical inventory of 1,312 French-language works published between 1917 and 1930, and relating to Russian and Soviet affairs. The seven main chapters are subdivided into sections which are arranged alphabetically. Seven indexes provide a variety of approaches to the contents.

12. Breslau. Osteuropa-Institut.   Osteuropäische Bibliographie. v. 1-4, 1920-1923. Breslau, Priebratschs Buchhandlung, 1921-1928. annual.

   In addition to a general chapter, each volume contains a section for Soviet Russia and for each of the East European countries, with subdivisions by subject. Entries refer to materials in Russian or other area languages as well as West European languages. One section of the volume for 1923 lists writings by Russian émigrés about Russia both before and after 1917. Author indexes. Length increased from 51 pages for the 1920 volume to 1,156 pages for the 1923 issue.

13. Kerner, Robert J.   Slavic Europe; a Selected Bibliography in the Western European Languages. Cambridge, Harvard University Press, 1918. 402 p. (Harvard Bibliographies. Library Series, v. 1)

   This bibliography retains substantial value as a guide to literature on historical and cultural topics. One chapter, with more than 1,700 entries, refers to Russia, while the remaining five chapters, containing almost 2,800 entries, are devoted to the Slavs in general and to individual Slavic peoples. Subject arrangement within each chapter. Author index.

14. Shapiro, David.   A Select Bibliography of Works in English on Russian History, 1801-1917. Oxford, Basil Blackwell, 1962. 106 p.

    Lists 1,070 books and articles considered relevant to the study of Russian history in its broadest sense. Hence, the scope of this bibliography is considerably wider than its title would suggest, and extends to the whole range of the political, economic, social, and intellectual aspects of the period covered. The material is presented in 21 main subject groups, most of which are subdivided. Crisp evaluative summaries precede many sections, and some of the entries are briefly annotated. References to critical reviews are given for books "that are important or possibly misleading." Index of authors and of persons mentioned in titles.

3. Of Periodicals and Newspapers

15. U.S. *Library of Congress.   Slavic and Central European Division.* The USSR and Eastern Europe; Periodicals in Western Languages. Compiled by Paul L. Horecky and Robert G. Carlton. Washington, 1964. 67 p.

    A selective bibliography, listing by country West European language periodicals published in the USSR and Eastern Europe (regardless of subject matter), and those published elsewhere if relevant to the study of the area. Brief annotations give bibliographical and subscription information. An earlier version was published in 1958. Abstract and translation journals which deal exclusively with science or technology are not included. For a list of such journals, see *List of Russian Serials Being Translated into English and Other Western Languages*, 4th rev. ed. (Washington, Science and Technology Division, Library of Congress, 1962, 53 p.)

16. U.S. *Library of Congress.   Slavic and Central European Division.* Newspapers of the Soviet Union in the Library of Congress (Slavic, 1954-1960; Non-Slavic, 1917-1960). Prepared by Paul L. Horecky with the assistance of John P. Balys and Robert G. Carlton. Washington, 1962. 73 p.

    This record of newspapers which are available in print and on microfilm lists a number of newspapers in West European languages.

17. Gazety i zhurnaly SSSR; Newspapers and Magazines of the USSR. 1930– Moscow, Vsesoiuznoe obshchestvo "Mezhdunarodnaya kniga." annual.

    A sales catalog of Soviet periodicals and newspapers available for foreign subscription, issued by the official Soviet book export agency, Mezhdunarodnaia kniga. Titles are in Russian and English, and prices are quoted in U.S. dollars and in other currencies. Titles are grouped by major subject fields and there are indexes giving the titles of serial publications in this list in Russian, English, and three other major languages. A number of serials in West European languages are included.

4. Of Dissertations

18. Buist, Eleanor. Soviet Dissertation Lists since 1934. The Library Quarterly, v. 33, April 1963: 192-207.

A thorough and well-informed discussion of the subject, which is followed by a checklist of such Soviet dissertation lists and bibliographies as were separately published in book or pamphlet form. The list consists of two parts: current bibliography and retrospective bibliography. The latter is organized by university, region, and subject.

19. Dossick, Jesse J. Doctoral Research on Russia and the Soviet Union. New York, New York University Press, 1960. 248 p.

A bibliography of 960 American, British, and Canadian doctoral dissertations on Russia and the Soviet Union, arranged by fields of learning. The individual sections contain: an analytical survey of the pertinent thesis material; an itemized alphabetical listing of dissertations; whenever applicable, "auxiliary theses" representing background material; and selected references for future research. No index. To be updated annually in the *Slavic Review* beginning with the December 1964 issue.

20. Hanusch, Gerhard. Osteuropa Dissertationen. Jahrbücher für Geschichte Osteuropas, Neue Folge. v. 1, 1953, no. 4, supplement: 1-44; v. 2, 1954, no. 2, supplement: 45-72; v. 3, 1955, no. 1, supplement: 73-114; v. 4, 1956, no. 3, supplement: 115-152; v. 6, 1958, no. 4, supplement: 153-194; v. 8, 1960, no. 2, supplement: 195-239.

A bibliography of dissertations and "Habilitationsschriften" on topics in the fields of the social sciences and humanities, relating to Eastern Europe and the Soviet Union, which were submitted to universities in the German-speaking areas of Europe, in Western and Northern Europe, and in North America in the years since 1945. Entries are grouped by major subject field, and author and subject indexes are provided.

Approximately 320 doctoral dissertations completed prior to 1933 and written in German are listed in *Doktorarbeiten über Russland, 1895-1933* (Leipzig, G. Fock, 1934, 11 p.), a price list of the firm Gustav Fock, booksellers, of Leipzig.

B. CATALOGS AND COLLECTION SURVEYS

21. Jena. Universität. *Bibliothek.* Slavica-Auswahl-Katalog der Universitätsbibliothek Jena; ein Hilfsbuch für Slawisten und Germanoslavica-

Forscher. v. 2, pt. 1: Russland und Sowjetunion. Weimar, H. Böhlaus Nachfolger, 1958. 263 p.

A catalog listing 2,585 titles held by the Jena University Library. Entries are grouped under broad subject headings and include works in German, Russian, and other languages. Also listed are works once held by the Jena Library, but lost as a result of military action in the years 1939-1945.

Slavic acquisitions of the Landesbibliothek Gotha from 1647 to 1945 are listed in Helmut Claus' *Slavica-Katalog der Landesbibliothek Gotha* (Berlin [East], Akademie-Verlag, 1961, 531 p.)

22. Leningrad. Publichnaia biblioteka (Imperatorskaia publichnaia biblioteka v Sanktpeterburgie). Catalogue de la Section des Russica, ou écrits sur la Russie en langues étrangères. St. Petersburg, Académie Impériale des Sciences, 1873. 2 v.

A catalog of books, the latest imprint of which is 1869, in European languages other than Russian, which refer to Russia or which were printed in Russia. Based upon the holdings of the St. Petersburg Public Library. Although this is not a complete catalog of all books of this nature, it offers a useful guide to material about Russia. A subject guide, which requires care in using, is included.

23. New York. Public Library. *Slavonic Division.* Dictionary Catalog of the Slavonic Collection. Boston, G. K. Hall, 1959. 26 v.

A photographic reproduction in bound volumes of approximately 550,000 entries in the card catalog of the Slavonic Collection of the New York Public Library. It includes materials in the Slavic and Baltic languages and publications in other languages about the Slavic and Baltic countries and their peoples. Many entries are for periodical articles not indexed elsewhere. Emphasis is given to belles lettres, social sciences, folklore, and — for the more recent period — to technology and economics. Medicine, theology, and law are not strongly represented.

24. Ruggles, Melville J., *and* Vaclav Mostecky. Russian and East European Publications in the Libraries of the United States. New York, Columbia University Press, 1960. 396 p.

A survey of USSR and East European library resources in the United States with emphasis on quantitative analysis. Discusses problems of acquisition, cataloging, and bibliographical control. Recommends possible improvements in the techniques employed in the handling of these materials. Contains many statistical data.

25. Unbegaun, Boris O. Catalogue des périodiques slaves et relatifs aux études slaves des bibliothèques de Paris. Paris, Champion, 1929. 221 p. (Travaux publiés par l'Institut d'Études Slaves, no. 9)

An alphabetically arranged catalog of serial publications of relevance to Slavic studies held by libraries in Paris through 1927. Materials in West European languages are also listed.

26. Union List of Russian Scientific and Technical Periodicals Available in European Libraries. Liste des périodiques scientifiques et techniques russes existant dans les bibliothèques européennes. Edited by L. J. van der Wolk and S. Zandstra. Amsterdam, Netherlands University Press, 1963–
> Volume one lists publications held by Netherlands libraries and includes on pages 314-398 journals containing Western-language translations.

C. TRANSLATIONS, ABSTRACTS, AND INDEXES

For a detailed listing of West European language translations of USSR periodicals, and of journals abstracting USSR literature, consult entry no. 15. Note also the widespread translation activities of the United States Joint Publications Research Service, as referred to in entries no. 29 and 32. Catalogs of recent Soviet books in English translation are issued from time to time by booksellers in the United States and England specializing in publications from the USSR, and by the Soviet book export firm, Mezhdunarodnaia kniga. A recent list by the latter is *Books Available in English Published in the U.S.S.R.* (Moscow, 1963, 86 p.), listing 340 such books.

27. British Broadcasting Corporation. *Monitoring Service.* Summary of World Broadcasts. Part 1: USSR. 1947– daily.
> Daily summaries of monitored Soviet broadcasts, divided into the following subject categories: General; Economic and Scientific; Broadcasting and Telecommunications. Weekly summaries digest the daily reports, and are sometimes accompanied by appendixes on international and/or internal affairs. From 1939 to 1947 such information was contained in the BBC's *Monitoring Report*, a publication of varying periodicity and format.

28. Current Digest of the Soviet Press. v. 1– February 1, 1949– New York, Joint Committee on Slavic Studies. weekly.
> Presents a knowledgeable selection of the contents of over 60 major Soviet newspapers and magazines, translated into English in full, or objectively condensed. Each issue groups the material translated according to broad subject headings — for which there is a table of contents — and offers weekly indexes to *Pravda* and *Izvestiia*. Quarterly cumulative indexes also cover the contents of major Soviet serial publications printed in English, as well as translations appearing in the journal *Soviet Studies* (*see* entry no. 43).

29. Soviet Periodical Abstracts. v. 1– May 1961– White Plains, N.Y., Slavic Languages Research Institute, Inc. quarterly.
> Published in two series, with subtitles: (1) *Soviet Society*; (2) *Asia, Africa, and Latin America*, providing English-language abstracts of selected articles on these subjects in over 50 Soviet publications. Entries indicate availability of translations in the *Current Digest of the Soviet Press* (*see* entry no. 28) or in the translation

series issued by the United States Joint Publications Research Service (*see* entry no. 32). Former title: *Selective Soviet Annotated Bibliographies.*

30. Soviet Press Translations. October 31, 1946– March 1953.   Seattle, University of Washington Press. biweekly.

Unabridged translations from Soviet journals and newspapers, principally upon foreign relations, with emphasis on events in Eastern Asia.

31. L'U.R.S.S. et les pays de l'Est; revue des revues.   1960– Paris, Centre National de la Recherche Scientifique. quarterly.

An abstracting and indexing journal consisting of two parts. The first section contains summaries, frequently at length, of major articles appearing in selected Soviet and East European journals on legal, economic, social, and cultural problems. The summaries are often followed by explanatory notes and comments written by the authors of the summaries. The second section is an index to the contents of the periodicals from which summarized articles are taken. Entries for articles not included in the first section are frequently supplied with short annotations. Sponsored by the University of Strasbourg's Center for Research on the USSR and the Eastern Countries.

32. U.S. *Joint Publications Research Service.*   Reports. no. 1– 1958–

The Joint Publications Research Service (JPRS) is an official agency serving the translation needs of agencies of the federal government. It produces, among other things, translations of materials on economic, political, cultural, and social developments in the Soviet Union. Since February 1, 1963, it has been possible to subscribe to the various series of these translations, as well as to acquire copies of individual reports. All JPRS publications and their prices are now listed in the *Monthly Catalog of United States Government Publications* which is available in most large libraries and on subscription from the Superintendent of Documents, United States Government Printing Office, Washington, D. C., 20402 ($4.50 domestic, $6.00 foreign). Each issue of this catalog contains a subject index, an annual cumulation of which appears in the December issue.

A Catalog of Current Joint Publications Research Service Publications, released by that organization in October 1963, is a useful source on its translation activities, on the possibilities of subscribing to translation series — in paper copy or in photoduplicated form, and on means of bibliographical access to this large body of materials.

JPRS translations and the sources from which they may be obtained in printed or photocopied form are discussed in an informative article, "Joint Publications Research Service Translations," published by Rita Lucas and George Caldwell in *College and Research Libraries*, v. 25, March 1964, p. 103-110.

D. GENERAL PERIODICALS

A detailed inventory of periodicals in West European languages dealing with Eastern Europe and the Soviet Union is given in *The USSR and Eastern Europe; Periodicals in Western Languages* (*see* entry no. 15). A number of periodicals of particular significance for the study of Soviet and Russian affairs are listed in this section. Indexing services which, according to Ulrich's *Periodicals Directory*, index a given periodical are shown at the end of the entry.

33. The Anglo-Soviet Journal. v. 1– 1940– London. quarterly.

    Produced by the British Society for Cultural Relations with the USSR. Takes a uniformly favorable view of Soviet affairs. Articles on the Soviet theater and other cultural subjects, some notices of new plays and films in Moscow, some abstracts from Soviet cultural journals.

34. Cahiers du monde russe et soviétique.   1959– Paris, École Pratique des Hautes Études, Section des Sciences Économiques et Sociales. quarterly.

    Scholarly articles upon a variety of subjects relating to Russian and Soviet history, culture, and social conditions. Frequent bibliographical surveys.

35. Institut zur Erforschung der UdSSR. Bulletin. 1954– Munich. monthly.

    English-language analyses of contemporary events and studies of Soviet history and culture by well-informed, principally émigré, writers. For other publications of the Institute for the Study of the USSR, *see* entry no. 15.

36. Osteuropa.   1951– Stuttgart, Deutsche Gesellschaft für Osteuropakunde e.V. monthly.

    Current political, economic, and cultural developments in the Soviet Union and in East-Central Europe are emphasized. Each issue contains a bibliography of recent literature, principally in German. The same organization also issues *Osteuropa-Naturwissenschaft, Osteuropa-Recht,* and *Osteuropa-Wirtschaft,* which appear semiannually and are devoted to problems of science, law, and economics in the Soviet Union and East Europe.

37. Problems of Communism.   1952– Washington, United States Information Agency. bimonthly.

    Articles and book reviews referring to the cultural, political, and economic problems arising in connection with the Communist movement, many of which report and interpret events within the Soviet Union from the point of view of serious and well-informed specialists. An edition in Spanish also appears. Indexed by Public Affairs Information Service.

38. Revue des études slaves.   1921– Paris, Institut d'Études Slaves de l'Université de Paris. annual.
See also entries no. 1255 and 1535.
> Concentrates on the study of culture, history, and linguistics. Each issue contains a lengthy bibliographical article, which lists books and articles on Russian language, literature, history, religion, art, and bibliography, in Russian and in other languages.

39. Russian Review.   1941– Hanover, N. H. quarterly.
> Places major emphasis on social, cultural, and historical problems relating to Russia, as distinguished from the Soviet Union. From 1942 to 1959 one issue of each year contained a bibliography of American books and articles on Russia (*see* entry no. 3). Annual index in last issue of each year. Cumulative index in last issue of each year. A *Cumulative Index to Volumes 1-20* (November 1941 — November 1961), arranged by author and subject, was compiled by Virginia L. Close (Hanover, N. H., 1962, 112 p.). Indexed by International Index and Public Affairs Information Service.

40. Slavic and East European Journal.   1943– Madison, Wisc., American Association of Teachers of Slavic and East European Languages. quarterly.
> Features articles on the problems of language training and on topics of literary and social history, reviews of general and specialized publications, and surveys of the position of Slavic studies in American education.

41. Slavic Review; American Quarterly of Soviet and East European Studies.   1940– Seattle, Wash., American Association for the Advancement of Slavic Studies. quarterly.
> A scholarly journal, which was formerly called *The American Slavic and East European Review*, devoted to problems of Slavic culture and history, with particular attention paid to Russian and Soviet affairs. Articles, discussion, reviews. Indexed by International Index and Public Affairs Information Service.

42. Slavonic and East European Review.   1922– London, School of Slavonic and East European Studies, University of London. semiannual.
> A scholarly journal stressing topics in cultural, political, and social history, and linguistics. Numerous authoritative reviews of books in these fields. Published in the U.S. in the period 1941-1944. Index for 1922-1932. Indexed by British Humanities Index.

43. Soviet Studies; a Quarterly Review of the Social and Economic Institutions of the U.S.S.R.   1949– London, Blackwell, for the Department for the Study of the Social and Economic Institutions of the USSR, University of Glasgow. quarterly.
See also entry no. 1148.

Major attention is given to topics of a sociological, economic, or legal nature. Numerous authoritative book reviews and frequent translations of relevant articles or excerpts from Soviet publications. Annual table of contents appearing in issue number four (April). Indexed by British Humanities Index and Public Affairs Information Service.

44. Survey; a Journal of Soviet and East European Studies. 1956– London, Congress for Cultural Freedom. quarterly.

Discusses literary, cultural, and political affairs, both in the Soviet Union and in East Europe. Translations from Soviet literary works also appear. Originally published as *Soviet Survey*. Indexed by Public Affairs Information Service.

E. ENCYCLOPEDIAS AND HANDBOOKS[2]

45. Holt, Robert T., *and* John E. Turner, *eds.*   Soviet Union: Paradox and Change. New York, Holt, Rinehart and Winston, 1962. 240 p.

Essays by a number of American scholars interpreting selected aspects of Soviet political, economic, and social life, including topics such as the Soviet city, education, youth, agriculture, and radio and television broadcasting. The authors base their conclusions both upon long study of the Soviet Union and upon their experiences in travel in that country. A short bibliography lists a number of recent publications devoted to each of the major topics discussed.

46. Maxwell, Robert, *ed.*   Information USSR; an Authoritative Encyclopaedia about the Union of Soviet Socialist Republics. Oxford, New York, Pergamon Press, 1962. 982 p.

A somewhat expanded and updated English-language version of the Soviet official handbook on the USSR as represented by volume 50 of the *Bol'shaia sovetskaia entsiklopediia* (2d ed., 1957). Contains additional appendixes: (1) statistical data relating to the national economy of the USSR (up to 1960); (2) a useful directory of establishments of higher learning in the USSR; (3) a select bibliography of recent books in English on the USSR (rather fragmentary); (4) data on trade with the Soviet Union; (5) a résumé of the program adopted at the Twenty-second Congress of the Communist Party of the Soviet Union, along with short biographies of leading officials of that party. Indexes of names and subjects are provided.

For a German translation of volume 50 of the *Bol'shaia sovetskaia entsiklopediia*, updated to 1959, *see*: Bol'shaia sovetskaia entsiklopediia. *Die UdSSR. Enzyklopädie der Union der sozialistischen Sowjetrepubliken*, edited by W. Fickenscher and others (Leipzig, Verlag Enzyklopädie, 1959, 1104 p.)

47. Mouskhély, Michel, *ed.*   L'U.R.S.S.; droit, économie, sociologie, politique, culture. v. 1. Paris, Éditions Sirey, 1962. 704 p.

[2] Entries are listed in reverse chronological order by period treated.

Articles by scholars from France, the Soviet Union, the United States, and other countries, on topics in Soviet legal, economic, social, and cultural affairs, and French translations of selected Soviet constitutional, legal, and cultural documents.

48.* Whiting, Kenneth R.   The Soviet Union Today; a Concise Handbook. New York, Praeger, 1962. 405 p.
See also entry no. 103.

An introduction to Soviet affairs for the reader seeking brief and basic information. The subject is presented in 14 chapters and a list of suggested reading in English is provided.

49. McGraw-Hill Encyclopedia of Russia and the Soviet Union.   Edited by Michael T. Florinsky. New York, McGraw-Hill, 1961. 624 p.

Some 3,500 entries in a dictionary-type arrangement, ranging from extensive essays to brief notes. The coverage, necessarily of varying quality, encompasses a wide spectrum of knowledge, and is particularly useful in biography, economics, science, and technology. Basic subject bibliographies of English-language publications and copious pictorial material. The editor is Professor of Economics at Columbia University.

50. Utechin, Sergej V.   Everyman's Concise Encyclopaedia of Russia. London, Dent; New York, Dutton, 1961. 623 p. Illus., maps.

Also the result of a co-operative effort and in dictionary form, though of lesser scope and reference usefulness than the McGraw-Hill encyclopedia (*see* entry no. 49). Substantial biographical material. Some entries supply bibliographic references.

51. Fitzsimmons, Thomas, *and others*.   USSR; Its People, Its Society, Its Culture. New Haven, HRAF Press, 1960. 590 p. Illus., maps. Bibliography: p. 521-548.
See also entries no. 92 and 1154.

A survey of the USSR, compiled by the Human Relations Area File, an organization affiliated with Yale University and assisted by the co-operation of 20 American universities. The book emphasizes chiefly the Great Russian social, economic, and political structure from a cultural-anthropological point of view. One chapter provides a concise account of the languages and peoples of the USSR.

52. Munich. Osteuropa-Institut.   Sowjetbuch. 2d enl. ed. Edited by Hans Koch. Cologne, Deutsche Industrieverlags-Gesellschaft, 1958. 687 p. Maps (part fold.)

A book of general and biographical information on the USSR prepared by German specialists. Part one surveys in a number of essays the principal sectors of contemporary Soviet life; part two provides rosters of leading officials in the Party, government, and religious organizations, as well as a 60-page biographical dictionary; part three consists of a good bibliography of West European literature on the USSR.

53. Strakhovsky, Leonid I., *ed.* A Handbook of Slavic Studies. Cambridge, Harvard University Press, 1949. 753 p.

> Twenty-eight major chapters, each prepared by a specialist, deal with the history and intellectual life, past and present, of the Slavic peoples. Nine chapters are devoted to Russia, the Ukraine, and the USSR. Very useful chapter bibliographies of West European publications. A comparative chronology of the historical development of the various Slavic peoples is appended.

54. Freund, Henry A.   Russia from A to Z; Revolution, State and Party, Foreign Relations, Economic System, Social Principles, General Knowledge. Sydney, London, Angus and Robertson, 1945. 713 p. Bibliography: p. 603-665.

> Written by a legal scholar and lifelong student of Russian affairs and sponsored by the Australian Institute of International Affairs, this concise handbook still remains a convenient source of information on the USSR up to 1945. The entries, arranged alphabetically under key words, focus primarily on political, economic, international, and legal affairs. Combined subject and name index.

55. The Russian Year Book.   1911-1916. London, Eyre and Spottiswoode. 6 v. Illus. (ports.), maps, diagrs.

> Each volume provides extensive general and statistical information. Much emphasis is given to British investment in the Russian economy.

56. Kovalevskii, Vladimir I.   La Russie à la fin du XIX siècle; ouvrage publié sous la direction de M. W. de Kovalevsky. Paris, P. Dupont, 1900. 989 p.

> A French translation of *Rossiia v kontsie XIX vieka* (St. Petersburg, Brokgauz-Efron, 1900, 968 p.). An official publication issued as part of the Russian participation in the Paris Exposition of 1900, containing articles surveying the major fields of government, economy, public finance, education, social conditions, and defense. Despite the promotional purpose of this volume, it retains its usefulness as a source of information on Russia at the turn of the century.
>
> A similar, though less extensive, work is *Statesman's Handbook for Russia* (St. Petersburg, E. Thiele, 1896, 2 v.), which was issued by the Committee of Ministers through its Chancellery (Komitet ministrov. Kantseliariia).

F. BIOGRAPHICAL MATERIALS [3]

For additional biographical information consult the encyclopedias and handbooks listed in Chapter I, E (entries no. 45 ff.)

57. Turkevich, John.   Soviet Men of Science; Academicians and Corre-

[3] Entries are listed in reverse chronological order by period treated.

sponding Members of the Academy of Sciences of the USSR. Princeton, N.J., Van Nostrand, 1963. 441 p.
See also entry no. 1788.

A biographical directory of members of the Academy of Sciences of the USSR. Included are persons working in fields of the humanities and social sciences, as well as natural science and technology.

For additional listings of those active in the social sciences and the humanities, *see* entry no. 61.

Other biographies of scientists are entered in *Who's Who in Soviet Science and Technology* (New York, Telberg Book Co., 1960, 119 l.), compiled by Ina Telberg on the basis of information contained in *Biograficheskii slovar' deiatelei estestvoznaniia i tekhniki* (Moscow, "Sovetskaia entsiklopediia," 1958, 2 v.)

The United States Joint Publications Research Service (*see* entry no. 32) has provided similar information in its serially issued *Soviet Scientific Personalities*, and in *Biographies of Soviet Scientists*. These publications are listed in the *Monthly Catalog of United States Government Publications*.

See also Institut zur Erforschung der UdSSR, *Prominent Personnel of the Academies of Sciences of the USSR and Union Republics* (Munich, 1963, 71 p.)

58. Who's Who in the USSR, 1961/1962. Edited by Heinrich E. Schulz and Stephen S. Taylor. Montreal, Intercontinental Book and Publishing Co., 1962. 963 p.

A biographical directory with approximately 4,000 entries for persons prominent in government, arts, sciences, and other walks of life. Lists information on careers and published works. Sponsored by the Institute for the Study of the USSR and prepared by its staff. Expands, though does not completely supersede, the Institute's *Biographic Directory of the USSR*, edited by Wladimir S. Merzalow (New York, Scarecrow Press, 1958, 782 p.)

The Institute's *Porträts der UdSSR Prominenz*, issued in looseleaf, contained longer articles and cited sources, but was discontinued with number 24, 1960.

59. Institut zur Erforschung der UdSSR. *Research Section*. Key Officials of the Government of the USSR and Union Republics. Munich, 1962. 111 p. (mimeographed)
See also entry no. 733.

A directory, reflecting the personnel situation as of February 1962. The section on the USSR offers a historical chart of posts and incumbents since 1917, and, from 1941, also the beginning and terminal dates of their tenure. Name index. Earlier versions of this list were issued as supplements to the Institute's *Bulletin*.

60. U.S. *Dept. of State. Division of Biographic Information*. Directory of Soviet Officials. Washington, 1960-1961. 2 v. (*Its* Biographic Directory, no. 272, 278)
See also entry no. 735.

A directory of officials in the USSR, union republic, autonomous republic, oblast', and krai governments and in various cultural and public organizations. Arrangement follows the organizational structure of government and other institutions. Date and source of information on which listing is based are indicated. Name index with each volume. Volume one lists persons in the USSR and RSFSR agencies as of July 30, 1960, and volume two, those in the other republics as of June 1, 1961.

61. Who's Who in Soviet Social Sciences, Humanities, Art, and Government. Compiled by Ina Telberg. New York, Telberg Book Co., 1961. 147 l.

Biographical data on 700 persons, based upon information contained in the third edition of the *Malaia sovetskaia entsiklopediia* (Moscow, "Sovetskaia entsiklopediia," 1958-1961, 10 v. plus index). A useful source of information, containing frequent bibliographical references to the works of those listed.

62. Koch, Hans, *ed.*   5,000 (i.e., Fünftausend) Sowjetköpfe; Gliederung und Gesicht eines Führungskollektivs. Cologne, Deutsche Industrieverlags-Gesellschaft, 1959. 862 p.

This amplification of the biographical section of *Sowjetbuch (see* entry no. 52) is a directory of Soviet personalities with details on careers and publications. More listings than in entry no. 58, though somewhat less elaborate and less detailed. Names are listed alphabetically according to a German system of transliteration which may complicate use.

63. Kleine slavische Biographie.   Wiesbaden, Otto Harrassowitz, 1958. 832 p.

A biographical directory listing eminent personalities, living and dead, of all the Slavic peoples, including many Russians. Emphasis is on representatives of cultural life. Frequent bibliographical references, including indications of West European language translations of the literary works of persons listed. Prepared by present and past staff members of the Slavische Seminar of Munich University.

64. Ikonnikov, Nikolai F.   NdR; la noblesse de Russie. Éléments pour servir à la reconstitution des registres généalogiques de la noblesse d'après les actes et documents disponibles, complétés grâce au concours dévoués des nobles russes. 2d ed. Paris, 1957–

A handbook for genealogists, providing information on birth, marriage, and death of members of the Russian gentry (*dvorianstvo*), both titled and untitled. Comparatively little information on the lives and careers of persons listed.

Additional genealogical data may be found in Roman I. Ermerin's *Annuaire de la noblesse de Russie; contenant les princes de l'empire augmenté d'un grand nombre de notices sur les familles alliées* (St. Petersburg, Librairie Impériale H. Schmitzdorff, 1889-1900, 3 v.) and in Petr V. Dolgorukov's *Notice sur les principales familles de la*

Russie, 2d ed. (Berlin, F. Schneider, 1858, 143 p.). The latter appeared in an English translation as *A Handbook of the Principal Families in Russia* (London, J. Ridgway, 1858, 192 p.)

65. Preev, Zinovy N. The Russian Revolution and Who's Who in Russia. London, John Bale, Sons and Danielsson, 1917. 119 p.

Although evidently compiled in haste and quite limited in scope, the biographical section of this book provides information about persons prominent at the time who may not be listed in standard sources.

66. Nikolai Mikhailovich, *grand duke of Russia*. Russkie portrety XVIII i XIX stoletii [Russian Portraits of the 18th and 19th Centuries]. St. Petersburg, Ekspeditsiia zagotovleniia gosudarstvennykh bumag, 1905-1909. 5 v. plus index. Illus., ports.

Engravings after paintings of several hundred persons of prominence in Russia from the time of Peter the Great. Each is accompanied by a short biographical note. Textual material and legends of plates are in both Russian and French.

Other portraits of some of the same persons, with biographical notes, may be found in Louis de St. Aubin's *Tridtsat' deviat' portretov, 1808-1815 g; fototipicheskiia vosproizvedeniia s biograficheskimi ocherkami. Trente-neuf portraits, 1808-1815; reproductions phototypiques avec notices biographiques* (St. Petersburg, Expédition pour la confection des papiers d'état, 1902, 39 p.). These portraits are more closely based on sketches from life and are perhaps less intentionally flattering to their subjects.

A number of bibliographical references to portraits published in other works may be found in Aleksandr I. Vasil'chikov's (Wassiltschikoff) *Liste alphabétique de portraits russes* (St. Petersburg, MM. Eggers, 1875, 2 v.)

67. Strahl, Philipp C. Das gelehrte Russland. Leipzig, F. Fleischer, 1828. 514 p.

Chronologically arranged biographical entries for writers in Russian (or Church Slavonic) from the ninth to the eighteenth centuries, all of whom were in holy orders. Based upon the *Slovar' istoricheskii o byvshikh v Rossii pisateliakh dukhovnago china greko-rossiiskoi tserkvi* (St. Petersburg, Tip. N. Grecha, 1818, 2 v. in 1) by Evgenii, Metropolitan of Kiev. Many of those listed in this work were also active in religious and political affairs.

68. Kostomarov, Nikolai I. Russische Geschichte in Biographien. v. 1: Die Herrschaft des Hauses Wladimirs des Heiligen; X bis XVI Jahrhundert. Leipzig, Verlag von Guillermo Levien, 1889. 695 p. No more published.

A translation of volume one of Kostomarov's *Russkaia istoriia v zhizneopisaniiakh eia glavnieishikh dieiatelei*, 2d ed. (St. Petersburg, Tip. M. M. Stasiulevicha, 1880). Contains 31 biographical articles about such persons as St. Vladimir, St. Aleksandr Nevskii, Maksim Grek, the false Dmitrii, and Filaret Nikitich Romanov.

G. OTHER REFERENCE TOOLS

1. Gazetteers

69. U.S. *Office of Geography.* U.S.S.R. and Certain Neighboring Areas; Official Standard Names Approved by the United States Board on Geographic Names. Washington, U.S. Government Printing Office, 1959. 7 v. (U.S. Board on Geographic Names. Gazetteer no. 42)
See also entry no. 195.

A gazetteer listing place names and geographic coordinates for regions, populated places, and topographic features within the Soviet Union. Entries under variant spellings and former names supply the spelling or name adopted by the Board on Geographic Names.

A retrospective survey of place name changes is offered by Wolfgang Meckelein in *Ortsumbenennungen und -neugründungen im europäischen Teil der Sowjetunion; nach dem Stand der Jahre 1910/ 1938/1951* (Berlin, Duncker und Humblot, 1955, 134 p.), covering 1,300 localities.

2. General Statistical Publications

70. Russia (*1923– U.S.S.R.*) *Tsentral'noe statisticheskoe upravlenie.* National Economy of the USSR in 1960; Statistical Yearbook. Washington, United States Joint Publications Research Service, 1962. 937 p. (JPRS Report no. 12137)
See also entry no. 334.

An English translation of *Narodnoe khoziaistvo SSSR v 1960 g.,* an official Soviet compilation of statistics on population, industry. agriculture, trade, education, health services, and other fields.

For previous years, materials in West European languages include the following:

Russia (*1923– U.S.S.R.*) *Tsentral'noe statisticheskoe upravlenie.* USSR in Figures for 1959; Brief Statistical Returns. Moscow, Foreign Languages Publishing House, 1961. 265 p.

Russia (*1923– U.S.S.R.*) *Tsentral'noe statisticheskoe upravlenie.* 1958 Statistical Yearbook on the National Economy of the USSR. Washington, United States Joint Publications Research Service, 1960. 818 p. (JPRS Report no. 6404)

Russia (*1923– U.S.S.R.*) *Tsentral'noe statisticheskoe upravlenie.* National Economy of the USSR; Statistical Returns. Moscow, Foreign Languages Publishing House, 1957. 230 p.

Russia (*1923– U.S.S.R.*) *Tsentral'noe statisticheskoe upravlenie.* The National Economy of the USSR; a Statistical Compilation. Moscow, State Statistical Publishing House, 1956. 270 p.

The data and conclusions presented in the above publication are discussed in Naum Jasny's *The Soviet 1956 Statistical Handbook; a Commentary* (East Lansing, Michigan State University Press, 1957. 212 p.). Another translation of this Soviet handbook, with additional tables and annotations by Harry Schwartz, appeared as *Studies in Business Economics*, v. 55 (New York, National Industrial Conference Board, 1957, 122 p.)

Russia (*1923– U.S.S.R.*) *Gosudarstvennaia planovaia komissiia.* Socialist Construction in the USSR; Statistical Abstract. Moscow, Soyouzorgutchet, 1936. 538 p.

Russia (*1923– U.S.S.R.*) *Tsentral'noe upravlenie narodno-khoziaistvennogo ucheta.* The USSR in Figures. Moscow, Soyouzorgutchet, 1934-1935. 2 v.

Russia (*1923– U.S.S.R.*) *Tsentral'noe statisticheskoe upravlenie.* Ten Years of Soviet Power in Figures, 1917-1927. Moscow, Central Statistical Board, 1927. 516 p.

71. Russia. *Tsentral'nyi statisticheskii komitet.*   Liste des publications du Comité central de statistique, Ministère de l'intérieur. St. Petersburg, 1914. 8 p.

A list of the statistical publications of the Russian Empire, grouped under very broad headings, with indication of publications issued in French.

More extensive details concerning publications issued before August 1, 1897, with annotations and summary of contents, may be found in:

Russia. *Tsentral'nyi statisticheskii komitet.* Aperçu bibliographique des publications du Comité central de statistique de l'Empire de Russie. St. Petersburg, 1895-1897. 2 v.

3. Libraries, Librarianship, and Publishing in the USSR

72. Gorokhoff, Boris I.   Publishing in the USSR. Bloomington, Indiana University Press, 1959. 306 p. (Indiana University Publications. Slavic and East European Series, v. 19)
Bibliography: p. 287-290.
See also entry no. 1010.

A survey of book, periodical, and newspaper publishing, including some related topics such as censorship, copyright, and the book trade. Generous coverage is given to publications in science and technology. The study is based chiefly on an analysis of Soviet sources. Numerous tables and statistical materials are added, as well as bibliographies of Russian and English sources.

The findings of a group of U.S. book publishers who visited the USSR in 1962 under the official U.S.–USSR exchange agreement are embodied in *Book Publishing in the USSR* (New York, American Book Publishers' Council, Inc., American Textbook Publishers Institute, Inc., 1963, 112 p.). Its 17 chapters include discussions of statistics on book production and prices, Soviet translations of works by foreign authors, authors' royalties in the USSR, and problems of copyright. Statistical tables are included.

73. Horecky, Paul L.   Libraries and Bibliographic Centers in the Soviet

Union. Bloomington, Indiana University Press, 1959. 287 p. (Indiana University Publications. Slavic and East European Series, v. 16)

A survey of libraries and their collections, librarianship, and bibliographic centers and their activities, as well as an appraisal of the ideological elements involved in this sector of Soviet cultural endeavor. Maps, charts, English translations of Soviet materials, a directory of principal library and bibliographic institutions, and a selective bibliography of sources in Russian and West European languages.

A report of the visit of the Delegation of U. S. Librarians to the Soviet Union in 1961, prepared by Melville J. Ruggles and Raynard C. Swank, has become available under the title *Soviet Libraries and Librarianship* (Chicago, American Library Association, 1962, 147 p.). The report is organized in eight sections, including one on "Advanced Mechanization and Automation." Four appendixes and a bibliography of recent English-language material on the subject are added. Illustrations.

The Saltykov-Shchedrin Library of Leningrad, one of the major libraries of the Soviet Union, is described by Nikolai I. Morachevskii in his *Guide to the M. E. Saltykov-Shchedrin State Public Library, Leningrad*, translated by Raymond H. Fisher (Los Angeles, University of California Library, 1963, 48 l.; UCLA Library Occasional Papers, no. 14).

4. American Organizations of Exiles from the USSR

74. East European Fund.   Directory of American Organizations of Exiles from the U.S.S.R. New York, 1952. 192 p.

Lists names and addresses of organizations in the United States formed by various persons formerly resident within the USSR. Background résumés concerning each national group precede the list of organizations.

H. RESEARCH ON THE USSR

1. In the U.S.A.

75. Fisher, Harold H., *ed.*   American Research on Russia. Bloomington, Indiana University Press, 1959. 240 p.

A collection of 13 essays written by scholars who review the state of the art in various fields of American research on the USSR since the Second World War, and who indicate areas of inquiry hitherto not sufficiently explored. Bibliographical references are included in "Notes" (p. 187-232).

The Joint Committee on Slavic Studies (appointed by the American Council of Learned Societies and the Social Science Research Council) sponsored both this study and the appraisal of the role of Russian studies in graduate, undergraduate, and secondary education in the United States which is given in *American Teaching about Russia*, edited by Cyril E. Black and John M. Thompson (Bloomington, Indiana University Press, 1959, 189 p.)

Language and Area Programs in American Universities, published by the External Research Staff, U.S. Department of State (Washington, 1964, 162 p.), a directory describing programs which offer graduate degrees in foreign language and area study, contains a chapter on the Soviet Union and Eastern Europe.

For data on publication programs and activities of major research institutions, *see*, inter alia: *Institute Publications, 1951-1962* (Munich, 1963, 100 p.), published by the Institute for the Study of the USSR and listing alphabetically titles in several languages, including English and German; *Ten Year Report, 1948-1959* (Russian Research Center, Harvard University, 1958, 106 p.); *The Russian Institute, 1946-1959* (Columbia University Bulletin, Series 59, August 22, 1959) and its continuation for 1960-1963 (Columbia University Bulletin, Series 64, December 21, 1964); "Les ressources du fonds slave et est-européen de la Bibliothèque du Congrès" by Paul L. Horecky published in *Cahiers du monde russe et soviétique,* v. 3, April–June 1962: 307-322; *Report on Research and Publication, 1947-1962* (Russian and East European Institute, Indiana University, 1963); and Roman Smal-Stocki's *The Slavic Institute of Marquette University 1949-1961* (Milwaukee, Wisc., Slavic Institute, Marquette University, 1962, 37 p.)

Articles by Adam Ulam, Robert F. Byrnes, and A. Gerschenkron in *Survey*, January 1964 (pages 53-68, 82-89) discuss the state of Soviet studies in the United States.

76. U.S. *Dept. of State. Bureau of Intelligence and Research.*   External Research; a List of Recently Completed Studies. 1952– Washington.

Published in 10 series, one of which is "USSR and Eastern Europe," issued annually from 1952 to 1953 and semiannually since April 1954. The spring issue bears the subtitle "A List of Studies Currently in Progress," and the fall issue, "A List of Recently Completed Studies." These lists are based on the catalog of social science research on foreign areas and international affairs compiled by the sponsoring unit from information furnished by private scholars. The entries, which describe both books and articles, are annotated. The publication is available, on request, to libraries, universities, and faculty members from the External Research Staff (INX/XR), Department of State, Washington, D. C., 20520.

2. In Other Countries

77. Hacker, Jens.   Osteuropa-Forschung in der Bundesrepublik. Das Parlament. Beilage "Aus Politik und Zeitgeschichte," September 14, 1960: 591-622.

An informative survey of research on the USSR and Eastern Europe in the German Federal Republic, reviewing academic and private institutions, their staffs and offices, activities, and publications, as well as the resources and facilities of libraries.

Analogous surveys for Switzerland ("Die Osteuropa-Forschung in der Schweiz") and Austria ("Ost- und Südosteuropa-Forschung in Österreich") are presented by the same author in the abovementioned publication (*Das Parlament*, Beilage "Aus Politik und

Zeitgeschichte," January 24, 1962: 21-27, and April 5, 1961: 181-192, respectively).

The work of two major German scholarly organizations in the field of Slavic studies is surveyed in *Fünfzig Jahre Osteuropa-Studien; zur Geschichte der Deutschen Gesellschaft zum Studium Osteuropas und der Deutschen Gesellschaft für Osteuropakunde* (Stuttgart, Deutsche Gesellschaft für Osteuropakunde, 1963, 48 p.)

Articles by Victor Frank, Basile Kerblay, and Jens Hacker in *Survey*, January 1964 (pages 90-118) discuss the state of Soviet studies in Great Britain, France, and Germany, respectively.

Danish research on Slavic and East European subjects is reviewed in Knud Rahbek Schmidt's "Slawistik und Ostforschung in Däne-mark," *Osteuropa*, v. 13, no. 7/8, July–August 1963: 465-479.

II

GENERAL
and
descriptive
works

by Wright W. Miller

A. PICTURE BOOKS

78. Abbe, James E.   I Photograph Russia; with 80 Photographs by the Author. New York, R. M. McBride, 1934. 324 p.

> Abbe's photographs, taken in 1932, still have great firsthand value and include many "forbidden" subjects, such as queues, accidents, railways, etc., besides portraits (taken with permission) of Stalin and other leaders. The text is of less significance.

79. Cartier-Bresson, Henri.   The People of Moscow. New York, Simon and Schuster, 1955.

> One of the world's outstanding "intimate" photographers conveys, in 163 photographs, a powerful impression of the Russian atmosphere, both public and personal.

80. Fichelle, Alfred.   Russia in Pictures, from Moscow to Samarkand. 178 photographs with an introduction translated from the French by Laetitia Gifford. London, Duckworth; New York, Studio Publications, 1956.

81. Hürlimann, Martin.   Moscow and Leningrad; 78 Pictures in Photo-

23

gravure, 9 Colour Plates, and 9 Line Drawings. Translated from the German by Daphne Woodward. New York, Studio Publications, 1958. 135 p.

> More than a picture book of architecture, this book also conveys a good deal of Russian atmosphere. Translation of *Moskau, Leningrad* (Zurich, Atlantis Verlag, 1958).

82. Kelly, Marie N., *Lady.*   The Country Life Picture Book of Russia. London, Country Life, 1952. (unpaginated)

> Contains about 100 excellent photographs by the author (wife of a British Ambassador). Subjects include Moscow and Leningrad, old art cities such as Vladimir, and Georgia, with many original subjects and some good photographs of individual types and of intimate Soviet life.

83. Martin, John S., *ed.*   A Picture History of Russia. New York, Crown Publishers, 1945. 376 p.

> Contains between one and two thousand photographs, most of them of considerable rarity, illustrating Russian history from prehistoric times to the end of the Second World War. Issued in consultation with members of the staff for the intensive study of contemporary Russian civilization at Cornell University.

84. Van der Post, Laurens.   A View of All the Russias. Holiday, v. 34, no. 4, October 1963: 58-172.

> An extensive article by a perceptive observer, which is accompanied by a number of striking color photographs. This issue also contains other, shorter articles on Russian music, literature, and history, and on travel in the Soviet Union, written by experienced critics and reporters.
>
> Similar coverage of the Soviet Union, relying to a greater extent on photography, may be found in *Life*, September 13, 1963, the whole issue of which is devoted to a survey of various facets of Soviet domestic affairs.

B. GUIDEBOOKS

85. Baedeker, Karl, *firm.*   Russia, with Teheran, Port Arthur, and Peking; Handbook for Travellers, with 40 Maps and 78 Plans. Leipzig, Karl Baedeker; New York, Charles Scribner's Sons, 1914. 590 p.
Bibliography: p. lxii-lxiv.

> A valuable source of general information which is still useful on the Russia of that time.

86. Levine, Irving R.   Travel Guide to Russia. Garden City, N. Y., Doubleday, 1960. 416 p.

> As a guide to travel in Russia (rather than a guidebook on Russia) this book provides excellent advice and information which the American visitor needs concerning customs and other restrictions

and the background and history of Russia. It deals at length with Moscow's sights and entertainments, and with most (though not all) of the other Soviet cities open to tourists. The author was correspondent in Moscow for the National Broadcasting Company for about 10 years from 1948.

87. Marabini, Lila, *and* Jean Marabini. Moscou, Léningrad (Iasnaia Poliana, Zagorsk, Pétrodvoretz). Paris, Hachette, 1963. 174 p. Maps, illus. (Les Guides bleus illustrés)

This guide follows the usual *Guide bleu* system of routes described in detail, with introductory matter on history, essential information, transportation, hotels, entertainment, restaurants, etc. Some dishes, and even wines, are recommended. Some telephone numbers are given. The map of Moscow is up to date as regards the Metro, less so for street names. There are few errors or misspellings. The most reliable full guide to Moscow and Leningrad in any Western language.

88. Rado, Alexander.   Guide-book to the Soviet Union. Berlin, Society for Cultural Relations of the Soviet Union with Foreign Countries, 1928. 855 p. Maps.

Covers the whole Soviet Union, but European Russia and the Ukraine receive much fuller treatment than the rest of the country, to which only 191 pages are assigned. While much of the general information is quite out of date, and many place names have been changed, the historical information is just what tourists need and cannot find in more recent guidebooks.

Translation of *Führer durch die Sowjet-Union* (Berlin, 1928, 897 p.)

C. GENERAL WORKS

89. Baring, *Hon.* Maurice.   The Russian People. London, Methuen, 1911 and 1914. 366 p.

Largely historical, but always related to contemporary events and attitudes. Contains a superb 70-page general essay on the country and the people.

The same author's *The Mainsprings of Russia* (New York and London, Thomas Nelson and Sons, 1914, 328 p.) is a classic essay on "what the Russians are like" and why — penetrating in observation, sound in fact, and sometimes poetic in the writing.

90. Braverman, Harry.   The Future of Russia. New York, Macmillan, 1963. 175 p.

An attempt to assess the forces which may break through as a result of economic progress. The author expects at least elementary and crude steps to be made toward more liberal ways. A stimulating though perhaps over-optimistic projection into the future.

91. Conquest, Robert.   Common Sense about Russia. London, Victor Gollancz; New York, Macmillan, 1960. 175 p.

A short outline of the differences between the USSR and Western countries and of the preconceptions and pitfalls in the way of arriving at a common sense view.

92. Fitzsimmons, Thomas, *and others.*   USSR; Its People, Its Society, Its Culture. New Haven, HRAF Press, 1960. 590 p. Illus., maps. Bibliography: p. 521-548.
See also entries no. 51 and 1154.

All important aspects of the USSR are dealt with, and although contributions from several hundred scholars were involved, the whole has been so skilfully edited that it can be read straight through. The editors rightly claim that many new relationships have been revealed as a result of collecting information from so many sources. Traditional and communist elements are adroitly blended in this examination, and the whole work may be regarded as the most comprehensive and reliable book yet published about the Soviet Union.

93. Fitzsimmons, Thomas, *ed.*   RSFSR, Russian Soviet Federated Socialist Republic. Contributors: Clifford Barnett and others. New Haven, Human Relations Area Files, 1957. 2 v. (681 p.) Illus., maps, tables.
Bibliography: v. 2, p. 611-633.

A fuller but earlier version of the material on the Russian Republic contained in the same editor's *USSR* (*see* entry no. 92).

94.* Gunther, John.   Inside Russia Today. Rev. ed. New York, Pyramid Publications, 1962. 604 p. Illus.
See also entry no. 1158.

A very useful "middlebrow" book, part fact and part impressions, covering what visitors to the USSR need to know about the country, and, among other themes, "What Has Russia Got?" Gunther naturally often orients his material specially for the American reader, but is not very often biased or unfair. This revised edition contains new information, added by the author and Gene Sosin, which makes it current to July 1962.

The same author's *Meet Soviet Russia* (New York, Harper and Row, 1962, 2 v.) is a "Meet the World" book for young readers, with brief sketches of political and social developments.

95. Harper, Samuel N.   The Russia I Believe In. Chicago, University of Chicago Press, 1945. 279 p.

Papers of Samuel Harper covering the years 1902-1941, edited by his brother Paul V. Harper and Ronald Thompson. The author had firsthand knowledge of the First Duma and was acquainted with many of its leaders. He also had firsthand experience of the Revolutionary period and later years. During his lifetime he was described by Sir Bernard Pares as "the first authority in the United States on things Russian."

96. Long, John. Modern Russia; an Introduction. London, Duckworth, 1957; New York, Philosophical Library, 1958. 180 p.

A sound, brief introduction to the geography, economics, and political features of the Soviet Union.

97.* Maynard, *Sir* John. Russia in Flux. Foreword by Sir Bernard Pares. New York, Macmillan, 1948. 564 p.

See also entries no. 270 and 1164.

A classic account of the Russian peasantry and Russia in the nineteenth century, with a wealth of illustration, leading to an equally solid account of the Soviet regime up to the time of writing. (Some of Maynard's judgments in the second part have become invalidated or superseded by events since his death.) Maynard had a great gift of social sympathy, and was one of the first to attempt to show that "Russia is in flux, but it is the same Russia, though with a new and important psychological addition made by the Revolution."

Edited and abridged by Stephen Haden Guest from *Russia in Flux, Before October* (London, Gollancz; New York, Macmillan, 1941, 301 p.) and *The Russian Peasant, and Other Studies* (London, Gollancz; New York, Macmillan, 1942, 512 p.)

98.* Miller, Wright W. The U.S.S.R. Oxford, Oxford University Press, 1963. 128 p. (The Modern World Series)

A brief and objective account, for the general reader, of Russian history and natural resources, the political, economic, and social aspects of the Soviet regime, the Soviet people, and some speculations about the future. Table of dates. Reading list.

99. Miller, Wright W. The Young Traveller in Russia. London, Phoenix House, 1958. 124 p. Map, illus.

A semi-fictional introduction to Russian life and atmosphere, which some adults as well as young readers have found presents a convincing picture.

100. Riha, Thomas, *ed.* Readings in Russian Civilization. Chicago, University of Chicago Press, 1964. 3 v.

Readings on Russian political, economic, and social life in past and present. Volume one covers the period 900-1700; volume two, 1700-1917; and volume three, the Soviet period, 1917-1963.

101. Schnitzler, Johann H. L'empire des tsars au point actuel de la science. Paris, Veuve Berger-Levrault, 1856-1866. 4 v.

A source of encyclopedic knowledge of all major aspects of life in the Russian Empire around the mid-nineteenth century.

102. Thayer, Charles W., *and* the Editors of *Life*. Russia. New York, Time, Inc., 1961. 176 p.

Thayer was at the American Embassy in Moscow from 1933 to 1937. The book is notable for its well-selected and often unusual photographs. The text is a useful essay covering, in an elementary but fundamental way, what Western readers might "need to know"

in 1961 about Russian history, Soviet industry, government, agriculture, education, and social relations, with some concluding speculations about the future.
Revised edition: London, Sunday Times, 1961.

103.* Whiting, Kenneth R.   The Soviet Union Today: a Concise Handbook. London, Thames and Hudson; New York, Praeger, 1962. 405 p.
See also entry no. 48.
An up-to-date handbook, covering geography, ethnology, history, ideology, the Soviet political and economic system, armed forces, and foreign relations. Includes bibliography. An objective book, in spite of a confessed "bias towards the democratic way of life."

D. CHARACTERISTICS OF THE PEOPLE [1]

104. Bauer, Raymond A.   The New Man in Soviet Psychology. Cambridge, Harvard University Press, 1952. 229 p.
See also entries no. 1229 and 1719.
An essay on the Soviet conception of man and on Soviet psychology and its interrelationship with the system.

105.* Bauer, Raymond A., Alex Inkeles, *and* Clyde Kluckhohn.   How the Soviet System Works. New York, Vintage Books, 1960. 312 p.
See also entry no. 1149.
Part of the Harvard Project on the Soviet Social System, drawing on evidence from refugees, scholars, and experts, this book aims at describing the characteristics of the Soviet people in general, of various groups among them, how the system operates on them, and the interaction between individuals and the system. Earlier printing: Cambridge, Harvard University Press, 1956.

106.* Berdiaev, Nikolai A.   The Russian Idea. Translated from the Russian by R. M. French. New York, Macmillan, 1948; London, Geoffrey Bles, 1947. 255 p.
See also entry no. 1609.
A brilliant essay on religious, philosophical, and national attitudes in Russia, contrasted with those of the West. Translation of *Russkaia ideia; osnovnye problemy russkoi mysli XIX veka i nachala XX veka* (Paris, YMCA Press, 1946, 258 p.). The Russian subtitle is: "fundamental problems of Russian thought in the nineteenth century and the beginning of the twentieth."

107. Black, Cyril E., *ed.*   The Transformation of Russian Society; Aspects of Social Change since 1861. Cambridge, Harvard University Press, 1960. 695 p.
See also entries no. 681 and 1238.
The result of the 1958 Arden House Conference, organized by

[1] For ethnic and sociological characteristics, *see also* Chapter V and Chapter VIII, B, respectively.

the Joint Committee on Slavic Studies of the American Council of Learned Societies and the Social Science Research Council. Scholars in economics, sociology, education, history, literature, philosophy, and politics contribute papers under the headings: society and change; law; politics and social change; social stratification; education, scholarship, and religion; family, youth, and human welfare; personal and social values. The editor, in a concluding essay, speculates on future possibilities in Soviet society.

108.* Gorer, Geoffrey, *and* John Rickman.   The People of Great Russia; a Psychological Study. New York, Chanticleer Press, 1950; London, Cresset Press, 1949. 235 p.
See also entry no. 1176.
The psychiatrist Rickman contributes valuable observations on the Russian character from his experience as a doctor in the early Soviet years. Gorer, who examined a large number of Russian refugees, puts forward interesting views on Russian character, particularly in relation to swaddling and early childhood training.
See also entry no. 109.

109. Grygier, Tadeusz.   The Psychological Problems of Soviet Russia. The British Journal of Psychology (General Section), v. 42, pts. 1 and 2, March and May 1951: 180-184.
A Polish psychiatrist who worked in Soviet Russia makes some criticisms of Geoffrey Gorer's and John Rickman's *The People of Great Russia* (*see* entry no. 108) and adds valuable evidence of his own.

110. Inkeles, Alex, *and* Raymond A. Bauer.   The Soviet Citizen; Daily Life in a Totalitarian Society. Cambridge, Harvard University Press, 1959. 533 p.
See also entry no. 1163.
Based mainly on evidence from Soviet refugees, this "presents the main body of statistical data" from the Harvard Project on the Soviet Social System as a book "about the social psychology of Soviet life," drawing parallels with life in other large-scale industrial societies. There is a useful introduction on the methods and methodology used in examining 3,000 refugees, and the questionnaires and scales employed are given in an appendix. There are sections on jobs, education, family life, news, the individual and the state, class and political cleavage, and nationality problems. Particularly valuable in indicating differences in attitude between age groups or between social classes, and in showing the "low level of active disaffection."

111. Jarintzov, Nadine.   The Russians and Their Language. Preface by Nevill Forbes. Oxford, B. H. Blackwell, 1916. 222 p.
A gossipy book which throws much light on subtler points of Russian character and habits and makes a good introduction for English-speaking readers.

112. Mead, Margaret.   Soviet Attitudes toward Authority; an Interdisci-

plinary Approach to Problems of Soviet Character. Santa Monica, Calif., The Rand Corporation, 1951. 148 p.

Through evidence from refugees, visitors, Soviet literature, films, and documents, an attempt is made to examine "patterns of behavior between those in authority and those over whom they have authority," and to see how far ideals and actual patterns are congruent.

113.* Miller, Wright W.   Russians as People. New York, Dutton, 1961; London, Phoenix House, 1960. 205 p.

See also entry no. 1179.

The author presents a picture (on the basis of two and a half years spent in Russia on five different occasions) of the character and habits bred by the Russian climate and landscape, by serfdom and peasant agriculture, by the tsars and the Russian Church, and by the impact of the Revolution on all these, as well as the impact of what the Revolution itself created.

114. Moore, Barrington, Jr.   Terror and Progress USSR: Some Sources of Change and Stability in the Soviet Dictatorship. Cambridge, Harvard University Press, 1954. 261 p.

See also entry no. 1246.

A well-documented, careful, and modest study of forces making for change and forces making for stability in the Soviet Union — totalitarian, traditional, and technological. Good chapters on the life of the Soviet scientist and creative artist.

115. Simmons, Ernest J., ed.   Continuity and Change in Russian and Soviet Thought. Cambridge, Harvard University Press, 1955. 563 p.

See also entry no. 1576.

The work of 30 scholars from many disciplines, who, after a year's preparation, discussed their papers at a conference at Arden House in 1954, under the auspices of the Joint Committee on Slavic Studies of the American Council of Learned Societies and the Social Science Research Council. Papers discuss the continuity, or lack of it, between Tsarist and Soviet Russia under the following heads: realism and Utopia; authoritarianism and democracy; collectivism and individualism; rationality and non-rationality; literature, state, and society; and Russia and the community of nations (messianic views and theory of action).

116.* Simmons, Ernest J., ed.   Through the Glass of Soviet Literature; Views of Russian Society. New York, Columbia University Press, 1953. 301 p.

See also entries no. 1168 and 1438.

Essays on the position of women and Jews, children, the theater, postwar ideology, and the writer Zoshchenko, based on the evidence of Soviet literature. The essays developed out of literature seminars at the Russian Institute of Columbia University.

117.* Weidlé, Wladimir.   Russia: Absent and Present. Translated from

the French by A. Gordon Smith. London, Hollis and Carter, 1953.
152 p.
See also entry no. 1578.

An essay on the history and "personality" of Russia, concluding
with the antinomy of the state machine and the "fluid" Russian man,
who belongs to a people which, in the words of Filaret, the Metropolitan of Moscow, as quoted by Gogol, has "little light, but plenty
of warmth." The essay is intended to be part one of the author's
European Triptych.

Translation of *La Russie absente et présente* (Paris, Gallimard,
1949, 238 p.)

118. Wortis, Joseph.   Soviet Psychiatry. Baltimore, Williams and Wilkins,
1950. 314 p.
See also entry no. 1234.

The non-specialist reader should find this a book which is easy
to read and sheds valuable light on the Russian view of human
nature.

E. TRAVEL ACCOUNTS AND DESCRIPTIONS

1. Pre-1917

119. Aleksinskii, Grigorii A.   Modern Russia. Translated by Bernard
Miall. London, T. F. Unwin; New York, Charles Scribner's Sons,
1913 and 1915. 361 p.

The author, a moderate Social Democrat, was a member of the
Duma. His book is especially useful on the development of industry,
capitalism, and urban life, and is in general interesting as a liberal
Russian view. Probably translated, with amplifications, from the
French *La Russie moderne*.

120. Baring, *Hon.* Maurice.   What I Saw in Russia. New York, London,
Thomas Nelson and Sons, 1913. 381 p.

Consists partly of the author's observations of the Russian people
and Russian institutions while acting as a war correspondent in
Manchuria during the Russo-Japanese War, and partly of observations during the disturbances of the years 1904-1906 in most regions
of European Russia. Like all Baring's work on Russia, a book of
great humanity.

121. Chamberlin, William H.   Russia under Western Eyes. Russian Review, v. 16, January 1957: 3-12.

A survey of Western writings on life in pre-Revolutionary Russia
and the USSR.

122.* Custine, Astolphe L. L., *marquis* de.   Journey for Our Time; Selections from the Journals of the Marquis de Custine. Edited and translated from the French by Phyllis Penn Kohler. Introduction by
Walter Bedell Smith. New York, Pellegrini and Cudahy, 1951. 338 p.

Custine "went to Russia to search for arguments against representative government, but returned as a partisan of constitutions." In consequence his book takes an almost exclusively political view of the despotism, backwardness, dirt, ignorance, etc., which he found. It contains much valuable information, but should be corrected to some extent by the arguments put forward by K. K. Labenskii (*see* entry no. 132).

Translation of *La Russie en 1839* (Paris, Amyot, 1843, 4 v.)

123. Dillon, Emile J. (*pseud.* E. B. Lanin).   Russian Characteristics. London, Chapman and Hall, 1892. 604 p.

The author, British but educated in Russia, was Professor of Comparative Philology at Kharkov University, adviser to Count Witte, and correspondent for the London *Daily Telegraph* 1886-1914, and was among those who carried the coffin of Dostoevski. His book was reprinted, with revisions from contributions to the *Fortnightly Review* during 1889-1892, and presents a full and convincing picture of "the demoralisation of the nation" — the misery, oppression, and superstition which burdened it. Dillon has no political or theoretical axe to grind but indicts the Tsarist despotism as responsible for almost all ills.

124.* Dostoevskii, Fedor M.   The Devils (The Possessed). Translated with an introduction by David Magarshack. London, Baltimore, Penguin Books, 1953. 669 p.

"A political melodrama" by one of the world's great novelists, revealing many of the extremes of which the Russian character is capable.

Also noteworthy for its psychological insight is Dostoevski's *The Idiot*, available in many editions, among them one translated with an introduction by David Magarshack (Harmondsworth, Middlesex, England, Penguin Books, 1958, 660 p.). "Idiot" does not mean a mental defective but a character of divine simplicity, the remarkable Prince Myshkin. Such persons can be peculiarly Russian and are respected even in Soviet society.

125. Forstetter, Michel, *comp.*   Voyageurs en Russie; textes choisis du Xe au XXe siècle. Vevey, Switzerland, La Table Ronde, 1947. 219 p.

126.* Gor'kii, Maksim (Aleksei Maksimovich Peshkov).   The Autobiography of Maxim Gorky: My Childhood; In the World; My Universities. Translated from the Russian by Isidor Schneider. New York, Citadel Press, 1949. 616 p.
See also entry no. 1497.

A unique picture of life among the Russian poor before the Revolution. Translation of *Detstvo*; *V liudiakh*; and *Moi universitety*, published in 1913, 1915, and 1923, respectively. Other editions also available.

127. Graham, Stephen.   Changing Russia. 3d ed. London, New York, John Lane, 1915. 309 p. Front. (port.), plates, map.

An educated Englishman who was drawn to the Russian Church and the simplicity of the Russian peasant, Graham describes in this book his tramps in the Urals and along the eastern shore of the Black Sea in 1912. There is a good deal about the intelligentsia and about the bourgeoisie, whom he disliked; he feared the results of "commercialism" on the simple Russians, whom he revered.

In his *Undiscovered Russia* (London and New York, John Lane, 1912, 337 p.), Graham reports on a hike from Archangel to Moscow, often in the company of pilgrims. His books give an idealized view of simple Russians but contain observations difficult to match elsewhere.

128. Haxthausen-Abbenburg, August F. L. M., *Freiherr* von.   The Russian Empire; Its People, Institutions and Resources. Translated from the German by Robert Farie. London, Chapman and Hall, 1856. 2 v. (432, 463 p.)
See also entry no. 265.

Translation of *Studien über die innern Zustände, das Volksleben und insbesondere die ländlichen Einrichtungen Russlands* (Hannover, Hahn, 1847-1852, 3 v.). The author, a specialist in rural institutions, received a commission from the Prussian government to study the German peasantry during 1830-1838. He found Slavonic survivals among the West Germans, and then turned to study European Russia, where he spent a year, and other Slavic countries. His book provides much valuable detail on Russian rural and agricultural life, but the German and French editions contain more of this than the Russian.

For eighteenth-century accounts by German travelers, *see also* the following:

Messerschmidt, Daniel G. *Forschungsreise durch Sibirien, 1720-1727.* Edited by E. Winter and A. Figurovskij. Berlin, Akademie Verlag, 1962.

Fries, Jakob. *Eine Reise durch Sibirien im achtzehnten Jahrhundert.* Edited and with commentary by Walther Kirchner. Munich, Isar Verlag, 1955. 126 p.

129. Kennan, George.   Siberia and the Exile System. New York, The Century Co., 1891. 2 v. Illus., ports., maps.
See also entries no. 315 and 807.

An account of the Tsarist prison and exile system by an astute observer, along with descriptions of Siberia's scenery, people, and customs.

130. Kohl, Johann G.   Russia and the Russians in 1842. Translated from the German. London, H. Colburn, 1842. 2 v. (also London, Chapman and Hall, 1842. 530 p.)

Kohl's travels appear to have been in the late 1830's. He was an assiduous traveler and author of books about many countries, including the U.S.A. His German thoroughness does not prevent him from being interesting and even amusing, and his work is full of valuable information of manners and customs, religion, the standard of living, etc., in European Russia and the Baltic countries, but particularly in St. Petersburg and Moscow. Although a German, he found much to admire in the Russians.

Translations of part of *Reisen im inneren von Russland und Polen* (Dresden and Leipzig, Arnold, 1841, 3 v.)

131. Kravchinskii, Sergei M. (*pseud.* Sergius Stepniak). The Russian Peasantry; Their Agrarian Condition, Social Life, and Religion. London, Swan, Sonnenschein; New York, Harper, 1888. 401 p.
See also entry no. 1189.

A classic work by the former editor of *Zemlia i volia*. Gives an intimate picture of all aspects of peasant life — economic, political, religious, superstitious, moral, and patriotic.

Another edition: New York, Dutton, 1905, 651 p.

132. Labenskii, Ksaverii K.   A Russian's Reply to the Marquis de Custine's "Russia in 1839." Edited (and translated?) by Henry J. Bradfield. London, T. C. Newby, 1844. 164 p.

Translation of *Un mot sur l'ouvrage de M. de Custine intitulé "La Russie en 1839"* (Paris, Firmin Didot, 1843).

Labenskii makes some apt criticisms of Custine's desire to find evidence of despotism in everything Russian, and reminds him of some of the geographical and historical facts of Russia's position at that time.

One may consult also Mikhail Ermolov, *Encore quelques mots sur l'ouvrage de M. de Custine, "La Russie en 1839"* (Paris, Ferra, 1843, 40 p.)

133. Leroy-Beaulieu, Anatole.   The Empire of the Tsars and the Russians. Translated from the third French edition by Zenaidé A. Ragozin. New York, London, Putnam, 1893-1896. 3 v. (588, 566, 601 p.)
See also entries no. 530, 619, and 1187.

A detailed picture of the Russian nation "in a state of change," taking account of historical influences and traditions as well as contemporary reactions. Useful chapters on rank, national character, institutions, and religion, but the author attributes too much to the effects of "the Slav character" and not enough to the despotism.

Translation of *L'empire des tsars et les russes* (Paris, Hachette, 1881-1889, 3 v.)

134.* Miliukov, Pavel N.   Russia and Its Crisis. With a foreword by Donald W. Treadgold. New York, Collier Books, 1962. 416 p.

The author, who was a leader of the Kadet Party and became Minister for Foreign Affairs in the Provisional Government, describes his book as "a result of long years of study devoted to the explanation of the Russian present by the Russian past." Basically the Crane Lectures which he delivered in 1903, his book contains chapters on nationalism, religion, politics, liberal ideas, socialist ideas, and the urgency of reform.

Original edition: Chicago, University of Chicago Press, 1905, 589 p.

135. Olearius, Adam. The Voyages and Travels of the Ambassadors Sent by Frederick, Duke of Holstein, to the Great Duke of Muscovy, and the King of Persia. Translated from the German by John Davies. London, Thomas Dring and John Starkey, 1662. 424 p.

> The author was secretary of the Embassy of the Duke of Holstein to the "Great Duke of Muscovy" and the King of Persia. His work has a German accuracy of record and absence of speculation, and is in great part geographical. The account of religious observance and its relation to the Greek Church (i.e., before the Schism) is of interest, as are some observations of secular customs.
>
> Translation of *Offt begehrte Beschreibung der newen orientalischen Reise*, 1647, 1656, 1663, 1696. New edition: *Moskowitische und persische Reise*, edited by Eberhard Meissner (Berlin, Rütten und Loening, 1959, 531 p.)

136.* Pares, *Sir* Bernard.   Russia and Reform. London, Archibald Constable, 1907. 576 p.

> A very privileged Englishman, once gentleman usher to the First Duma, Pares writes on "What to know, to form an intelligent judgment of events in Russia now." Much of his book is based on first-hand testimony ("written down immediately afterwards"), but it is far more than reportage and presents a valuable view of Russian history and the Russian character which throws light on the flux and change of 1905-1906.
>
> Republished as *Russia: between Reform and Revolution,* edited and with an introduction by Francis B. Randall (New York, Schocken Books, 1962, 425 p.)

137. Pinkerton, Robert.   Russia; or Miscellaneous Observations on the Past and Present State of That Country and Its Inhabitants, Compiled from Notes Made on the Spot. London, Seeley, 1833. 486 p.

> The author was an agent of the British and Foreign Bible Society, and has much of value to say on the standard of living, customs and habits, and particularly the state of the Church in European Russia, the Baltic States, and Russian Poland. Translations of seven sermons are appended as "specimens of the Russian style of preaching."

138. Polunin, Vladimir.   Three Generations; Family Life in Russia, 1845-1902. Translated from the Russian by A. F. Birch-Jones, London, Hill, 1957. 397 p. Illus.

> The well-known stage designer, a refugee in England, gives a picture of bourgeois life among his ancestors and their associates in Kursk, Moscow, St. Petersburg, Kiev, etc., with the intention that the reader shall "learn how natural and human is the real Russian."

139. Putnam, Peter, *ed.*   Seven Britons in Imperial Russia, 1698-1812. Princeton, Princeton University Press, 1952. 424 p.

> The editor describes the reports of the seven Britons as "often prejudiced and inaccurate," but there is much to be gleaned by discerning readers from the writings of: John Perry, engineer to Peter the Great, 1698-1712; Jonas Hanway, merchant of the Russia

Company, 1743-1750; William Richardson, tutor and secretary to the ambassador, 1768-1772; Sir James Harris, ambassador, 1777-1783; William Coxe, traveling tutor, 1778-1789; Robert Ker Porter, court painter, 1805-1807; Sir Robert Thomas Wilson, military emissary who accompanied the Russian armies against Napoleon, 1812.

140. Radishchev, Aleksandr N.   A Journey from St. Petersburg to Moscow. Translated from the Russian by Leo Wiener, with introduction and notes by R. P. Thaler. Cambridge, Harvard University Press, 1958. 286 p.

Written over the period 1780-1790, this is not a description of a real journey, but a "literary travelogue," "sentimental" in the eighteenth-century sense, providing a base for the author's attacks on Russian institutions. Radishchev, a high civil servant, was disgraced as a result of his book.

Translation of *Puteshestvie iz Peterburga v Moskvu* (St. Petersburg, 1790, 453 p.)

141. Stevens, Thomas.   Through Russia on a Mustang. New York, Cassell, 1891. 334 p.

Stevens, a New York *World* correspondent, rode from Moscow to Sevastopol and back along the Don and Volga to Nizhni in 1890, for the most part with a Russian-speaking companion. He said he "wanted to see the better side," but became "compelled to admit that matters were very bad indeed." His book includes some penetrating observations on Russian attitudes and on standards of living.

142. Tikhomirov, Lev A.   Russia, Political and Social. Translated from the French by Edward Aveling. London, Swan, Sonnenschein, 1888. 2 v. (311, 299 p.)

Treats "Russia as a social organism." Chapters on classes, development of the intelligentsia, economic growth, political events, etc.

143.* Tolstoi, Lev N., *graf*.   Anna Karenina. Newly translated with a foreword by David Magarshack. New York, New American Library, 1961. 807 p.

There is still no better introduction to the "broad" Russian nature than this great novel — particularly the scenes involving Kitty and Levin. Several other editions available. Written in 1875-1877.

144. Tooke, William.   A View of the Russian Empire during the Reign of Catherine II and to the End of the Present Century. London, T. N. Longman and O. Rees, 1799. 3 v. (564, 612, 693 p.)

Tooke lived in Russia during most of Catherine's reign, and compiled his book from the accounts of the academicians (many of whom he knew personally) whom Catherine sent out to investigate her Empire. An uncritical book, but full of useful geographical and economic information, with much detail about habits, customs, and ranks.

145. Troyat, Henri.   Daily Life in Russia under the Last Tsar. Trans-

lated from the French by Malcolm Barnes. New York, Macmillan, 1962; London, Allen and Unwin, 1961. 242 p.

The author is a distinguished French writer who was born in Russia in 1911. For his richly colored portrait of old Russia he draws not only on family recollections but on over 70 books (listed), many of them rarely met. Most of the illustrations are also rare specimens.

Translation of *La vie quotidienne en Russie* (Paris, Hachette, 1959, 319 p.)

146.* Turgenev, Ivan S.   A Sportsman's Notebook. Translated by Charles and Natasha Hepburn. New York, Chanticleer Press, 1950. 397 p.

Sketches of Russian country and peasant life, first published in 1852. A classic picture of Russia not long before the Emancipation. Another edition: *A Sportsman's Sketches*, translated by Constance Garnett (London, Heinemann, 1895, 2 v.)

Translations of *Zapiski okhotnika*, first published in 1852 (Moscow, Univ. tip., 2 v. in 1).

147. Vodovozova, Elizaveta N. (Tsevlovskaia).   A Russian Childhood. Translated from the Russian by Anthony Brode and Olga Lane. London, Faber and Faber, 1961. 216 p.

The authoress (1844-1923), who came from an impoverished country family, tells of the isolation and miseries of country life just before the emancipation, and later of her schooldays at the terrible Smolny. An educationist of considerable power, her unsentimental memoirs have a Russian simplicity and directness.

Translation of *Istoriia odnogo detstva* (Moscow, Gos. izd-vo detskoi lit-ry, 1939, 238 p.)

148.* Wallace, *Sir* Donald M.   Russia; on the Eve of War and Revolution. Edited and with an introduction by Cyril E. Black. New York, Vintage Books, 1961. 528 p.
See also entries no. 275, 529, and 1192.

The classic work on all aspects of Russia in the period 1870-1905, by the correspondent of the London *Times*, whose visits covered the whole period and most of European Russia as well as Central Asia. Particularly full on peasants and sects.

Abridgement of an earlier edition (New York, Henry Holt, 1905, 672 p.)

149. Walling, William E.   Russia's Message; — the True World Import of the Revolution. New York, Doubleday, Page, 1908. 476 p.

Walling spent two years in Russia soon after the disturbances of 1905-1906, knew the leaders of the reformist and revolutionary parties, and refers to Lenin and Trotsky at this early stage. He seems to have anticipated the successful revolution, and writes of both workers and peasants with unusual inside knowledge and insight. Cast within the framework of history and with some analysis of national character, the whole makes a study of the "state of the people" which is of particular value today.

150. Wiener, Leo.   An Interpretation of the Russian People. Introduction by Sir Donald Mackenzie Wallace. New York, McBride, Nast and Co., 1915. 248 p.
Bibliography: p. 239-248.
> The author was born and educated in Russia and became Professor of Slavic Languages and Literatures at Harvard. His book comprises essays on the continuity of Russian characteristics, and on the position of women, the nature of Russian art, music, and religion, etc.

151. Williams, Harold.   Russia of the Russians. New York, Charles Scribner's Sons; London, Pitman, 1914. 430 p.
> A comprehensive, popular account of Russia just before the Revolution, including much about the arts, institutions, religion, trade, and peasants, with sufficient historical and geographical information to make an enlightening whole picture of a country in a state of change.

152. Wright, Richardson L.   The Russians; an Interpretation. New York, Frederick A. Stokes, 1917. 288 p.
> The author attempts, after seven years' study of Russia, to show American readers the potentialities of the Russian people at a time when they had already suffered serious defeats at the hands of the Germans. A useful chapter is entitled "The Things [the Russian] Revolts Against." Chapters on the working man, business ways, religion, and folksongs convey a powerful impression of actuality.

2. Soviet Period

153. Belfrage, Sally.   A Room in Moscow. New York, Reynal, 1958. 186 p.
> A young Englishwoman of Soviet sympathies, who spent her youth in the United States, writes a light-hearted, unexaggerated account of several months spent in Moscow, partly working and partly mixing with students. Her political attitude makes her account of restrictions on liberty the more compelling in its honesty.

154. Carlisle, Olga A.   Voices in the Snow. New York, Random House; London, Weidenfeld and Nicolson, 1963. 224 p.
> The granddaughter of the writer Andreev visited Russia in 1960 and interviewed leading Soviet writers and painters. Her impressions of the country, as a native speaker of Russian, are of great value, and her account of Soviet cultural life shows both the continuity and the differences of outlook between the generations.

155. Chamberlin, William H.   Russia's Iron Age. Boston, Little, Brown, 1934. 400 p. Front., plates, port.
> The author was correspondent of the *Christian Science Monitor* in the USSR from 1922 to 1932 and again later. In this book he gives a vivid and reliable account of the country in the later years of the First, and the earlier years of the Second Five-Year Plan.

156. Crankshaw, Edward.   Russia and the Russians. New York, Viking Press, 1948. 223 p.

The most brilliant of this author's essays on Russia at various periods. Written at the beginning of the Cold War, it attempts to look at Russia "through the eyes of a stranger to this planet, to whom one set of people, one nation, is as good as another until the contrary is proved." In spite of the lapse of time since 1946-1947, this is still a very good introduction to Soviet Russia and the influences which have formed the Soviet nation.

For a vivid account of the situation at the time of the Twentieth Party Congress, as well as a general and forward-looking view of the potentialities and possibilities which had been liberated in 1956, see also Crankshaw's *Russia without Stalin; the Emerging Pattern* (New York, Viking Press, 1956, 264 p.). Includes eight pages of cartoons from *Krokodil* and many translated extracts from the Soviet press.

157. Dillon, Emile J.   Russia Today and Yesterday. Garden City, N.Y., Doubleday, Doran, 1930. 325 p.
>   For the author's qualifications see his *Russian Characteristics* (entry no. 123). As an elderly man he revisited Russia in 1928, and in spite of having lost all in the Revolution, found a good deal to praise in the new regime by contrast with the old. Another edition: London, Dent, 1929, 338 p.

158. Dreiser, Theodore.   Dreiser Looks at Russia. New York, H. Liveright, 1928. 264 p. Illus.
>   Dreiser, who declared himself "an incorrigible individualist," spent 11 weeks in Russia in 1927 as a rather unrestricted guest of the Soviet Government. While many of his political observations were too simple or too optimistic, his dramatic sketches of Russian scenes and people remain as a vivid evocation of much in this early period.

159. Duranty, Walter.   Duranty Reports Russia; Selected and Arranged by Gustavus Tuckerman, Jr. New York, Viking Press, 1934. 401 p.
>   Described by Duranty as "a mosaic made out of isolated fragments," this compilation from his dispatches to the New York *Times* has considerable value as a picture of the period 1921-1933.

160. Farson, Negley.   Black Bread and Red Coffins. New York, London, The Century Co., 1930. 316 p. Col. front., col. plates.
>   Farson covered a great deal of European Russia during 1926-1929 and conveys vividly those chaotic years. His book includes 23 exceptional illustrations — reproductions in full color of political posters of the time.
>   Another London edition with slight differences in the text is entitled *Seeing Red; Today in Russia* (Eyre and Spottiswoode, 1930, 275 p.)

161. Gide, André P. G.   Return from the USSR. Translated from the French by Dorothy Bussy. New York, A. A. Knopf, 1937. 94 p.
>   ———— Afterthoughts, a Sequel to "Return from the USSR." Translated from the French by Dorothy Bussy. London, Martin Secker and Warburg, 1937. 142 p.

These two books should be taken together; the second contains some replies to criticisms of the first, some additional thoughts, and some useful supporting letters from third parties. *Return from the USSR* shows a great writer received and fêted in Moscow, charmed in a hundred ways, especially by the people, but in spite of all, penetrating to fundamental grave defects in a very shrewd manner.

Translations of *Retour de l'URSS* (Paris, Gallimard, 1936, 125 p.) and *Retouches à mon retour de l'URSS* (Paris, Gallimard, 1937, 125 p.)

162. Gordey, Michel.   Visa to Moscow. Translated from the French by Katherine Woods. New York, Knopf, 1952. 419 p.

Gordey is of Russian parentage and speaks the language perfectly. In 1950 he visited Russia for some months as correspondent of *France-Soir* — the first French journalist to receive a visa since 1945. His analysis of the standard of living is informative and well-balanced, and his "Inventory of Mistaken Ideas" in both Soviet and Western views is excellent. Translation of *Visa pour Moscou* (Paris, Gallimard, 1953, 445 p.)

163. Gouzenko, Svetlana.   Before Igor; My Memories of a Soviet Youth. New York, Norton, 1960. 252 p.

Mrs. Gouzenko is the wife of the Soviet cipher clerk who defected to the Canadians in 1945. She is also a remarkable woman in her own right, and has written an autobiography extraordinarily free from both nostalgia and bitterness. A most convincing picture of Soviet life and of real people.

164. Hindus, Maurice G.   House without a Roof; Russia after 43 Years of Revolution. Garden City, N.Y., Doubleday, 1961. 562 p.
See also entry no. 1159.

Born a Belorussian Jewish peasant, Hindus returned to the Soviet Union in 1958 and 1960, after a long absence, and was still convinced that the Revolution was "national and peasant, not international and proletarian." He found "dramatic improvement" in peasant conditions, which he describes at length and from a background of unusually intimate knowledge. His book is also useful for its account of conditions in Siberia and for its estimate of the position of the Jews, which he found "disappointing," though improved since Stalin's death.

165. Hindus, Maurice G.   Humanity Uprooted. Rev. ed. New York, Jonathan Cape and H. Smith, 1930. 369 p.
See also entry no. 1160.

Hindus "never saw a train or electric light until he was fourteen." He returned to Russia as a correspondent in 1923 and thereafter almost annually until the postwar years. His view of the upheaval in his native country was found "objective and impartial, moving and vivid" by John Dewey.

Hindus' story of the collectivization is told, with an inside understanding and sympathy possessed by no other correspondent, in his *Red Bread* (New York, Jonathan Cape and H. Smith, 1931, 372 p.)

166. Jones, Mervyn. The Antagonists. New York, Clarkson N. Potter, 1962. 328 p.

A British journalist's penetrating comparison of Russia and America, based on visits paid to both countries in 1961 (and on earlier experience of the U.S.). His pointing of similarities and contrasts between the geography, history, institutions, and attitudes of the two countries is not merely vivid and surprising but extremely informative. (His own preferences, revealed in conclusion, are for neither America nor Russia, but for Europe.)

British edition: *Big Two; Life in America and Russia* (London, Jonathan Cape, 1962).

167. Kalb, Marvin L.   Eastern Exposure. New York, Farrar, Straus and Cudahy, 1958. 332 p.

Extracts from the journal of 13 months spent by a Harvard graduate researching in Moscow into the life and work of a nineteenth-century educationist. Kalb was resident during the period of the first exposure of Stalin in 1956, regards Communism skeptically, as "a period of transition," and reports from firsthand on the Russian desire for peace and on the efficiency, on the whole, of the Soviet economic and educational systems.

168.* Levine, Irving R.   Main Street, USSR. Garden City, N.Y., Doubleday, 1959. 408 p. Illus.

The author was correspondent in Moscow for the National Broadcasting Company for about 10 years from 1948, also contributing frequently to the London *Times*. His book covers nearly every aspect of everyday Soviet life in a combination of personal impression and official information, and opens with the refreshing reminder that "Russians change no easier than other peoples."

169. Liberman, Simon I.   Building Lenin's Russia. Chicago, University of Chicago Press, 1945. 228 p.

Liberman, a Menshevik businessman with much experience in the timber industry, served the Bolsheviks as manager of their timber trade from 1918 until 1926, when he was expelled as a non-Communist. His book includes information of rare interest about the early Soviet period, and he writes optimistically of the Soviet future in spite of his hatred of dictatorship.

170. Littlepage, John D., *and* Demaree Bess.   In Search of Soviet Gold. New York, Harcourt, Brace, 1938. 310 p.

See also entry no. 1105.

Littlepage worked on contract as an engineer in the gold mines of Siberia from 1928 to 1937. His indictment of inefficiency, ignorance, and tyranny is the more telling in that he speaks almost entirely from the point of view of his profession, "immune from artificial pro- or anti-Communist terminology," "speaking the language of an American producer."

171. Lyons, Eugene.   Moscow Carrousel. New York, A. A. Knopf, 1935. 357 p.

> Lyons writes with understanding of the enthusiasms, tyranny, disorder, and ignorance of the years 1928-1934, when he was United Press correspondent in Moscow. Nearly all of his book concerns Moscow, where "one lives intensely."

> British edition: *Modern Moscow* (London, Hurst and Blackett, 1935, 286 p.)

172. Makarenko, Anton S.   The Road to Life; an Epic of Education. Moscow, Foreign Languages Publishing House, 1955. 3 v.

See also entry no. 1750.

> The story of a delinquent colony in early Soviet days. Makarenko was its leader, and few books illustrate better the broad humanity of which Russians, in spite of all restrictions, are capable. Makarenko's teachings are today recommended throughout Soviet education. Translation of *Pedagogicheskaia poema* (Moscow, "Khudozhestvennaia literatura," 1935-1937, 3 v. in 2).

173.*Mehnert, Klaus.   Soviet Man and His World. Translated from the German by Maurice Rosenbaum. New York, Praeger, 1962. 310 p.

See also entry no. 1165.

> The author, of German parentage but born in Moscow, lived in Russia from 1906 to 1914, and paid 13 visits, totaling about six years, between 1929 and 1959. Covers national character, home life, prosperity, education, the press, industry and the state, Soviet man and his world — rather thin in places, but sound. Translation of *Der Sowjetmensch* (Stuttgart, Deutsche Verlags-Anstalt, 1958).

174. Novak, Joseph (*pseud.*)   "The Future Is Ours, Comrade!": Conversations with the Russians. Introduction by Irving R. Levine. Garden City, N.Y., Doubleday, 1960. 286 p.

See also entry no. 1180.

> A citizen of one of the satellite countries describes, under an ironic title, the most depressing features of contemporary Russia. Traveling more widely in the USSR than Western visitors, he provides important evidence from his meetings with those who support or tolerate the regime, though he lacks the background to put these into perspective.

175. Ostrovskii, Nikolai A.   The Making of a Hero. Translated by Alec Brown. New York, Dutton, 1937. 440 p.

> The classic novel about the Civil War by a young Communist workingman who took part in it, helped in the early stages of the Soviet regime, and only later found a talent for writing. Translation of *Kak zakalialas' stal'* (Moscow, Molodaia gvardiia, 1932-1934, 2 v.)

Another edition: *How the Steel Was Tempered*, translated by R
Prokofieva (Moscow, Foreign Languages Publishing House, 1952
2 v.)

176.*Pasternak, Boris L.   Doctor Zhivago. Translated from the Russian
by Max Hayward and Manya Harari. London, Collins and Harvill
Press, 1958. 510 p.
See also entry no. 1514.
> This poetic novel conveys an irresistible impression of Russian
> sensibility, Russian humanity, and country life, but lacks any reflec-
> tion of the enthusiasms which helped to build modern industrial
> Russia. *Dr. Zhivago* has not been published in Russia but appears to
> have been read by a number of the intelligentsia. American edition:
> New York, Pantheon Books, 1958, 558 p.

177. Prishvin, Mikhail M.   The Lake and the Woods, or Nature's Calendar. Translated by W. L. Goodman. New York, Pantheon Books,
1952. 258 p.
> Prishvin is a writer of distinction whose subjects are always nature,
> country life, or hunting. Translation of *Kalendar' prirody*, published
> in 1925.

178. Rama Rau, Santha.   My Russian Journey. New York, Harper, 1959.
300 p.
> An Indian writer, the wife of Faubion Bowers, writes an objective
> account of her three months' residence in Moscow with her husband
> and small boy, moving mostly in cultured and artistic circles.

179. Reswick, William.   I Dreamt Revolution. Chicago, H. Regnery,
1952. 328 p.
> The author, a Russian-born American, was Associated Press cor-
> respondent in Moscow during the "purge" years, and a trusted friend
> of Rykov, Bukharin, Chicherin, Yagoda, and other leaders who
> were executed. He tells from firsthand knowledge how Stalin de-
> stroyed the opposition, whom he labeled "the Right."

180. Salisbury, Harrison E.   American in Russia. New York, Harper,
1955. 328 p.
> As New York *Times* correspondent in Russia during the difficult
> years 1949-1954, Salisbury writes with objectivity and good judg-
> ment, avoiding guesswork. His book includes some good character
> sketches of Soviet leaders. Published in a British edition (London,
> Macmillan, 1955) as *Stalin's Russia and After*.
> For one of the liveliest and most penetrating, if slightly optimistic,
> of the books on post-Stalin Russia, *see also* Salisbury's *To Moscow
> — and Beyond* (New York, Harper, 1960, 301 p.). The author spent
> the better part of a year in the USSR in 1959, visiting Siberia twice,
> meeting Soviet leaders, and also accompanying Mr. Khrushchev
> and Mr. Mikoyan on their tours of the United States. The sketch
> of Mr. Khrushchev's life and character and the account of the con-
> troversy over *Dr. Zhivago* are impressive and original. The author

visited Mongolia and has some speculations on the possibilities of Sino-Russian conflict.

181. Scott, John.   Behind the Urals; an American Worker in Russia's City of Steel. Boston, Houghton Mifflin, 1942. 279 p.
See also entry no. 1200.

    The author is an American welder who, failing to find work at home, spent the years 1932-1937 in Magnitogorsk. He is unusual in seeing the hardships and low standards as essentially inevitable in the circumstances, but he does not shirk unpleasant features, and his firsthand judgments on such matters as "wrecking" are valuable. He wrote his book in 1942, "to show how it is the Russians resist so well."

182. Sholokhov, Mikhail A.   Virgin Soil Upturned. v. 1: Seeds of Tomorrow. Translated by Stephen Garry. New York, Knopf, 1959. 404 p.
—— Virgin Soil Upturned. v. 2: Harvest on the Don. Translated by H. C. Stevens. New York, Knopf, 1961. 367 p.
See also entry no. 1521.

    A large, untidy novel which conveys better than anything else the turmoil and robust life of a Don Cossack village through the collectivization of the First Five-Year Plan.

    Translations of volumes one and two of *Podniataia tselina*, first published in 1935.

183. Steinbeck, John.   A Russian Journal; with Pictures by Robert Capa. New York, Viking Press, 1948. 220 p.

    Books of personal impressions in the immediate postwar years are very few, and Steinbeck's is of much interest for the honesty and accuracy of its observation. The author says of his book that "it will not be satisfactory either to the ecclesiastical Left nor the lumpen Right. . . . It is superficial, and how could it be otherwise? . . . We have no conclusions to draw except that Russian people are like all other people in the world."

184. Stevens, Leslie C.   Life in Russia. New York, London, Longmans, Green, 1954. 403 p.

    Vice-Admiral Stevens was United States Naval Attaché in Moscow from 1947 to 1949. His long and well-written book contains a mass of interesting fact and personal experience, with very little speculation, and reveals an author who clearly loved Russia and the Russian people in spite of the frustrations he continually met.

    An earlier edition: *Russian Assignment* (Boston, Little, Brown, 1953, 568 p.)

185. U. S. *Dept. of State. Library Division.*   American Correspondents and Journalists in Moscow, 1917-1952; a Bibliography of Their Books on the USSR. Washington, 1953. 52 l. (*Its* Bibliography no. 73)

    A selective listing of 695 books by 190 journalists and other observers of the Soviet scene. Authors' dates of residence in the USSR are given.

186. Van der Post, Laurens.   Journey into Russia. New York, Morrow; London, Hogarth, 1964. 307 p. Map.

> A gifted South African writer, familiar with many African peoples and with the Japanese, brings an original mind and sensibility to his three months' journey through Russia, Siberia, and the Soviet East. This book seems likely to become one of the classic works on the Russian people, through its author's great powers of sympathy and empathy, in spite of the fact that he spoke little Russian.
> *See also* his *A View of All the Russias* (entry no. 84).

187. Werth, Alexander.   The Khrushchev Phase; the Soviet Union Enters the "Decisive" Sixties. London, Robert Hale, 1961. 284 p.

> The best and most solid of this Russian-born correspondent's books on Russia at various periods. He chooses to say "phase" rather than "epoch" in order to indicate the state of flux and transition which he describes. He reports conversations more intimate than those of almost any correspondent, paints a somewhat unusual picture of Khrushchev on the strength of his speeches in Siberia, and has valuable chapters on music, literature, and the Jewish question.

188. Williams, Albert R.   The Russian Land. New York, New Republic, 1927. 293 p.

> A romantic writer with little sense of the injustices of the Soviet regime, Williams paints vivid pictures of life "among real Russians" in out-of-the-way villages, and adds a warmly appreciative preface by the peasant Yarkov, who was writing, of course, before the collectivization.

189.* Zoshchenko, Mikhail M.   Scenes from the Bathhouse, and Other Stories of Communist Russia. Translated with an introduction by Sidney Monas. Stories selected by Marc Slonim. Ann Arbor, University of Michigan Press, 1961. 245 p.
See also entry no. 1532.

> The artless humor and sophisticated naïveté of this Soviet writer illustrate a traditional and important aspect of Russian character. Other similar editions are available.

III

the land[1]

by Chauncy D. Harris

A. GENERAL REFERENCE AIDS

190. U. S. *Library of Congress. Reference Department.* Soviet Geography; a Bibliography. Edited by Nicholas R. Rodionoff. Washington, 1951. 2 v.

> Extensive bibliography of Soviet geography up to 1950, covering geography as a science, general geography, exploration, historical geography, physical geography, economic geography, political and military geography, atlases and cartography, bibliography and bio-bibliography, and the individual regions of the Soviet Union in 4,421 entries. Holdings and call numbers of the Library of Congress and known holdings of other American libraries are indicated. Indexes for authors and subjects.

191. Soviet Geography; Accomplishments and Tasks. A Symposium of 50 Chapters, Contributed by 56 Leading Soviet Geographers and Edited by a Committee of the Geographic Society of the USSR, Academy of Sciences of the USSR, Innokenti P. Gerasimov, Chairman. Translated from the Russian by Lawrence Ecker. English edition edited by Chauncy D. Harris. New York, American Geographical Society, 1962. 409 p. Maps, diags., bibliographies at ends of chapters, appendix of serials cited.

> An inventory and appraisal of modern scholarly work in the geographical sciences in the Soviet Union. It briefly traces the rise and development of Russian geography and then examines in considerable detail each of the major fields of Soviet geography, some of the principal problems on which geographers work, the methods of geographical research, and the teaching of and dissemination of

[1] Arrangement is by order of emphasis.

46

knowledge about geography. Translation of *Sovetskaia geografiia; itogi i zadachi* (Moscow, Geografgiz, 1960, 634 p.)

192. American Geographical Society of New York. Research Catalogue. Boston, G. K. Hall, 1962. 15 v.

A major research bibliography including books, periodical articles, monographs, and documents in all forms of publication and in all languages, mainly since 1923. Contains about 7,000 entries for the Soviet Union, under the following headings:
The USSR as a Whole, v. 9, p. 6608-6687.
USSR with Other Countries, v. 9, p. 6605-6608.
European USSR, v. 9, p. 6687-6803.
Estonia, Latvia, v. 9, p. 6569-6589.
Lithuania, v. 10, p. 6813-6819.
Soviet Middle Asia, v. 12, p. 8697-8745.
Siberia and the Soviet Far East, v. 12, p. 8749-8820.
USSR with Other Asiatic Countries, v. 12, p. 8745-8749.

193. Bibliographie géographique internationale. Paris, Association de géographes français. v. 1– 1891– annual. Index.

Each annual volume of this great geographic bibliography has a section devoted to works on the Soviet Union.

194. Geographisches Jahrbuch. Gotha.

Schultz, Arved. "Europäisches Russland (1929-1936)." v. 52, 1937, p. 75-248.
Leimbach, Werner. "Nordasien, Westturkistan und Innerasien (1926-1937)." v. 53, 1938, no. 2: 437-565; v. 54, 1939, no. 1: 303-352; v. 54, 1939, no. 2: 555-596. Indexes.
Detailed and articulated bibliography with critical comments for the years covered.

195. U. S. *Office of Geography*. U.S.S.R. and Certain Neighboring Areas; Official Standard Names Approved by the United States Board on Geographic Names. Washington, U. S. Government Printing Office, 1951. 7 v. (U. S. Board on Geographic Names. Gazetteer no. 42)
See also entry no. 69.

Lists latitude and longitude for 350,000 places in the Soviet Union.

196. The Columbia Lippincott Gazetteer of the World. Edited by Leon E. Seltzer with the geographic research staff of Columbia University Press and with the co-operation of the American Geographical Society. New York, Columbia University Press, 1962. 2,148 p.

The best Western gazetteer for information on places in the Soviet Union. Earlier printing: 1952.

197. Meckelein, Wolfgang. Ortsumbenennungen und -neugründungen im europäischen Teil der Sowjetunion; nach dem Stand der Jahre 1910/1938/1951 mit einem Nachtrag für Ostpreussen 1953. Berlin, Duncker und Humblot, 1955. 134 p. Bibliography, index, folded map

in pocket. (Osteuropa-Institut an der Freien Universität Berlin. Wirtschaftswissenschaftliche Veröffentlichungen, Band 2)

An analysis and listing of 1,363 name changes and newly founded places in the European part of the Soviet Union between 1910 and 1951, with listing of names as of 1910, 1938, and 1951.

198. Harris, Chauncy D., *and* Jerome D. Fellmann.   International List of Geographical Serials. Chicago, 1960. 189 p. (University of Chicago, Department of Geography. Research Paper no. 63)

A listing of all known Russian and Soviet geographical periodicals and non-periodical serials is on pages 109-134.

199. Soviet Geography; Review and Translation. v. 1– 1960– New York, American Geographical Society. monthly, except July and August.

English translations of selected significant articles from Soviet geographical periodicals and serials, and news notes.

200. Petermanns geographische Mitteilungen. v. 1– 1855– Gotha. quarterly.

Since 1953 this leading German geographical periodical has included a special section devoted to Soviet geography.

B. ATLASES

201. The Economist (London).   The U.S.S.R. and Eastern Europe. Prepared by the Economist Intelligence Unit and the Cartographic Department of the Clarendon Press. London, Oxford University Press, 1956. 134 p. Colored maps, text, tables, bibliography, index. (Oxford Regional Economic Atlases)

Primarily a topical atlas covering physical geography, agriculture, minerals, manufacturing, and human geography for the Soviet Union as a whole, but with a number of regional reference maps. Particularly valuable as a reference atlas for economic geography. Also available as a paperback.

202. Soviet Union in Maps.   Edited by Harold Fullard. London, G. Philip; Chicago, Denoyer-Geppert, 1961. 32 p. Colored maps and text.

Inexpensive paperbound atlas covering historical, physical, economic, and regional geography. Suitable for general student use.

203. Kish, George, *with the assistance of* Ian M. Matley *and* Betty Bellaire. Economic Atlas of the Soviet Union. Ann Arbor, University of Michigan Press, 1960. 96 p. Bibliography, index.

A regional atlas with four maps (agriculture and land use; mining and minerals; industry; transportation and cities) for each of 15 regions and five general maps for the country as a whole, with accompanying text. Useful mainly for regional geography.

C. GENERAL GEOGRAPHY

204.* Cressey, George B.   Soviet Potentials; a Geographic Appraisal. Syracuse, N.Y., Syracuse University Press, 1962. 232 p. Illus., maps, tables, bibliography, index.

A readable and stimulating introduction to the resources, peoples, economy, and regions.

205. Jorré, Georges.   The Soviet Union; the Land and Its People. 2d ed. Translated from the French and revised by E. D. Laborde. London, Longmans; New York, Wiley, 1961. 372 p. Illus., maps, index.

A general geography, covering physical, historical, economic, and regional geography.

206. Lydolph, Paul E.   Geography of the U.S.S.R. New York, Wiley, 1964. 451 p. Illus., maps, tables, reading lists, index.

A combination of a general regional geography and a systematic economic geography for the country as a whole.

207. Shabad, Theodore.   The Soviet Union. *In* George W. Hoffman, *ed.* A Geography of Europe, Including Asiatic U.S.S.R. 2d ed. New York, Ronald Press, 1961. p. 638-728.

A succinct summary of the geography of the Soviet Union.

208. George, Pierre.   L'U.R.S.S. 2d ed. Paris, Presses Universitaires de France, 1962. 497 p. Illus., maps, tables, bibliography.

Systematic physical and economic geography of the country as a whole with rich detail and numerous interesting discussions.

209. Leimbach, Werner.   Die Sowjetunion; Natur, Volk und Wirtschaft. Stuttgart, Franckh, 1950. 526 p. Illus., maps, tables, bibliography, index.

Physical, cultural, and economic geography of the country as a whole. Rich detail.

210. Gregory, James S., *and* D. W. Shave.   The U.S.S.R.; a Geographical Survey. London, Harrap, 1944; New York, Wiley, 1946. 636 p. Maps, tables, bibliography, index.

The first geography of the Soviet Union written in England, now somewhat dated, but still valuable as a reference, especially for the regional geography.

211. Gray, G. D. B.   Soviet Land; the Country, Its People, and Their Work. London, A. and C. Black, 1947. 324 p. Illus., maps, bibliography, index.

An introductory account of the physical features, peoples, and economy, now somewhat dated.

212. Cressey, George B.   The Basis of Soviet Strength. New York, McGraw-Hill, 1945. 287 p. Illus., maps, bibliography, index.

The first geography of the Soviet Union to be written by an American geographer and therefore of historical interest. Now largely superseded by the author's *Soviet Potentials* (*see* entry no. 204).

213. Cressey, George B.   How Strong Is Russia? A Geographic Appraisal. Syracuse, N.Y., Syracuse University Press, 1954. 146 p. Illus., maps, bibliography, index.
    A brief popular introduction.

D. PHYSICAL GEOGRAPHY (INCLUDING MINERALS)

214. Berg, Lev S.   Natural Regions of the USSR. Translated from the Russian by Olga Adler Titelbaum. Edited by John A. Morrison and C. C. Nikiforoff. New York, Macmillan, 1950. 436 p. Illus., tables, maps, bibliography, glossary, indexes of plants, animals, places. (American Council of Learned Societies. Russian Translation Project. Series 6)
    A one-volume, authoritative, university textbook surveying the climate, relief, vegetation, and fauna of the landscape (vegetation) zones.
    Translation of *Priroda SSSR*, 2d ed. (Moscow, Uchpedgiz, 1938, 311 p.)

215. Mirov, Nicholas T.   Geography of Russia. New York, Wiley, 1951. 362 p. Maps, index.
    A physical geography by vegetation zones, shorter than Berg's (*see* entry no. 214), and designed specifically for American readers.

216. Suslov, Sergei P.   Physical Geography of Asiatic Russia. Translated from the Russian by Noah D. Gershevsky and edited by Joseph E. Williams. San Francisco, W. H. Freeman, 1961. 594 p. Photographs, maps, bibliography, index to plants, animals, and places.
    Scholarly and detailed description of the physical geography of the Asiatic part of the Soviet Union, covering relief, climate, permafrost, geology, hydrography, soils, vegetation, and fauna, by regional subdivisions.
    Translation of *Fizicheskaia geografiia SSSR; aziatskaia chast'* (Moscow, Uchpedgiz, 1st ed., 1947, 543 p.; 2d ed., 1954, 710 p.)

217. Berg, Lev (Leo) S.   Die geographische Zonen der Sowjetunion. Leipzig, B. G. Teubner, 1958-1959. 2 v. (v. 1, 1958, 437 p. and 48 plates; v. 2, 1959, 604 p. and 52 plates). Illus., maps, tables, bibliographies at end of each chapter, indexes of subjects, places, plants, and animals.
    A detailed and authoritative synthesis of the physical geography of the main landscape zones of the Soviet Union: the tundra, coniferous forests, mixed forests, broadleaf forests of the Far East, and the forest steppe, in volume one; and the steppe, half desert, desert, subtropical, and mountain zones, in volume two. Translation of *Geograficheskie zony Sovetskogo Soiuza* (Moscow, Geografgiz, v. 1, 3d ed., 1947, 397 p.; v. 2, 1952, 510 p.)

218. Hodgkins, Jordan A.   Soviet Power; Energy Resources, Production, and Potentials. Englewood Cliffs, N. J., Prentice-Hall, 1961. 190 p. Tables, maps, bibliographical footnotes.
    Distribution of the reserves, production, and consumption of coal, oil shale, petroleum, and natural gas. Valuable reference.

219. Hassmann, Heinrich.   Oil in the Soviet Union; History, Geography, Problems. Translated from the German with the addition of much new information by Alfred M. Leeston. Princeton, Princeton University Press, 1953. 173 p.
    Detailed examination of the development, regions, and problems of Soviet petroleum resources and their utilization.
    Original title: *Erdöl in der Sowjetunion: Geschichte, Gebiete, Probleme* (Hamburg, 1951, 176 p.)
    For a more recent treatment, *see* Alexander Mirtsching, *Erdöl- und Gaslagerstätten der Sowjetunion und ihre geologische Bedeutung* (Stuttgart, 1964, 195 p.)

220. Kazakov, George.   Soviet Peat Resources; a Descriptive Study. New York, Research Program on the USSR, 1953. 201 p. Tables, maps, bibliography, index.
    Detailed survey of peat reserves.

E. ECONOMIC GEOGRAPHY [2]

221. Cole, John P., *and* F. C. German.   A Geography of the USSR; the Background to a Planned Economy. London, Butterworth, 1961. 290 p. Maps, tables, bibliography, index.
    Up-to-date survey of branches of the economy and the economic planning regions at the beginning of the Seven-Year Plan (1959-1965). Solid and objective.

222. Zimm, Alfred.   Industriegeographie der Sowjetunion. Berlin, VEB Deutscher Verlag der Wissenschaften, 1963. 226 p. Illus., maps, tables, bibliography.
    A systematic survey of the economic geography of the coal, oil, gas, electric power, iron, machine, chemical, light, and food industries.

223. Bal'zak, S. S., Vasilii F. Vasiutin, *and* Iakov G. Feigin, *eds.*   Economic Geography of the USSR. American edition edited by Chauncy D. Harris. Translated from the Russian by Robert M. Hankin and Olga Adler Titelbaum. New York, Macmillan, 1949. 620 p. 84 maps, statistical appendixes, indexes to citations and of persons, plants and animals, and place names. (American Council of Learned Societies. Russian Translation Project. Series 3)
    Although out of date in various respects and doctrinaire and tendentious in places, this is still in some ways the best general systematic survey of the economic geography of the USSR. Excels in

[2] *See also* Chapter VIII, A.

the large number of maps and the discussions of actual distribution of branches of the economy. Reflects viewpoints and programs of the Third Five-Year Plan.

Translation of *Ekonomicheskaia geografiia SSSR*, v. 1 (Moscow, Sotsekgiz, 1940, 406 p.)

224. Baranskii, Nikolai N.   Economic Geography of the U.S.S.R. Moscow, Foreign Languages Publishing House, 1956. 412 p. Illus., maps.

An economic geography, primarily regional, for many years (until 1957) the basic textbook used in high schools in the Soviet Union.

Translation of *Ekonomicheskaia geografiia SSSR* (Moscow, Uchpedgiz, 1955, 391 p.)

225. Saushkin, Iulian (Y.) G.   Economic Geography of the Soviet Union. Oslo, Norway, Oslo University Press, 1956. 148 p. Mimeographed.

Eight lectures, March–April 1956, at the Department of Geography, University of Oslo, on selected topics of economic geography — resources, population, productive forces, agricultural and economic regions — by the Head of the Department of Economic Geography of the USSR, Moscow State University.

226. Mikhailov (Mikhaylov), Nikolai N.   Soviet Geography; the New Industrial and Economic Distributions of the U.S.S.R. London, Methuen, 1935. 232 p. Maps, tables, index.

The first account of the geography of the Soviet Union by a Soviet citizen to appear in English, and therefore something of a sensation at the time of its publication. Now dated. Transformation of the economy of the country as a whole under Soviet planning.

227. Mikhailov, Nikolai (Nicholas) N.   Land of the Soviets; a Handbook of the U.S.S.R. Translated from the Russian by Nathalie Rothstein. New York, Lee Furman, 1939. 351 p.

A regional economic geography of the Soviet Union on the eve of the Second World War.

228. Mikhailov, Nikolai (Nicholas) N., *in collaboration with* Vadim V. Pokshishevskii (Pokshishevsky).   Soviet Russia; the Land and Its People. Translated from the Russian by George H. Hanna. New York, Sheridan House, 1948. 374 p. Illus., index.

Highlights of the geography of the Soviet Union shown by a series of journeys on a map.

229. Mikhailov, Nikolai N.   Glimpses of the U.S.S.R.; Its Economy and Geography. Moscow, Foreign Languages Publishing House, 1960. 196 p. Illus.

Popular account of resources, economy, regions.

F. REGIONS

230. Shabad, Theodore.   Geography of the USSR; a Regional Survey. New York, Columbia University Press, 1951. 584 p. Maps, tables, bibliography, index.

A detailed regional survey by republics and *oblasts*. Valuable as a reference work.

231. Camena d'Almeida, Pierre J. États de la Baltique; Russie. Paris, Colin, 1932. 355 p. Illus., maps, bibliographies at the end of each chapter, index. (Géographie Universelle, edited by P. Vidal de la Blache and L. Gallois, v. 5)

A classic French geography with excellent regional descriptions, but badly outdated on all aspects of economic geography.

232. Handbuch der geographischen Wissenschaft. Edited by Fritz Klute. Potsdam, Athenaion. Illus., maps, bibliography, index.

Friedrichsen, Max. "Das europäische Russland." v. 4 (*Mitteleuropa ausser Deutsches Reich; Osteuropa in Natur, Kultur und Wirtschaft* [1933]), p. 321-434.

Plaetschke, Bruno. "Kaukasusländer." *Ibid.*, p. 435-464.

Anger, Helmut. "Sibirien." v. 9 (*Nordasien, Zentral- und Ostasien in Natur, Kultur und Wirtschaft* [1937]), p. 125-210.

Schultz, Arved. "Russisch-Turkestan." *Ibid.*, p. 211-244.

Lavishly-illustrated, solid regional geography.

233. Thiel, Erich. The Soviet Far East; a Survey of Its Physical and Economic Geography. Translated from the German by Annelie and Ralph M. Rookwood. New York, Praeger, 1957. 388 p. Tables, maps, bibliography, index.

Detailed scholarly account of the physical background, population, economy, and regions of the Soviet Far East and of southeastern Siberia east of Lake Baikal.

Translation of *Sowjet-Fernost: eine landes- und wirtschaftskundliche Übersicht* (Munich, Isar Verlag, 1953, 329 p.)

234. Taaffe, Robert N. Rail Transportation and the Economic Development of Soviet Central Asia. Chicago, 1960. 186 p. Illus., tables, maps, bibliography. (University of Chicago, Department of Geography. Research Paper no. 64)

Development of the rail pattern and its role in the rise of interregional trade between Middle Asia and the rest of the Soviet Union.

235.* Jackson, William A. D. The Russo-Chinese Borderlands; Zone of Peaceful Contact or Potential Conflict? Princeton, N. J., Van Nostrand, 1962. 126 p. Maps, tables, bibliography, index.

A political geography of the boundary with China.

G. EXPLORATION (INCLUDING THE NORTHERN SEA ROUTE)

236. Berg, Lev S. Geschichte der russischen geographischen Entdeckungen; gesammelte Aufsätze. Leipzig, Bibliographisches Institut, 1954. 283 p. Illus., maps, bibliography, index.

A general overview of Russian geographical exploration and research.

Translation of *Ocherki po istorii russkikh geograficheskikh otkry-tii*, 2d ed. (Moscow, Izd-vo Akademii nauk SSSR, 1949, 465 p.)

237. Armstrong, Terence E.   The Russians in the Arctic; Aspects of Soviet Exploration and Exploitation of the Far North, 1937-1957. London, Methuen, 1958. 182 p. Illus., maps, bibliography, index.
      Account of exploration and research expeditions, with chapters on the peoples of the Arctic and on archeology.

238. Armstrong, Terence E.   The Northern Sea Route; Soviet Exploitation of the North East Passage. Cambridge, England, The University Press (for the Scott Polar Research Institute), 1952. 162 p.
      Appraisal of the development of the Northern Sea Route from 1933 to 1949, including its characteristics, traffic, and administration.

IV

the people
ethnic and
demographic
features

A. ETHNOLOGY

by Lawrence Krader

1. Bibliographies, Encyclopedia Articles, Journals

239. Arctic Institute of North America. Arctic Bibliography. Prepared for and in co-operation with the Department of Defense under the direction of the Arctic Institute of North America. Washington, 1953– Indexes, v. 3– Maps.

> Ethnographic references *passim*. Latest published, volume 11, 1963.

240. COWA Bibliography. Current Publications in Old World Archaeology. Area 18. Northern Asia. Edited by Chester S. Chard. Cambridge, Council for Old World Archaeology.

> Bibliography of archeological sources. Editor is American specialist in Siberian archeology. Published so far: number one (1957) and number two (1960).

241. Central Asian Review. Edited by Geoffrey Wheeler. London Central Asian Research Centre, in association with St. Antony's College, Oxford. 1953– quarterly.
See also entry no. 1684.

Journal devoted primarily to current political, social, religious, national, and economic developments in Soviet Central Asia, Kazakhstan, and Azerbaijan. Questions of religious (Islamic), ethnic, and national minorities policies in the area *passim*. Soviet sources are directly, critically applied.

See also Stefan A. Wurm, *Turkic Peoples of the USSR* (London, Central Asian Research Centre, 1954, 51 p.), and *The Turkic Languages of Central Asia: Problems of Planned Culture Contact* (London, Central Asian Research Centre, 1952, 52 p.), a translation of an article entitled "Razvitie iazykov i pis'mennosti narodov SSSR," by Nikolai A. Baskakov in *Voprosy iazykoznaniia*, no. 3, May–June 1952: 19-44, with commentary by Stefan Wurm.

See also G. E. Wheeler, *Racial Problems in Soviet Muslim Asia* (London, New York, Oxford University Press, 1962, 67 p.), a brief historical and political survey of Central Asia and Azerbaijan by a British specialist.

242. Encyclopaedia Britannica. Chicago, London, Toronto. 1963–
Krader, L. Altaic Peoples, v. 1, p. 683-684; Asia. General Ethnology, v. 2, p. 587-594; Buryat, v. 4, p. 464-465; Chukchi, v. 5, p. 736; Circassians, v. 5, p. 780-781; Kalmuck, v. 13, p. 246; Ostyak, v. 16, p. 958; Tunguses, v. 22, p. 550.
Krader, L. Biographical notices of Russian ethnographers: W. Bogoraz, v. 3, p. 845; L. Sternberg, v. 21, p. 399.
Wheeler, G. E. Tatars, v. 21, p. 833.

243. Encyclopaedia of Islam. Edited by A. J. Wensinck, J. H. Kramers, and others. 1st ed. Leiden, E. J. Brill, 1913-1938. 4 v. and supplement.
Matters of ethnographic interest:
Barthold, W. (Bartol'd, Vasilii V.). Daghestan: v. 1, p. 887–892; Karakalpaks: v. 2, p. 736-737; Kazakhs: v. 2, p. 836; Kirgiz: v. 2, p. 1025-1026; Sarts: v. 4, p. 175-176; Tadjiks: v. 4, p. 598-599; Tartars: v. 4, p. 700-702; Turkistan: v. 4, p. 895-896; Turkmens (Turkomans): v. 4, p. 896-897; Turks (history and ethnography): v. 4, p. 900-908.
Minorsky, V. Kurdistan, Kurds: v. 2, p. 1130-1155; Tats: v. 4, p. 697-700.
Streck, M. Armenia: v. 1, p. 435-449.
Contributions by Barthold to ethnography and ethnic history of Islamic peoples of Russia and Russian Asia not otherwise available in English.

244. Encyclopedia of Religion and Ethics. Edited by James Hastings. New York, Charles Scribner's Sons, 1908-1926. 13 v. Index.
Batchelor, J. Ainus: v. 1, p. 239-252.
Chamberlain, A. F. Aleuts: v. 1, p. 303-305.
Czaplicka, Marie A. Ostyaks: v. 5, p. 575-581; Samoyeds: v. 11, p. 172-177; Siberians: v. 11, p. 488-496; Slavs: v. 11, p. 586-595; Tungus: v. 12, p. 476-483; Yakuts: v. 12, p. 826-829.
Klementz, Demetrius. Buryats: v. 3, p. 1-17; Gilyaks: v. 6, p. 221-226.

Radin, P., *and* L. H. Gray.   Eskimos: v. 5, p. 391-395.

Sayce, A. H., M. H. Ananikian, *and* F. Macler.   Armenia: v. 1, p. 793-807.

Contributions by Czaplicka and Klementz to Siberian ethnography outstanding for materials in English relating to the pre-1917 period.

245. Eurasia Septentrionalis Antiqua; bulletin et mémoires consacrés à l'archéologie et l'ethnographie de l'Europe orientale et de l'Asie du Nord.   Edited by U. T. Sirelius, A. M. Tallgren, and others. Helsinki, Archeological Society of Finland, 1926 (1927)-1939. 13 v.

Contributions in English, French, and German.

246. Jakobson, Roman, G. Hüttl-Worth, *and* J. F. Beebe.   Paleosiberian Peoples and Languages; a Bibliographic Guide. New Haven, HRAF Press, 1957. 222 p.

Bibliographic coverage: ethnography and linguistics of Chukchi, Kamchadal, Koryak, Yukagir, Gilyak, Ket, Kot, Arin, and Asan, and of Siberian ethnology and linguistics generally. Published works, archival sources, unpublished materials. Appendix sketch of peoples and languages.

247. Kerner, Robert J.   Northeastern Asia, a Selected Bibliography; Contributions to the Bibliography of the Relations of China, Russia, and Japan, with Special Reference to Korea, Manchuria, Mongolia, and Eastern Siberia, in Oriental and European Languages. Berkeley, University of California Press, 1939. 2 v.

Ethnographic materials *passim.*

248. Royal Central Asian Society.   Journal. 1914– London. quarterly.

Cultural, geographical, political, topical coverage of Central Asia and neighboring areas.

2. General Works

249. Beiträge zur Kenntniss des russischen Reiches und der angränzenden Länder Asiens.   Edited by Karl E. von Baer and G. V. Helmersen. St. Petersburg, Kaiserliche Akademie der Wissenschaften, 1839-1871. 26 v. Maps.

Fundamental publication of primary and translated materials. Contributions made in German or translated into German, except as noted. Issued by Russian Academy of Sciences. Natural history and ethnography of Russian Empire covered. Matters of ethnographic interest:

Volume 1: Wrangell, Ethnography of Alaska.

Volume 2: G. V. Helmersen, Notices on Khiva, Bukhara, Kokand.

Volume 3: J. de Hagemeister, Economy and trade of West Asia, Turkestan, Afghanistan, etc. (in French).

Volume 5/6: Helmersen, Urals and North Kazakhstan in 1833 and 1835.

Volume 7: W. F. Dahl, Notes on Kumis; Siberia; agriculture in

Yakutia; demography of Siberia; hunting in Siberia and Russian Empire; Alexander Schrenck, Kazakhs (1840).

Volume 9, part 1: General ethnography of Russian Empire; bibliography of source materials.

Volume 10: M. Pogodin, Nestor Chronicle; Danilovich, Lithuanian Chronicle. Both translated into German by F. Lowe.

Volume 11: Ethnographic notes: South Russia, Lappland.

Volume 12: E. Hofmann, Siberian goldfields.

Volume 13: P. Köppen, Travels in East and Central Russia (Kazan', Vyatka, Vologda).

Volume 14: Helmersen, Altay journey, 1834.

Volume 17: Alexander Lehmann, Travel to Bukhara and Samarkand in 1841-1842.

Volume 18: Von Baer, Forests of European Russia.

Volume 19: A. Bode, Lumbering in the Russian Empire.

Volume 20: Vlangali's travels in Eastern Kazakhstan.

Volume 22: Antipov, Mining in the Urals.

Volume 24: Gerstfeldt, Russian trade with Western Asia.

250. Bogoraz, Vladimir G. (Waldemar Bogoras). The Folklore of Northeastern Asia as Compared with That of Northwestern America. American Anthropologist (Menasha, Wisc.), n.s., v. 4, 1902: 577-683.

> See also his "Ideas of Space and Time in the Conception of Primitive Religion." Ibid., v. 27, 1925: 205-266. Studies of Siberian and North American folklore and religion by Russian ethnologist, revolutionary exile, poet, and educator.

251. Buschan, Georg, ed. Illustrierte Völkerkunde. v. 2, pts. 1-2. Stuttgart, Strecker und Schröder, 1923-1928. Illus., plates, maps, index. Also published separately, Berlin, n.d.

> General ethnography of peoples of Europe and Russian Asia. Arranged by peoples and by topics. Part of world ethnographic survey. Relevant items:

> Part one: Arthur Byhan, North Asia, Central Asia, Geographic introduction, p. 273-276; North Asia, p. 276-341; Central (Middle) Asia, p. 341-376.

> Part two: Michael Haberlandt, General introduction, p. 1-22; Baltic peoples, p. 23-27; Eastern Slavs, p. 37-40; Great Russians, p. 41-53; Belorussians, p. 53-54; Ukrainians, p. 55-62; Finno-Ugrian and Turkic peoples of Russia and Eastern Europe, introduction, p. 659-661; Finnic peoples, p. 661-677; Turks of East and South Russia, p. 678. General ethnographic coverage.

> Part two: Arthur Haberlandt, data on Russian and East European economy settlement, house utensils and crafts, folk art, social organization, spiritual culture, pages 305-658, passim.

252. Cahiers d'histoire mondiale. Contributions à l'histoire russe. Studies on Russian History. Special publication. Neuchâtel, La Baconnière, 1958. 335 p.

> A collection of papers by Soviet specialists on various aspects of

pre-history, proto-history, and related themes within boundaries of the USSR:

Debetz, G. F. "Palaeoanthropolical Finds on the Territory of the U.S.S.R. (Palaeolithic and Mesolithic)," p. 17-22.

Brioussov, A. I. "Les tribus néolithiques du territoire européen de l'U.R.S.S. et de la Sibérie occidentale," p. 23-43.

Piotrovsky, B. B. "L'étude des antiquités d'Urartu en U.R.S.S.," p. 44-54.

Sakharov, A. M. "Les Mongols et la civilisation russe," p. 77-97.

Khachikyan, L. S. "Mongols in Transcaucasia," p. 98-125.

See also M. E. and V. M. Masson, "Archaeological Cultures of Central Asia of the Aeneolithic and Bronze Age," *Cahiers d'histoire mondiale*, v. 5, 1959, no. 1: 17-40, a survey of archeological investigations by Soviet specialists.

253. Castrén, Matthias A. Nordische Reisen und Forschungen. Edited by Anton Schiefner. St. Petersburg, Buchdr. der Kaislerlichen Akademie der Wissenschaften, 1853-1862. 12 v.

v. 1: Reiseerinnerungen aus den Jahren 1838-1844, 1853, 308 p.

v. 2: Reiseberichte und Briefe aus den Jahren 1845-1849, 1856, 527 p.

v. 3: Vorlesungen über die finnische Mythologie, 1853, 340 p.

v. 4: Ethnologische Vorlesungen über die altaischen Völker nebst samojedischen Märchen und tatarischen Heldensagen, 1857, 257 p.

v. 5: Kleinere Schriften, 1862, 382 p.

v. 6: Versuch einer ostjakischen Sprachlehre, 1858, 125 p.

v. 7: Grammatik der samojedischen Sprachen, 1855, 608 p.

v. 8: Wörterverzeichnisse aus den samojedischen Sprachen, 1855, 404 p.

v. 9: Grundzüge einer tungusischen Sprachlehre, 1856, 139 p.

v. 10: Versuch einer burjatischen Sprachlehre, 1857, 244 p.

v. 11: Versuch einer koibalischen und karagasischen Sprachlehre, nebst Wörterverzeichnissen aus den tatarischen Mundarten des minussinschen Kreises, 1857, 210 p.

v. 12: Versuch einer Jenissei-Ostjakischen und kottischen Sprachlehre, 1858, 264 p. (Ket is designation of Yenisey-Ostyak).

Castrén was a great nineteenth-century Finnish ethnographer and linguist, specializing in Uralic and neighboring peoples of northern Eurasia. Traveled for many years, studying Uralic peoples of Eurasia.

254. Georgi, Johann G. Beschreibung aller Nationen des russischen Reichs, Ihrer Lebensart, Religion, Gebräuche, Kleidungen und übrigen Merkwürdigkeiten. St. Petersburg, C. W. Müller, 1776-1780. 4 pts., 1 v. plates, index.

Compendium of ethnographic coverage by the eighteenth-century academician and traveler, noted both as naturalist and ethnographer. *See also* his *Geographisch-physikalische und naturhistorische Beschreibung des russischen Reichs* (Königsberg, F. Nicolovius, 1797-1802): v. 1; v. 2, pts. 1-3; v. 3, pts. 1-7, for geography, ethnography, demography of Russia organized by political divisions, and related themes and coverage.

255. Manninen, Ilmari.   Die finnisch-ugrischen Völker. Leipzig, Harrassowitz, 1932. 384 p. Illus., maps, plans.

> See also his *Führer durch die ethnographischen Sammlungen* (Tartu, Estonian National Museum, 1928, 154 p.). Both are works by an Estonian ethnographer and museum curator on the language family to which Estonian belongs. The *Führer* focuses on the material culture.

256.*Mongait, Aleksandr L.   Archeology in the U.S.S.R. Translated and adapted by M. W. Thompson. London, Baltimore, Penguin Books, 1961. 320 p. Illus., maps, index.

> Another edition: *Archaeology of the U.S.S.R.*, translated by D. Skvirsky (Moscow, Foreign Languages Publishing House, 1959, 428 p., illus., maps, index). The Penguin edition translates the text of the Russian original but omits some of the indexes. The Moscow edition retains both. Survey of expeditions, excavations, publications, activities of Soviet archeologists. History of Soviet archeology, reference guide, summary of results.

257. Niederle, Lubor.   Manuel de l'antiquité slave. Collection de manuels publiée par l'Institut d'Études Slaves. Paris, E. Champion, 1923-1926. 2 v.

> History of proto-Slavs and formation of separate peoples. Russian social economics, material and spiritual culture in the medieval period, *passim*. By a Czech authority.

258. Pallas, Peter S.   Reise durch verschiedene Provinzen des russischen Reichs. St. Petersburg, Kayserliche Academie der Wissenschaften, 1771-1776. 3 v. in 5.

> Monumental work of exploration by eighteenth-century ethnographer and naturalist. In French as *Voyages dans plusiers provinces de l'empire de Russie et dans l'Asie septentrionale*, translated by C. Gauthier de la Peyronie (Paris, Maradan, 1789-1793, 5 v. text, 1 v. plates).
> See also his *Travels Through the Southern Provinces of the Russian Empire* (entry no. 287).

259. Pauli, Fedor Kh. (T. de).   Description ethnographique des peuples de la Russie. St. Petersburg, F. Bellizard, 1862. 5 pts. in 1 v. Illus., map, statistical table.

> Indo-European peoples: 154 p.; Caucasus: 30 p.; Uralic and Altaic peoples: 78 p.; East Siberian peoples: 13 p.; peoples of Russian America: 15 p. Encyclopedic survey, compendious in coverage. Ethnography, languages, demographic tables. Systematic presentation of materials. Richly illustrated.

260. Radlov, Vasilii V. (Wilhelm Radloff).   Aus Sibirien. Leipzig, T. O. Weigel, 1884. 2 v.

Volume one: Ethnographic travel notes and systematic survey of Western Siberia, Kazakhstan, Altay, Southern Siberia, Dzungaria, Kirgizia; volume two: Shamanism, Siberian antiquities, ethnographic survey of the Ili and Zeravshan valleys. By an outstanding Turkologist, folklorist, linguist, historian. Volumes of travel description and research materials. Second edition: 1893.

261. Riazanovskii (Riasanovsky), Valentin A.   Fundamental Principles of Mongol Law. Tientsin, 1937. 338 p.

Bibliography: p. 327-338.

Buryat, Kalmuk, Khalkha, Mongol imperial medieval law. Sources and records; customary, canonical, public law; institutions, comparative law. Revision of his *Customary Law of the Mongol Tribes* (Harbin, 1929, 3 pts., 306 p.)

See also his *Customary Law of the Nomadic Tribes of Siberia* (Tientsin, 1938, 151 p.): Buryat, Kazakh, Kuznetsk, Tartar, Ostyak (Khant), Samoyed, Tungus, Vogul (Mansi) customary practice in law.

262. Stralenberg (Strahlenberg), Philip J. von.   An Historico-Geographical Description of the Northern and Eastern Parts of Europe and Asia; but More Particularly of Russia, Siberia, and Great Tartary, both in Their Ancient and Modern State, together with an Entire New Polyglot-Table of the Dialects of 32 Tartarian Nations. London, W. Innys and R. Manby, 1738. 463 p. Illus., tables, map.

Translated from the German, *Das nord- und östliche Theil von Europa und Asien, in so weit solches das gantze ruszische Reich mit Siberien und der grossen Tartarey begreiffet, in einer historisch-geographischen Beschreibung der alten und neurern Zeiten, und vieler andern unbekannten Nachrichten, vorgestellet, nach niemals ans Licht gegebenen tabula polyglotta von zwey und dreyssigerley Arten tartarischer Völcker Sprachen und einem Kalmuckischen Vocabulario* (Stockholm, 1730, 438 p., illus., tables, map). By a Swedish war prisoner sent to Siberia; collections of ethnographic and linguistic data systematically drawn up. Yeniseyan materials not later available. Of fundamental importance, both for scope and for rarity of data.

3. European Russia

263. Chuprov, Aleksandr I. (Alexander Tschuprow).   Die Feldgemeinschaft; eine morphologische Untersuchung. Strassburg, Trübner, 1902. 304 p. (Abhandlungen aus dem Staatswissenschaftlichen Seminar zu Strassburg, v. 18)

The rural community in Russia under survey. Social and economic change, peasant institutions. Author was recognized authority on subject.

See also Jan St. Lewinski, *The Origin of Property and the Village Community* (London, 1913), a brief summary of controversy on peasant and land question, policy, economics.

264. Gimbutas, Marija.   The Prehistory of Eastern Europe. Edited by H. Hencken. Cambridge, Peabody Museum, 1956. 241 p. Illus., plates, maps. (Harvard University. American School of Prehistoric Research. Bulletin no. 20)

> Systematic survey of archeological materials. Mesolithic, neolithic, and copper age cultures in Russia and the Baltic area.

265. Haxthausen-Abbenburg, August F. L. M., *Freiherr* von.   The Russian Empire; Its Peoples, Institutions and Resources. Translated from the German by Robert Farie. London, Chapman and Hall, 1856. 2 v. (432, 463 p.)
See also entry no. 128.

> Translated and abridged from *Studien über die innern Zustände, das Volksleben und inbesondere die ländlichen Einrichtungen Russlands* (Hannover, Hahn, 1847-1852, 3 v.). By a specialist in contemporary problems of rural Russia.
> *See also* his *Transcaucasia* (entry no. 281).

266. Köppen, Petr I. (Peter von).   Statistische Reise in's Land der donischen Kosaken durch die Gouvernements Tula, Orel, Woronesh im Jahre 1850. St. Petersburg, Kaiserliche Akademie der Wissenschaften, 1852. 253, 107 p. Map, tables.

> By a nineteenth-century Russian administrator and specialist. Social conditions, economic data. Comparative materials, travel data, library research.

267. Kovalevskii, Maksim M. (Maxime Kovalevsky).   Modern Customs and Ancient Laws of Russia. London, D. Nutt, 1891. 260 p. Index.

> Russian rural family and village. Marriage, family organization, village life and authority. Serfdom in Russia. Oxford lectures, 1889-1890 by Russian cultural historian, ethnographer, political reformer, law specialist.
> *See also* his *Coutume contemporaine et loi ancienne* (entry no. 283), a comparable work on the Ossetians.

268. Le Play, Pierre G. F.   Les ouvriers européens. 2d ed., v. 2. Tours, A. Mame et fils, 1877. 560 p.
See also entry no. 1207.

> A series of studies, based on fieldwork in various parts of the world, relative to life under rural farm, rural industrial, and urban conditions. Family organization and economy, village life, budgets. Five studies of peoples of Russia included in the series "Russian Life Before Reforms of 1860's" (titles translated into English): (1) "Semi-Nomadic Bashkir Pastoralists of Eastern Russia," p. 1-46; (2) "Serfs (Corvée Peasants) of Orenburg, South Urals," p. 47-98; (3) "Smith of Ironworks in the Urals," p. 99-141; (4) "Carpenter of Goldfields of the Urals," p. 142-178; (5) "Freed Peasants (Obrok) of the Oka Basin, Central Russia," p. 179-230.
> See also *Les ouvriers des deux mondes*, second series, v. 1 (Paris, 1877), which has further data of same nature.

269. Masaryk, Tomáš G.   The Spirit of Russia; Studies in History, Literature, and Philosophy. Translated from the German by Eden and Cedar Paul. London, G. Allen and Unwin, 1919. 2 v.
See also entry no. 1596.
> The author was a scholar and the first president of Czechoslovakia. The work is a comprehensive survey of Russian spiritual culture. Significant for exploration of values of Russian culture. Second edition: London, G. Allen and Unwin; New York, Macmillan, 1955.

270.* Maynard, *Sir* John.   Russia in Flux; Before October. London, Victor Gollancz, 1941. 301 p. Index.
See also entries no. 97 and 1164.
> *See also* his *The Russian Peasant, and Other Studies* (London, Victor Gollancz, 1942, 512 p., index). Peasantry in Tsarist and Soviet periods. Life, customs, political movements. Author traveled widely in Russia during both eras; combined personal observation and reading. The two works are interrelated.

271. Meitzen, August.   Siedelung und Agrarwesen der Westgermanen und Ostgermanen, der Kelten, Römer, Finnen und Slawen. Berlin, W. Hertz, 1895. 3 v. plus atlas supplement.
> Volume two, pages 141-270: settlement, migrations, agrarian life of Slavs and Finns, including Estonians, Karelians, Livonians, South Slavs, Russians. Atlas supplement, figures 97-103, pages 321-338. Meitzen was an authority on European village forms and settlement patterns, their histories and present systems.

272. Simkhowitsch, Vladimir G.   Die Feldgemeinschaft in Russland. Jena, G. Fischer, 1908. 399 p.
> Peasant property in north Russia, central Russia, Ukraine, Moscow region. Communal land ownership under serfdom and after. Author was trained in Russia and Germany, later taught in United States.
> *See also* Alexander Kaufmann, "Beiträge zur Kenntnis der Feldgemeinschaft in Sibirien." *Archiv für soziale Gesetzgebung und Statistik* (Tübingen), v. 9, 1896: 108-154, by a Russian expert on peasant questions, and entry no. 263.

273. Smirnov, Ivan N.   Les populations finnoises des bassins de la Volga et de la Kama; études d'ethnographie historique. Translated from the Russian and edited by Paul Boyer. Paris, E. Leroux, 1898. 486 p. Index.
> Translation of part one, "Cheremis and Mordvins," of the Russian original, which also includes Votyaks and Permians. History, economy, family, death, religion, folklore. Based on fieldwork in 1888 and attendant studies.
> For an appreciation by a Finnish specialist, *see* E. N. Setälä, "I. N. Smirnovs Untersuchungen über die Ostfinnen." *Suomalais-Ugrilaisen Seuran. Aikakauskirja*, v. 17, no. 4 (Helsinki, 1900, 52 p.)

274. Tikhomirov, Mikhail N.   The Towns of Ancient Rus'. Translated by Y. Sdobnikow. Moscow, Foreign Languages Publishing House, 1959. 502 p. Index, maps.
See also entry no. 492.
  Translation of *Drevnerusskie goroda* (Ancient Russian Towns) (Moscow, 1956). Economic and social system of towns; rural-urban relations. Rise of towns, cultural history. Period covered is ninth to thirteenth centuries. By a Russian social and cultural historian.

275.* Wallace, *Sir* Donald M.   Russia. Rev. and enl. ed. London, New York, Cassell, 1912. 788 p.
See also entries no. 148, 529, and 1192.
  Systematic social observations by Scottish traveler and student of rural and urban Russia after liberation of the serfs. Social and economic change, religious, commercial, political life. First published in 1877.

276. Zelenin, Dmitrii K.   Russische (Ostslavische) Volkskunde. Berlin, Leipzig, de Gruyter, 1937. 424 p. Illus., plates, map. (Grundriss der slavischen Philologie und Kulturgeschichte, v. 3)
  Ethnography of Great Russians (northern and southern), Ukrainians, Belorussians. Agriculture, animal husbandry, fishing, beekeeping, food, transportation, household utensils, clothing, body care, housing, family life, social life, rituals, and beliefs. By a leading Russian ethnographer.

4. South Russia and Caucasus

277. Baddeley, John F.   The Rugged Flanks of Caucasus. London, Oxford University Press, 1940. 2 v. Illus., plates, ports., maps.
  Published at the end of his life by a British traveler, journalist, and scholar, author of historical and ethnographic account of Russia, Siberia, Mongolia. This work is both ethnographic and historical, based on travels in the nineteenth and twentieth centuries, and on later library research.
  See also his *The Russian Conquest of the Caucasus* (London, Longmans, Green, 1908, 518 p.), which covers history to 1859.

278. Demidov (Demidoff), Anatolii N.   Voyage dans la Russie méridionale et la Crimée, par la Hongrie, la Valachie et la Moldavie, exécuté en 1837. Paris, E. Bourdin, 1841-1842. 4 v. Illus., plates, maps, tables. Album of plates, atlas separately bound.
  Ethnography, natural history. Abridged English translation from second edition: *Travels in Southern Russia* (London, J. Mitchell, 1855, 2 v., maps, plates).

279. Erckert, Roderich von.   Der Kaukasus und seine Völker. Leipzig, P. Frohlberg, 1887. 385 p. Illus., plates, map, tables.
  General ethnographic survey of Caucasus peoples. Language groups, ethnographic classifications.

280. Geiger, Bernhard, *and others*.   Peoples and Languages of the Caucasus. The Hague, Mouton, 1959. 77 p. Illus. (Janua linguarum, no. 6)

> Brief ethnographic and linguistic characterizations. Issued previously (1955) by the Language and Communication Research Center, New York.

281. Haxthausen-Abbenburg, August F. L. M., *Freiherr* von.   Transcaucasia; Sketches of the Nations and Races between the Black Sea and the Caspian. Translated from the German by J. E. Taylor. London, Chapman and Hall, 1854. 448 p.

> An abridged translation of *Transkaukasia; Andeutungen über das Familien- und Gemeindeleben und die socialen Verhältnisse einiger Völker zwischen dem Schwarzen und Kaspischen Meere. Reiseerinnerungen und gesammelte Notizen* (Leipzig, F. A. Brockhaus, 1856, 2 v.). By a traveler and scholar, a specialist in ethnography of Russia.
>
> *See also* his *Russian Empire* (entry no. 265). The English version of *Transcaucasia* appeared before the German because of publishing difficulties in Germany.

282. Klaproth, Julius H.   Travels in the Caucasus and Georgia, Performed in the Years 1807 and 1808. Translated from the German by F. Shoberl. London, H. Colburn, 1814. 421 p.

> In German as *Reise in den Kaukasus und in Georgien* (Halle, 1812, 2 v.). French translation with language notes from second edition: 1826, 2 v., map. Notes of travels from St. Petersburg to Moscow, the Oka River, Donets, Black Sea Armenians, Kalmuks, Cossacks, Georgians, Turks of Caucasus, Cherkess, Kabardians, Ingush. Ethnography, relations with Russians, languages. By early leading orientalist, ethnographer, geographer, linguist. Appendix to German edition: *Kaukasische Sprachen* (Halle, Berlin, 1814, 7 pts.), with sketches of Lezgian, Checken, Ossetian, Cherkess, Abkhazian, Svanetian, and Tataric (Nogay, Karachay, Kumyk).
>
> *See also* his *Beschreibung der russischen Provinzen zwischen dem Kaspischen und Schwarzen Meere* (Berlin, 1814, 269 p., map). Ethnography, history, linguistic notes.
>
> *Consult also* his *Tableau historique, géographique, ethnographique et politique du Caucase* (Paris, Ponthieu, 1827, 187 p.)

283. Kovalevskii, Maksim M. (Maxime Kovalevsky).   Coutume contemporaine et loi ancienne. Droit coutumier ossétien, éclairé par l'histoire comparée. Paris, L. Larose, 1893. 520 p.

> The author was a Russian ethnographer and cultural historian and comparative law specialist. Ossetians are an Iranic people of the north Caucasus; their language is related to ancient Scythian.
>
> *See also* his *Modern Customs and Ancient Laws of Russia* (entry no. 267).

284. Luzbetak, Louis J.   Marriage and the Family in the Caucasus. Vien-

na, St. Gabriel's Mission Press, 1951. 272 p. Tables, maps. (Studia Instituti Anthropos, v. 3)

> Library study by a contemporary ethnologist with good knowledge of data.

285. Merzbacher, Gottfried. Aus den Hochregionen des Kaukasus. Leipzig, Duncker und Humblot, 1901. 2 v. Illus., plates.

> Ethnography of the north Caucasus, v. 1, p. 149-218; Svanetia (in Georgia) and the Svaneti, v. 1, p. 349-391; Ethnography of Kartveli (Georgians, Gruzins), v. 2, p. 39-127. Other ethnographic notes *passim*. Work of an explorer, naturalist, and ethnographer. Compendium of geology, geography, peoples, customs.

286. Minns, Ellis H. Scythians and Greeks; a Survey of Ancient History and Archaeology on the North Coast of the Euxine, from the Danube to the Caucasus. Cambridge, England, Cambridge University Press, 1913. 720 p. Illus., plates, maps, index.

> *See also* his "Art of the Northern Nomads." *Proceedings of the British Academy*, v. 27 (London, 1942, 54 p., map, plates); and Mikhail I. Rostovtsev (Rostowzew), *Skythen und der Bosphorus*, v. 1: *Kritische Übersicht der schriftlichen und archäologischen Quellen* (Berlin, 1931, 651 p., bibliography, maps, index). Minns was a British specialist on civilizations of the Black Sea in classical antiquity. Rostovtsev studied in Russia, later taught in United States.

287. Pallas, Peter S. Travels through the Southern Provinces of the Russian Empire in the Years 1793 and 1794. Translated from the German by F. W. Blagdon. London, T. N. Longman and O. Rees, 1802-1803. 2 v. Plates.

> In German: *Bemerkungen auf eine Reise in die südlichen Statthalterschaften des russischen Reichs* (Leipzig, 1799-1801, 2 v., illus., plates, maps). Itinerary: volume one: Volga–Caspian–Caucasus (Circassia, Taganrog)–Don–Black Sea–Kuban. Ethnographic information concerning Volga Germans, Kundur Tartars, Kalmuks, Turkmens (Trukhmen), Caucasus Cossack lines, Cherkessians, Nogay, Ossetians, Ingush, Svani, Don Cossacks, Armenians, Kazakhs. Towns: Moscow, Penza, Tsaritsyn (Volgograd), Zarepta, Astrakhan, Cherkassk, Taganrog. Volume two: Crimea. Ethnographic information on Crimean Tartars; Russians of the Crimea; relations of the two groups. Perekop, Bakhchiserai, Simferopol (Akmechet), Sebastopol. North shore of Black Sea.
>
> Notes of travels, ethnography, social conditions. By eighteenth-century ethnographer, explorer, naturalist, historian. *See also* his *Reise durch verschiedene Provinzen des russischen Reichs* (entry no. 258).

5. Central Asia

288. Bartol'd (Barthold), Vasilii V. Zwölf Vorlesungen über die Geschichte der Türken Mittelasiens. Hildesheim, Georg Olm, 1962. 278 p. (Photomechanical reproduction of 1935 ed.)

> German translation of lectures on Turks of Russian Turkestan by

a Russian cultural historian of Turks and Turkestan. Proto-history down to modern times (beginning of Soviet period). Linguistic, cultural, historical divisions of Turks. Notes appended by H. H. Schaeder. Appeared in a French adaptation by M. Donskis as *Histoire des Turcs d'Asie Centrale* (Paris, Adrien-Maisonneuve, 1945, 202 p.)

See also Bartol'd's *Four Studies on the History of Central Asia* (Leiden, E. J. Brill, 1956-1962, 3 v.), translated by V. and T. Minorsky: v. 1, Short History of Turkestan, History of the Semirechye; v. 2, Ulugh-Begh and His Times (Turkic khan, fifteenth-century Turkestan); v. 3, Mir 'Alī-Shīr (poet), History of the Turkmen People.

289. Burnes, Alexander.   Travels into Bokhara. London, J. Murray, 1834. 3 v. Plates.

British army officer and explorer. Among the first to travel and report extensively on the region. Valuable early source.

290. Castagné, Joseph.   Étude sur la démonologie des Kazak-Kirghizes. L'Ethnographie (Paris), n.s., v. 21-22, 1930: 1-23; Le culte des lieux saints de l'Islam au Turkestan. *Ibid.*, v. 46, 1951: 46-124; Magie et exorcisme chez les Kazak-Kirghizes et autres peuples turques orientaux. Revue des études islamiques, v. 21-22, 1930: 53-151.

Three studies of religious beliefs and practices by French ethnologist and political specialist in Islamic peoples of Central Asia.

291. Czaplicka, Marie A.   The Turks of Central Asia in History and at the Present Day. London, Clarendon Press, 1918. 242 p. Map, index.

Brief survey. Most useful for bibliographic material, pages 121-134.

See also her *Aboriginal Siberia* (entry no. 307).

292. Karutz, Richard.   Unter Kirgisen und Turkmenen. Leipzig, Klinkhardt und Biermann, 1911. 218 p.

German ethnologist on Kazakhs of Caspian littoral and neighboring Turkmens of Russian Turkestan. Fieldwork report.

293. Khanykov, Nikolai V.   Bokhara; Its Amir and Its People. Translated from the Russian by Clement de Bode. London, J. Madden, 1845. 316 p.

By Russian administrator, student, explorer of Central Asia.

294. Krader, Lawrence.   Peoples of Central Asia. Bloomington, University of Indiana Press, 1963. 319 p. (Uralic and Altaic Series, v. 20)

Ethnology, history, geography, languages, religions, demography, cities of Central Asia and Kazakhstan. Indigenous peoples: Uzbeks, Kazakhs, Kirgiz, Turkmens, Tajiks, Karakalpaks. In-migrants: Russians, Dungans, Uygurs.

See also his *Social Organization of the Mongol-Turkic Pastoral Nomads* (The Hague, Mouton, 1963, 412 p.; Uralic and Altaic Series, v. 26). Traditional organization of family, village, lineage, clan, principality, and empire, sixth to twentieth centuries. Orkhon-Yenisey Turks; ancient and medieval Mongols; Ordos, Buryat, Kalmuk Mongols; Monguors; Kazakhs.

295. Krader, Lawrence.   Principles and Structures in the Organization of the Asiatic Steppe-Pastoralists. Southwestern Journal of Anthropology (Albuquerque, N.M.), v. 11, 1955: 67-92; Ecology of Central Asian Pastoralism. *Ibid.*: 301-326.

> Two studies in traditional cultures of Central Asia. Latter item reprinted in *Studies in Human Ecology*, edited by G. A. Theodorson (Evanston, Ill., Row, Peterson, 1961), p. 471-487.

296. Levshin (Levchine), Aleksei I.   Description des hordes et des steppes des Kirghiz-Kazaks ou Kirghiz-Kaissaks. Translated from the Russian by Ferry de Pigny. Paris, Imprimerie royale, 1840. 514 p. Illus., plates.

> Ethnography, history, demography of Kazakhs, by Russian ethnographer, traveler, historian.

297. Majerczak, R.   La justice chez les Kirghizes-Kazaks. Revue du monde musulman (Paris), v. 35, 1917-1918: 193-272.

> *See also* his "Renseignements historiques sur les Kazaks ou Kirghizes-Kazaks, depuis la formation de la horde Kazaks jusqu'à la fin du XIXe siècle." *Ibid.*, v. 43, 1921: 54-220. Useful as an account, and for references to sources for further study.

298. Meiendorf, Egor F. (Georges de Meyendorff).   Voyage d'Orenbourg à Boukhara, fait en 1820. Paris, Dondey-Dupré, 1826. 508 p. Illus.

> An early account of high quality by Russian soldier and traveler. Ethnographic, statistical data.

299. Murav'ev, Nikolai N.   Voyage en Turcomanie et à Khiva fait en 1819 à 1820. Translated from the Russian by G. Lecointe de Laveau. Paris, 1823. 398 p. Illus., map.

> Russian officer and traveler. Ethnography, economy, polity, demography of the regions.

300. Nalivkin, Vladimir P.   Histoire du khanat de Khokand. Translated by August Dozon. Paris, E. Ledoux, 1889. 272 p.

> By Russian official and scholar. Virtually the sole source on the subject for that period.

301. Schuyler, Eugene.   Turkistan. New York, Scribner, Armstrong, 1876. 2 v.
See also entry no. 1692.

> Outstanding ethnographic, political analysis by American diplomat and scholar. Especially useful for data of period immediately after Russian conquest. Third edition: 1885.

302. Tolstov, Sergei P.   Auf den Spuren der altchoresmischen Kultur. Translated from the Russian by O. Mehlitz. Berlin, Verlag Kultur und Fortschritt, 1953. 361 p. Illus., plates, maps. (Sowjetwissenschaft, Beiheft 14)

Archeology of Central Asian proto-historical, early historical, and medieval culture. Translation of *Po sledam drevnekhorezmiiskoi tsivilizatsii* (Moscow, 1948, 322 p.)

303. Ujfalvy de Mező-Kövesd, Károly J. (Charles E. de).   Les aryens au nord et au sud de l'Hindu-Kouch. Paris, G. Masson, 1896. 488 p.

By a scholar and traveler. Incorporates earlier observations with later systematic library research on Mountain Tajiks.

See also his *Le Kohistan, le Ferghanah et Kouldja* (Paris, 1878), and *Le Syr-Darya, le Zarafchane, le pays des Sept-rivières et la Sibérie-occidentale* (Paris, 1879), both of which contain ethnographic materials synthesized in the 1896 work.

304. Vámbéry, Ármin.   Travels in Central Asia. London, J. Murray, 1864. 443 p. Illus.

Hungarian linguist, traveler, historian, nineteenth-century authority, much quoted in his day. Also in German as *Reise in Mittelasien* (Leipzig, 1873).

See also his *History of Bokhara*, 2d ed. (London, 1873), and *Die primitive Cultur des Turko-Tatarischen Volkes* (Leipzig, 1879).

6. Siberia

305. Bogoraz, Vladimir G. (Waldemar Bogoras).   The Chukchee. Leiden, E. J. Brill; New York, J. E. Stechert, 1904-1909. 3 pts. (Publications of the Jesup North Pacific Expedition, no. 7; Memoirs of the American Museum of Natural History, v. 11)

See also his "Chukchee Tales." *Journal of American Folklore*, v. 41, 1928: 297-452; "Chukchee." *Handbook of American Indian Languages*, edited by Franz Boas (Washington, 1922), pt. 2, p. 631-903. Fundamental works on Chukchi culture, folklore, language, by the great Russian ethnologist.

306. Chodzidło, Theophil.   Die Familie bei den Jakuten. Freiburg in der Schweiz, Paulusverlag, 1951. 462 p. Map. (Internationale Schriftenreihe für sozial- und politische Wissenschaften. Ethnologische Reihe, Bd. 1)

Family, kinship organization of the Yakuts, based on library materials.

307. Czaplicka, Marie A.   Aboriginal Siberia; a Study in Social Anthropology. Oxford, Clarendon Press, 1914. 374 p. Bibliography, illus., maps.

Preface by R. R. Marett. Ethnological survey, important for its period.

See also her *My Siberian Year* (London, Mills and Boon, 1916,

315 p., plates, map), an account of fieldwork in western Siberia in 1914-1915, under joint expedition of Oxford and Pennsylvania universities.

308. Donner, Kai. Among the Samoyed in Siberia. Translated from the German by R. Kyler. New Haven, Human Relations Area Files, 1954. 176 p. Illus., map.

> Translation of *Bei den Samojeden in Sibirien* (Stuttgart, 1926). Travel notes, 1911-1914, in northwestern Siberia. By Finnish ethnologist and linguist.
>
> For further data on indigenous cultures of western Siberia by this scholar of long standing in the field, *see* his *La Sibérie; la vie en Sibérie, les temps anciens,* translated from the Finnish by Léon Froman (Paris, Gallimard, 1946, 243 p., illus., plates, maps).

309. Finsch, Otto. Reise nach West-Siberien im Jahre 1876. Berlin, E. Wallroth, 1879. 663 p.

> Travel notes, ethnography of Urals, Ishim Steppe, Irtysh, Semipalatinsk, Ala-Kul, Kazakhstan, Altay, Ob, North Siberian tundra. Ethnography of Kazakhs, Ostyaks, Samoyeds.

310. Harva (Holmberg), Uno. Finno-Ugric, Siberian Mythology. Boston, Archaeological Institute of America, Marshall Jones, 1927. 587 p. (The Mythology of All Races, v. 4)

> *See also* his *Die religiösen Vorstellungen der Mordwinen* (Helsinki, Suomalainen Tiedeakatemia, 1952, 453 p.; FF Communications no. 142). Gods, spirits, cults, rites. Mordvins are a Finno-Ugric group living in Northeastern European Russia.
>
> *See also* Harva's *Die religiösen Vorstellungen der altaischen Völker* (entry no. 311).

311. Harva, Uno. Die religiösen Vorstellungen der altaischen Völker. Translated from the Finnish by Erich Kunze. Helsinki, Suomalainen Tiedeakatemia, 1938. 634 p. Illus., map. (FF Communications, no. 125)

> Based on long study by a Finnish ethnologist. Primarily concerned with Altaic peoples of Siberia (Buryats, Yakuts, Altay-Turks, South Siberian Turks). French translation: *Les représentations religieuses des peuples altaïques,* translated from the German by Jean-Louis Perret (Paris, Gallimard, 1959, 438 p., plates).

312. Jochelson, Vladimir I. (Waldemar). The Koryak. Leiden, E. J. Brill; New York, G. E. Stechert, 1908. 842 p. Illus., plates. (Publications of the Jesup North Pacific Expedition, no. 6; Memoirs of the American Museum of Natural History, v. 10)

> *See also* Vladimir G. Bogoraz (W. Bogoras), *Koryak Texts* (Leiden, E. J. Brill; New York, G. E. Stechert, 1917. 153 p. Publications of the American Ethnological Society, no. 5).
>
> *See also* Jochelson's *The Yukaghir and the Yukaghirized Tungus* (entry no. 313).

313. Jochelson, Vladimir I. (Waldemar). The Yukaghir and the Yuka-ghirized Tungus. Leiden, E. J. Brill; New York, G. E. Stechert, 1910-1926. 3 pts. 469 p. (Publications of the Jesup North Pacific Expedition, no. 9; Memoirs of the American Museum of Natural History, v. 13)

By a Russian ethnologist and political exile in Siberia, later resident in United States. Like Bogoraz and Sternberg, Jochelson did work while in exile, gathering otherwise unavailable data.

See also his "Essay on the Grammar of the Yukaghir Language," *Annals of the New York Academy of Sciences*, v. 16, pt. 2, 1905 Reprinted in *American Anthropologist*, n. s., v. 7, 1905, supplement p. 369-424.

314. Karjalainen, Kustaa F. Die Religion der Jugra-Völker. Translated from the Finnish by Oskar Hackman and Arno Bussenius. Helsinki, Suomalainen Tiedeakatemia, 1921-1927. 3 pts. (FF Communications no. 41, 1921, 204 p.; no. 44, 1922, 386 p.; no. 63, 1927, 350 p.)

Yugra peoples: Voguls (Khants) and Ostyaks (Mans), of the Finno-Ugrian (Uralic) language family. Copious treatment of the theme by a Finnish scholar.

315. Kennan, George. Siberia and the Exile System. New York, The Century Co., 1891. 2 v. Illus., ports., maps.
See also entries no. 129 and 807.

Notes of travels, exiles, Siberian Russians, indigenes, by an American traveler and early student of Russia.

316. Krader, Lawrence. Buryat Religion and Society. Southwestern Journal of Anthropology, v. 10, 1954, no. 3: 322-351.

Analysis of Buryat social organization, religious organization and doctrine.

317. Leroi-Gourhan, André. La civilisation du renne. 2d ed. Paris, Gallimard, 1936. 178 p. Illus., plates, maps.

French study of traditional cultures of indigenous contemporary Siberian peoples.

See also Berthold Laufer, "The Reindeer and Its Domestication," *Memoirs of the American Anthropological Association*, v. 4, 1917, no. 2: 91-147; Gudmund Hatt, "Notes on Reindeer Nomadism," *Ibid.*, v. 6, 1919, no. 2: 75-133.

Further discussion by B. Laufer in *American Anthropologist*, n. s., v. 22, 1920: 192-197; G. Hatt, *Ibid.*, v. 23, 1921: 97-101.

318. Michael, Henry N., *ed.* Studies in Siberian Ethnogenesis. Toronto, University of Toronto for the Arctic Institute of North America, 1962. 313 p. (Anthropology of the North: Translations from Russian Sources, no. 2)

Translations of Soviet works on origins and ethnic histories of indigenous peoples of Yakutia, Amur region; Buryats, Kirgiz, Koybals, Altayans, and Finno-Ugrian speakers of West Siberia and

European Russia. Transition from kin to territorial groups. Selected by Lawrence Krader.

Also published in this series: S. I. Rudenko, *The Ancient Culture of the Bering Sea and the Eskimo Problem*, translated by P. Tolstoy (Toronto, 1961, 186 p., illus., maps, plates; Translations from Russian Sources, no. 1).

319. Montandon, George.   La civilisation aïnou et les cultures arctiques. Paris, Payot, 1937. 272 p. Illus., maps, plates, index.

Part one, Ainu culture, pages 46-176; part two, relations with circum-Arctic cultures, pages 181-252. Bibliographies. French specialist on circum-Arctic cultures.

See also Lev Ia. Shternberg, "The Ainu Problem," *Anthropos* (Salzburg), v. 24, 1929: 755-799.

320. Müller, Ferdinand F.   Unter Tungusen und Jakuten; Erlebnisse und Ergebnisse der Olenék-Expedition der Kaiserlich russischen geographischen Gesellschaft in St. Petersburg. Leipzig, F. A. Brockhaus, 1882. 326 p. Illus., map.

By ethnologist and geographer. Fieldwork, travel account of indigenous peoples of Olenek district, Yakutia.

321. Patkanov (Patkanoff), Serafim K.   Geographie und Statistik der Tungusenstämme Sibiriens, nach den Angaben der Volkszählung von 1897. Budapest, Magyar Tudományos Akademia, 1905. 204 p. (Keleti Szemle, v. 4-6)

Survey of population data of all Manchu-Tungus-speaking peoples living in Siberia.

See also his *Essai d'une statistique et d'une géographie des peuples paleo-asiatique de la Sibérie* (St. Petersburg, 1903), which has ethnic data from 1897 census of Russian Empire (text is in Russian, statistical table titles and headings in French and Russian).

322. Sanzheev (Sandschejew), Garma.   Weltanschauung und Schamanismus der Alaren-Burjaten. Anthropos (Salzburg), v. 23, 1928: 576-613; v. 24, 1929: 538-560, 967-986. Plates.

The author is of Buryat origin, Russian trained. Combination of personal knowledge and research.

323. Schrenck, Leopold von.   Reisen und Forschungen im Amur-Lande in den Jahren 1854-1856. St. Petersburg, K. Akademie der Wissenschaften, 1856-1895. 4 v.

Volume three (3 pts., 77 p., 1881-1895) contains ethnography, has maps and tables. Supplement: Wilhelm Grube, *Linguistische Ergebnisse.* (1) *Giljakische Wörterverzeichniss nebst grammatischen Bemerkungen* (1892, 150 p.); (2) *Goldisch-Deutsches Wörterverzeichniss* (1900, 149 p., German-Goldi index). Expedition for purposes of natural history, ethnography, linguistics. Amur tribes, reports on their material and spiritual culture, social organization, physical anthropology.

324. Shimkin, Demitri B.   A Sketch of the Ket, or Yenisei "Ostyak."
Ethnos (Stockholm), v. 4, 1939: 147-176. Illus., map.
Study of a traditional culture by an American ethnologist.

325. Shirokogorov, Sergei M.   Social Organization of the Northern
Tungus. Shanghai, The Commercial Press, 1929. 427 p.
Introductory chapters on geographic distribution and history of
the Tungus. Social structure, family, clan, village forms and func-
tions. By investigator who studied Tungus over many years.
See also his *Psychomental Complex of the Tungus* (London, Ke-
gan Paul, Trench, Trubner, 1935, 469 p.); "Northern Tungus Mi-
grations. The Goldi and Their Ethnical Affinities." *Journal of the
Royal Asian Society*, North China Branch, v. 57, 1926; *Tungus
Dictionary* (Tokyo, 1944, 258 p.)

326. Shternberg, Lev Ia. (Leo Sternberg).   Die Religion der Giljaken.
Translated from the Russian by A. V. Peters. Archiv für Religions-
wissenschaft (Leipzig), v. 8, 1905: 244-274, 456-473.
Author of many Gilyak studies, of which few have been published outside Russia. Ethnologist, Siberian exile.
See also his "Divine Election in Primitive Religion (Including Material on Different Tribes of N. E. Asia and America)," *Proceedings
of the Twenty-first International Congress of Americanists* (Gothen-
burg, 1925), pt. 2, p. 472-512. Includes material on Gilyak religion
and on other indigenous peoples of Siberia.
See also his "The Turano-Ganowanian System and the Nations of
North-East Asia," *Proceedings of the Eighteenth International Congress of Americanists* (London, 1912), p. 319-333. Gilyak social
organization, developed in the light of L. H. Morgan; systems of
consanguinity.

B. DEMOGRAPHY

by Michael Roof

1. Basic Sources and Methodology

327. Kantner, John F., *and* Lydia W. Kulchycka.   The USSR Population
Census of 1926: a Partial Evaluation. Washington, 1957. 142 p.
(U. S. Bureau of the Census.[1] International Population Reports. Series P-95, no. 50)
The most exhaustive study yet undertaken of certain aspects of the
1926 USSR census, including age-heaping and the problem of the
underregistration of infants generally and of women in the Central Asian republics.

328. Kaufman, A.   The History and Development of the Official Russian
Statistics. *In* The History of Statistics; Their Development and Prog-

[1] All reports attributed in this section to the U. S. Bureau of the Census were prepared by its Foreign Manpower Research Office, now the Foreign Demographic Analysis Division. Those not published in a series are available in processed form.

ress in Many Countries, edited by John Koren. New York, Macmillan, 1918. p. 467-534.

Provides excellent general background concerning the earliest Russian statistics, including those of a demographic nature. Of especial interest is the discussion of population counts before the first census of 1897, the program of the 1897 census, vital statistics, and the origin and early development of the statistical yearbooks.

329. Kuczynski, Robert R.   The Balance of Births and Deaths. v. 2: Eastern and Southern Europe. Washington, The Brookings Institution, 1931. 164 p.

On pages 8-28 there is a chapter on the Russian Empire which includes a discussion of fertility, birth rates, abortions, and average life expectancy, up to 1929. An appendix describes registration of vital statistics in the former Baltic States (Estonia, Latvia, and Lithuania) and other parts of the Russian Empire. Of special interest is the description of ecclesiastical registers, which in pre-Revolutionary Russia formed the main source of information on vital events.

330. Lorimer, Frank.   The Nature of Soviet Population and Vital Statistics. American Statistician, v. 7, no. 2, April–May 1953: 13-18.

Brief survey of current registration statistics in the Soviet Union. Unfortunately, it is now out of date in terms of some points of detail. *See* entry no. 348 for a characterization of current statistics on labor force.

331. Lorimer, Frank.   The Population of the Soviet Union; History and Prospects. Geneva, League of Nations, 1946. 287 p.

The most generally useful work on Soviet demography. Covers historical development, geographic distribution, vital statistics, ethnic groups, and labor force. The book focuses on 1926, working backward to 1897 and forward to 1939.

332. Pod"iachikh, P. G.   The All-Union Census of Population of 1939. Translated by Arthur Saul. Washington, Bureau of the Census, 1959. 257 p.

This is the most complete and detailed manuscript in English describing the techniques and procedures of the 1939 USSR population census, all the more important because this census (like the 1959 census) represented a basic deviation from previous Russian censuses and embodied new concepts and methods which depart from the main Western patterns of evolution in census-taking.

Translation of *Vsesoiuznaia perepis' naseleniia 1939 goda* (Moscow, Gosstatizdat, 1953, 147 p.)

333. Russia. *Tsentral'nyi statisticheskii komitet.*   Premier recensement général de l'Empire de Russie, 1897. St. Petersburg, 1899-1905. 89 v.

A French translation of the 1897 census results (*Pervaia vseobshchaia perepis' naseleniia Rossiiskoi imperii 1897 g.*; St. Petersburg, 1899-1905, 89 v. in 24).

The Russian-language report of the results of the 1926 census also has titles and subtitles in French: Russia. Tsentral'noe statisticheskoe upravlenie. Otdel perepisi. *Vsesoiuznaia perepis' naseleniia 1926 g.* (Moscow, 1928-1933, 56 v.)

334. Russia (*1923– U.S.S.R.*) *Tsentral'noe statisticheskoe upravlenie.* The National Economy of the USSR in 1960; Statistical Yearbook. Washington, U. S. Joint Publications Research Service, 1962. 937 p. (JPRS Report no. 12,317)
See also entry no. 70.

   An English translation of pages 1-902 and 919-943 of *Narodnoe khoziaistvo SSSR v 1960 godu; statisticheskii ezhegodnik* (Moscow, Gosstatizdat, 1961, 937 p.). It includes selected results from the 1939 and 1959 population censuses.

335. Selegen, Galina, *and* Michael Roof.   Begriffe und Methoden russischer Volkszählungen. Osteuropa, no. 2, January–February 1958: 112-122.

   A general history of censuses in Russia and the USSR, including plans for the 1959 census.

336. Starodubsky, Lev.   Das Volkszählungswesen in der Union der Sozialistischen Sowjetrepubliken; eine statistisch-methodologische Untersuchung. Vienna, Deuticke, 1938. 141 p. (Schriften des Institutes für Statistik insbes. der Minderheitsvölker. Reihe C, no. 3)

   A methodological inquiry into the various types of Soviet population and family statistics. Excellent bibliography of early French and German works.

337. Ullman, Morris B.   The 1939 USSR Census of Population: Organization and Methodology; with Notes on Plans for the 1959 Census of Population. Washington, Bureau of the Census, 1959. 199 p.

   A critical examination essentially of Pod"iachikh's study (*see* entry no. 332). An appendix brings together most of the limited and widely scattered published results of the 1939 USSR census available at the time of the study.

   A shortened version of this processed study was published in the *American Statistician*, v. 13, no. 5, December 24, 1959: 14-17.

338. U. S. *Bureau of the Census.*   Materials on the Preparation and Conduct of the USSR All-Union Population Census of 1959. Washington, 1959. 131 p. (Bureau of the Census Working Paper, no. 8)

   The best single English-language guide to the conduct of the 1959 census. Contents include texts of official decrees and supporting measures, enumerator instructions and census forms, census publicity, timetable of operations, tabulating plans, and some cautious criticisms of official plans by Soviet scholars.

   Translation of *Materialy po Vsesoiuznoi perepisi naseleniia 1959 goda* (Moscow, Gosstatizdat, 1958), and other official materials.

2. Census Interpretations and Analyses

339. Brackett, James W.   Demographic Trends and Population Policy in the Soviet Union. *In* U. S. Congress. Joint Economic Committee. Dimensions of Soviet Economic Power. Washington, 1962. p. 487-589.

> A survey of the most general results of the 1959 Soviet population census, particularly as these relate to the size, age-sex composition, and residence of population, with projections into the future. The analysis of the quality of certain Soviet statistics, as well as of the impact of official population policy, is necessarily tentative.

340. Eason, Warren W.   The Soviet Population Today; an Analysis of the First Results of the 1959 Census. Foreign Affairs, v. 37, no. 4, July 1959: 598-606.

> One of the first reactions in the West to the preliminary 1959 Soviet census returns, with special reference to imputed wartime population losses. Eason's results concerning war losses are with few exceptions consistent with our best knowledge of these matters at the present moment, although we have a much greater volume of data now than he possessed.

341. Eisendrath, Ernst.   Das Bevölkerungspotential der Sowjetunion. Berlin, Duncker und Humblot, 1960. 56 p. (Deutsches Institut für Wirtschaftsforschung. Sonderhefte, N.F., no. 53)

> A survey of statistics on the general characteristics of the population with some international comparisons.

342. Ptukha, M. V.   La population de l'Ukraine jusqu'en 1960. *In* International Statistical Institute. Bulletin, v. 25, 1931, no. 3: 59-88.

> The author's projections for the population of the Ukraine up to 1960 are of less interest than his consideration of various technical demographic problems, including misstatement of age and under-reporting of infants in Russia's censuses and registries of vital events. In this study, Ptukha's work is clearly in line with the developing mainstream of Western demography.

343. Roof, Michael.   Soviet Population Trends. Eugenics Quarterly, v. 8, no. 3, September 1961: 123-134.

> A general evaluation of the 1959 census concepts, including an analysis of the census results pertaining to the total, urban, and rural population, age-sex distribution, educational attainment, and ethnic national composition.
>
> Reprinted from *Survey*, no. 37, July–September 1961: 34-42.

344. Selegen, Galina.   The First Report on the Recent Population Census in the Soviet Union. Population Studies, v. 14, no. 1, July 1960: 17-27.

> An analysis of the natural increase of population, its age and sex composition, geographical distribution, and migration from rural

to urban areas. The author argues for much lower war losses than do other observers.

Other significant articles by the author, who had firsthand experience with Soviet statistical procedures, are: "Changing Features in the Soviet Population Census Programme." *Population Studies*, v. 13, no. 1, July 1959: 40-45, which compares the census schedules for 1926 and 1959; and "Economic Characteristics of the Population in the Soviet Census Questionnaire." *Soviet Studies*, v. 11, no. 4, April 1960: 353-362.

345. U. S. *Bureau of the Census.*   Results of the USSR Population Census of 1959 and Related Data. Washington, 1960. 25 p.

A translation of the preliminary results of the All-Union Population Census of 1959, and a second official release pertaining to the educational level, ethnic composition, age structure, and distribution of the population by administrative-territorial subdivision.

Since the basic returns of the 1959 census remain untranslated, the reader may wish to refer to the following sources for preliminary returns: *Current Digest of the Soviet Press*, v. 12, no. 5: 3-7; v. 12, no. 13: 308; v. 13, no. 6: 25-30; v. 11, no. 12: 22; v. 12, no. 9: 18-19; and *Population Bulletin*, v. 15, no. 4, July 1959: 65-78.

3. Labor Force

346. Eason, Warren W.   The Agricultural Labor Force and Population of the USSR, 1926-41. Santa Monica, Calif., The Rand Corporation, 1954. 210 p. (Rand Corporation Research Memorandum RM-1248)

A unique work covering primarily the period of agricultural collectivization before the Second World War. In particular, an attempt is made to integrate a diversity of Soviet technical works concerning the participation of various age-sex groups in the labor force.

347. Eason, Warren W.   Soviet Manpower; the Population and Labor Force of the USSR. Ann Arbor, Mich., University Microfilms, 1959. 484 l.

The author's doctoral dissertation at Columbia University, consisting of a presentation and examination of earlier statistical information on the participation of USSR population in the labor force by age and sex, and the size and composition of the labor force. In addition, broad relations of population and labor force growth and economic and social change are delineated.

See also the author's "Population and Labor Force," in *Soviet Economic Growth: Conditions and Perspectives*, edited by Abram Bergson (Evanston, Ill., Row, Peterson, 1953), p. 101-122.

348. Feshbach, Murray.   The Soviet Statistical System; Labor Force Recordkeeping and Reporting. Washington, U. S. Government Printing Office, 1960. 151 p. (U. S. Bureau of the Census. Foreign Manpower Research Office. International Population Statistics Reports, Series P-90, no. 12)

A thorough investigation of labor force reporting practices, including the structure and functions of regulatory agencies, record-keeping in individual establishments, and national labor accounts. The practices described were those in use before the administrative reorganization of mid-1957. A supplement to this study dealing with changes induced by the reorganization, together with additional material, is available in the same series (P-90, no. 17, 1962, 99 p.) under the title *The Soviet Statistical System; Labor Force Record-keeping and Reporting since 1957.*

349. Sonin, Mikhail Ia.   The Reproduction of Labor Power in the USSR and the Balance of Labor. Washington, U. S. Joint Publications Research Service, 1960. 391 p. (JPRS Report no. 6,231)

A systematic examination of the complex problems of maximizing the size of the labor force and of influencing its redistribution as required by industrialization. The various means of achieving redistribution are clearly set forth, including organized recruitment and family resettlement programs. Of considerable interest are the methodological comments and illustrative planning forms. Translation of *Vosproizvodstvo rabochei sily v SSSR i balans truda* (Moscow, Gosplanizdat, 1959, 367 p.)

For a more technical discussion of the same general subject, see *Planning, Training and Allocation of Manpower in the USSR*, by N. N. Zabelin and others. Washington, U. S. Joint Publications Research Service, 1961. 230 p. (JPRS Report no. 8,916. Translation of *Planirovanie podgotovki i raspredeleniia rabochikh kadrov v SSSR* [Moscow, Gosplanizdat, 1960, 150 p.])

See also *Labor Resources of the USSR*, edited by N. I. Shishkin. Washington, U. S. Joint Publications Research Service, 1962. 295 p. (JPRS Report no. 13,945. Translation of *Trudovye resursy SSSR* [Moscow, Ekonomizdat, 1962, 246 p.])

350. Weitzman, Murray S., *and* Andrew Elias.   The Magnitude and Distribution of Civilian Employment in the U.S.S.R., 1928-1959. Washington, U. S. Government Printing Office, 1961. 193 p. (U. S. Bureau of the Census. Foreign Manpower Research Office. International Population Reports, Series P-95, no. 58)

A detailed statistical analysis of employment in the USSR. Much attention is devoted to Soviet statistical concepts and methodology. Contains glossary of terms and annotated bibliography.

351. Weitzman, Murray S., Murray Feshbach, *and* Lydia Kulchycka. Employment in the USSR: Comparative USSR-USA Data. *In* U. S. Congress. Joint Economic Committee. Dimensions of Soviet Economic Power. Washington, 1962. p. 591-667.

The most comprehensive survey of labor supply, management, and utilization. In particular, the USSR-USA comparisons are carefully worked out and only cautious conclusions drawn.

The article is followed (pages 671-744) by an excellent bibliography of recent Russian-language monographs, compiled by Murray Feshbach, and a statistical appendix, including population and labor force data.

4. Population Projections and Special Studies

352. Kulischer, Eugene M.   Europe on the Move; War and Population Changes, 1917-47. New York, Columbia University Press, 1948. 377 p.
Bibliography: p. 327-357.

The chapters devoted to Russia and the Soviet Union trace the often intimate association between war and migration from the turn of the century to the outbreak of the Second World War. In this respect it is a continuation of the Kulischer brothers' study of earlier European demographic history: Alexander and Eugene M. Kulischer, *Kriegs- und Wanderzüge; Weltgeschichte als Völkerbewegung* (Berlin and Leipzig, W. de Gruyter, 1932, 230 p.)

The treatment of migration during the Second World War is also a continuation of the author's earlier study entitled *The Displacement of Population in Europe* (Montreal, International Labor Office, 1943, 171 p.), which includes displacement of population from and within the USSR.

353. Mauldin, W. Parker.   Fertility Control in Communist Countries: Policy and Practice. *In* Milbank Memorial Fund. Population Trends in Eastern Europe, the USSR, and Mainland China. New York, 1960. p. 179-215.

A survey of policy and practice on fertility control in Communist countries, including the USSR. An appendix lists Soviet legislation on abortion, awards to mothers, and differential taxation on the basis of family status.

Discussion of the article on pages 216–223.

354. Natalité, mortalité en Union Soviétique.   Population (Paris), v. 14, no. 2, April–June 1959: 345-349.

Presentation and discussion of birth, death, and natural increase rates for the Soviet Union as a whole and for many of its subdivisions, as available in 1959. Rates which have been released subsequently have not, unfortunately, been published outside the USSR.

The sequence of earlier vital statistics can be traced by consulting the standard works cited herein, and Stanislas Kohn, "The Vital Statistics of European Russia during the World War, 1914–1917," in *The Cost of the War to Russia* (New Haven, Yale University Press, 1932, p. 3–154; [Carnegie Endowment for International Peace. Economic and Social History of the World War, Russian Series]).

355. Pradigou, Yves.   L'évolution démographique de l'U.R.S.S. et les problèmes de répartition de la main-d'oeuvre. Cahiers du monde russe et soviétique, v. 2, no. 1, January–March 1961: 5-36.

A general discussion of Soviet population trends with emphasis upon the changing patterns of internal migration.

356. Pressat, Roland. Les premières tables de mortalité de l'Union Soviétique (1958-1959). Population (Paris), v. 18, no. 1, January–March 1963: 65-92.

Analysis of life tables published in connection with the 1959 Soviet population census, including the data by age and sex and urban-rural residence. Systematic differences among death rates in rural and urban areas could, as the author makes clear, reflect imperfections in registration of vital events.

357. Princeton University. *Office of Population Research.* The Future Population of Europe and the Soviet Union; Population Projections, 1940-1970. By Frank W. Notestein, Irene B. Taeuber, Dudley Kirk (and others). Geneva, League of Nations, 1944. 315 p.

Includes a selected bibliography, some basic data, and population projections for the USSR and the former Baltic States.

For more recent population projections to 1980, *see also* entry no. 339.

358. Roof, Michael. The Russian Population Enigma Reconsidered. Population Studies, v. 14, no. 1, July 1960: 3-16.

A reconsideration of the major premises of the debate in the late 1940's and early 1950's among three outstanding Russian émigré scholars — Prokopovich, Timasheff, and Kulischer — concerning the postwar size of the USSR's population. One cardinal factual point is stressed: the Soviet government as early as 1950 possessed authentic data showing the size of the country's population to be about 20 million less than generally believed in the West.

359. Sauvy, Alfred. La population de l'Union Soviétique. Population (Paris), no. 3, July–September 1956: 461-480.

Sauvy's method consists of working backward from the official Soviet estimates for 1956, and his approximations of the year by year changes in births and deaths result in figures which are among the best available for the size of the USSR's population during the war and immediate postwar years.

360. Schechtman, Joseph B. Postwar Population Transfers in Europe, 1945-1955. Philadelphia, University of Pennsylvania Press, 1963. 408 p.
Bibliography: p. 399-410.

Chapters in this book are devoted to transfers of German and non-German minorities into, out of, and within the Soviet Union in the specified period.

361. Smulevich, Boleslav Ia. Morbidity, Mortality, and the Physical Development of the Populace: USSR. New York, U. S. Joint Publications Research Service, 1959. 140 p. (JPRS Report no. 1,632-N)

Primarily a methodological treatise designed to introduce the types of forms utilized in the collection of health statistics. Actual data are often given for illustrative purposes. Other Soviet reports have indicated that morbidity statistics are still collected on a sample basis rather than in the manner described by Smulevich.

Translation of *Zabolevaemost', smertnost', i fizicheskoe razvitie naseleniia* (Moscow, Medgiz, 1957, 132 p.)

V

the nations civilizations and politics

A. THE NATIONAL QUESTION

by Lawrence Krader

362. Barghoorn, Frederick C.   Soviet Russian Nationalism. New York, Oxford University Press, 1956. 330 p. Index.

> National sentiments and nationalism of individual Soviet peoples, *passim*.
>
> *See also* Boris Nikitine and Pierre George, *Contribution à l'étude du problème national en URSS* (Paris, P.U.F., 1948, 86 p.), for an earlier treatment of the same general theme; and Demetrio Boersner, *The Bolsheviks and the National and Colonial Questions, 1917-1928* (Geneva, E. Droz, 1957, 285 p.), for a discussion of the history of the nationalities policy in the USSR.

363. Gurian, Waldemar, *ed.*   Soviet Imperialism; Its Origins and Tactics. Notre Dame, Ind., University of Notre Dame Press, 1953. 166 p.

> Development of the problem of nationalities. Contrast of Tsarist and Soviet practices. See particularly the chapters by M. Pap, "The Ukrainian Problem," p. 43-74; and Richard Pipes, "Russian Moslems before and after the Revolution," p. 75-90.

364. Kolarz, Walter. Russia and Her Colonies. New York, Praeger, 1952. 334 p.

Compendious survey of minority peoples of USSR and Soviet policy toward them.

See also his *Peoples of the Soviet Far East* (New York, Praeger, 1954, 193 p., illus., map) for the Soviet Russian Far East. Indigenous peoples: Yakuts, Buryats, Mongols, Tuvans.

365. Pipes, Richard. The Formation of the Soviet Union; Communism and Nationalism, 1917-1923. Cambridge, Harvard University Press, 1954. 355 p.

Bibliography: p. 293-318.

See also entry no. 557.

National problem in Russia and Soviet approach to a solution. Peoples of Ukraine, Belorussia, Moslem areas, Caucasus.

See also his "Nationalism and Nationality," in *The USSR and the Future* (Munich, Institute for the Study of the USSR, 1963).

366. Studies on the Soviet Union. 1957– Munich, Institute for the Study of the USSR. quarterly.

Occasional articles by émigrés on nationalities questions in the USSR. Journal absorbed *Belorussian Review, Caucasian Review, East Turkic Review, Ukrainian Review. See also* the Institute's *Sowjet Studien* (Munich, 1956–).

B. UKRAINICA [1]

by Ivan L. Rudnytsky and O. Danko

1. General Aids and Bibliographies

367. Pelens'kyi, Ievhen Iu. (Eugene J. Pelenskyj). Ucrainica; Selected Bibliography on Ukraine in Western-European Languages. Munich, Bystrycia, 1948. 111 p. (Memoirs of the Ševčenko Scientific Society, v. 158)

Most authoritative bibliography of publications on the Ukraine, containing 2,600 entries (books and articles in learned journals) in English and other West European languages.

For a bibliography covering the period after 1947, *see* Roman Weres, *The Ukraine; Selected References in English Language* (Kalamazoo, Western Michigan University, 1961, 233 p.), and *Richnyk ukrains'koi bibliografii*, since 1957 published in New York by the Ukrainian Academy of Arts and Sciences in the United States.

368. Ukraine; a Concise Encyclopaedia. Prepared by Ševčenko Scientific Society. Edited by Volodymyr Kubijovyč. Foreword by Ernest J. Simmons. Toronto, published for the Ukrainian National Association, Toronto University Press, 1963– 2 v.

The best single up-to-date reference work available in English that deals exclusively with Ukrainian affairs. Volume one (1,185 pages) is arranged in sections according to subjects such as: general infor-

[1] Arrangement combines topical and chronological criteria.

mation, physical geography and natural history, population, ethnography, Ukrainian language, literature, history, Ukrainian culture, etc. Signed articles are prepared by specialists and include up-to-date bibliographies. The second, and last, volume — in preparation — will include material on economics, law, politics and government, religion, etc.

2. Serials

369. Digest of the Soviet Ukrainian Press. v. 1– July 1957– New York, "Prolog" Research and Publishing Association. monthly.
    Contains full text or extensive excerpts from original articles in English translation. Covers over 30 newspapers and journals published in the Ukrainian SSR.

370. Ukrainian Academy of Arts and Sciences in the U.S. Annals. v. 1– Winter 1951– New York.
    Scholarly serial publication devoted mainly to the study of the history and social and cultural problems of the Ukraine.

371. The Ukrainian Quarterly. v. 1– 1944– New York, Ukrainian Congress Committee of America.
    A journal devoted mainly to problems of the Soviet Union, and particularly the Ukraine. Intended for both general reader and specialist.

3. History

372. Doroshenko, Dmytro, *and* Olexander Ohloblyn. A Survey of Ukrainian Historiography, by Dmytro Doroshenko. Ukrainian Historiography, 1917-1956, by Olexander Ohloblyn. New York, 1957. 458 p. (The Annals of the Ukrainian Academy of Arts and Sciences in the U.S., v. 5/6, 1957)
    Comprehensive outline of the development of Ukrainian historiography, beginning with its oldest sources — chronicles of the eleventh century — to 1956. Includes a vast bibliographical apparatus. An indispensable guide for research in Ukrainian and general East European history.

373. Borshchak, Il'ko (Élie Borschak). L'Ukraine dans la littérature de l'Europe occidentale. Paris, 1935. 202 p.
    This study presents a basic critical analysis of all major Western European sources and writings which have any relevance to the Ukraine, from the fifteenth century to 1930. Originally published in *Le monde slave*, 1933, no. 3-4; 1934, no. 1-2, 4; 1935, no. 1.

374. Hrushevs'kyi, Mykhailo (Michael Hrushevsky). A History of Ukraine. Edited by O. J. Frederiksen. Preface by George Vernadsky. New Haven, Yale University Press, 1941. 629 p.
    Based on a one-volume popular work (*Iliustrovana istoriia Ukrainy*, L'viv, 1911), covering the whole period of the history of Ukraine to 1940. Concluding chapter, which deals with events in the Ukraine from 1918 to 1940, was prepared by Professor Frederiksen.

375. Doroshenko, Dmytro.   History of the Ukraine. Translated from the Ukrainian and abridged by Hanna Chikalenko-Keller. Edited with an introduction by G. W. Simpson. 2d ed. Edmonton, Alberta, The Institute Press, 1941. 686 p.
Bibliography: p. 665-672.
See also entry no. 480.
> Perhaps the best survey of the course of Ukrainian history up to the Second World War. By a distinguished scholar. A condensed translation of a two-volume work in Ukrainian: *Narys istorii Ukrainy* (Warsaw, 1932-1933).

376. Krupnitzky (Krupnyckyj), Borys.   Geschichte der Ukraine von den Anfängen bis zum Jahre 1917. 3d rev. ed. Wiesbaden, Otto Harrassowitz, 1963. 307 p.
> An excellent brief history of the Ukraine by a prominent historian. Earlier editions: 1939, 1943.

377. Rostovtsev, Mikhail I. (Michael I. Rostovtzeff).   Iranians and Greeks in South Russia. Oxford, Clarendon Press, 1922. 260 p.
Bibliography: p. 223-238.
> A study of the civilization in the lands of the present-day Ukraine from the ninth century B.C. Connections between the heritage of antiquity and the rise of the Kievan State are traced.

378. Hrushevs'kyi, Mykhailo (Michael Hrusevs'kyj).   Geschichte des ukrainischen (ruthenischen) Volkes. v. 1: Urgeschichte des Landes und des Volkes, Anfänge des Kijever Staates. Authorized translation from the second Ukrainian edition. Leipzig, B. G. Teubner, 1906. 753 p.
> A standard work on the early history of the Ukraine, up to and including the formation of the Kievan state; an authorized translation of the first volume of *Istoriia Ukrainy-Rusy* (L'viv, 1898-1936, 10 v.) by a renowned historian.

379. Bächtold, Rudolf.   Südwestrussland im Spätmittelalter; territoriale, wirtschaftliche und soziale Verhältnisse. Basel, Helbing und Lichtenhahn, 1951. 211 p. (Basler Beiträge zur Geschichtswissenschaft, Bd. 38)
Bibliography: p. 207-211.
> A study of the social and political conditions in the Ukrainian provinces of the Grand Duchy of Lithuania (Lithuanian-Ruthenian State) in the fourteenth to sixteenth centuries.

380. O'Brien, Carl B.   Muscovy and the Ukraine; from the Pereiaslavl Agreement to the Truce of Andrusovo, 1654-1667. Berkeley, University of California Press, 1963. 138 p.
Bibliography: p. 135-138.
> A study of a turbulent chapter in the history of the Cossack Ukraine, beginning with the acceptance of the suzerainty of Moscow by Hetman Khmelnytsky (1654), and ending with the division of the Ukrainian lands between Russia and Poland (1667).

381. Vernadsky, George. Bohdan, Hetman of Ukraine. New Haven, Yale University Press; London, H. Milford, Oxford University Press, 1941. 150 p.

> A biography of Bohdan Khmelnytsky, the leader of the Cossack revolution against Poland and the founder of the Ukrainian Cossack state in the middle of the seventeenth century.

382. Krupnitzky (Krupnyckyj), Borys. Hetman Mazepa und seine Zeit, 1687-1709. Leipzig, Otto Harrassowitz, 1942. 260 p.

> A biography of the famous and controversial Cossack leader, originally a friend of Peter I, and later an ally of the Swedish king, Charles XII, by an eminent student of that period. The work also includes chapters on social and cultural conditions in the Ukraine during Mazepa's administration.

383. Polons'ka-Vasylenko, Nataliia D.   The Settlement of the Southern Ukraine (1750-1775). New York, 1955. 350 p. (The Annals of the Ukrainian Academy of Arts and Sciences in the U.S., v. 4/5, Summer–Fall 1955)

> An extensive treatise on the colonization of the Southern Ukraine in the second half of the eighteenth century.

384. Borshchak, Il'ko (Élie Borschak). La légende historique de l'Ukraine: Istorija rusov. Paris, Institut d'Études Slaves, 1949. 195 p. (Collection historique de l'Institut d'Études Slaves, 13)

> A monograph on a landmark of Ukrainian historical-political thought, written at the turn of the nineteenth century.

385. Kostomarov, Nikolai I. (Nicolas).   Le livre de la genèse du peuple Ukrainien. Translated from the Ukrainian, with an introduction and notes, by Georges Luciani. Paris, Institut d'Études Slaves de l'Université de Paris, 1956. 149 p. (Collection historique de l'Institut d'Études Slaves, 17)

> An exhaustive analysis of N. Kostomarov's "Books of Genesis of the Ukrainian People" (Knyhy bytiia ukrains'koho narodu), the programmatic work of the Cyril-and-Methodius Society, 1846-1847, the parental organization of the modern Ukrainian national movement, written by its leader, an eminent historian. The program advocated the creation of a democratic federation of all Slavic peoples, including a free Ukraine.
>
> For an English version, *see* Nicolas Kostomarov, *Books of Genesis of the Ukrainian People*, with commentary by B. Yanivs'kyi (New York, Research Program on the USSR, 1954, 45 p.; [East European Fund, Mimeographed Series, no. 60]).

386. Rudnytsky, Ivan L.   The Role of the Ukraine in Modern History. Slavic Review, v. 22, June 1963: 201-216.

> A discussion of the key problems of nineteenth- and twentieth-century Ukrainian history. The essay is followed by comments by Arthur E. Adams, Omeljan Pritsak, and John S. Reshetar.

387. Rudnytsky, Ivan L., *ed.*   Mykhailo Drahomanov; a Symposium and Selected Writings. New York, 1952. 225 p. (The Annals of the Ukrainian Academy of Arts and Sciences in the U.S., v. 2, Spring 1952)

> A symposium of studies devoted to an outstanding scholar and representative political thinker of the second half of the nineteenth century. Included are selections from his writings and an annotated bibliography of his major works.

388. Manning, Clarence A.   Twentieth-Century Ukraine. New York, Bookman Associates, 1951. 243 p.
Bibliography: p. 211-216.

> A review of the history of the Ukraine since 1914.

389. Reshetar, John S.   The Ukrainian Revolution, 1917-1920; a Study in Nationalism. Princeton, Princeton University Press, 1952. 363 p.
Bibliography: p. 333-347.
See also entry no. 558.

> A standard survey of the Ukrainian effort to attain and defend independent statehood.

390. Kuchabs'kyi, Vasyl' (W. Kutschabsky).   Die Westukraine im Kampfe mit Polen und dem Bolschewismus in den Jahren 1918-1923. Berlin, Junker und Dünnhaupt, 1934. 439 p. Bibliography. (Schriften der Kriegsgeschichtlichen Abteilung im Historischen Seminar der Friedrich-Wilhelms-Universität Berlin. Allgemeine Reihe, Heft 8)

> The contribution of Galicia to the struggle of the Ukraine for independent nationhood. Contains an excellent general discussion of the problems of the history of the Ukrainian revolution.

4. Diplomatic History and Foreign Relations

391. Markus, Vasyl.   L'Ukraine soviétique dans les relations internationales et son statut en droit international, 1918-1923. Preface by Charles Rousseau. Paris, Les Éditions Internationales, 1959. 326 p.

> A study of the role of the Ukrainian SSR in international relations prior to its entrance into the Soviet Union (1923), written from a historical and legal point of view.

392. Text of the Ukraine "Peace."   Washington, U.S. Government Printing Office, 1918. 160 p.

> Includes texts of the Ukraine Peace Treaties of 1918 and a collection of documents on the Ukraine, 1917-1918.

393. Beyer, Hans.   Die Mittelmächte und die Ukraine, 1918. Munich, Isar Verlag, 1956. 58 p. (Jahrbücher für Geschichte Osteuropas, Beiheft 2)

> A study of the policies of the Central Powers towards the Ukraine at the time of the Brest-Litovsk peace negotiations and the German occupation of the Ukraine in 1918.

394. Ilnytzkyj, Roman.   Deutschland und die Ukraine, 1934-1945; Tatsachen europäischer Ostpolitik, ein Vorbericht. 2d ed. Munich, Osteuropa-Institut, 1958. 2 v. Bibliography.

   A survey of political relations between Germany and the Ukraine from 1934 to 1945. Numerous documents are appended to each volume.

395. Shul'hyn, Oleksander (Alexandre Choulguine).   L'Ukraine contre Moscou, 1917. Paris, Félix Alcan, 1935. 220 p.

   Memoirs on the revolutionary events of 1917 by the first minister of foreign affairs of the Ukrainian People's Republic.

5. Politics, Government, and Law

396. Iakovliv (Jakowliw), Andrii.   Das deutsche Recht in der Ukraine und seine Einflüsse auf das ukrainische Recht im 16.-18. Jahrhundert. Leipzig, S. Hirzel, 1942. 220 p.
   Bibliography: p. 4-9.

   A study of the German Magdeburg Law in the Ukraine and its influence on Ukrainian law in the sixteenth to seventeenth centuries.

397. Schumann, Hans.   Der Hetmanstaat (1654-1764). Jahrbücher für Geschichte Osteuropas, v. 1, 1936, no. 4: 499-548.

   A survey of the constitutional structure of the Ukrainian Cossack state, 1654-1764, and of its political institutions.

398. Lawrynenko, Jurij.   Ukrainian Communism and Soviet Russian Policy toward the Ukraine; an Annotated Bibliography, 1917-1953. Edited by David I. Goldstein. Foreword by John S. Reshetar, Jr. New York, Research Program on the USSR, 1953. 454 p. (Studies on the USSR, no. 4)

   An extensive guide to literature on Ukrainian communism and Soviet Russian policy in the Ukraine from 1917 to 1953. Its incisive annotations provide invaluable assistance for the student of these topics.

399. Sullivant, Robert S.   Soviet Politics and the Ukraine, 1917-1957. New York, Columbia University Press, 1962. 438 p.

   A broad survey of Russian Communist nationality policies in regard to the Ukraine, stressing the close ties between the industrial-agrarian question and the nationality question. Based on a doctoral dissertation at the University of Chicago.

400. Dmytryshyn, Basil.   Moscow and the Ukraine, 1918-1953; a Study of Russian Bolshevik Nationality Policy. New York, Bookman Associates, 1956. 310 p.
   Bibliography: p. 287-302.

   A comprehensive treatment of the Russian Bolshevik nationality policy in the Ukraine and an analysis of social and political changes in the country, particularly in the 1920's and 1930's.

401. Borys, Jurij.   The Russian Communist Party and the Sovietization
of Ukraine; a Study in the Communist Doctrine of the Self-Determination of Nations. Stockholm, 1960. 374 p.
Bibliography: p. 356-368.
A competent and well-documented analysis of Bolshevik policies
in the Ukraine, with particular reference to the doctrine of self-
determination of nations as applied in the Ukraine up to the sovietization of the country.

402. Adams, Arthur E.   Bolsheviks in the Ukraine; the Second Campaign,
1918-1919. New Haven, Yale University Press, 1963. 440 p. Illus.
A survey of one of the most complex periods of modern Ukrainian
history, with an emphasis on political and social factors during the
Civil War.

403. Kostiuk, Hryhory.   Stalinist Rule in the Ukraine; a Study of the
Decade of Mass Terror, 1929-39. New York, Praeger, 1961. 162 p.
Bibliography: p. 153-157.
See also entry no. 778.
An account, based on all presently accessible sources and the author's firsthand knowledge, of the 10 tragic years of modern Ukrainian history during which time forced collectivization and industrialization of the country were accomplished. Concentrates on the policy
of mass terror and forced Russification by Stalin and his lieutenants.

404. Armstrong, John A.   Ukrainian Nationalism. 2d ed. New York,
Columbia University Press, 1963. 361 p. Bibliography.
A thorough study of the Ukrainian independence movement during the Second World War. Based on widely scattered published
and unpublished documents as well as firsthand accounts of persons
who played key roles during the period. First published in 1955.

6. Economics

405. Czyrowski (Chirovsky), Nicholas L.   Old Ukraine: Its Socio-Economic History prior to 1781. Madison, N. J., The Florham Park
Press, 1963. 432 p.
An outline of socio-economic history of the Ukraine from the
pre-historic period to the end of the Cossack state.

406. Kononenko, Konstantyn.   Ukraine and Russia; a History of the Economic Relations between Ukraine and Russia, 1654-1917. Milwaukee, Marquette University Press, 1958. 257 p.
Bibliography: p. 245-250.
A study of the Ukraine's economic position in the Russian Empire, particularly in the nineteenth century. The "colonialist" aspects
of Russian economic policies towards the Ukraine are stressed.
The work is based on research done in the Ukrainian SSR in the
1920's by economic historians who have subsequently been purged.

407. Holubnychy, Vsevolod.   The Industrial Output of the Ukraine,

1913-1956; a Statistical Analysis. Munich, Institute for the Study of the USSR, 1957. 63 p.
Bibliography: p. 54-63.

7. Language

408. Andrusyshen, C. H., *and* J. N. Krett.   Ukrains'ko-anhliis'kyi slovnyk. Ukrainian-English Dictionary. Saskatoon, University of Saskatchewan, 1955. 1,163 p.
Contains some 95,000 Ukrainian words, their English equivalents and definitions, and about 35,000 idiomatic phrases and expressions.

409. Rudnyts'kyi, Iaroslav B. (Jaroslav B. Rudnyckyj).   An Etymological Dictionary of the Ukrainian Language. Winnipeg, Ukrainian Free Academy of Sciences, 1962–
Explanatory notes in English. In progress.

410. Luckyj, George S. N., *and* Jaroslav Rudnyckyj.   A Modern Ukrainian Grammar. 3d ed. Winnipeg, Ukrainian Free Academy of Sciences, 1958. 186 p.

411. Shevelov, George Y.   The Syntax of Modern Literary Ukrainian: the Simple Sentence. The Hague, Mouton, 1963. 319 p. (Slavistic Printings and Reprintings, no. 38)
Most competent and detailed treatment of the subject, with the main emphasis on a presentation of wide factual data from contemporary literary Ukrainian.

8. Literature

412. Manning, Clarence A.   Ukrainian Literature; Studies of the Leading Authors. With a foreword by Watson Kirkconnell. Jersey City, N. J., Ukrainian National Association, 1944. 126 p.
Bibliography: p. 123-126.
A brief history of Ukrainian literature, including sketches of lives and works of 13 leading Ukrainian authors.

413. Luzhnyts'kyi, Hryhor (Gregory Luznycky).   Ukrainian Literature within the Framework of World Literature; a Short Outline of Ukrainian Literature from Renaissance to Romanticism. Philadelphia, "America" Publishing House, 1961. 80 p.

414. Luckyj, George S. N.   Literary Politics in the Soviet Ukraine, 1917-1934. New York, Columbia University Press, 1956. 323 p.
Bibliography: p. 273-292.
A penetrating inquiry into Ukrainian literature during the first 17 years of the Soviet period, and its subsequent stifling through Party controls. Considerable attention is devoted to literary organizations, their histories and conflicts. Indispensable. Based on a doctoral dissertation at Columbia University.

415. Mijakows'kyj, Volodymyr, *and* George Y. Shevelov. Taras Ševčenko, 1814-1861; a Symposium Edited on Behalf of the Ukrainian Academy of Arts and Sciences in the United States. The Hague, Mouton, 1962. 302 p. (Slavistic Printings and Reprintings, no. 31)

> A symposium of nine essays by different authors presenting various aspects of the work and life of the most eminent Ukrainian poet: sources of his world view, peculiarities of his poetry, and his impact on later generations.

416. The Ukrainian Poets, 1189-1962. Selected and translated into English verse by C. H. Andrusyshen and Watson Kirkconnell. Toronto, published for the Ukrainian Canadian Committee by the University of Toronto Press, 1963. 500 p.

> This anthology begins with the translation of *The Tale of Ihor's Campaign* and covers the whole period of Ukrainian poetry to the present day. Biographical sketches of the authors precede the selections of poetry.

417. Franko, Ivan. Beiträge zur Geschichte und der Kultur der Ukraine; ausgewählte deutsche Schriften des revolutionären Demokraten 1882-1915. Berlin, 1963. 577 p. (Quellen und Studien zur Geschichte Osteuropas, v. 14)

> Important contributions to the social and cultural history of the Ukraine by the eminent Ukrainian scholar and author.

9. History of Thought

418. Mirchuk (Mirtschuk), Ivan. Geschichte der ukrainischen Kultur. Munich, Isar Verlag, 1957. 284 p. (Veröffentlichungen des Osteuropa-Institutes München, Bd. 12)
Bibliography: p. 253-274.

> A general outline of the history of Ukrainian civilization, treating such fields as religion, literature, theater, music, education, philosophical thought, etc.

419. Oljančyn, Domet. Hryhorij Skovoroda, 1722-1794; der ukrainische Philosoph des XVIII. Jahrhunderts und seine geistig-kulturelle Umwelt. Berlin, Osteuropa-Verlag, 1928. 168 p. (Osteuropäische Forschungen, N.F., Bd. 2)

> A study of the life and works of the eighteenth-century Ukrainian philosopher.

10. Religion

a. General

420. Winter, Eduard. Byzanz und Rom im Kampf um die Ukraine, 955-1939. Leipzig, Otto Harrassowitz, 1942. 227 p.

> A stimulating survey of Ukrainian ecclesiastical history by a German scholar. Stresses the interaction of Byzantine and Western ele-

ments and strivings towards their synthesis as the outstanding features of the Ukrainian cultural tradition.

b. Ukrainian Orthodox Church

421. Vlasovs'kyi (Wlasowsky), Ivan.   Outline History of the Ukrainian Orthodox Church. Translated from the Ukrainian by M. J. Diakowsky. New York, Bound Brook, Ukrainian Orthodox Church of U.S.A., 1956–

> A general outline of the history of the Ukrainian Orthodox Church for non-specialists, to be published in four volumes. The first volume covers the period from Christianization to the Union of Brest in 1596. Translation of *Narys istorii ukrains'koi pravoslavnoi tserkvy* (New York, 1955-1961, 4 v.)

422. Heyer, Friedrich.   Die Orthodoxe Kirche in der Ukraine von 1917 bis 1945. Cologne-Braunsfeld, R. Müller, 1953. 259 p.
Bibliography: p. 246-248.
See also entry no. 1660.

> The only comprehensive survey of the history of the Ukrainian Orthodox Church during these stormy years of revolutions, wars, factional struggles, and persecutions. By a German Protestant theologian.

c. Ukrainian Catholic Church

423. Halecki, Oscar.   From Florence to Brest, 1439-1596. Rome, Sacrum Poloniae Millenium; New York, Fordham University Press, 1958. 444 p.

> A substantial survey, based on archival sources, of the relations between the Holy See and the Orthodox Church of the Polish-Lithuanian Commonwealth in the fifteenth and sixteenth centuries. The central problem is one of the gradual rapprochement of the Ukrainians and Belorussians with the Catholic Church, leading to the Union of Brest, 1596.

424. Hrynioch, Ivan.   The Destruction of the Ukrainian Catholic Church in the Soviet Union. Prologue (New York), v. 4, Spring–Summer 1960: 1-51.

> A brief but comprehensive survey. German translation in *Ostkirchliche Studien*, v. 12, March 1963: 1-38.

425. Analecta Ordinis Sancti Basilii Magni; Sectio 3, Series 2: Documenta Romana Ecclesiae Catholicae in Terris Ucrainae et Bielarusjae. Edited by Athanasius G. Welykyj. Rome, PP. Basiliani, 1953–

> A series of volumes of documents from the Vatican archives concerning the history of the Eastern Church, especially that of the Ukraine and White Russia. Over 35 volumes have been published to date.

C. BALTICA

by John P. Balys

1. The Baltic Countries

426. Baltic Review.   1945– New York. irregular.
Chiefly devoted to current political affairs concerning the Baltic countries. In the period 1945-1949, published in Stockholm by Baltic Humanitarian Association. Since 1953, published in New York by Committees for a Free Estonia, Latvia, and Lithuania.

Acta Baltica, an annual published since 1962 by Institutum Balticum in Königstein im Taunus (German Federal Republic), deals with the situation of the Baltic countries under Soviet rule. Each volume contains studies in German on a variety of topics of current interest.

427. Balys, John P.   The Baltic States: a 10-Year Survey. *In* U.S. Library of Congress. Quarterly Journal of Current Acquisitions, v. 20, no. 1, Dec. 1962: 80-92.
Described are the more important works received at the Library of Congress in the preceding decade. A somewhat expanded version entitled "The More Important Works on the Baltic States: a Survey of the Last Ten Years," was published in *Lituanus*, v. 8, 1962, no. 4: 110-119.

428. Commentationes Balticae.   Jahrbuch des Baltischen Forschungsinstituts. v. 1– 1953– Bonn. annual.
The field of interest of the Institute embraces the humanities and the social sciences, and its yearbook contains a number of scholarly studies, usually in German, but occasionally also in English. The authors, members of the Institute, are exiled professors and intellectuals from the three Baltic countries.

429. Fraenkel, Ernst.   Die baltischen Sprachen; ihre Beziehungen zu einander und zu den indogermanischen Schwesteridiomen als Einführung in die baltische Sprachwissenschaft. Heidelberg, C. Winter, 1950. 126 p.
Bibliography: p. 125-126.
An introduction to Baltic linguistics. Relations of the Baltic languages, i.e., Latvian, Lithuanian, and Ancient Prussian, among themselves, and affinities with other Indo-European languages, especially the Slavonic languages, are discussed.

430. Gimbutas, Marija.   The Balts. New York, Praeger, 1963. 286 p. Illus., maps.
Bibliography: p. 214-223.
A survey of the origin, history and pre-history, linguistic background, and ancient religion of the Baltic peoples, based chiefly on archeological materials.

431. Royal Institute of International Affairs. *Information Dept.* The

Baltic States; a Survey of the Political and Economic Structure and the Foreign Relations of Estonia, Latvia, and Lithuania. London, Oxford University Press, 1938. 194 p. Folded map.

A very informative survey of the three Baltic States from the First World War to 1937, consisting of two main parts: historical and political, and economic and financial, respectively. Included are 56 statistical tables in the text, and two appendixes on vital statistics and communications.

432. Tarulis, Albert N.   Soviet Policy toward the Baltic States, 1918-1940. Notre Dame, Ind., University of Notre Dame Press, 1959. 276 p. Maps.

A well-documented survey of the struggle of the Baltic nations for self-determination and political independence after the First World War, and their conquest and annexation by the Soviet Union in 1940.

The history of the relations between the Baltic States and the USSR in 1939-1940 from the viewpoint of international law is discussed in Boris Meissner's *Die Sowjetunion, die baltischen Staaten und das Völkerrecht* (Cologne, Verlag für Politik und Wirtschaft, 1956, 377 p.)

The same problem is treated in a rather popular way by John A. Swettenham in *The Tragedy of the Baltic States; a Report Compiled from Official Documents and Eyewitnesses' Reports* (New York, Praeger, 1954, 216 p.)

For French readers, the same subject is covered by Henry de Chambon, author of several books on the Baltic countries, in his *La tragédie des nations Baltiques* (Paris, Éditions de la Revue parlementaire, 1946, 226 p.)

433. Weiss, Helmuth, *comp.* Baltische Bibliographie, 1945-1952; Schrifttum über Estland und Lettland in Auswahl. Zeitschrift für Ostforschung, v. 3, 1954, no. 2: 305-320.

Continuations of this bibliography have been published annually since 1955 in the same periodical.

Baltische Bibliographie 1945-1956 by Erik Thomson (Würzburg, Holzner-Verlag, 1957, 218 p.) lists only works of authors of Baltic German origin, published in German or translated into other languages.

2. Estonia

434. Aspects of Estonian Culture.   Edited by Evald Uustalu. London, Boreas Publishing Co., 1961. 332 p. Illus., maps.

A reference book by 19 authors who "confine themselves chiefly to those achievements of Estonian cultural activities by which the national characteristics are best expressed." Contains chapters on history, religious life, schools and education, humanities, research in science and technology, language and literature, fine arts, press, etc.

435. Harms, Robert T.   Estonian Grammar. Bloomington, Indiana University Press, 1962. 175 p. (Indiana University Publications. Uralic and Altaic Series, 12)

This is the most recent Estonian grammar in English.

Another practical grammar of conversational Estonian is Percy J. Cook's *Estonian Self-Taught by Natural Method, with Phonetic Pronunciation* (London, E. Marlborough, 1933, 182 p.)

436. Kangro, Bernard, *and* Valev Uibopuu, *comps.*   The Face of Estonia; Estonia in Picture and Word. Foreword by Ants Oras. Translated by Hillar Kallas. Lund, Eesti Kirjanike Kooperatiiv, 1961. 120 p. Illus.

A pictorial book of landscapes, cities, and architectural monuments, most of which were destroyed during the Second World War, with an essay on "Estonia — the Country, Her People and Their Culture."

A similar album of landscapes, flora and fauna is *Eesti kaunis loodus* (Estonian Beautiful Nature), edited by E. Varep and others under the sponsorship of the Academy of Sciences of the Estonian SSR (Tallinn, 1957). Introduction and picture captions are given in English and German as well as Estonian.

437. Raud, Villibald.   Estonia, a Reference Book. New York, Nordic Press, 1953. 158 p. Illus., map.

A book of general information, with emphasis on economic conditions during the period of independence, including 33 statistical tables, supplemented with chapters on Estonia under Soviet rule and on Estonians abroad.

438. Saagpakk, Paul F.   Eesti-inglise sõnaraamat. An Estonian-English Dictionary. New York, Nordic Press, 1955–

A practical dictionary published in parts. Volume one covers the letters A-Gra, with an English-language introduction, "A Grammatical Survey of the Estonian Language."

Another useful dictionary is J. Silvet's *Inglise-eesti sõnaraamat; an English-Estonian Dictionary*, 2d ed. (Toronto, Eesti Kirjastus Orto, 1956, 1,205 p.)

439. U. S. *Library of Congress. Slavic and Central European Division.* Estonia: a Selected Bibliography. Compiled by Salme Kuri. Washington, 1958. 74 p.

Contains 491 entries. "This bibliography is designed primarily to help the nonspecialist find information on Estonia and its people. . . . Preference in the selection of titles was given to publications in English. . . . Very few works published in Soviet Estonia . . . are included."

440. Uustalu, Evald.   The History of Estonian People. London, Boreas Publishing Co., 1952. 261 p. Illus., maps.

Chiefly a political history with important data and figures.

John H. Jackson's *Estonia* (2d ed., London, Allen and Unwin, 1948, 272 p.) places more emphasis on cultural history.

In *Histoire de l'Estonie* (Paris, Payot, 1935, 271 p.), Hans Kruus, an outstanding Estonian historian, outlines Estonian history from the thirteenth century until the end of the War of Independence and the peace treaty with Soviet Russia on February 2, 1920.

3. Latvia

441. Andersons, Edgars, *ed.* Cross Road Country: Latvia. Waverly, Iowa, Latvju Grāmata, 1953. 386 p. Illus.
Bibliography: p. 371-384.
    A collection of well-documented and illustrated articles on the country, people, and history of Latvia during its 22 years of independence. An extensive bibliography of books and articles in English on Latvia is appended.

442. Chicago. University. Bibliography of Latvia. New Haven, Human Relations Area Files, 1956. 45 p.
    Contains a selection of 161 annotated entries for books and articles in various languages. Included are some works published in Soviet Latvia.

443. Chicago. University. *Division of the Social Sciences.* Latvia: an Area Study. Edited by George B. Carson. New Haven, Human Relations Area Files, 1956. 2 v. (667 p.) Maps, plans.
    "This study . . . seeks to trace the historical background and geographical setting for the existence of the contemporary ethnic group, and describe its society, politics, and economy under present conditions."

444. Prince, John D. Practical Grammar of the Lettish Language for the Use of Students. London, Toronto, J. M. Dent, 1925. 81 p.
Bibliography: p. xiv.

445. Spekke, Arnolds. History of Latvia; an Outline. Translated from Latvian by H. Kundziņš and others. Stockholm, M. Goppers, 1951. 436 p. Illus., ports., maps.
Bibliography: p. 415-422, 429-436.
    A popular political, social, and cultural history of the Latvian nation from prehistoric times to 1944, with numerous illustrations and maps in text and on plates. An extensive bibliography is included.

446. Turkina, Eiženija. Latviešu-angļu vārdnica. Latvian-English Dictionary. Edited by M. Andersone. 2d ed. Riga, Latvian State Publishing House, 1962. 775 p.
Bibliography: p. 7.
    Contains about 31,000 words.

4. Lithuania

447. Balys, Jonas (John P.). Lithuania and Lithuanians; a Selected Bibliography. New York, published for the Lithuanian Research Institute by F. A. Praeger, 1961. 190 p. (Studia Lituanica, 2)

Contains about 1,200 entries for books and articles, primarily in Western languages; short annotations often are included; titles in Lithuanian and in Slavic languages are translated into English. Includes the more important books published in Soviet Lithuania.

448. Jungfer, Victor.   Litauen, Antlitz eines Volkes; Versuch einer Kultursoziologie. 2d ed. Tübingen, Patria-Verlag, 1948. 341 p. Illus. "Anmerkungen" (Bibliographical references): p. 315-341.

Contains chapters on language, folklore, literature, art, theater, and other aspects of intellectual life in independent Lithuania.

449. Lituanus; Lithuanian Quarterly. v. 1– Nov. 1954– Chicago.

An English-language journal, published by Lituanus Foundation, Inc., featuring well-documented articles and studies on a variety of aspects of Lithuanian affairs in the past and present.

450. Péteraitis, Vilius.   Lietuviškai angliškas žodynas. Lithuanian-English Dictionary. 2d ed. Chicago, Lietuviškos knygos klubas, 1960. 586 p. A 30,000-word dictionary.

Other useful bilingual dictionaries published in recent years are, e.g.: *Anglų lietuvių kalbų žodynas* (English-Lithuanian Dictionary), compiled by V. Baravykas and edited by A. Laučka and A. Dantaitė (Chicago, Terra, 1959, 538 p.); *Lietuvių-anglų Kalbų žodynas* (Lithuanian-English Dictionary), compiled by B. Piesarskas and B. Svecevičius (Vilnius, Valstybinė politinės ir mokslinės literatūros leidykla, 1960, 511 p.)

451. Senn, Alfred E.   The Emergence of Modern Lithuania. New York, Columbia University Press, 1959. 272 p.

Examines the realization of Lithuanian national aspirations and the establishment of an independent national state, as well as the backstage struggle in international affairs and military operations from September 1917 through May 1920.

452. Simutis, Anicetas, *ed.*   Pasaulio lietuvių žinynas. Lithuanian World Directory. 2d ed. New York, Lithuanian Chamber of Commerce, 1958. 464 p. Bibliography: p. 112-116.

Contains informative articles in English on various Lithuanian subjects (language, history, etc.), written by specialists, as well as lists of names and addresses of persons and institutions active in Lithuanian affairs.

D. OTHER NATIONS[2]

by Lawrence Krader

453. Bennigsen, Alexandre.   Les peuples musulmans de l'URSS et les Soviets. L'Afrique et l'Asie (Paris), 1952, no. 4: 10-26; 1953, no. 1: 13-30; 1953, no. 2: 21-32; 1953, no. 4: 15-35.

[2] *See also* the sections on Ethnology, Islam and Buddhism, and Judaism.

An account of political and social conditions of the Moslems of Central Asia and neighboring regions of the USSR.

454. Caroe, Olaf K.   Soviet Empire; the Turks of Central Asia and Stalinism. London, Macmillan, 1953. 300 p. Maps, index.

By a British diplomat, long active in Central and South Asian affairs. Political critique of Soviet rule in Central Asia. For early period, draws upon *Bugünkü Türkili* (Turkestan Today) by Zeki Validi Togan, Turkish politician and scholar.

455. Castagné, Joseph A.   Le bolchévisme et l'Islam. Paris, 1922. 254 p.

Part one: *Les organisations soviétiques de la Russie musulmane. See also* his *Russie slave et Russie turque* (Paris, 1923, 261 p.) and *Les musulmans et la politique des Soviets en Asie Centrale* (Paris, E. Leroux, 1925, 125 p.). Three studies by a French ethnographer and official specializing in this area. Originally published in *Revue du monde musulman*, same dates and pagination. Important source for the period.

The author's *Les basmatchis* (Paris, E. Leroux, 1925, 88 p.) deals with a nationalist movement of Central Asia.

456. Lang, David M.   A Modern History of Soviet Georgia. New York, Grove Press, 1962. 298 p. Illus., maps.

Georgia and Georgians in the Soviet period. Nationalities questions in historical development.

457. Matossian, Mary A. K.   The Impact of Soviet Policies in Armenia. Leiden, E. J. Brill, 1962. 239 p.
Bibliography: p. 228-239.

Survey and analysis of political and social problems of the Armenian SSR.

458. Park, Alexander G.   Bolshevism in Turkestan, 1917-1927. New York, Columbia University Press, 1957. 428 p.
Bibliography: p. 389-412.

Published as a Study of the Russian Institute, Columbia University. Introduction of Soviet system in Central Asia; nationalities questions discussed in historical context.

See also Richard A. Pierce, *Russian Central Asia, 1867–1917* (Berkeley, University of California Press, 1960, 359 p.) for a study of preceding historical period.

459. Sarkisyanz, Emanuel. Geschichte der orientalischen Völker Russlands bis 1917. Munich, Oldenbourg, 1961. 422 p. Illus.

Discussion of historical background of Russian policy regarding oriental peoples. Introduction by Berthold Spuler.

460. Spuler, Berthold.   Die Wolga-Tataren und Baschkiren unter russischer Herrschaft. Der Islam (Berlin), v. 29, 1949-1950: 142-216.

See also his "Die Lage der Muslime in Russland seit 1942." *Ibid.*,

v. 29, 1949-1950: 296-300. By a German specialist in Turkic affairs and Asian history.

461. Vakar, Nicholas P.   A Bibliographical Guide to Belorussia. Cambridge, Harvard University Press, 1956. 63 p.

462. Zenkovsky, Serge A.   Pan-Turkism and Islam in Russia. Cambridge, Harvard University Press, 1960. 345 p. Illus., maps, index.
See also entry no. 1695.
   Cultural politics of Turks in relation to Islam, 1905-1920.
   See also Baymirza Hayit, *Turkestan im XX Jahrhundert* (Darmstadt, Leske, 1956, 406 p., maps), and his *Sowjetrussische Orientpolitik am Beispiel Turkestans* (Cologne, Kiepenheuer und Witsch, 1962, 289 p.), for further treatment of the same theme.

VI

history[1,2]

by Richard Pipes

A. GENERAL SURVEYS

463. Miliukov, Pavel N., Ch. Seignobos, *and* L. Eisenmann. Histoire de Russie. Paris, E. Leroux, 1932-1933. 3 v.

An excellent, well-organized survey written from a liberal point of view. The principal contributions are by outstanding pre-Revolutionary historians headed by Miliukov, and including A. Kizevetter for the eighteenth century and V. Miakotin for part of the nineteenth. A good supplement to Platonov (*see* entry no. 464).

464. Platonov, Sergei F. Histoire de la Russie des origines à 1918. Paris, Payot, 1929. 991 p.

Probably the best general history of Russia available in a Western language. Written by an eminent Russian historian from a conservative, nationalistic point of view. Its particular strength resides in the discussion of the Muscovite period; the nineteenth and the twentieth centuries are sketchily treated. A translation of the tenth edition of the author's *Lektsii po russkoi istorii* (Petrograd, Senatskaia tipografiia, 1917, 743 p.). The English edition, *History of Russia* (New York, Macmillan, 1929, 435 p.), and the German, *Geschichte Russlands vom Beginn bis zur Jetztzeit* (Leipzig, Quelle und Meyer, 1927, 461 p.), are mere précis.

465. Stählin, Karl. Geschichte Russlands von den Anfängen bis zur Gegenwart. Graz, Akademische Druck- u. Verlagsanstalt, 1961. 4 v. in 5. Illus.

Stählin disposes of Russian history before the establishment of the Romanov dynasty in one volume, and then proceeds to provide a very detailed account of the remaining three centuries, stopping with

---

[1] The arrangement within the sections of this chapter combines chronological and topical criteria, general treatments preceding those of a more specialized nature.

[2] For diplomatic history, *see* Chapter VII, C; for histories of other special topics, see the pertinent sections.

1917. The emphasis throughout is on military and diplomatic events. Particularly valuable for the eighteenth century. This edition is an unaltered reprint of the earlier work of the same title (Stuttgart, Deutsche Verlagsanstalt, 1923-1939, 4 v. in 5).

466. Stökl, Günther.   Russische Geschichte von den Anfängen bis zur Gegenwart. Stuttgart, A. Kröner, 1962. 824 p. Illus.

An up-to-date account based on recent research. Two-thirds of the narrative covers the period preceding the accession of Alexander II, with the consequence that the period 1855-1917 is gone over rapidly. Attention is given to social conditions, political institutions, and thought.

467. Florinsky, Michael T.   Russia; a History and an Interpretation. New York, Macmillan, 1953. 2 v.
Bibliography: v. 2, p. 1482-1511.

The most thorough narrative of pre-Revolutionary Russian history available in English. Particularly strong on the nineteenth and early twentieth centuries. Very hostile to the old regime, it has been criticized for overemphasizing the "road to disaster" theme.

468. Riasanovsky, Nicholas V.   A History of Russia. New York, Oxford University Press, 1963. 711 p. Illus.

A lucid and balanced one-volume textbook for college students. From earliest times to the present.

469. Russian Thought and Politics.   Edited by Hugh McLean and others. The Hague, Mouton, 1957. 513 p. (Harvard Slavic Studies, 4)

Essays, principally on Russian intellectual history of the eighteenth to twentieth centuries, by 26 historians, students of Professor Michael Karpovich.

B. GENERAL MONOGRAPHS

470. Kovalevskii (Kovalevsky), Maksim M.   Russian Political Institutions; the Growth and Development of These Institutions from the Beginnings of Russian History to the Present Time. Chicago, University of Chicago Press, 1902. 299 p.

The only work in a Western language to provide a general picture of Russian constitutional history. Written by an eminent sociologist, it is little more than an outline.

471. Diakonov, Mikhail A.   Skizzen zur Gesellschafts- und Staatsordnung des alten Russlands. Breslau, Priebatsch, 1931. 436 p.

A translation of *Ocherki obshchestvennago i gosudarstvennago stroia drevnei Rusi*, a standard work on pre-Petrine political, social, and legal institutions. Judicious, comprehensive, and well-organized, it has not yet been surpassed in any language.

472. *Miliukov, Pavel N. (Paul).   Outlines of Russian Culture. Edited by Michael Karpovich. Translated by Valentine Ughet and Eleanor Davis. Philadelphia, University of Pennsylvania Press, 1942. 3 v. Illus.
See also entries no. 1569, 1638, and 1815.
 A partial translation of the second volume of the "jubilee edition" of Miliukov's great work, *Ocherki po istorii russkoi kul'tury* (Paris, "Sovremennyia zapiski," 1930-1937, 3 v. in 4). Deals with religion and church, literature, architecture, painting, and music from the earliest times to the Revolution. Probably still the best introduction to the subject. An earlier German translation, including a greater part of Miliukov's first edition, appeared as *Skizzen russischer Kulturgeschichte* (Leipzig, O. Wigand, 1898-1901, 2 v.)

473. Ammann, Albert M.   Abriss der ostslawischen Kirchengeschichte. Vienna, Thomas Morus Presse, 1950. 748 p.
See also entry no. 1628.
 The author, a Jesuit, gives a full account of Russian church history from the beginning to the present, utilizing a wealth of Russian and Western sources.
 Paul Pierling's *La Russie et le Saint-Siège; études diplomatiques* (Paris, Plon-Nourrit, 1896-1912, 5 v.) is a history, by a Jesuit scholar, of Russian diplomatic relations with Rome from the Council of Florence to the accession of Nicholas I. It is based on Italian archives, including those of the Vatican.

474. Liashchenko, Petr I.   History of the National Economy of Russia, to the 1917 Revolution. Translated by L. M. Herman. New York, Macmillan, 1949. 880 p. (American Council of Learned Societies. Russian Translation Project. Series 4)
See also entry no. 1026.
 A Marxist-Leninist interpretation. The book is a translation (with omissions) of the first edition of the author's standard Soviet text, *Istoriia russkogo narodnogo khoziaistva* (Moscow, Sotsekgiz, 1939, 674 p.)

475. Grekov, Boris D.   Die Bauern in der Rus von den ältesten Zeiten bis zum 17. Jahrhundert. Berlin, Akademie-Verlag, 1958-1959. 2 v.
 An exhaustive study by a leading Soviet social historian, with emphasis on social conditions and conflicts. Translation of *Krest'iane na Rusi s drevneishikh vremen do XVII veka* (2d rev. and enl. ed.; Moscow, Izdatel'stvo Akademii nauk SSSR, 1952-1954, 2 v.)

476. Blum, Jerome.   Lord and Peasant in Russia from the Ninth to the Nineteenth Century. Princeton, Princeton University Press, 1961. 656 p.
Bibliography: p. 623-645.
See also entries no. 1022 and 1184.
 A comprehensive study of rural Russia from earliest times to the

emancipation of serfs in 1861. Social as well as economic conditions are treated.

477. Tugan-Baranovskii, Mikhail I.   Geschichte der russischen Fabrik. Berlin, E. Felber, 1900. 626 p.

The author, a prominent economist of Marxist leanings, traces the history of Russian industrialization from the seventeenth century to the end of the nineteenth. Originally written as a polemical work against non-Marxist socialists who denied the feasibility of capitalist industrialism in Russia. A translation of *Russkaia fabrika v proshlom i nastoiashchem; istoriko-ekonomicheskoe izsliedovanie* (St. Petersburg, Izdanie L. F. Pantelieeva, 1898, 496 p.)

478. Jelavich, Barbara.   A Century of Russian Foreign Policy, 1814-1914. Philadelphia, New York, Lippincott, 1964. 308 p.
See also entry no. 854.

A succinct and judicious account which emphasizes the successes of Russian diplomatic and military policies.

479. Nol'de, Boris E., *baron*.   La formation de l'Empire russe; études, notes et documents. Paris, Institut d'Études Slaves, 1952-1953. 2 v.
Bibliography: v. 1, p. 275-293; v. 2, p. 389-401.

The uncompleted work of an excellent émigré scholar, intended as a general history of Russian expansion and empire building. Volume one deals with the penetration into the Volga-Ural region from the fifteenth to the eighteenth centuries; volume two discusses expansion toward the Black Sea and Caucasus from the sixteenth to the nineteenth centuries.

480. Doroshenko, Dmytro.   History of the Ukraine. Translated from the Ukrainian and abridged by Hanna Chikalenko-Keller. Edited with an introduction by G. W. Simpson. Edmonton, Alberta, The Institute Press, 1939. 686 p.
Bibliography: p. 665-672.
See also entry no. 375.

Emphasis on the seventeenth and eighteenth centuries. Written from a nationalistic point of view, but less so than Michael Hrushevsky's *A History of Ukraine* (*See* entry no. 374).

481. Dubnov (Dubnow), Semen M.   History of the Jews in Russia and Poland from the Earliest Times until the Present Day. Philadelphia, The Jewish Publication Society of America, 1916-1920. 3 v.
Bibliography: v. 3, p. 171-203.
See also entry no. 1700.

An original work, written especially for this edition. Dubnov was the outstanding historian of Russian Jewry, moderate in national matters and a liberal in politics. The work nevertheless suffers from a bias characteristic of what has been called the "lachrymose school" of Jewish historiography, for which the course of Jewish history is an uninterrupted tale of woe.

C. KIEVAN AND MUSCOVITE RUS'

482. Povest' vremennykh let. *English.*   The Russian Primary Chronicle: Laurentian Text. Translated and edited by Samuel H. Cross and Olgerd P. Sherbowitz-Wetzor. Cambridge, Mediaeval Academy of America, 1953. 313 p. (Mediaeval Academy of America. Publication no. 60)
Bibliography: p. 288-295.
See also entry no. 1391.
> A translation of the most important Russian chronicle with a historical and historiographical introduction.

483. Medieval Russian Laws. Translated by George Vernadsky. New York, Columbia University Press, 1947. 106 p.
Bibliography: p. 97-99.
See also entry no. 587.
> A translation of *Russkaia pravda* and of several other legal documents from the Dvina land, Pskov, and Novgorod.

484. Vernadsky, George, *and* Michael Karpovich.   A History of Russia. New Haven, Yale University Press, 1943–
> Unquestionably the most comprehensive account of early Russian history available in any Western language. Stresses heavily Russia's relations with Asian cultures. In progress, with four volumes published so far (*Ancient Russia, Kievan Russia, The Mongols and Russia,* and *Russia at the Dawn of the Modern Age*), all written by Professor Vernadsky.

485. Paszkiewicz, Henryk.   The Origin of Russia. London, Allen and Unwin, 1954. 556 p.
Bibliography: p. 470-519.
> A collection of essays concerned with some critical problems of early Russian history (ninth to fourteenth centuries), such as the Norman dispute and the authenticity of the *Slovo o polku Igoreve* (*see* entry no. 1395). Especially useful for its extensive treatment of the Polish and Lithuanian aspects.

486. Eck, Alexandre.   Le moyen âge russe. Preface by Henri Pirenne. Paris, Maison du livre étranger, 1933. 569 p.
Bibliography: p. 495-505.
> A survey of political and social institutions from the beginning of the thirteenth to the sixteenth century. Resembles Diakonov's work (*see* entry no. 471) in its approach.

487. Fedotov, Georgii P., *ed.*   A Treasury of Russian Spirituality. New York, Sheed and Ward, 1948. 501 p.
Bibliography: p. 500-501.
See also entries no. 1380 and 1635.

A collection of sources on early Russian religion, including excerpts from the writings of the saints.

488.*Fedotov, Georgii P.   The Russian Religious Mind. v. 1: Kievan Christianity. Cambridge, Harvard University Press, 1946. 438 p.
Bibliography: p. 413-424.
See also entries no. 1373 and 1634.
An evocation of the religious spirit of Kievan Rus' which combines a high degree of religious empathy with excellent knowledge of the literature.

489. Goetz, Leopold K.   Deutsch-russische Handelsgeschichte des Mittelalters. Lübeck, O. Waelde, 1922. 572 p.
An important study which treats in great detail, on the basis of numerous archival and printed sources, the whole long history of Russia's commercial relations with Germany. Much information on Novgorod, including its internal conditions.
See also the same author's *Deutsch-russische Handelsverträge des Mittelalters* (Hamburg, L. Friederichsen, 1916, 394 p.), which contains sources.

490. Spuler, Berthold.   Die goldene Horde; die Mongolen in Russland, 1223-1502. Leipzig, O. Harrassowitz, 1943. 556 p.
Bibliography: p. 455-516.
The best history of the Golden Horde, with much information on its rule over the Russian principalities.
See also Boris D. Grekov and A. Iakubovskii, *La horde d'or* (Paris, Payot, 1939, 251 p.), an account of the same subject by eminent Soviet Slavic and Oriental historians.

491. Schaeder, Hildegard.   Moskau, das Dritte Rom; Studien zur Geschichte der politischen Theorien in der slavischen Welt. 2d ed. Darmstadt, Gentner, 1957. 215 p.
Bibliography: p. 172-197.
See also entry no. 1377.
A study of the "Third Rome" concept from its Bulgarian sources, through Filofei, Krizhanich, and Nikon, down to Konstantin Leont'ev. A republication of the author's first edition of the same title (Hamburg, Friederichsen, De Gruyter, 1929, 140 p.)

492. Tikhomirov, Mikhail N.   The Towns of Ancient Rus'. Translated by Y. Sdobnikow. Moscow, Foreign Languages Publishing House, 1959. 502 p. Index, maps.
See also entry no. 274.
The author is a leading Soviet medievalist. In this book, which traces one by one the histories of the major urban centers, nationalism often supersedes Marxism. Translation of *Drevnerusskie goroda* (Moscow, Gospolitizdat, 1956, 476 p.)

493. Fennell, John L. I.   Ivan the Great of Moscow. London, Macmillan; New York, St. Martin's Press, 1961. 386 p. Illus.
> A study of the reign of Ivan III, with emphasis almost entirely on diplomatic relations and foreign policy. Its purpose is to analyze the expansion of Moscow under a ruler for whose statesmanship the author has much praise.

494. Herberstein, Sigmund, *Freiherr* von.   Notes upon Russia: Being a Translation of the Earliest Account of That Country, Entitled Rerum Moscoviticarum Commentarii. Translated and edited, with notes and an introduction, by R. H. Major. London, Printed for the Hakluyt Society, 1851-1852. 2 v.
> Herberstein traveled to Russia in 1517 and 1526 as a representative of the Holy Roman Emperor. His account was the first relatively reliable description of Muscovy available to Western Europeans.

495. Kurbskii, Andrei M., *kniaz'*. The Correspondence between Prince A. M. Kurbsky and Tsar Ivan IV of Russia, 1564-1579. Edited with a translation and notes by J. L. I. Fennell. Cambridge, England, Cambridge University Press, 1955. 275 p.
Bibliography: p. 266-267.
See also entry no. 1406.
> The original Russian text and its English translation, with notes but without introduction.

496. Bond, *Sir* Edward A., *ed.*   Russia at the Close of the Sixteenth Century. London, Printed for the Hakluyt Society, 1856. 392 p.
> Contains Giles Fletcher's *Of the Russe Commonwealth* and the travels of Jerome Horsey, both important sources.

497. Platonov, Sergei F.   Boris Godounov, tsar de Russie (1598-1605). Paris, Payot, 1929. 269 p.
> The great authority on seventeenth century Russia endeavors to rehabilitate the reputation of the tsar. Translation of the Russian original.

498. Palmer, William.   The Patriarch and the Tsar. London, Trubner, 1871-1876. 6 v.
> Mainly sources (in English) bearing on Nikon's conflict with Aleksei Mikhailovich, some of which have not yet been published in the original Russian. The editor, who advocated the unification of the Anglican and Orthodox Churches, spent much time studying in Russia, where he obtained these documents.

499. Pascal, Pierre.   Avvakum et les débuts du Raskol; la crise religieuse au XVIIe siècle en Russie. Paris, Istina, 1938. 618 p.
Bibliography: p. 575-598.
See also entry no. 1639.

A major study which, using Avvakum as a subject, provides the best account of the schism available in a Western language. Based on thorough knowledge of the literature. Stresses the disastrous effects of the schism on the destiny of the Russian Orthodox Church.

D. EIGHTEENTH CENTURY

500. Schuyler, Eugene.   Peter the Great, Emperor of Russia; a Study of Historical Biography. New York, C. Scribner's Sons, 1884. 2 v. Illus., plates, ports., fold. geneal. tab., fold. map.

An old work, rather popular and somewhat old-fashioned, it nevertheless retains its value. Based on Russian and Western sources.

501.* Kliuchevskii, Vasilii O.   Peter the Great. Translated by Liliana Archibald. New York, St. Martin's Press, 1958. 282 p.

A new translation of part of volume four of the most celebrated work in Russian historical literature, Kliuchevskii's *Kurs russkoi istorii*, which has appeared in a number of editions. The integral English translation by C. J. Hogarth, *A History of Russia* (London, J. M. Dent; New York, E. P. Dutton, 1911-1931, 5 v.; reprinted, New York, Russell and Russell, 1960, 5 v.), is notoriously bad. There is a French translation of volume one, *Histoire de Russie* (Paris, Gallimard, 1956), and a German one of volumes four and five, *Russische Geschichte von Peter dem Grossen bis Nikolaus I* (Zurich, Artemis-Verlag, 1945, 2 v.)

502. Bil'basov, Vasilii A.   Geschichte Katharina II. Berlin, Norddeutsches Verlags-Institut, Berend und Jolowicz, 1891-1893. 4 pt. in 3 v.
Bibliography: v. 1, pt. 2, p. 166-172; v. 2, pt. 1, p. 587-589.

Traces the life and politics of Catherine to 1764. Documents. Translation from Russian of the author's ambitious, but uncompleted, biography.

503. Catharine II, *Empress of Russia*.   Documents of Catherine the Great; the Correspondence with Voltaire and the Instruction of 1767, in the English Text of 1768. Edited by W. F. Reddaway. Cambridge, England, Cambridge University Press, 1931. 349 p.

504. Haumant, Émile.   La culture française en Russie (1700-1900). Paris, Hachette, 1910. 571 p.
Bibliography: p. 531-549.

A thorough investigation of Russian-French cultural contacts, including Russians in France and the French in Russia, manners, education, literature, political ideas, and religion.

505. Rogger, Hans.   National Consciousness in Eighteenth-Century Russia. Cambridge, Harvard University Press, 1960. 319 p.
Bibliography: p. 285-295.
See also entries no. 1181 and 1574.

Traces in literature, historiography, political thought, etc., the emergence of a sense of national identity among the cosmopolitan elite.

E. 1801-1855

506. Kornilov, Aleksandr A.   Modern Russian History from the Age of Catherine the Great to the End of the Nineteenth Century. Translated by Alexander S. Kaun, with a bibliography by John S. Curtiss. New York, Knopf, 1943. 2 v. in 1 (310, 284 p.)
Bibliography: v. 2, p. 273-284.
> A well-informed narrative from the reign of Catherine the Great to the end of the nineteenth century. Foreign affairs are neglected, and the author — a staunch liberal — is very critical of the old regime. Probably no work in a Western language, however, gives so excellent a picture of internal policies in the nineteenth century. There are earlier editions of this translation (New York, Knopf, 1916-1917 and 1924, 2 v.)

507. Karpovich, Michael.   Imperial Russia, 1801-1917. New York, H. Holt, 1932. 106 p.
Bibliography: p. 97-102.
> A tour de force. In 97 pages of text the author surveys Russian history from 1801 to 1917, judiciously criticizing its failures and praising its achievements.

508. Leontovitsch, Victor.   Geschichte des Liberalismus in Russland. Frankfurt a/M, V. Klostermann, 1957. 425 p.
See also entry no. 633.
> Not so much a history of liberalism, in the usual sense of the word, as a stimulating essay on the gradual transformation of Russia by the monarchy into a *Rechtsstaat*. Covers the period from 1762 to 1917.

509. Karamzin, Nikolai M.   Memoir on Ancient and Modern Russia. Translated and with commentary by Richard Pipes. Cambridge, Harvard University Press, 1959. 266 p.
Bibliography: p. 255-259.
> A translation of Karamzin's *O drevnei i novoi Rossii* with notes and an introduction tracing the historical roots of the author's conservatism and the sources of this text.

510. Nikolai Mikhailovich, *grand duke of Russia*.   Le tsar Alexandre Ier. Translated by Baroness N. Wrangel. Paris, Payot, 1931. 358 p.
> An account of the character and reign of Alexander I by a member of the imperial family who enjoyed access to archives closed to other historians. A source book rather than a historical monograph. An abbreviated version of the sumptuously illustrated *Imperator Aleksandr I; opyt istoricheskago izsliedovaniia* (St. Petersburg, Expeditsiia zagotovleniia gosudarstvennykh bumag, 1912, 2 v.), the

second volume of which consists of the correspondence (in French) and other papers of Alexander I.

511. Pypin, Aleksandr N.   Die geistigen Bewegungen in Russland in der ersten Hälfte des XIX Jahrhunderts. v. 1: Die russische Gesellschaft unter Alexander I. Berlin, S. Cronbach, 1894. 690 p.

A liberal treatment of reform and oppositional movements in the reign of Alexander I, including Speranskii, Karamzin, the Masonic lodges, and the Decembrists. Very critical of the monarchy. A translation of the second edition of *Obshchestvennoe dvizhenie v Rossii pri Aleksandrie I* (St. Petersburg, Tip. M. M. Stasiulevicha, 1885, 543 p.)

512. Raeff, Marc.   Michael Speransky, Statesman of Imperial Russia, 1772-1839. The Hague, M. Nijhoff, 1957. 387 p.
Bibliography: p. 368-375.

A biographical study, with extensive analyses of the political activities and projects of Count Mikhail M. Speranskii. Mildly critical.

513. Tarle, Evgenii (Eugene) V.   Napoleon's Invasion of Russia, 1812. Translated by Norbert Guterman and Ralph Mannheim. New York, Toronto, Oxford University Press, 1942. 422 p.
See also entry no. 848.

Translation of a Soviet work originally published in 1938, *Nashestvie Napoleona na Rossiiu, 1812 god* (Moscow, Sotsekgiz, 1938, 279 p.). It is imbued with patriotism and often alludes to parallels between the Napoleonic invasion and the threatened attack by Nazi Germany. Still, Tarle was once a great historian, and retained to the end his gift of vivid narrative.

514. Mazour, Anatole G.   The First Russian Revolution, 1825; the Decembrist Movement, its Origins, Development, and Significance. Stanford, Calif., Stanford University Press, 1961. 328 p.

The most detailed history of the Decembrist Uprising in a Western language. It summarizes the findings of Russian historians. This study first appeared in 1937.

515. Schiemann, Theodor.   Geschichte Russlands unter Kaiser Nikolaus I. Berlin, G. Reiner, 1904-1919. 4 v.

Volume one deals with the reign of Alexander I. In the remaining three volumes, which cover the reign of Nicholas I, attention is centered almost exclusively on foreign and military affairs. Domestic events and policies are treated in passing.

516. Riasanovsky, Nicholas V.   Nicholas I and Official Nationality in Russia, 1825-1855. Berkeley, University of California Press, 1959. 296 p.
Bibliography: p. 273-292.

An outline of the ideology of the reign of Nicholas I in terms of its principles, the personalities who implemented them, and their effects.

517. Hertzen (Gertsen, Herzen), Aleksandr I.   My Past and Thoughts. London, Chatto and Windus, 1924-1927. 6 v.

A classic autobiography and an unsurpassed source of information and insight into the life of the Russian intelligentsia in the reign of Nicholas I. A translation of *Byloe i dumy* (Berlin, Slovo, 1921–, 5 v.). American edition: New York, Knopf, 1924-1926, 5 v.

518. Baddeley, John F.   The Russian Conquest of the Caucasus. London, New York, Longmans, Green, 1908. 518 p.

A vivid account of the wars for the possession of the Caucasian range, including the campaigns against Shamil.

F. 1855-1900

519. Fischer, George.   Russian Liberalism, from Gentry to Intelligentsia. Cambridge, Harvard University Press, 1958. 240 p.
Bibliography: p. 209-226.
See also entries no. 629 and 1586.

An essay which traces the evolution of liberal forces from 1855 to 1905 in terms of transition from domination by the gentry to domination by professional groups.

520. Robinson, Geroid T.   Rural Russia under the Old Régime. New York, Longmans, Green, 1932. 342 p.
Bibliography: p. 312-326.
See also entries no. 1091 and 1190.

The peasant question from the Emancipation Act to the Revolution. Begins where J. Blum's book stops. (*See* entry no. 476.)

521.* Seton-Watson, Hugh.   The Decline of Imperial Russia, 1855-1914. New York, Praeger, 1956. 406 p.
See also entry no. 865.

Thorough and well-balanced, this book surveys both internal and foreign policies.

522.* Kropotkin, Petr A., *kniaz'*.   Memoirs of a Revolutionist. Boston, New York, Houghton Mifflin, 1899. 502 p.

Lively and honest, these recollections by a leading anarchist theoretician, a participant in the "going to the people" movement, convey an impression of the radical movement of the 1860's and 1870's in Russia and Western Europe. Originally appeared in the *Atlantic Monthly* (September 1898 to September 1899). Reprinted in 1930.

523. Kulczycki, Ludwik.   Geschichte der russischen Revolution. Gotha, F. A. Perthes, 1910-1914. 3 v.

Translation from Polish of a very well-informed account of Russian revolutionary movements from the Decembrists to 1900. Based on a thorough knowledge of the sources.

524. Venturi, Franco. Roots of Revolution; a History of the Populist and Socialist Movements in Nineteenth Century Russia. Introduction by Isaiah Berlin. New York, Knopf, 1960. 850 p.
See also entry no. 641.

A history of "Populism," narrative rather than analytical, but the most thorough treatment in any language. Contains much on the leading radical thinkers: Hertzen, Chernyshevskii, Bakunin. Ends with the assassination of Alexander II in 1881. Originally appeared as *Il populismo russo* (Turin, Giulio Einaudi, 1952, 2 v.)

525. Spiridovich, Aleksandr I. (Alexandre Spiridovitch). Histoire du terrorisme russe, 1886-1917. Paris, Payot, 1930. 668 p.

The author, one-time chief of the emperor's personal guard, traces the history of the Socialist-Revolutionary Party. Based on rich source materials.

526. Sumner, Benedict H. Russia and the Balkans, 1870-1880. Oxford, Clarendon Press, 1937. 724 p.
Bibliography: p. 675-698.
See also entry no. 866.

A diplomatic and military narrative of the antecedents, course, and consequences of the Balkan War. Based on English archival sources and Balkan, as well as Russian, printed ones. An appendix contains documents, including the texts of the treaties of San Stefano and Berlin. Reprinted in 1962 (Hamden, Conn., Archon Books, 724 p.)

527. Langer, William L. The Franco-Russian Alliance, 1890-1894. Cambridge, Harvard University Press; London, H. Milford, Oxford University Press, 1929. 455 p.
Bibliography: p. 421-439.

A thorough study based on Western as well as Russian sources.
See also Boris E. Nol'de, *L'alliance franco-russe; les origines du système diplomatique d'avantguerre* (Paris, Droz, 1936, 700 p.)

528. Witte (Vitte), Sergei Iu., *graf*. The Memoirs of Count Witte. Translated and edited by Abraham Yarmolinsky. Garden City, N. Y., Toronto, Doubleday, Page, 1921. 445 p.

An abbreviated version of his *Vospominaniia*. Although often criticized as partisan and inaccurate, these memoirs provide a good picture of the man and his times. The German translation, with an introduction by Otto Hoetzsch, appeared as *Erinnerungen* (Berlin, Ullstein, 1923, 580 p.), and there is also a French translation, *Les mémoirs du Comte Witte (1849-1915)* (Paris, Plon-Nourrit, 1921, 387 p.)
See also Theodore H. von Laue, *Sergei Witte and the Industrialization of Russia* (New York, Columbia University Press, 1963, 360 p.)

G. 1900-1917

529.* Wallace, *Sir* Donald M.   Russia.   Rev. and enl. ed. London, New York, Cassell, 1912. 788 p.
See also entries no. 148, 275, and 1192.

A classic description of Russia by a *Times* correspondent who had spent, on and off, some 40 years in the country. A lively and well-informed account of institutions, social and ethnic groups, and political developments at the turn of the century, with their historical background. First published in 1877 (London, Paris and New York, Cassell, Petter and Galpin, 1877, 2 v.) and later extensively revised.

530. Leroy-Beaulieu, Anatole.   The Empire of the Tsars and the Russians. Translated from the third French edition by Zenaidé A. Ragozin. New York, London, Putnam, 1893-1896. 3 v. (588, 566, 601 p.)
See also entries no. 133, 619, and 1187.

A sympathetic panorama of Russian life and institutions toward the end of the nineteenth century, translated from the French (*L'empire des tsars et les russes*; Paris, Hachette, 1881-1889, 3 v.). Volume one deals with the land and its inhabitants, volume two with institutions, and volume three with religion. Optimistic about the outlook for the monarchy.

531. Keep, J. L. H.   The Rise of Social Democracy in Russia.   London, Oxford University Press, 1963. 334 p.
Bibliography: p. 304-322.
See also entry no. 632.

A history of the origins of Marxist parties, with stress on organization rather than ideology, and centered on the 1905 Revolution.

See also Dietrich Geyer, *Lenin in der russischen Sozial-demokratie; die Arbeiterbewegung als Organisationsproblem der revolutionären Intelligenz, 1890-1903* (Cologne, Böhlau, 1962, 447 p.), and Richard Pipes, *Social Democracy and the St. Petersburg Labor Movement, 1885-1897* (Cambridge, Harvard University Press, 1963, 154 p.)

532. Lederer, Ivo J., *ed.*   Russian Foreign Policy; Essays in Historical Perspective. New Haven, Yale University Press, 1962. 620 p.
See also entry no. 834.

Eighteen historians discuss various aspects of Russian foreign policy before and after the Revolution: its formulation, its agencies, and its application to various territories. The emphasis is on "continuity" and "change" between tsarism and communism.

533. Curtiss, John S.   Church and State in Russia; the Last Years of the Empire, 1900-1917. New York, Columbia University Press, 1940. 442 p.
Bibliography: p. 411-425.
———. The Russian Church and the Soviet State, 1917-1950. Boston, Little, Brown, 1953. 387 p.
Bibliography: p. 371-378.

See also entry no. 1653.

A detailed history of church-state relations and of the church establishment in the twentieth century. Religious life, insofar as it does not bear on relations with the state, is ignored. So are the non-Orthodox groups.

534. Hoetzsch, Otto. Russland; eine Einführung auf Grund seiner Geschichte von 1904 bis 1912. Berlin, G. Reimer, 1913. 550 p. Bibliography: p. 521-527.

A well-informed analysis of early twentieth-century Russia, with particular stress on the constitutional regime, its achievements and its shortcomings. Deals with political parties, the agrarian question, administration, social classes and local government, schooling and church, finances, armed forces, and the nationalities.

535. Walkin, Jacob. The Rise of Democracy in Pre-Revolutionary Russia; Political and Social Institutions under the Last Three Czars. New York, Praeger, 1962. 320 p. Bibliography.
See also entries no. 625 and 1171.

A stimulating essay on the question of whether the Soviet government is a logical continuation or an aberration of Russian pre-Revolutionary historical development. The author opts for the second alternative, stressing the rapid growth of democratic forces and institutions in pre-1917 Russia. No literature published after 1953 has been utilized.

536. Preyer, Wilhelm D. Die russische Agrarreform. Jena, G. Fischer, 1914. 415 p. Bibliography: p. 403-415.

The best Western account of the so-called Stolypin reforms. Discusses the legal and economic aspects, as well as the reaction of public opinion.

537.* Florinsky, Michael T. The End of the Russian Empire. New Haven, Yale University Press; London, Oxford University Press, 1931. 272 p. (Carnegie Endowment for International Peace. Division of Economics and History. Economic and Social History of the World War. Russian Series)
See also entry no. 617.

An analytical study of Russia during the First World War. Concentrates on politics and social conditions, and points to excessive strains put on the Russian state by the exigencies of war as the cause of the Revolution. Later edition: New York, Collier Books, 1961, 254 p.

538. Golovin (Golovine), Nikolai N. The Russian Army in the World War. New Haven, Yale University Press; London, Oxford University Press, 1931. 287 p. (Carnegie Endowment for International Peace. Division of Economics and History. Economic and Social History of the World War. Russian Series)

Not a military narrative, but an analysis of the condition of the Russian army by a Tsarist general and theoretician, who planned it as a part of a larger work on the "sociology of war." Among other topics, it discusses the conscription and supply systems, losses of manpower, munitions, transport, and the morale of the army, ending with the Bolshevik coup.

H. REVOLUTION AND CIVIL WAR

539. Treadgold, Donald W.   Twentieth Century Russia. Chicago, Rand McNally, 1959. 550 p.

A lucid, well-organized account, the bulk of which is devoted to the post-1917 period; in effect, a history of the Soviet Union and international communism.

540. Carr, Edward H.   A History of Soviet Russia. London, New York, Macmillan, 1951–
See also entries no. 896 and 1024.

A broadly-conceived, multi-volume work. The first three volumes are *The Bolshevik Revolution, 1917-1923*; the fourth, *The Interregnum, 1923-1924*; and the next three, *Socialism in One Country, 1924-1926*. The treatment is topical rather than narrative and frequently affected by the author's political convictions. No other work contains a comparable wealth of information.

541.* Kennan, George F.   Russia and the West under Lenin and Stalin. Boston, Little, Brown, 1961. 411 p.
See also entry no. 901.

An excellent history of Soviet foreign policy and the West's reaction to it. The author discounts the chiliastic element in communism.

542. Golder, Frank A., *ed.*   Documents of Russian History, 1914-1917. New York, London, The Century Co., 1927. 663 p.

A useful selection of documents (many of an official nature), largely from *Riech'* and *Izvestiia*, dealing with the First World War and the Revolution until the Bolshevik coup. The bulk of the material deals with 1917.

543. Browder, Robert P., *ed.*   The Russian Provisional Government, 1917; Documents, Selected and Edited by Robert Paul Browder and Alexander F. Kerensky. Stanford, Calif., Stanford University Press, 1961. 3 v. (477, 1-1193, 1195-1875 p.)
See also entry no. 616.

A collection of documents chosen and edited by the head of the Provisional Government with the assistance of an American scholar. It has been criticized for its selectivity as well as for its failure to give documents in full. It is useful as a source for understanding the assumptions and aims of the Provisional Government.

544. Bunyan, James, *and* Harold H. Fisher, *comps.*   The Bolshevik Revo-

lution, 1917-1918; Documents and Materials. Stanford, Calif., Stanford University Press, 1934. 735 p.

Bunyan, James, *ed.*   Intervention, Civil War and Communism in Russia, April–December 1918; Documents and Materials. Baltimore, Johns Hopkins Press, 1936. 594 p.
> Both volumes are excellently edited, and supply translations of important documents, including unpublished ones from the Hoover Library.
> See also *The Testimony of Kolchak and Other Siberian Materials*, edited and translated by Elena Varneck and Harold H. Fisher (Stanford, Calif., Stanford University Press; London, H. Milford, Oxford University Press, 1935, 466 p.), in the same collection.

545. Radkey, Oliver H.   The Election to the Russian Constituent Assembly of 1917. Cambridge, Harvard University Press, 1950. 89 p. Bibliography: p. 81-83.
See also entry no. 623.
> The best available analysis of the election procedures and results and of the abortive Constituent Assembly.

546. Chamberlin, William H.   The Russian Revolution, 1917-1921. New York, Macmillan, 1935. 2 v. Bibliography: v. 2, p. 505-524.
> Still the best general history of the Revolution and Civil War. Based on thorough study of the literature, Communist and non-Communist. Emphasizes political and military events rather than ideological and social aspects. Reprinted in 1952.

547.* Sukhanov, Nikolai N.   The Russian Revolution, 1917; a Personal Record. Edited, abridged, and translated by Joel Carmichael. London, New York, Oxford University Press, 1955. 691 p.
> A condensation containing approximately one-half of Sukhanov's seven-volume *Zapiski o revoliutsii* (Berlin, Izd-vo Z. I. Grzhebina, 1922-1923, 7 v.). The author, a Socialist Revolutionary turned Social Democrat, participated in important capacities in the revolutionary events. A critic, and at the same time an admirer, of the Bolshevik movement.

548.* Trotskii, Lev (Leon Trotsky).   The History of the Russian Revolution. Translated by Max Eastman. New York, Simon and Schuster, 1932. 3 v.
> Trotsky's verbal pyrotechnics cannot quite conceal his polemical intent and unscholarly methodology. His objections to "treacherous impartiality" and preference for "scientific conscientiousness," rooted not in the "good intentions of the historian but the natural laws revealed to him by the historic process itself" (Introduction, v. 1, p. xxi), will hardly convince scholarly readers. But as a well-written personal account of 1917, it has its place in the memoir literature. Reissued in 1957 (Ann Arbor, University of Michigan Press, 1957,

3 v. in 1.). A translation of *Istoriia russkoi revoliutsii* (Berlin, Izd-vo Granit, 1932-1933, 2 v. in 3).

549. Denikin, Anton I.   The Russian Turmoil; Memoirs: Military, Social, and Political. London, Hutchinson, 1922. 344 p.

This is a translation of volume one of *Ocherki russkoi smuty* (Paris, J. Povolzky, 1921-1926, 5 v.), which deals with events up to July 1917. The author's *The White Army* (London, J. Cape, 1930, 367 p.) is a summary of all five volumes. Clearly partisan, Denikin's work is an indispensable source.

550. Vrangel' (Wrangel), Petr N., *baron*.   The Memoirs of General Wrangel, the Last Commander-in-Chief of the Russian National Army. New York, Duffield, 1930. 356 p.

Honestly written, with important documents cited verbatim. Centers on 1920. Reissued under the title *Always with Honour; Memoirs of General Wrangel* (New York, R. Speller, 1957, 356 p.). A translation of *Zapiski; noiabr' 1916 — noiabr' 1920*, which originally appeared in *Bieloe dielo*, v. 6 (Berlin, Mednyi Vsadnik, 1928, 320 p.)

551.*Shub, David.   Lenin; a Biography. Garden City, N. Y., Doubleday, 1948. 438 p.
See also entry no. 737.

A study of the man rather than the statesman, it is vivid and often psychologically true, but also partisan and rather superficial. For three recent biographies of Lenin, *see* the annotation to entry no. 737.

552. Schapiro, Leonard B.   The Communist Party of the Soviet Union. New York, Random House; London, Eyre and Spottiswoode, 1960. 631 p.
Bibliography: p. 591-603.
See also entry no. 745.

The best treatment of the subject. Includes an extensive account of the pre-Revolutionary history of Russian Social Democracy.

553. Deutscher, Isaac.   The Prophet Armed; Trotsky, 1879-1921. New York, Oxford University Press, 1954. 540 p.
Bibliography: p. 523-528.
————. The Prophet Unarmed; Trotsky, 1921-1929. London, New York, Oxford University Press, 1959. 490 p.
————. The Prophet Outcast; Trotsky, 1929-1940. London, New York, Oxford University Press, 1963. 543 p.
See also entry no. 739.

A lively, well-written biography of Trotsky by an ardent admirer, to whom Trotsky was both a prophet and a hero. The best study of any Soviet leader presently available.

554. Kritzmann (Kritsman), Lev N.   Die heroische Periode der grossen

russischen Revolution; ein Versuch der Analyse des sogenannten "Kriegskommunismus." Vienna, Berlin, Verlag für Literatur und Politik, 1929. 439 p.

A scholarly Bolshevik study of the period of so-called "War Communism" (1918-1921) which pays much attention to economic policies and conditions. A translation of *Opyt analiza t. n. "voennogo kommunizma,"* 2d ed. (Moscow, Gosizdat, 1926, 272 p.)

555. Batsell, Walter R.   Soviet Rule in Russia. New York, Macmillan, 1929. 857 p.
Bibliography: p. 807-825.
See also entry no. 679.

A useful account of Soviet constitutional developments. Contains translations of many important documents not available elsewhere.

556. Daniels, Robert V.   The Conscience of the Revolution: Communist Opposition in Soviet Russia. Cambridge, Harvard University Press, 1960. 526 p.
Bibliography: p. 439-448.
See also entry no. 754.

A serious historical study of the "difference within the Communist movement in Russia and of all groups that disputed with the movement's leaders" from 1903 to the late 1930's.

557. Pipes, Richard.   The Formation of the Soviet Union; Communism and Nationalism, 1917-1923. Cambridge, Harvard University Press, 1954. 355 p.
Bibliography: p. 293-318.
See also entry no. 365.

A history of the disintegration of the Russian Empire and emergence on its ruins of new national states, followed by an account of their reconquest and incorporation into what became the Union of Soviet Socialist Republics. A second, revised edition is scheduled for publication in late 1964.

558. Reshetar, John S.   The Ukrainian Revolution, 1917-1920; a Study in Nationalism. Princeton, Princeton University Press, 1952. 363 p.
Bibliography: p. 333-347.
See also entry no. 389.

An impartial study of the successive Ukrainian national governments and their eventual collapse under Soviet pressure.

559. Kazemzadeh, Firuz.   The Struggle for Transcaucasia, 1917-1921. New York, Philosophical Library, 1951. 356 p.
Bibliography: p. 332-345.
See also entry no. 1686.

Transcaucasia in the course of the Russian Revolution and Civil War.

560. Hayit, Baymirza.   Turkestan im XX. Jahrhundert. Darmstadt, C. W. Leske, 1956. 406 p.
Bibliography: p. 379-385.
See also entry no. 1685.

> A history of the national movement in Russian Central Asia, written by a well-informed sympathizer.

I. RECENT HISTORY

561. Souvarine, Boris.   Stalin; a Critical Survey of Bolshevism. New York, Longmans, Green, 1939. 690 p.
See also entry no. 709.

> Although written in mid-stream of Stalin's career, it is still the best study of the man. Appeared in French as *Staline: aperçu historique du bolchévisme* (Paris, Plon, 1935, 574 p.). Preferable to Isaac Deutscher's *Stalin, a Political Biography* (London, New York, Oxford University Press, 1949, 600 p.)

562.* Fainsod, Merle.   Smolensk under Soviet Rule. Cambridge, Harvard University Press, 1958. 484 p.
See also entries no. 775 and 811.

> A detailed account covering the period 1917-1938. Based on 200,000 pages of Soviet materials which fell into German hands in 1941, and which, at the end of the Second World War, were captured by United States forces. A unique insight into the effect of Soviet political practice on the ordinary citizen.

563. Schwarz, Solomon M.   The Jews in the Soviet Union. Syracuse, Syracuse University Press, 1951. 380 p.
See also entry no. 1712.

> Emphasizes the evolution of Communist feeling from friendship for the Jewish minority to more or less overt anti-Semitism.

564. Dallin, Alexander.   German Rule in Russia, 1941-1945; a Study of Occupation Policies. New York, St. Martin's Press; London, Macmillan, 1957. 695 p.

> A very comprehensive and objective study of the Nazis in Russia. Based on captured German documents. Deals mainly with dissent within the Nazi civil and military commands over the policies toward Russians and minorities.

565. Philippi, Alfred, *and* Ferdinand Helm.   Der Feldzug gegen Sowjetrussland, 1941 bis 1945; ein operativer Überblick. Stuttgart, W. Kohlhammer, 1962. 293 p.

> A history of military operations based on both German archives and Soviet printed works.

566. Gruliow, Leo, *ed*.   Current Soviet Policies. v. 2: The Documen-

tary Record of the XX Communist Party Congress and Its Aftermath. New York, Praeger, 1957. 247 p.

See also entry no. 668.

Contains the text of Khrushchev's speech on Stalin, as well as other important historical documents released on this occasion.

567.* Black, Cyril E., *ed.*   Rewriting Russian History; Soviet Interpretations of Russia's Past. New York, Published for the Research Program on the U.S.S.R. by Praeger, 1956. 413 p.

Essays by various authors, including refugees from the Soviet Union, tracing the changing attitude of Soviet authorities toward certain historical problems.

See also Konstantin F. Shteppa, *Russian Historians and the Soviet State* (New Brunswick, N. J., Rutgers University Press, 1962, 437 p.), which is informative, but carelessly edited.

VII

the state

A. LAW

by *John N. Hazard and William B. Stern*

1. Texts

568. Akademiia nauk SSSR. *Institut gosudarstva i prava.* International Law; a Textbook for Use in Law Schools. Translated from the Russian by Dennis Ogden. Moscow, Foreign Languages Publishing House, 1961. 477 p.

> An English translation of the 1957 textbook used in Soviet law schools to introduce the subject to Marxist-oriented students (*Mezhdunarodnoe pravo;* Moscow, Gosiuridizdat, 1957, 471 p.). Authors include Ia. A. Korovin, S. B. Krylov, and F. I. Kozhevnikov, who was the editor of the volume.

569.* Berman, Harold J. Justice in Russia; an Interpretation of Soviet Law. Cambridge, Harvard University Press, 1950. 322 p.
See also entry no. 1150.

> A pioneer study indicating the influence of Marxist theory and Russian legal history upon Soviet law and concluding that the Russian revolution had settled down by 1950 and had found, of necessity, a place for law in social control. A major portion of the book treats planning as the mainspring of legal development, and the parental approach of the judge as the explanation of legal procedure. A revised and enlarged edition was published in 1963 under the title *Justice in the U.S.S.R.* (New York, Vintage Books, 450 p.)

570. Berman, Harold J., *and* Miroslav Kerner, *eds.* Documents on Soviet Military Law and Administration. Cambridge, Harvard University Press, 1955. 164 p.

Berman, Harold J., *and* Miroslav Kerner. Soviet Military Law and Administration. Cambridge, Harvard University Press, 1955. 208 p.

Documents and explanatory text describing the specialized subject of military law.

571. Boguslavskii, Mark M., *and* A. Rubanov.   The Legal Status of Foreigners in the U.S.S.R.   Translated from the Russian by Julius Katzer. Moscow, Foreign Languages Publishing House, 1961. 122 p.

A popularized discussion for foreigners dwelling within the USSR of the extent to which Soviet law governs their activities. Also considers the Soviet conflict of law rules applicable. Translation of *Pravovoe polozhenie inostrantsev v SSSR* (Moscow, Institut mezhdunarodnykh otnoshenii, n.d., 122 p.)

572. Calvez, Jean Y.   Droit internationale et souveraineté en U.R.S.S.; l'évolution de l'idéologie juridique soviétique depuis la Révolution d'octobre. Paris, Colin, 1953. 299 p. (Cahiers de la Fondation Nationale des Sciences Politiques, no. 48)

A pioneering study in French of the development of Soviet legal theory, with extensive citation from Soviet authors.

Paralleled for international law by Ivo Lapenna, *Conceptions soviétiques de droit international public* (Paris, Pedone, 1954, 324 p.)

573. David, René, *and* John N. Hazard.   Le droit soviétique. Paris, Librairie générale de droit et de jurisprudence, 1954. 2 v. (367, 409 p.) (Les systèmes de droit contemporains, no. 7-8)

David's volume (*Les données fondamentales du droit soviétique*) presents a Romanist jurist's thinking on the history and philosophical base of Soviet law. Hazard's volume is a translation of his *Law and Social Change in the U.S.S.R.* Contains an exhaustive bibliography of books in French, English, German, Spanish, and Italian on Soviet law, as of publication date. A Spanish-language edition, revised to 1962, is to be published by La Ley, Buenos Aires, in 1964.

574. Denisov, Andrei I., *and* M. Kirichenko.   Soviet State Law. Moscow, Foreign Languages Publishing House, 1960. 459 p.
See also entry no. 678.

A translation, with the original criticisms of law in the United States expunged, of the authors' *Sovetskoe gosudarstvennoe pravo* (Moscow, Gosiuridizdat, 1957), explaining the Soviet state structure and the role of the constitution.

575. El'iashevich, Vasilii B. (Basile El'iachevitch), Paul Tager, *and* Boris Nol'de.   Traité de droit civil et commercial des soviets. Paris, Librairie générale de droit et de jurisprudence, 1930. 3 v. (323, 462, 467 p.)

An early and exhaustive treatise, by former Russian Imperial jurists, of civil law in effect during the period of the New Economic Policy of the 1920's. Brought up to date regarding property in K. Stoyanovitch, *Le régime de la propriété en U.R.S.S.* (Paris, Librairie générale de droit et de jurisprudence, 1962, 312 p.)

576. Greyfié de Bellecombe, Louis.   Les conventions collectives de travail en Union Soviétique. Preface by René David. Paris, Mouton,

1958. 172 p. (Études sur l'économie et la sociologie des pays slaves, v. 3)
Bibliography: p. 165-172.
> An account of collective bargaining in the USSR written by a French exchange student in Moscow after study in the U.S. An attempt to determine its role and legal status in labor-management relations.

577. Grzybowski, Kazimierz.   Soviet Legal Institutions; Doctrines and Social Functions. Ann Arbor, University of Michigan Press, 1962. 285 p.
> Erudite study, documenting well the thesis that the law of Communist-oriented states in Europe is structured upon a Romanist base. Cohesion in discussion of a wide variety of matters is provided by focus on the effect of law on the life of the individual. Finds a post-Stalin trend away from litigation toward mass mediation, suggested, perhaps, by Chinese ideas.

578. Gsovski, Vladimir.   Soviet Civil Law; Private Rights and Their Background under the Soviet Regime. Comparative Survey and Translation. Ann Arbor, University of Michigan Law School, 1948-1949. 2 v. (909, 907 p.)
> A collection of translations, not only of the RSFSR Civil Code of 1922 as amended to date of publication, but of other pertinent codes and statutes, preceded by a volume of historical commentary especially rich in comparison with the law of other Romanist countries.

579. Gsovski, Vladimir, *and* Kazimierz Grzybowski, *eds.*   Government, Law and Courts in the Soviet Union and Eastern Europe. New York, Praeger; London, Stevens, 1959. 2 v. (917, 921-2067 p.)
> Description of law in European Communist-oriented states by a group of former lawyers of these countries. Great detail, but uneven coverage of subject matter. Includes extensive treatment of the steps taken by Communists in these countries to achieve power. Dr. Gsovski contributed all material on the USSR.

580. Guins, George C.   Soviet Law and Soviet Society. The Hague, M. Nijhoff, 1954. 457 p.
> A comparison, by a former Imperial Russian judge, of Soviet law with that of the West, compressing much material into a small space to prove that increasing centralization of authority is reducing personal freedom.

581. Hazard, John N.   Law and Social Change in the U.S.S.R. London, Stevens and Sons, 1953. 310 p.
> An analysis of substantive Soviet law, utilizing over 100 judicial decisions to sketch the nature of the legal component in molding a new society.

582. Hazard, John N.   Settling Disputes in Soviet Society; the Formative

Years of Legal Institutions. New York, Columbia University Press, 1960. 534 p.

An account of the development of Soviet legal institutions from the simple tribunals of 1917, functioning without a labyrinth of rules of procedure and without prosecution or bar, to the complicated courts of 1925 applying a codified legal system. Utilizes extensive judicial materials. Points briefly to post-1925 development.

583. Hazard, John N.   Soviet Housing Law. New Haven, Yale University Press, 1939. 178 p.

The law on ownership and distribution of housing in the USSR from 1917 to the reforms of 1937. Brought up to date by Bernard Rudden in *International and Comparative Law Quarterly,* v. 12, 1963: 591-630.

584. Kelsen, Hans.   The Communist Theory of Law. London, Stevens; New York, Praeger, 1955. 203 p.

An analysis of Soviet legal philosophy as evidenced in translations appearing in *Soviet Legal Philosophy* (20th Century Legal Philosophy Series, v. 5). Concludes that Marxism is not scientific, nor based on accurate appraisal of the causes for the emergence of law, and that Soviet philosophers are attempting to make of it a new type of natural law with development of Vyshinsky's normativism.

585. Konstantinovsky, Boris A.   Soviet Law in Action; the Recollected Cases of a Soviet Lawyer. Edited by Harold J. Berman. Cambridge, Harvard University Press, 1953. 77 p.

The practice of Soviet law as seen by the former legal adviser to the Odessa Bread Trust, providing much otherwise unavailable information, including the influence of local Communist Party functionaries on the courts. Professor Berman's annotations place the material in the framework of the Soviet legal system.

In George Feifer's *Justice in Moscow* (New York, Simon and Schuster, 1964), an American student reports on 55 trials witnessed in 1961-1962.

586. Kucherov, Samuel.   Courts, Lawyers, and Trials under the Last Three Tsars. Foreword by Michael Karpovich. New York, Praeger, 1953. 339 p.

An account by a former member of the bar in Imperial Russia of the activities of lawyers and the milieu of the legal profession from 1864 to 1917. Concludes that the Imperial bar was on the road to independence and was one of the primary institutions of Imperial Russia through which democracy was growing.

587. Medieval Russian Laws.   Translated by George Vernadsky. New York, Columbia University Press, 1947. 106 p.
See also entry no. 483.

A translation of the *Pravda Russkaia,* together with a 25-page introductory statement of the early origins of law in what became Russia, and translations of the earliest city charters.

588. Morgan, Glenn G.   Soviet Administrative Legality; the Role of the Attorney General's Office. Stanford, Calif., Stanford University Press, 1962. 281 p.

Historical development, in the light of practice, of the Procuracy's function in protecting citizens from arbitrary action of administrators, concluding that the function is performed least well during campaigns to force citizens along unpopular paths of social organization. Compares Tsarist practices and the *ombudsman* of Scandinavian states.

589. Riazanovskii (Riasanovskii), Valentin A.   Customary Law of the Nomadic Tribes of Siberia. Tientsin, 1938. 151 p.

Description of the law of indigenous peoples who were permitted to proceed unmolested by Tsarist authorities.

590. Romaskin, Petr S., *ed.*   Fundamentals of Soviet Law. Moscow, Foreign Languages Publishing House, 1960. 516 p.

A co-operative work prepared by senior Soviet specialists for foreigners. Elementary, but useful in providing authoritative Soviet views in English.

591. Schlesinger, Rudolf, *ed.*   Changing Attitudes in Soviet Russia; Documents and Readings. v. 1: The Family. London, Routledge and Paul, 1949. 408 p.
See also entry no. 1209.

Translations of Soviet sources with commentary.

592. Schlesinger, Rudolf, *ed.*   Changing Attitudes in Soviet Russia. v. 2: The Nationalities Problem and Soviet Administration; Selected Readings on the Development of Soviet Nationalities Policies. Translated by W. W. Gottlieb. London, Routledge and Paul, 1956. 299 p.

Material useful for understanding the character of the Soviet federation.

593. Schlesinger, Rudolf.   Soviet Legal Theory, Its Social Background and Development. London, Kegan Paul; New York, Oxford University Press, 1945. 299 p.

The first non-Soviet treatment of Soviet legal thought. Written by a former Central European Marxist. Concludes that the recalcitrance of the peasantry, the need to overcome underdevelopment rapidly, and the resistance of national minorities served as retarding elements in the evolution of society toward socialism, and hence of Soviet law. Expects that the Soviet pattern will serve as a model for other societies seeking to establish socialism, and that the principal lessons are in economic organization and the suppression of political antagonists. A second edition was published in London in 1951 (Routledge and Paul, 312 p.)

594. Soviet Legal Philosophy.   Translated by Hugh W. Babb with an introduction by John N. Hazard. Cambridge, Harvard University Press, 1951. 456 p. (20th Century Legal Philosophy Series, v. 5)

Translations of the principal statements made by Soviet legal theorists in search of a distinctive Soviet approach to law in evolution of Marxist fundamentals. The introduction provides the historical setting. Contains the principal texts of E. B. Pashukanis.

595. Sverdlov, Grigorii M.   Legal Rights of the Soviet Family; Marriage, Motherhood and the Family in Soviet Law. London, "Soviet News," 1945. 55 p.

Explanatory treatment by the principal Soviet authority on Soviet family law. Popularized.

596. Taracouzio, Timothy A.   The Soviet Union and International Law; a Study based on the Legislation, Treaties and Foreign Relations of the Union of Socialist Soviet Republics. New York, Macmillan, 1935. 530 p.

The first non-Soviet study of Soviet attitudes toward, and practice of, international law, with a calendar of treaties.

597. Triska, Jan F., *and* Robert M. Slusser.   The Theory, Law, and Policy of Soviet Treaties. Stanford, Calif., Stanford University Press, 1962. 593 p. Bibliography.

See also entry no. 878.

A detailed analysis of Soviet treaty practice, attempting to determine the extent to which other states may rely on the USSR's good faith in observance of her treaties.

Preceded by an exhaustive *Calendar of Soviet Treaties, 1917-1957* with indexes (Stanford University Press, 1959, 530 p.)

598. Vyshinskii (Vyshinsky), Andrei Ia., *ed.*   The Law of the Soviet State. Translated by Hugh W. Babb. New York, Macmillan, 1948. 749 p.

Translation of the 1938 edition of *Sovetskoe gosudarstvennoe pravo,* written by a group of which Vyshinsky was chairman. It is the primary text of the late Stalin epoch after the denunciation of E. B. Pashukanis in 1937. Treats only the matter of public law in spite of the broad title.

599. Zaitsev, Evgenii (Yevgeny), *and* Arkady Poltorak.   The Soviet Bar. Moscow, Foreign Languages Publishing House, 1959. 255 p.

A popularized account designed to prove that the Soviet bar is organized to assure due process of law in Soviet courts. Contains some abstracts of cases in which lawyers figured prominently.

600. Zelitch, Judah.   Soviet Administration of Criminal Law. Philadelphia, University of Pennsylvania Press, 1931. 418 p. (University of Pennsylvania Law School Series, v. 5)

The earliest American study of Soviet law, describing the origin of the Soviet courts and their procedures. Written on the basis of Soviet documentation and field interviews.

601. Zigel' (Sigel), Feodor F.   Lectures on Slavonic Law; Being the

Ilchester Lectures for the Year 1900. London, Henry Frowde; New York, Oxford University Press, 1902. 152 p.

> The classic statement in English of the origins of law among the Slavs: Bulgaria, Serbia, Russia, Bohemia, Poland, and Croatia.

2. Documentation

602.* Hazard, John N., *and* Isaac Shapiro. The Soviet Legal System; Post-Stalin Documentation and Historical Commentary. Dobbs Ferry, N.Y., Oceana Publications, 1962. 3 v. in 1 (186, 235, 174 p.) (Parker School Studies in Foreign and Comparative Law)

> Translations of statutes, judicial decisions, doctrine, and Communist Party documents, presented with historical essays by the editors to provide a framework for understanding by Americans. Contains translations of legal forms and extensive bibliography of Soviet works in English translation and of non-Soviet commentary in English.

603. Meisel, James H., *and* Edward S. Kozera, *eds.* Materials for the Study of the Soviet System; State and Party Constitutions, Laws, Decrees, Decisions, and Official Statements of the Leaders in Translation. 2d rev. and enl. ed. Ann Arbor, Mich., Wahr Publishing Co., 1953. 613 p.
Bibliography: p. 581-589.
See also entry no. 647.

> Compendium of translations of primary sources from 1917 on. Without commentary. Well selected for teaching purposes to show historical development.

604. Russia (*1923– U.S.S.R.*) *Laws, statutes, etc.* Fundamentals of Soviet Criminal Legislation, the Judicial System and Criminal Court Procedure; Official Texts and Commentaries. Translated by George H. Hanna. Moscow, Foreign Languages Publishing House, 1960. 102 p.

> Translations of the fundamentals with brief commentary by Soviet specialists.

3. Periodicals

605. Bibliographie für Staats- und Rechtsfragen. v. 1-8. 1955-1962. Potsdam. bimonthly.

> An index to legal periodicals published in the German Democratic Republic, the Soviet Union, and the countries of the people's democracies. Contains lists of unpublished German translations in the library of the East German Academy for State and Legal Sciences. Merged in 1963 with *Rechtswissenschaftliche Dokumentation; Referatzeitschrift für die Staats- und Rechtswissenschaft.*
>
> Published East German translations are listed in *Bibliographie deutscher Übersetzungen aus den Sprachen der Völker der Sowjetunion und der Länder der Volksdemokratie* (1952– Leipzig).

606. Institut für Ostrecht, *Munich.*   Studien. v. 1– 1958– Herrenalb.
Monographs by scholars of note.

607. Jahrbuch für Ostrecht.   v. 1– 1960– Herrenalb. semiannual.
Published by Institut für Ostrecht, Munich. Articles, expert opinions, German translations of East European laws, and court decisions.

608. Law in Eastern Europe; a Series of Publications Issued by the Documentation Office for East European Law, University of Leiden.
no. 1– 1958– Leiden.
Monographs and translations of codes and statutes. Edited by Z.
Szirmai.

609. Osteuropa-Recht.   v. 1– 1955– Stuttgart.   v. 1-5, semiannual;
v. 6–, quarterly.
Published in German, with English and Russian contributions.
Articles, bibliographies, documents.

610. Soviet Law and Government.   v. 1– 1962– New York, International
Arts and Sciences Press. quarterly.
Unabridged translations of selected articles in the foremost Soviet
legal periodicals.

611. Wiener Quellenhefte zur Ostkunde, Reihe Recht.   1958– Vienna.
loose-leaf.
Published by Arbeitsgemeinschaft Ost and edited by Helmut Slapnicka. German translations and digests of laws of East European
countries, book reviews, etc.

4. Bibliographies

612. Akademiia nauk SSSR.   *Institut gosudarstva i prava.*   Literature
on Soviet Law; Index of Bibliography. Moscow, 1960. 279 p.
A selected English-language bibliography prepared by Soviet
specialists for foreigners, indicating primary sources and treatises.
Reproduced copies available from Los Angeles County Law Library.

613. Meissner, Boris.   Sowjetunion und Völkerrecht 1917-1962. Cologne,
Verlag Wissenschaft und Politik, 1963. 622 p.
Contains translations of V. N. Durdenevskii's bibliography "Sowjetische Literatur des Internationalen Rechts 1917-1957," and a
supplement for the years 1958-1962 by Aleksandr Ushakov, with
commentary by the compiler.

614. Szladits, Charles.   A Bibliography on Foreign and Comparative
Law: Books and Articles in English. New York, Oceana Publications, 1955. 508 p. (Parker School Studies in Foreign and Comparative Law)
A systematized bibliography including materials on Soviet law and
on the law of other Communist-oriented states. A second volume,

published in 1962 (599 p.), continued the series to 1959, compiling the annual supplements to the first volume as they had appeared in the *American Journal of Comparative Law,* beginning with volume five (1956).

B. POLITICS AND GOVERNMENT

by John A. Armstrong

(except for the section on "The Police Power")

Introductory note: It is extraordinarily difficult to compile a systematic bibliography on the government and politics of Russia. As a totalitarian system, the Soviet regime tends to make all aspects of life political; even in the Russian Empire, politics and government impinged on far wider aspects of life than is usual in Western societies. Consequently, books listed elsewhere in this bibliography, while not concerned directly with political affairs, may be more enlightening for the student of Russian politics than many an item listed in this section. Moreover, books which do explicitly treat government and politics in Russia vary widely in reliability; many of the most important are in no sense scholarly studies. As a result, choice of works has been difficult, and it has been necessary to include an unusual number of critical comments in the annotations.

There are hundreds of useful articles on Soviet government and politics. With rare exceptions, however, these articles treat specific episodes or periods rather than monographic themes. Therefore, it has seemed appropriate to list only those articles of unique importance which have appeared in journals not generally devoted to East Europe, while referring the reader for additional articles to the tables of contents of the many important journals which devote major attention to Russian and Soviet politics.[1] Similarly, few chapters from books are included.

The large number of general works now available on Soviet government — frequently by the authors of the better Soviet government sections in comparative government textbooks — makes it unlikely that the student would find it profitable to seek out such comparative government texts; consequently, none have been included.

1. Before the Bolshevik Revolution

a. Institutions of the Russian Empire and the Provisional Government

615. Badaev (Badayev), Aleksei E.   The Bolsheviks in the Tsarist Duma, with an Article by Lenin on the Work and Trial of the Bolshevik Group in the Duma and an Introduction by Em. Yaroslavsky. New York, International Publishers, 1932. 250 p.

[1] Especially *Slavic Review* (formerly *American Slavic and East European Review*); *Russian Review*; *Problems of Communism*; *Current Digest of the Soviet Press*; *Soviet Studies*; *Survey*; *Bulletin* of the Institute for the Study of the USSR; *Studies on the Soviet Union*; *Ost-Probleme*; *Osteuropa*; *Osteuropa-Recht*; *Cahiers du monde russe et soviétique; Est et Ouest* (formerly *Bulletin d'études et d'information politiques internationales*).

The official Communist version of the activities of the Bolshevik faction in the Fourth Duma from the time of its election (1912) to the arrest of the Bolshevik delegates in 1914. While biased, the account is important, especially because it has been a constantly cited source for more recent Soviet accounts. Ostensibly the book is the memoir of a Bolshevik Duma delegate of worker background.

616. Browder, Robert P., *ed.* The Russian Provisional Government, 1917; Documents, Selected and Edited by Robert Paul Browder and Alexander F. Kerensky. Stanford, Calif., Stanford University Press, 1961. 3 v. (477, 1-1193, 1195-1875 p.)
See also entry no. 543.

This series represents an effort to overcome the tendentious interpretation of the year of revolution in Russia (1917) in Soviet historiography by presenting a massive selection from the collection of documents in the Hoover Institution. A vast number of important political documents issued by the Provisional Government are included, but the collection also includes memoir accounts, military communications, and other items which are outside the scope of customary official documentation. The bibliography and annotations greatly enhance the value of the work.

617.* Florinsky, Michael T.   The End of the Russian Empire. New Haven, Yale University Press; London, Oxford University Press, 1931. 272 p. (Carnegie Endowment for International Peace. Division of Economics and History. Economic and Social History of the World War. Russian Series, 10)
See also entry no. 537.

A summary volume which brings together and interprets the data in this comprehensive series. From the standpoint of the study of government and politics, the most valuable portions are those dealing with the court, the bureaucracy, the Duma, and the class structure. The analysis of the relation of the classes to the downfall of the Imperial system is especially valuable.

618. Harper, Samuel N.   The New Electoral Law for the Russian Duma. Chicago, University of Chicago Press, 1908. 56 p.

The first systematic treatise on Russian political institutions by an American, with an analysis of the law which was promulgated for elections to the Imperial legislature after the Tsar had dissolved the first two Dumas for proving recalcitrant. The book, written shortly after the election which was carried out under the new law, also discusses very briefly the actual results of the voting.

619. Leroy-Beaulieu, Anatole.   The Empire of the Tsars and the Russians. Part II: The Institutions. Translated from the third French edition by Zenaïde A. Ragozin. New York, London, Putnam, 1894. 566 p.
See also entries no. 133, 530, and 1187.

The author was perhaps the most systematic nineteenth-century Western observer of Russia; though much of his data is antiquated, the work is still useful. Other parts of this three-volume work deal with "The Country and Its Inhabitants" (1893), and "Religion" (1896). Part two treats a number of topics directly related to the political system: the peasant commune, the bureaucracy, the zemstvo system, the press, and the radical movements. The first edition appeared as *L'empire des tsars et les russes* (Paris, Hachette, 1881-1889, 3 v.) and the third edition, revised and enlarged, in 1890-1896.

620. Levin, Alfred.   The Second Duma; a Study of the Social-Democratic Party and the Russian Constitutional Experiment. New Haven, Yale University Press, 1940. 414 p.

One of the best monographic treatments of any phase of politics under the Tsarist regime, this book is an intensive examination of the election, organization, and activities of the legislative body elected in the summer of 1906 and dissolved a year later. While the Social Democrats (especially the Mensheviks) are stressed, the analysis of the other parties is very good. There are extensive bibliographical notes.

621. Maurach, Reinhart.   Der russische Reichsrat. Introduction by Freiherr von Freytagh-Loringhoven. Berlin, Junker und Dünnhaupt, 1939. 247 p.

A history of the Gosudarstvennyi Soviet, which was, before 1905, the highest legislative body of the Empire, and after 1905, co-ordinate with the Imperial Duma. Although this book provides only a slim bibliography and reflects the conditions of its date and place of origin, it is among the few studies of a major governmental institution of the Tsarist period which are available in a Western European language.

622. Polner, Tikhon I.   Russian Local Government during the War and the Union of Zemstvos. New Haven, Yale University Press; London, Oxford University Press, 1930. 317 p. (Carnegie Endowment for International Peace. Division of Economics and History. Economic and Social History of the World War. Russian Series, 9) Bibliography: p. 308-309.

This volume is devoted entirely to the zemstvo organizations, which were semi-representative councils at the provincial and district level. By attracting vigorous and dedicated volunteer workers, in marked contrast to the professional bureaucrats, the zemstvos were able to develop an efficient organization which assumed much of the responsibility for care of the military as well as the civilian population during the war. The volume includes numerous statistics.

623. Radkey, Oliver H.   The Election to the Russian Constituent Assembly of 1917. Cambridge, Harvard University Press, 1950. 89 p. Bibliographical note: p. 81-83.
See also entry no. 545.

A very important analysis of the only free election held in Russia.

While the author presents some material concerning the conduct of the election and the historical framework in which it took place, his main service was in painstakingly compiling and assessing the very scattered (and still incomplete) reports on the results of the voting, and analyzing their significance.

624. Russian Public Finance during the War. New Haven, Yale University Press; London, Oxford University Press, 1928. 461 p. (Carnegie Endowment for International Peace. Division of Economics and History. Economic and Social History of the World War. Russian Series, 1)

> This volume includes sections by Alexander Michelson on "Revenue and Expenditure"; by Paul N. Apostol on "Credit Operations"; and by Michael W. Bernatzky on "Monetary Policy." Foreign exchange and credit operations are covered. While most of the discussion is fairly technical and relies heavily on statistical presentation, the general subject is an important aspect of government operations.

625. Walkin, Jacob. The Rise of Democracy in Pre-Revolutionary Russia; Political and Social Institutions under the Last Three Czars. New York, Praeger, 1962. 320 p. Bibliography.
See also entries no. 535 and 1171.

> A study of Russian social and governmental institutions prior to 1917, with emphasis on factors of similarity and dissimilarity between the Tsarist and the Soviet regimes. The contrast between the growing capacity of Russian society for autonomous action and the rigidity of the Imperial government forms the principal theme of the author's argument.

626. The War and the Russian Government: The Central Government, by Paul P. Gronsky. The Municipal Government and the All-Russian Union of Towns, by Nicholas J. Astrov. New Haven, Yale University Press; London, Oxford University Press, 1929. 331 p. (Carnegie Endowment for International Peace. Division of Economics and History. Economic and Social History of the World War. Russian Series, 4)

> Composed of essays of approximately equal length on the central government (Imperial and Provisional) from 1914 to 1917 by Gronsky, a former Duma member, and on municipal government (particularly the All-Russian Union of Towns, but excluding the zemstvos) by Astrov, former mayor of Moscow. Both portions are richly documented and contain numerous statistical tables; a highly useful bibliography of Russian sources is appended. While the focus is institutional and descriptive, considerable attention is directed to the effectiveness of the governmental structure.

627. Zagorskii (Zagorsky), Semen O. State Control of Industry in Russia during the War. New Haven, Yale University Press; London,

Oxford University Press, 1928. 351 p. (Carnegie Endowment for International Peace. Division of Economics and History. Economic and Social History of the World War. Russian Series, 2)
"Sources": p. 270-272.

A large portion of this volume is concerned with technical questions of an economic nature, supported by voluminous statistical appendixes. Parts three and four, however, are concerned with the organizational framework and methods employed by the government in its effort to control the economy; in addition, part four contains a summary discussion of the economic programs of the various revolutionary groups.

b. Political movements and personalities [2]

628. Anweiler, Oskar.   Die Rätebewegung in Russland 1905-1921. Leiden, Brill, 1958. 344 p.
Bibliography: p. 326-342.

A detailed account, primarily historical in approach, of the development of workers' councils ("soviets") in modern Western Europe and Russia, and of their adoption by the Bolsheviks as the form of the revolutionary state. Nearly half of the book is devoted to the spontaneous soviets of the 1905 revolutionary period and to the aftermath of these events; the remainder is principally concerned with the revival of the soviets in 1917 and their capture and utilization by the Bolsheviks.

629. Fischer, George.   Russian Liberalism, from Gentry to Intelligentsia. Cambridge, Harvard University Press, 1958. 240 p.
Bibliography: p. 209-226.
See also entries no. 519 and 1586.

Although the focus is never very clearly defined, this is a study of the middle and upper class elements in Russia which desired moderate, democratic reform, in contrast to the traditional autocracy and the revolutionary extremists. The treatment extends from the reforms (connected with the liberation of the serfs) of the 1860's to the 1905 Revolution.

630. Haimson, Leopold H.   The Russian Marxists and the Origins of Bolshevism. Cambridge, Harvard University Press, 1955. 246 p.
Bibliography: p. 235-240.
See also entry no. 1587.

This study in intellectual history traces the formative influences (Russian and non-Russian) on those sections of the nineteenth-century intelligentsia which turned to Marxism. Much of the author's focus is biographical: on Lenin, G. V. Plekhanov, P. B. Akselrod, and Iu. O. Martov. After examining the development of the Bolshevik and Menshevik factions of the Russian Social Democratic Party, the book closes on the eve of the 1905 Revolution.

[2] Only those works which are directly relevant to internal political activities have been included here. References to more general works on the history of ideas will be found under "History" or "History of Thought and Culture."

631. Hare, Richard.   Pioneers of Russian Social Thought; Studies of Non-Marxian Formation in Nineteenth Century Russia and of Its Partial Revival in the Soviet Union. London, New York, Oxford University Press, 1951. 307 p.
See also entry no. 1588.
>An examination of the "Westernizers" and "Slavophils" of the early nineteenth century, and of a few later reformers such as N. G. Chernyshevskii, A. Hertzen, and the conservative K. Leontiev. Uses primarily the biographical approach to the history of ideas.

632. Keep, J. L. H.   The Rise of Social Democracy in Russia. London, Oxford University Press, 1963. 334 p.
Bibliography: p. 304-322.
See also entry no. 531.
>A study of Social Democracy, in both its Bolshevik and its Menshevik forms, from its origins to the "ebbing tide" after 1905. Based on a wide range of materials, published and unpublished, and written with noteworthy clarity.

633. Leontovitsch, Victor.   Geschichte des Liberalismus in Russland. Frankfurt a/M, V. Klostermann, 1957. 425 p.
See also entry no. 508.
>A history of civil liberty rather than of liberal movements. Within a general chronological treatment the development of legal codes relating to personal freedom is stressed. The first part deals rather summarily with the period 1762-1855. The second part, treating the "development of civil freedom" in 1856-1914, is almost entirely concerned with laws affecting peasant status. The third part, treating the "development of political freedom" in the same period, discusses matters more directly related to political institutions and movements such as the zemstvo system, the Duma, and moderate political parties.

634. Malia, Martin E.   Alexander Herzen and the Birth of Russian Socialism, 1812-1855. Cambridge, Harvard University Press, 1961. 486 p.
Bibliography: p. 427-428.
See also entry no. 1594.
>A biographical study of one of the greatest nineteenth-century Russian writers and social thinkers. Much of the work is devoted to examining the Western European intellectual sources of Hertzen's thought.

635. Mendel, Arthur P.   Dilemmas of Progress in Tsarist Russia; Legal Marxism and Legal Populism. Cambridge, Harvard University Press, 1961. 310 p.
Bibliography: p. 255-263.
See also entry no. 1597.
>The treatment of legal populism, the movement which was one successor to the violently revolutionary *Narodnaia Volia*, revolves around the biography and writings of N. K. Mikhailovskii. Legal

Marxists discussed include P. Struve, N. Berdiaev, and S. Bulgakov. Essentially a study in social thought, with a good bibliography.

For further treatment of Mikhailovskii, *see* James H. Billington, *Mikhailovsky and Russian Populism* (Oxford, Clarendon Press, 1958, 217 p.), which contains additional bibliographic material on pages 197-211.

636. Pipes, Richard.   Social Democracy and the St. Petersburg Labor Movement, 1885-1897. Cambridge, Harvard University Press, 1963. 154 p.
Bibliography: p. 143-149.

A study of the relationship between various revolutionary movements, dominated largely by the intelligentsia, and the labor force in the Russian capital between 1885 and 1897. The author concludes that the labor movement was largely independent of the Social Democrats, who (to the extent to which any intelligentsia movements influenced the working men) were outdistanced by the populist *Narodnaia Volia.*

637. Pobedonostsev, Konstantin P.   Reflections of a Russian Statesman. London, G. Richards, 1898. 271 p.

As Procurator of the Holy Synod and, even more, as a close personal associate of Alexander III and Nicholas II, Pobedonostsev played an important role in bolstering the unswerving attitude of the Russian government in the face of public pressure for reform. These essays constitute a strong and earnest criticism of many of the views of liberals both in Russia and in Europe, and help to explain the reaction of the Imperial government to all signs of public expression of such liberal hopes. A translation of *Moskovskii sbornik* (Moscow, Sinodal'naia tipografiia, 1896, 304 p.)

638. Radkey, Oliver H.   The Agrarian Foes of Bolshevism; Promise and Default of the Russian Socialist Revolutionaries, February to October, 1917. New York, Columbia University Press, 1958. 521 p.
Bibliography: p. 486-500.

This is a study of Russian populism at the moment of its greatest strength and opportunity, between the overthrow of the Tsarist regime and the Bolshevik seizure of power. The author briefly traces the origin and development of the Socialist Revolutionary Party, and analyzes in great detail the internal conflicts and the mistakes in tactics and policy which prevented the SR's from presenting a viable alternative to communism in 1917.

639. Treadgold, Donald W.   Lenin and His Rivals; the Struggle for Russia's Future, 1898-1906. New York, Praeger, 1955. 291 p.

A study of the political forces struggling for change in Russia in the decade before the 1905 Revolution and during that revolution. These forces, the author considers, were the extreme (Bolshevik) and moderate (Menshevik) factions of Marxism; the Populists (Socialist Revolutionaries); and the Liberals (Constitutional Democrats). Much of the approach centers on the roles of the leaders of these groups — Lenin, V. M. Chernov, Iu. O. Martov, and P. N. Miliukov.

640. Utechin, Sergej V.   Russian Political Thought; a Concise History. New York, Praeger, 1964. 320 p.
Bibliography: p. 279-306.
See also entry no. 1607.

Russian political thought from medieval times to the present, but emphasizing the period from 1825 to 1917, and "primarily intended for students of politics rather than of Russian history."

641. Venturi, Franco.   Roots of Revolution; a History of the Populist and Socialist Movements in Nineteenth Century Russia. Introduction by Isaiah Berlin. New York, Knopf, 1960. 850 p.
See also entry no. 524.

The fullest treatment of the development of nineteenth-century Russian thought since Tomáš G. Masaryk's *The Spirit of Russia* (*see* entry no. 269). The present volume, unlike Masaryk's, is focused upon a single aspect of this great body of thought. The treatment begins with A. I. Hertzen and M. A. Bakunin in the 1830's and ends with the assassination of Alexander II by the *Narodnaia Volia* in 1881. Sir Isaiah Berlin has contributed a lengthy and illuminating introduction. The work is copiously documented but, unfortunately, this translation has no bibliography. The Italian original, which appeared as *Il populismo russo* (Turin, Giulio Einaudi, 1952, 2 v.), provides a bibliography (v. 2, p. 1163-1165).

642. Wolfe, Bertram D.   Three Who Made a Revolution; a Biographical History. New York, Dial Press, 1948. 661 p.

The background of the Bolshevik Revolution in the form of a composite biography of three of its principal protagonists — Lenin, Trotsky, and Stalin. The book is a high literary achievement, incorporating a wealth of detail derived from many years of research. It provides excellent biographies of its subjects, and is probably the most authoritative history of the Bolshevik movement prior to the February (March) Revolution.

643.* Yarmolinsky, Avrahm.   Road to Revolution; a Century of Russian Radicalism. London, Cassell, 1957; New York, Macmillan, 1959. 369 p.

Nineteenth-century revolutionary movements in the Russian Empire, from Alexander Radishchev's *A Journey from Petersburg to Moscow* of 1790 (*see* entry no. 140) through the Decembrists and mid-century revolutionaries such as Chernyshevskii and Hertzen, to the *Narodnaia Volia*. Primarily a history of social thought.

2. The Soviet Regime

a. Soviet materials in translation

(1) Source books

644.* Daniels, Robert V., *ed.*   A Documentary History of Communism. New York, Random House, 1960. 321, 393 p.

A useful collection of documents, focused on internal Soviet developments, but including many relating to international communism, the East European satellites, and the Far East, primarily for the post-Stalin period. While Lenin's and Stalin's writings and speeches occupy a prominent place, selections from such sources as speeches of other leaders, the press, and purge trial records are included.

645. Hendel, Samuel, *ed.*   The Soviet Crucible; Soviet Government in Theory and Practice. Princeton, N. J., Van Nostrand, 1959. 594 p. Bibliography: p. 579-587.

A book of readings on the ideological, political, and economic aspects of the Soviet system. About one-fourth of the annotated selections are from Soviet documents or authors; the majority are by non-Soviet observers.

646.* Kommunisticheskaia partiia Sovetskogo Soiuza.   Soviet Communism; Programs and Rules; Official Texts of 1919, 1952 (1956), and 1961. Edited by Jan F. Triska. San Francisco, Chandler, 1962. 196 p.

A useful compilation of the following texts: the program of the Soviet Communist Party adopted in 1961, with interlinear indications of changes between the draft program and the final version and of variations between the Russian and the official English texts; the program of 1919; the 1961 Party rules, with changes from the draft and variations in the Russian and English texts indicated; and the juxtaposed text of the 1952 Party rules, including minor changes made in 1956. A lengthy introduction enhances the value of the collection.

647. Meisel, James H., *and* Edward S. Kozera, *eds.*   Materials for the Study of the Soviet System; State and Party Constitutions, Laws, Decrees, Decisions, and Official Statements of the Leaders in Translation. 2d rev. and enl. ed. Ann Arbor, Mich., Wahr Publishing Co., 1953. 613 p.

Bibliography: p. 581-589.

See also entry no. 603.

Although now partially obsolete, this collection is much the best and most comprehensive source book for the period up to Stalin's death. The general arrangement is chronological; but the usability of the volume is somewhat reduced by the fact that some items are included in a supplement at the end of the book, while an additional supplement (on 1952 items) appears at the beginning.

648. U. S. *Congress. House. Committee on Un-American Activities.* The Communist Conspiracy: Strategy and Tactics of World Communism. Part 1: Communism Outside the United States. Section B: The U.S.S.R. Washington, U. S. Government Printing Office, 1956. 528 p. (84th Congress, 2d Session. Report no. 2241)

    A useful compilation of a wide variety of documents on Soviet internal affairs from 1917 on. The materials are otherwise available only in widely scattered sources, and some had not previously been translated into English.

(2) Writings by major Soviet leaders [3]

649. Khrushchev, Nikita S.   Khrushchev Speaks; Selected Speeches, Articles, and Press Conferences, 1949-1961. Edited with commentary by Thomas P. Whitney. Ann Arbor, University of Michigan Press, 1963. 466 p.

    Of the 18 items included in this collection, 14 were statements made by Khrushchev after Stalin's death, and all were made after Khrushchev's return to Moscow in 1949. Even for this later period, the selection is necessarily somewhat arbitrary, but it includes most of his major pronouncements. Their significance is described in substantial and judicious introductions by the editor, a journalist with long experience in Moscow. Half of the translations are from the *Current Digest of the Soviet Press* (*see* entry no. 28), with omitted passages filled in by the editor's translations. Most of the remaining translations are of Soviet origin, but appear to contain no major changes from the originals.

650. Lenin, Vladimir I.   Collected Works. Moscow, Foreign Languages Publishing House, 1960– Illus., ports., diagrs., facsims.

    A translation of the fourth, enlarged Russian edition, prepared by the Institute of Marxism-Leninism of the Central Committee of the Communist Party of the Soviet Union. So far, 19 volumes of this edition have been published.

    An earlier, incomplete edition appeared as *Collected Works* (New York, International Publishers, 1929-1945, 7 v. in 10 pts., i.e.: v. 4 [pts. 1 and 2], 13, 18, 19, 20 [pts. 1 and 2], 21 [pts. 1 and 2], 23). This is a translation of the second Russian edition, *Sochineniia* (Moscow, Gosizdat, 1926-1932, 30 v.) and, according to Alfred G. Meyer who has compared it with the original, the translation is "faulty, misleading, and therefore useless."

651.* Lenin, Vladimir I.   Imperialism. The State and Revolution. New York, The Vanguard Press, 1927. 225 p.

    Two of the basic writings of Lenin, handily available in this com-

---

[3] For Stalin and Lenin, only the most important editions of collected works plus major works not included in the series and a few especially handy small collections are listed. Selected major statements by Communist leaders from Marx to Khrushchev are presented in topical arrangement in *Soviet World Outlook, a Handbook of Communist Statements* (*see* entry no. 652).

pact edition. "Imperialism" offers the theory that in its last, or "monopoly" stage, capitalism produces international tension and war through "exporting exploitation." In "The State and Revolution" Lenin argues the need of a tightly disciplined party to bring about the "dictatorship of the proletariat."

Both works are also available in separate editions: *The State and Revolution* (New York, International Publishers, 1935, 104 p.; Little Lenin Library, v. 14); *Imperialism, the Highest Stage of Capitalism* (New York, International Publishers, 1933, 127 p.; Little Lenin Library, v. 15). The former is a translation of *Gosudarstvo i revoliutsiia* (Petrograd, Zhizn' i znanie, 1918, 113 p.), and the latter of *Imperializm, kak novieishii etap kapitalizma* (Petrograd, Zhizn' i znanie, 1917, 130 p.)

652. Soviet World Outlook; a Handbook of Communist Statements. 3d ed. Washington, U. S. Government Printing Office, 1959. 247 p. (U. S. Dept. of State. Publication no. 6836)

Contains selected major statements by Communist leaders from Marx to Khrushchev in topical arrangement.

653. Stalin, Iosif (Joseph) V. Works. New York, International Publishers, 1952-1955. 13 v.

A translation based on a heavily-edited and expurgated edition of Stalin's works in Russian, which was begun in 1949 and terminated shortly after his death in 1953. Since the final volume goes only to January 1934, Stalin's most vitriolic writings — and those which are most controversial from the standpoint of his successors — do not appear in this collection.

654. Stalin, Iosif (Joseph) V. Mastering Bolshevism. New York, New Century Publishers, 1946. 48 p.

Two very important speeches made by Stalin at the March 1937 plenary session of the Soviet Communist Central Committee, which marked a major intensification of the Great Purge. These speeches contain Stalin's most elaborate presentation of the thesis that the farther "socialism" advances in the USSR, the more fiercely the domestic and foreign opponents of the Soviet regime will combat it. The speeches also contain important directives on personnel selection and training.

Stalin's major public statements during the Second World War are contained in his *On the Great Patriotic War of the Soviet Union* (Moscow, Foreign Languages Publishing House, 1946, 209 p.). Also included are Stalin's replies to four letters from British and American correspondents, but his brief, very significant address at the victory reception of Red Army commanders on May 23, 1945, is *not* included.

655. Stalin, Iosif (Joseph) V. Problems of Leninism. Moscow, Foreign Languages Publishing House, 1953. 803 p.

A voluminous collection of Stalin's speeches and articles from the period after 1924. The vast majority are available in his *Collected*

Works, but this collection provides a handy reference to the most important ones. The dominant theme is his vindictive attitude toward his opponents and critics.

Earlier, less extensive editions in English appeared in Moscow in 1945 and 1947, and an American edition was published as *Leninism: Selected Writings* (New York, International Publishers, 1942, 479 p.)

656. Trotskii, Lev (Leon Trotsky). The Basic Writings of Trotsky. Edited and with an introduction by Irving Howe. New York, Random House, 1963. 427 p.

Selected writings which provide a survey of Trotsky's political-intellectual career. Part one follows roughly the main events of his life and part two offers examples of Trotsky's views on literature and social structure.

657. Trotskii, Lev (Leon Trotsky). Diary in Exile, 1935. Translated from the Russian by Elena Zarudnaya. Cambridge, Harvard University Press, 1958. 218 p. Illus.

A small part of the voluminous Trotsky papers at Harvard University. This volume contains interesting details on Stalin's views and on the fate of his opponents in the USSR.

658.* Trotskii, Lev (Leon Trotsky). Lenin. New York, Capricorn Books, 1962. 216 p.

Articles and speeches of Trotsky about Lenin, collected shortly after Lenin's death, which are as revealing of Trotsky himself as they are of Lenin. Translated from *O Lenine; materialy dlia biografa* (Moscow, Gosizdat, 1924, 168 p.)

Previous English editions appeared as *Lenin* (New York, Minton, Balch, 1925, 216 p., and Garden City, N. Y., Garden City Books, 1959, 216 p.)

659.* Trotskii, Lev (Leon Trotsky). My Life; an Attempt at an Autobiography. New York, C. Scribner's Sons, 1930. 599 p.

Trotsky's account of his life up to the time of his exile from the USSR, stressing, however, his career prior to the Bolshevik Revolution and his service under Lenin after 1917; his role in the Revolution and his struggle with Stalin are more amply treated in other books he wrote. An indispensable source, in spite of the fact that the careful student will be annoyed by the "total recall" of conversations — which the author notes, however, often are meant to have "symbolic" significance.

Translation of *Moia zhizn'; opyt avtobiografii* (Berlin, Granit, 1930, 2 v. in 1).

660. Trotskii, Lev (Leon Trotsky). The Real Situation in Russia. Translated by Max Eastman. New York, Harcourt, Brace, 1928. 364 p.

Trotsky's effort to overcome the power of Stalin's regime, which had deprived him of office and exiled him, by appealing to public opinion in the USSR and, indirectly, abroad. The book is a compilation of a number of speeches and programs (particularly the one known as the "Opposition Platform" in the Communist Party Central Committee meeting in September 1927) reflecting the views of Trotsky and his adherents.

661. Trotskii, Lev (Leon Trotsky). The Revolution Betrayed. What Is the Soviet Union and Where Is It Going? Translated by Max Eastman. Garden City, N. Y., Doubleday, Doran, 1937. 308 p.
See also entry no. 1249.

Trotsky's most extended and coherent criticism of Soviet development under Stalin. He identifies the villain in what he considers to be the corruption of the revolutionary system primarily as the bureaucracy, rather than Stalin, the individual dictator who personifies it. Nevertheless, Trotsky argues, the Soviet system represents a genuine historical achievement because it overcame the class divisions of capitalism, and therefore the bureaucratic group can only delay the ultimate victory of the revolutionary principles.

662.* Trotskii, Lev (Leon Trotsky). Stalin; an Appraisal of the Man and His Influence. Edited and translated from the Russian by Charles Malamuth. New York, Harper, 1941. 516 p.

A voluminous examination of Stalin's career to 1939, in the framework of the development of the Bolshevik party and the Soviet state. Trotsky is obviously not an unbiased biographer, but he is an exceptionally well-informed one.

663.* Trotskii, Lev (Leon Trotsky). Terrorism and Communism; a Reply to Karl Kautsky. Introduction to the second English edition by Leon Trotsky, with a foreword by Max Schachtman. Ann Arbor, University of Michigan Press, 1961. 191 p.

Trotsky's most vehement defense of the ruthless tactics used by the Bolsheviks to consolidate their power, written in 1920 as a reply to the German Social Democrat Kautsky. The shorter pieces by Trotsky, published after his exile from the USSR, reaffirm his belief in revolutionary violence.

Translation of *Terrorizm i kommunizm* (Peterburg, Gosizdat, 1920, 178 p.)

(3) Party meetings and decisions [4]

664. Socialism Victorious, by Stalin, Molotov, Kaganovich and Others. London, M. Lawrence, 1935. 719 p.

The only extended translation of material from the Seventeenth Congress of the Soviet Communist Party. The selection is the official Soviet version.

665. Zhdanov, Andrei A. Organizational Problems of the Communist Party, and Decisions of the Central Committee of the Communist Par-

[4] Arrangement is chronological by date of meeting or decision.

ty of the Soviet Union, February, 1937. New York, Workers Library Publishers, 1937. 47 p.

Zhdanov's speech, the decisions on organizational matters (only a small part of the work of the crucial February–March plenary session of the Central Committee), and two *Pravda* editorials on the same matters. Zhdanov's principal point was the need to invigorate "internal party democracy," an anomalous emphasis in view of the increasing momentum of the Great Purge.

666. Kommunisticheskaia partiia Sovetskogo Soiuza.   *18. s"ezd, Moscow, 1939.* The Land of Socialism Today and Tomorrow; Reports and Speeches at the Eighteenth Congress of the Communist Party of the Soviet Union (Bolsheviks), March 10-21, 1939. Moscow, Foreign Languages Publishing House, 1939. 488 p.

Contains the speeches of Politburo members, Congress resolutions (including Party rules and amendments), and a list of Central Committee and Central Inspection Committee members. While this material is only a small portion of the proceedings of the Congress, it is the only extensive translation of these proceedings available, and even the Russian stenographic record is difficult to obtain.

667. Decisions of the Central Committee, C.P.S.U.(B.) on Literature and Art (1946-1948). Moscow, Foreign Languages Publishing House, 1951. 38 p.

The drastic decrees (attributed to Andrei Zhdanov) enforcing conformity in belletristic literature, the theater, motion pictures, and the opera. The Soviet translation is non-literal, but reflects the basic content of the decrees.

668. Gruliow, Leo, *ed.*   Current Soviet Policies; the Documentary Record of the Communist Party Congress. 1952– New York, Praeger.
See also entry no. 566.

A volume of this series has been published for each of the congresses of the Communist Party of the Soviet Union held since 1952. The volume for the Nineteenth Congress provides the only comprehensive record apart from the daily reports in the Soviet press and the translations in the weekly *Current Digest of the Soviet Press* (*see* entry no. 28). It also includes some of the most important documents on the period between the Congress, which was held in the fall of 1952, and the reorganization of the Soviet government following Stalin's death in March 1953. The second volume, reporting the proceedings of the Twentieth Congress in February 1956, contains, in addition to the published speeches, a version of N. S. Khrushchev's "secret speech," and a number of documents relating to the crises in the East European Communist parties later in 1956. The Extraordinary Twenty-first Congress is reported in the third volume, while the fourth volume contains extensive portions of the proceedings of the Twenty-second Congress. Each volume provides data concerning members of the Central Committee and of other organs of the Party.

(4) Political trial records [5]

669. Ramzin, Leonid K., *defendant*. Wreckers on Trial; a Record of the Trial of the Industrial Party Held in Moscow, Nov.–Dec., 1930. Edited with a foreword by Andrew Rothstein. New York. Workers' Library Publishers, 1931. 214 p.

> A summary record (rather than a stenographic report) of the trial of a group of former Mensheviks and members of the "Industrial Party" charged with sabotaging Soviet industry. While the charges were not as fantastic as those in the Great Purge trials of subsequent years, the reliance upon "confessions" and the attempts to implicate "bourgeois" states were already present.

670. Vitvitskii, Nikolai P., *defendant*. The Case of N. P. Vitvitsky (and others) Charged with Wrecking Activities at Power Stations in the Soviet Union, Heard before the Special Session of the Supreme Court of the U.S.S.R. in Moscow, April 12-19, 1933. Moscow, State Law Publishing House, 1933. 2 v. (234 p.)

> Stenographic report of testimony in the trial of 18 Soviet and British citizens accused of sabotage. The main attempt of the prosecution was to show that representatives of Metropolitan-Vickers, Ltd., a British firm engaged in contract work in the USSR, had contributed to breakdowns in power stations and arsenals by engaging in a conspiracy for sabotage.

671. Zinov'ev, Grigorii, *defendant*. Report of Court Proceedings; the Case of the Trotskyite-Zinovievite Terrorist Centre, Heard before the Military Collegium of the Supreme Court of the U.S.S.R., Moscow, August 19-24, 1936 . . . Moscow, People's Commissariat of Justice of the U.S.S.R., 1936. 180 p.

> A summary version (not even purportedly a *stenographic* report) of the testimony in the first trial ("the 16") of the Great Purge. The principal defendants were Grigorii Zinoviev and Lev Kamenev, but Stalin's evident intention was to convict Leon Trotsky *in absentia* for plotting against the Soviet regime. Even the published proceedings (aside from later revelations) indicated that the charges, supported almost entirely by "confessions," were fabrications.

672. Piatakov, Georgii L., *defendant*. Report of Court Proceedings in the Case of the Anti-Soviet Trotskyite Centre, Heard before the Military Collegium of the Supreme Court of the U.S.S.R., Moscow, January 23-30, 1937 . . . Moscow, People's Commissariat of Justice of the U.S.S.R., 1937. 580 p.

> Testimony (purportedly a stenographic report) in the second public trial (of the "17") in the Great Purge. The best-known defendants were G. L. Piatakov and K. B. Radek, but, as in the other trials, the principal accusations were directed, unconvincingly, against Leon Trotsky. The theme of treasonable plotting with German and Japanese "Fascists" was much enlarged.

[5] Arrangement is chronological by date of trial.

673. Bukharin, Nikolai I., *defendant*.   Report of Court Proceedings in the Case of the Anti-Soviet "Bloc of Rights and Trotskyites," Heard before the Military Collegium of the Supreme Court of the U.S.S.R., Moscow, March 2-13, 1938 . . . Moscow, People's Commissariat of Justice of the U.S.S.R., 1938. 799 p.

> The purported stenographic report of the third, and last, public trial (of the "21") in the Great Purge. The "Rights" were headed by N. I. Bukharin and A. I. Rykov. G. G. Iagoda, former NKVD chief, several Communist Party leaders from the non-Russian areas, and other important figures were also linked to the "Trotskyite" plot. A sensational aspect of the accusations was the alleged "medical murder" plot.

(5) Party histories and textbooks on government [6]

674. Popov, Nikolai N.   Outline History of the Communist Party of the Soviet Union. Moscow, Cooperative Publishing Society of Foreign Workers in the U.S.S.R., 1934. 2 v. (414, 460 p.)

> The first major official history of the Communist Party to be translated into English. Written after Stalin's attainment of power, but before the Great Purge, it tendentiously criticizes Trotsky and the other "opposition" leaders and praises Stalin. Since, however, it lacked the fulsome and lavish praise which Stalin demanded, it was soon replaced as the official history. Translation of *Ocherk istorii Vsesoiuznoi kommunisticheskoi partii* (*bol'shevikov*) (Moscow, Gosizdat, 192?).

675. Knorin, Vil'gel'm G., *ed*.   Communist Party of the Soviet Union; a Short History. Moscow, Cooperative Publishing Society of Foreign Workers in the U.S.S.R., 1935. 516 p.

> One of several "short histories" of the Soviet Communist Party, prepared in the middle thirties, which were rejected by Stalin in favor of the "short course" version (*see* entry no. 676). The work is now of interest principally as a reflection of the evolution of the distortion of history in the USSR. Translation of *Kratkaia istoriia VKP* (*b*) (Moscow, Partizdat, 1935?).

676. Kommunisticheskaia partiia Sovetskogo Soiuza.   *Tsentral'nyi Komitet*. The History of the Communist Party of the Soviet Union (Bolsheviks); Short Course. New York, International Publishers, 1939. 364 p.

> As the official Party history under Stalin, this book had enormous influence as an indoctrination manual, for, in accord with the Leninist principle of the "unity of theory and practice," the Party's history is regarded as the unfolding of the ideology. Some years after the book appeared, the authorship was attributed to Stalin personally; apparently he did write the logically obscure but historically important section two, chapter four, "Dialectical and Historical Materialism." The book is marked throughout by adulation of Stalin and savage vilification of his opponents.

[6] Arrangement is chronological.

Translation of *Istoriia Vsesoiuznoi kommunisticheskoi partii* (*bol'shevikov*); *kratkii kurs* (Moscow, Gospolitizdat, 1938, 350 p.)

677. History of the Communist Party of the Soviet Union. By B. N. Ponomaryov and others. Moscow, Foreign Languages Publishing House, 1960. 765 p.

A massive Soviet official text, designed to replace the *Short Course* (*see* entry no. 676) which had made Party history revolve around Stalin. The new history practically eliminated references to Khrushchev's many rivals; since the decision to condemn Stalin severely and openly had not yet been taken, the net result was a bland "history" in which there are no actors, good or bad. Consequently, while the book is an interesting example of transitional indoctrinational technique, it adds virtually nothing to our historical knowledge.

Translation of *Istoriia Kommunisticheskoi partii Sovetskogo Soiuza* (Moscow, Gospolitizdat, 1959, 742 p.)

678. Denisov, Andrei I., *and* M. Kirichenko.   Soviet State Law. Moscow, Foreign Languages Publishing House, 1960. 459 p.
See also entry no. 574.

A translation of *Sovetskoe gosudarstvennoe pravo* (Moscow, Gosiuridizdat, 1957, 334 p.). Aside from its strong pro-Soviet bias, the book follows the traditional European pattern of formal analysis of legal institutions. Useful mainly as a recent example of Soviet text treatments.

b. Critical studies

(1) General works on the Soviet political system

679. Batsell, Walter R.   Soviet Rule in Russia. New York, Macmillan, 1929. 857 p.
Bibliography: p. 807-825.
See also entry no. 555.

In spite of its early date, this book is a massively documented treatise based on Russian sources gathered in the USSR; some of the more important of these are translated in the appendix or the text. The treatment of the Communist Party is slight, and overlooks the crucial power struggle then going on. On the other hand, the discussion of governmental institutions, primarily in a historical context, is still useful. The book presents a better picture of the nationalities problem in the USSR than do many more recent general treatments.

680. Biscaretti di Ruffia, Paolo.   Lineamenti generali dell'ordinamento costituzionale sovietico; dottrina, legislazione e prassi. Con in "appendice" il testo, aggiornato, al luglio 1956 della Costituzione federale. Milan, Giuffre, 1956. 207 p.

An examination of the legal philosophy on which the Soviet constitution rests, viewed in historical development, with attention given

further to the topics of federalism, the principal organs of state
power, the system of justice, the role of the CP, and the rights of
the citizen. Conclusions are drawn regarding development of Soviet
constitutional law and practice in recent years, the varying interpretations given in the Soviet Union, and the views which may be
formed on this subject among Western students of jurisprudence.

681. Black, Cyril E., *ed.* The Transformation of Russian Society; Aspects of Social Change since 1861. Cambridge, Harvard University
Press, 1960. 695 p.
See also entries no. 107 and 1238.
        This large collection of scholarly articles contains six items espe-
cially relevant to government and politics: "The Patterns of Autoc-
racy" by Zbigniew K. Brzezinski; "The Parties and the State: the
Evolution of Political Attitudes" by Leopold H. Haimson; "The
State and the Local Community" by Alexander Vucinich; "The State
and the Economy" by Theodore H. von Laue; "Social Classes and
Political Structure" by Robert A. Feldmesser; and "Summary and
Review" by Merle Fainsod.

682.* Brumberg, Abraham, *ed.*   Russia under Khrushchev; an Anthology
from Problems of Communism. New York, Praeger, 1962. 660 p.
See also entry no. 1239.
        A substantial number of the articles on the USSR in the United
States Information Agency publication *Problems of Communism*
from 1959 to 1961, and a few from earlier years. Includes pieces
on a wide range of subjects, but the general focus is on analysis of
political trends.

683. Chambre, Henri.   Le pouvoir soviétique; introduction a l'étude
de ses institutions. Paris, Librairie générale de droit, 1959. 168 p.
        A brief but very lucid survey of the Soviet political system by a
leading French scholar. The bulk of the treatment relates to the
Soviet state and its organs.

684.* Daniels, Robert V.   The Nature of Communism; an Analysis of the
Most Threatening Political, Social and Military Movement of Our
Times. New York, Random House, 1962. 398 p.
        An extended essay attempting to analyze and show the insights
of a number of the major interpretations of communism in the
Soviet Union and abroad. These interpretations include communism
as a "strategy of struggle"; as an outgrowth of Russian national
traditions; as a movement especially related to Eastern reactions to
the West; as a response to the industrial revolution; as totalitarianism; and as a faith movement.

685.* Deutscher, Isaac.   Russia in Transition, and Other Essays. New
York, Coward-McCann, 1957. 245 p.
See also entry no. 1243.
        A collection of short essays concerning the immediate post-Stalin
period, interesting mainly as the expression of a long-time observer

of the Soviet scene. The author takes the position (based on alleged evidence which subsequent events have partially contradicted) that this period is the "twilight of totalitarianism."

686.* Deutscher, Isaac.   Stalin: a Political Biography. New York, Oxford University Press, 1949. 600 p.
Bibliography: p. 571-575.
   One of the most influential interpretations of the Soviet political system ever written. While written as a "biography," it is essentially a history of Soviet politics in which Stalin is viewed as necessary to the successful consolidation of the system. Recent revelations have refuted much of the evidence adduced and cast strong doubt on the basic interpretation.

687. Fainsod, Merle.   How Russia Is Ruled. 2d ed. Cambridge, Harvard University Press, 1963. 684 p.
See also entry no. 1730.
   Probably the best single volume on the Soviet political system ever written. The treatment, primarily within a historical and institutional framework, stresses the development of the Soviet Communist Party, but the state, police, military, and economic institutions are also included. The book is fully annotated and accompanied by an excellent selective bibliography of works in Russian and Western languages.
   First edition: Cambridge, Harvard University Press, 1953, 575 p.

688. Florinsky, Michael T.   Towards an Understanding of the USSR; a Study in Government, Politics, and Economic Planning. Rev. ed. New York, Macmillan, 1951. 223 p.
Bibliography: p. 209-214.
   A lucid introduction to the Soviet system under Stalin. The author considers it an "attempt to appraise the evolution of the Soviet state from 1917 to the end of 1950," but actually (like most other analysts) he focuses upon the party and ideology in his treatment of the Soviet political system. The book also contains an extended discussion of the economic aspects of the system.

689.* Friedrich, Carl J., *and* Zbigniew K. Brzezinski.   Totalitarian Dictatorship and Autocracy. Cambridge, Harvard University Press, 1956. 346 p.
   An analytical comparative study of the Soviet Union, Fascist Italy, and Nazi Germany. The authors tend to see the political systems of these three countries as basically similar, compared to non-totalitarian governments. The authors also see a similarity between modern totalitarianism and traditional autocracies, but note that technology has sharply modified the former.

690. Graham, Malbone W., Jr.   New Governments of Eastern Europe. New York, H. Holt, 1927. 826 p.
   This pioneering work deals exclusively with governments of coun-

tries which were part of the Russian Empire, and which are now wholly or in part in the USSR. About two-thirds of the text is devoted to a description of the status of the areas under the Empire; a history of their development toward new forms of government during the First World War, the Bolshevik Revolution, and the Civil War; and an analysis of the governmental and political institutions of the mid-1920's. While much of the factual information is dated, this part of the book still has some reference value. In addition, there are useful charts and 240 pages of documents, many of which are not otherwise available in translation.

691. Grottian, Walter.   Das sowjetische Regierungssystem. Die Grundlagen der Macht in der Sowjetunion. Leitfaden und Quellenbuch. Cologne, Westdeutscher Verlag, 1956. 2 v. (175, 170 p.)

    The first volume is a systematic and fairly up-to-date general treatment of Soviet government and politics. For much of the statistical data, however, the author draws on Towster's *Political Power in the USSR* (*see* entry no. 710), and Fainsod's *How Russia Is Ruled* (*see* entry no. 687), which are more easily accessible to the English-speaking student. The second volume is a collection of sources topically arranged.

692.* Gurian, Waldemar.   Bolshevism; an Introduction to Soviet Communism. Notre Dame, Ind., Notre Dame University Press, 1953. 189 p. Bibliography: p. 177-180.

    An interpretation of communism as a secular, social, and political religion. The discussion is primarily within a historical framework, in which the development of the Soviet regime is treated as an aberration arising from fundamental weaknesses in Western civilization. The text is accompanied by a 50-page appendix of remarkably cogent quotations (from Marx to Soviet writers as late as 1950).

693. Harper, Samuel N., *and* Ronald Thompson.   The Government of the Soviet Union. 2d rev. and enl. ed. New York, Van Nostrand, 1949. 369 p.

    A revision of one of the earliest and most influential general treatments of the Soviet political system, this book retains a certain interest as an example of pioneering American scholarship on the USSR. The main emphasis is on factual description and historical narrative rather than analytical or theoretical aspects.

694. Hazard, John N.   The Soviet System of Government. 3d rev. and enl. ed. Chicago, University of Chicago Press, 1964. 282 p.

    A concise survey developed around the theme that the Soviet political system is a blending of popular, democratic institutional forms and totalitarian dictatorial content. In addition to the usual emphasis on Party and state structure, the author provides an extended account of administrative and legal institutions. The Soviet constitution, Rules of the Communist Party, and an annotated bibliography are appended.

695.*Kulski, Władisław W.   The Soviet Regime; Communism in Practice. 4th ed. Syracuse, Syracuse University Press, 1963. 444 p. Bibliography: p. 417-434.

> The most massive textbook treatment of Soviet political affairs. The text includes innumerable translations of important passages from little-known materials. Unfortunately, the polemic tone and rather loose organization make the volume somewhat hard to use.

696. McClosky, Herbert, *and* John E. Turner.   The Soviet Dictatorship. New York, McGraw-Hill, 1960. 657 p.

> An encyclopedic coverage of the Soviet political system, with the statute of the Soviet Communist Party and the Soviet constitution appended. At the time of its publication this book was the most complete and accurate treatment of the subject available, though it lacked the thorough integration of Merle Fainsod's *How Russia Is Ruled* (*see* entry no. 687). Much space is devoted to aspects of the Soviet system peculiar to the Stalin regime.

697. McNeal, Robert H.   The Bolshevik Tradition; Lenin, Stalin, and Khrushchev. Englewood Cliffs, N. J., Prentice-Hall, 1963. 181 p.

> An examination of the main issues in each stage of development of the Communist Party in Russia, and of the predominant influence of its three chief leaders.
>
> This volume is supplemented by *Lenin, Stalin, and Khrushchev; Voices of Bolshevism*, edited by Robert H. McNeal (Englewood Cliffs, N. J., Prentice-Hall, 1963, 180 p.), an anthology of writings and speeches which illustrate the course of Communist development.

698. Maurach, Reinhart.   Handbuch der Sowjetverfassung. Staat, Partei, Recht, Wirtschaft und Gesellschaft in Theorie und Praxis. Munich, Isar Verlag, 1955. 429 p. (Veröffentlichungen des Osteuropa-Instituts München, Bd. 14)

> An annotated edition of the Soviet constitution, providing notes, article by article, on the varying interpretations given to each, on the institutional and practical expression of each provision, and on the legal relationships arising therefrom. References are made to relevant Soviet legislation and to legal practices followed in the USSR.

699. Maxwell, Bertram W.   The Soviet State; a Study of Bolshevik Rule. Topeka, Kansas, Steves and Wayburn, 1934. 377 p. Bibliography: p. 373-377.

> Considering the date of publication, a remarkably good survey of Soviet government. Most of the information has become obsolete, either through the march of events or through the availability of new data, but the book (especially the selected bibliography of Russian sources) is valuable as an indication of information available to American specialists three decades ago.

700. Meissner, Boris.   Russland im Umbruch; der Wandel in der Herrschaftsordnung und sozialen Struktur der Sowjetunion. Frankfurt am Main, Verlag für Geschichte und Politik, 1951. 91 p.

A pioneering effort to analyze political alignments in the late Stalin period, with particular attention to personnel and organizational changes. Organized in handbook form, it was very useful for reference when it appeared. Though now partly obsolete, the book contains many useful insights.

701.* Meyer, Alfred G.   Communism. New York, Random House, 1960. 217 p.

This little book is an effort to describe and analyze in an introductory fashion the three major aspects of communism: the theory (which receives the main emphasis); Soviet rule in Russia; and world communism. The author draws an interesting parallel between the diversifying types of present-day communism and the Puritan sects of the post-Reformation period. An excellent bibliography accompanies each chapter.

702. Mosely, Philip E., ed.   Russia since Stalin; Old Trends and New Problems. The Annals of the American Academy of Political and Social Science, v. 303, Jan. 1956. 198 p. Index.

While this volume deals with many aspects of the USSR besides the political, the focus is on the post-Stalin Soviet internal and foreign policies. Articles by John N. Hazard on governmental developments and by Merle Fainsod on the Communist Party are especially relevant to this section of the bibliography.

703. Mosely, Philip E., ed.   The Soviet Union since World War II. The Annals of the American Academy of Political and Social Science, v. 263, May 1949: 1-211.

One of the best surveys of Soviet developments in the immediate postwar period. Articles by John N. Hazard on the "Political, Administrative, and Judicial Structure"; by Merle Fainsod on "The Communist Party"; and by Percy E. Corbett on "Ideology" are especially pertinent.

704. Mouskhély, Michel, and Zygmunt Jedryka.   Le gouvernement de l'U.R.S.S. Paris, Presses Universitaires de France, 1961. 429 p.

The lengthiest recent French text on Soviet political institutions. Very little space is devoted to the Communist Party, and what is said on this subject is for the most part historical rather than analytical. Treatment of such topics as constitutional theory, the federal structure, and the judiciary is fuller, but also tends to be concerned with form rather than substance.

705.* Rostow, Walt W.   The Dynamics of Soviet Society. New York, Norton, 1953. 282 p.

See also entry no. 1167.

A careful effort by an outstanding social scientist, who is not a research scholar in Russian affairs, to synthesize information in works by specialists on the Soviet Union. On the whole a well-balanced and readable account of Soviet society immediately following Stalin's death. However, many of the generalizations are so hedged as to be of little value; when predictions are offered, there is an overemphasis on some features of the Soviet system, such as the police, and underestimation of its ability to survive a struggle for succession without undergoing widespread conflict.

706.* Schuman, Frederick L.   Government in the Soviet Union. New York, Crowell, 1961. 190 p.

While the primary focus of this concise book is Soviet government and politics, it contains a good deal on Russian history and Soviet foreign policy. The author stresses what he considers the accomplishments of the Soviet regime, and has an extraordinary confidence in his own ability to assess the favorable reaction of the Soviet citizenry to these "accomplishments." A translation of the Soviet constitution and a select bibliography are appended.

707. Schuman, Frederick L.   Soviet Politics at Home and Abroad. New York, Knopf, 1946. 663 p.

As the author writes in the preface, "this work is frankly intended to foster unity through a fuller understanding of the USSR." Many critics have felt that this purpose prevented him from facing up to many of the harsher realities of the Soviet regime. Essentially an interesting, even dramatic, account of the evolution of the Soviet political system; although the author is intent upon pointing out the relation to international affairs, Soviet foreign policy receives relatively slight direct consideration.

708.* Scott, Derek J. R.   Russian Political Institutions. New York, Rinehart, 1958. 265 p.

A concise discussion of the Soviet political system by a British political scientist. The treatment of the constitutional framework, the Soviet legislative bodies, administration, and mass organizations, is particularly good; in comparison, the Communist Party and its ideology are treated rather slightly.

709. Souvarine, Boris.   Stalin; a Critical Survey of Bolshevism. New York, Longmans, Green, 1939. 690 p.

See also entry no. 561.

A highly critical account by a Polish ex-Communist of Stalin's first decade and a half of power. While much that the author reports was speculative when he wrote it, a remarkably high proportion has been confirmed by subsequent revelations.

Published originally as *Staline; aperçu historique du bolshevisme* (Paris, Plon, 1935, 574 p.), with a valuable bibliography on pages 545-570.

710. Towster, Julian.   Political Power in the USSR, 1917-1947; the Theory and Structure of Government in the Soviet State. New York, Oxford University Press, 1948. 443 p.

Bibliography: p. 419-430.

At the time of its publication this book was the most systematic and useful treatise on the Soviet political system. It contains a considerable amount of material on the functioning and organization of the Soviet Communist Party, social groups and nationalities, and military-civil relations which is now obsolete. The main emphasis, however, is on the development of Soviet public law theory and the structure of the Soviet state; this material remains highly relevant.

711.* Tucker, Robert C.   The Soviet Political Mind; Studies in Stalinism and Post-Stalin Change. New York, Praeger, 1963. 238 p.
See also entry no. 921.

A collection of essays dealing with a wide range of topics on Soviet political life. The first essay presents a theory of the Soviet Communist Party as an example of a "revolutionary mass movement regime," while the third section of the book contains several essays on foreign policy. The rest is more directly concerned with the Soviet political system: the influence of the historical heritage on it, the transition following Stalin's death, Stalin's use of psychology, and the author's direct observation of Soviet local government.

712. Webb, Sidney, *and* Beatrice Webb.   Soviet Communism: a New Civilization? London, New York, Longmans, Green, 1935. 2 v.
See also entry no. 1172.

This book, written by two eminent British Fabian socialists and public administration experts after a brief trip to the USSR, is now mainly of interest as an example of how highly intelligent specialists in their own field could be misled by superficial observation of the Soviet system. Though the work was written at a time when the famine following collectivization had hardly ended, and when the Great Purge was beginning, the treatment is essentially an apologia. There are, however, a number of interesting and useful details, primarily on aspects of the Soviet social service which the Webbs observed personally.

713. Wolfe, Bertram D.   Communist Totalitarianism; Keys to the Soviet System. Boston, Beacon Press, 1961. 328 p.

A somewhat expanded version of *Six Keys to the Soviet System* (Boston, Beacon Press, 1956). The articles which make up the book were published over a span of 20 years; consequently, their factual relevance to present Soviet politics varies. The author's main concern is the impact of totalitarianism; he shows how this constant feature of the Soviet political system has affected many aspects of policy and behavior.

(2) Soviet Communist ideology

714. Bell, Daniel.   One Road from Marx; on the Vision of Socialism, and the Fate of Workers' Control, in Socialist Thought. World Politics, v. 11, July 1959: 491-512.

A study of the rapid change from Lenin's concept (1917) that ordinary workers could carry on the principal functions of government and economic management, to his position, after confronting the realities of power, that strict direction by specialists was needed.

Some introductory remarks on the view of Marx and early Marxists on this question are included.

715.* Berdiaev (Berdyaev), Nikolai A.   The Origin of Russian Communism. Translated by R. M. French. Ann Arbor, University of Michigan Press, 1960. 191 p.
See also entry no. 1581.

This essay, first published in English in 1937, is perhaps the most profound and influential exposition of the view that Soviet communism is a secular religion. The importance of the work is enhanced by the fact that Berdiaev, an anti-Communist émigré, was one of the greatest philosophical and religious thinkers that Russia has produced.

716.* Brzezinski, Zbigniew K.   Ideology and Power in Soviet Politics. New York, Praeger, 1962. 180 p.
See also entry no. 873.

Five essays (reprinted from various periodicals) analyzing the relation between the ideology and the political behavior of Communists. While two of the essays are devoted to Soviet foreign policy and the Communist bloc, the bulk of the book deals with Soviet internal politics. The author writes that his purpose is to stimulate rather than to convince; hence, his work concentrates upon theoretical analysis and definition rather than the presentation of evidence.

717. Chambre, Henri.   Le Marxisme en Union Soviétique; idéologie et institutions, leur évolution de 1917 à nos jours. Paris, Éditions du Seuil, 1955. 509 p.
See also entry no. 1583.

This is the most comprehensive examination of the relation of Marxist-Leninist ideology to specific spheres of social development in the USSR. Under "legal ideology," the author considers marriage, labor, property, penology, and general legal theory; under "moral and anti-religious ideology," the nationality question is discussed as well as the subjects indicated in the title; the section on "economic theory" contains an interesting discussion of Stalin's *Economic Problems of Socialism* (*see* entry no. 1073). The treatment throughout tends to be sociological rather than philosophical.

718. Eastman, Max.   Marx and Lenin; the Science of Revolution. New York, A. and C. Boni, 1927. 267 p.

While no longer very significant as a factual account of Soviet ideology, the work is interesting as an early interpretation by one of the principal American adherents of Trotsky. Essentially Eastman rejects the dialectical aspects of Marxism in favor of a straight materialist interpretation based on a "pragmatic" and "scientific" approach. He feels that this was really Lenin's fundamental position; there is some evidence to suggest that the present Soviet regime, while retaining the dialectic in principle, is approaching Eastman's position on it in practice.

719.* Hunt, Robert N. C.   The Theory and Practice of Communism; an Introduction. New York, Macmillan, 1957. 286 p.

> Perhaps the best survey of Communist doctrine from Marx and Engels through Stalin ever written. The presentation is simple enough to be used by the intelligent beginner in the study of Marxist doctrine. Discussion of "practice" is much slighter, and requires supplementing from other sources.

720. Ideology and Reality in the Soviet System.   Proceedings of the American Philosophical Society, v. 99, no. 1, Jan. 27, 1955. 38 p.

> Papers by Sidney Hook (relating historical determinism to Soviet ideology), Geroid T. Robinson (discussion of Stalin's concept of complete communism), and Calvin B. Hoover (on the relation of ideology to economics). A very useful survey of the relation of ideology to Soviet practice at the end of the Stalin era.

721.* Labedz, Leopold, *ed.*   Revisionism; Essays on the History of Marxist Ideas. London, Allen and Unwin; New York, Praeger, 1962. 404 p.

See also entry no. 1592.

> A very far-ranging collection dealing, in effect, with interpretations of Marxism which have deviated from the official Soviet position. Thus, even though a large proportion of the discussions treat "revisionism" outside the USSR (including several studies of Marxist thought before the Bolshevik Revolution), the book is essentially an indirect examination of the nature of Soviet Communist ideology.

722. Laqueur, Walter Z., *and* Leopold Labedz, *eds.*   The Future of Communist Society. New York, Praeger, 1962. 196 p.

See also entry no. 1244.

> A series of essays centering around the new Soviet Communist Party program adopted in 1961. While many of the pieces deal with economic or foreign policy implications, or with the historical background of revolutionary "utopian" thought, the focus of the book is upon the implications for the political development of the Soviet system.

723. Leites, Nathan C.   A Study of Bolshevism. Glencoe, Ill., The Free Press, 1953. 639 p.

Bibliography: p. 630-634.

See also entry no. 1177.

> A massive effort to determine the objectives and techniques of Soviet communism by intensive examination of all the works of Lenin and Stalin. The author's focus is somewhat obscured by the juxtaposition of Communist quotations and passages from the nineteenth-century classics of Russian literature; he denies that the passages are intended to show that Soviet psychology is an outgrowth of Russian national character, but maintains that these passages represent what the Bolshevik leaders might have said if they had spoken without inhibition.

The author follows essentially the same approach in his *The Operational Code of the Politburo* (New York, McGraw-Hill, 1951, 100 p.). However, the brevity and preliminary nature of the book make the presentation more schematic and consequently less flexible and convincing than the author's expanded version.

724. Low, Alfred D.   Lenin on the Question of Nationality. New York, Bookman Associates, 1958. 193 p.

A useful summary of Lenin's views on nationality and nationalism, mainly in chronological order. While the study is not rich in theoretical or comparative insights, evaluations are generally sound. The work is accompanied by a very useful analytical bibliography.

725.* Marcuse, Herbert.   Soviet Marxism; a Critical Analysis. New York, Columbia University Press, 1958. 271 p.
See also entry no. 1595.

A very provocative thesis rather than a systematic description. The approach is what the author calls an "immanent critique" — initial acceptance of the theoretical premises of Marxism, followed by a re-examination in the light of their ideological and sociological consequences. The result, in fact, is a highly individual interpretation of Soviet ideology.

726.* Meyer, Alfred G.   Leninism. Cambridge, Harvard University Press, 1957. 324 p.
See also entry no. 1598.

One of the best concise interpretations of Lenin's doctrine. Political rather than philosophical aspects are emphasized, but the operational and organizational sides of the doctrine are not allowed to overshadow the elements of sociological interpretation and historical prophecy in Lenin's thought. The attempt to relate changes in doctrine after the Bolshevik Revolution to practical circumstances is less complete.

727. Monnerot, Jules.   Sociology and Psychology of Communism. Translated from the French by Jane Degras and Richard Rees. Boston, Beacon Press, 1953. 339 p.
See also entries no. 1232 and 1599.

A partial translation (omitting part two) of *Sociologie du communisme* (Paris, Gallimard, 1949, 510 p.). The change of title in translation is apparently meant to suggest that the work is not sociology in the sense of analysis of communism in terms of social phenomena such as class structure and membership, but in the sense of sociology of ideas. Basically the work is a most elaborate exposition of the thesis that communism is a secular religion.

728. Moore, Barrington, Jr.   Soviet Politics: the Dilemma of Power. Cambridge, Harvard University Press, 1950. 503 p.
Bibliography: p. 467-485.
See also entry no. 1245.

A very interesting sociological examination of the changes induced in Communist ideology by the practical requirements and temptations which arose when the Bolsheviks attained power. The whole range of activity of the regime — decision-making, bureaucracy, promotion of world revolution and national expansion, collectivization, social stratification, and industrialization — is considered. The author concludes that many of the goals of the original ideology have been indefinitely postponed or ritualized, though some have been achieved.

729. Morgan, George (*pseud.* "Historicus"). Stalin on Revolution. Foreign Affairs, v. 27, Jan. 1949: 175-214.

A succinct but penetrating demonstration of the consistency of Stalin's position that the ultimate aim of communism is world revolution. Contains numerous quotations from Stalin's works prior to *Marksizm i voprosy iazykoznaniia.*

730. Page, Stanley W. Lenin and World Revolution. New York, New York University Press, 1959. 252 p.

A study of the evolution of Lenin's concept of Communist revolution as a world phenomenon. While there is a brief introduction on the earlier phases of Lenin's thought, the bulk of the study deals with the period between the overthrow of the Tsarist regime and the Second Comintern Congress in 1920. The account presents no major new conclusions, but it does provide abundant and detailed documentation for Lenin's changing views.

731.*Schapiro, Leonard B., *ed.* The U.S.S.R. and the Future; an Analysis of the New Program of the CPSU. Published for the Institute for the Study of the USSR. New York, Praeger, 1963. 324 p.

A collection of essays by many non-Soviet observers, analyzing the program adopted at the Twenty-second Party Congress in 1961. While the international, social, economic, and cultural implications are considered, the primary focus is on the program as a political document.

732. Ulam, Adam B. The Unfinished Revolution; an Essay on the Sources of Influence of Marxism and Communism. New York, Random House, 1960. 307 p.
See also entry no. 922.

An extended essay on the thesis that every modernizing society has a period when Marxist ideas are relevant. The author traces the origin of Marxism in the intellectual traditions of nineteenth-century Europe, the development of the Marxist movement in Europe and Russia, and the attempt to apply Marxism in the USSR. The last portion of the book deals with the present international implications of Marxism.

(3) Political biographic directories [7]

733. Institut zur Erforschung der UdSSR. *Research Section.* Key Offi-

[7] For additional biographical material, *see* Chapter I.

cials of the Government of the USSR and Union Republics. Munich, 1962. 111 p. (mimeographed)
See also entry no. 59.

A list of several hundred major central offices of the Soviet state and the persons occupying each office from 1917 to 1958. For the period after 1941 the dates of each incumbency are given. There is also a list of major regional officials in 1958, but this is inferior to the lists in the Department of State directories of Soviet officials (*see* entries no. 60 and 735).

734. U. S. *Dept. of State. Division of Biographic Information.* Biographic Directory of Soviet Political Leaders. Washington, 1957. 375 p. (*Its* Biographic Directory, no. 251)

A very useful guide to officials occupying major posts in the Soviet government and Communist Party (at the central and Union Republic levels) during the period 1953-1957. The main body of the directory was completed just before the major changes arising from industrial reorganization and the defeat of the "anti-Party" group, but many of the new offices and appointments are indicated in a supplement.

735. U. S. *Dept. of State. Division of Biographic Information.* Directory of Soviet Officials. Washington, 1960-1961. 2 v. (v. 1: Personnel in the Communist Party, Government, and Mass Organizations of the USSR and RSFSR; v. 2: Personnel in the Communist Party, Government, and Mass Organizations of the Soviet Union Republics [excluding RSFSR]) (*Its* Biographic Directory, no. 272, 278)
See also entry no. 60.

A detailed and extremely useful roster of officials in government, Party, the military, and in diplomatic, cultural, and educational posts. Names of incumbents are entered in tables of organization of the respective agencies and institutions. An index permits easy cross-reference. The second volume, covering the union republics other than the RSFSR, is less detailed than the first.

(4) Political biographies [8,9]

736. Pistrak, Lazar. The Grand Tactician; Khrushchev's Rise to Power. New York, Praeger, 1961. 296 p.

The best book on Khrushchev's career before he attained supreme power in the USSR, although in some respects William Medlin's series of articles ("Khrushchev; a Political Profile" in the *Russian Review*, v. 17, Oct. 1958: 278-291; v. 18, Jan. 1959: 23-24; v. 18, Apr. 1959: 131-144; v. 18, July 1959: 173-183) is more judicious. The account is divided into sections on Khrushchev's early career as a minor official in the Ukraine; his rise to prominence (under L. M. Kaganovich) in Moscow in the late 1920's and early 1930's;

[8] For works (especially those concerning Stalin) which are predominantly studies of periods of Soviet political history, rather than autobiographies of individual leaders, *see* Chapter VII, B, 2, a (2), entries no. 649-663.
[9] Arrangement is alphabetical by the subject of the biography.

and his emergence as a major Soviet proconsul in the Ukraine (1938-
1949). His subsequent career in the Central Committee Secretariat
up to Stalin's death is treated more briefly.

737.* Shub, David.   Lenin; a Biography. Garden City, N. Y., Doubleday,
1948. 438 p.
See also entry no. 551.

The most detailed and systematic treatment of Lenin's life. The
author is, however, more concerned with biography in the narrow
sense of the word than with the development of political ideas and
forces. Thus he presents a great deal of important information on
Lenin's personal activity, with an adequate background of the external course of events, but does not systematically analyze the development of Lenin's thought. A lengthy bibliography is appended.

As the present bibliographic guide was being readied for publication, the following three biographies of Lenin appeared: Louis
Fischer, *The Life of Lenin* (New York, Harper and Row, 1964, 703
p.); Robert Payne, *The Life and Death of Lenin* (New York, Simon
and Schuster, 1964, 672 p.); and Stefan T. Possony, *Lenin: the
Compulsive Revolutionary* (Chicago, Regnery, 1964, 418 p.)

738. Ebon, Martin.   Malenkov: Stalin's Successor. Introduction by Harry
Schwartz. New York, McGraw-Hill, 1953. 284 p.

Actually only 154 pages of this book are devoted to a biography of
G. M. Malenkov; the remainder consists of translations of several
of his speeches and other incidental information. This division of
space was reasonable, since little was known of Malenkov's personal
background at the time; a certain amount of additional information
appeared in subsequent years, mainly as a result of Khrushchev's
castigation of his defeated rival. Unfortunately, however, the author
did not even assemble much of the available information on Malenkov's career in the 1930's and during the Second World War.

739. Deutscher, Isaac.   The Prophet Armed; Trotsky, 1879-1921. The
Prophet Unarmed; Trotsky, 1921-1929. The Prophet Outcast; Trotsky, 1929-1940. London, New York, Oxford University Press, 1954-
1963. 3 v. (540, 490, 543 p.)
See also entry no. 553.

Based upon the unpublished Trotsky archives in the United States,
these three volumes provide a detailed examination of Trotsky's career as a revolutionary leader, military organizer, and unsuccessful
opponent of Stalin. The author sympathizes with Trotsky, yet he
apparently regards his protagonist's defeat as unavoidable in terms
of the Leninist system.

(5) Studies on the Party

740. Armstrong, John A.   The Politics of Totalitarianism; the Commu-
nist Party of the Soviet Union from 1934 to the Present. New York,
Random House, 1961. 458 p.
Bibliography: p. 349-427.

This third volume in a detailed history sponsored by the Research Program on the History of the Communist Party of the Soviet Union summarizes available evidence and conflicting interpretations for the period 1934-1960. Organized around the central theme of the power struggle, it deals with Party organization and policy, the political police, the military, and the Soviet state. Most revealing on the Second World War period.

The author's *An Essay on Sources for the Study of the Communist Party of the Soviet Union, 1934-1960* (n.p., 1961, 41 p.) extends the bibliography of the larger work.

741. Avtorkhanov, Abdurakhman.   Stalin and the Soviet Communist Party; a Study in the Technology of Power. New York, Praeger, 1959. 379 p.

A substantial treatment of the entire period of Stalin's dictatorship; must be used with caution because the author often relies on his memory and on unsubstantiated rumors he heard while still in the USSR.

A translation of his *Tekhnologiia vlasti; protsess obrazovaniia KPSS. Memuarno-istoricheskie ocherki* (Munich, Tsentral'noe ob"edinenie politicheskikh emigrantov iz SSSR, 1959, 418 p.)

742.* Reshetar, John S., Jr.   A Concise History of the Communist Party of the Soviet Union. New York, Praeger, 1960. 331 p.

A highly useful brief treatment of the entire history of the party from the origins of Marxism to the post-Stalin struggle for power (although the latter period is treated summarily). A useful selected reading list is appended.

743. Rosenberg, Arthur.   History of Bolshevism; from Marx to the First Five Years' Plan. London, Oxford University Press, 1934. 250 p. Bibliography: p. 241-246.

This edition is translated from the unaltered German version of 1932: *Geschichte des Bolschewismus von Marx bis zur Gegenwart* (Berlin, Rowohlt, 1932, 239 p.). The author, a German Communist who resigned from the party in 1927 but maintains that he did not adhere to any opposition group, presents a systematic historical study rather than a memoir. After a very brief introduction on Marxism and Russian Bolshevism prior to the First World War, the book provides a concentrated examination of Soviet communism during the Revolution, Civil War, and the 1920's, intertwined with the history of the Third International.

744. Rutych, N.   Le Parti communiste au pouvoir, en URSS 1917-1960. Paris, La Table ronde, 1961. 522 p.

A full-scale history of the Soviet Communist Party; like Leonard Schapiro's (*see* entry no. 745), it deals very lightly with the period following the end of the Great Purges (1938), but unlike Schapiro's, this book does not discuss the pre-Revolutionary origins of Bolshevism. The focus is upon personages and incidents rather than upon organizational development or sociological analysis, but the treatment of some social questions (particularly the peasant problem) is excellent. On the other hand, the author appears occasionally to be led astray by his extreme opposition to communism, e.g., in his overemphasis on the importance of the German subsidies to the Bolsheviks.

A translation of his *KPSS u vlasti; ocherki po istorii Kommunisticheskoi partii, 1917-1957* (Frankfurt am Main, Posev, 1960, 464 p.)

745. Schapiro, Leonard B.   The Communist Party of the Soviet Union. New York, Random House; London, Eyre and Spottiswoode, 1960. 631 p.
Bibliography: p. 591-603.
See also entry no. 552.

The most comprehensive treatment of the central aspect of the Soviet political system. The author discusses in authoritative detail the origins and development of the pre-Revolutionary Bolsheviks, the Revolutionary and Civil War periods, the struggle for power in the 1920's, and Stalin's purges in the 1930's. The coverage of the period from 1939 to 1959 is summary. In addition to organizational charts and a bibliographical essay, the book contains lists of Party congresses and conferences and of members of the Politburo and the Party Presidium.

(6) Power conflicts within the regime

746. Bernaut, Elsa, *and* Melville J. Ruggles.   Collective Leadership and the Political Police in the Soviet Union. Santa Monica, Calif., The Rand Corporation, 1956. 56 l. (Rand Corporation. Research Memorandum, RM-1674)

Contains some interesting sidelights on the struggle between Lavrentii Beria and other Soviet leaders in the months immediately following Stalin's death. Evidently based in part upon information from defectors which is not available elsewhere.

747. Brzezinski, Zbigniew K.   The Permanent Purge: Politics in Soviet Totalitarianism. Cambridge, Harvard University Press, 1956. 256 p.
Bibliography: p. 191-199.
See also entry no. 819.

The thesis is that radical renewal of membership in the Soviet political elite is a fundamental technique of the totalitarian system. By "purge" the author understands both the bloody decimation of real or suspected opposition elements and the periodical replacement of officials. Data drawn from a wide variety of areas of Soviet political life between 1929 and 1953.

748. Conquest, Robert.   Power and Policy in the U.S.S.R.; the Study of Soviet Dynasties. New York, St. Martin's Press, 1961. 485 p.

A complex but clearly presented theory of "Kremlinology" — the interpretation of power alignments in the USSR through close examination of the phraseology of published statements and of personnel changes. The author applies the theory to the years after the Second World War, with considerable assurance down to 1957 and more speculatively for the period 1957-1960.

749. Embree, George D.   The Soviet Union between the 19th and 20th Party Congresses, 1952-1956. The Hague, Nijhoff, 1959. 365 p. Bibliography: p. 341-359.

    A detailed compendium of developments, mainly political, in the unsettled period just before and after Stalin's death. Both Soviet and non-Soviet sources were used, but nearly all Soviet sources were apparently used in translation. Moreover, the author frequently fails to relate subsequent revelations (from either type of source) to the events he describes.

750.* Leonhard, Wolfgang.   The Kremlin since Stalin. Translated by Elizabeth Wiskemann. New York, Praeger, 1962. 403 p.

    A stimulating survey of Soviet developments (mainly political) since 1953. The author's insight is undoubtedly heightened by the fact that he is a former German Communist trained in the USSR. At times he seems rather overconfident of his speculations, however. Translated and revised from *Kreml ohne Stalin* (Cologne, Verlag für Politik und Wirtschaft, 1959, 646 p.)

751. Meissner, Boris.   Russland unter Chruschtschow. Munich, R. Oldenbourg, 1960. 699 p.

    The first part of this book is a detailed analysis of political rivalries and policies in the six years following Stalin's death. The second part consists of German translations of major Soviet published documents and articles from this period. Most of the latter have appeared in English translation, usually in the *Current Digest of the Soviet Press* (*see* entry no. 28), but the collection is convenient.

752. Rush, Myron.   The Rise of Khrushchev. Washington, D.C., Public Affairs Press, 1958. 116 p.

    A detailed analysis of the steps by which Khrushchev sought and attained predominance in the Soviet leadership. The study is distinguished by its skillful use of "esoteric language" (references in published Soviet statements which are intelligible only to the initiated) and its clear explanation of the significance of these clues. The effort to demonstrate that Khrushchev was following almost precisely in Stalin's footsteps appears exaggerated, however.

(7) Opposition political movements

753. Commission of Inquiry into the Charges Made Against Leon Trotsky in the Moscow Trials. *Preliminary Commission, Coyoacan, Mexico, 1937*. The Case of Leon Trotsky; Report of Hearings . . . Edited by John Dewey. New York, Harper, 1937. 617 p.

    During the period April 10-17, 1937, John Dewey headed a commission of prominent persons who felt a public service would be performed by investigating the extreme charges which had been made against Trotsky in the first two trials of the Great Purge. This is a verbatim record of the testimony which the committee took from Trotsky and others.

The Commission's report, entitled *Not Guilty* (New York, Harper, 1938, 422 p.) makes use of materials and publications in Trotsky's hands and elsewhere outside the USSR, as well as of discrepancies and contradictions in Soviet publications on the subject. The conclusion is that Trotsky was not guilty of charges of directing terror and sabotage against the USSR.

754. Daniels, Robert V.   The Conscience of the Revolution; Communist Opposition in Soviet Russia. Cambridge, Harvard University Press, 1960. 526 p.
Bibliography: p. 439-448.
See also entry no. 556.

A detailed and fully-documented history of the elements in the Soviet Communist Party which opposed the leadership (in part of Lenin, but primarily of Stalin) down to the end of the 1920's. The author maintains that these elements represented tendencies which, if triumphant, would have made the Soviet regime more liberal and less totalitarian and dictatorial.

755. Fischer, George.   Soviet Opposition to Stalin; a Case Study in World War II. Cambridge, Harvard University Press, 1952. 230 p.
Bibliography: p. 218-222.

Primarily an account of the group around Soviet General Andrei Vlasov, who collaborated with the Germans after his capture in 1942. The author analyzes the group and its program as one of the most prominent symptoms of disaffection with the Soviet system. Based on extensive Russian and German written records (more of the latter have come to light since the book's publication) and on numerous interviews with Vlasov's surviving followers and the Germans who dealt with them.

756. Leites, Nathan C., *and* Elsa Bernaut.   Ritual of Liquidation; the Case of the Moscow Trials. Glencoe, Ill., The Free Press, 1954. 515 p.

An interesting attempt to explain the trials of the Great Purge (1936-1938) through a complex psychological interpretation of Communist mentality. More recent revelations (as in Khrushchev's secret speech of 1956) suggest, however, that sheer force was more of a factor in securing confessions from Communists accused by Stalin than were the elaborate motivations advanced by the authors.

757. Radkey, Oliver H.   The Sickle under the Hammer; the Russian Socialist Revolutionaries in the Early Months of Soviet Rule. New York, Columbia University Press, 1963. 525 p.
Bibliography: p. 497-509.

A continuation of Professor Radkey's magisterial work on the struggle of the Bolsheviks with the populist-minded Socialist Revolutionaries (*see* entry no. 638). This volume discusses in great detail the crucial period from the Bolshevik Revolution in November 1917 to the outlawing of the SR's in March 1918. The principal thesis is that the divided, intellectualistic SR's, although enjoying widespread support, were no match for Lenin's well-organized and skillfully led party.

758. Schapiro, Leonard B.   The Origin of the Communist Autocracy; Political Opposition in the Soviet State, First Phase, 1917-1922. Cambridge, Harvard University Press, 1955. 397 p.
Bibliography: p. 369-387.
   The most authoritative study of the left-wing opponents (mainly Socialist Revolutionaries, Mensheviks, and "left" Communists) of Bolshevism during Lenin's lifetime, and of the devices he and his supporters used to suppress them. The "White" groups which opposed the Bolsheviks by force (and, in general, conservative opposition elements) are not treated. The book is most interesting in its demonstration that the repressive aspects of Soviet communism were already well developed under Lenin.

759. Sedov, Lev.   Livre rouge sur le Procès de Moscou. Paris, Éditions populaires, 1936. 128 p.
   A polemical but useful analysis, by Trotsky's son, of the testimony in the first Great Purge public trial ("The case of the Trotskyite-Zinovievite terrorist centre"). The author conclusively demonstrates the inconsistencies and factual inaccuracies in the confessions upon which the prosecution relied. He also offers some significant clues to reasons for the holding of the trial in August 1936, and the nature of Stalin's preparation for it.

(8) Political control mechanisms [10]

760. Brzezinski, Zbigniew K., *ed.*   Political Controls in the Soviet Army. New York, Research Program on the USSR, 1954. 93 p. Illus.
See also entry no. 949.
   A collection of accounts by former members of the Soviet armed forces (Vyacheslav P. Artemyev and others). Mainly useful on controls and indoctrination, but information (which for the most part dates back to the Second World War) is somewhat slight and partly obsolete.

761. Carson, George B.   Electoral Practices in the U.S.S.R. New York, Praeger, 1955. 151 p. Illus.
   Historical description of the legal provisions governing elections under the various Soviet constitutions, with some introductory remarks on pre-Revolutionary Russian elections. The author notes the extreme limitations upon the voter, as well as the significance even "rigged" elections may have for unsophisticated Soviet citizens.

[10] Only those works are included here which focus upon mechanisms of control rather than the subjects controlled.

The study does not, however, provide analysis in depth of the important use of electoral campaigns as propaganda devices. Charts illustrate the various electoral procedures; a translation of the 1947 law on local elections is appended.

762. Dinerstein, Herbert S., *and* Leon Gouré.   Communism and the Russian Peasant by Herbert S. Dinerstein. Moscow in Crisis by Leon Gouré and Herbert S. Dinerstein. Two Studies in Soviet Controls. Foreword by Philip E. Mosely. Glencoe, Ill., The Free Press, 1955. 254 p.
Bibliography: p. 247-254.
The first study, by Dinerstein alone, focuses on Soviet agricultural policy and the peasants' reaction during the last years of Stalin's life, prior to the considerable changes introduced by Khrushchev. The second study (by both authors) is a very illuminating day-by-day account (based on interviews with defectors as well as on published sources) of the reaction of the Soviet regime and the Moscow population to the threat of German capture of the city.

763. Fisher, Ralph T., Jr.   Pattern for Soviet Youth; a Study of the Congresses of the Komsomol, 1918-1954. New York, Columbia University Press, 1959. 452 p.
See also entry no. 1733.
A comprehensive history of the organization and programs of the Komsomol (Communist Youth League), not of its "grass roots" activity. Based primarily on the records of the 12 Komsomol Congresses, the work provides a systematic chronological account except, unfortunately, for the long period (1936-1949) when no congresses were held.

764. Harper, Samuel N.   Civic Training in Soviet Russia. Chicago, University of Chicago Press, 1929. 401 p.
Bibliography: p. 382-394.
This book, by the foremost American academic authority on Russia of his time, is a massive attempt to analyze the relationship between politics, education, and youth in the formative period of the Soviet system. While the work does not take full account of the specifically totalitarian nature of Soviet communism, and consequently tends to overrate its accomplishments in Western terms, it is still valuable.
The same author's *Making Bolsheviks* (Chicago, University of Chicago Press, 1931, 167 p.) focuses upon the results, rather than the mechanisms, of indoctrination of Soviet youth in the late 1920's. Though the growing rigidity and bureaucratization of the Soviet regime quickly rendered many of the book's conclusions obsolete, it is still useful for its insights into the appeals of Soviet communism during its first decade.

765. Institut zur Erforschung der UdSSR.   Soviet Youth: Twelve Komsomol Histories. Edited by Nikolai K. Novak-Deker. Translation

edited by Oliver J. Frederiksen. Munich, Institute for the Study of the USSR, 1959. 256 p. (*Its* Research and Materials, Ser. 1, no. 51)
> Contains reports by former members of the Komsomol who left the Soviet Union during the years 1941-1945.

766. Laird, Roy D.   Collective Farming in Russia; a Political Study of Soviet Kolkhozy. Lawrence, Kansas, University of Kansas Publications, 1958. 176 p.
Bibliography: p. 161-173.
> The only full-scale analysis of the political aspects of Soviet agricultural development. Covers the period down to the abolition of the machine tractor station system.

767. Lavroff, Dmitri-Georges.   Les libertés publiques en Union Soviétique. Paris, Pedone, 1960. 217 p.
> A systematic but very superficial examination of the state of civil liberties in the USSR. The author claims to examine his subject from "inside" the presuppositions of Marxist-Leninist doctrine, and does provide a detailed analysis of the significance of "liberty" in the writings of Marx, Engels, and Lenin. In examining concrete liberties (particularly personal freedom, religious freedom, and freedom of labor) he neglects Soviet practice, relying for his interpretation almost entirely upon the constitution, penal codes, and a few legal theorists.

768. Mirkine-Guetzévitch, Boris.   La théorie générale de l'État soviétique. Paris, M. Giard, 1928. 203 p.
> A detailed analysis of Soviet constitutional law theory. French translations of the (1923) constitution of the USSR and the (1925) constitution of the RSFSR are appended. The study is an interesting early effort to analyze Soviet constitutional thought in terms of traditional Western public law.
>
> First appeared as a series of articles in *Revue du droit public* (1925-1927).

769. Mouskhély, Michel.   Le système soviétique de contrôle. Revue du droit public et de la science politique en France et à l'étranger, v. 75, 1959, no. 3: 484-514.
> This well-documented article by a Strasbourg professor of law is almost the only scholarly work to deal extensively with the concept. The author is primarily concerned with analyzing Soviet discussions of how "control" should be understood and implemented. He has little to say about the sociological aspects of the control system or the Party organizations for control; his discussion of the control functions of state agencies (particularly the procuracy) devotes more attention to the institutional and legal aspects.

770. Swayze, Harold.   Political Control of Literature in the USSR, 1946-1959. Cambridge, Harvard University Press, 1962. 301 p.
See also entry no. 1442.
> A systematic examination of the control of literature by the Soviet

regime, from Andrei Zhdanov's campaign for ideological control following the Second World War through the first years of Khrushchev's ascendancy. The emphasis is on the doctrinal significance of ideological conformity and the institutional mechanisms for enforcing it, rather than on the intrinsic content of literature, but the historical development of controlled literary expression is well treated.

771. U. S. *Congress. Senate. Committee on Government Operations.* National Policy Machinery in the Soviet Union. Report of the Committee on Government Operations, Made by Its Subcommittee on National Policy Machinery, pursuant to S. Res. 115, 86th Cong. Washington, U. S. Government Printing Office, 1960. 70 p. Illus., map. (86th Congress, 2d Session, Report no. 1204)

An analytical survey of the principal bodies of the Soviet Communist Party and the Soviet state, including special sections on agencies involved in foreign policy formation, economic policy, scientific policy, and military policy. The numerous and detailed organizational charts, the data on Central Committee plenary sessions in 1956-1959, and the lists of key officials are especially useful.

(9) Regional organization and case studies of particular areas [11]

772. Armstrong, John A.   The Soviet Bureaucratic Elite; a Case Study of the Ukrainian Apparatus. New York, Praeger, 1959. 174 p. Bibliography: p. 152-162.

An intensive study of personnel turnover and career patterns in the middle levels (down to the provincial officials) in the Ukraine between the end of the Great Purge (1938) and 1957. Based on regional newspapers and Soviet dissertations.

773. Barfivala, C. D.   Local Government in the U.S.S.R. Bombay, All-India Institute of Local Self-Government, 1958. 94 p.

The only book-length treatment of Soviet local government in a Western language, but unfortunately a very uncritical discussion which relies primarily on Soviet sources taken at face value and on the work of Sidney and Beatrice Webb (*see* entry no. 712). The book is highly misleading on such subjects as elections, but of some use for its description of the structure of Soviet local government.

774. Chambre, Henri.   L'aménagement du territoire en URSS; introduction à l'étude des régions économiques soviétiques. Paris, Mouton, 1959. 250 p. (Études sur l'économie et la sociologie des pays slaves, 4)
See also entry no. 1059.

A detailed examination of the treatment of territorial subdivision in Soviet thinking and practice. The focus is upon the economic significance of regionalization, but the matter is highly important from the point of view of political administration as well. Among the special topics considered are basic economic regions, agricultural regions, transportation, and distribution of industry.

[11] *See also* the sections "Baltica" and "Ukrainica" in Chapter V.

775.* Fainsod, Merle.   Smolensk under Soviet Rule. Cambridge, Harvard University Press, 1958. 484 p.
See also entries no. 562 and 811.

An examination, in the microcosm of a single province, of nearly all facets of Soviet political affairs between 1917 and 1938. Based on the voluminous provincial Party archives captured by the German army during the Second World War, the book provides irrefutable proof for numerous generalizations about the operation of the Soviet system which could be advanced earlier only on the basis of émigré accounts or indirect inference. The work provides the best base line for interpreting the course of Soviet political development in subsequent decades.

776. Harcave, Sidney.   The Structure and Functioning of the Lower Party Organizations in the Soviet Union. Maxwell Air Force Base, Alabama, Air Research and Development Command, 1954. 58 p. (Human Resources Research Institute. Technical Research Report no. 23)

Apart from Fainsod's Smolensk under Soviet Rule (see entry no. 775), this is the most detailed study in print on Soviet party organization and operation below the province level. It is based on a considerable sample of articles from Soviet newspapers and periodicals of the late 1940's and early 1950's and on interviews with over two dozen Soviet defectors; the study is one of the most valuable undertaken in connection with the interviews of the Harvard Project on the Soviet Social System.

777. Kaelas, Aleksander.   Das sowjetisch besetzte Estland. Stockholm, Eesti Rahvusfond, 1958. 134 p.

The only recent systematic examination of the political and economic conditions in a single union republic (other than the Ukraine) in book form, although extensive surveys of the Baltic Republics frequently appear in such periodicals as Osteuropa (see entry no. 36). The author, an anti-Soviet émigré Estonian, presents the subject in a manner which is generally reliable and objective. The book contains much useful information on administration and personalities.

778. Kostiuk, Hryhory.   Stalinist Rule in the Ukraine; a Study of the Decade of Mass Terror, 1929-39. New York, Praeger, 1961. 162 p. Bibliography: p. 153-157.
See also entry no. 403.

An examination of the especially severe impact of purges (inside and outside of the Communist Party) in the Ukraine. While some of the émigré Ukrainian author's conclusions are affected by his over-emphasis on his own country, the general approach is cautious and objective. Perhaps the most valuable feature of the book is the author's demolition of many of the extreme versions of Ukrainian resistance activities furthered (for different purposes) by Stalin's police and by certain émigré sources.

779. Schultz, Lothar.   Die Verfassungsentwicklung der baltischen Staaten

seit 1940. Commentationes Balticae (Bonn), v. 6/7, 1959, no. 7: 273-313.

About half of this well-documented article is devoted to a description and critique of recent Soviet efforts (in works in Russian and in the Baltic languages) to demonstrate that there is a continuity between the Soviet regimes which attempted to gain power in Latvia, Estonia, and Lithuania in 1917-1919 and those established in 1940. The second portion deals with changing Soviet interpretations of the periods of the Baltic republics' development after 1940 (especially the question of when the stage of "socialism" was attained).

780. Simon, Ernest D. S., *and others*. Moscow in the Making. New York, Longmans, Green, 1937. 252 p. Front., fold. maps.

A detailed examination of the operation of the Moscow city administration by four British administrators and academic specialists. Among the subjects examined are industry, finance, education, housing, construction, and planning. Most of the information was obtained during a four-week visit to Moscow. Because of the brevity of the visit, the lack of background studies, and the inability of the authors to speak Russian, many aspects of the study are superficial. Nevertheless, it contains many remarkably hard-headed observations.

c. Personal accounts

(1) From the Soviet or Communist point of view

781.* Boffa, Giuseppe.   Inside the Khrushchev Era. New York, Marzani, 1959. 226 p.

Translation of a book, *La grande svoltà* (Rome, Editori Riuniti, 1959, 287 p.), by the Moscow correspondent of the Italian Communist newspaper, *Unità*. Boffa's account is valuable particularly for its revelation of the contents of secret letters of the Central Committee of the CPSU which are otherwise known only through the accounts of defectors. The English version is marred by non-literal translations and some serious deletions.

782. Dedijer, Vladimir.   Tito.   New York, Simon and Schuster, 1953. 443 p.

A biography of Josef Broz-Tito, the leader of the Yugoslav Communists, written in 1949 by one of his principal lieutenants (who has since broken with the Yugoslav regime). Most of the information concerns internal Yugoslav developments, but there are important items of information concerning the Soviet regime, based on the author's personal contacts.

783. Fedorov (Fyodorov), Aleksei.   The Underground R. C. Carries On. Moscow, Foreign Languages Publishing House, 1952. 518 p.

Memoir of a first secretary of a provincial party organization who went underground during the German invasion (Second World War) and led a partisan band. Though he distorts the historical facts to some extent, his book is a highly useful source for the background, values, and attitudes of the Party elite. Translation of *Podpol'nyi obkom deistvuet* (Moscow, Voenizdat, 1947, 2 v.). Later Russian editions are considerably expanded and somewhat altered in emphasis.

784. Partito comunista italiano.   Problemi e realtà dell'URSS; relazione sul viaggio della delegazione del PCI nell'Unione Sovietica. Rome, Editori Riuniti, 1958. 368 p. Fold. map.

The principal value of this book lies in the detailed reports of conversations between the Italian Communist leaders and major officials of the Soviet Communist Party and state. A considerable amount of important information (unpublished in the USSR) concerning the organization and functioning of these Soviet bodies was elicited. Though much of this information is now obsolete, portions are still very valuable.

(2) By disillusioned sympathizers other than Soviet citizens

785. Burmeister, Alfred.   Dissolution and Aftermath of the Comintern; Experiences and Observations, 1937-1947. New York, Research Program on the U.S.S.R., 1955. 43 p. (East European Fund. Mimeographed Series, no. 77)

Account of a former Polish Communist who spent a number of years in the USSR. Important especially for information on the fate of Polish Communist leadership, mechanisms used by the Soviet Communist Party to control non-Soviet Communists, and training of Communist agents for work in their home countries.

786. Ciliga, Anton.   Dix ans derrière le rideau de fer. Paris, Plon, 1950, 2 v. (v. 1: Au pays du mensonge déconcertant; v. 2: Sibérie, terre de l'exil et de l'industrialisation)
See also entry no. 827.

This memoir of a Yugoslav Communist is very important for its insights into the relationship between Stalin and the opposition forces in 1926-1933. A large part of the material is derived from the author's conversations, as a concentration camp inmate, with imprisoned members of various opposition factions.

Volume one appeared first as *Au pays du grand mensonge* (Paris, Gallimard, 1938, 252 p.), with an English translation, *The Russian Enigma* (London, George Routledge, 1940, 304 p.). The second edition omits about 30 pages of obsolete observations and includes a greatly expanded chapter on Stalin's and Lenin's policies (showing how Lenin's actions prepared the way for tyranny).

787.* Ðilas (Djilas), Milovan.   Conversations with Stalin.   Translated from the Serbo-Croat by Michael B. Petrovich. New York, Harcourt, Brace and World, 1962. 211 p.
See also entry no. 885.

A memoir by a former leader of the Yugoslav Communists, subsequently imprisoned, emphasizing his negotiations with the Soviet leaders during and immediately after the Second World War. In addition to interesting general insights into the mentality of the Soviet leadership, the book provides information on several important details of Soviet political history.

788. Fischer, Louis.   Men and Politics; an Autobiography. New York, Duell, Sloan, and Pearce, 1941. 672 p.

A wide-ranging personal account by a major left-wing journalist of the years between the wars. From the standpoint of Soviet politics, the volume is interesting mainly because of the author's intimate contacts with a generation of Soviet officials and writers. He is candid in discussing his early attraction to the Soviet system and his growing disillusionment in the purge period.

789.*Leonhard, Wolfgang.   Child of the Revolution. Translated by C. M. Woodhouse. Chicago, Regnery, 1958. 447 p.

See also entry no. 889.

Memoir of a German who spent his adolescence as an émigré in the USSR, was trained in a secret school for foreign Communist agents in Ufa (in the Urals), and was sent to the Soviet zone of Germany as part of the cadre of German pro-Communists. He later defected to West Germany. The book is valuable for its information on the organizational and propaganda techniques developed by the Soviet regime to maintain control over international communism after the dissolution of the Comintern. A translation of *Die Revolution entlässt ihre Kinder* (Cologne, Kiepenheuer und Witsch, 1955, 557 p.)

790. Moreno Hernández, Ramón.   Rusia al desnudo; revelaciones del comisario comunista español Rafael Pelayo de Hungría, comandante del Ejército ruso. Madrid, Mundial, 1956. 406 p.

Memoir (in third-person form) of a Spanish Republican who returned to Spain after many years in the Soviet military service. Most of the book is trivial in content, but the portions dealing with Soviet "advisers" to the Republican guerrillas and with Soviet "scorched-earth" plans in the Caucasus in 1942 (the memoirist was personally involved in both affairs) are significant.

791. Reale, Eugenio.   Avec Jacques Duclos au banc des accusés à la réunion constitutive du Kominform à Szklarska Poręba (22-27 septembre 1947). Translated by Pierre Bonuzzi. Paris, Plon, 1958. 203 p.

See also entry no. 932.

By a former high Italian Communist official who represented his party at the first Cominform session. While most of the information (based on his notes taken at the session) relates to international and East European communism, rather than to the USSR, there are important observations concerning Soviet delegates Andrei Zhdanov and Georgii Malenkov and their relations to Stalin.

Originally appeared in Italian as *Nascita del Cominform* (Milan, A. Mondadori, 1958, 174 p.)

(3) By Soviet defectors

792. Avtorkhanov, Abdurakhman (Alexander Uralov, *pseud.*).   The Reign of Stalin. London, Bodley Head, 1953. 256 p.

The account of a North Caucasian who held posts in the Soviet Communist Party apparatus during the 1930's, was purged, and escaped from the USSR during the Second World War. Much of the information is based on the author's personal experiences and observations in the USSR. Unfortunately, this information is mingled with his speculations, some of which are demonstrably incorrect.

Originally published as *Staline au pouvoir* (Paris, Les Iles d'or, 1951, 318 p.)

793. Barmine, Alexander.   One Who Survived; the Life Story of a Russian under the Soviets. New York, Putnam, 1945. 337 p.

Memoir of an official who defected in 1937 after nearly 20 years' service to the Soviet regime as a soldier, an industrial director, and a diplomat. Substantive revelations on Soviet politics are few, but the tone of political life is conveyed in a remarkably dispassionate manner.

794. Bazhanov (Bajanov), Boris G.   Avec Staline dans le Kremlin. Paris, Les Éditions de France, 1930. 262 p.

An interesting account by a defector who claims to have served as the recording secretary for the Politburo in the early 1920's. While it is quite possible that some of the author's claims are exaggerated and his information secondhand, there appears to be a core of information based on direct observation of the Soviet leadership during the period when Stalin was attaining power.

795. Kravchenko, Viktor A.   I Chose Freedom; the Personal and Political Life of a Soviet Official. New York, C. Scribner's Sons, 1946. 496 p.

Because of the dramatic manner of the author's defection (from the wartime Soviet Purchasing Commission in Washington), this became one of the best-known Soviet émigré memoirs. However, while there is no reason to doubt the basic accuracy of the account (part of which was verified in the course of a libel trial in France), the revelations are less important than those of several other memoirs. Most interesting is the account of the impact of the Great Purge upon industrial managers (including the author) in Moscow and the Dnepropetrovsk area.

796. Krivitsky, Walter G.   In Stalin's Secret Service; an Exposé of Russia's Secret Policies by the Former Chief of the Soviet Intelligence in Western Europe. New York, Harper, 1939. 273 p.
See also entry no. 813.

Probably the most important memoir by a defector from the Stalin regime. The author, who was a key official in the Soviet military (later NKVD) intelligence network in Western Europe until his flight in 1937, is especially good on Soviet intervention in the

Spanish Civil War and on personalities and attitudes in the NKVD
and the Comintern apparatus. His interpretation of Stalin's foreign
policy, which is based (at best) on secondhand sources, is much
more dubious.

British edition: *I Was Stalin's Agent* (London, Hamilton, 1939,
297 p.)

797. Lermolo, Elizabeth.   Face of a Victim. Translated by I. D. W. Tal-
madge. Foreword by Alexandra Tolstoy. New York, Harper, 1955.
311 p.

Account of the experiences of a Leningrad woman who was acci-
dentally involved in the fierce repression following the assassination
of Sergei Kirov in 1934. After her arrest she met many prominent
Soviet political figures who were also accused of participation in the
assassination "plot." While some of her memories appear to be distorted, she provides important items of information on the political
developments of the mid-1930's.

798. Murray, Nora K.   I Spied for Stalin. Foreword by Lt. Gen. Sir Noel
Mason-Macfarlane. New York, Funk, 1951. 256 p.
See also entry no. 814.

A melodramatic but significant memoir by the daughter of a high
NKVD official who, after her father was purged, was compelled to
act as a secret police agent among foreign diplomats. Her book (written some years after she escaped by marrying one of the latter) contains little of significance on spying, but has important sidelights on
official and personal relations in top secret police circles at the end
of the 1930's.

799. Nicolaevsky, Boris I.   Letter of an Old Bolshevik; the Key to the
Moscow Trials. New York, Rand School Press, 1937. 62 p.

A famous anti-Stalin tract, long thought to be the work of N. I.
Bukharin. In 1959 Nicolaevsky revealed (in *Novoe russkoe slovo*,
December 6) that he had written the Letter, drawing on conversations with Bukharin in 1936 and on other sources. While the work
undoubtedly contains many important items of information on Stalin's rise to dictatorship, it is hard to tell how much of the general
interpretation should be ascribed to Soviet opposition circles and
how much is Nicolaevsky's own concept.

800. Orlov, Alexander.   The Secret History of Stalin's Crimes. New
York, Random House, 1953. 366 p.

A sensational memoir by a man who was, until his flight to the
United States in 1938, a high NKVD official and director of the
Soviet secret police in Republican Spain. Despite the undoubted au-
thenticity of its author's background, the book must be used with
reserve because of the incredibly detailed conversations which the
author recounts — after a lapse of 15 years — and his evident omission of portions of his own record, particularly his activities in
Spain.

801. Serge, Victor (*pseud.* of Viktor L. Kibalchich). Russia Twenty Years After. Translated by Max Schachtman. New York, Hillman-Curl, 1937. 298 p.

The most complete analysis (translated from the French original of 1937) of the Soviet system which Serge (a confidant of Lenin, later imprisoned and exiled by Stalin) wrote. It is one of the most lucid arguments for the thesis that the Soviet system developed from a true social revolution to control by a totalitarian bureaucracy. It is still interesting as an "inside" view.

British edition: *Destiny of a Revolution* (London, Jarrolds, 1937, 287 p.)

802. Slusser, Robert, *ed.* Soviet Economic Policy in Postwar Germany; a Collection of Papers by Former Soviet Officials. New York, Research Program on the USSR, 1953. 184 p.
Bibliography: p. 168-172.

These carefully organized papers by seven defectors from the Soviet administration in East Germany are valuable to this section of the bibliography, not because of what they have to say about Soviet economic policy or Soviet policy in Germany, but because of the remarkable information they contain on policy differences within the Soviet regime in the middle 1940's. Although this information is admittedly based on rumor or indirect inference, much of it appears to be plausible.

3. The Police Power

by Robert M. Slusser

a. Tsarist Russia

(1) The secret police

803. Laporte, Maurice. Histoire de l'Okhrana, la police secrète des tsars, 1880-1917. Preface by Vladimir Bourtzev. Paris, Payot, 1935. 245 p.

The best available, general historical account of the Tsarist secret police in its final form.

The following shorter or more specialized works help provide a fuller picture:

Bienstock, J. W. "La révolution russe; l'Okhrana." *Mercure de France*, v. 123, 1917: 626-652; v. 124, 1917: 77-97.

Gerasimov, A. V. *Tsarisme et terrorisme: souvenirs du général Guérassimov, ancien chef de l'Okhrana de Saint-Pétersbourg, 1909-1912.* Paris, Plon, 1934.

Koshko, A. F. *Souvenirs d'un detective russe.* Paris, Payot, 1930. 243 p.

Kurlov, P. G. *Das Ende des russischen Kaisertums; persönliche Erinnerungen des Chefs der russischen Geheimpolizei Generals der Kavallerie Komaroff-Kurloff.* Berlin, Scherl, 1920. 367 p.

Veselago, Nikolai V. "The Department of Police, 1911-1913, from the recollections of Nikolai Vladimirovich Veselago." Translated by

E. E. Smith. Unpublished manuscript, Hoover Institution, Stanford University, 1963.

Zavardzin, P. P. "Police et révolutionnaire au temps des tsars." *Monde slave*, May 1929: 224-251.

804. Monas, Sidney. The Third Section; Police and Society in Russia under Nicholas I. Cambridge, Harvard University Press, 1961. 354 p. Bibliography: p. 297-314.

A study of the foundation and development of the organization in which the Tsarist Russian secret police received its classic embodiment in the first half of the nineteenth century. Based on extensive research, restrained and judicious in its evaluations; indispensable for understanding the later development of the Tsarist secret police.

805. Nicolaevsky (Nikolajewsky), Boris I. Aseff, the Spy, Russian Terrorist and Police Stool. Translated from the Russian by George Reavey. Garden City, N. Y., Doubleday, Doran, 1934. 307 p.

A classic account of a major cause célèbre in the complex and intertwined relations between the Tsarist secret police and the terrorist organizations in the first decade of the twentieth century. Translation of *Istoriia odnogo predatelia; terroristy i politicheskaia politsiia* (Berlin, Petropolis, 1932, 250 p.). British edition (London, Hurst and Blackett, 1934, 285 p.) has the title *Aseff, the Russian Judas*.

For a contemporary report, *see* J. Longuet and G. Silber, *Les dessous de la police russe; terroristes et policiers* (Paris, 1909).

806. Vasilev, Aleksei T. The Ochrana: the Russian Secret Police. Edited and with an introduction by Rene Fülöp-Miller. Philadelphia, Lippincott, 1930. 305 p.

The only book on the Okhrana in English, but far from adequate, despite the fact that its author was the last head of the institution. Noteworthy chiefly for its revelation of the limited mental scope and prejudiced outlook of its author. An adequate historical analysis of the Okhrana, an urgent necessity for the study of the revolutionary movement before 1917, has now become feasible, thanks to the opening of the Maklakov archives of the Paris headquarters of the Okhrana, housed in the Hoover Institution, Stanford University.

A useful related volume, by the former head of the Kiev Okhrana and chief of security for Nicholas II, is Aleksandr I. Spiridovich's *Histoire du terrorisme russe, 1886-1917*, translated from the Russian by Vladimir Lazarevski (Paris, Payot, 1930, 668 p.)

(2) The exile system

807. Kennan, George. Siberia and the Exile System. New York, The Century Co., 1891. 2 v. Illus., ports., maps.

See also entries no. 129 and 315.

A classic account of the Russian exile system as it existed towards the end of the nineteenth century, based on personal observations and interviews made during the author's extensive travels in European Russia and Siberia. Abridged edition: Chicago, University of Chicago Press, 1958, 243 p.

For a valuable unpublished supplement, *see* Kennan's *Portraits of Russian Political Exiles and Convicts, with Some Additional Photographs Depicting the Life of Both Political and Common Criminals in Siberia* (New York, unpublished manuscript, New York Public Library, 1920).

b. Soviet Union

(1) The secret police

808. Agabekov, Grigorii S.   OGPU, the Russian Secret Terror. Translated from the French by H. W. Bunn. New York, Brentano, 1931. 277 p.

   The most valuable of the early memoirs by secret police defectors, particularly informative on espionage in Central Asia and on the transformation of the secret police following Dzerzhinsky's death in 1926. The English version is a much-abbreviated and unreliable rendering, at one remove, of the Russian original (*G.P.U.: zapiski chekista*; Berlin, Strela, 1930, 247 p.)

   A second, partially overlapping work by the author exists in a somewhat shortened German translation by A. Chanoch, *Die Tscheka bei der Arbeit* (Stuttgart, Union Deutsche Verlagsgesellschaft, 1932): a translation of *Ch. K. za rabotoi* (Berlin, Strela, 1931).

809. Brunovskii (Brunovsky), Vladimir Kh.   The Methods of the OGPU. Translated from the German. London, Harper, 1931. 255 p.

   Translation of *In Sowjetkerkern: Erlebnisse eines ehemaligen Sowjetfunktionärs* (Stuttgart, Union Deutsche Verlagsgesellschaft, 1930), which in turn is translated from *Eto bylo v SSSR; stranichka iz vospominanii byvshego "smertnika"* (Berlin, Slovo, 1928 [*Arkhiv russkoi revoliutsii*, v. 19, 1928: 5-156]).

   Covers the period between the author's arrest on charges of espionage in May 1923 and his release in December 1926. The author, a Latvian agricultural specialist, has attempted, with a considerable degree of success, not only to record his own experiences but to understand the structure of the secret police and its motivating principles.

810. Dzerzhinskii (Dzierzynski), Feliks E.   Ausgewählte Artikel und Reden, 1908-1926. Berlin, Dietz, 1953. 384 p.

   This translation of *Izbrannye stat'i i rechi, 1908-1926* (Moscow, Gospolitizdat, 1947, 2 v.) is the only fairly extensive selection in translation from the writings of the founder and the first head of the Soviet secret police, the man who laid the basis for its structure and code of action, and who is still regarded by Soviet Chekists as the normative exemplar of their profession.

   The Russian original has since been superseded by the following fuller selections: *Dnevnik. Pis'ma k rodnym* (2d rev. and enl. ed.; Moscow, Molodaia gvardiia, 1958, 268 p.) and *Izbrannye proizvedeniia v dvukh tomakh* (Moscow, Gospolitizdat, 1957).

811.*Fainsod, Merle.   Smolensk under Soviet Rule. Cambridge, Harvard
University Press, 1958. 484 p.
See also entries no. 562 and 775.
    An analytical study of a cross-section of Soviet society in the
period up to the middle thirties, based on the Smolensk Party
archives which fell into Western hands after the Second World War.
The most valuable source available for an understanding of the
operations of the secret police in their total societal context. Of particular interest are Chapter 8, "The Organs of State Security"; Chapter 9, "The Machinery of Justice — the Procuracy and the Courts";
Chapter 10, "Crime in Smolensk — out of the Police Records"; and
Chapter 11, "Purges and People."

812. Kaznacheev, Aleksandr Iu.   Inside a Soviet Embassy; Experiences
of a Russian Diplomat in Burma. Edited with an introduction by
Simon Wolin. Philadelphia, Lippincott, 1962. 250 p.
See also entry no. 887.
    One of the best, as well as most recent, firsthand descriptions of
secret police activities in the fields of espionage, foreign policy implementation, and control of Soviet diplomatic personnel abroad.

813. Krivitsky, Walter G.   In Stalin's Secret Service; an Exposé of Russia's Secret Policies by the Former Chief of the Soviet Intelligence
in Western Europe. New York, Harper, 1939. 273 p.
See also entry no. 796.
    The most famous, and probably the most valuable, account by a
secret police defector. Krivitsky in general limits himself to describing what he actually experienced or knew at firsthand. His analysis
of the part played by the secret police in Soviet foreign policy, particularly the background of the Soviet-Nazi pact of 1939, is an essential part of history.
    Another book by a highly-placed secret police defector, which
despite its valuable details on the mechanism of the purges, suffers
by comparison with Krivitsky's, particularly in the author's tendency
to unfounded speculation presented as fact, is Alexander Orlov's
The Secret History of Stalin's Crimes (New York, Random House,
1953, 366 p.)

814. Murray, Nora K.   I Spied for Stalin. Foreword by Lt. Gen. Sir Noel
Mason-Macfarlane. New York, Funk, 1951. 256 p.
See also entry no. 798.
    Despite its sensational and misleading title, one of the most valu-
able accounts available of the special world of the Soviet secret
police. The author was the daughter of a prominent Old Chekist and
grew up in the secret police milieu. Her account ends with the
disappearance of her father during the final stage of the Great Purge.

815. Petrov, Vladimir M., *and* Evdokia Petrov.   Empire of Fear. New
York, Praeger, 1956. 351 p. Illus.
    Among books by former secret police officials, that of the Petrovs

is outstanding for the intelligence and insight with which it describes the functioning of the police regime, both inside Russia and in Soviet diplomatic headquarters abroad.

See also an article by V. Petrov, "Aims and Methods of Soviet Terrorism," in *The Soviet Union: Background, Ideology, Reality; a Symposium*, edited by Waldemar Gurian (Notre Dame, Ind., University of Notre Dame Press, 1951), p. 137-152.

816. Scott, E. J.   The Cheka. Oxford, St. Antony's College, 1953. 23 p. (St. Antony's Papers on Soviet Affairs, no. 9)

A valuable presentation of the known facts concerning the establishment of the Soviet secret police. Reprinted in *Soviet Affairs* (Oxford), no. 1, 1956: 1-23.

A fuller study, particularly good for the period 1917-1922, which unfortunately remains in manuscript, is Ernest V. Hollis, Jr's *Development of the Soviet Police System, 1917-1946* (unpublished doctoral dissertation, Department of Public Law and Government, Columbia University, 1955).

817. Wolin, Simon, *and* Robert M. Slusser, *eds.*   The Soviet Secret Police. New York, Praeger, 1957. 408 p. Bibliography: p. 355-368.

An attempt to present an objective picture of the historical evolution, structure, and functions of the secret police, using published and unpublished documentary sources as well as analytical studies by former members and victims of the secret police.

The historical introduction, written by the editors, is extended in two articles:

Slusser, R. M.   "The Budget of the OGPU and the Special Troops from 1923-4 to 1928-9." *Soviet Studies*, v. 10, April 1959: 375-383.

Wolin, Simon.   "Russia 5 Years after Stalin: the Secret Police." *New Leader*, v. 41, April 28, 1958: 17-19.

(2) The purges

818. Beck, F. (*pseud.*), *and* W. Godin (*pseud.* of K. F. Shteppa).   Russian Purge and the Extraction of Confession. Translated from the German by Eric Mosbacher and David Porter. New York, Viking, 1951. 277 p.

The authors — one a scientist, the other a historian — were arrested and imprisoned during the Great Purge. As prisoners, they applied their training to the attempt to understand the purges as a sociological, historical, and psychological phenomenon. A milestone in the analytical study of the Soviet social system under Stalin, although its major value lies in the evidence compiled by the authors rather than in their theories.

Shteppa, at the time of his death in 1958, had begun work on a long study of Dzerzhinsky and the principles of "Chekism" (the operating principles of the secret police), a trial sketch for which, in the form of an article on Dzerzhinsky, is included in Wolin and Slusser, *The Soviet Secret Police* (*see* entry no. 817).

819. Brzezinski, Zbigniew K. The Permanent Purge: Politics in Soviet Totalitarianism. Cambridge, Harvard University Press, 1956. 256 p. Bibliography: p. 191-199.
See also entry no. 747.

A noteworthy attempt to analyze the purge as a functional mechanism of change in Soviet society. Although the hypothesis is presented in terms relevant to any totalitarian society, the focus of the author's attention and the major part of his evidence concern Soviet Russia.

820. Chernov, Viktor M., *ed.* Tché-ka. Matériaux et documents sur la terreur bolchéviste recueillis par le Bureau Centrale du Parti Socialiste Révolutionnaire Russe. Translated from the Russian by E. Pierremont. Paris, Povolotzky, 1922. 307 p.

A collection of materials of varied origin and reliability, with emphasis on political repression, particularly that involving members of the Socialist Revolutionary party. Translation of *Ch-Ka; materialy po deiatel'nosti Chrezvychainykh Komissii* (Berlin, Izdanie Biuro Partii Sotsialistov-Revoliutsionerov, 1922).

821. Khrushchev, Nikita S. The Crimes of the Stalin Era. Special Report to the 20th Congress of the Communist Party of the Soviet Union. Annotated by Boris I. Nicolaevsky. The New Leader, v. 39, July 16, 1956, Section two.

Khrushchev's secret speech to the Twentieth Party Congress in February 1956 is a cardinal document for the history of the secret police and the purges, made even more valuable in this version by the annotations of the veteran analyst of Soviet affairs, Mr. Nicolaevsky. Reprinted subsequently as a 67-page pamphlet.

Uncollected articles by Mr. Nicolaevsky, dealing among other things with secret police developments, which have appeared principally in the *New Leader* over a period of years, constitute as a body perhaps the most penetrating analysis available of the role of the secret police and its leaders in Soviet internal affairs.

822. Mel'gunov, Sergei P. The Red Terror in Russia. London, Dent, 1925. 271 p.
Bibliography: p. 267-271.

The author, a trained historian and member of a small socialist party at the time of the 1917 Revolution, remained in Russia until 1922 and was then deported, having undergone arrest, imprisonment, and trial. The book is not an account of the experiences of the author but a compilation from various sources of varying reliability, assembled for the avowed purpose of documenting the secret police's misdeeds. It is a translation of *Krasnyi terror v Rossii, 1918-1923,* 2d ed. (Berlin, Vataga, 1924, 312 p.). The file of original materials collected by the author is now at the Hoover Institution, Stanford University.

823. Weissberg, Alexander. The Accused. Translated by Edward Fitz-

gerald. Preface by Arthur Koestler. New York, Simon and Schuster, 1951. 518 p.

The author, a physicist of Austrian and Jewish origin but a Communist by conviction, was arrested in the Soviet Union in 1937, forced to confess to various terrorist and sabotage acts, and then, after trial and imprisonment, handed over to the Gestapo under the Nazi-Soviet pact. Perhaps the finest, certainly one of the most revealing of the many personal accounts of the experiences of victims of the secret police, both for its detailed picture of the entire cycle from arrest to confession and for its penetrating analysis of the social and political conditions which made the purges possible.

British edition has the title *Conspiracy of Silence* (London, Hamilton, 1952, 509 p.)

(3) The system of repression: prisons, concentration camps, forced labor

824. American Federation of Labor.   Slave Labor in Russia; the Case Presented by the American Federation of Labor to the United Nations. Washington, D.C., 1949. 179 p.

An appendix presents in translation the texts of corrective labor laws, decrees, and ordinances through March 1940.

A useful supplement is the Massachusetts Institute of Technology's *Forced Labor in the Soviet Union* (Cambridge, 1955) — a selective bibliography.

825. Barton, Paul, *pseud.*   L'institution concentrationnaire en Russie (1930-1957). Paris, Plon, 1959. 519 p. (Les documents de "Tribune libre," 6)

A broad, yet detailed, survey of the entire system of Soviet concentration camps during the period of their most extensive development. Based on a wide variety of materials, carefully evaluated, effectively integrated, and presented with restraint.

826. Belomor; an Account of the Construction of the New Canal between the White Sea and the Baltic Sea.   Edited by Maxim Gorky, L. Auerbach, and S. G. Firin. New York, Smith and Haas, 1935. 344 p.

An official account of one of the large-scale construction projects carried out in the Soviet Union during the thirties with the use of forced labor. Notwithstanding its official character, it includes much material of value in assessing the role of forced labor in Soviet penology during the thirties. Translation of *Belomorsko-Baltiiskii Kanal imeni Stalina; istoriia stroitel'stva* (Moscow, Istoriia fabrik i zavodov, 1934, 613 p.)

Two books which present an uncritical and generally laudatory account of Soviet penal practice at this period are:

Callcott, Mary S. *Russian Justice.* New York, Macmillan, 1935. 265 p.

Koerber, Helene. *Soviet Russia Fights Crime; a Study of the Soviet Prison System.* New York, Dutton, 1934. 240 p.

827. Ciliga, Anton.   The Russian Enigma. Translated from the French by

Fernand G. Renier and Anne Cliff. London, Routledge, 1940. 304 p.
See also entry no. 786.

Translation of *Au pays du grand mensonge* (Paris, Gallimard, 1938, 252 p.). Ciliga, a Yugoslav Communist, went to Russia as a Comintern functionary in 1926, was arrested on charges of association with the Left Opposition in 1930, and thereafter underwent imprisonment in a series of police installations until his release in 1936. His account is particularly valuable for the light it throws on secret police techniques for the suppression of political opposition.

A sequel has been published in French: *Sibérie, terre de l'exil et de l'industrialisation* (Paris, Plon, 1950, 310 p.)

828. Claudius, W.   A Soviet Isolator. Oxford, St. Antony's College, 1956. 19 l.

A brief but informative account of the experience of the author, a German arrested on charges of espionage in 1950 and released under an amnesty in 1955. The system of "isolators" or "polit-isolators" constitutes an inner security network within the concentration camp structure, and because of the special care taken to prevent escapes, as well as the high degree of improbability of release, little reliable information on these camps has been published.

For a fuller study, *see* Jean-Paul Serbet, *Polit-isolator* (Paris, Laffont, 1961, 443 p.)

829. Dallin, David J., *and* Boris I. Nicolaevsky.   Forced Labor in Soviet Russia. New Haven, Yale University Press, 1947. 331 p.

A massive treatment of the development of forced labor in the Soviet system and of its geographical and economic aspects. Despite their strong moral condemnation of the institution, the authors make a determined and generally successful effort to evaluate the evidence, drawn from Soviet as well as émigré sources, and to present an objective account. A bibliography (pages 309-319) surveys the most important literature through 1946.

830. International Commission Against Concentrationist Regimes.   Police-State Methods in the Soviet Union. Prepared under the direction of David Rousset. Translated from the French by Charles R. Joy. Edited by Jerzy G. Gliksman. Boston, Beacon Press, 1953. 64 p.

A survey covering the late years of Stalin's rule. The editor, Jerzy Gliksman, is the author of *Tell the West* (New York, Gresham Press, 1948, 358 p.), one of the best personal accounts of imprisonment in Soviet concentration camps.

831. Jasny, Naum.   Labor and Output in Soviet Concentration Camps. Journal of Political Economy, v. 59, Oct. 1951: 405-419.

A pioneering analysis of the role of forced labor in the Soviet economy, based on the secret official plan for 1941 (*Gosudarstvennyi plan razvitiia narodnogo khoziaistva SSSR na 1941 god*. American Council of Learned Societies Reprints: Russian Series no. 30. Baltimore, Universal Lithographers, n.d.)

See also Solomon M. Schwarz, "Russia's Planned Slavery." *New Leader*, v. 34, Feb. 12, 1951.

For a critical analysis of Jasny's estimate, *see* Alexander M. Baykov, "A Note on the Economic Significance of Compulsory Labour in the U.S.S.R.," *Bulletins on Soviet Economic Development* (University of Birmingham), Series 2, no. 7, December 1952.

832. U. S. *Dept. of State. Office of International Information.* Inside Soviet Slave Labor Camps, 1939-1942; an Analysis of Written Statements by 9,200 Former Prisoners. Based on research prepared by the U. S. Library of Congress. Washington, U. S. Information Service, 1952. 71 p. Illus., map.

Based on statements by Polish citizens who were arrested and imprisoned by the Soviet police in 1939 but who were subsequently released. The original documents are now in the Hoover Institution, Stanford University.

Noteworthy personal narratives dealing with the experiences of Polish prisoners during the same period include the following:

Anonymous. *The Dark Side of the Moon*. Preface by T. S. Eliot. London, Faber and Faber, 1946. 232 p.

Czapski, Józef (Joseph). *The Inhuman Land*. Translated from the French by Gerard Hopkins. New York, Sheed and Ward, 1952. 301 p.

Herling, Gustaw. *A World Apart*. Translated from the Polish by Joseph Marek. London, Heinemann, 1951. 262 p.

C. DIPLOMACY AND FOREIGN RELATIONS

by Alexander Dallin

1. General and Reference Materials

833. Foreign Affairs Bibliography; a Selected and Annotated List of Books on International Relations, 1952-1962.   Edited by Henry L. Roberts. New York, Bowker, 1964.   750 p.

This volume, the fourth such bibliography prepared under the auspices of the Council on Foreign Relations, comprises chiefly books published in the decade 1953-1962. While the emphasis is on foreign affairs, principal works on the domestic life, politics, and economy are also included. The majority of the titles are in English and other Western languages. Pages 491-543 are devoted to the USSR, in addition to pertinent books listed in other contexts.

World Communism; a Selected Annotated Bibliography (Washing, U. S. Government Printing Office, 1964, 394 p.), was compiled by Joseph G. Whelan of the Legislative Reference Service, Library of Congress. Pages 81-204 and 358-371 list English-language materials dealing with communism in the USSR, with considerable space devoted to foreign relations. The bibliography was prepared at the request of the Subcommittee To Investigate the Administration of the Internal Security Act and Other Internal Security Laws of the U. S. Senate Committee on the Judiciary.

Soviet Foreign Relations and World Communism; a Selected, An-

notated Bibliography of 7,000 Books in 30 Languages, edited by Thomas T. Hammond, is scheduled for publication in 1965 by Princeton University Press.

834. Lederer, Ivo J., *ed.*   Russian Foreign Policy; Essays in Historical Perspective. New Haven, Yale University Press, 1962. 620 p.
See also entry no. 532.

Papers by leading American specialists on a variety of topics related to the assessment of continuity and change in Russian foreign policy during the past century. The most comprehensive recent effort, uneven in quality, in part excellent. The problems discussed include Russian objectives, modernization, nationalism and communism, policy formation, instruments of foreign policy, and policy in action in different geographic settings.

835. Potemkin, Vladimir P., *ed.*   Histoire de la diplomatie. Translated by Xenia Pamphilova and Michel Eristov. Paris, Médicis, 1946-1947. 3 v.

The standard Soviet work in diplomatic history produced during the Stalin era. Uneven, at times substantial, often misleading, these three volumes cover not only Russian but all diplomacy, from antiquity to modern times. Translation of *Istoriia diplomatii* (Moscow, Sotsekgiz, 1941-1945, 3 v.)

Of the thoroughly revised edition of *Istoriia diplomatii* (1959–), no English or French translation is as yet available.

2. Diplomacy and Foreign Relations before 1917

a. General

In view of the paucity of over-all studies of Russian diplomatic history, attention is invited to some of the general histories of Russia which devote considerable space and attention to problems of foreign relations, such as the history by Michael Florinsky (entry no. 467) and similar works listed in Chapter V, B, and Chapter VI.

836. Bailey, Thomas A.   America Faces Russia; Russian-American Relations from Early Times to Our Day. Ithaca, Cornell University Press, 1950. 375 p.
Bibliography: p. 357-368.

A readable and soundly documented account of Russo-American relations since 1775. The author, though concerned primarily with diplomatic problems, writes in considerable detail of public opinion and attitudes, including the role of the press.

837. Grunwald, Constantin de.   Trois siècles de diplomatie russe. Paris, Calmann-Lévy, 1945. 272 p. Illus.

One of the few book-length accounts of Tsarist foreign policy, this somewhat superficial history covers the period from 1613 to 1917. Concentrating heavily on personalities, political developments, and "high society," it provides a not entirely reliable framework, which some readers will wish to supplement from other sources.

838.* Laserson, Max M.   The American Impact on Russia, Diplomatic and Ideological, 1784-1917. New York, Macmillan, 1950. 441 p. Illus., ports.

> A perceptive and well-documented study of American influences in Russia from the American Revolution to the Russian Revolution, by a political scientist with sympathies for both countries and cultures. Stresses social thought and liberal currents, along with "official" contacts and influence.

839. Seton-Watson, Robert W.   Main Currents in Russian Foreign Policy. *In* Transactions of the Royal Historical Society (London), Fourth Series, v. 29, 1947: 167-186.

> One of the few attempts at brief synthesis and interpretation of Russian foreign policy, by a renowned British historian of Southeastern Europe, who here stresses Russian interests abroad in the eighteenth and nineteenth centuries. Reviewing the course of Anglo-Russian relations, the author finds no causes for a necessary conflict between the two powers.

840. Vernadsky, George.   Political and Diplomatic History of Russia. Boston, Little, Brown, 1936. 499 p.

> An accurate and generally conventional one-volume history by a prominent historian, paying considerable attention to foreign relations. Somewhat "old-fashioned" in its heavy emphasis on political events, border problems, and chronology, this is nonetheless a standard text.

b. Before 1700

841. Fleischhacker, Hedwig.   Die staats- und völkerrechtlichen Grundlagen der moskauischen Aussenpolitik (14.-17. Jahrhundert). Würzburg, Holzner, 1959. 247 p.

> Eleven essays dealing with different aspects of the international and legal status of the Muscovite state and the foreign activities of various Russian rulers, from the appanage princes to the Romanovs. Republication of a dissertation originally printed in 1938.

842. Forstreuter, Kurt.   Preussen und Russland von den Anfängen des Deutschen Ordens bis zu Peter dem Grossen. Göttingen, Musterschmidt, 1955. 257 p.

> A study, based on archival research, of the political, military, diplomatic, commercial, and cultural ties between Russia and Prussia — or more properly, between Muscovy, Pskov, and Novgorod and the Teutonic Order, Old Prussia, and Brandenburg. Considerable stress is placed on the convergence or divergence of their objectives regarding third powers, such as Poland and Lithuania, the Ottoman Empire, and Sweden.

843. Stökl, Günther.   Russland und Europa vor Peter dem Grossen. Historische Zeitschrift, v. 184, December 1957: 531-554.

> The perennial problem of "Russia and the West" reexamined by a

prominent historian, with emphasis on the period of Muscovy. Contains references to other recent studies and interpretations.

c. 1701-1815

844. Doerries, Heinrich.   Russlands Eindringen in Europa in der Epoche Peters des Grossen; Studien zur zeitgenössischen Publizistik und Staatenkunde. Königsberg, Berlin, Ost-Europa-Verlag, 1939. 188 p.

An investigation of the place of Muscovy in the European state system of the sixteenth and seventeenth centuries; Europe's image of Russia and Russia's image of Europe; the scope of contacts, education, political propaganda, and forms of co-operation between Russia and the West under Peter the Great; a reassessment of his purposes and legacy; the place of mercantilism; and the continuing gap between Russia and the European West.

845. Hurewitz, Jacob C.   Russia and the Turkish Straits: a Revaluation of the Origins of the Problem. World Politics, v. 14, July 1962: 605-632.

This recent reexamination of the vexatious Eastern question offers some new documentation on the Russo-Ottoman Treaty of 1805 and presents a sharp critique of many standard works on the Straits problem. Despite the voluminous literature on the subject, no balanced and exhaustive treatment appears to be available.

See, in addition to entry no. 858, the older "pro-Russian" version, Sergei M. Goriainov, *Le Bosphore et les Dardanelles* (Paris, Plon, 1910, 392 p.); and *Constantinople et les détroits* . . . (Paris, Les éditions internationales, 1930-1932, 2 v.)

846. Mediger, Walther.   Moskaus Weg nach Europa; der Aufstieg Russlands zum europäischen Machtstaat im Zeitalter Friedrichs des Grossen. Braunschweig, Westermann, 1952. 744 p. Illus.

A massive tome on Russia's place in the European state system from 1710 to 1762. Based on extensive archival research but not footnoted throughout, this volume includes detailed discussions of Russian goals and motives, as well as of the policy options open to statesmen such as Bestuzhev. Special attention is paid to Anglo-Russian relations in the middle of the eighteenth century and to Russia's place in the plans and calculations of Frederick the Great.

847.* Sumner, Benedict H.   Peter the Great and the Emergence of Russia. New York, Macmillan, 1951. 216 p.

A political biography for the non-specialist by an outstanding historian, with a considerable part devoted to foreign and military affairs. Sumner argues that "the greatness of Peter lies in the fact that to a large extent he gave shape to needs and aspirations growing within Muscovite society of the late seventeenth century."

For an admirable miniature monograph, *see* the same author's *Peter the Great and the Ottoman Empire* (Oxford, Blackwell, 1949, 80 p.)

848. Tarle, Evgenii (Eugene) V.   Napoleon's Invasion of Russia, 1812.

Translated by Norbert Guterman and Ralph Mannheim. New York, Toronto, Oxford University Press, 1942. 422 p.
See also entry no. 513.

A readable account of the dramatic story of Napoleon's Russian campaign, by a prominent Russian historian. One of several successive versions, each related to changing political requirements of the day, this edition reflects a "patriotic" reconsideration of the evidence. Translation of *Nashestvie Napoleona na Rossiiu: 1812 god* (Moscow, Sotsekgiz, 1938, 279 p.)

849. Vandal, Albert. Napoléon et Alexandre Ier; l'alliance russe sous le premier empire. Paris, Plon, 1891-1896. 3 v.

A prize-winning classic on Napoleon's grand policy "between Tilsit and Moscow." The author considers Napoleon's failure to effect a reconciliation with Russia, after rousing her ambitions, as his fatal error, pivotal in consequences for Europe's history. Though politically opportune at the time of its publication, this is a solid study.

d. 1815-1917

850. Bolsover, George H. Aspects of Russian Foreign Policy, 1815-1914. *In* Essays Presented to Sir Lewis Namier, edited by Richard Pares and A. J. P. Taylor. London, Macmillan; New York, St. Martin's, 1956. p. 320-356.

One of the most concise yet substantial summaries of Russian foreign policy in the century between the Napoleonic Wars and the First World War, by a noted British historian. The chapter discusses, among other things, foreign policy making; the role of the Tsar and the foreign minister; the major geographical areas to which St. Petersburg addressed itself; and the changes of emphasis placed upon these areas.

851. Carlgren, W. M. Iswolsky und Aehrenthal vor der bosnischen Annexionskrise. Russische und österreichische Balkanpolitik 1906-1908. Uppsala, Almkvist und Wiksell, 1955. 334 p.
Bibliography: p. 319-329.

A thorough and informed study of the background of one of the most dramatic crises prior to the First World War. The author makes use of unpublished sources as well as printed materials to investigate both the diplomatic and the domestic antecedents, paying considerable attention to views and differences within the Russian elite.

852. Columbia University. *Russian Institute.* Russian Diplomacy and Eastern Europe, 1914-1917. Introduction by Henry L. Roberts. New York, King's Crown Press, 1963. 305 p.
Bibliography: p. 277-288.

A series of essays by different authors on Russian war aims and Tsarist policy during the First World War toward Poland, Rumania, Austria-Hungary, Bulgaria, Germany, and the future Yugoslavia.

853. Dallin, David J.   The Rise of Russia in Asia. New Haven, Yale University Press, 1949. 293 p.

A survey of Russian policy in Asia, from the middle of the nineteenth century to 1931 (continued in the same author's *Soviet Russia and the Far East*; New Haven, Yale University Press, 1948, 398 p.). Individual chapters deal with the major developments such as the background and consequences of the Russo-Japanese War; Russia's dilemmas in dealing with China, before and after the 1917 Revolution; the problem of the Russo-Chinese borderlands — Manchuria, Mongolia, Sinkiang; and the Communist disputes over China policy in the 1920's.

854. Jelavich, Barbara.   A Century of Russian Foreign Policy, 1814-1914. Philadelphia, New York, Lippincott, 1964. 308 p.
See also entry no. 478.

A narrative history of Russian involvement in world affairs in the century preceding the First World War, assessing the principal goals of Russian foreign policy and the degree to which they were attained.

855. Jelavich, Charles, *and* Barbara Jelavich, *eds.*   Russia in the East, 1876-1880; the Russo-Turkish War and the Kuldja Crisis As Seen through the Letters of A. G. Jomini to N. K. Giers. Leiden, Brill, 1959. 173 p.

A sample of painstaking monographic work currently being done on individual facets of Russian diplomatic history, based on unpublished letters and archival materials.

856.*Kohn, Hans.   Pan-Slavism; Its History and Ideology. 2d rev. ed. New York, Vintage, 1960. 468 p.

This richly documented volume by an acknowledged authority, in surveying pan-Slavism "from Herder to Stalin," deals with Russian sentiments — particularly between 1861 and 1917 — along with the attitude of the Western Slavs. With debatable propriety, it also applies the pan-Slav label to certain phenomena of the Stalin era.

857. Lensen, George A.   The Russian Push toward Japan; Russo-Japanese Relations, 1697-1875. Princeton, Princeton University Press, 1959. 553 p. Illus.

The most recent and most painstaking account of Russo-Japanese contacts and relations prior to their confrontation as major world powers. Based in part on unpublished sources.

858. Mandelstam, Andrei N.   La politique russe d'accès à la Méditerrannée au XXe siècle. *In* The Hague. Academy of International Law. Recueil des cours. v. 47, 1934, no. 1: 603-802. Bibliography.

An informed cycle of lectures by an "insider" who exhibited some detachment and scholarship in assessing the evidence. Even so, his presentation may be judged somewhat defensive or official. While he concentrates on the period between 1908 and 1917, he provides an expert background of the problem, going back into the nineteenth century.

859. Nol'de, Boris E., *baron*. L'alliance franco-russe; les origines du système diplomatique d'avant-guerre. Paris, Droz, 1936. 700 p.

A brilliant review of Russian and French diplomacy between 1871 and 1893 against the background of the European power system, with particular emphasis on individual actors, groups, publications, and institutions, rather than on "state" policies. Significantly different in interpretation from the Langer volume (*see* entry no. 527).

860. Okun', Semen B.   The Russian-American Company. Edited with an introduction by Boris D. Grekov. Translated by Carl Ginsburg. Preface by Robert J. Kerner. Cambridge, Harvard University Press, 1951. 311 p. (American Council of Learned Societies. Russian Translation Project, Series 9)

A detailed account of "Russian America," from the early Russian settlers to the exploits in California and Hawaii, and finally the sale of Alaska. Based on Russian archives and other sources. The standard work on the subject. A translation of *Rossiisko-amerikanskaia kompaniia* (Moscow, Sotsekgiz, 1939, 258 p.)

861. Romanov, Boris A.   Russia in Manchuria, 1892-1906. Translated from the Russian by Susan Wilbur Jones. Ann Arbor, Mich., J. W. Edwards, 1952. 549 p. (American Council of Learned Societies. Russian Translation Project, Series 15)

The most authoritative work on a controversial subject, by a serious diplomatic historian having access to the Tsarist archives. Translation of *Rossiia v Man'chzhurii, 1892-1906* gg. (Leningrad, Vostochnyi institut, 1928, 605 p.)

For a later, though in part unfinished, study which refreshingly questions (but not always disproves) some accepted assumptions about Russian objectives and intentions, *see* Andrew Malozemoff, *Russian Far Eastern Policy 1881-1904; with Special Emphasis on the Causes of the Russo-Japanese War* (Berkeley, University of California Press, 1958, 358 p.), and in particular its "Bibliographical Essay" (p. 317-331).

Another study, based in part on unpublished sources and focusing more particularly on relations with the United States, is Edward H. Zabriskie, *American-Russian Rivalry in the Far East; a Study in Diplomacy and Power Politics, 1895-1914* (Philadelphia, University of Pennsylvania Press, 1946, 226 p.)

862. Rosen, Roman R.   Forty Years of Diplomacy. London, Allen and Unwin; New York, Knopf, 1922. 2 v.

The political autobiography of an astute, independent-minded Russian diplomat. Full of insights, these memoirs are at times marred by the author's strong personal and political biases.

For another autobiography dealing with substantially the same period, but only in part with diplomatic questions, *see* Count Sergei

Witte's *Memoirs* (Garden City, N. Y., Doubleday, 1921, 445 p.), which, like Rosen's, are of particular interest in regard to Russia's policy in the Far East.

863. Schaeder, Hildegard.   Die Dritte Koalition und die Heilige Allianz; nach neuen Quellen. Königsberg, Berlin, Ost-Europa-Verlag, 1934. 100 p.

A reexamination of the alliance policy of Alexander I, using new sources, and focusing on the seeming conflict between "revolutionary" and "reactionary" purposes.

864. Sazonov, Sergei D.   Fateful Years, 1909-1916; the Reminiscences of Serge Sazonov. London, Jonathan Cape, 1928. 327 p.

One of the most valuable memoirs of Russian officials concerned with foreign affairs under Nicholas II. Useful for an assessment of the contending pressures within the Tsarist government in the years prior to, and at the beginning of, the First World War. Sazonov's account stands up as honest, but suffers from having been written without access to archives or documents. Translation of *Vospominaniia* (Paris, Siial'skaia, 1927, 398 p.)

The memoirs of Sazonov's predecessor, Aleksandr Izvol'skii (Alexander Iswolsky), are but a fragment of what he had planned to write. His *Recollections of a Foreign Minister* (Garden City, N. Y., Doubleday, 1921, 303 p.; British edition published as *Memoirs,* London, Hutchinson, 1920, 288 p.) do not cover the years when he was foreign minister, but do deal with various incidents of 1905-1906.

Among the memoirs of foreign envoys serving in St. Petersburg, the most valuable are Maurice Paléologue, *An Ambassador's Memoirs* (London, Hutchinson, 1923-1925, 3 v.) and Sir George Buchanan, *My Mission to Russia . . .* (Boston, Little, Brown, 1923, 2 v.)

865.* Seton-Watson, Hugh.   The Decline of Imperial Russia, 1855-1914. New York, Praeger, 1956. 406 p.

See also entry no. 521.

This informed and readable survey of Russia between the Crimean War and the First World War devotes several chapters to foreign relations and ably places them in the context of domestic developments.

On the final phases of the Tsarist order, *see also* Florinsky's *End of the Russian Empire* (entries no. 537 and 617).

866. Sumner, Benedict H.   Russia and the Balkans, 1870-1880. Oxford, Clarendon Press, 1937. 724 p.

Bibliography: p. 675-698.

See also entry no. 526.

A massive and masterly examination of one of the most complex situations in European diplomacy, with special attention to the Russian aspects. Though in its detail overwhelming to the non-specialist, this classic provides pithy syntheses and beautiful vignettes of personalities and situations, and introduces a consideration of other trends — social, ideological, military — to enrich an understanding of diplomatic developments. With a documentary appendix.

Another edition: Hamden, Conn., Archon Books, 1962, 724 p.

867. Sumner, Benedict H.   Tsardom and Imperialism in the Far East and Middle East, 1880-1914. London, H. Milford, Oxford University Press, 1942. 43 p.

A separate print from the *Proceedings of the British Academy*, before which the author delivered this paper as a Raleigh Lecture in 1940. An outstanding summation of Russian objectives in Asia during the final phases of the Tsarist Empire, with a fine sensitivity to the diversity of interests pursued by various socio-economic and political groups in pre-1917 Russia.

868. Taylor, Alan J. P.   The Struggle for Mastery in Europe, 1848-1918. Oxford, Clarendon Press, 1954. 638 p.

Bibliography: p. 569-601.

A brilliant, often "revisionist" and idiosyncratic reinvestigation of European diplomacy, which pays considerable attention to Russian policy and conduct. Valuable also for its general setting of diplomatic developments and for an expert review of available sources and studies (for instance, the various series of diplomatic documents and the literature on the origins of the First World War).

In view of the lack of comprehensive studies of Russian nineteenth-century diplomacy (as distinguished from monographs), it is advisable to consult other standard works on European diplomacy, such as William L. Langer, *European Alliances and Alignments 1871-1890* (2d ed., New York, Knopf, 1950, 510 p.), and his *Diplomacy of Imperialism 1890-1902* (2d ed., New York, Knopf, 1950, 2 v.)

3. Soviet Diplomacy and Foreign Relations

a. General

Readings from this section should be supplemented by general treatments of the Soviet period which also deal at length with foreign affairs, such as Leonard Schapiro's *Communist Party of the Soviet Union* (entries no. 552 and 745), John A. Armstrong's *Politics of Totalitarianism* (entry no. 740), and other pertinent books listed in Chapter VII, B.

869.* Adams, Arthur E., *ed.*   Readings in Soviet Foreign Policy; Theory and Practice. Boston, Heath, 1961. 420 p.

A selection of narrative, documentary, and analytical readings "to provide the college student or intelligent layman with a coherent introduction to Soviet foreign policy since late 1917." Represented among the authors are Lenin, Stalin, Khrushchev; E. H. Carr, Isaac Deutscher, Max Beloff; Cordell Hull, James F. Byrnes, and Walt W. Rostow. A useful bibliography (pages 409-420) is provided.

870.* Aspaturian, Vernon V.   Soviet Foreign Policy. *In* Macridis, Roy C., *ed.* Foreign Policy in World Politics. Rev. ed. Englewood Cliffs, N. J., Prentice-Hall, 1962. p. 133-199.

>One of the most systematic and informed summaries of Soviet foreign policy, which is here discussed in terms of ideology, historical and geographical setting, policy formulation and implementation, and interaction with social and political forces at home.

871. Aspaturian, Vernon V.   The Union Republics in Soviet Diplomacy; a Study of Soviet Federalism in the Service of Soviet Foreign Policy. Geneva, Droz, 1960. 228 p.

>An astute investigation of the formal and actual roles played by constituent Union Republics of the USSR in international affairs and international law.

872. Barghoorn, Frederick C.   The Soviet Image of the United States; a Study in Distortion. New York, Harcourt, Brace, 1950. 297 p.
See also entry no. 1718.

>A comprehensive examination of how the United States is depicted in official Soviet media, and why. A pioneering study undertaken at the height of Stalinism.

873.* Brzezinski, Zbigniew K.   Ideology and Power in Soviet Politics. New York, Praeger, 1962. 180 p.
See also entry no. 716.

>This series of essays, by one of the outstanding political scientists dealing with Soviet affairs, includes a sophisticated reexamination of "Communist Ideology and International Affairs" against a background of changing politics and military technology.

874. Dallin, Alexander, *comp.*   Soviet Conduct in World Affairs; a Selection of Readings. New York, Columbia University Press, 1960. 318 p.

>A collection of 15 interpretive essays by Western specialists on a wide range of problems, from the role of ideology to "continuity and change" in Soviet foreign policy. Among the authors represented are Daniel Bell, Alex Inkeles, George F. Kennan, Philip E. Mosely, Nathan Leites, Richard Löwenthal, Barrington Moore, Robert C. Tucker, and Bertram D. Wolfe.

875. Goodman, Elliot R.   The Soviet Design for a World State. New York, Columbia University Press, 1960. 512 p.
Bibliography: p. 489-493.

>A thorough and conscientious collection of statements, writings, and pronouncements by Soviet leaders and spokesmen on the future of nationalities, states, sovereignties, and languages under communism. The evidence does not necessarily bear any relation to actual trends or Soviet practices.

876.* Mosely, Philip E., *ed.*   The Soviet Union, 1922-1962; a Foreign Affairs Reader. New York, Praeger, 1963. 497 p.

A rewarding collection of articles on Soviet affairs, culled from the pages of the quarterly *Foreign Affairs*. It includes significant articles — mostly on foreign relations — by Soviet spokesmen of the day, such as Khristian Rakovskii, Karl Radek, Nikolai Bukharin, and Nikita Khrushchev; exiles and émigrés, such as Viktor Chernov and Lev Trotsky; and critical observers, such as George Kennan, Isaiah Berlin, and Philip Mosely.

877.* Strausz-Hupé, Robert, *and others.*   Protracted Conflict. New York, Harper, 1959. 203 p.

An over-all interpretation of Communist world strategy by a leading academic proponent of an uncompromisingly "hard" line. The contents are suggested by chapter headings such as "The Communists' View of Conflict," "The Indirect Approach," "Deception and Distraction," "Monopoly of the Initiative," "Attrition," and "Communist Psychological Warfare."

878. Triska, Jan F., *and* Robert M. Slusser.   The Theory, Law and Policy of Soviet Treaties. Stanford, Calif., Stanford University Press, 1962. 593 p. Bibliography.
See also entry no. 597.

A thorough and thoughtful academic examination of Soviet treaty law, policy, and behavior, with massive annotations. The authors describe their work as a study of diplomatic history "from the point of view of Soviet international treaties and agreements," including a consideration of the circumstances under which they were concluded, carried out, and terminated; the motives and objectives pursued; their place in Soviet foreign policy; the way they were made; and the statements made about them by Soviet political leaders and scholars.

The companion volume by Robert M. Slusser and Jan F. Triska, *A Calendar of Soviet Treaties, 1917-1957* (Stanford, Calif., Stanford University Press, 1959, 530 p.), containing a chronological listing of international agreements as well as bibliographical data on the treaties listed, is a useful reference tool.

879. Warth, Robert D.   Soviet Russia in World Politics. New York, Twayne, 1963. 544 p.

One of the few one-volume, one-man efforts to digest the entire history of Soviet foreign policy and provide an interpretive scheme. While the conceptual aspects are apt to arouse controversy, the evidence is reliably marshaled and ably presented. The volume contains a most useful bibliography (pages 475-525).

880. Wolfe, Bertram D.   Communist Ideology and Foreign Policy. Foreign Affairs (New York), v. 41, October 1962: 152-170.

An able exposition, by a seasoned expert, of the view which stresses the continuing and essential motivating role of Communist ideology in Soviet foreign policy, and minimizes the substantive significance of changes in the post-Stalin period.

b. Memoirs and sources

For views and statements of past Soviet leaders on foreign affairs, consult also works listed in Chapter VII, B, 2, a(2), entries no. 649-663.

881. Byrnes, James F.   Speaking Frankly. New York, Harper, 1947. 324 p.
The political memoirs of the former U. S. Secretary of State, dealing in large measure with his handling of the Soviet problem and his encounters with Soviet leaders and diplomats in 1945-1947. Though at times revealing more about the author than about Soviet policy, the volume does provide some unique information.

882. Deane, John R.   The Strange Alliance. New York, Viking, 1947. 344 p.
The most reliable and readable account by a senior U. S. officer in Russia during the Second World War. General Deane, who headed the United States Military Mission to the USSR, relates his negotiations with Soviet officialdom on a variety of matters and conveys something of the atmosphere of wartime alliance and suspicion.

883. Degras, Jane T., *ed*.   Soviet Documents on Foreign Policy, 1917-1941. London, New York, Oxford University Press, 1951-1953. 3 v.
The most adequate English-language collection of primary sources on Soviet foreign policy between the wars, sponsored by the Royal Institute of International Affairs. Does not profess to be complete and needs to be supplemented with other documentation made available since these volumes appeared.

884. Dennett, Raymond, *and* Joseph E. Johnson, *eds*.   Negotiating with the Russians. Boston, World Peace Foundation, 1951. 310 p.
An interesting collection of papers by individuals who dealt with Soviet officials toward the end of the Second World War and in the years following it, on a wide variety of problems, such as trade, cultural exchanges, international law, and territorial settlements. Presents a revealing tableau of Soviet negotiating behavior in the Stalin era.

885.*Ðilas (Djilas), Milovan.   Conversations with Stalin. Translated from the Serbo-Croat by Michael B. Petrovich. New York, Harcourt, Brace and World, 1962. 211 p.
See also entry no. 787.
A unique volume of memoirs by the famous Yugoslav who was a leading Communist during and immediately after the Second World War.
Other important retrospective accounts of the war years by former Communists include:
Dedijer, Vladimir.   *Tito*. New York, Simon and Schuster, 1953. 443 p.

Hernández, Jesús. *Yo fuí un ministro de Stalin.* Mexico, Editorial América, 1953. 365 p.

Castro Delgado, Enrique. *J'ai perdu la foi à Moscou.* Paris, Gallimard, 1950. 350 p.

886. Eudin, Xenia J., *and* Robert C. North, *eds.* Soviet Russia and the East, 1920-1927; a Documentary Survey. Stanford, Calif., Stanford University Press, 1957. 478 p.
Bibliography: p. 405-455.

Eudin, Xenia J., *and* Harold H. Fisher, *eds.* Soviet Russia and the West, 1920-1927; a Documentary Survey. Stanford, Calif., Stanford University Press, 1957. 450 p.
Bibliography: p. 419-442.
Two useful, though necessarily incomplete, collections of documents regarding Soviet views on diplomacy and revolution and the actual conduct of foreign policy in the NEP era, with helpful annotations and comments. The first volume in particular contains some hard-to-find materials and a most useful bibliography (pages 405-455).

887. Kaznacheev, Aleksandr Iu. Inside a Soviet Embassy; Experiences of a Russian Diplomat in Burma. Edited with an introduction by Simon Wolin. Philadelphia, Lippincott, 1962. 250 p.
See also entry no. 812.
One of the few recent accounts by a young Soviet diplomat who defected. Here he describes both his training for the foreign service and his assignment to Burma.
For a somewhat comparable account dealing with the years prior to the Second World War, *see* Alexander Barmine, *One Who Survived* (New York, Putnam, 1945, 337 p.)

888. Khrushchev, Nikita S. Communism — Peace and Happiness for the Peoples. Moscow, Foreign Languages Publishing House, 1962. 2 v.
The speeches, interviews, and broadcasts of Khrushchev on the international situation and Soviet foreign policy, delivered in 1961. Similar materials for other years are available, among other sources, in the *Current Digest of the Soviet Press*, and in writings such as:
Khrushchev, Nikita S. "On Peaceful Coexistence." *Foreign Affairs*, v. 38, October 1959: 1-18.
————. *For Victory in Peaceful Competition with Capitalism.* New York, Dutton, 1960. 784 p. (Speeches and statements of 1958)
————. *World without Arms; World without Wars.* Moscow, Foreign Languages Publishing House, 1960. 2 v. (Speeches, interviews, and broadcasts of 1959)
————. *Speeches and Interviews on World Problems, 1957.* Moscow, Foreign Languages Publishing House, 1958. 386 p.

889.* Leonhard, Wolfgang. Child of the Revolution. Translated by C. M.

Woodhouse. Chicago, Regnery, 1958. 447 p.
See also entry no. 789.

A unique volume of memoirs (somewhat abridged in the English version) by a prominent German analyst of Soviet affairs who received his education in the USSR, was close to Comintern circles, and served with Ulbricht in East Germany from 1945 to 1948, when he broke with the Stalin system. Translation of *Die Revolution entlässt ihre Kinder* (Cologne, Kiepenheuer und Witsch, 1955, 557 p.)

890. Litvinov, Maksim M.   Against Aggression; Speeches by Maxim Litvinov. New York, International Publishers, 1939. 208 p.

An official Communist collection of speeches by the Soviet People's Commissar for Foreign Affairs, who was a leading advocate of "collective security" in the middle 1930's, and was later shelved by Stalin.

891. Rubinstein, Alvin Z., *ed.*   The Foreign Policy of the Soviet Union. New York, Random House, 1960. 457 p.

An examination of Soviet foreign policy as it evolved in time, seen through a series of excerpts from Soviet documents and pronouncements, with comments and notes by the editor. A final chapter provides five selections by representative Western observers.

892. Russia (*1923– U.S.S.R.*) *Komissiia po izdaniiu diplomaticheskikh dokumentov.*   Stalin's Correspondence with Churchill, Attlee, Roosevelt and Truman, 1941-45. New York, Dutton, 1958. 2 v. (400, 301 p.)

The English-language version of a Soviet compilation of the letters exchanged between Stalin and the British and American leaders in the Second World War, apparently authentic, and inviting some fascinating insights.

Translation of *Perepiska Predsedatelia Soveta Ministrov SSSR s prezidentami SShA i prem'er-ministrami Velikobritanii vo vremia Velikoi Otechestvennoi voiny, 1941-1945* (Moscow, Gospolitizdat, 1957, 2 v.)

Other editions: Moscow, Foreign Languages Publishing House; London, Lawrence and Wishart, 1957.

893. U. S. *Dept. of State.*

The Soviet Union, 1933-1939.   Washington, U. S. Government Printing Office, 1952. 1034 p.

The Conferences at Malta and Yalta (1945).   Washington, U. S. Government Printing Office, 1955. 1032 p.

The Conferences of Berlin [Potsdam] (1945).   Washington, U. S. Government Printing Office, 1960. 2 v.

The Conferences at Cairo and Teheran, 1943.   Washington, U. S. Government Printing Office, 1961. 932 p.

These are some of the key volumes from the invaluable *United*

States Foreign Relations documentary series, consisting largely of dispatches by U. S. diplomats, notes taken at international conferences, State Department staff memoranda, and other official materials.

c. 1917-1939

894. Beloff, Max.   The Foreign Policy of Soviet Russia, 1929-1941. London, New York, Oxford University Press, 1947-1949. 2 v.
Bibliography: v. 2, p. 402-417.

> Perhaps the most detailed Western account of Soviet foreign policy from the end of the NEP to the German invasion (1929-1941). The author himself recognized (see his "Notes," in *Soviet Studies*, no. 2 [July 1950]: 123-137) that some subsequent reconsideration and amplification were in order. Nonetheless, as a sequel to the Louis Fischer volumes on the preceding 12 years (*see* entry no. 899), this factual study provides an essential body of evidence with a minimum of partisanship.

895. Browder, Robert P.   The Origins of Soviet-American Diplomacy. Princeton, Princeton University Press, 1953. 256 p.
Bibliography: p. 239-247.

> An able study of the years between Revolution and recognition, with emphasis on the period from 1929 to 1933. While the nature of the sources, including unpublished archives, leads the author to emphasize questions of U. S. motives and techniques in dealing with the Soviet problem, the volume also deals in some detail with Soviet conduct and with the negotiations leading to the establishment of diplomatic relations.

896. Carr, Edward H.   A History of Soviet Russia. The Bolshevik Revolution, 1917-1923. v. 3: Soviet Russia and the World. London, New York, Macmillan, 1953. 614 p.
See also entries no. 540 and 1024.

> A part of the multi-volume effort by a leading British writer on Soviet affairs, this study ably traces Soviet foreign outlook and policies during the Lenin years of Soviet rule. Despite its occasionally controversial character, this is in many respects a valuable guide and an interesting synthesis.

897. Cattell, David T.   Soviet Diplomacy and the Spanish Civil War. Berkeley, University of California Press, 1957. 204 p.
Bibliography: p. 179-190.

> "The second part of a study of the Soviet Union's most consistent attempt to apply the doctrine of collective security as a means to her own defense." A conscientious reconstruction.

898.* Craig, Gordon A., *and* Felix Gilbert, *eds*.   The Diplomats, 1919-1939. Princeton, Princeton University Press, 1953. 700 p.

> Included in this superb collection are two chapters on Soviet diplomats: Theodore von Laue, "Soviet Diplomacy: G. V. Chicherin, People's Commissar for Foreign Affairs, 1918-1930"; and Henry L. Roberts, "Maxim Litvinov."

899.* Fischer, Louis.   The Soviets in World Affairs; a History of Relations between the Soviet Union and the Rest of the World [1917-1929]. Princeton, Princeton University Press, 1951. 2 v. (892 p.)

> The "classic" account of Soviet foreign policy under War Communism and the New Economic Policy, by a veteran journalist who then enjoyed the confidence of leading Soviet statesmen and journalists such as Chicherin, Litvinov, and Karakhan. While the books, originally published in 1930, require comparison with other more recent studies, they are a mine of unique information. Abridged edition: New York, Vintage, 1960, 616 p.

900. Freund, Gerald.   Unholy Alliance; Russo-German Relations from the Treaty of Brest-Litovsk to the Treaty of Berlin. New York, Harcourt, Brace; London, Chatto and Windus, 1957. 283 p.
Bibliography: p. 261-270.

> Perhaps the soundest of the many studies of Russo-German relations before and after Rapallo.
>
> For other accounts, partly amplifying, partly differing from the above, see, e.g., Gustav Hilger and Alfred G. Meyer, *The Incompatible Allies* (New York, Macmillan, 1953, 350 p.); Lionel Kochan, *Russia and the Weimar Republic* (Cambridge, England, Bowes and Bowes, 1954, 190 p.); Hans Gatzke, "Russo-German Military Collaboration during the Weimar Republic," *American Historical Review*, April 1958; and Günter Rosenfeld, *Sowjetrussland und Deutschland*, 1917-1922 (Berlin [East], Akademie-Verlag, 1960, 423 p.)

901.* Kennan, George F.   Russia and the West under Lenin and Stalin. Boston, Little, Brown, 1961. 411 p.
See also entry no. 541.

> Deservedly the best-known English-language survey of Soviet relations with the Western world from 1917 to 1945. Though somewhat episodic and at times quite controversial in interpretation, it reflects the competence and authority of its author, an outstanding scholar and diplomat.

902. Kennan, George F.   Soviet-American Relations, 1917-1920.
v. 1: Russia Leaves the War. Princeton, Princeton University Press, 1956. 544 p.
v. 2: The Decision to Intervene. Princeton, Princeton University Press, 1958. 513 p.

> The first two of a contemplated three-volume set reexamining in considerable detail the years of civil war and intervention in Russia. While focusing on Soviet-American relations, this literate and thought-provoking work contains numerous comments on other aspects of Soviet and Western policies.
>
> In addition to the bibliography in these two volumes, *see also* the somewhat complementary study by Richard H. Ullman, *Anglo-Soviet Relations, 1917-1921* (Princeton, Princeton University Press, 1961–), and the stimulating view of European politics in Arno J. Mayer's

Political Origins of the New Diplomacy, 1917-1918 (New Haven, Yale University Press, 1959, 435 p.)

903. Taracouzio, Timothy A.   War and Peace in Soviet Diplomacy. New York, Macmillan, 1940. 354 p.

A thoroughly documented examination of the Leninist view of war and peace, just and unjust war, the evolution of attitudes toward violence, and changing foreign policy strategies until 1939. This study still provides a helpful background for an understanding of the later evolution of Soviet doctrine and behavior.

904. Whiting, Allen S.   Soviet Policies in China, 1917-1924. New York, Columbia University Press, 1954. 350 p.
Bibliography: p. 327-337.

A valuable study of early Soviet dealings with China and, more generally, Communist views of the "East." It includes a concise and competent analysis of the Lenin-Roy dispute and the policy of the Comintern toward Asian nationalist movements, as well as a survey of conflicting ideological, territorial, political, and other Soviet objectives.

d. Since 1939

905. Barghoorn, Frederick C.   The Soviet Cultural Offensive; the Role of Cultural Diplomacy in Soviet Foreign Policy. Princeton, Princeton University Press, 1960. 353 p.

A systematic examination of the use of cultural, scientific, and educational activities and exchanges in Soviet propaganda and foreign policy, especially in the post-Stalin period.

See also the same author's *Soviet Foreign Propaganda* (Princeton, Princeton University Press, 1964, 329 p.)

906. Beloff, Max.   Soviet Policy in the Far East, 1944-1951. London, New York, Oxford University Press, 1953. 278 p.

Though somewhat dated in the light of later evidence, this volume still provides a valuable framework for the interpretation of Soviet goals and policies in Asia in the years after the Second World War. The study, based on rich factual materials, is supplemented by a survey of Soviet policy toward Southeast Asia.

907. Brzezinski, Zbigniew K., *ed.*   Africa and the Communist World. Stanford, Calif., Stanford University Press, 1963. 272 p.

This collection of informed papers, well documented, includes chapters on Soviet political and economic policy in Africa, the impact of the Sino-Soviet conflict on Africa, and "the African challenge" to the Communist camp.

908.*Dallin, Alexander.   The Soviet Union at the United Nations; an Inquiry into Soviet Motives and Objectives. New York, Praeger, 1962. 244 p.

An assessment of the place of the United Nations in Soviet world strategy in the context of historical antecedents for Soviet participation in international organizations, its record in the UN, changing Soviet perception of political opportunities open to it through the UN, and Soviet attitudes and behavior in respect to such issues as national sovereignty, the veto, and disarmament.

For a more intensive study of one aspect of the problem, *see* Harold K. Jacobson, *The USSR and the UN's Economic and Social Activities* (Notre Dame, Ind., University of Notre Dame Press, 1963, 309 p.), and Alvin Z. Rubinstein, *The Soviets in International Organizations: Changing Policy toward Developing Countries, 1953-1963* (Princeton, Princeton University Press, 1964).

909. Dallin, David J.   Soviet Foreign Policy after Stalin. Philadelphia, Lippincott, 1961. 543 p.

A well-documented study of Soviet policy, largely in the period from Stalin's death to the consolidation of power by Khrushchev in 1957. Includes examinations of conflicting Communist assessments of the world scene; Soviet policy toward Germany, the underdeveloped areas, and the United States; and relations within the Communist Bloc.

910.*Deutscher, Isaac.   The Great Contest; Russia and the West. New York, London, Oxford University Press, 1960. 86 p.
See also entry no. 1241.

A highly optimistic series of lectures by a well-known and prolific writer on Soviet affairs, summarizing his views on the prospects of Soviet evolution and Soviet foreign policy.

911.*Feis, Herbert.   Churchill, Roosevelt and Stalin; the War They Waged and the Peace They Sought. Princeton, Princeton University Press, 1957. 692 p.

A major study of the relations of the Big Three during 1941-1945. Making extensive use of diplomatic and personal archives, the author reconstructs the dealings among the leaders, the wartime conferences held by them and by their deputies, and their conflicting motives and varying competence and comprehension.

On the same subject, *see also* William H. McNeill, *America, Britain and Russia: Their Cooperation and Conflict, 1941-46* (London and New York, Oxford University Press, 1953, 818 p.), and John L. Snell, *ed., Wartime Origins of the East-West Dilemma over Germany* (New Orleans, La., Hauser, 1959, 268 p.)

912. Fiedler, Heinz.   Der sowjetische Neutralitätsbegriff in Theorie und Praxis; ein Beitrag zum Problem des Disengagement. Cologne, Verlag für Politik und Wirtschaft, 1959. 301 p.
Bibliography: p. 278-288.

A systematic and documented examination of the concept of neutrality as used and interpreted by the Soviet Union in international relations and law, including the change in Soviet attitude in the Khrushchev era.

913. Gromyko, A. A., *ed.* Die friedliche Koexistenz — der Lenin-

sche Kurs der Aussenpolitik der Sowjetunion. Berlin [East], Staatsverlag, 1964. 299 p.

A series of essays exploring the official content of "peaceful coexistence" in its current Soviet meaning. The original volume was sponsored by the Moscow Institute of International Relations, which is linked with the USSR Ministry of Foreign Affairs. A translation of *Mirnoe sosushchestvovanie — leninskii kurs vneshnei politiki Sovetskogo Soiuza* (Moscow, IMO, 1962, 303 p.)

914. Laqueur, Walter Z. The Soviet Union and the Middle East. New York, Praeger, 1959. 366 p.

Like the same author's *Communism and Nationalism in the Middle East* (New York, Praeger, 1956, 362 p.), this volume presents rich documentation and interesting hypotheses on Soviet views and prospects in the Arab world and the neighboring countries.

On Iran, see George Lenczowski's *Russia and the West in Iran, 1918-1948* (Ithaca, Cornell University Press, 1949, 383 p.)

For another volume, containing some additional bibliographical and documentary materials, see Ivar Spector, *The Soviet Union and the Muslim World, 1917-1958* (Seattle, University of Washington Press, 1959, 328 p.)

915. Mackintosh, John M. Strategy and Tactics of Soviet Foreign Policy. Rev. ed. London, New York, Oxford University Press, 1963. 353 p.

Virtually the only serious volume covering the evolution of Soviet policy from the end of the Second World War to the present. In spite of its various shortcomings, such as the heavy emphasis on military capabilities and intentions, this book by a recognized British specialist fills a genuine need.

916. Meissner, Boris. Russland, die Westmächte und Deutschland; die sowjetische Deutschlandpolitik 1943-53. Hamburg, Nölke, 1953. 372 p.

A heavily documented examination of Soviet and Allied policy toward Germany in the Stalin era, by a leading West German specialist.

In addition to relevant chapters in general studies of Soviet policy, see also Walter P. Davison, *The Berlin Blockade* (Princeton, Princeton University Press, 1958, 423 p.); and Werner Erfurt, *Moscow's Policy in Germany* (Esslingen, Germany, Bechtle, 1959).

917. Meissner, Boris. Die Sowjetunion, die baltischen Staaten und das Völkerrecht. Cologne, Verlag für Politik und Wirtschaft, 1956. 377 p. Bibliography: p. 318-347.

The relations between the Soviet Union and the Baltic States analyzed by a leading German scholar specializing in Soviet government and law. After a survey of their diplomatic relations between the two World Wars, the study examines the incorporation of Lithuania, Latvia, and Estonia into the USSR as a problem of international politics as well as international law.

918.*Roberts, Henry L.   Russia and America; Dangers and Prospects. New York, Harper, 1956. 251 p.

A broad-gauged survey of Soviet motives and conduct, and a perceptive examination of the implications for United States policy. By a leading American expert, based on a study sponsored by the Council on Foreign Relations in New York.

919. Rozek, Edward J.   Allied Wartime Diplomacy: a Pattern in Poland. New York, Wiley, 1958. 481 p.
Bibliography: p. 465-470.

A detailed and documented account of the dealings among the Western Allies, the Soviet Union, and the Polish government-in-exile during the Second World War regarding the future frontiers and government of Poland. While it is not free of partisan convictions, the study is based on a variety of otherwise inaccessible sources.

For a review of the evidence on the single most critical incident, the Katyn massacre, *see* J. K. Zawodny, *Death in the Forest* (Notre Dame, Ind., University of Notre Dame Press, 1962, 235 p.)

920. Shulman, Marshall D.   Stalin's Foreign Policy Reappraised. Cambridge, Harvard University Press, 1963. 320 p.
Bibliography: p. 275-282.

A sophisticated and provocative examination of Soviet foreign policy, primarily from 1949 to 1952. The author reviews the final years of Stalin's rule to determine the rationality of his policies, the incipient elements of a shift toward "peaceful coexistence," and more generally the elements of change and continuity between the Stalin and the post-Stalin eras.

921.*Tucker, Robert C.   The Soviet Political Mind; Studies in Stalinism and Post-Stalin Change. New York, Praeger, 1963. 238 p.
See also entry no. 711.

A series of essays, written between 1953 and 1963, on various aspects of Soviet policy and politics. Included are several interpretive pieces on foreign policy, on changing ideological and personal influences in the Soviet leadership, and on the Soviet view of the West and of the underdeveloped areas.

922. Ulam, Adam B.   The Unfinished Revolution; an Essay on the Sources of Influence of Marxism and Communism. New York, Random House, 1960. 307 p.
See also entry no. 732.

――――. The New Face of Soviet Totalitarianism. Cambridge, Harvard University Press, 1963. 233 p.

Two sophisticated interpretations by a Harvard political scientist which include, among other subjects, thoughtful and informed comments on the role of Marxist thought in Soviet foreign policy and on relations among Communist parties and states.

923. Weinberg, Gerhard L.   Germany and the Soviet Union, 1939-1941. Leiden, Brill, 1954. 218 p.
Bibliography: p. 183-208.

Factually, perhaps the most balanced of the various books on the Nazi-Soviet Pact, despite the author's primary concern with German rather than Soviet motives and behavior.

For a different assessment, see Angelo Rossi (pseud.), The Russo-German Alliance, translated by John and Micheline Cullen (Boston, Beacon Press, 1951, 218 p.; translation of Deux ans d'alliance germano-soviétique, Paris, Fayard, 1949).

For the documentation from captured German records, see Raymond J. Sontag, ed., Nazi-Soviet Relations, 1939-1941 (Washington, U. S. Government Printing Office, 1948, 362 p.)

On the Russo-Finnish conflict of 1939-1940, see also Max Jakobson, The Diplomacy of the Winter War (Cambridge, Harvard University Press, 1961, 281 p.)

e. International communism

924. Boersner, Demetrio.   The Bolsheviks and the National and Colonial Question, 1917-1928. Geneva, Droz, 1957. 285 p.
Bibliography: p. 277-285.

An examination of the Communist view of, and policy toward, the national movements in non-Western countries, as seen largely through the eyes of the Comintern from its First to its Sixth World Congress in 1928. Also includes a review of Marx's, Engels', and Lenin's views on the subject.

925.*Borkenau, Franz.   World Communism; a History of the Communist International. Ann Arbor, University of Michigan Press, 1962. 442 p.

Widely considered the most incisive and knowledgeable general history of the Comintern from its beginnings to 1938 (when this volume was originally written), this book by a former "right-wing" Communist and later prominent anti-Communist journalist has a healthy awareness of varieties and variations within the Communist fold. While necessarily inadequate for developments in other than the major countries, it remains valuable, primarily for the period down to 1933.

926. Brandt, Conrad.   Stalin's Failure in China, 1924-1927. Cambridge, Harvard University Press, 1958. 226 p.
Bibliography: p. 181-188.

A highly-compressed study, making excellent use of the Trotsky Archives, of Soviet policy toward the Chinese revolution and the Stalin-Trotsky conflict.

Probably the best of the many books on this dramatic crisis, it may be supplemented by Robert C. North and Xenia J. Eudin, M. N. Roy's Mission to China: the Communist-Kuomintang Split of 1927 (Berkeley, University of California Press, 1963, 399 p.)

927. Degras, Jane T., ed.   The Communist International, 1919-1943. London, New York, Oxford University Press, 1956–

The first two volumes (published in 1956 and 1960, covering the period to 1928) of a documentary series consisting largely of selections, in English, of statements, debates, editorials, and official reports from Comintern sources and individual Communist parties.

928. Lazić (Lazitch), Branko, *pseud.* Lénine et la IIIe Internationale. Geneva, Kundig; Neuchâtel, Baconnière, 1951. 285 p.

An examination of Lenin's views which led to the establishment of the Communist International, by an émigré Yugoslav journalist. Interesting also for its discussion of whether the Comintern was the improvised product of momentary circumstances and pressures, or the implementation of a design antedating the seizure of power.

929. McKenzie, Kermit E.   Comintern and World Revolution, 1928-1943; the Shaping of Doctrine. New York, Columbia University Press, 1964. 356 p.

A thorough examination of continuity and changes in explicit Communist ideology, strategy, and tactics regarding the prospects of world revolution, the ways and means of seizing and holding power, and the role of the USSR in the process. This volume concentrates on the period from the Sixth World Congress to the dissolution of the Comintern during the Second World War.

930. McLane, Charles B.   Soviet Policy and the Chinese Communists, 1931-1946. New York, Columbia University Press, 1958. 310 p.

A basic study, though without the use of Chinese sources, of one of the most puzzling periods in Sino-Soviet relations, including an assessment of the Mao-Stalin relationship prior to 1946, the likelihood of tension, lack of co-ordination, and divergence of policies between Moscow and the Chinese Communists.

For a somewhat broader sweep, *see* Robert C. North, *Moscow and the Chinese Communists* (rev. ed., Stanford, Calif., Stanford University Press, 1963, 310 p.)

931. Nollau, Günther.   International Communism and World Revolution. Translated by Victor Andersen. New York, Praeger, 1961. 357 p.

Perhaps the most concise, if rigid, survey of the international Communist movement, from its origins to the present, with a strong emphasis on organizational aspects. A revised translation of *Die Internationale; Wurzeln und Erscheinungsformen des proletarischen Internationalismus* (Cologne, Verlag für Politik und Wirtschaft, 1959, 343 p.)

932. Reale, Eugenio.   Avec Jacques Duclos au banc des accusés à la réunion constitutive du Kominform à Szklarska Poręba (22-27 septembre 1947). Translated by Pierre Bonuzzi. Paris, Plon, 1958. 203 p.
See also entry no. 791.

A former Communist who was one of the two Italian delegates to the conference which established the so-called Cominform in 1947 tells of his experiences there. If true, revealing of Andrei Zhdanov's outlook and expectations and of relations among the Communist delegates, and interesting for information on the speeches given at the conference. Translation of *Nascita del Cominform* (Milan, Mondadori, 1958, 174 p.)

933. Trotskii, Lev.   The First Five Years of the Communist International. Translated and edited by John G. Wright. New York, Pioneer Publishers, 1945-1953. 2 v.

————. The Third International after Lenin. Translated by John G. Wright. 2d ed. New York, Pioneer Publishers, 1957. 400 p.

Essays, articles, and comments by one of the giants of the Bolshevik movement and one of its best writers and speakers. At times more revealing of Trotsky's outlook than of the state of the world movement.

Translations of *Piat' let Kominterna* (Moscow, Gosizdat, 1924, 612 p.), and of an unpublished Russian manuscript.

f. The Communist Bloc; Sino-Soviet relations

934.*Brzezinski, Zbigniew K.   The Soviet Bloc; Unity and Conflict. Rev. ed. New York, Praeger, 1961. 543 p.

A rounded and sophisticated interpretation of Soviet policy in Eastern Europe and the response to it by Communists and non-Communists alike, from the Second World War to 1961. Interesting, among other things, for its assessment of the roles of Communist doctrine and organization, and the problems of diversity within a totalitarian   framework.

935.* Columbia University. *Russian Institute*. The Anti-Stalin Campaign and International Communism. Rev. ed. New York, Columbia University Press, 1956. 342 p.

The text (released by the U. S. State Department from a clandestine copy) of the so-called "secret" speech delivered by Khrushchev in February 1956, containing the first open denunciation of Stalin; also the reaction of the major East European and Western Communist parties to the shock of de-Stalinization in the summer of 1956.

936.*Dallin, Alexander, *and others, eds*. Diversity in International Communism; a Documentary Record, 1961-1963. New York, Columbia University Press, 1963. 867 p.

Some 120 documents, or excerpts therefrom, from the Twenty-second CPSU Congress (October 1961) to the eve of the open Sino-Soviet split (May 1963). Included are pronouncements of individual leaders, party resolutions, and editorials from the various Communist parties around the globe on a wide range of issues over which Communists have differed, from coexistence to de-Stalinization. An introductory chapter discusses these issues and some of the clues which permit their detection in Communist documents.

937. Griffith, William E.   Albania and the Sino-Soviet Rift. Cambridge, Massachusetts Institute of Technology Press, 1963. 423 p.

A careful monograph, supported by extensive documentation, offering both a broad framework for understanding the Albanian rift with the Soviet-oriented Communist camp, and a painstaking, detailed analysis of the evolution of the conflict, particularly in 1960-1962.

938.*Laqueur, Walter Z., *and* Leopold Labedz, *eds*.   Polycentrism: the New Factor in International Communism. New York, Praeger, 1962. 259 p.

A collection of articles and essays of uneven value, including some excellent ones, compiled by the two editors of the British quarterly *Survey*, where most of the pieces originally appeared.

For another collection of articles from *Survey*, *see* Leopold Labedz, *ed., Revisionism; Essays on the History of Marxist Ideas* (New York, Praeger, 1962, 404 p.)

939. Löwenthal, Richard.   Chruschtschew und der Weltkommunismus. Stuttgart, Kohlhammer, 1963. 245 p.

A series of essays and articles by one of the outstanding Western commentators on Soviet and international Communist affairs, at present professor at the Free University in Berlin. The author has an enviable record of sound and brilliant analysis.

940. Mehnert, Klaus.   Peking and Moscow. Translated by Lelia Vennewitz. New York, Putnam, 1963. 522 p.

A massive synthesis by a veteran German writer with extensive background in both Russia and China. This volume includes a comparison of the two countries and cultures as well as a reconstruction of their uneven relationship in recent years. Translation of *Peking und Moskau* (Stuttgart, Deutsche Verlags-Anstalt, 1962, 605 p.)

941. The Soviet-Yugoslav Dispute; Text of the Published Correspondence. London, New York, Royal Institute of International Affairs, 1948. 79 p.

The fascinating exchange of letters between Stalin and Tito in 1948, which led to the break between the Soviet and Yugoslav Communists, sheds a revealing light on top-level relations among bloc leaders.

In addition to Djilas and Dedijer (*see* entry no. 885), *see also* Adam Ulam, *Titoism and the Cominform* (Cambridge, Harvard University Press, 1952, 243 p.), and Ernst Halperin, *The Triumphant Heretic* (London, Heinemann, 1958, 324 p.)

942. Zagoria, Donald S.   The Sino-Soviet Conflict, 1956-1961. Princeton, Princeton University Press, 1962. 484 p.

The most thoroughly documented study of Sino-Soviet differences. Since its publication the evidence has been overwhelmingly confirmed by Chinese and Soviet pronouncements. Valuable particularly for the actual evolution of the "ideological" conflict in 1957-1960.

For additional documentation on developments in 1960-1961, *see* G. F. Hudson, Richard Löwenthal, and Roderick MacFarquhar, *eds., The Sino-Soviet Dispute* (New York, Praeger, 1961, 227 p.), and Edward Crankshaw, *The New Cold War; Moscow v. Pekin* (Baltimore, Penguin Books, 1963, 167 p.)

The more recent developments are included in the following general surveys of Sino-Soviet relations:

Floyd, David. *Mao against Khrushchev; a Short History of the Sino-Soviet Conflict*. New York, Praeger, 1964. 456 p.

Schwartz, Harry. *Tsars, Mandarins and Commissars: a History of Chinese-Russian Relations*. New York, Lippincott, 1964. 252 p.

Griffith, William E. *The Sino-Soviet Rift*. Cambridge, MIT Press, 1964. 512 p.

g. Serials

943. The Communist International. 1919-1943. Moscow, London, etc.

The central organ of the Communist International, published in different languages, including English, French, German, Russian, and Spanish, with varying frequency, in variant editions, and under somewhat varying titles.

944. International Affairs. v. 1– 1955– Moscow. monthly.

The English-language edition of a quasi-official Soviet monthly devoted to foreign affairs, often revealing of the official outlook and argument. On the whole, heavily politicized and non-academic, but intended for the serious general reader.

The weekly world-affairs magazine, *New Times* (Moscow, 1944–), is generally more propagandistic but no less official.

945. World Marxist Review; Problems of Peace and Socialism. v. 1– September 1958– Toronto. monthly.

The only "official" mouthpiece of the Khrushchev-oriented international Communist movement, produced in Prague by an international staff under Soviet editorship. The English-language edition, under the above title, appears both in London and in Toronto. Though often dull and obscure, the monthly is a revealing source of insight and information, since it is the only centrally-produced publication aimed at Communist followers throughout the world.

D. MILITARY AFFAIRS

by Raymond L. Garthoff

1. General Works

946. Basseches, Nikolaus. The Unknown Army. Translated from the German by Marion Saerchinger. New York, Viking, 1943. 239 p.

A perceptive, if impressionistic, interpretation of the nature and broad development of the Russian army under Imperial Russia and under the Soviet regime to the Second World War. Translation of *Die unbekannte Armee* (Zürich, Europa-Verlag, 1942, 177 p.)

947. Berchin, Michel, *and* Eliahu Ben-Horin.   The Red Army. New York, Norton, 1942. 277 p.

A general account of the development of the Red Army in the 1930's, and of its operations in the first year of the Soviet-German war. It was well-based for the information available at that time, but has been overtaken by fuller data since the war.

948. Berman, Harold J., *and* Miroslav Kerner.   Soviet Military Law and Administration. Cambridge, Harvard University Press, 1955. 208 p.

The only study of this subject available in Western literature, the book is useful for its analysis of Soviet military law and its application in practice.

949. Brzezinski, Zbigniew K., *ed.*   Political Controls in the Soviet Army. New York, Research Program on the USSR, 1954. 93 p. Illus. *See also* entry no. 760.

In part written by, and based almost entirely upon the experiences of, six former Soviet officers. Presents a useful description of political indoctrination and police surveillance in the Soviet army during the war and postwar years of the Stalin regime.

950. Dixon, Cecil A., *and* Otto Heilbrunn.   Communist Guerrilla Warfare. London, Allen and Unwin; New York, Praeger, 1954. 229 p.

A useful general account of Soviet partisan warfare techniques in the Second World War (as well as of German anti-partisan warfare).

951. Friedl, Berthold C.   Les fondements théoriques de la guerre et de la paix en U.R.S.S. Paris, Éditions Médicis, 1945. 203 p.

A good theoretical study of Soviet military doctrine, especially useful for making available in full Lenin's annotations on Clausewitz.

952. Garder, Michel.   Histoire de l'armée soviétique. Paris, Plon, 1959. 308 p.

A competent general account of the development of the Soviet armed forces, with particular attention to the late 1950's. The best general history in French.

953. Garthoff, Raymond L.   The Military as a Social Force. *In* Cyril E. Black, *ed.* The Transformation of Russian Society; Aspects of Social Change since 1861. Cambridge, Harvard University Press, 1960. p. 323-338.

A study of the military institution in the Russian society and polity since 1861.

954. Garthoff, Raymond L.   Soviet Military Doctrine. Glencoe, Ill., Free Press, 1953. 587 p. Illus., maps.

A comprehensive and definitive study of Soviet military thought, strategy and tactics, and doctrine in the period up to 1953. Based on wide use of Soviet as well as other sources, it contains an extensive bibliography. Doctrinal developments in the Second World War are covered, but a historical account of the course of that war is not provided.

British edition: *How Russia Makes War* (London, Allen and Unwin, 1954). Also available in other languages.

955. Goudima, Constantin (Robert).   L'Armée rouge dans la paix et la guerre. Paris, Éditions Défense de la France, 1947. 428 p.

A general account of the development of the Red Army from the Russian Civil War through the Second World War. One of the better available works in French, though there are a number of factual inaccuracies of detail.

956. Guillaume, Augustin L.   Soviet Arms and Soviet Power. Washington, D. C., Infantry Journal Press, 1949. 212 p.

A frequently misleading and inaccurate work, excessively credulous of Soviet accounts and explanations. Written by the former French chief military representative in Moscow.

French edition: *Pourquoi l'Armée rouge a vaincu* (Paris, R. Julliard, 1948, 258 p.)

957. Liddell Hart, Basil H., *ed.*   The Soviet Army. London, Weidenfeld and Nicolson, 1956. 480 p. Illus., maps.

A collective work written by a number of British, American, German, ex-Soviet, and other authors. Of uneven quality, it does include a number of informative and useful chapters on various historical and current aspects of the Soviet ground forces.

American edition published as *The Red Army* (New York, Harcourt, Brace, 1956, 480 p.)

958. Pruck, Erich F.   Der rote Soldat; sowjetische Wehrpolitik. Munich, Gunter Olzog, 1961. 331 p.

A historical and topical survey of the Soviet military structure. Among the problems considered are the Party's control of the army, training of officers, military law, the Soviet army's position in the Warsaw Pact system, the level of Soviet military science, etc. Multilanguage bibliography.

959. U. S. *Dept. of the Army. Army Library.*   Soviet Russia; Strategic Survey. Washington, 1963. 217 p. (Dept. of the Army Pamphlet no. 20-64)

An extensive and useful bibliography of works on Soviet military affairs, especially complete for Western studies, though weaker on Russian areas. Includes periodical articles as well as books.

Supersedes an earlier publication titled *Soviet Military Power* and issued as Department of the Army Pamphlet no. 20-65 of 1959.

960. Whiting, Kenneth R.   Readings in Soviet Military Theory. Montgomery, Ala., Air University, 1952. 80 p.

A useful compilation in English of a number of the more indicative

Soviet military doctrinal writings, chiefly of the prewar period, on the general role of war and the army in Communist policy.

2. Military Affairs prior to 1917

961. Caulaincourt, Armand A. L. de.   With Napoleon in Russia. New York, Grosset and Dunlap, 1959. 422 p.
    The best Western account of the Napoleonic campaigns in Russia. Another edition: New York, William Morrow, 1935, 422 p.

962. Greene, Francis V.   Sketches of Army Life in Russia. New York, Scribner's Sons, 1880. 326 p.
    Useful impressions of the Russian army in the reform period of the latter nineteenth century by an American military observer.

963. Kinglake, Alexander W.   The Invasion of the Crimea. 4th ed. New York, Harper and Bros., 1868. 3 v. (v. 1, 702 p.; v. 2, 632 p.; v. 3, 344 p.)
    A dry but informative source book on the Crimean Campaign, chiefly as seen from the Western side.
    Other editions also available.

964. Parry, Albert.   Russian Cavalcade, a Military Record. New York, Washburn, 1944. 334 p.
    A well-written and interesting account of Russian military history. About half the book deals with the Russian army prior to 1917, and the remainder with the period from 1917 to 1943. Undocumented.

3. Military Affairs, 1917-1939

965. Erickson, John.   The Soviet High Command; a Military-Political History, 1918-1941. New York, St. Martin's; London, Macmillan, 1962. 889 p. Port., maps, diagrs.
    Bibliography: p. 809-834.
    A comprehensive, penetrating, and thorough study of Soviet military policy and relations of the military chiefs with the Soviet political leadership in the period up to the Soviet-German war in 1941. A very useful contribution to the field of Soviet history.

966. Fedotoff White, Dimitri.   The Growth of the Red Army. Princeton, Princeton University Press, 1944. 486 p.
    This book is a valuable contribution on the general development of the Soviet armed forces from 1917 to 1940. Based on wide use of Soviet and other sources, it examines in considerable detail many facets of the Soviet military establishments.

967. Makhine, Théodore H.   L'armée rouge; la puissance militaire de l'URSS. Paris, Payot, 1938. 356 p. Maps.
    A very good study based on Soviet published sources and other data, by an objective former White officer. One of the better works available in French on the Red Army in the 1920's and 1930's.

968. Schiffrin, Alexander (Max Werner, *pseud.*) The Military Strength of the Powers. London, Gollancz, 1939. p. 34-133 and 262-303.

> Contains a considerable review of Western estimates and views on the Red Army in the 1930's, and a more limited but well-selected summary of Soviet statements and information as well.

969. Wollenberg, Erich. The Red Army; a Study of the Growth of Soviet Imperialism. Translated from the German by Claud W. Sykes. London, Secker and Warburg, 1940. 400 p.

> A worthwhile general account and evaluation of the development of the Red Army during the Russian Civil War and on to the late 1930's. The author himself served in that army in the early years of the Soviet regime. The chief value of the book today lies in the general impression it gives of the Red Army at that time, rather than in its utility as a source of the details of the army's development.
>
> Parts of this book were published earlier as *The Red Army* (London, Secker and Warburg, 1938, 283 p.)

4. Military Affairs, 1939-1945

970. Allen, William E. D., *and* Paul Muratoff. The Russian Campaigns. London, Penguin, 1944-1946. 2 v. (v. 1, 1941-1943, 192 p.; v. 2, 1944-1945, 332 p.)

> A useful, contemporary, general chronicle and account of the Soviet-German war, but limited to materials available during the war.

971. Anders, Władysław. Hitler's Defeat in Russia. Chicago, Regnery, 1953. 267 p.

> A useful account of the German-Soviet campaigns by the former Polish general. Translation of *Klęska Hitlera w Rosji, 1941-1945* (London, Gryf, 1952, 137 p.)

972. Armstrong, John A., *and others*. The Soviet Partisan Movement in World War II; Summary and Conclusions. New York, War Documentation Project, Bureau of Applied Social Research, Columbia University, 1955. 48 p.

> The summary and conclusions of a project which examined in some detail the major Soviet partisan operations. Reference is made to the other supporting studies.

973. Garder, Michel. Une guerre pas comme les autres; la guerre germano-soviétique. Paris, La Table ronde, 1962. 344 p. Illus.

> A good study of Second World War Soviet campaigns, well-written and informative, by a French officer specializing in Soviet military affairs.

974.* Gouré, Leon. The Siege of Leningrad. Stanford, Calif., Stanford University Press; London, Oxford, 1962. 363 p. Illus., maps.

> An excellent study of the impact of prolonged pressure on the people of Leningrad and on the Soviet system.

975. Guillaume, Augustin L.   La guerre germano-soviétique, 1941-1945. Paris, Payot, 1949. 219 p. Illus., maps.
Bibliography: p. 217.
    A fairly comprehensive chronicle of military operations on the Soviet-German front, by a former French general serving in Moscow during the war.

976. Halder, Franz.   The Halder Diaries. Campaign in Russia. v. 6 and 7, February 1941 through September 1942. Washington, D. C., Infantry Journal Press, 1950.
    The diary of the former Chief of the German General Staff during the first months of the war with the USSR. A very valuable source on that campaign.

977. Howell, Edgar M.   The Soviet Partisan Movement, 1941-1944. Washington, U. S. Department of the Army, 1956. 217 p. Maps, diagrs.
Bibliography: p. 215-217.
    Based on a thorough study of captured German documents and other sources, this is a good military analysis of the Soviet partisan movement.

978. Kerr, Walter B.   The Russian Army; Its Men, Its Leaders and Its Battles. New York, Knopf, 1944. 250 p.
    A good journalistic account of the first year and a half of the Soviet-German war by an American correspondent in Russia. It gives an observer's impression of the war, though of course access to information was largely limited to Soviet propaganda.

979. Léderrey, Ernest.   La défaite allemande à l'Est; les armées soviétiques en guerre de 1941 à 1945. Lausanne, Payot; Paris, Charles-Lavauzelle, 1951. 270 p.
    A good general historical chronicle of the combat record of the Red Army in the Soviet-German war, by Colonel Léderrey, Swiss specialist on Soviet military affairs.

980.*Liddell Hart, Basil H.   The German Generals Talk. New York, Morrow, 1948. 308 p.
    A work based on extensive conversations with German generals, presenting their view of operations in the German-Soviet campaigns of the Second World War. An interesting and useful source of information.

981. U. S. *Dept. of the Army*.   Russian Combat Methods in World War II; a Historical Study. Washington, 1950. 116 p. (Dept. of the Army Pamphlet no. 20-230)
    Based directly on interviews in depth, and writings by former German generals and other officers with wide experience on the Soviet front, this is a very useful source for the Red Army as seen by its opponent in the field.

982. Werth, Alexander. Russia at War, 1941-1945. New York, Dutton, 1964. 1100 p.
A comprehensive but not definitive study based on Soviet and other sources, as well as the author's own personal observations in the USSR.

983. Werth, Alexander. The Year of Stalingrad. New York, Knopf, 1947. 475 p. Maps.
A very good report on the USSR during 1942, with fine use of Soviet sources on the military operations of that year, especially at Stalingrad.
British edition: London, H. Hamilton, 1946, 478 p.

5. Military Affairs, 1945-1963

984. Crane, Robert D., ed. Soviet Nuclear Strategy; a Critical Appraisal. Washington, D. C., Center for Strategic Studies, Georgetown University, 1963. 82 p.
A report of a study seminar on recent developments in Soviet military thinking and strategy, by 18 leading U. S. and UK authorities in the field. A useful collection of differing views and speculations.

985. Dinerstein, Herbert S. The Soviet Military Posture as a Reflection of Soviet Strategy. Santa Monica, Calif., The Rand Corporation, 1958. 22 p. (Rand Corporation Research Memorandum RM-2102)
A thoughtful essay on the relationship of possible Soviet strategic attitudes and intentions to the Soviet military forces in recent years.

986.* Dinerstein, Herbert S. War and the Soviet Union; Nuclear Weapons and the Revolution in Soviet Military and Political Thinking. New York, Praeger, 1959. 268 p.
An interpretation of the effect of differing strategic conceptions attributed by the author to the competing Malenkov and Khrushchev political factions in the 1953-1955 period. It clearly makes the point that apparent strategic differences may be but weapons used in political infighting.

987. Ely, Louis B. The Red Army Today. Harrisburg, Pa., Military Service, 1949. 256 p. Illus., maps.
A good account, based largely on interrogations of former Soviet and German officers, with attention paid to early postwar developments too. It has been overtaken by more recent events, but remains a useful study.

988. Garthoff, Raymond L. Sino-Soviet Military Relations. Annals of the American Academy of Political and Social Science, v. 349, September 1963: 81-93.
A survey and analysis of the changing development of military relations between the USSR and Communist China from 1945 through 1963.

989. Garthoff, Raymond L.   The Soviet Image of Future War. Washington, D. C., Public Affairs Press, 1959. 137 p.

A brief study of the role of military power in Soviet strategy and of Soviet theory regarding the role of surprise and of large armies in the nuclear age. Several leading Soviet doctrinal articles are appended in full translation.

990.* Garthoff, Raymond L.   Soviet Strategy in the Nuclear Age. Rev. ed. New York, Praeger, 1962. 301 p.

A thorough and comprehensive account of Soviet military thinking in the period from 1953 to 1962, which marked the adjustment in the post-Stalin period to the implications of the nuclear age. Also includes discussion of Soviet views on limited war, and views of Western military concepts.

Earlier editions: New York, Praeger; London, Allen and Unwin, 1958. Also available in other languages.

991.* Gouré, Leon.   Civil Defense in the Soviet Union. Berkeley, University of California Press, 1962. 207 p.

The one major book to appear on the problem, this work by a senior staff member of the Rand Corporation is based on firsthand observations in the USSR and on the limited data available in Soviet publications. Its highly debated conclusion is that the Soviet Union has been covertly engaged for 10 years in a massive program of civil defense, designed to protect its administration, population, and economy against enemy attacks from all types of weapons.

992.* Sokolovskii, Vasilii D., ed.   Military Strategy. Translation with introduction by R. L. Garthoff. New York, Praeger, 1963. 395 p.

This is probably the most significant postwar Soviet work on military affairs, prepared by collective efforts of a group of officers headed by the former Chief of the General Staff, Marshal Sokolovskii.

Another edition: Soviet Military Strategy, translated and with an analytical introduction, annotations, and supplementary material by H. S. Dinerstein, L. Gouré, and T. W. Wolfe (Englewood Cliffs, N. J., Prentice-Hall, 1963, 544 p.)

Translations of Voennaia strategiia (Moscow, Voenizdat, 1962, 457 p.)

993. Tokaev, Grigori A.   Stalin Means War. London, Weidenfeld and Nicolson, 1951. 214 p.

Recollections of a former Soviet aviation engineer and lieutenant colonel, who participated in high-level Soviet discussions and actions to acquire German technical specialists in aviation and rocketry.

994. U. S. Dept. of the Army.   Handbook on the Soviet Army. Washington, 1959. 260 p. Illus., fold. map, diagrs. (Dept. of the Army Pamphlet no. 30-50-1)

An excellent descriptive survey of the Soviet army, its organization, tactics, weapons, and strength. Authoritative and comprehensive. It is not an historical review, but deals with the current state of the Soviet army.

6. Air and Rocket Forces

995. Kilmarx, Robert A.   A History of Soviet Air Power. New York, Praeger, 1962. 359 p.

The published version of a dissertation written at Georgetown University, this well-documented study traces the development of Russian air power from Tsarist days to the missile age.

996. Lee, Asher.   The Soviet Air Force. Rev. ed. New York, John Day, 1962. 288 p.

A good historical review of the development of the Soviet air forces and of Soviet aviation in general. Not documented, but generally accurate and sound. This revised version is much more useful than the original (New York, Harper, 1950, 207 p.)

997. Lee, Asher, *ed.*   The Soviet Air and Rocket Forces. New York, Praeger; London, Duckworth, 1959. 311 p. Illus.

A collective volume by a number of Western students of Soviet aviation and military affairs. It is good on general development of aviation and air weapons and on the Soviet air force as an institution, but weak on missiles and on current and future strategy. In all, the best collection on the subject.

998. Parry, Albert.   Russia's Rockets and Missiles. New York, Doubleday, 1960. 382 p.

A popularized account of Russian and Soviet interest in, and development of, rocketry and space flight. It is not documented, and the parts on military applications are weak and frequently in error.

999. Pokrovskii, Georgii I.   Science and Technology in Contemporary War. Translated and annotated by R. L. Garthoff. New York, Praeger, 1959. 180 p. Illus.

An annotated translation of a book, an article, and a pamphlet by a Soviet technical general, surveying the role of various fields of science in contemporary weaponry and warfare.

Translations of:

Nauka i tekhnika v sovremennykh voinakh (Moscow, Voenizdat, 1956, 87 p.)

Rol' nauki i tekhniki v sovremennoi voine (Moscow, Znanie, 1957, 23 p.)

An article in the newspaper *Sovetskii patriot*, Sept. 11, 1957.

7. The Navy

1000. Isakov, Ivan S.   The Red Fleet in the Second World War. Translated from the Russian by Jack Hural. New York, London, Hutchinson, 1947. 124 p. Ports., maps.

A history of the operations of the Soviet navy in the Second

World War by the former naval commander-in-chief. It is not a detailed account, but it does trace the main activities.

Translation of *Voenno-morskoi flot SSSR v Otechestvennoi voine* (Moscow, Voenizdat, 1946, 101 p.)

1001. Meister, Jürg.   Soviet Sea Power. The Navy (London). 12 pts. v. 62, nos. 6-12, and v. 63, nos. 1-6 (June 1957–June 1958).

A useful series of articles with much information on many aspects of Soviet naval affairs, though in many cases the accuracy of the information cannot be judged.

1002. Mitchell, Mairin.   The Maritime History of Russia, 848-1948. London, Sidgwick and Jackson, 1949. 544 p. Illus., maps. Bibliography: p. 455-480.

A long discursive history of a millennium of growth of Russian maritime affairs, including a number of useful chapters on the prewar development of the Soviet navy.

1003. Saunders, Malcolm G., *ed.*   The Soviet Navy. New York, Praeger; London, Weidenfeld and Nicolson, 1958. 340 p. Illus.

A collective, comprehensive work on the Soviet navy by a number of Western specialists. There is relatively little historical background and the work is focused on the postwar naval establishment. It is uneven in treatment, and weak on naval doctrine, but on balance the best general survey available.

E. PUBLIC OPINION, PROPAGANDA, AND COMMUNICATIONS

by Abraham Brumberg

1004. Barghoorn, Frederick C.   Soviet Foreign Propaganda. Princeton, Princeton University Press, 1964. 329 p.

Whatever this book lacks in freshness of insight is more than amply made up by its scrupulous scholarship, impressive scope, and refreshing sobriety. Chapter by chapter, Professor Barghoorn analyzes, with copious documentation, the ideological principles underlying Soviet propaganda, its basic themes (peace, the Soviet model of industrialization, anti-Americanism, etc.), and its techniques, as well as its effectiveness and limitations. One interesting chapter deals with the Soviet exploitation of nationalism, especially in former colonial areas, and its attempt to prove that the USSR has solved the problems of a multi-national society. Altogether a most valuable book.

The same author's *The Soviet Cultural Offensive* (Princeton, Princeton University Press, 1960, 353 p.) is a valuable, if somewhat pedantic, survey of the Soviet Union's efforts to project a favorable image of its system through the communication media as well as cultural exchange programs.

1005. Bauer, Raymond A., *and* David B. Gleicher. Word-of-Mouth Communication in the Soviet Union. Maxwell Air Force Base, Ala.,

Air Research and Development Command, Human Resources Research Institute, 1953. 18 p. (Human Resources Research Institute. Research Memorandum no. 15)

A study of the place of word-of-mouth communication in the Soviet Union, with an estimate of its importance as a means of conveying information.

1006. Clews, John C.   Communist Propaganda Techniques. New York, Praeger, 1964. 326 p.

A well-informed and up-to-date treatment of Communist propaganda concepts and techniques, devoting considerable space to the Soviet Union.

A brief account of the propaganda drive undertaken in the Soviet Union in 1960, stressing the important role assigned to the communication media in the new indoctrination effort, is provided by Abraham Brumberg in "New Formula for Soviet Propaganda," *The New Leader*, v. 43, August 15-22, 1960: 16-20.

1007. Counts, George S., *and* Nucia Lodge.   The Country of the Blind; the Soviet System of Mind Control. Boston, Houghton Mifflin, 1949. 378 p.

The most comprehensive collection of documents comprising the *Zhdanovshchina* — that period in Soviet history when all rational stops seemed to have been pulled out in an attempt to regiment the "Soviet man" and remove him completely from any links with the Western world. The various decrees issued in the Soviet Union between 1946 and 1949 — on literature, drama, music, genetics, education, and so on — are fully reproduced, and the introductions by the authors are as astute as they are just.

1008. Dizard, Wilson P.   Television in the Soviet Union. Problems of Communism (Washington), v. 12, no. 6, November–December 1963: 38-45.

The author provides a general account of the history and present status of television in the USSR, and speculates on the reasons why the Soviet propaganda apparatus has not emphasized this particular medium of information in the past, and is not likely to do so in the future.

1009. Dunham, Donald C.   Kremlin Target: U.S.A.; Conquest by Propaganda. New York, I. Washburn, 1961. 274 p.

While this book contains some useful information on the organization and methods of Soviet anti-American propaganda, its value is lessened considerably by its emotional tone and questionable thesis, according to which the aim of Soviet propaganda is "to create neurosis on a global scale" as a prelude to "world domination."

1010. Gorokhoff, Boris I.   Publishing in the USSR. Bloomington, Indiana University Press, 1959. 306 p. (Indiana University Publications. Slavic and East European Series, v. 19)

Bibliography: p. 287-290.
See also entry no. 72.

Somewhat deficient with regard to belles lettres, this book is otherwise a most comprehensive compendium of information on the organization of book and press publishing in the Soviet Union. The accent is on the technical aspects, such as types of publications, publishing procedures, and circulation, rather than on content.

Book Publishing in the USSR (New York, American Book Publishers' Council, Inc., American Textbook Publishers' Institute, Inc., 1963, 112 p.) is a well-informed eyewitness account by six American book publishers who visited the Soviet Union as members of an official U. S. delegation.

1011. Grolier, E. de.   Information et propagande en URSS; théorie, organisation, moyens; essai de psychopolitique. Paris, Institut d'Études Politiques et Sociales, n.d. 179 p.

A multigraphed study published by Section Division et Propagande, Institut d'Études Politiques et Sociales.

1012. Howell, W. S., *and* E. W. Ziebarth.   The Soviet Airwaves. *In* Soviet Union; Paradox and Change. Edited by Robert T. Holt and John E. Turner. New York, Holt, Rinehart and Winston, 1962. p. 184-207.

A trenchant and lively account of Soviet broadcasting and television, covering domestic auditions as well as those beamed to the outside world. For English-language summaries of Soviet broadcasts, *see* entry no. 27.

1013. Inkeles, Alex.   Public Opinion in Soviet Russia; a Study in Mass Persuasion. Cambridge, Harvard University Press, 1958. 393 p. *See also* entries no. 1161 and 1739.

A reissue of a classic — indeed, probably the best — study of the principles and techniques of Soviet propaganda, covering relevant Leninist theories, oral agitation, the press, broadcasting, and the cinema. Published originally in 1950, the book is inevitably dated, dealing as it does with Stalinist society. In a penetrating postscript, however, the author notes that "to revisit the Soviet press, radio, and cinema, to read again its propaganda or hear the speech of its agitator, is to renew acquaintance with thoroughly familiar terrain."

1014. Just, Artur W.   Die Presse der Sowjetunion; Methoden diktatorischer Massenführung. Berlin, C. Duncker, 1931. 304 p. Illus. (Zeitung und Zeit; Fortschritte der internationalen Zeitungsforschung, herausgegeben vom Deutschen Institut für Zeitungskunde in Berlin, Band 1)
Bibliography: p. 284-303.

A survey of the Soviet press, including its relations with state and Party, the characteristics of the central and provincial newspapers, the training of Soviet journalists, treatment of news, and the effectiveness of the press as an agency of communication. The author

visited the Soviet Union both as a student of journalism and as a
practicing journalist.

1015. Kalnins, Bruno. Der sowjetische Propagandastaat. Stockholm,
Tiden, 1956. 276 p.

A detailed study of the techniques of Soviet propaganda and indoctrination in the Communist Party, in the Soviet armed forces,
and in mass organizations, with solid chapters on the Soviet press,
radio, and cultural and education media. Contains an excellent
bibliography on pages 269-276.

1016.* Kruglak, Theodore E. The Two Faces of TASS. Minneapolis,
University of Minnesota Press, 1962. 263 p.

The title stems from the author's thesis that TASS is at once an
organ of the government of the USSR and an ostensibly independent
news-gathering agency. The examination of the "two faces," while
rendered in readable English, is somewhat breezy. The author's analysis of the tendentiousness of Soviet news reporting is frequently
vitiated by questionable comparisons with various American public
relations and (non-U.S. government controlled) publicity media.

1017. Out of the Crocodile's Mouth. Edited by William Nelson. Washington, D. C., Public Affairs Press, 1949. 116 p. Illus.

A collection of anti-American cartoons taken from the Soviet
satirical journal *Krokodil*, mostly from the years 1947-1949, when
anti-American propaganda in the USSR had reached its virulent cli-
max. There is a simple but informed introduction by the editor, plus
short introductions to the various chapter headings dealing with
the distorted image of American life.

1018.* Qualter, Terrence H. Propaganda and Psychological Warfare.
New York, Random House, 1962. 176 p.

A valuable, if somewhat elementary, account of the history of
psychological warfare, with special emphasis on American propaganda during the "cold war." The sections on Soviet techniques are
of a rather general nature, with all concrete data drawn from secondary sources.

1019. The Soviet Propaganda Program. Washington, U. S. Government
Printing Office, 1952. 23 p. (U. S. Congress. Senate. Committee on
Foreign Relations. Staff Study of the Subcommittee on Overseas
Information Programs of the United States, no. 3)

A sober, if somewhat spotty and by now largely outdated, survey
of the Soviet propaganda apparatus, including brief sections on
films, radio, and cultural exchanges.

1020. U. S. *Information Agency. Research and Reference Service.* Communist Propaganda around the World; Apparatus and Activities in
1961. Edited by Murray G. Lawson. Washington, 1962. 427 p.
Illus.

Contains useful information on the volume and character of Soviet broadcasting activities in 1961.

1021. U. S. *Information Agency. Research and Reference Service.* Twelve Years of Communist Broadcasting, 1948-1959. Prepared by Simon Costikyan. Washington, n.d. 78 p.

Very valuable for statistics on Communist broadcasting, both within Communist-controlled countries and outside, less so as far as content analysis is concerned. Data on clandestine radio stations is particularly interesting.

VIII

the economic and social structure

A. THE ECONOMY

by Leon M. Herman

1. Economic History

1022. Blum, Jerome. Lord and Peasant in Russia from the Ninth to the Nineteenth Century. Princeton, Princeton University Press, 1961. 656 p.
Bibliography: p. 623-645.
See also entries no. 476 and 1184.

The volume traces the history of relations between the Russian landed nobility and their enserfed peasants over a period of a thousand years and against the background of the country's political and economic evolution. The author systematically relates the changing trends in agrarian institutions to the impact of evolving developments in commerce, manufacturing, market expansion, and entrepreneurial activity.

1023. Bowden, Witt, Michael Karpovich, *and* Abbott P. Usher. An Economic History of Europe since 1750. New York, American Book Co., 1937. 948 p.
Bibliography: p. 885-924.

Contains several chapters by Michael Karpovich devoted to the economic-commercial history of Russia from the pre-reform period through the collectivization of agriculture during the First Five-Year Plan.

1024. Carr, Edward H. A History of Soviet Russia. The Bolshevik Revolution, 1917-1923. v. 2. London, New York, Macmillan, 1952. 397 p.
See also entries no. 540 and 896.

This volume in the author's distinguished account of the Bolshevik Revolution is devoted to "the economic order." In the work's six chapters, he deals with Marxist economic doctrine, economic policies, and experiments with organizational forms during the five year period of Revolution, War Communism, and the first stage of N.E.P.

1025. Goldsmith, Raymond W. The Economic Growth of Tsarist Russia, 1860-1913. Economic Development and Cultural Change (Chicago, Research Center in Economic Development), v. 9, no. 3, April 1961: 441-475.

A rigorous statistical account of the economic growth of Russia between the liberation of the serfs and the First World War, written by a prominent specialist in the field of international income and wealth. Computations of rates of growth, including parallel international comparisons, cover the areas of agriculture, industry, transportation, trade, and national income.

1026. Liashchenko, Petr I. History of the National Economy of Russia, to the 1917 Revolution. Translated by L. M. Herman. New York, Macmillan, 1949. 880 p. (American Council of Learned Societies. Russian Translation Project, Series 4)
See also entry no. 474.

A translation from the Russian original (*Istoriia narodnogo khoziaistva SSSR*; Moscow, Sotsekgiz, 1939) of this major work by the prominent Soviet economic historian whose writings spanned a period of 40 years, including the last decade of the Tsarist period. Thoroughly permeated with the Marxist-Leninist-Stalinist economic and political doctrine, the volume begins with the prehistoric period, devotes one-half of its coverage to the period of "capitalism," and concludes with the collapse of the Tsarist regime.

1027. Mavor, James. An Economic History of Russia. New York, Dutton, 1914. 2 v. (614, 630 p.)

Comprehensive, documented survey of Russia's economic history by a professor of political economy. First volume covers the early centuries to the reform of 1861. Second volume concentrates on more recent developments in industry, agriculture, labor, and the revolutionary movement up to the First World War.

1028.*Maynard, *Sir* John. The Russian Peasant and Other Studies. London, Victor Gollancz, 1942. 512 p.

A companion volume to the author's *Russia in Flux*, published in 1941 (*see* entries no. 97, 270, and 1164). The latter title was also used for an abridged version of the two volumes, published in 1948. The main qualities of this penetrating study, attractively blended, are social sympathy for the Russian peasant, broad personal experience, and serious historical scholarship. In the village community dominated by the collective farm committee, the author finds "an example of democracy on the lower plane which may yet prove to be one of the germs of democracy on the higher."

1029. Miller, Margaret S.   The Economic Development of Russia, 1905-1914. London, P. S. King and Son, 1926. 311 p.
Bibliography: p. 301-307.

A study of developments in the major sectors of Russia's economy (manufacturing, mining, finance, transportation, and foreign trade) during a crucial decade. The author, a British academic economist, is persuaded that "the story of Russia is a story of continuity, in the economic sphere at least."

1030. Mossé, Robert.   L'économie collectiviste. Paris, Librairie générale de droit et de jurisprudence, 1939. 210 p.

A study of the administrative mechanism of the Soviet economy and of planning during the period of the First Five-Year Plan.

1031. Prokopovich (Prokopovicz), Serge N.   Histoire économique de l'URSS. Paris, au Portulan, 1952. 627 p.

The economic evolution of the USSR from 1917 to 1950. Attention is given to demographic and agrarian problems, as well as to the monetary system, real wages, foreign commerce, and the national income. The author is a pioneer in the study of the Russian national income. Translated from the Russian manuscript which appeared as *Narodnoe khoziaistvo SSSR* (New York, Izdatel'stvo im. Chekhova, 1952, 2 v.). A German edition appeared as *Russlands Volkswirtschaft unter den Sowjets* (Zurich, New York, Europa, 1944, 459 p.)

1032. Russian Agriculture during the War. By Alexis N. Antsiferov (Antsyferov) and others.   New Haven, Yale University Press; London, H. Milford, Oxford University Press, 1930. 394 p.

One of the series of 10 monographs dealing with the effects of the First World War on the economic and social life of Russia. The series was planned by Sir Paul Vinogradoff, written by prominent Russian scholars in exile, and sponsored by the Carnegie Endowment for International Peace under the general editorship of James T. Shotwell. The individual volumes are admittedly written on the basis of inadequate statistical and other factual material. They do, however, shed useful light on a critical period in Russian history. The authors, contemporary scholars, were also active participants in the practical affairs of the country. For other volumes in this series *see* entries no. 537, 538, 617, 622, 624, 626, and 627.

1033. Von Laue, Theodore H.   Sergei Witte and the Industrialization of Russia. New York, Columbia University Press, 1963. 384 p.

A historian's account of the impact of the important economic reforms enacted during the influential decade 1892 to 1903 by the energetic Minister of Finance. The author examines the Witte system in the context of the economic, social, and cultural environment of Tsarist Russia, as well as in the larger perspective of the politics of underdevelopment.

1034. Voznesenskii (Voznesensky), Nikolai A. The Economy of the USSR during World War II. Washington, D. C., Public Affairs Press, 1948. 103 p.

A translation of *Voennaia ekonomika SSSR v period Otechestvennoi voiny* (Moscow, Gospolitizdat, 1947, 190 p.), the well-known Soviet treatise on the subject by the chief of the State Planning Commission. The volume provides selected official data, not otherwise available, on levels of production and related economic matters for the critical war years.

Another edition: *The Soviet Economy during the Second World War* (New York, International Publishers, 1949, 160 p.)

1035. Zaleski, Eugène. Planification de la croissance et fluctuations économiques en URSS. v. 1: 1918-1932. Paris, Société d'Édition d'Enseignement Supérieur, 1962. 369 p. (Développement économique, 3)

A history of the formative years of the system of Soviet planning and of the First Five-Year Plan (1928-1932). Contains a systematic analysis of the various types of plans, their projection and execution, with the purpose of studying the specific kinds of economic fluctuation in a planned economy of the Soviet type.

2. General Economic Studies

1036. Baykov, Alexander M. The Development of the Soviet Economic System. Cambridge, England, Cambridge University Press; New York, Macmillan, 1947. 514 p.
Bibliography: p. 480-495.

This prominent Western study published during the early post-World War II period is subtitled "an essay on the experience of planning in the USSR." It provides a good chronological account of the administrative structure erected for the management of the national economy of the Soviet Union. The evaluation of Soviet economic policy, performance, and goals follows quite closely the official version contained in the abundant original sources underlying this study.

1037. Bergson, Abram. The Real National Income of Soviet Russia since 1928. Cambridge, Harvard University Press, 1961. 472 p.
Bibliography: p. 449-460.

The concluding volume in an extended and influential series of research studies aimed at reconstructing and analyzing the national income of the USSR. On the basis of the previous work of several associates in this undertaking, the author presents his results in the form of a series of Soviet national income data in constant as well as current prices for a number of bench mark years (1928, 1937, 1940, 1944, 1950, and 1955).

1038. Bergson, Abram, *ed.* Soviet Economic Growth: Conditions and Perspectives. Evanston, Ill., Row, Peterson, 1953. 376 p.

The full, revised record of proceedings of a conference held in 1952 on the conditioning factors and future prospects of Soviet economic development. Major topics covered by 31 specialists are: national income, capital formation, population and labor force, transportation, industry, agriculture, and foreign trade.

1039. Bergson, Abram, *and* Simon Kuznets, *eds.* Economic Trends in the Soviet Union. Cambridge, Harvard University Press, 1963. 392 p.

This collection of research papers read before a conference on Soviet economic growth, held from May 6-8, 1961, is presented by its editors as a "sequence" to *Soviet Economic Growth*, edited by Professor Bergson and published in 1953 (*see* entry no. 1038). The eight broad areas covered in this symposium are: national income, labor force, capital stock, industrial production, agriculture, consumption, foreign trade, and an international comparative appraisal of Soviet economic growth.

1040. Bettelheim, Charles. L'économie soviétique. Paris, Receuil Sirey, 1950. 472 p. (Traité d'économie politique sous la direction de Gaëtan Picon, 12)

Broad panorama of the economic institutions of the USSR in the period prior to the death of Stalin, with a survey of the functions of the major sectors of activity as revealed in their historical evolution.

1041. Bordaz, Robert. La nouvelle économie soviétique, 1953-1960. Paris, Grasset, 1960. 286 p.

A clear, serviceable synthesis of the economic evolution of the USSR from 1953 to 1960 in the light of the administrative reforms, of foreign economic relations, and of the theoretical discussions during this period. M. Bordaz was economic and financial counselor of the French Embassy in Moscow.

1042. Bornstein, Morris, *and others.* Soviet National Accounts for 1955. Ann Arbor, Mich., Center for Russian Studies, University of Michigan. 1961. 142 l.

The product of a systematic and vigorous research undertaking directed by a leading specialist in the field. All figures are in 1955 rubles, and the method employed is a modification of the accounting system recommended by the Organization for European Economic Cooperation and the United Nations.

1043. Calvez, Jean Y. Revenu national en URSS, problèmes théoriques

et description statistique. Paris, Société d'Édition d'Enseignement Supérieur, 1956. 264 p.
Bibliography: p. 255-263.

An explanation of Soviet concepts and practices, particularly of the methods of analysis of services as a component of national income.

1044.* Campbell, Robert W.   Soviet Economic Power. Boston, Houghton Mifflin, 1960. 209 p.

A compact, non-technical but serious account of how the Soviet economy functions and how well it performs its job. Basic Soviet economic institutions, concepts, procedures, and problems are discussed with evident skill and clarity of expression within an abridged format.

1045. Collette, J. M.   Le taux de croissance du revenu national soviétique. Paris, Institut de Science Économique Appliquée, 1961. 126 p. (Institut de Science Économique Appliquée. Cahiers, Série G, no. 12)

An attempt to calculate the rate of growth, differentiated by the contributions of productive and service sectors, for the year 1957, with details concerning the method used to determine the imputation of the surplus product and the weights for each sector before determining the total rate.

1046. Dobb, Maurice H.   Soviet Economic Development since 1917. London, Routledge and Kegan Paul, 1948. 474 p.

A revised and expanded version of a serious scholarly study written 20 years earlier. The approach to the subject is based on the acceptance of Marxist economic doctrine, Communist political goals, and the Soviet version of recent history. Distinguished for its clear and elegant style of presentation, the study examines a vast body of original source material published during the first decade of the Soviet period.

1047. Gerschenkron, Alexander.   Economic Backwardness in Historical Perspective; a Book of Essays. Cambridge, Belknap Press of Harvard University Press, 1962. 456 p.

A collection of 15 essays (plus three lesser pieces in the appendix) representing the recent periodical writings of a distinguished economic historian who has long specialized in Russian and Soviet industrial history. The underlying theme of the collection is concerned with the prerequisites for industrialization, with Russia, Italy, and Bulgaria serving as case studies. Several of the longer essays deal with Soviet economic growth and industrial organization.

1048. Holzman, Franklyn D., ed.   Readings on the Soviet Economy. Chicago, Rand McNally, 1962. 763 p.

A collection of 41 of the "best and most representative" articles and extracts from books dealing with 10 major problem areas of the Soviet economy.

Other volumes of readings recently published are:

Bornstein, Morris, *and* David Fulfeld, *eds.   The Soviet Economy; a Book of Readings.* Homewood, Ill., Richard D. Irwin, 1962. 382 p.

Shaffer, Harry G.   *The Soviet Economy.* New York, Appleton-Century-Crofts, 1963. 456 p.

1049. Jasny, Naum.   The Soviet Economy during the Plan Era. Stanford, Calif., Stanford University Press, 1951. 116 p.

The author critically examines published Soviet data on national income, evaluates the work of several Western scholars, and computes independent series of data for several bench mark years in terms of "real 1926-27 prices."

First of a series of three consecutive monographs by the author, the other two being *The Soviet Price System* (Stanford, 1951, 179 p.), and *Soviet Prices of Producers' Goods* (Stanford, 1952, 180 p.)

1050.* Nove, Alec.   The Soviet Economy. New York, Praeger, 1961. 328 p.

Described in the subtitle as "an introduction" to the subject, this thoughtful and well-written work covers the whole spectrum of problems related to Soviet economic development. Among its unique features are excellent accounts of the issues in the current discussions on economic theory in the Soviet Union and of the relevance of Soviet experience to the world problem of economic underdevelopment.

1051. Schwartz, Harry.   Russia's Soviet Economy. 2d ed. New York, Prentice-Hall, 1954. 682 p.

Though both of its editions appeared during the years of the "great drought" in economic data, the volume is generally regarded as the first successful textbook on the subject for college use. The treatment of the subject matter is extensive and statistical, providing in addition to the hard core topics (industry, agriculture, labor, internal trade, finance), chapters dealing with the mineral resources, history, ideology, transportation, and foreign economic relations of the USSR.

1052. Spulber, Nicolas.   The Soviet Economy. New York, W. W. Norton, 1962. 311 p.

A detailed analytical survey of the main features of the Soviet economic system, focusing on the principles and administrative structure of the Soviet "system" of central planning. The author is concerned primarily with presenting a contemporary model of the "mature" centrally-planned Soviet socialist economy, rather than with the historical stages and geographical and ideological factors related to Soviet economic development.

1053. U. S. *Congress. Joint Economic Committee.* Dimensions of

Soviet Economic Power. Washington, U.S. Government Printing Office, 1962. 744 p.

A compendium of 26 studies prepared by specialists, dealing with economic policy, national product, planning, industry, agriculture, labor productivity, etc.

Previous surveys made by the Committee were: *Comparisons of the U.S. and Soviet Economies*, 1959; *Soviet Economic Growth*, 1957; and *Trends in Economic Growth*, 1955.

The work of the Joint Economic Committee in this field is continued in its *Annual Economic Indicators for the U.S.S.R.* (Washington, U.S. Government Printing Office, 1964, 218 p.), which continues basic Soviet statistical series through 1962 and includes a variety of bibliographical data.

1054. Varga, Eugen.   Two Systems: Socialist Economy and Capitalist Economy. Translated from the German by R. Page Arnot. New York, International Publishers, 1939. 268 p.

A tendentious presentation of contemporary economic issues and the manner of their resolution in the USSR and in the West during the 1920's and the 1930's. The author, a prominent Soviet specialist in international economics, presents selected statistics and broad judgments to support his thesis that "capitalism has become 'overripe,' is historically surpassed, has become an obstacle to the development of the productive forces."

1055. Vucinich, Alexander S.   Soviet Economic Institutions. Stanford, Calif., Stanford University Press, 1952. 150 p.
Bibliography: p. 138-150.
See also entry no. 1202.

A study focused on the Soviet factory and other production units as social organizations functioning as integral parts of Soviet society. In the five types of economic bodies studied the author finds distinct and unequal groups, each with its own pattern of values and behavior.

3. Economic Theory and the Planning System

1056. Bobrowsky, Czesław.   Formation du système soviétique de planification. Paris, Mouton, 1956. 92 p. (Études sur l'économie et la sociologie des pays slaves, 1)

A study of the historical stages which have contributed to the formation of the present system of planning in the USSR, including examinations of the influence of the wartime economy, of the market, and of theoretical and methodological debates on the problems of industrial planning.

1057. Brutzkus, Boris.   Economic Planning in Soviet Russia. Translated from the German by Gilbert Gardiner. Foreword by F. A. Hayek. London, Routledge and Sons, 1935. 234 p.

This important early discussion of the economic problems of socialism is the work of a prominent anti-Marxist Russian academic economist, a professor of agricultural economics at St. Petersburg from 1907 to 1922.

1058. Campbell, Robert W.   Accounting in Soviet Planning and Management. Cambridge, Harvard University Press, 1963. 315 p.

This study evolved from a doctoral dissertation at Harvard, with the basic approach recast and brought up to date to reflect the changes in a number of areas of accounting. Author explores the use of accounting information in the process of planning and management, on the assumption that the flow of such information in the management and control of the giant corporation constituted by the Soviet economy plays a much more crucial role than in any capitalist economy.

1059. Chambre, Henri.   L'aménagement du territoire en URSS; introduction a l'études des régions économiques soviétiques. Paris, Mouton, 1959. 250 p. (Études sur l'économie et la sociologie des pays slaves, 4)

See also entry no. 774.

A study of economic doctrine and of the plans for regionalization of the Soviet economic area prior to the creation of the *sovnarkhozy* in 1957. An analysis of the Soviet criticism of the theories of A. Weber, and a consideration of the influences of the factor of transport on the location of industry.

1060. Chambre, Henri, *and* Alec Nove.   Rationalité et croissance économiques soviétiques. Paris, Institut de Science Économique Appliquée, 1960. 135 p. (Institut de Science Économique Appliquée. Cahiers, Série G, no. 9)

An analysis of the criteria influencing the choice of objects of investment (Chambre) and of the problems of economic rationality as viewed from the standpoint of the reconciliation of the needs of organization and of growth (Nove).

1061. Collette, J. M.   Recherche, développement et progrès économique en URSS. Paris, Institut de Science Économique Appliquée, 1962. 152 p. (Institut de Science Économique Appliquée. Cahiers, Série G, no. 15)

Evolution of Soviet policy on research and a consideration of its role in economic growth in the years 1935-1955, as well as an examination of the reforms envisaged since 1955 for the better co-ordination of relations among fundamental research, production, and teaching.

1062. Degras, Jane, *and* Alec Nove, *eds.*   Soviet Planning; Essays in Honour of Naum Jasny. Oxford, Basil Blackwell, 1964. 225 p.

Collection of 10 essays on a variety of subjects generally related to Soviet planning, past and present, by a group of eminent economists in Britain and the United States.

1063. Erlich, Alexander.   The Soviet Industrialization Debate, 1924-

1928. Cambridge, Harvard University Press, 1960. 214 p. Bibliography: p. 195-201.

An illuminating account of the divergent economic views, forecasts, and policy recommendations contending for official acceptance in the USSR on the eve of the adoption of the First Five-Year Plan. The author reconstructs in vivid detail the historical setting of this remarkable debate between two groups of leading Communist theoreticians over the problem of the appropriate speed and pattern for the economic development of the country.

1064. Evenko (Yevenko), Ivan A.   Planning in the USSR. Translated from the Russian by Leo Lempert. Moscow, Foreign Languages Publishing House, 1963. 250 p.

A rather general description and analysis, by a major Soviet specialist in the field, of the organization and methodology of economic planning on the national level. In the main, the treatment of the subject relates to the "central sector" of the national economic plan, namely industry. Translation of *Voprosy planirovaniia v SSSR na sovremennom etape* (Moscow, Gosplanizdat, 1959, 207 p.)

1065. Grossman, Gregory, *ed.*   Value and Plan. Berkeley, University of California Press, 1960. 370 p.

This volume grew out of a conference on economic development in Eastern Europe (chiefly the USSR, Poland, and Yugoslavia). Contains 13 papers under the general heading "Economic Calculation and Organization in Eastern Europe," grouped into a comprehensive analysis of the growing concern in that area with the problems of price formation, cost determination, and economic decision-making.

1066. Haensel, Paul.   The Economic Policy of Soviet Russia. London, King, 1930. 190 p.

A study of economic conditions and policies at the beginning of the First Five-Year Plan by a specialist on public finance who taught at the University of Moscow for 25 years prior to his departure from the USSR in 1928. Based on official statistical series considered by the author to be trustworthy, the survey covers agriculture, industry, labor, internal trade, foreign commerce, transportation, and public finance.

1067. Hirsch, Hans.   Quantity Planning and Price Planning in the Soviet Union. Translated from the German by Karl Scholz. Edited by William N. Loucks. Philadelphia, University of Pennsylvania Press, 1961. 272 p.

Translated from the German original *Mengenplanung und Preisplanung in der Sowjetunion* (Basel, Kyklos-Verlag, 1957, 195 p.), this monograph is devoted to a searching analysis of principles of price formation and the dual guidance system (physical and financial) used by planners to communicate their objectives to the enterprise managers and to verify their performance.

1068. Hoff, Trygve J. B.   Economic Calculation in the Socialist Society. Translated from the Norwegian by M. A. Michael. London, Wm. Hodge, 1949. 264 p.
Bibliography: p. 252-257.

> Translation of *Okonomisk kalkulasjon i socialistiske samfund* (Oslo, H. Aschehoug, 1938, 373 p.). The study investigates the possibilities of economic calculation in socialist societies. The volume is devoted to an encyclopedic examination of the theoretical literature in the field, to test existing economic theory in a climate lacking markets and prices set by demand and supply. Appendix (32 pages) relates the author's conclusions to the experience of Soviet Russia.

1069. Kantorovich, Leonid V.   Mathematical Methods of Organizing and Planning Production. Management Science, v. 6, July 1960: 366-422.

> Enlarged stenographic record of a pioneer report made by the eminent Soviet mathematician to a meeting of Leningrad University and industrial specialists in May 1939. The author has been recognized as having broken new ground in the application of mathematical methods to solving problems in organization and planning in industry, construction, and transport.

1070. Lange, Oscar.   The Working Principles of the Soviet Economy. *In* Robert J. Kerner, *ed.* USSR Economy and the War. New York, Russian Economic Institute, 1943. p. 22-47.

> A lucid analysis of the "physiology" of the Soviet economy, written by the well-known Polish economist and Marxist while he was teaching in the United States. The essay, containing references to other studies by the author, reflects his basic sympathy with the economic goals of socialism, as well as the mood of the times looking forward to the co-operation of the Soviet Union with the free democratic nations of the world.

1071. Obolenskii, Valerian V., *and others.*   Social Economic Planning in the USSR. The Hague, New York, International Industrial Relations Association, 1931. 158 p.

> Collective report of the delegation from the USSR to the World Social Economic Congress at Amsterdam, held in August 1931. Four officials and economists from the USSR present substantial papers on the organization and operation of the Soviet planning system in general, as well as in the spheres of industry, agriculture, and labor relations.

1072. Le plan septennal soviétique; études et documents.   Paris, Institut de Science Économique Appliquée, 1960. 367 p. (Institut de Science Économique Appliquée. Cahiers, Série G, no. 10)

> The French translation of an internal document of Gosplan, not issued in the Soviet Union, the French title of which is *Recueil des données comptables et indicateurs destinés à servir de base au projet de plan perspectif 1959-1965.* It does not include statistical ma-

terials. This document is preceded by two commentaries by Henri Chambre and Basile Kerblay which set forth the characteristics of the methods of drawing up the regional and national plans.

1073. Stalin, Iosif V. (Joseph).   Economic Problems of Socialism in the USSR. New York, International Publishers, 1952. 71 p.

Part one of this important last-published political essay by the author is made up of his far-ranging "remarks" on a draft of a textbook on political economy prepared by a group of prominent Soviet authors. Part two consists of the author's replies to questions from several participants in the discussion.

Translation of *Ekonomicheskie problemy sotsializma v SSSR* (Moscow, Gospolitizdat, 1952, 93 p.)

1074. Strumilin, Stanislav G.   Planning in the Soviet Union. London, Soviet News, 1957. 56 p. (Soviet News Booklet, no. 17)

A highly compressed, orthodox survey of the objectives, methods, and results of economic planning in the USSR. By a leading protagonist of central planning whose experience has spanned five decades of active work in the administrative and academic organs of the country.

1075. Wiles, Peter J. D.   The Political Economy of Communism. Oxford, Basil Blackwell, 1962. 404 p.

An advanced treatment of economic theory intended to introduce the graduate student to the analytical study of Communist theory and practice. The main emphasis of this stimulating discussion falls on problems and policies in the Soviet Union as related to planning models, planners' criteria, pricing practices, investment, rationality, distribution, measurement criteria, and rate of growth.

4. Statistics

1076. Appraisals of Russian Economic Statistics.   Review of Economics and Statistics, v. 29, no. 4, November 1947: 213-246.

Five experts offer their appraisals of principal Soviet statistical series (national income, industry, labor) in the interest of a more realistic approach to Russian economic accomplishments. The authors find much evidence of impressive economic results, but they also conclude that the manner of collecting statistics is suspect, and that concepts are not clearly defined, suggesting an intent to present a biased statistical record.

1077. Clark, Colin.   A Critique of Russian Statistics. London, Macmillan, 1939. 76 p.

An influential, pioneer undertaking in the effort of Western economists to recalculate official Soviet national income data (and other aggregative series) upon the basis of real costs, in order to exclude the effect of the arbitrary Soviet system of valuation. The basic method used is to express reported quantities of physical goods and services at their 1934 market value in Great Britain.

1078. Ezhov (Yezhov), A. I.   Soviet Statistics. Moscow, Foreign Languages Publishing House, 1957. 131 p.

A translation from the Russian by V. Shneerson of a study originally titled *Organizatsiia gosudarstvennoi statistiki v SSSR* (Moscow, Gosstatizdat, 1957, 131 p.), by a high official of the Central Statistical Administration (Ts.S.U.). The volume describes the evolution of statistical agencies in the USSR, the procedures for the collection of data, and the concepts underlying the major statistical indicators.

1079. Grossman, Gregory.   Soviet Statistics of Physical Output of Industrial Commodities. Princeton, Princeton University Press, 1960. 151 p.

Bibliography: p. 137-148.

An evaluative study of the agencies, the method of compilation, and the quality of industrial statistics in the USSR. The volume is the first in a series of publications on Soviet economic growth initiated by the National Bureau of Economic Research in 1954.

1080. Jasny, Naum.   The Soviet 1956 Statistical Handbook; a Commentary. East Lansing, Michigan State University Press, 1957. 212 p.

A detailed critical examination of the reliability of the statistical series contained in the first compendium of official economic data published in the USSR since 1939. The main aim of the author is to distinguish between the substantial real growth that has in fact occurred in heavy industry, transport, capital investment, and the claimed gains in the areas of agriculture and the real income of workers and peasants.

1081. Reliability and Usability of Soviet Statistics.   The American Statistician, April–May and June–July, 1953: 8-21, 8-16.

A symposium of five papers describing Soviet statistical practices and evaluating their reliability in the spheres of population, industry, national income, and agriculture.

1082. Russia (*1923– U.S.S.R.*) *Ministerstvo vneshnei torgovli.*   Foreign Trade of the USSR in 1961; a Statistical Survey. Washington, D. C., 1962. 230 p. (U. S. Joint Publications Research Service. Report no. 16,086)

Official statistical compilation of Soviet foreign trade returns, by country and by commodity, for the years 1960 and 1961. Translation of *Vneshniaia torgovlia SSSR za 1961 god* (Moscow, 1962, 232 p.). Similar translations are available for earlier years.

1083. Russia (*1923- U.S.S.R.*) *Tsentral'noe statisticheskoe upravlenie.* Forty Years of Soviet Power in Facts and Figures. Moscow, Foreign Languages Publishing House, 1958. 319 p.

A translation of an official handbook issued in conjunction with the fortieth anniversary of the Bolshevik Revolution. The volume contains selected statistical series, through 1956, on the major sectors of the economy for bench mark years, including some 1913 data. Translation of *Dostizheniia Sovetskoi vlasti za 40 let v tsifrakh* (Moscow, Gosstatizdat, 1957, 370 p.)

5. Agriculture

1084. Belov, Fedor.   The History of a Soviet Collective Farm. New York, Praeger, 1955. 237 p. (East European Fund. Research Program on the USSR. Studies, no. 13)
See also entry no. 1194.

A detailed chronicle of events experienced by a Ukrainian village since the beginning of the drive for collectivization. The author, a native of the village, who served as chairman of the local collective farm during the years 1947-1949, presents a detailed account, based on his diaries, of the organization, economic relations, planning activities, field operations, and household problems on his farm.

1085. Chombart de Lauwe, Jean.   Les paysans soviétiques. Paris, Éditions du Seuil, 1961. 427 p.

The author, who occupies the Chair of Rural Economy in the École Nationale d'Agriculture at Grignon, visited the USSR in 1955 and 1960 to study the results of the industrialization of agriculture in its economic and social aspects, without neglecting either the historical factors or the institutional mechanisms. His conclusions also touch upon the lessons of this experience for any policy on the industrialization of agriculture.

1086. Hubbard, Leonard E.   The Economics of Soviet Agriculture. London, Macmillan, 1939. 315 p.

Popular factual account of the coming of collectivization, sketched against the broad historical background of the role of the peasantry in the Russian state. Author aims at examining the advantages and disadvantages of collectivization from the peasants' point of view.

1087. Jasny, Naum.   The Socialized Agriculture of the USSR. Stanford, Calif., Stanford University Press, 1949. 837 p.
Bibliography: p. 799-813.

Comprehensive pioneer work devoted to a searching examination of the policies pursued and the production level achieved by the Stalin regime through forced collectivization of agriculture. Author achieved a major statistical tour de force by adjusting the official Soviet grain figures (based on "biological yield") downward to a level very close to the revised official figures (based on "barn yield") published seven years later.

1088. Laird, Roy D., *ed.*   Soviet Agricultural and Peasant Affairs. Lawrence, University of Kansas Press, 1963. 335 p.

A compendium of 10 papers and six commentaries by prominent specialists, dealing with the economic record and the geographic, social, administrative, and political problems of Soviet agriculture. Contributors include Naum Jasny, Lazar Volin, Alec Nove, Luba Richter, H. Swearer, Demitri Shimkin, and others.

1089. Owen, Launcelot A.   The Russian Peasant Movement, 1906-1917. New York, Russell and Russell, 1963. 267 p.
Bibliography: p. 251-257.
    Re-issue of a work in economic history first published in 1937, recording the course of events that led to the agrarian revolution of 1917, in which the peasants changed the course of history by their own direct appropriation of all farm land. The author suggests that by means of this fait accompli the peasants assured both the success of the Bolsheviks in the civil war and the stabilization of the Soviet regime.

1090. Pavlovskii (Pavlovsky), George A.   Agricultural Russia on the Eve of the Revolution. London, Routledge, 1930. 340 p.
    A monograph based on a doctoral thesis (University of London) exploring the economic forces at work in the agricultural economy of Russia in the early twentieth century. The study uses statistical and other documentary material available outside of Russia.

1091. Robinson, Geroid T.   Rural Russia under the Old Régime. New York, Longmans, Green, 1932. 342 p.
Bibliography: p. 312-326.
See also entries no. 520 and 1190.
    Distinguished scholarly history of the tension-laden economic relations between landlord and peasant in Russia, covering the centuries between the establishment of serfdom and the First World War. The author finds that despite the clear trend to independent farming after 1905, the system of peasant tenure was still in flux and the new ways of farming had not yet become habitual.

1092. Schiller, Otto.   Das Agrarsystem der Sowjetunion; Entwicklung seiner Struktur und Produktionleistung. Tübingen, Böhlau, 1960. 172 p.
    A compact but authoritative survey of the organizational forms and production record of Soviet agriculture by a lifelong student of the subject, containing a large body of quantitative material through 1958.

1093. Timoshenko, Vladimir P.   Agricultural Russia and the Wheat Problem. Stanford University, Calif., published jointly by the Food Research Institute and the Committee on Russian Research of the Hoover War Library, 1932. 571 p.
    A painstaking study of contemporary conditions in Soviet Russian agriculture against a solid background of developments prior to the First World War. The author, a well-known student of world agricultural problems who left Russia in 1919, uses official sources of information critically, especially the more controlled flow of

statistical information after the beginning of the collectivization drive in 1928.

1094. Volin, Lazar.   A Survey of Soviet Russian Agriculture. Washington, U. S. Government Printing Office, 1951. 194 p. (U.S. Dept. of Agriculture. Agriculture Monograph no. 5)

Documented account of the evolution of the agricultural economy of the USSR through 1950, by a distinguished Western specialist on this subject. The volume contains a balanced précis of the mass of available knowledge in the field, along with a thoughtful evaluation of the accomplishment of the Soviet system of collectivized farming.

6. Industry and Transport

1095. Berliner, Joseph S.   Factory and Manager in the USSR. Cambridge, Harvard University Press, 1957. 386 p.

Bibliography: p. 337-345.

See also entry no. 1195.

A major study of the industrial enterprise system and of managerial behavior in the USSR, by the established specialist in the field. The study is based primarily on information gathered through interviewing former Soviet citizens with specific personal experience in this field prior to the Second World War. The basic material is effectively integrated with a scholarly analysis of published sources on the subject through 1956.

1096. Bienstock, Gregory, Solomon M. Schwartz, *and* Aaron Yugow. Management in Russian Industry and Agriculture. New York, Oxford University Press, 1944. 198 p.

See also entry no. 1196.

An early and enduring exemplar of research monographs on management in the USSR, written by three Russian-trained scholars. The individual contributions of the three are identified, and the work is accompanied by an extensive, helpful introduction by J. Marschak.

1097. Buchholz, Erwin.   Die Waldwirtschaft und Holzindustrie der Sowjetunion. Munich, BLV Verlagsgesellschaft, 1961. 233 p.

A broad survey of the Soviet timber industry by a competent student of forestry developments in the USSR who has followed the subject for more than three decades.

1098. Clark, Mills G. (M. Gardner).   The Economics of Soviet Steel. Cambridge, Harvard University Press, 1956. 400 p.

Bibliography: p. 329-341.

A monograph based on a thorough examination of the economic and technical literature of the USSR devoted to this basic Soviet industry. In addition to dealing with production, investment, location, development, specialization, and scale, the study (based on the author's doctoral dissertation) hazards some forecasts on future prospects of the steel industry in the USSR.

Of related interest is a volume edited by the same author, *Steel in the Soviet Union* (New York, American Iron and Steel Institute, 1960, 376 p.)

1099. Gerschenkron, Alexander.   The Rate of Industrial Growth in Russia since 1885. Journal of Economic History, Supplement 7, 1947: 144-174.

A compact analytical essay that spans the pre- and post-Revolutionary periods of Russian history, featuring a comparison of the rates of industrial growth during various intervals of a period that begins in the middle of the 80's and ends with the coming of the Second World War. The essay explores thoroughly the relevant literature on the subject and describes briefly the specific facts that both impelled and hindered the process of industrialization.

1100. Granick, David.   Management of the Industrial Firm in the USSR. New York, Columbia University Press, 1954. 346 p.
Bibliography: p. 305-328.
See also entry no. 1197.

A closely documented study exploring the Soviet economic planning system, with particular reference to the management of state enterprises in heavy industry. The period covered in depth is 1934-1941, and the bulk of the material treated is derived from the daily and periodical press, which reflect actual operations and cite specific case histories, as compared with books and legal materials, which present a generalized and theoretical picture of Soviet industry.

1101. Hodgman, Donald R.   Soviet Industrial Production, 1928-1951. Cambridge, Harvard University Press, 1954. 241 p.
Bibliography: p. 185-188.

Influential study of the quantitative aspects of Soviet industrial development, in which a critique of the official measures of Soviet industrial output is combined with an imaginative construction of an independent index of the annual industrial product. In devising his index, the author used as weights Soviet data on wage payrolls in individual branches of industry.

1102. Hunter, Holland.   Soviet Transportation Policy. Cambridge, Harvard University Press, 1957. 416 p.
Bibliography: p. 283-293.

Detailed scholarly examination, based on a wealth of statistical material, of the role of transportation in the economic history of the USSR, devoted mainly to the period 1928-1955. The study, based on a doctoral dissertation, suggests that Soviet policies toward transportation provide valid lessons for other countries in quest of rapid industrial growth.

1103. Jasny, Naum.   Soviet Industrialization, 1928-1952. Chicago, University of Chicago Press, 1961. 467 p.

An important contribution by the "senior western student of the Soviet economy," providing an interpretive analysis, supported by his own statistical measurements, of all major aspects of the economic development of the USSR during the Stalin era. His skepticism of Soviet statistics and his criticism of official policies do not prevent the author from recognizing the results achieved in terms of growth. A brief "postscript" deals with the events of the post-Stalin era.

1104. Lehbert, Ben.   Die Entwicklung der Stahlwirtschaft in den Vereinigten Staaten von Amerika und in der Sowjetunion. Kiel, 1961. 200 p., 12 tables. (Forschungsberichte des Instituts für Weltwirtschaft an der Universität Kiel, 57)

A closely documented survey of the basic steel industry in the leading world economies, amply illustrated with tabular material, technical characteristics, and locational data. No index.

1105. Littlepage, John D., *and* Demaree Bess.   In Search of Soviet Gold. New York, Harcourt, Brace, 1938. 310 p.
See also entry no. 170.

Firsthand, systematic account of the production experience of an American engineer who served as chief technical adviser to the Soviet Gold Trust in Asia between 1928 and 1937. Written with the aid of an experienced journalist, the volume is representative of an interesting body of literature by engineers from the West who were engaged in the technical modernization of Soviet industry during the inter-war period.

Other books of this general type are: Walter A. Rukeyser, *Working for the Soviets* (New York, 1932, 286 p.), and Alcan Hirsch, *Industrialized Russia* (New York, 1934, 309 p.)

1106. Nutter, G. Warren, *assisted by* Israel Borenstein *and* Adam Kaufman.   The Growth of Industrial Production in the Soviet Union. Princeton, Princeton University Press, 1962. 706 p.
Bibliography: p. 635-686.

The second study to appear in print as part of a comprehensive research project on Soviet economic growth undertaken in 1954 by the National Bureau of Economic Research. This volume, including 400 pages of appendixes, contains extensive tabulations and calculations of Soviet production and growth rates. A number of the author's calculations and conclusions have caused several prominent scholars in the field to state their disagreement in print.

1107. Shimkin, Demitri B.   Minerals, a Key to Soviet Power. Cambridge, Harvard University Press, 1953. 452 p.
Bibliography: p. 393-418.

Systematic survey of the deposits, production, and consumption of minerals in the Soviet Union, intended to provide a guide to the operation of the national economy. In connection with the six major groups of minerals covered, the author provides detailed data and assessment for the period 1926 through 1937.

1108. Shimkin, Demitri B.   The Soviet Mineral-Fuels Industries, 1928-1958; a Statistical Survey. Washington, U.S. Dept. of Commerce, Bureau of the Census, 1962. 183 p.

A largely statistical report which presents the characteristics and performance of the basic Soviet fuel industries since the beginning of the planning period. This report also contains selected comparisons with the United States and an assessment of Soviet goals for 1965 and 1972.

1109. Williams, Ernest W., *assisted by* George Novak *and* Holland Hunter. Freight Transportation in the Soviet Union, Including Comparisons with the United States. Princeton, Princeton University Press, 1962. 221 p.
Bibliography: p. 209-214.

A systematic inquiry into the role played by transportation in the growth of Soviet economy. The analysis, concerned primarily with the railroads, uses comparisons with the U. S. experience and characterizes the transportation system of the USSR as a "starved but sturdy agent" of economic growth.

7. Labor

1110. Anstett, Marcel.   La formation de la main-d'oeuvre qualifiée en Union Soviétique de 1917 à 1954. Paris, Marcel Rivière, 1958. 245 p.

History of the formation of the labor force in the USSR, set in the framework of the economy's requirements.

1111. Association nationale des directeurs et chefs du personnel. Conditions de travail en URSS. Paris, Les Éditions d'Organisation, 1961. 276 p.

Report of a study mission to the USSR on the problems of plant organization, the role of the trade unions, the conditions of labor, and the training of workers. Also provides some indications of wage levels.

1112. Bergson, Abram.   The Structure of Soviet Wages; a Study in Socialist Economics. Cambridge, Harvard University Press, 1944. 255 p.
Bibliography: p. 241-249.

A systematic examination of wage statistics in the USSR, mainly for the period 1928-1934, with some coverage through 1937. The author, a leading U.S. scholar in the field, traces the effect of the official abandonment of wage egalitarianism in 1931 to discover a system of relative wages in the USSR that "reveals striking uniformity in results" with the system of differentiated wages in capitalist countries.

1113. Chapman, Janet G.   Real Wages in Soviet Russia since 1928. Cambridge, Harvard University Press, 1963. 395 p.

A detailed presentation and analysis of available statistical data on the movement of wages and the cost of living in the USSR through 1954. Less detailed data are included for several years thereafter, through 1960. In addition, valuable material on the collective farm market, ration prices, the cost of services, and social insurance benefits is included in an extensive appendix of 181 pages.

1114. Deutscher, Isaac.   Soviet Trade Unions; Their Place in Soviet Labour Policy. London, Royal Institute of International Affairs, 1950. 156 p.

A brief description and selective analysis of the role of the Soviet trade unions, the function they perform in the planned economy, and their relationship with the Communist Party (1917 to 1950). In the author's view, a systematic historical treatment for the post-1929 period is precluded by the fact that the institution became surrounded by a thick web of legend and myth.

1115. Dewar, Margaret.   Labour Policy in the USSR, 1917-1928. London, New York, Royal Institute of International Affairs, 1956. 286 p.
Bibliography: p. 278-280.

A closely documented study tracing the evolution of Soviet labor policy on the basis of the abundant published official material of that period. The author describes in detail the methods employed by the Soviet government in putting Bolshevik theory into practice by way of strengthening discipline in order to increase the productivity of the labor force. In the author's view, "there has been no essential modification" in the basic structure of Soviet labor policy since 1928. The appendix includes an extensive summary of official decrees on the subject (pages 160-276).

1116. Galenson, Walter.   Labor Productivity in Soviet and American Industry. New York, Columbia University Press, 1955. 273 p.
Bibliography: p. 265-273.

A product of the research program of the Rand Corporation, including 86 tables, devoted to a comparative analysis of the average output per worker in Soviet industry. The study is based largely on the available data for the period before the Second World War, and is further handicapped by the lack of dependable Soviet output data in value terms and by the problem of computing an exchange rate for the ruble.

1117. Gliksman, Jerzy G., *and others*.   The Control of Industrial Labor in the Soviet Union. Santa Monica, Calif., The Rand Corporation, 1960. 172 p. (Rand Corporation Research Memorandum, no. RM-2494)

A carefully documented account of the use, by Soviet state authorities, of various systems of material incentives to raise existing levels of industrial production. The study reviews in detail material on more flexible methods of labor control employed since the death of Stalin, and arrives at the conclusion that the "basic nature of the system has remained unchanged in that the authorities have retained complete control over industrial labor."

1118. Schwarz, Solomon M.   Labor in the Soviet Union. New York, Praeger, 1952. 364 p.

Documented survey of the growth, transformation, wages, and living standards of the industrial working class in the USSR. The author, a prominent specialist on labor conditions in the USSR, concentrates his study on the period following the adoption of comprehensive planning.

8. Money, Finance, Commerce, and Housing

1119. Arnold, Arthur Z.   Banks, Credit, and Money in Soviet Russia. New York, Columbia University Press, 1937. 559 p.
Bibliography: p. 525-543.

A pioneer study in English, dealing comprehensively with the development of Soviet banks, credit, and money. Includes three chapters on the financial institutions of Tsarist Russia. The treatment of the material is sufficiently broad to interest the general student of economic conditions.

1120. Davies, Robert W.   The Development of the Soviet Budgetary System. Cambridge, England, Cambridge University Press, 1958. 372 p.
Bibliography: p. 344-352.

A study, employing the historical approach, of the role of finance and of the budgetary system in particular, in the execution of the established general economic policy of the Soviet government. The volume, an adaptation of a Ph.D. thesis, offers some suggestions on the extent to which the budget system in use was conditioned by Soviet industrialization and on its applicability to directly planned economies in general.

1121. Goldman, Marshall I.   Soviet Marketing; Distribution in a Controlled Economy. New York, Free Press of Glencoe, 1963. 229 p.
Bibliography: p. 209-223.

An up-to-date survey of the marketing process for consumer goods in the domestic economy of the Soviet Union by an experienced academic specialist in the field. The study concerns itself with a description of the organization of distribution and an examination of the operation of demand estimation, product assortment, and consumer sovereignty within the setting of a centrally controlled system of production goal decisions.

1122. Grossman, Gregory.   Union of Soviet Socialist Republics. *In* Benjamin H. Beckhart, *ed.* Banking Systems. New York, Columbia University Press, 1954.   p. 733-768.

A concise and illuminating account of how the institutions and practices of the Soviet banking system serve as both the executive and the controlling arm of the vast planning and operational economic apparatus of the state.

1123. Haensel, Paul.   Die Finanz– und Steuerverfassung der Union der Sozialistischen Sowjet-Republiken. Jena, G. Fischer, 1928. 285 p. Appendix and index, 40 p.

A systematic and complete account of the financial policy and tax structure of the Soviet Union on the eve of the First Five-Year Plan by a distinguished former professor of economics at the Moscow State University.

1124. Holzman, Franklyn D.   Soviet Taxation; the Fiscal and Monetary Problems of a Planned Economy. Cambridge, Harvard University Press, 1955. 376 p.

Documented study of the fiscal and monetary problems confronting the Soviet planned economy, based on a doctoral dissertation at Harvard. Generally considered to be the first systematic survey of taxation in the USSR. Subject is traced from the early Soviet period, with detailed treatment of turnover tax, income tax, and various agricultural taxes.

1125. Lavigne, Marie-L.   Le capital dans l'économie soviétique. Paris, Société d'Édition d'Enseignement Supérieur, 1962. 351 p. (Développement économique, 7)

A study of the concept of "capital" viewed — on the one hand — from the standpoint of the evaluation of productive factors and the costs of production, and — on the other — from that of the management of capital (reevaluation of balances, policies of amortization, financing of modernization), all in the light of theoretical discussions and of the realities of economic activity.

1126. Pasvolsky, Leo, *and* Harold G. Moulton.   Russian Debts and Russian Reconstruction. New York, McGraw-Hill, 1924. 247 p.

This volume examines the relationship between indebtedness of Soviet Russia and the problem faced in economic reconstruction. Pre-Soviet statistical data are examined to determine Russia's capacity to pay outstanding debts if and when, with the aid of reconstruction loans, stable economic conditions should be restored.

1127. Reddaway, William B.   The Russian Financial System. London, Macmillan, 1935. 106 p.

Brief analytical essay on the nature and functions of the monetary and financial system of the USSR. This rigorous discussion is based on material gathered in a series of interviews with competent officials in 1934 and may profitably be used to introduce a reader to the principles governing financial relations in the Soviet economy.

1128. Sosnovy, Timothy.   The Housing Problem in the Soviet Union. New York, Research Program on the USSR, 1954. 300 p. Bibliography: p. 277-290.
See also entry no. 1225.

A systematic examination of the housing situation in the USSR with special stress on the socio-economic impact of rapid industrialization on the living conditions of the expanded urban population. The author draws upon the wealth of available published material as well as on his personal observations of Soviet housing policy in practice during the inter-war period.

9. Foreign Economic Relations

1129. Allen, Robert L.   Soviet Economic Warfare. Washington, D.C., Public Affairs Press, 1960. 293 p. Bibliography.

A work based on three years of research conducted between 1956 and 1959 in which more than 20 scholars participated. The study, parts of which had been previously published, examines in detail and by region the course of recent Soviet activities and motives in international commerce, technical assistance, military credits, and foreign economic aid.

1130. Aubrey, Henry G., *assisted by* Joel Darmstadter. Coexistence: Economic Challenge and Response. Washington, D.C., National Planning Association, 1961. 323 p.

A comprehensive, balanced review of the problems created for the West as a result of the Soviet change to a policy of active economic diplomacy after the death of Stalin. The volume summarizes the findings of several monographs dealing with the political economy of the East-West contest for influence in the newly developing regions of the world.

1131. Baykov, Alexander M.   Soviet Foreign Trade. Princeton, Princeton University Press; London, Oxford University Press, 1946. 100 p. Appendix (tables), 24 p.

A concise history of the foreign commercial relations of the USSR, including a brief account of pre-Soviet developments, and a large body of representative statistics, showing the geographic distribution and commodity composition of this trade. The author has included in his survey "interpretations commonly accepted in Soviet literature on the subject as well as the point of view of Soviet authors and government leaders."

1132. Berliner, Joseph S.   Soviet Economic Aid; the New Aid and Trade Policy in Underdeveloped Countries. New York, Praeger, 1958. 232 p.
Bibliography: p. 224-228.

This volume, published for the Council on Foreign Relations, covers the early phase of the Soviet program of economic aid to neutral underdeveloped nations. The author, a prominent student of internal economic developments in the USSR, considers the subject analytically, in a framework of maturing Soviet economic capabilities and rising pressures to participate in the international division of labor.

1133. Condoide, Mikhail V.   Russian-American Trade. Columbus, Ohio State University Press, 1946. 160 p.
Bibliography: p. 150-154.
    A survey of trade relations between the two countries during the inter-war period which includes, in addition to abundant detailed statistical data, background material on the pre-1914 trade of Russia, global Soviet trade data, and texts of bilateral commercial treaties.

1134. Conolly, Violet.   Soviet Economic Policy in the East: Turkey, Persia, Afghanistan, Mongolia, Tana Tuva, Sin Kiang. London, Oxford University Press, 1933. 168 p.
Bibliographical note: p. 147-152; bibliography: p. 153-161.
    One of several studies by the author which examine the special system of economic relations cultivated by the USSR with the small nations on its Asian border during the inter-war period. The special treatment of this group of states, including exemptions from the total monopoly of foreign trade, is described as a unique Soviet experiment in seeking political influence through a combination of commercial preference and revolutionary pressure.

1135. Dewar, Margaret.   Soviet Trade with Eastern Europe, 1945-1949. London, New York, Royal Institute of International Affairs, 1951. 123 p.
    A well-documented account of the early phase in the reorientation of the trade of Eastern Europe toward the USSR at the end of the Second World War. Six chapters deal with the problems of the individual countries, including Yugoslavia but excluding East Germany. The study contains abundant statistical material, including data on the prewar period, and several texts of bilateral commercial agreements.

1136. Gerschenkron, Alexander.   Economic Relations with the USSR. New York, Committee on International Economic Policy, 1945. 73 p.
    A concise, documented, and readable discussion of the outlook for economic collaboration between Russia and its wartime Western allies, from the pen of an eminent student of Soviet economic development and Russian history. The discussion, seeking to find an international framework for the operation of Russian trade along multilateral lines, is based on two major assumptions: (1) Russia will retain its planned economy and foreign trade monopoly; (2) Russia may be prepared to reduce the degree of autarky pursued in the early decades.

1137. Herman, Leon M.   Foreign Trade. *In* George B. de Huszar, *ed.* Soviet Power and Policy. New York, Crowell, 1955.   p. 335-369.

Provides a brief survey of Soviet foreign trade developments between the time of the establishment of the foreign trade monopoly and the aftermath of the 1952 Moscow Economic Conference. Included at the end of the chapter is a useful bibliography of the pre-1955 literature in English on the subject.

1138. Kovner, Milton.   The Challenge of Coexistence; a Study of Soviet Economic Diplomacy. Washington, D.C., Public Affairs Press, 1961. 130 p.
Bibliography: p. 113-128.
Broad survey of the evolution and direction of recent foreign economic policy of the USSR, in which foreign trade is treated as an integral part of foreign policy. The main concern of the author is with the reversal by the post-Stalin leadership of the classical concept of trade following the flag. Instead, an attempt is made to use trade and aid to influence political institutions in the underdeveloped areas.

1139. Lewery, Leonard J.   Foreign Capital Investments in Russian Industries and Commerce. Washington, U.S. Government Printing Office, 1923. 28 p. (U.S. Dept. of Commerce. Bureau of Foreign and Domestic Commerce. Miscellaneous Series, no. 124)
A summary of official information published in Soviet Russia during 1920-1922 on the private investments made by the Western nations during the Tsarist period. Detailed statistical data are presented by country of the capital's origin and by branch of industry or type of commerce in which it was invested.

1140. Mikesell, Raymond F., *and* Jack N. Behrman.   Financing Free World Trade with the Sino-Soviet Bloc. Princeton, Princeton University Press, 1958. 109 p. Appendix (tables), 145 p.
After reviewing briefly the structure and organization of trade within the countries of the Communist Bloc, the study examines the motives of all countries concerned in negotiating bilateral trade and payments agreements, and offers an assessment of the operation of the East-West bilateral trade arrangements.

1141. Nove, Alec, *and* Desmond Donnelly.   Trade with Communist Countries. London, Institute of Economic Affairs, 1960. 183 p.
In this two-part book, Mr. Nove (in part one) provides a brief but incisive comment on the influence economic principles and planning institutions have on the conduct of Soviet-bloc trade. Mr. Donnelly furnishes a commentary on the political and practical issues involved in trading with the individual Communist countries. The work is addressed primarily to businessmen, and contains valuable reference and statistical data.

1142. Pisar, Samuel.   A New Look at Trade Policy toward the Communist Bloc; the Elements of a Common Strategy for the West. Materials Prepared for the Subcommittee on Foreign Economic Policy of the Joint Economic Committee. Washington, U.S. Government Printing Office, 1961. 103 p.

A collection of research papers devoted to an analysis of the issues and the data relative to the state of trade relations between the Communist-governed nations and the commercial communities of the rest of the world. The study contains a large body of statistical material illustrating the significance of East-West trade for various participants, by region and by individual country.

1143. State Trading.   Law and Contemporary Problems (Durham, N. C., Duke University), nos. 2-3. Spring and Summer, 1959.

The two issues embody a series of 14 articles by prominent experts, devoted to the theory, legal framework, and practice of state trading, including specific discussions dealing with the foreign trade of the USSR.

1144. U. S. *Dept. of State.*   The Sino-Soviet Economic Offensive in the Less Developed Countries. Washington, May 1958. 111 p. (Publication 6,632. European and British Commonwealth Series, 51)

A broad survey, by country, of the trade and credit relations of the USSR with the world's less developed countries since 1953. The account includes abundant statistical data as a basis for an official analysis of the motives and objectives of the Communist bloc of nations in their post-1953 drive to use their growing economic and industrial capacities as a means of gaining political influence in new areas.

1145. U. S. *Library of Congress. Legislative Reference Service.*   Soviet Oil in the Cold War. Washington, U.S. Government Printing Office, 1961. 26 p.

A summary of major developments in the petroleum export policy and of USSR trade transactions during the late 1950's. These activities are examined against the backdrop of stated official Soviet views regarding the importance of oil concessions to Western political influence in the less developed countries.

10. Serials

1146. Economics of Planning. 1961– Oslo, Norway. quarterly.

Main area of interest is the theory and practice of centrally planned economies and their relations with market economies.

1147. Problems of Economics.   1958– New York. monthly.

Selected English translations of Russian-language material published in the periodical press of the USSR.

1148. Soviet Studies.   v. 1– 1949– Glasgow. quarterly.

A quarterly review of the social and economic institutions of the USSR, edited at the University of Glasgow and published by Basil Blackwell, Oxford.

Other serials which carry with some regularity articles in English on Soviet economic topics include:
Problems of Communism. v. 1– 1952– Washington. bimonthly.
Slavic Review. v. 1– 1940– Seattle. quarterly.
American Economic Review. v. 1– 1911– Evanston, Ill. 5 no. a year.

B. THE SOCIETY

by Kent Geiger

1. Overview of Society

1149.* Bauer, Raymond A., Alex Inkeles, *and* Clyde Kluckhohn.   How the Soviet System Works. Cambridge, Harvard University Press, 1956. 274 p.
See also entry no. 105.
Emphasis is on the "operating characteristics" of the system and their impact, but attention is given also to institutional contexts, basic personality structure, and the goals and problems of the Soviet leadership.

1150.* Berman, Harold J.   Justice in Russia; an Interpretation of Soviet Law. Cambridge, Harvard University Press, 1950. 322 p.
See also entry no. 569.
A historical and analytical account, tracing the origins and special features of Soviet law and paying particular attention to the matter of how law has served the purposes of the Party as a socializing as well as a control agency.

1151. Bruford, Walter H.   Chekhov and His Russia; a Sociological Study. London, K. Paul, Trench, Trubner, 1947. 233 p. Bibliography.
See also entry no. 1484.
The writing of Chekhov is used as a primary source of information about Russian society, affording chapters on the peasant, the landowner, the official class, the church, etc. The results, tempered and enhanced by reference to historians' and travelers' accounts, are quite evocative.

1152. Cherniavsky, Michael.   Tsar and People; Studies in Russian Myths. New Haven, Yale University Press, 1961. 258 p.
Myths and sacred symbols are traced through Russian history in relation to political and social developments. The treatment of myths and myth-making includes the Christlike "Blessed Tsar," "Holy Russia," and the "Russian soul."

1153.* Đilas (Djilas), Milovan.   The New Class; an Analysis of the Communist System. New York, Praeger, 1957. 214 p.
Characterization of contemporary Communist society, with special reference to the USSR and Yugoslavia, in terms of its shortcomings when compared with the aspirations of democratic social-

ism. The keystone is seen as the "new ruling class" — the Communist Party bureaucracy.

1154. Fitzsimmons, Thomas, *and others*. USSR; Its People, Its Society, Its Culture. New Haven, HRAF Press, 1960. 590 p. Illus., maps. Bibliography: p. 521-548.
See also entries no. 51 and 92.
   A comprehensive survey which also manages to give a good deal of attention to informal patterns of value and behavior.

1155. Fülöp-Miller, René. The Mind and Face of Bolshevism; an Examination of Cultural Life in Soviet Russia. Translated from the German by F. S. Flint and D. F. Tait. New York, London, Knopf, 1928. 433 p. Plates, ports.
Bibliography: p. 411-421.
See also entry no. 1808.
   A broad canvas of cultural and social life in the NEP period, with particular attention to the arts. Bolshevism is treated as a "new way of life or a new religion." Translation of *Geist und Gesicht des Bolschewismus* (Zurich, Amalthea-Verlag, 1926, 490 p.)

1156. Gibian, George. Interval of Freedom; Soviet Literature during the Thaw, 1954-1957. Minneapolis, University of Minnesota Press, 1960. 180 p.
See also entry no. 1423.
   A record, with examples, of Soviet belletristic contributions and theoretical and political controversies in the period 1954-1957. Particular attention is given to the three topics which most preoccupied writers inclined toward genuine social criticism in this time: science and scientists, love and sexuality, and the traits of the "negative character" or literary villain. Valuable and rarely documented insights into the social realities of Soviet life are provided. Chapter five is on *Doctor Zhivago* and the Pasternak affair.

1157. Guins, George C. Communism on the Decline. New York, Philosophical Library, 1956. 287 p.
   A view of Soviet Communist society 40 years after the Revolution. The author concludes that the Communist social order has reached a stage of progressive decay: the regime's promises no longer raise enthusiasm, its achievements no longer satisfy the people, etc. A chapter entitled "Inner Conflicts" analyzes the dissensions within Soviet society.

1158.* Gunther, John. Inside Russia Today. Rev. ed. New York, Pyramid Publications, 1962. 604 p. Illus.
See also entry no. 94.
   A general survey of a large assortment of data plus personal observations. Probably the best and most readable journalistic portrait of its time. First published in 1958.

1159. Hindus, Maurice G.   House without a Roof; Russia after 43 Years of Revolution. Garden City, N.Y., Doubleday, 1961. 562 p. *See also* entry no. 164.

An up-to-date general survey with much useful information on social patterns, written by a man with an intimate knowledge of the people.

1160. Hindus, Maurice G.   Humanity Uprooted. Rev. ed. New York, Jonathan Cape and H. Smith, 1930. 369 p. *See also* entry no. 165.

A systematic interpretation of the "new civilization." The book went through 20 printings, 1929-1934.

1161. Inkeles, Alex.   Public Opinion in Soviet Russia; a Study in Mass Persuasion. Cambridge, Harvard University Press, 1958. 393 p. *See also* entries no. 1013 and 1739.

How the Soviet regime has used the mass media for its own purposes. Particularly valuable for its concise description of the Bolshevik view of public opinion in relation to the role of the Party, and for its analysis of personal oral agitation and radio broadcasting as devices of mass persuasion and control. Earlier edition: 1950, 379 p.

1162. Inkeles, Alex, *and* Kent Geiger, *eds.*   Soviet Society; a Book of Readings. Boston, Houghton Mifflin, 1961. 703 p.

A collection of articles designed to give a coherent total picture of Soviet society.

1163. Inkeles, Alex, *and* Raymond A. Bauer.   The Soviet Citizen; Daily Life in a Totalitarian Society. Cambridge, Harvard University Press, 1959. 533 p. *See also* entry no. 110.

Social psychological data gathered from Soviet refugees, with a general interpretation of Soviet man and society. Virtually the only substantial volume making use of modern sociological research methods to study informal patterns of behavior and belief.

1164.*Maynard, *Sir* John.   Russia in Flux. Foreword by Sir Bernard Pares. New York, Macmillan, 1948. 564 p. *See also* entries no. 97 and 270.

A reprint of the author's *Russia in Flux: Before October* (London, Gollancz, 1941, 301 p.), and the "main substance" of his *The Russian Peasant, and Other Studies* (London, Gollancz, 1942, 512 p.). This book is a landmark, a sympathetic interpretation of the Soviet scene with a great deal of intellectual and social history woven in, by a man well acquainted with Tsarist Russia.

1165.*Mehnert, Klaus.   Soviet Man and His World. Translated from the German by Maurice Rosenbaum. New York, Praeger, 1962. 310 p. *See also* entry no. 173.

An authoritative topical account stressing everyday life and what it means to the individual to live in the USSR. Probably as objective a survey of Soviet society as can be found. Translation of *Der Sowjetmensch* (Stuttgart, Deutsche Verlags-Anstalt, 1958, 497 p.)

1166.* Morton, Henry W.   Soviet Sport; Mirror of Soviet Society. New York, Collier Books, 1963. 221 p.

An examination of the organization of Soviet sport, its methods, and the role it plays in Soviet society.

1167.* Rostow, Walt W.   The Dynamics of Soviet Society. New York, Norton, 1953. 282 p.

See also entry no. 705.

A general survey giving special attention to sources of cohesion, tension, and instability. The central role of power and leadership is stressed.

1168.* Simmons, Ernest J., *ed.*   Through the Glass of Soviet Literature; Views of Russian Society. New York, Columbia University Press, 1953. 301 p.

See also entries no. 116 and 1438.

A series of essays in which Soviet belles lettres are used to investigate the changing role of women, and other subjects. In the introductory essay the editor sets forth the case for developing insights into Soviet social and psychological life by taking fictional literature as primary data.

1169. Smith, Robert E. F.   A Russian-English Dictionary of Social Science Terms. London, Butterworth, 1962. 495 p.

Several thousand words and terms in the fields of sociology, politics, economics, accounting, public administration, welfare, and education.

1170. Vakar, Nicholas P.   The Taproot of Soviet Society. New York, Harper, 1962. 204 p.

Soviet society is seen as greatly influenced by the "Third Russian Revolution," namely the infiltration of the Communist Party by a "peasant element." This occurrence reached a point of consolidation around 1938 and thenceforth the Communist leadership, headed by Stalin, a "true primitive," acted according to the peasant cultural heritage, rather than abstract ideology or middle-class culture. Many innovations are seen as a revival of "paternalistic relationships . . . borrowed from the traditional village and applied to the nation."

1171. Walkin, Jacob.   The Rise of Democracy in Pre-Revolutionary Russia; Political and Social Institutions under the Last Three Czars. New York, Praeger, 1962. 320 p. Bibliography.

See also entries no. 535 and 625.

An interpretation of the interplay between the state and the politically important institutions of society, giving a good picture of Tsarist social structure in terms of social classes, voluntary associations, and other sociological categories. Bolshevism and the Soviet order are seen as an "aberration in Russian constitutional history . . . finding its origin in the unique situation arising out of Russia's participation in World War I."

1172. Webb, Sidney, *and* Beatrice Webb.   Soviet Communism: a New Civilization? London, New York, Longmans, Green, 1935. 2 v. *See also* entry no. 712.

A classic and detailed study of Soviet institutional and cultural innovations in terms of Soviet-approved viewpoints.

2. National Character, Social Types, Human Relations

1173. Bauer, Raymond A.   Nine Soviet Portraits. New York, Wiley, 1955. 190 p.

Soviet social types and life experiences, based on refugee accounts and organized into quasi-fictitious portraits of a Party secretary, factory manager, housewife, etc.

1174.* Cantril, Hadley.   Soviet Leaders and Mastery over Man. New Brunswick, N. J., Rutgers University Press, 1960. 173 p.

Discusses the assumptions made by Soviet leaders about human nature, as well as techniques and rationale for manipulation and guidance of public opinion and effort. Also a discussion of weaknesses and problems linked with Soviet assumptions about man, and recent accommodation and relaxation in regard to some of them.

1175. Dicks, Henry V.   Observations on Contemporary Russian Behavior. Human Relations (London), v. 5, 1952: 111-175.

Report by a British psychiatrist of his clinical examinations of postwar refugees, documenting basic character trends and conflicts, and showing in particular the divergence between the officially desired personality type and that which is modal. Also good on the emotions and images generated among the people by the behavior of their rulers.

1176.* Gorer, Geoffrey, *and* John Rickman.   The People of Great Russia; a Psychological Study. New York, Chanticleer Press, 1950; London, Cresset Press, 1949. 235 p. *See also* entry no. 108.

The statement of the swaddling hypothesis: an attempt to link Soviet adult behavior and socio-cultural institutions to the custom of swaddling infants. The first part, by Rickman, tells of his experiences and impressions among the peasantry in 1916-1918. New edition: New York, Norton, 1962.

1177. Leites, Nathan C.   A Study of Bolshevism. Glencoe, Ill., The Free Press, 1953. 639 p.
Bibliography: p. 630-634.
See also entry no. 723.

An assessment of the code of behavior and character structure of the Bolshevik leadership, based on a psychoanalytic interpretation of literature and political documents. Bolsheviks are interpreted as reacting against the preoccupations of the nineteenth-century intelligentsia; much of the unique content of their behavior can be traced to defenses against the fear of death and the fear of passive homosexual impulses. Submergence in the Party, for example, is seen as a defense against the fear of death.

1178. Mead, Margaret, *and* Rhoda Métraux, *eds.*   The Study of Culture at a Distance. Chicago, University of Chicago Press, 1953. 480 p.

Selected documentary and theoretical materials on cultural images and themes and on psychological characteristics of Great Russians: the swaddling hypothesis; Russian sensory images; and analysis of the content of cultural products, folklore, films, etc.

1179.* Miller, Wright W.   Russians as People. New York, Dutton, 1961; London, Phoenix House, 1960. 205 p.
See also entry no. 113.

An analysis of the Russian national character, based on observations made on several visits and on a general familiarity with Russian and Soviet history. Considerable stress is placed on the collectivist or communal spirit.

1180. Novak, Joseph (*pseud.*)   "The Future Is Ours, Comrade!": Conversations with the Russians. Introduction by Irving R. Levine. Garden City, N.Y., Doubleday, 1960. 286 p.
See also entry no. 174.

A down-to-earth account of everyday, as well as more exalted, Soviet citizens and their experiences and opinions, with much quoted material. The author, who writes under a pseudonym, is an East European who paid an extended visit to the USSR about five years after Stalin's death. Full of interesting ideas and good insight and analysis, but of suggestive rather than solid scholarly value.

1181. Rogger, Hans.   National Consciousness in Eighteenth-Century Russia. Cambridge, Harvard University Press, 1960. 319 p.
Bibliography: p. 285-295.
See also entries no. 505 and 1574.

An effort to delineate national consciousness, "striving for common identity, character and culture by the articulate members of a given community," as expressed in Russian letters of the time. Valuable for the light it sheds on the developing attitudes toward the West, the origin of adoration of the plain folk, and other components of the Russian ethos.

1182. Winter, Ella.   Red Virtue; Human Relationships in the New Russia. New York, Harcourt, Brace, 1933. 332 p.
Bibliography: p. 319-324.
> A general survey, with emphasis on manners, morals, personal relations, art, and cultural life. Many revealing excerpts from the author's interviews with Soviet officials and ordinary people.

3. Social Strata

1183. Bill, Valentine T.   The Forgotten Class; the Russian Bourgeoisie from the Earliest Beginnings to 1900. New York, Praeger, 1959. 229 p.
> A topical history of the commercial and industrial middle classes which seeks to fill an important gap in Russian social history and to redress the distorted picture of this social level gained from the writings of the nineteenth-century intelligentsia. There is a chapter on the Morozov family, one on the nineteenth-century way of life, and one on the possible link between economic discipline and the religious zeal of the Old Believers.

1184. Blum, Jerome.   Lord and Peasant in Russia from the Ninth to the Nineteenth Century. Princeton, Princeton University Press, 1961. 656 p.
Bibliography: p. 623-645.
See also entries no. 476 and 1022.
> The first complete history in English of the Russian peasantry to the nineteenth century, with a considerable amount of material on the gentry. Especially strong on social and economic history.

1185. Borders, Karl.   Village Life under the Soviets. New York, Vanguard Press, 1927. 191 p.
> A sympathetic view of what peasant and village looked like during the NEP period by an American relief worker who spent almost three years there in the mid-twenties.

1186. Dallin, David J.   The Changing World of Soviet Russia. New Haven, Yale University Press, 1956. 422 p.
Bibliography: p. 396-403.
> Part one, "Social Revolution in Russia," contains a detailed analysis of the Soviet class structure as of 1930, in comparison with the Russia of the pre-World War I era. A general interpretation of the Soviet system in terms of its principal institutional complexes, state economy, political dictatorship, and its class system is offered. The intelligentsia is seen as destined to play a decisive role in introducing internal social changes.

1187. Leroy-Beaulieu, Anatole.   The Empire of the Tsars and the Russians. Translated from the third French edition by Zenaïde A. Ragozin. New York, London, Putnam, 1893-1896. 3 v. (588, 566, 601 p.)
See also entries no. 133, 530, and 619.

Useful for accurate information on the society and many other aspects of the Tsarist order. Volume one has sections on the "Social Hierarchy," "Peasantry and Emancipation," "*Mir*, Family and Village Communities," etc. Translation of *L'empire des tsars et les russes* (Paris, Hachette, 1881-1889, 3 v.)

1188. Pipes, Richard, *ed.*   The Russian Intelligentsia. New York, Columbia University Press, 1961. 234 p.
See also entries no. 1571 and 1783.

Essays on pre-Soviet Russian and Soviet intellectuals. Several of the articles deal with the social composition and attitudes of special groups, e.g., writers, university students. Reprinted from *Daedalus*, v. 89, Summer 1960.

1189. Kravchinskii, Sergei M. (*pseud.* Sergius Stepniak).   The Russian Peasantry; Their Agrarian Condition, Social Life, and Religion. London, Swan, Sonnenschein; New York, Harper, 1888. 401 p.
See also entry no. 131.

An essay stressing the worsening plight of the peasantry and arguing that only socialism could solve their problems.

1190. Robinson, Geroid T.   Rural Russia under the Old Régime. New York, Longmans, Green, 1932. 342 p.
Bibliography: p. 312-326.
See also entries no. 520 and 1091.

A scholarly study of the history and role of the peasant, an invaluable background for an understanding of the revolution of 1917. Reissued: New York, Macmillan, 1949.

1191. Voinov, Nicholas (*pseud.*)   The Waif. New York, Pantheon, 1955. 291 p.

Autobiography of an orphan in the USSR who joined up with homeless children and young criminals. Excellent worms-eye view of life in Stalin's Russia as experienced by a real "down-and-outer," who somehow emerged from it well enough off to write this book.

1192.* Wallace, *Sir* Donald M.   Russia. Rev. and enl. ed. London, New York, Cassell, 1912. 788 p.
See also entries no. 148, 275, and 529.

A famous work on the people and institutions of Tsarist Russia at the turn of the century by a keen British traveler, with especially good material on peasant life.

4. Occupational Strata

1193. Ashby, Eric.   Scientist in Russia. New York, Penguin Books, 1947. 252 p.
See also entry no. 1769.

The organization of science and the personal experiences of an Australian scientist.

1194. Belov, Fedor.   The History of a Soviet Collective Farm. New York, Praeger, 1955. 237 p. (East European Fund. Research Program on the USSR. Studies, no. 13)
See also entry no. 1084.

> The author was chairman of the kolkhoz about which he writes from 1947 through 1949. The account is both historical and analytical, especially valuable for its depiction of grass roots administrative behavior. The first chapter has a succinct sketch of both "dekulakization" and collectivization. The main themes are exploitation from above, and theft, bribery, "every man for himself" on the grass roots level.

1195. Berliner, Joseph S.   Factory and Manager in the USSR. Cambridge, Harvard University Press, 1957. 386 p.
Bibliography: p. 337-345.
See also entry no. 1095.

> How middle-level industrial personnel conduct their work in a planned economy and a totalitarian polity. Rewards, punishments, conditions of work, and informal adaptive mechanisms such as *blat* in the individual enterprise, with special attention to the factory manager.

1196. Bienstock, Gregory, Solomon M. Schwartz, *and* Aaron Yugow. Management in Russian Industry and Agriculture. New York, Oxford University Press, 1944. 198 p.
See also entry no. 1096.

> Good for its analysis of conflicting forces in decision-making, and also valuable for its treatment of collective farms and their managers.

1197. Granick, David.   Management of the Industrial Firm in the USSR. New York, Columbia University Press, 1954. 346 p.
Bibliography: p. 305-328.
See also entry no. 1100.

> Assessment of the role of the manager and the effectiveness of bureaucratic organization in Soviet industry in the period 1934-1941. One of the conclusions is that Soviet heavy industry is less "bureaucratic" than some of the giant firms in capitalist societies. Another is that the factory manager has retained considerable autonomy in decision-making.

1198.* Granick, David.   The Red Executive; a Study of the Organization Man in Russian Industry. Garden City, N.Y., Doubleday, 1960. 334 p.

> Wide-ranging and comparative with the U.S.A., this book treats industry, factory life, managers, education, and other topics.

1199. Pondoev, Gavriil S.   Notes of a Soviet Doctor.   2d rev. and enl. ed. Translated from the Russian by Basil Haigh. New York, Consultants Bureau, 1959. 238 p.

A handbook for young Soviet doctors, written in didactic style by an "honored physician" of the Georgian SSR. Chapter titles include "The Vocation of the Doctor," "At the Patient's Bedside," "The Doctor's Mistakes," "The Quack," etc.

1200. Scott, John.   Behind the Urals; an American Worker in Russia's City of Steel. Boston, Houghton Mifflin, 1942. 279 p.
See also entry no. 181.

An account of experiences undergone by the author, between 1932 and 1937, while helping to build up the steel center of Magnitogorsk. A vivid, firsthand picture of his life and observations as electric welder, foreman, chemist, and husband of a Russian girl. As close to life itself, with all its turmoil, enthusiasm, and sacrifice, as anything available for the period.

1201. Vucinich, Alexander S.   The Soviet Academy of Sciences. Stanford, Calif., Stanford University Press, 1956. 157 p.
Bibliography: p. 143-150.
See also entry no. 1795.

Science and scientists and how they fit with the Soviet system, in the form of an intensive analysis of the center of organized research. A historical as well as analytical study.

1202. Vucinich, Alexander S.   Soviet Economic Institutions. Stanford, Calif., Stanford University Press, 1952. 150 p.
Bibliography: p. 138-150.
See also entry no. 1055.

Description of the basic Soviet production units, factory, MTS, state farm, collective farm, and urban producers' cooperatives. The emphasis is on the central hierarchies and on the methods used to ensure that they follow the directions set by plan.

5. Women and Family

1203. Elnett, Elaine P.   Historic Origin and Social Development of Family Life in Russia. New York, Columbia University Press, 1926. 151 p.

This study of family life is divided into two periods — the primitive era before Peter the Great, and the modern era ushered in by his reign. The third part is an effort to capture custom, folklore, and wit, through examples of Russian proverbs.

1204. Halle, Fannina W.   Woman in Soviet Russia. Translated from the German. London, Routledge, 1934. 409 p.

Women, sexual and family relations, the abolition of prostitution, etc. A lively and thorough survey by a Russian-born and Russian-speaking Austrian. Translation of *Die Frau in Sowjetrussland* (Berlin, P. Zsolnay, 1932, 567 p.)

For a recent French treatment, *see* André Pierre's *Les femmes en Union Soviétique* (Paris, Spes, 1960, 314 p.)

1205. Halle, Fannina W.   Women in the Soviet East. Translated from the German by Margaret M. Green. London, Secker and Warburg; New York, Dutton, 1938. 363 p.

A valuable account, with much case material, of the changing position of women in the Islamic areas of the USSR. Emphasis is on the changing pattern of daily life and the resistance to it on the part of men, older people, and the *mullahs*. Translation of *Frauen des Ostens* (Zurich, Europa-Verlag, 1938, 319 p.)

1206. Kingsbury, Susan M., *and* Mildred Fairchild.   Factory, Family and Women in the Soviet Union. New York, Putnam, 1935. 334 p.

A survey emphasizing the institutions and patterns clustering around work and domestic life, written by two Bryn Mawr professors who were in the USSR in 1929-1930 and in 1932. Relatively non-critical and with some surprising omissions and unsound generalizations, it is nevertheless a useful source of information on Soviet institutions of the time.

1207. Le Play, Pierre G. F.   Les ouvriers européens. 2d ed., v. 2. Paris, A. Mame et fils, 1877. 560 p.
See also entry no. 268.

Five chapters, pages 1-230, are on worker and peasant family life in Tsarist Russia, with good descriptions of everyday patterns and special attention to budgets.

1208. Mace, David R., *and* Vera Mace.   The Soviet Family. Garden City, N. Y., Doubleday, 1963. 367 p.

A sympathetic account, based in part on a tour of inquiry made by the authors. Chapters on sex, the "new Soviet woman," marriage, divorce, the housing situation, etc.

1209. Schlesinger, Rudolf, *ed.*   Changing Attitudes in Soviet Russia; Documents and Readings. v. 1: The Family. London, Routledge and Paul, 1949. 408 p.
See also entry no. 591.

Translations of family law and important Soviet writings, with an essay by the editor.

1210. Serebrennikov, Georgii N.   The Position of Women in the USSR. London, Gollancz, 1937. 288 p.

The official Soviet version of what happened to women as a result of the Revolution and in the two decades after it. Advances in the political, economic, social, physical health, and other domains are discussed, with a good deal of statistical evidence adduced.

1211. Smith, Jessica.   Woman in Soviet Russia. New York, Vanguard Press, 1928. 216 p.

A sympathetic, if not enthusiastic, depiction of the position of women, the family, housing conditions, "revolutionary morality," etc., by an American who spent several years in Russia in the 1920's.

6. Children and Youth

1212. Institut zur Erforschung der UdSSR.   Youth in Ferment. Munich, Institute for the Study of the USSR, 1962. 101 p.

Fourteen essays by émigré scholars on the psychological unrest found in the Soviet younger generation. The essays are based on analysis of Soviet literary and periodical materials.

1213. Meek, Dorothea L., *ed. and trans.*   Soviet Youth; Some Achievements and Problems; Excerpts from the Soviet Press. London, Routledge and Paul, 1957. 251 p.

Forty articles appearing in the Soviet press during the decade preceding publication and treating various aspects of the interest of Soviet authorities in children and young people.

1214. Mehnert, Klaus.   Youth in Soviet Russia. Translated from the German by Michael Davidson. New York, Harcourt, Brace, 1933. 270 p.

The life and atmosphere of youth, from the firsthand impressions of this correspondent and scholar. Translation of *Die Jugend in Sowjetrussland* (Berlin, S. Fischer, 1932, 273 p.)

1215. Zenzinov, Vladimir M.   Deserted: the Story of the Children Abandoned in Soviet Russia. Translated from the Russian by Agnes Pratt. London, H. Joseph, 1931. 216 p.

A classic story of one group of the Revolution's victims. The information comes mainly from Soviet sources, but the author is very critical of the regime's efforts to deal with the problem. Translation of *Bezprizornye* (Paris, Sovremennyia Zapiski, 1929, 318 p.)

7. Medicine, Health, Welfare, Insurance, Housing, Social Security

1216. Alt, Herschel, *and* Edith Alt.   Russia's Children; a First Report on Child Welfare in the Soviet Union. New York, Bookman Associates, 1959. 240 p.
See also entry no. 1716.

The report of what two social workers were able to find out in a summer visit. The authors discuss discipline, the child and his family, education, health services, delinquency, etc., and also carefully, and sometimes amusingly, record the obstacles they met in their efforts to investigate the Soviet Union's program for its children.

1217. Field, Mark G.   Approaches to Mental Illness in Soviet Society:

Some Comparisons and Conjectures. Social Problems, v. 7, no. 4, Spring 1960: 277-297.

> Nature and size of the problem, facilities available, and methods of treatment are compared for the Soviet Union and the United States, and an assessment is made of some links between types of society and aspects of mental illness.

1218. Field, Mark G.   Doctor and Patient in Soviet Russia. Cambridge, Harvard University Press, 1957. 266 p.

> Sociological analysis of the medical profession and its role in the Soviet social system, greatly enriched by interview and questionnaire data from Soviet refugees.

1219. Gordon, Manya.   Workers before and after Lenin. New York, Dutton, 1941. 524 p.

> A careful and informed comparison of the fate of the workers under the tsar and under the Soviet order. It is concluded that in terms of wages, living standards, and in most other respects, they were better off before the Revolution.

1220. Haines, Anna J.   Health Work in Soviet Russia. New York, Vanguard Press, 1928. 177 p.

> A standard account of the scene in terms of the work of the Commissariat of Health in the 1920's, by an American who represented the Red Cross and the American Friends' Service Committee.

1221. Kovrigina, Mariia D., *ed.*   Forty Years of Soviet Public Health. New York, U. S. Joint Publications Research Service, 1959. 139 p. (JPRS Report no. 880-D)

> Articles on various branches of Soviet medicine and public health by Mme. Kovrigina, then Minister of Public Health, and others. A partial translation of *Sorok let sovetskogo zdravookhraneniia; k 40-letiiu Velikoi Oktiabr'skoi sotsialisticheskoi revoliutsii, 1917-1957* (Forty Years of Soviet Public Health; on the Fortieth Anniversary of the Great October Socialist Revolution, 1917-1957; Moscow, Medgiz, 1957, 661 p.)

1222. Maistrakh, Ksenia V.   The Organization of Public Health in the USSR. Translated by the U.S. Joint Publications Research Service. Washington, U.S. Department of Health, Education and Welfare, 1959. 200 p.

> Principles and history of public health, medical and vital statistics, organization of medical-prophylactic facilities, education in hygiene, financing of public health, etc. Translation of *Organizatsiia zdravookhraneniia* (4th ed.; Moscow, Medgiz, 1956, 266 p.)

1223. Parkins, Maurice F.   City Planning in Soviet Russia, with an Interpretative Bibliography. Chicago, University of Chicago Press, 1953. 257 p.

History of city planning in the USSR by stages ("initial," 1922-1931; "transitional," 1931-1944; and "reconstruction," 1944-1950), planning principles, and the structure of administration, research, and training. A very substantial annotated bibliography, pages 127-240.

1224. Sigerist, Henry E.   Medicine and Health in the Soviet Union. New York, Citadel Press, 1947. 364 p.

The standard "sociological study" of Soviet socialized medicine, stressing principles, administrative structure, and historical and social perspective. The book is strong on Soviet achievements and weak on Soviet shortcomings.

Originally published as *Socialized Medicine in the Soviet Union* (New York, Norton, 1937, 378 p.)

1225. Sosnovy, Timothy.   The Housing Problem in the Soviet Union. New York, Research Program on the USSR, 1954. 300 p.
Bibliography: p. 277-290.
See also entry no. 1128.

A historical and descriptive account in which Soviet sources are analyzed to demonstrate the steady deterioration of urban housing which the Soviet leaders have allowed to occur.

1226. U.S. *Public Health Mission to the Union of Soviet Socialist Republics.*   Report of the United States Public Health Mission to the Union of Soviet Socialist Republics. Washington, U.S. Department of Health, Education and Welfare, 1959. 67 p.
See also entry no. 1765.

Impressions of medicine and public health from the Mission's tour in 1957. Important for the conscious effort made by the five team members to give a critical and comparative evaluation of what they found.

1227. U.S. *Social Security Administration.*   A Report on Social Security Programs in the Soviet Union. Washington, U.S. Department of Health, Education and Welfare, 1960. 157 p.

A result of observations and discussions with Soviet officials by an American team of social security experts during a visit to the USSR, August–September 1958. Includes information about pensions; sickness, maternity, industrial injury and disease benefits; determination of disability for disablement programs; etc.

1228. World Health Organization.   Health Services in the USSR; Report Prepared by Participants in a Study Tour. Geneva, 1960. 58 p. (Public Health Papers, no. 3)

A general survey by representatives of 21 countries and territories who visited the USSR in October 1958. A relatively accurate, impartial, and useful, though quite brief, appraisal.

8. Psychology and Psychiatry

1229. Bauer, Raymond A.   The New Man in Soviet Psychology. Cambridge, Harvard University Press, 1952. 229 p.
See also entries no. 104 and 1719.

A discussion of what happened to psychology as an academic discipline. Traces the interaction of psychology, the emerging forces in Soviet society, and the needs of the Soviet leadership. Also shows how Marxist determinism gave way to Stalinist voluntarism.

1230. Bauer, Raymond A., *ed.*   Some Views on Soviet Psychology. Washington, D.C., American Psychological Association, 1962. 285 p.

Eight essays on different aspects of Soviet psychological work and theory by eight noted American psychologists. An introductory essay by Alexander Mintz offers historical perspective and a broad overview of recent developments. The intent of the volume, like that of the 1960 exchange visits from which the participants gained much of the information for their essays, is to open up communication between American and Soviet psychology.

1231. Lustig, Bruno.   Therapeutic Methods in Soviet Psychiatry. New York, Fordham University, 1963. 63 p.

Originally appeared as *Berichte des Osteuropa-Instituts an der Freien Universität Berlin,* Heft 51.

1232. Monnerot, Jules.   Sociology and Psychology of Communism. Translated from the French by Jane Degras and Richard Rees. Boston, Beacon Press, 1953. 339 p.
See also entries no. 727 and 1599.

The development of Bolshevism is treated as a "twentieth century 'Islam'." Also discussed are the nature and sources of twentieth-century totalitarianism, a "secular religion," and its influence on the West.

Translation of part one of *Sociologie du communisme* (Paris, Gallimard, 1949, 510 p.)

1233. Simon, Brian, *and* Joan Simon, *eds.*   Educational Psychology in the USSR. Stanford, Calif., Stanford University Press, 1963. 283 p.
See also entry no. 1759.

Translations of recent works on the psychology of learning by leading Soviet psychologists. Topics include the relation between learning and development; the nature of concept formation and problem solving; and conditions bearing on the formation of skills and habits, etc.

1234. Wortis, Joseph.   Soviet Psychiatry. Baltimore, Williams and Wilkins, 1950. 314 p.
See also entry no. 118.

An admiring and often overly enthusiastic discussion, to be read with caution.

9. Social Problems

1235. Callcott, Mary S. Russian Justice. New York, Macmillan, 1935. 265 p.

Soviet crime and judicial and penal systems as they appeared to an American criminologist who made tours of prisons and courts in the USSR. The generally quite favorable impressions of the author are based on her reliance on official publications, interviews with Vyshinsky, etc.

1236. Koerber, Helene (Lenka von). Soviet Russia Fights Crime. Translated from the German. London, Routledge, 1934; New York, Dutton, 1935. 240 p.

A very favorable account of prison conditions and reform treatment by a German who visited many prisons in all parts of the USSR in 1932.

Translation of *Sowjetrussland kämpft gegen das Verbrechen* (Berlin, Rowohlt, 1933, 212 p.)

1237. Symposium on Social Problems in the Soviet Union. Social Problems, v. 7, no. 4, Spring 1960.

Articles by specialists on a variety of social problems — mental illness, alcoholism, etc., and Soviet methods of combating them.

10. Social Change

1238. Black, Cyril E., *ed.* The Transformation of Russian Society; Aspects of Social Change since 1861. Cambridge, Harvard University Press, 1960. 695 p.
See also entries no. 107 and 681.

A variety of papers written by specialists for a conference held in 1958. The main theme, social change, is treated from several perspectives, and the efforts of the contributors are summarized and enhanced by review articles from leading scholars of Soviet affairs at the end of each section. Professor Black also contributed a useful introduction and conclusion.

1239.* Brumberg, Abraham, *ed.* Russia under Khrushchev; an Anthology from Problems of Communism. New York, Praeger, 1962. 660 p.
See also entry no. 682.

A selection of articles originally published in *Problems of Communism*, published by the U.S. Information Agency, and treating internal developments and trends during the Khrushchev era.

1240.* Crankshaw, Edward. Khrushchev's Russia. Baltimore, Penguin Books, 1959. 175 p.

An imaginative interpretation of the historical role of Stalin and his posthumous dethronement in the Soviet system. The author argues that Stalin's ironhanded methods became outmoded, that he died "in the nick of time," and that the reforms of the past decade have been substantial and permanent.

1241.*Deutscher, Isaac.   The Great Contest; Russia and the West. New York, London, Oxford University Press, 1960. 86 p.
See also entry no. 910.

> Post-Stalinist developments, the mood in the USSR, and implications for the future. Mr. Deutscher here develops further his thesis that the contemporary USSR is now on the way toward a truly "democratic-socialist" society, from the point of view of both personal freedom and material welfare, and predicts further far-reaching political and social reforms. This evolution is seen as an embodiment of the original Marxist-Socialist dream.

1242. Deutscher, Isaac.   Russia: What Next? New York, Oxford University Press, 1953. 230 p.

> An analysis and forecast of the breakup of Stalinism, with an inevitable trend toward democracy posited. The author's frame of reference is quite heavily deterministic in the Marxist tradition: the new conditions, especially technological development plus socialist institutions, make Stalinism outmoded.

1243.*Deutscher, Isaac.   Russia in Transition, and Other Essays. New York, Coward-McCann, 1957. 245 p.
See also entry no. 685.

> Fourteen essays and reviews, on various topics. Several of them deal directly or peripherally with the author's view of how to interpret the post-Stalin changes. The key concept is "bureaucratic self-determination," by which Stalin's successors instituted de-Stalinization. The "twilight of totalitarianism" is his term for the present period, and the USSR is seen as approaching "the formation of a new political consciousness . . . and the inception or regeneration of a spontaneous mass movement."
> Revised edition: New York, Grove Press, 1960, 265 p.

1244. Laqueur, Walter Z., *and* Leopold Labedz, *eds*.   The Future of Communist Society. New York, Praeger, 1962. 196 p.
See also entry no. 722.

> A collection of articles analyzing the CPSU Program of 1961 from various points of view.

1245. Moore, Barrington, Jr.   Soviet Politics: the Dilemma of Power. Cambridge, Harvard University Press, 1950. 503 p.
Bibliography: p. 467-485.
See also entry no. 728.

> An account of what happened to the pre-Revolutionary ideology of the Bolsheviks after they gained power. In general, a wide-ranging treatment of social change from a sociological perspective.

1246. Moore, Barrington, Jr.   Terror and Progress, USSR: Some Sources of Change and Stability in the Soviet Dictatorship. Cambridge, Harvard University Press, 1954. 261 p.
See also entry no. 114.

The Soviet system is seen in terms of areas of tension, and of its strengths and weak points, with discussions of the polity, industry, agriculture, and the arts. A final chapter sets out a forecast for the future.

1247. Timasheff, Nicholas S.   The Great Retreat; the Growth and Decline of Communism in Russia. New York, Dutton, 1946. 470 p.

A sociological interpretation of the drastic shift in Soviet policy in the 1930's. One of the few efforts to deal sociologically with the changing make-up of Soviet society. In general, change is interpreted as the working out of conflict between the traditional culture and society and the new institutions and plans of the Bolsheviks. Developments since Stalin's death have suggested that the story is not yet finished.

1248. Tomašić, Dinko A.   The Impact of Russian Culture on Soviet Communism. Glencoe, Ill., Free Press, 1953. 287 p.

Among the influences discussed are the nomads from the Eurasian steppes, the Byzantine Church, the village community, and the intelligentsia. Events, ideologies, and characteristic patterns of personality development have all contributed toward making contemporary Soviet Russia what it is — a land characterized by economic dependency and regimentation, and political conformity.

1249. Trotskii, Lev (Leon Trotsky).   The Revolution Betrayed. What Is the Soviet Union and Where Is It Going? Translated by Max Eastman. Garden City, N.Y., Doubleday, Doran, 1937. 308 p.
See also entry no. 661.

A critical account of the economic, social, cultural, and political developments through 1935, with special attention to "contradictions," the new bureaucratic upper class, and mistakes made by Stalin and colleagues. Also interesting for its critique of the work of Sidney and Beatrice Webb (*see* entries no. 712 and 1172).

IX

the intellectual and cultural life

A. LANGUAGE [1]

by Boris O. Unbegaun

1. Bibliography

1250. Unbegaun, Boris O., *with the collaboration of* John S. G. Simmons. A Bibliographical Guide to the Russian Language. Oxford, Clarendon Press, 1953. 174 p.

> A fully annotated, critical, and selective bibliography of 1,073 works dealing with all aspects of the Russian language, modern and old.

1251. Hille, Annemarie. Bibliographische Einführung in das Studium der slawischen Philologie. Halle (Saale), VEB Max Niemeyer Verlag, 1959. 149 p.

> An unannotated bibliography of Slavic philology which includes a section on Russian linguistics (pages 50-61).

1252. Rocznik slawistyczny; Revue slavistique. 1908– Cracow.

> Each volume contains an annotated bibliography of works on Slavic linguistics. Does not cover the period from 1918 to 1928.

[1] Arrangement is by order of emphasis.

Fairly exhaustive; omissions are insignificant in the more recent volumes.

1253. Permanent International Committee of Linguists. Bibliographie linguistique. Utrecht, Antwerp, Spectrum, 1949–
>   The first volume covers the years 1939-1947. A reasonably complete, general bibliography which includes Russian material.
>   *See also* the bibliography in volume one of *Current Trends in Linguistics*, edited by Thomas A. Sebeok (The Hague, Mouton, 1963, 606 p.)

1254. Indogermanisches Jahrbuch.   v. 1-55. 1914-1955. Strassburg, Berlin, Leipzig, Berlin.
>   An annotated bibliography of Indo-European linguistics. Covers publications of the years 1912 to 1948. Though not exhaustive, it omits nothing of importance.

1255. Revue des études slaves.   1921– Paris, Institut d'Études Slaves de l'Université de Paris. annual.
>   *See also* entries no. 38 and 1535.
>   Each volume contains a bibliographical survey which covers all the more important publications.

2. Modern Russian Language

a. General description and grammar

1256. Unbegaun, Boris O.   Russian Grammar. Oxford, Clarendon Press, 1962. 319 p.
>   A concise analytical and descriptive grammar. The material is presented according to grammatical categories and special attention is paid to inflection and word formation.

1257. Whitfield, Francis J.   A Russian Reference Grammar. Cambridge, Harvard University Press, 1944. 222 p.
>   Provides full lists of words arranged in classes according to accent and morphological characteristics.

1258. Mazon, André.   Grammaire de la langue russe. 4th ed., revised with the assistance of José Johannet and Jacques Lépissier. Paris, Institut d'Études Slaves, 1963. 368 p.
>   A well-balanced grammar, which discusses the verb in great detail. Includes an elementary treatment of syntax and word formation. Earlier edition: 1949, 301 p.

1259. Isačenko, Aleksandr V.   Die russische Sprache der Gegenwart. Part I: Formenlehre. Halle (Saale), VEB Max Niemeyer Verlag, 1962. 706 p.
>   An original, full, and stimulating description of Russian morphology. The structure of Russian is compared throughout with that of German.

1260. Forbes, Nevill.   Russian Grammar. rev. 2d ed. Oxford, Clarendon Press, 1916. 275 p.
>Gives a sound but not very systematic description of the language. A new edition is in preparation.

1261. Forbes, Nevill.   Elementary Russian Grammar. 2d ed., revised by Elizabeth Hill. Oxford, Clarendon Press, 1943. 174 p.
>A shortened version of the author's *Russian Grammar* (*see* entry no. 1260).

1262. Semeonoff, Anna H.   A New Russian Grammar, in Two Parts. 13th rev. ed. London, J. M. Dent; New York, Dutton, 1960. 323 p.
>————. Key to A New Russian Grammar. London, J. M. Dent; New York, Dutton, 1959. 63 p.
>————. Russian Syntax, Being Part III of A New Russian Grammar. London, J. M. Dent; New York, Dutton, 1962. 251 p.
>A convenient textbook on traditional lines.

1263. Boyanus, Simon C., *and* N. B. Jopson.   Spoken Russian, a Practical Course; Written and Spoken Colloquial Russian with a Pronunciation, Intonation, Grammar, English Translation and Vocabulary. 3d ed. London, Sidgwick and Jackson, 1952. 366 p.
>A very thorough manual which is based on viva-voce instruction, special attention being paid to pronunciation and intonation. It is illustrated by 35 texts recorded by S. C. Boyanus on 12 HMV 78-rpm records.

1264. Lunt, Horace G.   Fundamentals of Russian; First Russian Course. The Hague, Mouton; New York, W. W. Norton, 1958. 320 p.
>An interesting attempt to introduce structural linguistics and phonemics into the practical teaching of Russian.

1265. Potapova, Nina F.   Russian; an Elementary Course. 4th ed. Moscow, Foreign Languages Publishing House, 1959. 2 v.
>A convenient practical manual.

1266.* Fennell, John L. I., *comp.*   The Penguin Russian Course; a Complete Course for Beginners. London, Penguin Books, 1961. 343 p.
>Based on Potapova's *Elementary Course* (*see* entry no. 1265), the textual material of which has been largely retained, while the explanations, grammatical rules, and exercises have been radically revised. One of the best introductory grammars.

b. Phonetics, pronunciation, and stress

1267. Halle, Morris.   The Sound Pattern of Russian; a Linguistic and Acoustical Investigation; with an Excursus on the Contextual Variants of the Russian Vowels, by Lawrence G. Jones. The Hague,

Mouton, 1959. 206 p. Plates. (Description and Analysis of Contemporary Standard Russian, 1)
Bibliography: p. 199-206.
> A thorough and scholarly investigation into the acoustic side of
> Russian speech.

1268. Fant, Gunnar.   Acoustic Theory of Speech Production; with Cal-
culations Based on X-Ray Studies of Russian Articulations. The
Hague, Mouton, 1960. 323 p. Plates. (Description and Analysis of
Contemporary Standard Russian, 2)
Bibliography: p. 313-323.
> A thorough description of Russian pronunciation on experimental
> lines.

1269. Jurgens Buning, J. E., *and* C. H. Van Schooneveld.   The Sentence
Intonation of Contemporary Standard Russian as a Linguistic Struc-
ture. The Hague, Mouton, 1961. 97 p. Tables. (Description and
Analysis of Contemporary Standard Russian, 3)
> An excellent analysis of Russian intonation by a linguist and a
> musicologist.

1270. Boyanus, Simon C.   Russian Pronunciation; the Russian System of
Speech Habits in Sounds, Stress, Rhythm, and Intonation, together
with a Russian Phonetic Reader. London, Lund Humphreys; Cambridge, Harvard University Press, 1955. 2 v. in 1.
> A convenient handbook which provides a concise and thorough
> treatment of the subject. Problems of intonation are given special
> attention.

1271. Ward, Dennis.   Russian Pronunciation; a Practical Course. Edinburgh, Oliver and Boyd, 1958. 90 p.
> An excellent and convenient guide to Russian pronunciation.

1272. Trofimov, Mikhail V., *and* Daniel Jones.   The Pronunciation of
Russian. Cambridge, England, The University Press, 1923. 252 p.
> An older, but still useful, description of Russian pronunciation.

1273. Trubetskoi (Trubetzkoy), Nikolai S.   Das morphonologische System der russischen Sprache. Prague, 1934. 94 p. (Travaux du Cercle
Linguistique de Prague, 5/2)
> Discusses Russian phonemics as a factor in the morphological
> system of the language.

1274. Kiparsky, Valentin.   Der Wortakzent der russischen Schriftsprache.
Heidelberg, Carl Winter Universitätsverlag, 1962. 396 p.
> A most useful study of stress in Russian words, which are classi-
> fied according to their grammatical and morphological character-
> istics. Historical evidence is adduced where available.

1275. Forsyth, James.   A Practical Guide to Russian Stress. Edinburgh, London, Oliver and Boyd, 1963. 160 p.

A convenient guide giving stress patterns in basic parts of speech and in suffixes, including those of proper names. Copious examples.

1276. Nahtigal (Nachtigall), Rajko.   Akzentbewegung in der russischen Form- und Wortbildung. I: Substantiva auf Konsonanten. Heidelberg, Carl Winter, 1922. 300 p. (Slavica, 7)

A historical and descriptive study dealing with mobile accent in Russian nouns ending in a consonant.

c. Morphology and syntax

1277. Dickenmann, Ernst.   Untersuchungen über die Nominalkomposition im Russischen. Part I: Einleitung und Material. Leipzig, Otto Harrassowitz, 1934. 377 p. (Veröffentlichungen des Slavischen Instituts an der Friedrich-Wilhelm-Universität Berlin, 12)

A comprehensive and well-arranged collection of compound nouns. Includes a bibliography.

1278. Daum, Edmund, *and* W. Schenk.   Die russischen Verben: Grundformen, Aspekte, Rektion, Betonung, deutsche Bedeutung. Mit einer Einführung in die Flexion und Aspektbildung des russischen Verbs von Rudolf Ruzicka. Leipzig, Bibliographisches Institut, 1954. 798 p.

A most useful reference book which includes an alphabetical list of about 14,000 Russian verbs with indication of their morphology, aspect, government, and stress. German translations of verbs are provided.

1279. Forbes, Nevill.   The Russian Verb, Being The Second Russian Book. Oxford, Clarendon Press, 1960. 336 p.

This is an offset reprint of the second edition of 1917. The book describes the structure of Russian verbs and illustrates their use by appropriate examples.

1280. Braun, Maximilian.   Das Kollektivum und das *Plurale tantum* im Russischen: ein bedeutungsgeschichtlicher Versuch. Leipzig, 1930. 119 p.

Discusses the semantic side of collectives and nouns which occur only in plural form.

1281. Mazon, André.   Emploi des aspects du verbe russe. Paris, Champion, 1914. 257 p. (Bibliothèque de l'Institut Français de Saint-Pétersbourg, 4)

The best and fullest collection of illustrative material on the use of the Russian aspects. Excellently annotated.

1282. Garde, Paul.   L'emploi du conditionnel et de la particule *by* en russe. Aix-en-Provence, Éditions Ophrys, 1963. 362 p. (Publications des Annales de la Faculté des Lettres d'Aix-en-Provence, nouvelle série, 36)

An excellent study of the expression of the conditional and the use of the particle *by* in modern Russian.

1283. Borras, F. M., *and* R. F. Christian.   Russian Syntax; Aspects of Modern Russian Syntax and Vocabulary. Oxford, Clarendon Press, 1959. 404 p.

The authors' aim was to help the student in translating Russian phrases and prepositional expressions into English. The book does not deal with the structure of the sentence.

d. Dictionaries and studies of vocabulary

1284. Lewanski, Richard C.   A Bibliography of Slavic Dictionaries. v. 3: Russian. New York, The New York Public Library, 1963. 400 p.

Lists 3,182 titles of dictionaries, both monolingual and bilingual. The fullest bibliography of its kind.

1285. Smirnitskii, Aleksandr I.   Russian-English Dictionary. 5th ed. Moscow, State Publishing House of Foreign and National Dictionaries, 1961. 951 p.

The best Russian-English dictionary.

1286. Miuller, Vladimir K.   Anglo-russkii slovar'; Anglo-Russian Dictionary. 10th ed. Moscow, Gos. izd-vo inostrannykh i natsional'-nykh slovarei, 1963. 1192 p.

The best English-Russian dictionary.

1287. Wolkonsky, Catherine A., *and* Marianna A. Poltoratzky.   Handbook of Russian Roots. New York, Columbia University Press, 1961. 414 p.

Lists over 500 of the most productive Russian roots with their derivatives and elements of phraseology. The Russian words are stressed throughout. The etymology is not given.

1288. Greve, Rita, *and* Bärbel Kroesche.   Russisches rückläufiges Wörterbuch. Prepared under the direction of Max Vasmer. Wiesbaden, Otto Harrassowitz, 1958-1959. 2 v. (Veröffentlichungen der Abteilung für slavische Sprachen und Literaturen des Osteuropa-Instituts [Slavisches Seminar] an der Freien Universität Berlin, 13)

This reverse dictionary is based on material included in the dictionaries of V. I. Dal', D. N. Ushakov, and I. Pavlovskii, as well as on that of seven other minor dictionaries. The words are not stressed.

1289. Bielfeldt, Hans H., *ed.*   Rückläufiges Wörterbuch der russischen Sprache der Gegenwart. Berlin, Akademie-Verlag, 1959. 392 p. (Deutsche Akademie der Wissenschaften. Veröffentlichungen des Instituts für Slawistik. Sonderreihe Wörterbücher)

This reverse dictionary is based on material included in the dictionaries of D. N. Ushakov and S. I. Ozhegov. The words are stressed.

1290. U. S. *Library of Congress. Reference Dept.* Russian Abbreviations; a Selective List. Compiled by Alexander Rosenberg. 2d rev. ed. Washington, 1957. 513 p.

1291. Scheitz, Edgar. Russische Abkürzungen und Kurzwörter, Russisch-Deutsch, mit etwa 20.000 Abkürzungen. Berlin, Verlag Technik, 1961. 727 p.

A dictionary of Russian abbreviations, with transcription and translation into German.

1292. Josselson, Harry H. The Russian Word Count and Frequency Analysis of Grammatical Categories of Standard Literary Russian. Detroit, Wayne University Press, 1953. 274 p.

The only Russian word-frequency list.

1293. Baecklund, Astrid. Die univerbierenden Verkürzungen der heutigen russischen Sprache. Inauguraldissertation. Uppsala, Almqvist und Wiksell, 1940. 141 p.

Bibliography: p. 127-132.

The best study of the structure of compound words by abbreviation in contemporary Russian. Good bibliography.

1294. Busch, Ulrich. Die Seinsätze in der russischen Sprache. Meisenheim am Glan, Anton Hain, 1960. 196 p. (Slavisch-Baltisches Seminar der Westfälischen Wilhelms-Universität, Münster. Veröffentlichung no. 4)

A thorough and most instructive study of sentences with the verb "to be" in old and modern Russian.

1295. Nowikowa, Irene. Die Namen der Nagetiere im Ostslavischen. Berlin, Wiesbaden, Otto Harrassowitz, 1959. 152 p. (Veröffentlichungen der Abteilung für slavische Sprachen und Literaturen des Osteuropa-Instituts [Slavisches Seminar] und der Freien Universität Berlin, 19)

A thorough investigation of over 800 names of rodents in East Slavic, concentrating on Russian material.

1296. New York University. *Committee for Russian-English Technical Dictionaries.* Russian-English Scientific and Technical Dictionaries; a Survey. New York, New York University, 1960. 20 p.

Discusses about 80 dictionaries and surveys future needs in specific fields.

e. Versification

1297. Unbegaun, Boris O. Russian Versification. rev. 2d ed. Oxford, Clarendon Press, 1963. 166 p.

Bibliography: p. 156-161.
See also entry no. 1445.
    A description of Russian versification with historical background.
French translation from the first edition (1956): *La versification
russe* (Paris, Librairie des cinq continents, 1958, 203 p.)

1298. Burgi, Richard.   A History of the Russian Hexameter. Hamden,
Conn., The Shoe String Press, 1954. 208 p.
    A reliable and well-informed study.

f. Scientific Russian

1299. Magner, Thomas F.   Manual of Scientific Russian. Minneapolis,
Burgess Publishing Co., 1958. 101 p.
    Presents the essentials of Russian grammar and scientific termi-
nology in concise tabular form.

1300. Ward, Dennis.   Russian for Scientists. London, University of London Press; New York, Macmillan, 1960. 204 p.
    Excellent presentation of the subject.

3. History of the Russian Language

a. Common Slavic and Old Church Slavonic

1301. Vaillant, André.   Grammaire comparée des langues slaves. Lyon,
IAC, 1950-1958. 2 v. in 3. (Collection "Les langues du monde."
Serie Grammaire, philologie, littérature, 6, 11, 12)
    Well-proportioned, up-to-date, and highly original comparative
grammar of Slavic languages. The three volumes published so far
include phonetics and declension.

1302. Meillet, Antoine.   Le slave commun. 2d ed., revised and enlarged
with the assistance of A. Vaillant. Paris, Champion, 1934. 538 p.
(Collection de manuels publiée par l'Institut d'Études Slaves, 2;
Collection linguistique de la Société de Linguistique de Paris, 15)
Bibliography: p. xiii-xix.
    A reliable account of the Common Slavic system, which is placed
in its Indo-European context.

1303. Stang, Christian S.   Slavonic Accentuation. Oslo, 1957. 192 p.
(Skrifter utgitt av Det Norske Videnskaps-Akademi i Oslo, I.
Hist.-Fil. Klasse, 1957, 3)
    In this comprehensive and clear book, Slavic accentuation is dis-
cussed mainly in its application to different morphological categories.

1304. Stang, Christian S.   Das slavische und baltische Verbum. Oslo,
1942. 280 p. (Skrifter utgitt av Det Norske Videnskaps-Akademi
i Oslo, II. Hist.-Fil. Klasse, 1942, 1)
    A convenient study of the Slavic (and Baltic) verb system.

1305. Handbook of Old Church Slavonic.   Part I: Old Church Slavonic Grammar, by G. Nandris; Part II: Texts and Glossary, by R. Auty. London, The Athlone Press, 1959-1960. 2 v.
    The most comprehensive handbook on Old Church Slavonic in English.

1306. Lunt, Horace G.   Old Church Slavonic Grammar. The Hague, Mouton, 1955. 143 p. (Slavistic Printings and Reprintings, 3)
    A reliable description of Old Church Slavonic into which elements of structural linguistics are introduced.

1307. Vaillant, André.   Manuel du vieux slave. Paris, Institut d'Études Slaves, 1948. 2 v. (Collection de manuels publiée par l'Institut d'Études Slaves, 6)
    The best handbook of Old Church Slavonic. Volume one (375 p.) contains a grammar; volume two (127 p.), texts and glossary.

1308. Miklosich, Franz, *Ritter* von.   Lexicon palaeoslovenico-graeco-latinum emendatum auctum. Vindobonae, Gulielmus Braumeller, 1862-1865. 1171 p.
    The only Old Church Slavonic dictionary which includes also later Church Slavonic material. Offset reprint: Leipzig, Frommhold und Wendler, 1923.

1309. Slovník jazyka staroslověnského.   Lexicon linguae palaeosloveni-cae. Prague, Československá akademie věd, 1959–
    This dictionary promises to be the fullest of those which limit themselves to the oldest stage of Old Church Slavonic. Translations in Czech, Russian, German, Latin, and Greek are given, and rich illustrative material is adduced. So far installments 1-6 (a-vušeliti) have been published.

b. General works and grammar

1310. Entwistle, William J., *and* William A. Morison.   Russian and the Slavonic Languages. London, Faber and Faber, 1949. 407 p. Maps.
    A historical and comparative study which sets Russian in its context among the other Slavic languages. The work is highly compressed, and provides a summary of current theories. Its frame of reference excludes original interpretation.

1311. Matthews, William K.   Russian Historical Grammar. London, The Athlone Press, 1960. 362 p.
    Bibliography: p. 321-334.
    The only historical grammar of Russian in English. Includes historical specimens of Russian prose, a history of Russian historical grammar, and an annotated bibliography.

1312. Matthews, William K.   The Structure and Development of Russian. Cambridge, England, The University Press, 1953. 225 p.

A description of the language, including dialects and history, which is too compressed to be wholly successful.

1313. Chernykh, Pavel Ia. (P. J. Tchernych). Historische Grammatik der russischen Sprache. German edition edited by H. H. Bielfeldt. Halle (Saale), VEB Max Niemeyer Verlag, 1957. 304 p. (Slawistische Bibliothek, 6)

A short and generally reliable historical grammar. Translation of *Istoricheskaia grammatika russkogo iazyka*; *kratkii ocherk* (2d rev. ed.; Moscow, Uchpedgiz, 1954, 311 p.)

1314. Vinokur, Grigorii O. La langue russe. Translated from Russian by Yves Millet. Paris, Institut d'Études Slaves, 1947. 158 p. (Bibliothèque russe de l'Institut d'Études Slaves, 22)

————. Die russische Sprache. Translated by R. von Trautmann. Leipzig, Otto Harrassowitz, 1949. 183 p. (Slawistische Studienbücherei, 2)

A brief résumé of the evolution of literary Russian, illustrated by well-chosen examples. Translations of *Russkii iazyk; istoricheskii ocherk* (Moscow, Goslitizdat, 1945, 189 p.)

1315. Kiparsky, Valentin. Russische historische Grammatik. v. 1: Die Entwicklung des Lautsystems. Heidelberg, Carl Winter, 1963. 171 p.

Thorough and clear treatment of the history of Russian phonology illustrated by convenient tables. On pages 30-67 there is a detailed list of Russian texts from the eleventh to the fourteenth centuries, with particulars of their editions and of studies devoted to them.

1316. Jakobson, Roman. Remarques sur l'évolution phonologique du russe comparée à celle des autres langues slaves. Prague, Jednota československých matematiků a fysiků, 1939. 118 p. (Travaux du Cercle linguistique de Prague, 2)

Ingenious theories based on the inherent necessities of phonemic structure. Textual control is almost entirely absent.

1317. Unbegaun, Boris O. La langue russe au XVIe siècle (1500-1550); la flexion des noms. Paris, Champion, 1935. 480 p. (Bibliothèque de l'Institut Français de Léningrad continuée par la Bibliothèque russe de l'Institut d'Études Slaves, 16)

Bibliography: p. 464-466.

The author attempts to establish the nature of sixteenth-century Russian declension on the basis of a personal examination of the texts. 'Sixteenth-century Russian' is throughout regarded as a single stage in the evolution of the language, and the study accordingly overlaps the chronological limitations of the title.

1318. Cocron, Frédéric. La langue russe dans la seconde moitié du

XVIIe siècle (morphologie). Paris, Institut d'Études Slaves, 1962.
278 p. (Bibliothèque russe de l'Institut d'Études Slaves, 33)
A penetrating analysis of Russian morphology of the late seventeenth century based on firsthand evidence.

1319. Stang, Christian S.   Die altrussische Urkundensprache der Stadt Polozk. Oslo, 1939. 148 p. (Skrifter utgitt av Det Norske Videnskaps-Akademi i Oslo, II. Hist.-Fil. Klasse, 1938, 9)
An excellent study, and the only full history of the language of Polotsk.

1320. Kirchner, Gottfried.   Die russischen Adjektivadverbien auf -*i*. Berlin, Akademie-Verlag, 1961. 81 p. (Deutsche Akademie der Wissenschaften zu Berlin. Veröffentlichungen des Instituts für Slawistik, 23)
A penetrating analysis of the form and history of Russian adjective-derived adverbs in -*i*.

1321. Schooneveld, Cornelis H. van.   A Semantic Analysis of the Old Russian Finite Preterite System. The Hague, Mouton, 1959. 171 p. (Slavistic Printings and Reprintings, 7)
A thorough study of the use of the past tense in Old Russian of the Kievan period.

1322. Ruzicka, Rudolf.   Der Verbalaspekt in der altrussischen Nestorchronik. Berlin, Akademie-Verlag, 1957. 107 p. (Deutsche Akademie der Wissenschaften zu Berlin. Veröffentlichungen des Instituts für Slawistik, 14)
A thorough study of the verbal aspect in the Russian Primary Chronicle.

1323. Janke, Gottfried.   Der Ausdruck des Passivs im Altrussischen. Berlin, Akademie-Verlag, 1960. 70 p. (Deutsche Akademie der Wissenschaften zu Berlin. Veröffentlichungen des Instituts für Slawistik, 22)
A good study of the development of the passive mood in Old Russian.

1324. Stang, Christian S.   La langue du livre "Uchenie i khitrost' ratnago stroeniia liudei," 1647; une monographie linguistique. Oslo, Jacob Dybwad, 1952. 86 p. (Skrifter utgitt av Det Norske Videnskaps-Akademi i Oslo, II. Hist.-Fil. Klasse, 1952, 1)
A thorough linguistic study of a representative seventeenth-century text.

1325. Birnbaum, Henrik.   Neuere Arbeiten über russische Syntax, I-II. Zur Erforschung der historischen Syntax des Russischen in den Jahren 1939-1959. Zeitschrift für slavische Philologie, v. 28, 1960: 416-431; v. 29, 1961: 151-172.

A critical survey of works on the history of Russian syntax published in 1939-1959.

1326. Bräuer, Herbert.   Untersuchungen zum Konjunktiv im Altkirchenslavischen und im Altrussischen. Part 1: Die Final- und Abhängigen Heischesätze. Wiesbaden, Otto Harrassowitz, 1957. 262 p. (Veröffentlichungen der Abteilung für Slavische Sprachen und Literaturen des Osteuropa-Instituts [Slavisches Seminar] an der Freien Universität Berlin, 11)
Bibliography: p. xi-xv.
A thorough study of the conjunctive in Old Church Slavonic and Old Russian. The Russian part, which occupies more than two-thirds of the book, is based mainly on chronicle material.

1327. Winkel, Hans Jürgen zum.   Über die Homophonie in der russischen Literatursprache. Meisenheim am Glan, Anton Hain, 1958. 148 p. (Slavisch-Baltisches Seminar der Westfälischen Wilhelms-Universität Münster. Veröffentlichung no. 1)
A good study of homophony both lexical and morphological in modern and Old Russian.

1328. Gunnarsson, Gunnar.   Studien über die Stellung des Reflexivs im Russischen. Uppsala, Almqvist und Wiksell, 1935. 105 p. (Uppsala Universitets Årsskrift, 1935, 9)
A historical study of the attachment of the particle *sia* to the reflexive verb.

1329. Widnäs, Maria.   La position de l'adjectif épithète en vieux russe. Helsingfors, 1952. 197 p. (Societas Scientiarum Fennica. Commentationes Humanarum Litterarum, 18/2)
A well-documented work on the position of the attributive adjective in Old Russian.

1330. Martel, Antoine.   Michel Lomonosov et la langue littéraire russe. Paris, Champion, 1933. 135 p. (Bibliothèque de l'Institut Français de Léningrad, 13)
A study of the part played by Michael Lomonosov in the creation of modern literary Russian.

1331. Shevelov, George Y., *and* Fred Holling, *eds.*   A Reader in the History of the Eastern Slavic Languages: Russian, Belorussian, Ukrainian. New York, Columbia University Press, 1958. 81 p.
See also entry no. 1384.
A collection of 60 texts reproduced photographically from various printed editions. Contains a glossary.

c. Dictionaries and studies of vocabulary

1332. Unbegaun, Boris O.   Où en sont les études d'histoire du vocabulaire russe? *In* Brussels. Université Libre. Institut de Philologie et d'Histoire Orientales et Slaves. Annuaire. v. 14, 1957: 263-284.

A bibliographical survey of studies dealing with the history of the Russian vocabulary.

1333. Vasmer, Max. Russisches etymologisches Wörterbuch. Heidelberg, Carl Winter, 1953-1958. 3 v.

> The best and fullest of Russian etymological dictionaries. Pays special attention to dialectal and foreign words.

1334. Hüttl-Worth, Gerta. Foreign Words in Russian; a Historical Sketch, 1550-1800. Berkeley, Los Angeles, University of California Press, 1963. 132 p.

> Gives a selected list (pages 55-123) of foreign words with dated examples which is intended to supplement Vasmer's etymological dictionary (*see* entry no. 1333). The list is preceded by a general study.

1335. Shakhmatov, Aleksei A. (Alexei A. Šachmatov), *and* George Y. Shevelov. Die kirchenslavischen Elemente in der modernen russischen Literatursprache. Wiesbaden, Otto Harrassowitz, 1960. 107 p. (Slavistische Studienbücher, 10)

> The book contains (pages 1-41) a German translation of the section on the Church Slavonic element in Russian in Shakhmatov's work *Ocherk sovremennogo russkogo literaturnogo iazyka* (Moscow, Uchpedgiz, 1941) and G. Shevelov's commentary on and supplements to it (pages 45-106).

1336. Trubetskoi (Trubetzkoy), Nikolai S. The Common Slavic Element in Russian Culture. Edited by Leon Stilman. New York, Columbia University Press, 1949. 39 p.

> A brief survey of the role played by Church Slavonic elements in the vocabulary of literary Russian. Translation of "Obshcheslavianskii element v russkoi kulture." *K probleme russkogo samopoznaniia; sobranie statei* (Paris, Evraziiskoe knigoizd., 1927), p. 54-94.

1337. Paschen, A. Die semasiologische und stylistische Funktion der *trat/torot* Alternationen in der altrussischen Literatursprache. Heidelberg, Carl Winter, 1933. 71 p. (Slavica, 10)

> A useful study of the semantic and stylistic value of words with and without pleophony in Old Russian of the Kievan period.

1338. Hüttl-Worth, Gerta. Die Bereicherung des russischen Wortschatzes im XVIII. Jahrhundert. Wien, Adolf Holzhausens Nfg., 1956. 232 p.
Bibliography: p. 223-231.

> A fully annotated, selective list of Russian neologisms of the eighteenth century (pages 80-222), preceded by a general study of the subject.

1339. Mazon, André. Lexique de la guerre et de la révolution en Russie

(1914-1918). Paris, Champion, 1920. 63 p. (Bibliothèque de l'Institut Français de Petrograd, 6)
> A study of neologisms which appeared in Russian during the First World War and the early Soviet period.

1340. Meulen, Reinder van der. De hollandsche zee- en scheepstermen in het Russisch. Amsterdam, 1909. 282 p. (Verhandelingen der Koninklijke Akademie van Wetenschappen, Afd. Letterkunde, nieuwe reeks, deel X, no. 2)
> A detailed study of the Dutch contribution to Russian maritime and naval terminology.

1341. Meulen, Reinder van der. Nederlandse woorden in her Russische. Amsterdam, N. V. Noord-Hollandsche Uitgevers Maatschappij, 1959. 117 p. (Verhandelingen der Koninklijke Nederlandse Akademie van Wetenschappen, Afd. Letterkunde, nieuwe reeks, deel LXVI, no. 2)
> Supplements the author's *Hollandsche zee- en scheepstermen in het Russisch* (entry no. 1340) and deals with borrowings from Dutch of other than naval and maritime terms.

1342. Thörnqvist, Clara. Studien über die nordischen Lehnwörter im Russischen. Uppsala, Almqvist und Wiksell, 1948. 284 p. (Études de philologie slave, 2)
> The fullest work on Russian loan-words of Scandinavian origin.

1343. Kalima, Jalo J. Die ostseefinnischen Lehnwörter im Russischen. Helsinki, Société Finno-Ougrienne, 1919. 265 p. (Memoires de la Société Finno-Ougrienne, 44)
> Bibliography: p. ix-xv.
> An exhaustive study of Russian borrowings from the West Finnic languages.

4. Onomastics

1344. Onoma: Bibliographical and Information Bulletin. 1950– Louvain.
> Each volume contains an annual bibliography of Russian onomastics, beginning with volume four (1953) for 1952. Number three of volume five (1954) contains a 77-page general bibliography of Russian onomastics by Rosemarie Richhardt.

1345. Unbegaun, Boris O. Où en sont les études d'anthroponymie russe; bibliographie critique. Revue internationale d'onomastique (Paris), v. 2, 1950: 151-160.
> A critical bibliographical survey of studies of Russian personal names.

1346. Vasmer, Max. Die alten Bevölkerungsverhältnisse Russlands im Lichte der Sprachforschung. Berlin, W. de Gruyter, 1941. 35 p. (Preussische Akademie der Wissenschaften. Vorträge und Schriften, 5)

A thorough and systematic interpretation of early ethnic developments in Russia based on place name evidence.

1347. Vasmer, Max., *ed.* Wörterbuch der russischen Gewässernamen. Prepared by A. Kerndl', R. Richhardt, and W. Eisold, under the direction of Max Vasmer. Berlin, Wiesbaden, Otto Harrassowitz, 1961– (Veröffentlichungen der Abteilung für slavische Sprachen und Literaturen des Osteuropa-Instituts [Slavisches Seminar] an der Freien Universität Berlin)

> Intended to be an exhaustive collection of hydronyms of European Russia. Based on Russian printed material. So far volume one (A-E, 1961, 710 p.) and installment one of volume two (Zh-Kamyshevakha, 1962, 240 p.) have appeared.

1348. Russisches geographisches Namenbuch. Prepared by Max Vasmer, with the assistance of I. Coper, I. Doerfer, J. Prinz, and R. Siegmann. Wiesbaden, Otto Harrassowitz, 1962– (Akademie der Wissenschaften und der Literatur, Mainz)

> Intended to be an exhaustive collection of place names of European Russia. Based on Russian printed material. So far installments one and two of volume one (A to Borisova Okolitsa, 1962-1963, 480 p.) have appeared.

1349. Dickenmann, Ernst.   Aufgaben und Methoden der russischen Ortsnamenforschung. Beiträge zur Namenforschung, v. 6, 1955: 120-138, 244-275.

> Discusses the tasks and methods of investigation in Russian toponymy.

1350. Baecklund, Astrid.   Personal Names in Medieval Velikij Novgorod. v. 1: Common Names. Stockholm, Almqvist und Wiksell, 1959. 195 p. (Acta Universitatis Stockholmiensis. Études de philologie slave, 9)

> A thorough study of the most frequent baptismal names in ancient Novgorod.

5. Dialectology

1351. Matthews, William K.   Modern Russian Dialects. Transactions of the Philological Society (London), 1950: 112-148. Maps.

A sound and convenient survey of the chief dialect divisions.

B. LITERATURE

1. Prior to the Nineteenth Century

by David Djaparidze

a. Bibliography [2]

1352. Harvard University. *Library*.   The Kilgour Collection of Russian Literature, 1750-1920. With notes on early books and manuscripts

[2] Arrangement is chronological by period covered.

of the 16th and 17th centuries. Cambridge, Harvard University
Press, 1959. unpaginated.
This work includes six pages of facsimiles, with 1,350 entries
and a 13-page index. The bulk of the volume is devoted to rare
books and first editions of literature of the eighteenth to twentieth
centuries, but there are references to earlier materials. The Bayard
Livingston Kilgour collection is housed at the Houghton Library of
Harvard University.

1353. Gudzii (Gudzij), Nikolai K.   Die altrussische Literaturgeschichte
in den Jahren 1914-1926. Zeitschrift für slavische Philologie, v. 5,
1928-1929: 153-175, 418-471; v. 6, 1929-1930: 258-269.

1354. Woltner, M.   Die altrussische und altukrainische Literaturfor-
schung in den Jahren 1926-1936. Zeitschrift für slavische Philologie,
v. 14, 1937: 105-161.

1355. Woltner, M.   Die altrussische Literaturgeschichte im Spiegelbild
der Forschung. Zeitschrift für slavische Philologie, v. 21, 1952-
1953: 159-193, 344-367; v. 23, 1954-1955: 189-200; v. 27, 1958-
1959: 179-198; v. 28, 1959-1960: 190-211.
An account which is to be continued.

1356. Kuz'mina, V. D.   Kritiko-bibliograficheskii obzor statei i zametok
po istorii drevnerusskoi literatury v zhurnale "Revue des études
slaves" (1932-1955) [Critical-bibliographical Survey of Articles and
Notes on Old Russian Literature in the Journal "Revue des études
slaves," 1932-1955]. In Akademiia nauk SSSR. Institut russkoi
literatury. Otdel drevnerusskoi literatury. Trudy, v. 13, 1957:
629-634.

1357. Raab, H.   Obzor rabot po drevnerusskoi literature, opublikovan-
nykh na nemetskom iazyke s 1945 g. [Survey of German-Language
Works on Old Russian Literature Published since 1945]. In Akademiia nauk SSSR. Institut russkoi literatury. Otdel drevnerusskoi
literatury. Trudy, v. 15, 1958: 474-485.

1358. Jakobson, Roman.   Izuchenie "Slova o polku Igoreve" v Soedinën-
nykh Shtatakh Ameriki [Research on "Slovo o polku Igoreve" in
the United States]. In Akademiia nauk SSSR. Institut russkoi literatury. Otdel drevnerusskoi literatury. Trudy, v. 14, 1958: 102-121.
Pages 112-116 include a bibliography of American works on the
Slovo for the years 1943-1956.

b. Histories and critical studies [3]

1359. Chyzhevs'kyi (Čiževskii), Dmytro.   History of Russian Literature

[3] Arrangement is chronological by period covered, proceeding within periods from
the general to the more specific.

from the Eleventh Century to the End of the Baroque. The Hague, Mouton, 1960. 451 p. (Slavistic Printings and Reprintings, 12)

This is the most significant contribution to this discipline published outside of Russia. The reader should bear in mind, however, that this work is primarily a history of Russian *literature* (*slovesnost'*) as distinguished from the history of *letters* (*pis'mennost'*) and that, consequently, writings not predominantly literary in nature are cursorily treated. Includes an index of proper names and an index of writings. The bibliography is to appear as a separate booklet.

A more detailed treatment of certain aspects of Eastern Slavic medieval literatures and, in some instances, a different approach, is to be found in this author's survey of Ukrainian literature and in his study of Old Russian literature of the eleventh to thirteenth centuries: *Geschichte der altrussischen Literatur im 11., 12. und 13. Jahrhundert; Kiever Epoche* (Frankfurt, V. Klostermann, 1948, 465 p., 16 pl., map, geneal. table).

1360. Chyzhevs'kyi (Tschižewskij), Dmytro.   Russische Geistesgeschichte. Hamburg, Rohwolt, 1959-1961. 2 v.
Bibliography: v. 1, p. 160-162; v. 2, p. 163-168.
See also entry no. 1566.

Volume one covers the tenth through seventeenth centuries; volume two, the eighteenth through twentieth centuries.

1361. Chyzhevs'kyi, Dmytro (D. Čiževsky).   On the Question of Genres in Old Russian Literature. Harvard Slavic Studies, v. 2, 1954: 105-115.

1362. Chyzhevs'kyi (Cizevsky), Dmytro.   Outline of Comparative Slavic Literatures. Boston, American Academy of Arts and Sciences, 1952. 143 p. (Survey of Slavic Civilizations, v. 1)
Bibliography: p. 137-138.

One of the most concise and comprehensive treatments of comparative Slavic literatures; more than half of the work is devoted to the medieval and baroque periods.

1363. Gudzii (Gudzij), Nikolai K.   Geschichte der russischen Literatur, 11.-17. Jahrhundert. Translated by F. V. Lilienfeld. Halle (Saale), Max Niemeyer Verlag, 1959. 650 p. (Slawistische Bibliothek, 10)

Contains an 82-page appendix of sample Old Russian texts.

An earlier edition, now outdated, was published in English as *History of Early Russian Literature*, translated by Susan Wilbur Jones (New York, Macmillan, 1949, 545 p.)

1364. Jakobson, Roman.   The Kernel of Comparative Slavic Literature. Harvard Slavic Studies, v. 1, 1953: 1-71.

1365. Lettenbauer, Wilhelm.   Russische Literaturgeschichte. 2d rev. and enl. ed. Wiesbaden, O. Harrassowitz, 1958. 336 p.
Bibliography: p. 317-326.

The most recent, and the best, general manual of Russian literature in German. First edition: Frankfurt am Main, Humboldt, 1955.
There is also an earlier, somewhat outdated work by Arthur
Luther, *Geschichte der russischen Literatur* (Leipzig, Bibliographisches Institut, 1924, 499 p.)

1366. Lo Gatto, Ettore.   Storia della letteratura russa. Rome, Anonima
romana editoriale, 1928-1944. 7 v.

> Volume one: Dalle origine a tutto il sec. XVI; Introduz. Lettera-
> tura orale. La letteratura scritta del periodo di Kiev. La letteratura
> scritta dei periodi mongolico e moscovito. 1928, 294 p.
> Volume two: Le origini della letteratura moderna. La letteratura
> del sec. XVII. Da Pietro il Grande a Caterina II. L'epoca di Cate-
> rina II. N. M. Karamzin. 1928, 292 p.
> Volumes three and four cover the literature of the nineteenth
> century.
> There is also a condensed edition of this work. First published in
> 1937, the fourth revised and corrected edition is available as *Storia
> della letteratura russa* (Florence, Sansoni, 1950, 590 p.)

1367.* Mirskii, Dmitrii P. (D. S. Mirsky).   A History of Russian Literature, Comprising "A History of Russian Literature" and "Contemporary Russian Literature." Edited and abridged by Francis J.
Whitfield. New York, Knopf, 1949. 518 p. Bibliography.

> An excellent concise survey of Russian literature. Chapter one,
> "The Literature of Old Russia"; chapter two, "The Passing of Old
> Russia"; and chapter three, "The Age of Classicism," are particu-
> larly relevant (pages 3-71). Later edition: New York, Vintage
> Books, 1958.

1368. Picchio, Riccardo.   Storia della letteratura russa antica. Milan,
Nuova accademia editrice, 1959. 416 p.

> Extremely well-informed treatment of Old Russian literature.
> The work is divided into four parts: the Kievan period (pages 11-
> 90); the local traditions, twelfth to fifteenth centuries (pages
> 93-229); the Muscovite period (pages 233-355); and the oral
> tradition (pages 359-380). Includes interesting discussions, useful
> bibliographies of pre- and post-Revolutionary works, and a chrono-
> logical index of Old Russian literature (pages 395-403).

1369. Raab, Harald.   Geschichte der altrussischen Literatur, 10. bis 17.
Jahrhundert. Berlin, Deutscher Verlag der Wissenschaften, 1957.
76 p.

1370. Stender-Petersen, Adolf.   Geschichte der russischen Literatur. v. 1.
Translated by Wilhelm Krämer. Munich, Beck, 1957. 472 p.
Bibliography: p. 438-462.

> First published in Danish under the title *Den Russiske litteraturs
> historie*.

1371. Trubetskoi, Nikolai S. (N. Trubetzkoy).   Introduction to the History of Old Russian Literature. Harvard Slavic Studies, v. 2, 1954: 91-103.

> Excellent approach to the major problems of Old Russian literature.
> For a further discussion of the subject, *see* the following two articles:
> Stender-Petersen, Adolf. "Die Problematik der russischen Literatur; vom Byzantinismus zum Europäismus." *Vorträge auf der Berliner Slawistentagung.* Berlin, 1956. p. 130-139.
> Gudzii, Nikolai K. "The Artistic Heritage of Old Russian Literature." *Oxford Slavonic Papers*, v. 7, 1957: 17-26.

1372. Dvornik, Francis. Byzantine Political Ideas in Kievan Russia. Dumbarton Oaks Papers, v. 9-10, 1956: 73-121.

> Based on an analysis of Russian literary, as well as historical, texts of the Kievan period.

1373.* Fedotov, Georgii P. The Russian Religious Mind. v. 1: Kievan Christianity. Cambridge, Harvard University Press, 1946. 438 p. Bibliography: p. 413-424.

> *See also* entries no. 488 and 1634.
> Later edition: New York, Harper and Row, 1960, 431 p. A second volume of this work is scheduled to appear at Harvard University Press in 1964.

1374. Slovo o polku Igoreve.   La Geste du Prince Igor'. Épopée russe du douzième siècle. Translated, with commentary, by Roman Jakobson and Marc Szeftel, with the assistance of J. A. Joffe, under the direction of Henri Grégoire. New York, 1948. 383 p. (École libre des hautes études à New York. Annuaire de l'Institut de philologie et d'histoire orientales et slaves, v. 8)

> Includes: R. Jakobson, "Remarques sur l'édition critique du *Slovo*, sur sa traduction en langues modernes et sur la reconstruction du texte primitif," p. 5-37; R. Jakobson, "Édition critique du *Slovo*," p. 38-78; H. Grégoire, "Traduction française du *Slovo*," p. 39-79; R. Jakobson, "Altérations du texte et leur corrections," p. 81-96; M. Szeftel, "Commentaire historique au texte du *Slovo*," p. 97-149; R. Jakobson, "Essai de reconstruction du *Slovo* dans sa langue originale"; S. H. Cross, "Traduction anglaise du *Slovo*"; R. Jakobson, "Traduction du *Slovo* en russe moderne," p. 181-200; J. Tuwim, "Traduction polonaise du *Slovo*," p. 201-216; G. Vernadsky, "La Geste d'Igor' au point de vue historique," p. 217-234; R. Jakobson, "L'authenticité du *Slovo*," p. 235-360; etc.

1375. Jakobson, Roman, *and* Ernest J. Simmons, *eds.* Russian Epic Studies. Philadelphia, American Folklore Society, 1949. 224 p. (Memoirs of the American Folklore Society, v. 42)

> Includes: "The Vseslav Epos," by Roman Jakobson and Marc Szeftel, p. 13-86; "Classical Influence on the *Slovo*," by Clarence Manning, p. 87-97; "Scandinavian Influence on the *Slovo*?" by M. Schlauch, p. 99-124; "On Alliteration in Ancient Russian Epic

Literature," by D. Čiževsky (Chyzhevs'kyi), p. 125-130; "Le Digénis russe," by Henri Grégoire, p. 131-169; "The First Polish Translation of the *Slovo*," by Manfred Kridl, p. 171-178; "Rainer Maria Rilke's Translation of the Igor Song (Slovo)," with introduction and notes by André von Gronicka, p. 179-202; "The *Slovo* in English," by A. Yarmolinsky, p. 203-224.

1376. Besharov, Justinia.   Imagery of the Igor' Tale in the Light of Byzantino-Slavic Poetic Theory. Leiden, E. J. Brill, 1956. 114 p. (Studies in Russian Epic Tradition, 2)

1377. Schaeder, Hildegard.   Moskau, das Dritte Rom; Studien zur Geschichte der politischen Theorien in der slavischen Welt. 2d ed. Darmstadt, Gentner, 1957. 215 p. Bibliography.
See also entry no. 491.
    First published in Hamburg in 1929. One of the most important works on the intellectual as well as political history of medieval Russia. Includes texts, such as the Epistles of the monk Filofei.

1378. Denissoff, Élie.   Maxime le Grec et l'Occident; contribution à l'histoire de la pensée religieuse et philosophique de Michel Trivolis. Paris, Desclée, De Brouwer; Louvain, Bibliothèque de l'Université, 1943. 460 p., 11 plates.
    The most fundamental contribution to the history of religious and philosophical thought in sixteenth-century Muscovy and its relations with Western Europe and Eastern Orthodoxy. For the first time Maxim the Greek is here identified as the Humanist Michael Trivolis and a detailed analysis of his life and activity in Italy, on Mount Athos, and in Russia is given.

1379. Harder, Hans-Bernd.   Studien zur Geschichte der russischen klassizistischen Tragödie, 1747-1769. Wiesbaden, O. Harrassowitz, 1962. 174 p. (Osteuropastudien der Hochschulen des Landes Hessen. Reihe 3, Bd. 6)

c. Anthologies

1380. Fedotov, Georgii P., *ed.*   A Treasury of Russian Spirituality. New York, Sheed and Ward, 1948. 501 p.
Bibliography: p. 500-501.
See also entries no. 487 and 1635.
    The only anthology of its kind in English, with translated and annotated selections from texts relating to St. Theodosius, St. Sergius, St. Nilus Sorskii, Avvakum, St. Tikhon, St. Seraphim, St. John of Kronstadt, and Father Alexander Elchaninov. Some items were translated by Helen Izvol'skii.

1381. Manning, Clarence A., *ed.*   Anthology of Eighteenth Century Russian Literature. New York, King's Crown Press, 1951-1953. 2 v.

1382.* Obolensky, Dimitri, *ed.*   The Penguin Book of Russian Verse. Harmondsworth, Baltimore, Penguin Books, 1962. 444 p.

See also entry no. 1466.
> Pages 1-67 are devoted to pre-Petrine poetry. Russian texts with English prose translations.

1383.* Reeve, Franklin D., *ed. and tr.*   An Anthology of Russian Plays. v. 1 (1790-1890). New York, Vintage Books, 1961. 454 p.
See also entry no. 1469.
> Includes a translation of Fonvizin's *Nedorosl'* (pages 21-83).

1384. Shevelov, George Y., *and* Fred Holling, *eds.*   A Reader in the History of the Eastern Slavic Languages: Russian, Belorussian, Ukrainian. New York, Columbia University Press, 1958. 81 p.
See also entry no. 1331.
> Intended primarily for students in philology and linguistics. Useful for the variety of texts it provides (Old Rus' language, Middle Russian, Middle Belorussian, Middle Ukrainian). No grammatical annotations, but includes a 10-page glossary.

1385. Slavische Geisteswelt.   Edited by Martin Winkler. v. 1: Russland. Darmstadt, Geneva, Holle, 1955. 340 p.
> Excellent anthology in German translation of the most important texts relating to the spiritual and intellectual evolution of the Russian people. Pages 1-157 cover the period from the earliest times to the end of the eighteenth century; pages 331-340 contain a selected bibliography; and pages 341-367, critical notes.

1386. Stender-Petersen, Adolf, *and* Stefan Congrat-Butler, *eds.*   Anthology of Old Russian Literature. New York, Columbia University Press, 1954. 542 p.
> Intended primarily for students of literature. Text in Old Russian. Includes excellent annotations and grammatical explanations, together with a glossary of Old Russian words, an index of authors and titles, an index of names, and genealogical tables.

1387. Trautmann, Reinhold.   Altrussisches Lesebuch. Part 1: 11.-14. Jahrhundert. Leipzig, Harrassowitz, 1949. 152 p. (Slavistiche Studienbücherei, 3)
> Annotations in German.

1388. Wiener, Leo, *ed.*   Anthology of Russian Literature from the Earliest Period to the Present Time. New York, London, G. P. Putnam's Sons, 1902-1903. 2 v.
> The first part covers the period from the tenth century to the close of the eighteenth.

1389.* Zenkovsky, Serge A., *ed. and tr.*   Medieval Russia's Epics, Chronicles and Tales. New York, Dutton, 1963. 436 p. Illus.
> Very well selected anthology of translated Old Russian texts from the eleventh to the seventeenth century. Includes a 40-page general introduction to the literature of Medieval Russia, as well

as short notes on each text, a glossary of Old Russian terms, a chronology of Russian history, and three maps. Recommended for students in both the history and literature of pre-Petrine Russia.

d. Texts and translations [4]

1390. Josephus, Flavius.   La prise de Jerusalem, de Joseph le Juif. Old Russian text published in full by V. Istrin. Printed under the supervision of A. Vaillant. Translated into French by Pierre Pascal. Paris, Institut d'Études Slaves, 1934-1938. 2 v. (Textes publiés par l'Institut d'Études Slaves)

The only existing translation of the Slavonic text into a Western language.

1391. Povest' vremennykh let. *English.*   The Russian Primary Chronicle; Laurentian Text. Translated and edited by Samuel H. Cross and Olgerd P. Sherbowitz-Wetzor. Cambridge, Mediaeval Academy of America, 1953. 313 p. (Mediaeval Academy of America. Publication no. 60)

Bibliography: p. 288-295.

See also entry no. 482.

The first edition of this translation, by S. H. Cross, appeared in *Harvard Studies and Notes in Philology and Literature*, v. 12, 1930. The translation is based upon the text edited by E. F. Karskii in 1926 in the second edition of the series *Polnoe sobranie russkikh letopisei.* A photomechanical reprint of E. F. Karskii's text of the Laurentian Chronicle was issued in 1962 by the Historical Institute of the Academy of Sciences of the USSR as part of the general reprinting program of the *Polnoe sobranie russkikh letopisei.*

For a German translation, *see* R. Trautmann's *Die altrussische Nestorchronik, Povest' vremennych let* (Leipzig, Market und Petters, 1931, 302 p.). *See also* Trautmann's excerpts, *Die altrussische Nestorchronik, in Auswahl* . . . (Leipzig, Harrassowitz, 1948, 76 p.), an abridged version in German.

1392. Novgorodskaia letopis'.   The Chronicle of Novgorod, 1016-1471. Translated from the Russian by Robert Michell and Nevill Forbes. With an introduction by C. Raymond Beazley, and an account of the text by A. A. Shakhmatov. London, 1914. 237 p. (Royal Historical Society. Publications. Camden Third Series, v. 25)

1393. Benz, Ernst, *and others, eds. and trs.*   Russische Heiligenlegenden. Zurich, Verlag Die Waage, 1953. 524 p. Illus. (48 pl.)

An extremely useful collection of translations into German including (1) texts relating to the oldest Russian saints and the penetration of Christianity into Kievan Russia (eleventh century); (2) narratives about Russian saints from the Kiev-Pecherskii paterikon; (3) Old Russian hagiography from the thirteenth to the fifteenth century; (4) Muscovite hagiography of the sixteenth and

° Arrangement is chronological by date of text.

seventeenth centuries; (5) popular religious narratives (such as the *Legend of Petr and Fevroniia, Merkurii Smolenskii,* and others).

1394. Müller, Ludolf, *ed.* Des Metropoliten Ilarion Rede über das Gesetz und die Gnade. Lobpreis auf dem Fürsten Vladimir. Gebet für das ganze Russische Land und das Glaubenkenntnis. New edition of the original 1844 edition, with new introduction and commentary. Word list by S. Kehrer and W. Seegatz. Wiesbaden, Harrassowitz, 1962. 229 p. (Slavistische Studienbücherei, 2)
> Old Russian text with introduction and notes.

1395. Slovo o polku Igoreve. *English.*   The song of Igor's Campaign; an Epic of the Twelfth Century. Translated from Old Russian by Vladimir Nabokov. New York, Vintage Books; London, Weidenfeld and Nicolson, 1960. 134 p.
> Excellent translation and critical foreword.
> Other translations: a previous English translation by S. H. Cross; a French translation by H. Grégoire; and a translation into modern Russian by R. Jakobson in the symposium *La Geste du Prince Igor'* (*see* entry no. 1374).

1396. Slovo o polku Igoreve.   Das Igor-Lied, eine Heldendichtung. Old Russian text, with the German translation of Rainer-Maria Rilke and a modern Russian prose version by D. S. Likhachev (Lichatschow). Leipzig, Insel-Verlag, 1960. 75 p.

1397. Slovo o polku Igoreve. *Italian.*   Cantare della Gesta di Igor. Epopea russa del XII secolo. Translated, with an introduction and commentary, by Renato Poggioli. Critical remarks by Roman Jakobson. Turin, Giulio Einaudi, 1954. 235 p.
> Includes a literary analysis of Old Russian epic style (pages 19-86) as well as most useful commentaries (pages 211-235).

1398. The Homily of Adam in Hades to Lazarus.   The Slavonic and East European Review, v. 10, no. 29, December 1931: 244-252.

1399. Müller, Klaus.   Sendschreiben Daniels des Verbannten. Zeitschrift für Slawistik, v. 5, 1960, no. 3: 432-445.
> An excellent German version of the *Molenie Daniila Zatochnika,* with a concise introduction describing the manuscripts in which this text is preserved.

1400. Zernov, Nicolas.   St. Sergius, Builder of Russia. London, The Society for Promoting Christian Knowledge; New York, Macmillan, 1939. 155 p.
> Includes an English translation of *The Acts and Miracles of our Dear and Holy Father, Sergius,* by Epiphanius the Wise.

1401. Pascal, Pierre.   Le "Digénis" slave ou la "Geste de Devgenij." Byzantion (Brussels), v. 10, 1935: 301-334.

1402. Nikitin, Afanasii.   Die Fahrt des Athanasius Nikitin über die drei Meere; Reise eines russischen Kaufmannes nach Ostindien, 1466-1472. Translated from Old Russian, with an introduction and notes, by Karl H. Meyer. Leipzig, Schraepler, 1920. 47 p. Illus. (Quellen und Aufsätze zur russischen Geschichte, 2)

> See also a recent German translation of this text, together with an excellent analysis and a bibliography: Paul Winter-Wirz, *Die Reise des russischen Kaufmannes Afanasii Nikitin über drei Meere und sein Aufenthalt in Indien 1466-1472* (Heidelberg, 1960, 209 p.)

1403. Sturm, Gottfried.   Übersetzung der "Zadonščina." Zeitschrift für Slawistik, v. 3, 1958, no. 5: 700-710.

> A German translation of the "Zadonshchina" epic.

1404. Duchesne, E., *tr.*   Le Stoglav ou les Cent Chapitres; recueil des décisions de l'assemblée ecclésiastique de Moscou, 1551. Paris, Champion, 1920. 292 p. (Bibliothèque de l'Institut Français de Pétrograd, 5)
Bibliography: p. xliii-xlvi.

1405. Duchesne, E.   Le Domostroi (Ménagier russe du XVI-ème siècle); traduction et commentaire. Paris, Picard, 1910.

1406. Kurbskii, Andrei M., *kniaz'*.   The Correspondence between Prince A. M. Kurbsky and Tsar Ivan IV of Russia, 1564-1579. Edited with a translation and notes by J. L. I. Fennell. Cambridge, England, Cambridge University Press, 1955. 275 p.
Bibliography: p. 266-267.
See also entry no. 495.

> Both Russian and English texts.
> For a German text, see *Der Briefwechsel Iwans des Schrecklichen mit dem Fürsten Kurbskij (1564-1579)*, translated by Karl H. Meyer and Karl Stählin (Leipzig, Schraepler, 1921, 175 p.)
> For an Italian translation, see *Le lettere di Ivan il Terrible a cura di Maria Olsufieff con i commentarii della Moscovia di A. Possevino* (Florence, 1958, 359 p., illus.)

1407. Liewehr, Ferdinand.   Kurbskijs "Novyj Margarit." Prague, 1928. 120 p. (Veröffentlichungen der slawistischen Arbeitsgemeinschaft an der Deutschen Universität Prag. II. Reihe, Heft 2)

1408. Avvakum, *Protopope*.   La vie de l'archiprêtre Avvakum écrite par lui-même, et sa dernière Epitre au Tsar Alexis. Translated from the Old Russian, with an introduction and notes, by Pierre Pascal. Paris, NRF-Gallimard, 1960. 250 p.

> The best translation into any West European language of Avvakum's *Zhitie*. Includes an excellent introduction and detailed bibliography. First edition: 1938.

1409. Avvakum, *Protopope*.   The Life of Archpriest Avvakum by Himself. Translated from the seventeenth century Russian by Jane Harrison and Hope Mirrlees. Preface by D. S. Mirsky. London, Hogarth Press, 1924. 155 p.

> Reprinted: Hamden, Conn., Archon Books, 1963.
>
> Excerpts from a more recent English translation of Avvakum's *Zhitie* by Helen Izvol'skii are to be found in G. P. Fedotov's *Treasury of Russian Spirituality* (*see* entry no. 1380).
>
> For a German translation, see *Das Leben des Protopopen Awwakum von ihm selbst niedergeschrieben*, translated from the Old Russian, with an introduction and commentary, by Rudolf Jagoditsch (Berlin, Ost-Europa Verlag, 1930, 227 p., illus.)

1410. Gregori, Iogann Gotfrid (Johann Gottfried Gregori).   La comédie d'Artaxerxès présentée en 1672 au Tsar Alexis par Gregorij le Pasteur. German and Russian texts, published by André Mazon and Frédéric Cocron. Paris, 1954. 296 p. (Bibliothèque russe de l'Institut d'Études Slaves, 28)

> The *Artakserksovo Deistvo* was the first dramatic work ever to be performed in Muscovy. Attributed to the Pastor Gregori, it was played before the Tsar Aleksei Mikhailovich on October 17, 1672. The text, however, was lost and was discovered only recently in the Library of Lyon, France, in an incomplete bilingual (German and Russian) manuscript. The above edition of the German original and its Russian adaptation thus represents a document marking the beginnings of theatrical art in Russia.

2. Nineteenth and Twentieth Centuries
by Hugh McLean

a. Survey studies, histories of literature, reference works, and general bibliographies

1411. Alexandrova, Vera (*pseud.* of Vera A. Schwarz).   A History of Soviet Literature. Translated by Mirra Ginsburg. Garden City, N.Y., Doubleday, 1963. 369 p.

> A useful survey, not technically scholarly, but well informed, competent, and often illuminating. The author has for many years written extensively on Soviet literature in the Russian émigré press, particularly the Menshevik organ *Sotsialisticheskii vestnik*.

1412. Baring, *Hon.* Maurice.   An Outline of Russian Literature. London, Williams and Norgate; New York, Holt, 1915. 256 p.

> A brief history of Russian literature from the early nineteenth century down to 1914. Somewhat antiquated, but occasionally enlightening.
>
> The same author's *Landmarks in Russian Literature* (London, Methuen; New York, Macmillan, 1910, 299 p.) contains essays on the major nineteenth-century authors. New edition: London, Methuen; New York, Barnes and Noble, 1960, 212 p.

1413. Borland, Harriet.   Soviet Literary Theory and Practice during the First Five-Year Plan, 1928-32. New York, King's Crown Press, 1950. 256 p.
Bibliography: p. 229-242.
   A very unliterary, but nevertheless useful and revealing, book about the harnessing of Russian literature to Communist propaganda machinery. Well-documented.

1414. Brown, Deming B.   Soviet Attitudes toward American Writing. Princeton, Princeton University Press, 1962. 338 p.
   A detailed history of Soviet criticism of American literature.

1415. Brown, Edward J.   The Proletarian Episode in Russian Literature, 1928-1932. New York, Columbia University Press, 1953. 311 p.
   A very careful and illuminating monograph on Russian literature in the period when it was dominated by the RAPP (Russian Association of Proletarian Writers).

1416.* Brown, Edward J.   Russian Literature since the Revolution. New York, Collier Books; London, Collier-Macmillan, 1963. 320 p.
   Not a discursive history, but an extended and stimulating essay on various aspects of Soviet literature, especially the revelation of the individual personality.

1417. Eastman, Max.   Artists in Uniform; a Study of Literature and Bureaucratism. New York, Knopf; London, Allen and Unwin, 1934. 261 p.
   An indignant and polemical treatise against the regimentation of literature in the Soviet Union in the early Stalinist period. Well-written; contains much interesting material.

1418. Erlich, Victor.   The Double Image: Concepts of the Poet in Slavic Literatures. Baltimore, Johns Hopkins Press, 1964. 160 p.
   Six urbane and illuminating essays on various poets' notions of what it means to be a poet. All but one of the poets are Russian.

1419. Erlich, Victor.   Russian Formalism; History, Doctrine. Preface by René Wellek. The Hague, Mouton, 1955. 276 p. Bibliography (Slavistic Printings and Reprintings, 4)
   An immensely interesting and scholarly monograph on the "formalist" school of Russian literary criticism, which flourished from about 1915 to 1930 and made many important contributions, not only to the study of Russian literature but to literary theory in general. Provides a judicious account of its history and an enlightening analysis of its theories.

1420. Ermolaev, Herman.   Soviet Literary Theories, 1917-1934; the Genesis of Socialist Realism. Berkeley, University of California Press, 1963. 261 p.
   An important monograph on the theoretical controversies of the early Soviet period.

1421. Ettlinger, Amrei, *and* Joan M. Gladstone. Russian Literature, Theatre and Art; a Bibliography of Works in English, Published 1900-1945. London, New York, Hutchinson, 1947. 96 p.
See also entry no. 1800.

A very useful bibliography, fairly complete, of books in English on Russian literature, art, and theater, including translations into English of Russian authors. Not free from errors and gaps, but still the only work of its kind for this period.

A similar bibliography for the period before 1900 is Maurice B. Line's *A Bibliography of Russian Literature in English Translation to 1900* (*Excluding Periodicals*) (London, The Library Association, 1963, 74 p.). It contains 426 entries representing translated works of 48 authors. A chronological list of first appearances of translations and an index of translators are provided.

For translations into English and other languages published after 1945, see *Proizvedeniia sovetskikh pisatelei v perevodakh na inostrannye iazyki*, for 1945-1953 (Moscow, 1954, 322 p.), and for 1954-1957 (Moscow, 1957, 277 p.), as well as *Index translationum* (Paris, UNESCO, 1949–).

French translations of Russian literature since the mid-eighteenth century are listed in Vladimir Boutchik, *Bibliographie des oeuvres littéraires russes traduites en français* (Paris, G. Orobitg, 1935-1936, 2 v.), with *Supplément* (Paris, J. Flory, 1938-1941, 2 v.)

Three major authors' works are entered in Boutchik's *Bibliographie des oeuvres littéraires russes traduites en français. Tourguénev, Dostoevski, Léon Tolstoi* (Paris, Messages, 1949, 110 p.)

1422. Friedberg, Maurice. Russian Classics in Soviet Jackets. New York, Columbia University Press, 1962. 228 p.
Bibliography: p. 207-211.

An interesting and well-documented study of the uses and abuses of the Russian classics in the Soviet period.

1423. Gibian, George. Interval of Freedom; Soviet Literature during the Thaw, 1954-1957. Minneapolis, University of Minnesota Press, 1960. 180 p.
See also entry no. 1156.

A judicious discussion of literary politics and production in the period immediately after Stalin's death.

1424.* Harkins, William E. Dictionary of Russian Literature. New York, Philosophical Library, 1956; London, Allen and Unwin, 1957. 439 p.

A compendium of short articles on authors, periods, schools, and other terms peculiar to Russian literature. Its usefulness is impaired by factual inaccuracies and failure to provide any bibliographical references.

1425. Hayward, Max, *and* Leopold Labedz, *eds*. Literature and Revolution in Soviet Russia, 1917-62. London, New York, Oxford University Press, 1963. 235 p.

An extremely interesting collection of essays by leading specialists on various aspects of Soviet literary life from its beginnings to the present.

1426. Jackson, Robert L.   Dostoevsky's Underground Man in Russian Literature. The Hague, Mouton, 1958. 223 p. (Slavistic Printings and Reprintings, 15)
Bibliography: p. 217-221.
An interesting attempt to trace the theme of the "underground man" through later Russian literature.

1427. Kaun, Alexander S.   Soviet Poets and Poetry. Berkeley, Los Angeles, University of California Press, 1943. 208 p.
A well-written, lively, and interesting monograph on the history of modern Russian poetry from the Symbolists to the Second World War. The earlier part of the book is much better than the latter, which is marred by gross over-optimism about the state of Soviet literature in the Stalinist period.

1428. Lednicki, Wacław.   Bits of Table-Talk on Pushkin, Mickiewicz, Goethe, Turgenev and Sienkiewicz. The Hague, Nijhoff, 1956. 263 p.
Literary essays by an outstanding scholar in the field of Russian and Polish literature.

1429. Mathewson, Rufus W., Jr.   The Positive Hero in Russian Literature. New York, Columbia University Press, 1958. 364 p.
A brilliant analysis of the intellectual and artistic antecedents of "socialist realism," tracing the demand for "positive heroes" in literature from Belinskii through Chernyshevskii and Lenin down to Andrei Zhdanov.

1430. Mirskii, Dmitrii P. (D. S. Mirsky).   Contemporary Russian Literature, 1881-1925. London, Routledge; New York, Knopf, 1926. 372 p.
Bibliography: p. 331-360.
A continuation of the *History of Russian Literature* (*see* entry no. 1431), actually written before it. The latter part of this volume suffered heavily at the hands of the editor of the 1949 version, which is inferior to this edition. Reprinted: London, Routledge, 1933.

1431. Mirskii, Dmitrii P. (D. S. Mirsky).   A History of Russian Literature from the Earliest Times to the Death of Dostoevsky (1881). London, Routledge; New York, Knopf, 1927. 388 p.
Bibliography: p. 371-377.
Perhaps the most brilliant and original inclusive work on the history of Russian literature in any language. Some of the judgments may be questionable, but the range, vitality, and freshness of the work are extraordinary. It is a great pity that only mutilated versions of this great book are now readily available.

This volume, combined with *Contemporary Russian Literature* (*see* entry no. 1430), was edited and abridged by Francis J. Whitfield and published in 1949 under the title *A History of Russian Literature* (New York, Knopf, 518 p.). A part of this abridged version was later reprinted under the title *A History of Russian Literature from Its Beginnings to 1900* (New York, Vintage, 1958, 383 p.)

1432. Muchnic, Helen.   An Introduction to Russian Literature. Garden City, N. Y., Doubleday, 1947. 272 p.

Not really an introduction at all, the book contains interesting essays on most of the major nineteenth-century Russian authors.

The same author's *From Gorky to Pasternak; Six Writers in Soviet Russia* (New York, Random House, 1961, 438 p.) has perceptive essays on Gor'kii, Blok, Maiakovskii, Leonov, Sholokhov, and Pasternak.

1433. Poggioli, Renato.   The Phoenix and the Spider; a Book of Essays about Some Russian Writers and Their View of the Self. Cambridge, Harvard University Press, 1957. 238 p.

Essays on Tolstoi, Bunin, Rozanov, and others.

1434. Poggioli, Renato.   The Poets of Russia, 1890-1930. Cambridge, Harvard University Press, 1960. 383 p.

Bibliography: p. 345-367.

Essays on the major figures in modern Russian poetry from Symbolism through Futurism, with an introduction on their antecedents in the nineteenth century.

1435. Reavey, George.   Soviet Literature Today. London, Drummond, 1946; New Haven, Yale University Press, 1947. 190 p.

Deals largely with the organization of Soviet literature, the Writers' Union, publishing houses, and Party controls. Loosely put together and occasionally naïve, it nevertheless contains useful information.

1436. Scott, H. G., *ed*.   Problems of Soviet Literature; Reports and Speeches at the First Soviet Writers' Congress. New York, International Publishers, 1935; London, Lawrence and Wishart, 1936. 278 p. Ports.

A collection of historically important speeches made at the First Congress of the Soviet Writers' Union in 1934, including an ominous official one by Andrei Zhdanov and somewhat less official, and literarily more interesting, addresses by Gor'kii, Bukharin, and others.

1437. Simmons, Ernest J.   Russian Fiction and Soviet Ideology. New York, Columbia University Press, 1958. 267 p. Illus.

Essays on the literary careers of Fedin, Leonov, and Sholokhov, largely from the point of view of their adaptation to the official ideology.

1438.*Simmons, Ernest J., *ed.*   Through the Glass of Soviet Literature; Views of Russian Society. New York, Columbia University Press, 1953. 301 p.
See also entries no. 116 and 1168.

A valuable collection of five essays, by various hands, on Soviet society as seen through its literature. Later edition: 1961.

1439. Slonim, Mark L. (Marc).   The Epic of Russian Literature, from Its Origins through Tolstoy. New York, Oxford University Press, 1950. 367 p.

Although very weak in its chapters on older Russian literature and generally careless about factual accuracy, this volume contains some interesting chapters on nineteenth-century literature, especially its social and ideological background.

Continued in the author's *Modern Russian Literature, from Chekhov to the Present* (New York, Oxford University Press, 1953, 467 p.), the first 10 chapters of which have been reprinted under the title *From Chekhov to the Revolution; Russian Literature, 1900-1917* (New York, Galaxy Books, 1962, 229 p.)

A condensed version of the two earlier volumes, carried up to the date of publication, was issued as *An Outline of Russian Literature* (New York, Oxford University Press, 1958, 235 p.)

1440. Strakhovsky, Leonid I.   Craftsmen of the Word; Three Poets of Modern Russia: Gumilyov, Akhmatova, Mandelstam. Cambridge, Harvard University Press, 1949. 114 p. Ports.
Bibliography: p. 111-114.

Badly written and trite, but the only monograph in English on these three important modern poets.

1441. Struve, Gleb.   Soviet Russian Literature, 1917-50. Norman, University of Oklahoma Press, 1951. 414 p.
Bibliography: p. 373-400.

A revised and expanded version of two earlier works: *Soviet Russian Literature* (London, Routledge, 1935, 270 p.) and *Twenty-Five Years of Soviet Russian Literature, 1918-1943* (London, Routledge, 1944, 347 p.)

Far and away the most careful, accurate, and dependable history of Russian literature in the Soviet period. The 1951 edition is greatly superior to the earlier ones. A German translation gives the most recent data: *Geschichte der Sowjetliteratur*, translated by Horst Neerfeld and Günter Schäfer (Munich, Isar Verlag, 1957, 595 p.)

1442. Swayze, Harold.   Political Control of Literature in the USSR, 1946-1959. Cambridge, Harvard University Press, 1962. 301 p.
See also entry no. 770.

A thorough and well-documented monograph on the relation between literature and Communist authority from the Zhdanov era up through the "thaw."

1443. Tertz, Abram, *pseud.*   On Socialist Realism. Translated by George Dennis. Introduction by Czesław Miłosz. New York, Pantheon Books, 1960. 95 p.

> An extremely interesting essay on the role of art in a totalitarian society, reportedly written by a young Russian living in the USSR, and smuggled out to be published abroad. Badly translated and edited.

1444.* Trotskii, Lev (Leon Trotsky).   Literature and Revolution. Translated from the Russian by Rose Strunsky. New York, International Publishers, 1925. 255 p.

> Partisan and intolerant, but nevertheless a brilliant display of critical insight and literary talent. Contains essays on most leading writers and poets of the Revolutionary period. New edition: Ann Arbor, University of Michigan Press; London, Cresset, 1960. Translation of *Literatura i revoliutsiia* (1924).

1445. Unbegaun, Boris O.   Russian Versification. rev. 2d ed. Oxford, Clarendon Press, 1963. 166 p.
Bibliography: p. 156-161.
See also entry no. 1297.

> An excellent brief outline of the subject.

1446. Vickery, Walter N.   The Cult of Optimism; Political and Ideological Problems of Recent Soviet Literature. Bloomington, Indiana University Press, 1963. 189 p.
Bibliography: p. 169-184.

> An informative analysis of Soviet literary politics in the most recent period.

1447. Vogüé, Eugène M. M., *vicomte* de.   The Russian Novel. Translated from the eleventh French edition by Colonel H. A. Sawyer. London, Chapman and Hall, 1913; New York, Knopf, 1916. 337 p., 6 ports.

> In many ways antiquated, but interesting for a contemporary Western reaction to nineteenth-century Russian literature. A pioneering work. Translation of *Le roman russe* (1886).

1448. Yarmolinsky, Avrahm.   Literature under Communism; the Literary Policy of the Communist Party of the Soviet Union from the End of World War II to the Death of Stalin. Bloomington, University of Indiana Press, 1960. 165 p.

> A well-documented chronicle of the fate of Russian literature during the bleak period of Zhdanovism.

1449. Zavalishin, Viacheslav.   Early Soviet Writers. New York, Praeger, 1958. 394 p.

> A useful monograph on Soviet literature, mostly of the 1920's. Discusses a very large number of writers, including many now

obscure or forgotten, and therefore has little detail on any one, but contains valuable information.

b. Anthologies

1450. Bakshy, Alexander, *comp. and tr.*   Soviet Scene: Six Plays of Russian Life. New Haven, Yale University Press, 1946. 348 p.

> Contains Konstantin Trenev's *Liubov' Iarovaia*, Nikolai Pogodin's *Chimes of the Kremlin*, and other plays.

1451. Blake, Patricia, *and* Max Hayward, *eds.*   Dissonant Voices in Soviet Literature. New York, Pantheon, 1962. 308 p.

> An interesting anthology of "nonconformist" literary pieces by Soviet writers from the 1920's to the present.

1452. Bowra, *Sir* Cecil M., *ed.*   A Book of Russian Verse. Translated into English by various hands. London, Macmillan, 1943. 127 p.

> ———. A Second Book of Russian Verse. Translated into English by various hands. London, Macmillan, 1948. 153 p.

> Verse translations, especially by amateur poets, are seldom satisfactory, but these are better than most.

1453. Bowring, *Sir* John.   Specimens of the Russian Poets. 2d ed. London, 1821-1823. 2 v.

> One of the first collections of translations from Russian into English ever published. Contains quite good translations, mostly of eighteenth-century Russian poets.

1454.* Cournos, John, *ed.*   A Treasury of Classic Russian Literature. New York, Capricorn Books, 1962. 580 p.

> Originally published as *A Treasury of Russian Life and Humor* (New York, Coward-McCann, 1943, 676 p.). A rather odd collection of short stories, verse, and snippets from novels, apparently designed to illustrate the "spirit of Russia" manifested during the war.

1455. Coxwell, Charles F., *ed. and tr.*   Russian Poems. Introduction by D. S. Mirsky. London, Daniel, 1929. 306 p.

> One of the best anthologies of nineteenth and early twentieth-century Russian poetry in English.

1456. Four Soviet Plays.   London, Lawrence and Wishart; New York, International Publishers, 1937. 427 p.

> Contains plays by Gor'kii, Vsevolod Vishnevskii, Nikolai Pogodin, and Ivan Kocherha.

1457. Graham, Stephen, *ed.*   Great Russian Short Stories. London, Benn, 1929. 1,008 p.

> A vast compendium of short stories from Zhukovskii to Valentin Kataev. Later edition: New York, Liveright, 1960, 1,021 p.

1458. Guerney, Bernard G., *comp. and tr.*   New Russian Stories. London, Owen; New York, New Directions, 1953. 240 p.

> A small selection of Soviet short stories from the 1920's onward.

1459.* Guerney, Bernard G., *ed.*   The Portable Russian Reader. New York, Viking, 1947. 658 p.

> A rather miscellaneous sampling of prose and verse from the nineteenth and twentieth centuries. Pleasant reading, but too "cutely" edited.

1460. Guerney, Bernard G., *ed.*   A Treasury of Russian Literature. New York, Vanguard, 1943; Philadelphia, Blakiston, 1945. 1,048 p.

> A vast compendium, mostly from Russian literature of the nineteenth and twentieth centuries. The editor is obtrusive, but not always informative or accurate.

1461. Kunitz, Joshua, *ed.*   Russian Literature since the Revolution. New York, Boni and Gaer, 1948. 932 p.

> Contains some verse, many short stories, and the complete texts of three novels: Kataev's *The Embezzlers*; Sholokhov's *Virgin Soil Upturned*; and Krymov's *Tanker Derbent*. Poorly edited and annotated.

1462. Lyons, Eugene, *ed.*   Six Soviet Plays. Boston, New York, Houghton Mifflin, 1934. 468 p.

> A good collection of plays, including Mikhail Bulgakov's *Days of the Turbins* and Valentin Kataev's *Squaring the Circle*. British edition: London, Gollancz, 1935, 608 p.

1463.* McLean, Hugh, *and* Walter N. Vickery, *eds. and trs.*   The Year of Protest, 1956; an Anthology of Soviet Literary Materials. New York, Vintage Books, 1961. 269 p.

> Short stories, verse, criticism, and a play published during the "thaw" year.

1464. Nabokov, Vladimir, *ed. and tr.*   Three Russian Poets; Selections from Pushkin, Lermontov and Tyutchev in New Translations. Norfolk, Conn., New Directions, 1944. 37 p.

> Excellent translations of selected lyrics. British edition published as *Pushkin, Lermontov, Tyutchev; Poems* (London, Drummond, 1947, 56 p.)

1465.* Noyes, George R., *ed. and tr.*   Masterpieces of the Russian Drama. London, New York, Appleton, 1933. 902 p.

> One of the best anthologies of the Russian drama, from Griboedov's *Woe from Wit* to Maiakovskii's *Mystery-Bouffe*. New editions: New York, Dover, 1960, 2 v.; Gloucester, Mass., P. Smith, 1961.

1466.* Obolensky, Dimitri, *ed.*   The Penguin Book of Russian Verse. Harmondsworth, Baltimore, Penguin Books, 1962. 444 p.
See also entry no. 1382.
　　The Russian texts with English prose translations.

1467. The Oxford Book of Russian Verse.   Edited by Maurice Baring. 2d ed. Supplemented by D. P. Costello. Notes by D. S. Mirsky. London, Oxford University Press, 1953. 311 p.
　　An agreeable anthology of Russian poetry. Russian text only, with English introduction and commentaries.

1468. Reavey, George, *and* Marc Slonim, *eds. and trs.*   Soviet Literature; an Anthology. London, Wishart, 1933, 430 p.; New York, Covici-Friede, 1934. 426 p.
　　One of the most representative collections of early Soviet literature, containing short stories, excerpts from novels, poetry, and criticism.

1469.* Reeve, Franklin D., *ed. and tr.*   An Anthology of Russian Plays. New York, Vintage Books, 1961-1963. 2 v.
See also entry no. 1383.
　　A basic collection of Russian plays, including the best-known classics from Fonvizin to Maiakovskii, and a few not so well known.

1470. Seven Soviet Plays.   Edited by Henry W. L. Dana. New York, Macmillan, 1946. 520 p.
　　Contains plays from the 1930's and 1940's by Leonov, Afinogenov, Simonov, Korneichuk, and others.

1471. Shelley, Gerard, *tr.*   Modern Poems from Russia. London, Allen and Unwin, 1942. 93 p.
　　Mostly poems of the Symbolist and post-Symbolist generations.

1472. Yarmolinsky, Avrahm, *ed.*   An Anthology of Russian Verse, 1812-1960. Garden City, N. Y., Doubleday, 1962. 292 p.
　　A "revised and expanded" version of earlier editions: *A Treasury of Russian Verse* (New York, Macmillan, 1949); *Russian Poetry, an Anthology* (New York, International Publishers; London, Lawrence, 1929); and *Modern Russian Poetry* (London, Lane, 1921).
　　A fairly comprehensive selection. Most of the translations, by Babette Deutsch, are smooth, but often stray rather far from the originals in style and diction.

1473. Yarmolinsky, Avrahm, *ed.*   Soviet Short Stories. Garden City, N. Y., Anchor Books, 1960. 301 p.
　　A collection of stories from the whole range of Soviet literature, from Zamiatin to Israel Metter.

1474. Yarmolinsky, Avrahm, *ed.*   A Treasury of Great Russian Short Stories, Pushkin to Gorky. New York, Macmillan, 1944. 1,018 p.
　　A large selection of classic stories, well presented.

c. Translations of works of individual authors, and works about them

Works in this section have been listed in the following order under each writer's entry: bibliographies, works by the writer, works about the writer. Not always are all three categories included.

1475. **Akhmatova, Anna A.**
Forty-seven Poems. Translated by Natalie Duddington. London, Cape, 1927. 64 p.
> Poems by one of the leading Acmeists, a major poet of the post-Symbolist generation.

1476. **Aksakov, Sergei T.**
A Russian Gentleman.* Translated by J. D. Duff. London, Edward Arnold, 1917. 209 p.
> A standard classic: a semi-fictionalized autobiography and vivid evocation of Russian provincial life at the end of the eighteenth century. Second edition: London and New York, Oxford University Press, 1923, 283 p. Translation of *Semeinaia khronika* (1856).

A Russian Schoolboy. Translated by J. D. Duff. London, Edward Arnold; New York, Longmans, Green, 1917. 216 p.
> Continuation of *A Russian Gentleman.* Second edition: London, Oxford University Press, 1924, 288 p. Translation of *Vospominaniia* (1856).

Years of Childhood.* Translated by J. D. Duff. London, Edward Arnold; New York, Longmans, Green, 1916. 340 p.
> Further recollections of the author's early childhood. Second edition: London and New York, Oxford University Press, 1923, 446 p. Translation of *Detskie gody Bagrova-vnuka* (1858).

1477. **Andreev, Leonid N.**
Plays: The Black Maskers; The Life of Man; The Sabine Women. Translated by Clarence L. Meader and Fred Newton Scott. Introduction by V. V. Brusyanin. New York, Scribners; London, Duckworth, 1915. 214 p.
> Representative examples of Andreev's work as a dramatist. Translations of *Chernye maski* (1909), *Zhizn' cheloveka* (1907), and *Prekrasnye sabinianki* (1912).

His Excellency the Governor. Translated by M. Magnus. London, Daniel, 1921. 96 p.
> One of Andreev's best stories. Translation of *Gubernator* (1906).

The Seven That Were Hanged, and Other Stories.* New York, Random House, 1958; New York, Vintage Books, 1961. 249 p.
> A good collection of Andreev's stories. Translations of *Rasskaz o semi poveshennykh* (1908) and other stories.

Kaun, Alexander S. Leonid Andreyev; a Critical Study. New York, B. W. Huebsch, 1924. 361 p. Bibliography.
> A scholarly and discriminating monograph.

1478. Babel', Isaak E.
The Collected Stories.* Edited and translated by Walter Morison. Introduction by Lionel Trilling. New York, Criterion Books, 1955. Harmondsworth, Penguin Books, 1961. 381 p.
> The complete fiction (no plays) of this important Soviet prose writer. Translations of *Konarmiia, Odesskie rasskazy,* and other stories.

1479. Belinskii, Vissarion G.
Selected Philosophical Works. Moscow, Foreign Languages Publishing House, 1948. 552 p.
> Articles and book reviews, rather tendentiously selected, by this leading nineteenth-century critic. Despite the title, the emphasis is literary, not "philosophical." Second edition: 1956, 583 p. Translation of *Izbrannye filosofskie proizvedeniia* (Moscow, Gospolitizdat, 1941).

Matlaw, Ralph E., *ed.* Belinsky, Chernyshevsky, and Dobrolyubov; Selected Criticism.* New York, Dutton, 1962. 226 p.
> A selection of basic texts by these three pillars of social criticism of literature in the nineteenth century.

Bowman, Herbert E. Vissarion Belinski, 1811-1848; a Study in the Origins of Social Criticism in Russia. Cambridge, Harvard University Press, 1954. 220 p.
> A useful and judicious, if somewhat pedestrian, survey of Belinskii's intellectual development.

1480. Blok, Aleksandr A.
Reeve, Franklin D. Aleksandr Blok: between Image and Idea. New York, Columbia University Press, 1962. 268 p. Ports., facsims.
> An interesting, if somewhat densely and even pretentiously written, monograph on Blok's poetry and ideas.

Bonneau, Sophie. L'univers poétique d'Alexandre Blok. Paris, Institut d'Études Slaves, 1946. 519 p.
> A substantial monograph on Blok's themes and style.

Berberova, Nina. Alexandre Blok et son temps, suivi d'un choix de poèmes. Paris, Éditions du Chêne, 1947. 248 p.
> A good introductory study, with a selection of poems translated into French.

1481. Briusov, Valerii Ia.
The Fiery Angel. A Sixteenth-Century Romance. Translated by Ivor Montagu and Sergei Nalbandov. London, H. Toulmin, 1930. 392 p.
> The most important novel by this leader of the Symbolists, a historical romance about sixteenth-century Germany. Translation of *Ognennyi angel* (1908).

The Republic of the Southern Cross, and Other Stories. Translated with an introduction by Stephen Graham. London, Constable, 1918; New York, McBride, 1919. 162 p.

Translation of *Respublika iuzhnogo kresta* and other stories.

1482. Bugaev, Boris N. (Andrei Belyi, *pseud.*)

St. Petersburg.* Translated with an introduction by John Cournos. Foreword by George Reavey. New York, Grove Press, 1959; London, Weidenfeld and Nicolson, 1960. 310 p.

A major novel by this important Symbolist.

Maslenikov, Oleg. The Frenzied Poets; Andrey Biely and the Russian Symbolists. Berkeley, University of California Press, 1952. 234 p. Bibliography, ports.

An informative monograph on the life of Belyi and his relations with other poets and writers of his time.

1483. Bunin, Ivan A.

The Village. Translated by Isabel F. Hapgood. New York, Knopf, 1923; London, Martin Secker, 1923. 291 p.

An important novel by a major figure of the early twentieth century. Mediocre translation of *Derevnia* (1910).

The Gentleman from San Francisco.* Translated by Bernard Guilbert Guerney. New York, Knopf, 1923. 313 p.

In addition to the title story, an acknowledged classic, the book contains some of Bunin's most memorable work in the short story form, including "A Goodly Life," "Brethren," and "The Dreams of Chang." Reprinted in 1927, 1933, and 1941. Translations of *Gospodin iz San-Frantsisko* and other stories.

Dark Avenues, and Other Stories. Translated by Richard Hare. London, Lehmann, 1949. 223 p.

Bunin's last collection of short stories. Translation of *Temnye allei* (1946).

1484. Chekhov, Anton P.

Heifetz, Anna S. Chekhov in English; a List of Works by and about Him. New York, New York Public Library, 1949. 35 p.

Covers the period through 1948.

Yachnin, Rissa. Chekhov in English; a Selective List of Works by and about Him, 1949-1960. New York, New York Public Library, 1960. 11 p.

The Tales of Tchehov. Translated by Constance Garnett. London, Chatto and Windus; New York, Macmillan, 1916-1923. 13 v.

The largest single collection of Chekhov's stories in English, but still far from complete.

The Plays of Tchehov. London, Chatto and Windus; New York, Macmillan, 1923. 2 v.

The Grasshopper, and Other Stories.   Translated with an introduction by A. E. Chamot. London, Paul; Philadelphia, McKay, 1926. 283 p.
>   Contains stories not in the Garnett edition.

Stories of Russian Life.   Translated by Marian Fell. New York, Scribner's; London, Duckworth, 1914. 314 p.

Russian Silhouettes; More Stories of Russian Life.   Translated by Marian Fell. New York, Scribner's; London, Duckworth, 1915. 318 p.

Bruford, Walter H.   Chekhov and His Russia; a Sociological Study. London, K. Paul, Trench, Trubner, 1947. 233 p. Bibliography.
See also entry no. 1151.
>   An interesting review of Chekhov's stories and plays from the point of view of the classes and social problems depicted in them.

Magarshack, David.   Chekhov; a Life. London, Faber and Faber, 1952; New York, Grove Press, 1953. 431 p.
>   A readable but rather unreliable biography.

Hingley, Ronald.   Chekhov; a Biographical and Critical Study. London, Allen and Unwin, 1950. 278 p. Bibliography.
>   A useful brief monograph on Chekhov's life and works. Contains a chronological list of all Chekhov's stories available in English.

Eekman, T., *ed.*   Anton Čechov, 1860-1960; Some Essays. Leiden, Brill, 1960. 335 p.
>   An excellent collection of essays, in various languages, by leading Chekhov scholars throughout the world.

Magarshack, David.   Chekhov, the Dramatist.* London, Lehmann; New York, Auvergne, 1952. 301 p. Illus.
See also entry no. 1922.
>   An analysis of the genesis and structure of Chekhov's plays. Later edition: New York, Hill and Wang, 1960.

Simmons, Ernest J.   Chekhov; a Biography. Boston, Little, Brown, 1962. 669 p. Illus.
>   A massive and detailed life.

1485. Chernyshevskii, Nikolai G.
Selected Philosophical Essays.   Moscow, Foreign Languages Publishing House, 1953. 610 p. Illus.
>   A large collection of articles, some of them literary criticism and theory, by this leading nineteenth-century radical and materialist.

What's To Be Done? Tales about New People.*   The Benjamin R. Rucker translation, revised and abridged by Ludmila B. Turke-

vich. Introduction by E. H. Carr. New York, Vintage Books, 1961.
354 p.

> Though artistically hopeless, this novel is important as an intellectual document and as a prototype of later didactic radical novels. Translation of *Chto delat'?* (1862).

1486. Dobroliubov, Nikolai A.
Selected Philosophical Essays. Translated by J. Fineberg. Moscow, Foreign Languages Publishing House, 1948. 650 p.

> A large collection of articles, mostly on literature, by this important radical critic of the late 1850's.

1487. Dostoevskii, Fedor M.
The Novels of Fyodor Dostoevsky. Translated by Constance Garnett. London, W. Heinemann; New York, Macmillan, 1912-1920. 12 v.

> This set includes all Dostoevski's fiction, plus *Notes from the House of the Dead*. There are more recent translations of some of the novels, but the Garnett version remains standard. Numerous reprints of the individual volumes of this translation exist.

The Diary of a Writer. Translated and annotated by Boris Brasol. New York, Scribner's; London, Cassell, 1949. 2 v. (1,079 p.)

> Not really a diary, but a collection of journalistic pieces Dostoevski wrote under this title on a wide variety of literary, cultural, and political topics. Inadequately annotated. Translation of *Dnevnik pisatelia* (1873-1880).

Berdiaev, Nikolai A. Dostoevsky.* Translated by Donald Attwater. New York, Meridian Books, 1957. 227 p.

> An important milestone among Russian Dostoevski studies. A philosophical and religious, rather than social or artistic, interpretation; interesting, if sometimes arbitrary. Translation of *Mirosozertsanie Dostoevskago* (Prague, YMCA Press, 1923).

Carr, Edward H. Dostoevsky, 1821-1881; a New Biography.* Preface by D. S. Mirsky. London, Allen and Unwin, 1931; Boston, New York, Houghton Mifflin, 1931. 331 p.

> A well-written life, based on thorough research. The tone of amused condescension, however, becomes irritating. Reprinted: London, Allen and Unwin, 1949.

Mochul'skii, Konstantin V. (Constantine Motchoulski). Dostoievski; l'homme et l'oeuvre. Translated by Gustave Welter. Paris, Payot, 1962. 552 p.

> One of the best single works on Dostoevski, skillfully treating the interrelation between his life, art, and ideas. Translation of *Dostoevskii; zhizn' i tvorchestvo* (Paris, YMCA Press, 1947).

Simmons, Ernest J. Dostoevski; the Making of a Novelist.* New York, London, Oxford University Press, 1940. 416 p.

> An informative monograph on the development of Dostoevski's

art. Later editions: London, Lehman, 1950; New York, Vintage, 1963.

Muchnic, Helen. Dostoevsky's English Reputation, 1881-1936. Northampton, Mass., 1939. 219 p. Bibliography. (Smith College Studies in Modern Languages, v. 20, no. 3-4)
>An excellent survey of English and American criticism of Dostoevski.

Seduro, Vladimir. Dostoyevski in Russian Literary Criticism, 1846-1956. New York, Columbia University Press, 1957. 411 p. Bibliography.
>A useful survey of the history of criticism and scholarship on the works of Dostoevski.

Passage, Charles E. Dostoevski the Adapter; a Study in Dostoevski's Use of the Tales of Hoffmann. Chapel Hill, University of North Carolina Press, 1954. 203 p.
>An interesting analysis of Dostoevski's use of themes from Hoffmann's tales.

Yarmolinsky, Avrahm. Dostoevskii; a Life. New York, Harcourt, Brace, 1934. 447 p.
>The most straightforward and satisfactory biography in English. Revised and enlarged edition published as *Dostoevsky, His Life and Art* (New York, Criterion Books, 1957, 434 p.)

Wellek, René, *ed.* Dostoevsky; a Collection of Critical Essays.* Englewood Cliffs, N. J., Prentice-Hall, 1962. 180 p.
>A collection of critical articles on Dostoevski, mostly by Western writers. Includes a valuable "History of Dostoevsky Criticism" by the editor.

Ivanov, Viacheslav I. Freedom and the Tragic Life; a Study in Dostoevsky.* Foreword by Sir Maurice Bowra. Translated by Norman Cameron. London, Harvill Press; New York, Noonday Press, 1952. 166 p.
>An important study by the noted Symbolist poet. Translation of *Dostoevskii i roman-tragediia* (1932).

1488. Ehrenburg, Il'ia G.
The Extraordinary Adventures of Julio Jurenito and His Disciples. Translated by Usick Vanzler. New York, Covici-Friede, 1930. 399 p.
>One of Ehrenburg's early satirical novels. Another edition: *Julio Jurenito*, translated by Anna Bostock and Yvonne Kapp (London, MacGibbon, 1958, 317 p.). Translations of *Neobychainye pokhozhdeniia Khulio Khurenito i ego uchenikov* (1922).

Out of Chaos. Translated by Alexander Bakshy. New York, Henry Holt, 1934. 391 p.
>Ehrenburg's "Five-Year-Plan" novel, a turning point in his career. Translation of *Den' vtoroi* (1931).

A Change of Season.   Translated by Manya Harari and Humphrey Higgins. London, MacGibbon and Kee, 1961; New York, Knopf, 1962. 299 p.

> Ehrenburg's most recent novel, which gave its name to the whole post-Stalin "thaw" in Soviet life. Translation of *Ottepel'*. Part one (1954) also translated separately as *The Thaw*, and part two (1956) as *The Spring*.

People and Life.   Translated by Anna Bostock and Yvonne Kapp. London, MacGibbon and Kee, 1962-1963. 3 v.

> The first three volumes of Ehrenburg's memoirs, extending from 1891 to 1933. A valuable source on Russian literature and literary life, and an epoch-making event in recent Soviet literature. Translation of *Liudi, gody, zhizn'* (1961-1963). Volumes one and two also published in one volume as *People and Life, 1891-1921* (New York, Knopf, 1962, 453 p.)

Eve of War, 1933-1941.   Translated by Tatiana Shebunina with Yvonne Kapp. London, MacGibbon and Kee, 1963. 286 p.

> The fourth volume of the controversial memoirs.

1489. Esenin, Sergei A.
Serge Essénine; une étude par Sophie Laffitte.   Choix de textes, bibliographie, portraits. Paris, P. Seghers, 1959. 219 p. Illus.

> A selection of Esenin's poetry translated into French, with a biographical and critical introduction.

1490. Fadeev, Aleksandr A.
The Nineteen.   Translated by R. D. Charques. London, Laurence; New York, International, 1929. 293 p.

> An important early Soviet novel, neo-Realist in style. Another edition: *The Rout*, translated by O. Gorchakov (Moscow, Foreign Languages Publishing House, n.d., 207 p.). Translations of *Razgrom* (1927).

The Young Guard; a Novel.   Translated by Violet Duff. Moscow, Foreign Languages Publishing House, n.d. 715 p.

> A 1945 Stalin Prize novel (*Molodaia gvardiia*) about the Second World War, drastically revised as a result of official criticism, and reissued in 1951.

1491. Fedin, Konstantin A.
Cities and Years; a Novel.*   Translated by Michael Scammell. New York, Dell, 1962. 415 p.

> Fedin's first, and in many ways his best, novel. Translation of *Goroda i gody* (1924).

No Ordinary Summer; a Novel in Two Parts.*   Translated by Margaret Wettlin. Moscow, Foreign Languages Publishing House, 1950. 2 v.

> One of the best postwar Soviet novels; deals with the period of the Revolution and Civil War. Translation of *Pervye radosti* (1945-

1946) and *Neobyknovennoe leto* (1948). The first volume is also available separately, in two editions, as *Early Joys* (Moscow, Foreign Languages Publishing House, 1948, 503 p.; New York, Vintage Books, 1960, 418 p.)

1492. Garshin, Vsevolod M.
The Signal, and Other Stories. Translated by Captain Rowland Smith. London, Duckworth; New York, Knopf, 1915. 356 p.
Stories by an interesting, if short-lived, fiction writer of the 1880's. Translations of *Signal* (1887) and other stories.

Parker, Fan. Vsevolod Garshin; a Study of a Russian Conscience. New York, King's Crown Press, 1946. 86 p. Bibliography.
A rather pedestrian monograph on Garshin.

1493. Gippius, Zinaida N. (Merezhkovskaia).
The Green Ring; a Play in Four Acts. Translated by S. S. Koteliansky. London, Daniel, 1920. 104 p.
A play by the noted Symbolist poet, the wife of D. S. Merezhkovskii. Translation of *Zelenoe kol'tso* (1916).

1494. Gladkov, Fedor V.
Cement; a Novel.* Translated by A. S. Arthur and C. Ashleigh. London, Lawrence and Wishart; New York, International, 1929. 311 p.
Not a very good novel, but important as a prototype of the "industrial novel" so characteristic of later Soviet literature. New edition: New York, Ungar, 1960. Translations of *Tsement* (1925).

1495. Gogol', Nikolai V.
Moscow. Vsesoiuznaia gosudarstvennaia biblioteka inostrannoi literatury. Bibliografiia perevodov na inostrannye iazyki proizvedenii N. V. Gogolia (Bibliography of Translations of Works of N. V. Gogol' into Foreign Languages). Moscow, 1953. 107 p.

The Works of Nikolay Gogol. Translated by Constance Garnett. London, Chatto and Windus; New York, Knopf, 1922-1929. 6 v.
Includes all of Gogol's completed fiction. There are numerous reprints of separate volumes of this edition, as well as later translations of various works contained in it. Of the latter the following is especially worthy of notice: *Chichikov's Journeys; or, Home Life in Old Russia* (Dead Souls). Translated by Bernard Guilbert Guerney. Foreword by Clifton Fadiman. New York, The Readers Club, 1942, 368 p. Second edition, with an introduction by Avrahm Yarmolinsky: New York, The Heritage Press, 1944, 484 p. Translation of *Mertvye dushi*, including the unfinished second volume.

Setschkareff, Vsevolod. N. V. Gogol; Leben und Schaffen. Berlin, O. Harrassowitz, 1953. 192 p. Bibliography. (Veröffentlichungen der Abteilung für Slavische Sprachen und Literaturen des Osteuropa-Instituts [Slavisches Seminar] an der Freien Universität Berlin, Bd. 2)

The most scholarly condensed monograph on Gogol' in any Western language.

Magarshack, David. Gogol; a Life. London, Faber and Faber; New York, Grove Press, 1957. 329 p. Illus.

A well-documented and readable biography.

Nabokov, Vladimir V. Nikolai Gogol.* Norfolk, Conn., New Directions, 1944. 172 p.

An extravagant and biased but stimulating monograph, dealing principally with *The Inspector-General, Dead Souls,* and *The Overcoat.*

1496. Goncharov, Ivan A.
A Common Story. Translated by Constance Garnett. London, William Heinemann, 1917. 283 p.

Goncharov's first novel, a milestone in the development of Russian realism. Translation of *Obyknovennaia istoriia* (1847).

Oblomov.* Translated by Natalie A. Duddington. London, G. Allen and Unwin; New York, Macmillan, 1929. 525 p.

Goncharov's greatest novel, a major Russian classic. Later editions: London, J. M. Dent; New York, Dutton, 1932 and 1953, 517 p. Translations of *Oblomov* (1859).

Mazon, André. Un maître du roman russe; Ivan Gontcharov, 1812-1891. Paris, Champion, 1914. 473 p. Bibliography.

A solid and thorough, but very pedestrian, "life and works."

1497. Gor'kii, Maksim.
Selected Short Stories. Introduction by Stefan Zweig. New York, F. Ungar, 1959. 348 p.

A representative selection of Gor'kii's work in the short story form.

Mother.* New York, Appleton, 1921. 498 p.

Probably Gor'kii's worst novel, but historically important since it is held up as a model of "socialist realism." Other editions, translated by Margaret Wettlin: Moscow, Foreign Languages Publishing House, 1950, 716 p.; 4th ed., n.d., 382 p.; New York, Collier Books, 1962, 352 p. Translations of *Mat'* (1907).

The Autobiography of Maxim Gorky: My Childhood; In the World; My Universities.* Translated from the Russian by Isidor Schneider. New York, Citadel Press, 1949. 616 p.
See also entry no. 126.

Though represented as a new translation, this version was actually produced by rewriting the following earlier translations: *My Childhood,* translated from *Detstvo* (1913) by Gertrude M.

Foakes (London, T. W. Laurie, 1915, 308 p.; New York, Century, 1916, 374 p.); *In the World*, translated from *V liudiakh* (1915) by Gertrude M. Foakes (London, T. W. Laurie, 1917, 464 p.; New York, Century, 1917, 507 p.); *Reminiscences of My Youth* (My Universities), translated from *Moi universitety* (1923) by Veronica Dewey (London, William Heinemann, 1924, 334 p.)

This autobiographical trilogy is undoubtedly Gor'kii's greatest work and a major classic.

Reminiscences of Tolstoy, Chekhov, and Andreev.* Translated by Katharine Mansfield, S. S. Koteliansky, and Leonard Woolf. London, Leonard and Virginia Woolf, 1934. 191 p.

A major work of literature, one of Gor'kii's very best, full of sensitivity and insight. New edition: London, Hogarth Press, 1949. Translation of *Lev Tolstoi* (1919), *A. P. Chekhov* (1904), and *L. Andreev* (1922).

A Book of Short Stories. Edited by Avrahm Yarmolinsky and Baroness Moura Budberg. New York, Henry Holt, 1939. 403 p.

A good, comprehensive selection of Gor'kii's short fiction.

Seven Plays of Maxim Gorky. Translated by Alexander Bakshy, in collaboration with Paul S. Nathan. New Haven, Yale University Press, 1945. 396 p.

Gor'kii's work as a dramatist, including *The Lower Depths* and *Egor Bulichev and the Others*. New edition with the title *The Lower Depths, and Other Plays*: 1959, 220 p.

Kaun, Alexander S. Maxim Gorky and His Russia. New York, J. Cape and H. Smith, 1931. 620 p.

The most scholarly biography, based on extensive research as well as personal contacts.

1498. Griboedov, Aleksandr S.
The Mischief of Being Clever. Translated by Bernard Pares. Introduction by D. S. Mirsky. London, Eyre and Spottiswoode, 1925. 67 p.

A major classic of the Russian theater. Translation of *Gore ot uma* (1822-1823). *See* entry no. 1465 for another translation.

1499. Grigor'ev, Apollon A.
My Literary and Moral Wanderings, and Other Autobiographical Material.* Translated with an introduction by Ralph E. Matlaw. New York, Dutton, 1962. 174 p.

One of the best autobiographical works in Russian, by an important critic and poet. Translation of *Moi literaturnye i nravstvennye skital'chestva* (1864).

1500. Il'f, Il'ia, *pseud.* (Il'ia Fainzil'berg), *and* Evgenii Petrov, *pseud.* (Evgenii Kataev).
The Twelve Chairs.* Translated by John H. C. Richardson. In-

troduction by Maurice Friedberg. New York, Vintage Books, 1961.
395 p.
>One of the best Soviet satirical novels. Translation of *Dvenad-tsat' stul'ev* (1928).

The Golden Calf.* Translated by John H. C. Richardson. New York, Random House, 1962. 390 p.
>A sequel to *The Twelve Chairs,* carrying the action into the First Five-Year Plan period. Translation of *Zolotoi telenok* (1931).
>*The Twelve Chairs* and *The Golden Calf* have been published in one volume under the title *The Complete Adventures of Ostap Bender* (New York, Random House, 1963, 785 p.)

Little Golden America; Two Famous Soviet Humorists Survey These United States. Translated by Charles Malamuth. New York, Farrar and Rinehart, 1937. 387 p. Illus.
>A witty and mildly satirical travelogue. Translation of *Odnoetazhnaia Amerika* (1936).

1501. Kataev, Valentin P.
The Embezzlers. Translated by Leonid Zarine. Introduction by Stephen Graham. New York, Dial Press, 1929. 300 p.; London, Benn, 1929. 254 p.
>An amusing satirical novel about the NEP period. Translation of *Rastratchiki* (1927).

Peace Is Where the Tempests Blow. Translated by Charles Malamuth. New York, Farrar and Rinehart, 1937. 341 p.
>A very well written novel, dealing with the experiences of two boys in Odessa during the revolution of 1905. Other editions: *Lonely White Sail, or Peace Is Where the Tempests Blow* (London, Allen and Unwin, 1937, 341 p.); *A White Sail Gleams*, translated by Leonard Stoklitsky (Moscow, Foreign Languages Publishing House, 1954, 294 p.). Translations of *Beleet parus odinokii* (1936).

Time, Forward! Translated by Charles Malamuth. New York, Farrar and Rinehart, 1933. 345 p.
>A characteristic "Five-Year-Plan" novel, much better than the average. Another edition: *Forward, Oh Time!* (London, Gollancz, 1935, 432 p.). Translations of *Vremia, vpered!* (1932).

1502. Khlebnikov, Velemir.
Markov, Vladimir. The Longer Poems of Velemir Khlebnikov. Berkeley, University of California Press, 1962. 273 p. Bibliography.
>A valuable monograph on this difficult and important poet, leader of the Futurists.

1503. Korolenko, Vladimir G.
The Blind Musician. Translated by Sergius Stepniak and William Westfall. London, Ward and Downey, 1890. 187 p.
>An excellent early story. Another edition, translated by Aline Delano, with an introduction by George Kennan: Boston, Little, Brown, 1890, 244 p. Translations of *Slepoi muzykant* (1886).

The Murmuring Forest, and Other Stories.   Translated by Marian
Fell. London, Duckworth, 1916. 297 p.

> A good collection of some of Korolenko's best stories. Another
> edition, with the title *Makar's Dream, and Other Stories*: New
> York, Duffield, 1916, 297 p. Translation of *Les shumit* (1886),
> *Son Makara* (1885), *V durnom obshchestve* (1885), and *Sudnyi
> den'* (1890).

In a Strange Land.   Translated by Gregory Zilboorg. New York,
Richards, 1925. 214 p.

> An amusing story of three Ukrainian immigrants in America.
> Translation of *Bez iazyka* (1895).

1504. Krylov, Ivan A.
Fables.   Translated with a preface by Bernard Pares. London,
Cape, 1926; New York, Harcourt, 1927. 271 p.

> The greatest Russian fabulist (1768-1844).

1505. Kuprin, Aleksandr I.
The River of Life, and Other Stories.   Translated by S. S. Koteliansky and J. M. Murry. London, Maunsel; Boston, Luce, 1916. 248
p.

> Another edition: London, Allen and Unwin, 1943.

Yama (The Pit); a Novel in Three Parts.*   Translated by Bernard
Guilbert Guerney. Foreword by Arthur Garfield Hays. New York,
The Modern Library, 1932. 442 p.

> A famous novel about prostitution. Another edition: London,
> Hamilton, 1924, 326 p. Translations of *Iama* (1910).

The Bracelet of Garnets, and Other Stories.   Translated by Leo
Pasvolsky. Introduction by William Lyon Phelps. New York, Scribners, 1917; London, Duckworth, 1919. 266 p.

> Another good collection of Kuprin stories. Translations of *Grana-
> tovyi braslet* (1911) and other stories. A similar collection: *The
> Garnet Bracelet, and Other Stories*, translated by Stepan Apresyan
> (Moscow, Foreign Languages Publishing House, 1960, 383 p.)

The Duel; and Selected Stories.*   Translated with an afterword
by Andrew R. MacAndrew. New York, New American Library,
1961. 256 p.

> A good collection of Kuprin's stories. Translation of *Poedinok*
> (1905) and other stories.

1506. Leonov, Leonid M.
Sot.   Translated by Ivor Montagu and S. S. Nolbandov. Foreword
by Maksim Gor'kii. London, Putnam, 1931. 387 p.

> Leonov's "First Five-Year Plan" novel. Another edition, with
> the title *Soviet River*: New York, Dial Press, 1932, 383 p. Transla-
> tions of *Sot'* (1931).

The Thief.*   Translated by Hubert Butler. London, Secker and
Warburg; New York, Dial Press, 1931. 566 p.

Probably Leonov's best novel, a psychological study of some human anomalies of the NEP period. New edition: New York, Vintage, 1960, 519 p. Translation of *Vor* (1927).

The Badgers.   Translated by Hilda Kazanina. London, New York, Hutchinson, 1947. 336 p.

Leonov's first, and one of his best novels, dealing with the theme of peasant opposition to the Bolsheviks during the Civil War. Translation of *Barsuki* (1925).

1507. Lermontov, Mikhail Iu.
A Hero of Our Own Times.* Translated by Eden and Cedar Paul. Introduction by Sir Maurice Bowra. London, New York, Oxford University Press, 1958. 284 p.

A major classic of Russian prose. A translation by Vladimir Nabokov and Dmitri Nabokov, entitled *A Hero of Our Time* (Garden City, N. Y., Doubleday, 1958, 210 p.), is better, but the edition is marred by the too obtrusive and self-indulgent presence of the translator and his opinions. Translations of *Geroi nashego vremeni* (1840).

Mersereau, John.   Mikhail Lermontov. Preface by Harry T. Moore. Carbondale, Southern Illinois University Press, 1962. 176 p.

A well-informed and judicious monograph on Lermontov's life and works, with emphasis on his prose.

1508. Leskov, Nikolai S.
The Cathedral Folk.   Translated by Isabel F. Hapgood. New York, Knopf; London, Lane, 1924. 439 p.

An important novel on the life of the clergy (*Soboriane*, 1872). The translation, unfortunately, is very poor.

Selected Tales.*   Translated by David Magarshack. Introduction by V. S. Pritchett. London, Secker and Warburg; New York, Farrar, Strauss and Cudahy, 1961. 300 p.

A fairly representative sampling of Leskov's shorter fiction, including *The Enchanted Wanderer* (*Ocharovannyi strannik*, 1874) and *The Left-Handed Craftsman* (*Levsha*, 1882).

The Musk-Ox, and Other Tales.   Translated by R. Norman. London, Routledge, 1944. 207 p.

Another good selection of Leskov's stories.

The Amazon, and Other Stories.   Translated by David Magarshack. London, Allen and Unwin, 1949. 282 p.

The Sentry, and Other Stories.   Translated by A. E. Chamot. London, Lane; New York, Knopf, 1923. 320 p. Port., illus.

Setschkareff, Vsevolod.   N. S. Leskov; sein Leben und sein Werk. Wiesbaden, O. Harrassowitz, 1959. 170 p.

Over-condensed and rather hostile to its subject, but the best monograph on Leskov in a Western language.

1509. Maiakovskii, Vladimir V.
Mayakovsky and His Poetry.   Compiled by Herbert Marshall. London, Pilot Press, 1942. 151 p.
    A fair sampling of Maiakovskii's verse, quite well translated, but accompanied by unpleasantly Party-line commentaries. Revised edition: London, 1945, 157 p.; New York, Transatlantic Arts, 1946, 157 p.

The Bedbug, and Selected Poetry.*   Translated by Max Hayward and George Reavey. Edited by Patricia Blake. Cleveland, Meridian Books, 1960; London, Weidenfeld and Nicolson, 1961. 317 p.
    Maiakovskii's best satirical play, plus a small selection of poetry, the latter in both English and Russian.

1510. Merezhkovskii, Dmitrii S.
Julian the Apostate. The Death of the Gods.   Translated by Bernard Guilbert Guerney. New York, The Modern Library, 1929. 473 p.
    The first part of the trilogy Christ and Antichrist by the noted Symbolist novelist, poet, and critic. Translation of Iulian Otstupnik, ili Smert' bogov (1894).

The Romance of Leonardo da Vinci.*   Translated by Bernard Guilbert Guerney. New York, The Modern Library, 1928. 637 p.
    Part two of Christ and Antichrist. Other editions: London, Cassell; New York, Random House, 1931, 574 p.; London, Nonesuch Press; New York, The Heritage Club, 1938, 580 p. Translation of Leonardo da Vinchi; ili Voskresshie bogi (1896).

Peter and Alexis; the Romance of Peter the Great.   Translated by Bernard Guilbert Guerney. New York, The Modern Library, 1931. 591 p.
    The final part of Christ and Antichrist. Translation of Petr i Aleksei (1902).

1511. Nekrasov, Nikolai A.
Poems.   Translated by Juliet M. Soskice. Introduction by Lascelles Abercrombie. London, Oxford University Press, 1929. 196 p.

Who Can Be Happy and Free in Russia?   Translated by Juliet M. Soskice. Introduction by David Soskice. London, H. Milford, Oxford University Press, 1917. 339 p.
    Nekrasov's great satirical poem, a panorama of Russian life in the 1870's. Translation of Komu na Rusi zhit' khorosho.

Corbet, Charles.   Nekrasov, l'homme et le poète. Paris, Institut d'Études Slaves, 1948. 465 p. Bibliography.
    A very thorough and scholarly monograph.

1512. Olesha, Iurii K.
The Wayward Comrade and the Commissars.*   Translated by

Andrew R. MacAndrew. New York, New American Library, 1960. 143 p.

> A sample of the work of one of the most talented and thoughtful early Soviet writers. Translation of *Zavist'*, *Liubov'*, *Liompa*, and *Aldebaran*.

1513. Ostrovskii, Aleksandr N.
Plays. Translated and edited by George R. Noyes. New York, Scribners, 1917. 305 p.

> A representative sample of the work of this major dramatist. Translation of *Vospitannitsa* (1859), *Bednost' ne porok* (1854), *Grekh da beda na kogo ne zhivet* (1863), and *Svoi liudi sochtemsia* (1850).

The Storm. Translated by Constance Garnett. London, Duckworth; Chicago, H. Sergel, 1899. 119 p.

> Ostrovskii's most famous and probably greatest play. Translation of *Groza* (1860).

Patouillet, Jules. Ostrovski et son théâtre de moeurs russes. Paris, Plon-Nourrit, 1912. 481 p.
See also entry no. 1906.

> The most substantial work on Ostrovskii in a Western language.

1514. Pasternak, Boris L.
Doctor Zhivago.* Translated from the Russian by Max Hayward and Manya Harari. London, Collins and Harvill Press, 1958. 510 p.
See also entry no. 176.

> This translation has been much criticized, but it is the only one in existence. New edition: 1961, 542 p. "Americanized" version of the same translation: New York, Pantheon, 1958, 558 p.

I Remember; Sketch for an Autobiography.* Translated with a preface and notes by David Magarshack. With an essay on translating Shakespeare, translated by Manya Harari. New York, Pantheon Books, 1959. 191 p. Illus.

> Two characteristic late prose works by the noted poet.

Selected Writings.* New York, New Directions, 1949. 288 p.

> Contains most of Pasternak's prose fiction (other than *Doctor Zhivago*) and a small selection of lyric poems. New edition, with the title *Safe Conduct, an Autobiography; and Other Writings*: 1958, 286 p.

Conquest, Robert. Courage of Genius: the Pasternak Affair; a Documentary Report on Its Literary and Political Significance. London, Collins and Harvill Press, 1961. 191 p.

> A collection of documents concerning the publication of *Doctor Zhivago*, the award to Pasternak of the Nobel Prize, and the repercussions of these events in the Soviet Union and elsewhere.

1515. Pisarev, Dmitrii I.

Selected Philosophical, Social and Political Essays.   Moscow, Foreign Languages Publishing House, 1958. 711 p. Illus.
> Selected articles, some of them literary, by the most extreme of the anti-aesthetic radical critics of the mid-nineteenth century. Translation of *Izbrannye filosofskie i obshchestvenno-politicheskie stat'i*, edited by V. S. Kruzhkov (Moscow, Gospolitizdat, 1944).

Coquart, Armand.   Dmitri Pisarev (1840-1868) et l'idéologie du nihilisme russe. Paris, Institut d'Études Slaves, 1946. 464 p. Bibliography. (Bibliothèque russe de l'Institut d'Études Slaves, v. 21)
See also entry no. 1584.
> A very thorough and scholarly monograph on the nature and sources of Pisarev's ideas.

1516. Pisemskii, Aleksei F.
One Thousand Souls.*   Translated by Ivy Litvinov. New York, Grove Press; London, Calder, 1959. 472 p.
> Probably the best novel of this important writer, too little known in the West. Translation of *Tysiacha dush* (1858).

The Simpleton.   Translated by Ivy Litvinova. Moscow, Foreign Languages Publishing House, 1960. 224 p.
> One of Pisemskii's early novels. Translation of *Tiufiak* (1850).

1517. Pushkin, Aleksandr S.
The Poems, Prose and Plays of Alexander Pushkin.   Selected and edited with an introduction by Avrahm Yarmolinsky. New York, The Modern Library, 1936. 896 p.
> The most comprehensive edition available. Contains all the prose fiction, *Evgenii Onegin*, some of the plays, and a selection of lyric poems. Unfortunately, the translations are mostly unsatisfactory, particularly that of *Evgenii Onegin*.
> A new translation by Vladimir Nabokov, *Eugene Onegin; a Novel in Verse* (New York, Pantheon; Toronto, Random House, 1964, 4 v.), is a novelist's effort to out-scholar the scholars, by producing, together with a careful prose translation, an exhaustive commentary, factual, historical, literary, biographical, and personal. Too bulky for the general reader, but a tour de force of its kind.

Simmons, Ernest J.   Pushkin. Cambridge, Harvard University Press, 1937. 435 p. Bibliography.
> A detailed biography.

Lednicki, Wacław.   Pushkin's Bronze Horseman; the Story of a Masterpiece. With an appendix including, in English, Mickiewicz's "Digression," Pushkin's "Bronze Horseman," and other poems. Berkeley, University of California Press, 1955. 163 p.
> A revealing and very scholarly study of Pushkin's *Mednyi vsadnik*.

Mirskii, Dmitrii P. (D. S. Mirsky).   Pushkin.*   Introduction by George Siegel. New York, Dutton, 1963. 288 p.

A brilliant and illuminating short monograph on Pushkin's life and works. Earlier edition: 1926.

Cross, Samuel H., *and* Ernest J. Simmons, *eds*. Centennial Essays for Pushkin. Cambridge, Harvard University Press, 1937. 226 p.

A collection of essays on various aspects of Pushkin's life and works, by such scholars as G. R. Noyes, Michael Karpovich, George Vernadsky, and others.

1518. Remizov, Aleksei M.

On a Field Azure. Translated by Beatrice Scott. London, Drummond, 1946. 125 p. Illus.

One of Remizov's best stories. Translation of *V pole blakitnom* (1922).

The Fifth Pestilence, together with The History of the Tinkling Cymbal and Sounding Brass, Ivan Semyonovitch Stratilatov. Translated with a preface by Alec Brown. London, Wishart, 1927; New York, Payson and Clarke, 1928. 235 p.

Two powerful stories by this important master. Translation of *Piataia iazva* (1909) and *Povest' o Stratilatove* (1912).

The Clock. Translated by John Cournos. London, Chatto and Windus, 1924. 212 p.

Translation of *Chasy* (1908) and other stories.

1519. Rozanov, Vasilii V.

Fallen Leaves. Bundle One. Translated by S. S. Koteliansky. Foreword by James Stephens. London, Mandrake, 1929. 166 p.

A translation of the first of two collections of essays with this title by this important critic and philosopher. Translation of *Opavshie list'ia* (1913).

Solitaria, with an Abridged Account of the Author's Life by E. Gollerbach, Other Biographical Material and Matter from The Apocalypse of Our Times. Translated by S. S. Koteliansky. London, Wishart, 1927. 188 p.

A characteristic example of Rozanov's best work. Translation of *Uedinennoe* (1912).

1520. Saltykov (Saltykov-Shchedrin), Mikhail E.

Tales from M. Saltykov-Shchedrin. Translated by Dorian Rottenberg. Moscow, Foreign Languages Publishing House, n.d. 198 p. Illus.

A collection of Saltykov's shorter pieces.

Fables. Translated by Vera Volkhovsky. London, Chatto and Windus, 1931. 257 p.

An important late work. Translation of *Basni* (1880-1885).

The Golovlyov Family.* Translated by Natalie Duddington. Introduction by Edward Garnett. London, Allen and Unwin; New York, Macmillan, 1931. 336 p.

One of the great novels of the nineteenth century. New edition: London, Dent; New York, Dutton, 1934, and later printings. Translation of *Gospoda Golovlevy*.

Sanine, Kyra.   Saltykov-Chtchédrine; sa vie et ses oeuvres. Paris, Institut d'Études Slaves, 1956. 358 p. Bibliography.
A very detailed and scholarly monograph.

Strelsky, Nikander.   Saltykov and the Russian Squire. New York, Columbia University Press, 1940. 176 p.
A rather unsatisfactory monograph on the sociology of Saltykov's work.

1521. Sholokhov, Mikhail A.
Tales from the Don.   Translated by H. C. Stevens. London, Putnam, 1961, 285 p.; New York, Knopf, 1962, 310 p.
Translation of *Donskie rasskazy* (1925), Sholokhov's first published work.

The Silent Don.   pt. 1: And Quiet Flows the Don. pt. 2: The Don Flows Home to the Sea.* Translated by Stephen Garry. London, Putnam, 1940, 868 p.; New York, Knopf, 1934, 1946, 2 v.
One of the most notable Soviet novels, an epic account of the Revolution and Civil War. Translation of *Tikhii Don* (1928-1940).

Virgin Soil Upturned.   v. 1: Seeds of Tomorrow. Translated by Stephen Garry. New York, Knopf, 1959. 404 p.
See also entry no. 182.
A characteristic Soviet novel, dealing with collectivization. Other editions: London, Putnam, 1935, 488 p.; New York, Knopf, 1934 and 1942, 404 p. Translation of the first part of *Podniataia tselina* (1931).

Virgin Soil Upturned. v. 2: Harvest on the Don.*   Translated by H. C. Stevens. New York, Knopf, 1961. 367 p.
See also entry no. 182.
A translation of the long-awaited conclusion of Sholokhov's second major novel (*Podniataia tselina*, part two, 1960). Another edition: London, Putnam, 1960, 399 p.

1522. Sukhovo-Kobylin, Aleksandr V.
Krechinsky's Wedding; a Comedy in Three Acts.   Translated by Robert Magidoff. Ann Arbor, University of Michigan Press, 1961. 104 p. Illus.
A classic of the Russian theater. Translation of *Svad'ba Krechinskogo* (1855).

1523. Teternikov, Fedor K. (Fedor Sologub, *pseud.*)
The Created Legend.   Translated by John Cournos. London, Secker; New York, Stokes, 1916. 318 p.
Translation of the first part of a trilogy by the distinguished Symbolist novelist and poet (*Tvorimaia legenda*, 1908-1912).

The Petty Demon.   Translated with a preface and notes by Andrew Field. Introduction by Ernest J. Simmons. New York, Random House, 1962. 355 p.

> Sologub's most famous novel. Translation of *Melkii bes* (1907).

The Sweet-Scented Name, and Other Fairy Tales, Fables and Stories. Translated by Stephen Graham. London, Constable; New York, Putnam, 1915. 239 p.

The Old House, and Other Stories.   Translated by John Cournos. London, Secker, 1915. 294 p.

1524. Tiutchev, Fedor I.
Izbrannye stikhotvoreniia. Poésies choisies.   Introduction and notes by Nicolas Otzoupe. Translated into French by Charles Salomon. Foreword by André Mazon. Paris, Institut d'Études Slaves, 1957. 166 p.

> A good selection of Tiutchev's lyrics, with Russian text and French translation.

Strémooukhoff, Dimitri.   La poésie et l'idéologie de Tiouttchev. Paris, Les Belles lettres, 1937. 184 p.

> A study of Tiutchev's intellectual and literary background.

1525. Tolstoi, Aleksei N., *graf.*
The Road to Calvary.   Translated by Edith Bone. New York, Knopf, 1946. 885 p.

> A vast trilogy dealing with the Revolution and Civil War. Another edition published as *Ordeal*, translated by Ivy and Tatiana Litvinova (Moscow, Foreign Languages Publishing House, 1953, 3 v.). Translations of *Khozhdenie po mukam* (1921-1940).

Peter the First.*   Translated by Tatiana Shebunina. London, Lawrence and Wishart, 1956. 795 p.

> One of the best Soviet historical novels (*Petr pervyi*, 1929-1945). This is the only complete translation.

Selected Stories.   Moscow, Foreign Languages Publishing House, 1949. 639 p.

> A large selection of Tolstoi's short stories.

1526. Tolstoi, Lev N., *graf.*
Moscow. Vsesoiuznaia gosudarstvennaia biblioteka inostrannoi literatury. Khudozhestvennye proizvedeniia L. N. Tolstogo v perevodakh na inostrannykh iazykakh, otdel'nye zarubezhnye izdaniia; bibliografiia (Bibliography of Foreign Editions of Translations of the Literary Works of L. N. Tolstoi). Moscow, 1961. 588 p.

The Works of Leo Tolstoy.   Translated by Aylmer and Louise Maude. London, New York, Oxford University Press, 1928-1937. 21 v.

Probably the best and most complete translation of Tolstoi; contains nearly all the fiction and most of the essays and tracts. Volumes one and two contain *The Life of Tolstoy* by Aylmer Maude. These volumes were included later under their individual titles in the Oxford World's Classics series.

The Complete Works of Count Tolstoy. Translated by Leo Wiener. Boston, Estes, 1904-1905. 24 v.

Poor translation, but contains some non-fiction items missing from the Maude edition.

Tolstoy; Literary Fragments, Letters, and Reminiscences Not Previously Published. Edited by René Fülöp-Miller. Translated by Paul England. New York, Dial Press, 1931. 330 p.

Contains some posthumously published work not found in either the Maude or the Wiener editions.

Simmons, Ernest J.   Leo Tolstoy. Boston, Little, Brown, 1946. 852 p. Bibliography.

An immensely detailed and scholarly biography. A 790-page "trade" edition, omitting the notes and bibliography included in the above "special" edition, was also published.

Berlin, *Sir* Isaiah.   The Hedgehog and the Fox; an Essay on Tolstoy's View of History.* New York, Simon and Schuster, 1953. 86 p. *See also* entry no. 1564.

A brilliant analysis of Tolstoi's philosophy of history.

Steiner, George.   Tolstoy or Dostoevsky; an Essay in the Old Criticism.* New York, Knopf, 1959, 354 p.; London, Faber, 1960, 355 p.

A stimulating, if somewhat overconfident and unbalanced, attempt to follow in Merezhkovskii's footsteps. British edition has the subtitle "An Essay in Contrast."

Christian, Reginald F.   Tolstoy's "War and Peace": a Study. Oxford, The Clarendon Press, 1962. 184 p.

A study of the sources, composition, structure, characterizations, and style of Tolstoi's great novel.

Kuz'minskaia, Tat'iana A. (Bers).   Tolstoy as I Knew Him; My Life at Home and at Yasnaya Polyana. Translated by Nora Sigerist and others. Introduction by Ernest J. Simmons. New York, Macmillan, 1948. 439 p.

A basic biographical source on Tolstoi, by his sister-in-law, a model for Natasha Rostova in *War and Peace*. Translation of *Moia zhizn' doma i v Iasnoi Poliane* (1925-1926).

Merezhkovskii, Dmitrii S.   Tolstoi as Man and Artist; with an Essay on Dostoievski. New York, London, Putnam, 1902. 310 p.

An abridged translation of a famous comparative study of the two writers (*Tolstoi i Dostoevskii*, 1901).

Noyes, George R.   Tolstoy. New York, Duffield, 1918. 395 p.
A sensible and illuminating introduction to Tolstoi.

1527. Turgenev, Ivan S.
Yachnin, Rissa, *and* David H. Stam, *comps.*   Turgenev in English;
a Checklist of Works by and about Him. New York, New York
Public Library, 1962. 55 p.

The Novels and Tales of Ivan Turgenev.   Translated by Constance
Garnett. London, Heinemann; New York, Macmillan, 1894-1899.
15 v.
The best complete edition of Turgenev's fiction. There are numerous later translations of individual works, but Mrs. Garnett's
remains standard. Library edition: 1919-1923, 17 v.

Literary Reminiscences and Autobiographical Fragments.   Translated with an introduction by David Magarshack, and an essay on
Turgenev by Edmund Wilson. New York, Farrar, Strauss and Cudahy, 1958. 309 p.
An important autobiographical source, translation of *Literaturnye
i zhiteiskie vospominaniia* (1869-1880), plus an interesting psychological study by Edmund Wilson.

Three Famous Plays.   A Month in the Country; A Provincial
Lady; A Poor Gentleman.*   Translated by Constance Garnett. In-
troduction by David Garnett. London, Duckworth; New York,
Scribner's, 1951. 235 p.
Three of Turgenev's best works for the theater. Earlier edition:
London, Cassell, 1934. Translation of *Provintsialka* (1851), *Mesiats
v derevne* (1855), and *Nakhlebnik* (1857).

Granjard, Henri.   Ivan Tourguénev et les courants politiques et
sociaux de son temps. Paris, Institut d'Études Slaves, 1954. 506 p.
The most substantial monograph on Turgenev's intellectual formation and ideology. Extensive bibliography.

Yarmolinsky, Avrahm.   Turgenev; the Man, His Art and His Age.*
Rev. ed. New York, Orion Press; London, Deutsch, 1959. 406 p.
A readable and competent biography.

Magarshack, David.   Turgenev; a Life. London, Faber and Faber;
New York, Grove Press, 1954. 328 p. Illus., bibliography.
A well-documented biography.

Freeborn, Richard.   Turgenev: the Novelists' Novelist; a Study.
London, Oxford University Press, 1960. 201 p.
An analysis of Turgenev's literary technique.

1528. Tynianov, Iurii N.
Death and Diplomacy in Persia.   Translated by Alec Brown. London, Boriswood, 1938. 357 p.

One of the best Soviet historical novels, dealing with the last years in the life of A. S. Griboedov. Abridged translation of *Smert' Vazir-Mukhtara* (1929).

1529. Vogau, Boris A. (Boris Pil'niak, *pseud.*)
The Volga Falls to the Caspian Sea.   Translated by Charles Malamuth. New York, Cosmopolitan Book Corp., 1931. 353 p.
> Pil'niak's attempt at a "Five-Year Plan" novel. British edition: London, Davies, 1932 and 1935, 322 p. Translation of *Volga vpadaet v Kaspiiskoe more* (1930).

The Naked Year.   Translated by Alec Brown. Introduction by D. S. Mirsky. Edited with a preface by George Soloveytchik. New York, Payson and Clarke; London, Putnam, 1928. 305 p.
> A famous "anti-novel" by a leading early Soviet writer, later purged. Translation of *Golyi god* (1922).

Tales of the Wilderness.   Translated by F. O'Dempsey. Introduction by D. S. Mirsky. London, Routledge, 1924; New York, Knopf, 1925. 223 p.
> A good selection of Pil'niak's shorter fiction.

1530. Zamiatin, Evgenii I.
We.*   Translated with a new foreword by Gregory Zilboorg. Introduction by Peter Rudy. Preface by Marc Slonim. Rev. ed. New York, Dutton, 1959. 218 p.
> The famous anti-utopian novel, still banned in the USSR. Translation of *My* (written in 1920).

Richards, David J.   Zamyatin: a Soviet Heretic. London, Bowes, 1962. 112 p.
> A monograph on Zamiatin's life and work.

1531. Zhukovskii, Vasilii A.
Ehrhard, Marcelle.   V. A. Jeukovski et le préromantisme russe. Paris, Institut d'Études Slaves, 1938. 442 p.
> A solid, scholarly monograph on Zhukovskii's life and literary works.

1532. Zoshchenko, Mikhail M.
Scenes from the Bathhouse, and Other Stories of Communist Russia.*
Translated with an introduction by Sidney Monas. Stories selected by Marc Slonim. Ann Arbor, University of Michigan Press, 1961. 245 p.
See also entry no. 189.
> A good selection of Zoshchenko's short fiction.

Nervous People and Other Satires.   Edited with an introduction by Hugh McLean. Translated by Maria Gordon and Hugh McLean. New York, Pantheon Books; London, Gollancz, 1963. 449 p.
> A comprehensive selection of Zoshchenko's fiction.

C. FOLKLORE [5]

by Barbara Krader

1. Bibliographies

1533. Volkskundliche Bibliographie. 1917-1938. Berlin. irregular.
Continued by *Bibliographie internationale des arts et traditions populaires* (Paris, 1939– irregular). Entries describe literature in many languages, including Slavic, arranged by subject. Probably the most complete bibliographical tool, but appears after considerable delay.

1534. The American Bibliography of Russian and East European Studies. 1957– Bloomington, Ind. annual. (Indiana University Publications. Russian and East European Series)
See also entry no. 3.
The section on folklore is especially useful for coverage of literature in English, and because of prompt publication.

1535. Revue des études slaves. 1921– Paris, Institut d'Études Slaves de l'Université de Paris. annual.
See also entries no. 38 and 1255.
Bibliographical section of the journal includes coverage of folklore, with valuable critical comment by specialists in the field, such as André Mazon and André Vaillant.

2. Periodicals

1536. Demos. v. 1– 1960– Berlin. semiannual.
Published in East Berlin, contains extensive abstracts in German of major folklore studies published in Eastern Europe, although these frequently appear several years after the original was published. Abstracts written by authors or their co-workers. Contributing editors from academy institutes of folklore of Albania, Bulgaria, Czechoslovakia, Hungary, Poland, Rumania, and the USSR.

1537. Deutsches Jahrbuch für Volkskunde. v. 1– 1955– Berlin.
Issued by the Institute of Folklore of the German Academy in East Germany, this annual contains important bibliographies and survey articles, some by Soviet specialists.
The following journals also contain occasional articles on folklore: *Archiv für slavische Philologie*; *Indiana Slavic Studies*; *International Journal of Slavic Linguistics and Poetics*; *Revue des études slaves*; *Russische Revue, Monatschrift für die Kunde Russlands* (St. Petersburg); *Slavische Rundschau* (Prague); *Slavonic and East European Review*; *Zeitschrift für slavische Philologie*.

3. Surveys

1538. Oinas, Felix J. Folklore Activities in Russia. Journal of American Folklore, v. 74, no. 294, October–December 1961: 362-379. Bibliography.

[5] Arrangement is by order of emphasis.

Balanced appraisal of research during the Soviet period.

See also Margaret Schlauch's "Folklore in the Soviet Union," in *Science and Society* (New York), v. 8, 1944: 205-222, which is a pro-Soviet survey of trends in European and Soviet folklore studies from the late nineteenth century to the Second World War, with bibliographical references.

A recent Soviet account in English translation is V. E. Gusev's "Folklore Research in the U.S.S.R.," in *Soviet Review*, v. 2, January 1961: 51-58.

1539. Sokolov, Iurii M.   Russian Folklore. Translated from the Russian by Catherine Ruth Smith. New York, Macmillan, 1950. 760 p. (American Council of Learned Societies. Russian Translation Project, Series 7)

> Translation in full of Soviet textbook covering pre-Revolutionary and Soviet folklore (*Russkii fol'klor*; Moscow, Uchpedgiz, 1938, 557 p.). Valuable historiography (pages 40-155), although chapters on *byliny* and others suffer from biases of 1930's. *See* review in *Midwest Folklore*, v. 2, 1952: 119-127.
>
> French edition, *Le folklore russe* (Paris, Payot, 1945), has been abridged and altered, with section on Soviet period and bibliographical apparatus wholly omitted.
>
> See also D. K. Zelenin's *Russische (Ostslavische) Volkskunde* (entry no. 276), in which chapters 9 through 12 (pages 290 ff.) deal with family customs, community customs, rituals observed at specific seasons of the year, and folk beliefs.

1540. Bogatyrev, Petr G. (Pierre).   Actes magiques, rites et croyances en Russie subcarpathique. Paris, H. Champion, 1929. 162 p. Bibliography. (Travaux publiés par l'Institut d'Études Slaves, 11)

> Synchronic, functional study of customs related to folk calendar, birth, marriage, and death, and supernatural beings, in what is now the Western Ukraine in the USSR.

1541. Karskii, Evfimii F.   Die weissrussische Volksdichtung. *In his* Geschichte der weissrussischen Volksdichtung und Literatur. Berlin, Leipzig, W. de Gruyter, 1926. p. 1-95. (Grundriss der slavischen Philologie und Kulturgeschichte, 2)

> Traces history of study, and discusses types of folklore, including incantations, calendar songs, songs at birth, wedding, and death, proverbs, riddles, tales, traces of epos, religious songs. Examples in original language, with sources indicated. Bibliographies at ends of chapters.

1542. Loorits, Oskar.   Grundzüge des estnischen Volksglaubens. Lund, C. Blom, 1949-1960. 3 v. Illus. (Skrifter utgivna av Kungl. Gustav Adolfs akademien för folklivsforskning, 18: 1-3)

4. Songs

1543. Chadwick, Hector M. (H. Munro), *and* Nora K. Chadwick.   Russian Oral Literature. *In their* The Growth of Literature. Cambridge,

England, Cambridge University Press, 1936. v. 2, p. 3-296. Bibliography.

Primarily devoted to *byliny*, but spiritual songs (*dukhovnye stikhi*), other narrative songs, and wedding ritual songs are also discussed. Long section on singers of *byliny* and spiritual songs.

Another account is Leonard Arthur Magnus' *The Heroic Ballads of Russia* (London, Kegan Paul, Trench, Trubner, 1921, 210 p.), which surveys the tradition and the subject matter with some comparative remarks.

1544. Chadwick, Nora K.   Russian Heroic Poetry. Cambridge, England, Cambridge University Press, 1932. 294 p.

Introduction of 32 pages, followed by English translations of *byliny*, with sources given for texts.

See also Reinhold Trautmann's *Die Volksdichtung der Grossrussen.* v. 1: *Das Heldenlied (Die Byline)* (Heidelberg, Carl Winter, 1935, 446 p.). Trautmann surveys carriers of tradition, the form and content of the heroic songs, and the place of the genre in history, following with prose translations of 65 song texts.

Still of importance is Alfred N. Rambaud's *La Russie épique; étude sur les chansons héroïques de la Russie, traduites ou analysées pour la première fois* (Paris, Maisonneuve, 1876, 504 p.), a pioneer study by the distinguished French historian of the *byliny*, spiritual songs, and historical songs up through Napoleon and Nicholas I, including a chapter on the Ukrainian epos, with summaries and translations.

1545. Jakobson, Roman, *and* Marc Szeftel.   The Vseslav Epos. *In* Russian Epic Studies, edited by Roman Jakobson and Ernest J. Simmons. Philadelphia, American Folklore Society, 1949. p. 13-86. (Memoirs of the American Folklore Society, v. 42)

Analysis of *byliny* texts concerning Vseslav, and comparison of themes with the Primary Chronicle and the *Slovo o Polku Igoreve.*

1546. Chettéoui, Wilfrid R.   Un rapsode russe; Rjabinin le père; la byline au XIXe siècle. Paris, Champion, 1942. 256 p. (Bibliothèque russe de l'Institut d'Études Slaves, 19)

Biography, study of repertoire, and poetic analysis of the earliest great *bylina* singer discovered, Trofim Grigor'evich Riabinin. Bibliography and map.

1547. Scherrer, Marie.   Les dumy ukrainiennes; épopée cosaque. Ukrainian texts and complete translations, with an introduction and notes. Paris, C. Klincksieck, 1947. 140 p. Bibliography, music.

For further analysis, see Paul Diels' "Die Duma; das epische Lied der Kleinrussen." *Mitteilungen des Schlesischen Gesellschaft für Volkskunde* (Breslau), v. 34, 1934: 26-67, which surveys the literature on the subject, gives a history of collection and study, analyzes subject matter, style, and performance, and adds comparative remarks.

1548. Stief, Carl.   Studies in the Russian Historical Song. Copenhagen, Rosenkilde and Bagger, 1953. 274 p.

Studies of the lyrical historical songs of Richard James' manuscript, the epic historical song, "new" historical songs, the historical songs of the Cossacks (Ermak), and songs of the fall of Kazan. Includes textual analysis. Significant original research. Bibliography in footnotes.

1549. Katzenelenbogen, Uriah, *comp.*   The Daina; an Anthology of Lithuanian and Latvian Folksongs. With a critical study and preface by the compiler. Chicago, Lithuanian News Publishing Co., 1935. 165 p. Bibliography.

In English translation only, with sources indicated. Introduction by Clarence A. Manning.

5. Tales

1550. Ralston, William R. S.   Russian Folk-Tales. New York, R. Worthington, 1880. 388 p.

Fifty-one tales taken from collections of Afanas'ev, Khudiakov, Erlenvein, Chudinskii, and Rudchenko, with sources indicated. Comments reflect views of the mythological school, no longer accepted.

For animal tales, this collection may be supplemented by an excellent work by Adolph Gerber, *Great Russian Animal Tales; a Collection of Fifty Tales with an Introduction, a Synopsis of the Adventures and Motives, a Discussion of the Same and an Appendix* (Baltimore, Modern Language Association of America, 1891, 112 p.). Gerber indicates source and region for each tale, with references to variants.

1551. Jakobson, Roman.   On Russian Fairy Tales. *In* Russian Fairy Tales. Translated by Norbert Guterman. New York, Pantheon, 1945. p. 631-656. Bibliography.

Authoritative history of collection and study, with analysis of characteristic features. Accompanying anthology is an excellent translation, but sources of tales are not identified. Some are from Afanas'ev.

A survey of subsequent study and publication on Russian tales is Erna V. Pomerantseva's "Die Erforschung des russischen Märchens in der UdSSR in den Jahren 1945-1959." *Deutsches Jahrbuch für Volkskunde*, v. 6, 1960: 444-451.

1552. Propp, Vladimir Ia.   Morphology of the Folktale. Edited with an introduction by Svatava Pirkova-Jakobson. Translated by Laurence Scott. Bloomington, Ind., 1958. 134 p. (Bibliographical and Special Series of the American Folklore Society, v. 9)

Formalist analysis of the magic tale by Soviet folklorist, based primarily on Russian tale materials. Translation of *Morfologiia skazki* (Leningrad, 1927).

See review article by Claude Lévi-Strauss, "L'analyse morphologique des contes russes," in *International Journal of Slavic Linguistics and Poetics*, v. 3, 1960: 122-149.

1553. Azadovskii, Mark K.   Eine Sibirische Märchenerzählerin. Helsinki, Suomalainen Tiedeakatemia, 1926. 70 p. (FF Communications, no. 68)

Biography, study of repertoire, and analysis of style of the gifted teller Natal'ia Osipovna Vinokurova of the Verkholensk region in Siberia, by an outstanding Soviet specialist.

1554. Andreev, Nikolai P.   A Characterization of the Ukrainian Tale Corpus. Fabula (Berlin), v. 1, 1958: 228-238.

Preliminary conclusions based on materials compiled for an index of types of Ukrainian tales. Materials believed lost after Andreev's death in Leningrad in the winter of 1942.

Translation of "K kharakteristike ukrainskogo skazochnogo materiala," in *Sergeiu Fedorovichu Ol'denburgu* (Leningrad, Izd-vo Akademii nauk SSSR, 1934), p. 61-72.

1555. Coxwell, Charles F., *ed.*   Siberian and Other Folk-Tales; Primitive Literature of the Empire of the Tsars, Collected and Translated with an Introduction and Notes. London, C. W. Daniel, 1925. 1056 p. Map.

Siberian nationalities include Chukchi, Yukagir, Gilyak, Tungus, Buriat, Kalmuk, and others. Also contains tales from the Caucasus and Central Asia, as well as nearly 70 Russian and several Ukrainian and Belorussian narratives. All sources are indicated. Many standard Russian ethnographic collections are used. Comments outline the culture or describe the customs of the groups telling the tales.

1556. Dirr, Adolf, *comp. and tr.*   Kaukasische Märchen. Jena, E. Diederichs, 1920. 294 p. (Die Märchen der Weltliteratur, 16)

Seventy-eight tales, of which 17 were collected by Dirr himself, a noted linguist. Sources of all are given. Includes Georgian, Avan, Agul, Imeretian, Ud, Zachur, Lak, Chechen, Kabardinian, Tat, Ossetian, Armenian, Kunik, Mingrelian, Abkhazian.

Collection translated from the German into English by Lucy Menzies as *Caucasian Folk-Tales* (London and Toronto, J. M. Dent, 1925, 306 p.). National origin of each tale is indicated, but one tale and Dirr's own sources are omitted.

1557. Boehm, Maximilian, *and* Franz Specht, *eds.*   Lettisch-litauische Volksmärchen. Jena, E. Diederichs, 1924. 333 p. Bibliography.

Sources are indicated and comments included.

See also John P. Balys' *Motif-Index of Lithuanian Narrative Folk-Lore* (Kaunas, 1936, 295 p.). A recent collection of importance, edited by Oskar Loorits, is *Estnische Volkserzählungen* (Berlin, W. de Gruyter, 1959, 227 p.)

6. Other Genres

1558. Mahler, Elsa. Die russischen dörflichen Hochzeitsbräuche. Berlin, Otto Harrassowitz, 1960. 508 p. (Veröffentlichungen der Abteilung für slavische Sprachen und Literaturen des Osteuropa-Instituts [Slavisches Seminar] an der freien Universität Berlin, Band 20)

Analysis, with texts of speeches and songs in original and in German translation. Includes previously unpublished texts collected by Mahler during 1937-1939 in the Pskov region and elsewhere.

See also descriptive account by Fedir Vovk (Theodore Volkov), "Rites et usages nuptiaux en Ukraine," *L'Anthropologie* (Paris), v. 2, 1891: 160-184, 408-437, 537-587; v. 3, 1892: 541-588.

1559. Mansikka, Viljo J. Über russische Zauberformeln, mit Berücksichtigung der Blut- und Verrenkungssegen. Helsinki, 1909. 309 p. Bibliography, subject index. (Suomalainen tiedeakademie toimituksia. Series B, tom 1, no. 3)

Scholarly study, with much comparative data from other Slavic traditions and an appendix of comparative Finno-Ugric materials.

1560. Graf, A. E. 6000 deutsche und russische Sprichwörter. 3d ed. Halle (Saale), Max Niemeyer, 1960. 294 p. Bibliography: p. 5-6.

Corresponding German and Russian proverbs, in original languages, arranged in parallel columns. Equivalent proverbs in English are often included, and some Russian proverbs translated literally into German. Serious comparative study. Sources indicated for German proverbs, and Russian originals mostly traceable in Dal's proverb collection.

See also a study by Andrew Guershoon, *Certain Aspects of Russian Proverbs* (London, Frederick Muller, 1941, 204 p.), which contains a discussion of subject matter, formal devices, and other aspects, appending 1,361 Russian proverbs in English translation only. General sources indicated.

7. Special Language Groups

1561. Radlov, Vasilii V. (W. Radloff). Proben der Volksliteratur der türkischen Stämme Süd-Siberiens, gesammelt und übersetzt. v. 1-6. St. Petersburg, Commissionäre der Kaiserlichen Akademie der Wissenschaften, 1866-1886.

Introduction to each volume describes circumstances of Radlov's collection. Tales and song texts of Altai Turks, Abakan Turks, Kazakhs, Tatars, Kirgiz, and Taranchis. Texts in Turkic and in Radlov's German translation.

1562. Sebeok, Thomas A., *ed.* Studies in Cheremis. Bloomington, Indiana University Press, 1952–

First volume, published in 1952, contains an analysis of the Cheremis folktale, and classifications and lists of proverbs and riddles. The second volume (New York, Wenner-Gren Foundation, 1956) concerns the supernatural. Volume six (Bloomington, 1958) contains descriptions of Cheremis games, with comparative references to games of other nationalities. Additional volumes are in preparation.

D. HISTORY OF THOUGHT AND CULTURE
by George L. Kline
1. Intellectual and Cultural Life

1563. Berdiaev (Berdyaev), Nikolai A.   Leontiev. Translated from the Russian by George Reavey. London, G. Bles, The Centenary Press, 1940. 229 p.

Close study of an important, but neglected, nineteenth-century Russian thinker, emphasizing his critique of religion and culture. Translated from the Russian original, *Konstantin Leont'ev; ocherk iz istorii russkoi religioznoi mysli* (Paris, YMCA Press, 1926, 268 p.)

1564.*Berlin, *Sir* Isaiah.   The Hedgehog and the Fox; an Essay on Tolstoy's View of History. New York, Simon and Schuster, 1953. 86 p. *See also* entry no. 1526.

Critical analysis of Tolstoi's philosophy of history, tracing its origins to the Slavophiles, Proudhon, and de Maistre.

1565. Christoff, Peter K.   An Introduction to Nineteenth-Century Russian Slavophilism. v. 1: A. S. Xomjakov (Khomiakov). The Hague, Mouton, 1961. 301 p.

Careful exposition of Khomiakov's philosophical and theological views, with special attention to the idea of "sobornost'."

1566. Chyzhevs'kyi (Tschiżewskij), Dmytro.   Russische Geistesgeschichte. Hamburg, Rowohlt, 1959-1961. 2 v.
Bibliography: v. 1, p. 160-162; v. 2, p. 163-168.
See also entry no. 1360.

A concise intellectual and cultural history of Russia. Volume one (*Das heilige Russland; Russische Geistesgeschichte 10. - 17. Jahrhundert*) covers the period from the tenth to the seventeenth century. Volume two (*Zwischen Ost und West; Russische Geistesgeschichte 18. - 20. Jahrhundert*) covers the period from the eighteenth to the twentieth century, with emphasis on the nineteenth century.

1567. Koyré, Alexandre.   Études sur l'histoire de la pensée philosophique en Russie. Paris, J. Vrin, 1950. 223 p.

A collection of articles on Kireevskii, Chaadaev, Hertzen, and "Hegel in Russia," the latter including discussion of the philosophical views of Stankevich, Bakunin, and Belinskii.

1568. Miliukov, Pavel N.   Le mouvement intellectuel russe. Translated from the second Russian edition by J. W. Bienstock. Paris, Bossard, 1918. 445 p.

A collection of articles on Stankevich, Granovskii, Belinskii, Hertzen, Danilevskii, Leont'ev, Vladimir Solov'ev, and others. The author was a noted liberal historian. Translated from *Iz istorii russkoi intelligentsii; sbornik statei i etiudov* (St. Petersburg, "Znanie," 1903, 308 p.)

1569.* Miliukov, Pavel N. (Paul).   Outlines of Russian Culture. Edited by Michael Karpovich. Translated by Valentine Ughet and Eleanor Davis. Philadelphia, University of Pennsylvania Press, 1942. 3 v. Illus.

See also entries no. 472, 1638, and 1815.

Informed essays on religion, literature, music, architecture, and painting in Russia and the Soviet Union (through the 1920's), with some attention to general cultural and intellectual trends.

A translated abridgment of *Ocherki po istorii russkoi kul'tury* (Paris, 1930-1937, 3 v.)

1570. Pascal, Pierre.   Les grands courants de la pensée russe contemporaine. *In* Les grands courants de la pensée mondiale contemporaine, edited by M. F. Sciacca. Part 1, v. 2. Milan, Marzorati, 1959.

Concise review of the major developments in Russian thought from 1855 through the 1950's, stressing philosophical theology and the philosophy of history, as related to such literary and cultural movements as symbolism and futurism. Reprinted in *Cahiers du monde russe et soviétique*, v. 3, January–March 1962: 5-89.

1571. Pipes, Richard, *ed.*   The Russian Intelligentsia. New York, Columbia University Press, 1961. 234 p.

See also entries no. 1188 and 1783.

Informed essays by various hands on the origin and development of the Russian intelligentsia, its transformation in the Soviet Union, and its similarities to and differences from the intelligentsias of contemporary Spain and Communist China. Originally published in the Summer 1960 issue of *Daedalus*, journal of the American Academy of Arts and Sciences.

1572. Pokrovskii, Mikhail N.   Historia de la cultura rusa. Translated by Andrés Nin. Madrid, Editorial España, 1932. 345 p.

Interpretations of the development of religious and political ideas in Russia, from the earliest times through the late nineteenth century, in terms of underlying economic factors. Translation of *Ocherk istorii russkoi kul'tury* (Moscow, Gosizdat, 1929, 2 v.)

1573. Riasanovsky, Nicholas V.   Russia and the West in the Teaching of the Slavophiles; a Study of Romantic Ideology. Cambridge, Harvard University Press, 1952. 244 p.

Close study of the influence of Schelling and Hegel upon the philosophy of history of such Slavophiles as K. Aksakov, Khomiakov, I. and P. Kireevskii, and Samarin.

1574. Rogger, Hans.   National Consciousness in Eighteenth-Century Russia. Cambridge, Harvard University Press, 1960. 319 p.
Bibliography: p. 285-295.
See also entries no. 505 and 1181.
   A concise account of the development of a Russian sense of national and cultural identity in the eighteenth century, its relation to dominant French influences, and its prefiguring of nineteenth-century Russian nationalism. Special attention is devoted to the views of such thinkers as Karamzin, Lomonosov, Novikov, Radishchev, Shcherbatov, and Tatishchev.

1575. Sarkisyanz, Emanuel.   Russland und der Messianismus des Orients; Sendungsbewusstsein und politischer Chiliasmus des Ostens. Tübingen, J. C. B. Mohr, 1955. 419 p.
   An unconventional interpretation of Soviet Marxism-Leninism in terms of the messianic "chiliasm" or historical utopianism of certain religious movements — particularly schismatic ones — in both Russia and Asia.

1576. Simmons, Ernest J., *ed.*   Continuity and Change in Russian and Soviet Thought. Cambridge, Harvard University Press, 1955. 563 p.
See also entry no. 115.
   Of particular interest is part four, "Rationality and Nonrationality," p. 283-377, with contributions by Theodosius Dobzhansky, Georges Florovsky, Waldemar Gurian, George L. Kline, and Herbert Marcuse, and a summary and review by Geroid T. Robinson.

1577. Venturi, Franco.   Esuli russi in Piemonte dopo il '48. Turin, Einaudi, 1959. 159 p.
   An account of the "agonizing reappraisal" on the part of such Russian emigres as Hertzen, Sazonov, and Engel'son (then living in Nice, Genoa, and Turin) of their views on the future of Western Europe and of Russia, following the failure of the French Revolution of 1848.
   See also the author's *Roots of Revolution* (entries no. 524 and 641).

1578.* Weidlé, Wladimir.   Russia: Absent and Present. Translated from the French by A. Gordon Smith. London, Hollis and Carter, 1953. 152 p.
See also entry no. 117.
   Philosophical reflections on central problems of Russian intellectual and cultural history, by a noted historian of art and literature. A translation of *La Russie absente et présente* (Paris, Gallimard, 1949, 238 p.)

1579. Zen'kovskii (Zenkovsky), Vasilii V.   Russian Thinkers and Europe. Translated from the Russian by Galia S. Bodde. Ann Arbor, Mich., J. W. Edwards, 1953. 199 p. (American Council of Learned Societies, Russian Translation Project, Series 21)

A survey of the philosophy of history of Gogol', Khomiakov, Hertzen, Danilevskii, Leont'ev, Tolstoi, Vladimir Solov'ev, and others, with special attention to their critiques of the civilization of Western Europe. A translation of *Russkie mysliteli i Evropa; kritika evropeiskoi kul'tury u russkikh myslitelei* (Paris, YMCA Press. 1926, 291 p.)

2. Social and Political Thought

1580. Baron, Samuel H.   Plekhanov; the Father of Russian Marxism. Stanford, Calif., Stanford University Press, 1963. 400 p.

A detailed account of Plekhanov's life and thought, his early acceptance of Populism, his turn to Marxism, and his final rejection of Leninism.

1581.* Berdiaev (Berdyaev), Nikolai A.   The Origin of Russian Communism. Translated by R. M. French. Ann Arbor, University of Michigan Press, 1960. 191 p.
See also entry no. 715.

A concise survey of the Russian roots of contemporary Marxism-Leninism in nineteenth-century Slavophilism, nihilism, populism, and anarchosocialism. First published in English in 1937; the original Russian text did not appear in print until 1955 (*Istoki i smysl russkogo kommunizma*; Paris, YMCA Press, 157 p.)

1582. Billington, James H.   Mikhailovsky and Russian Populism. Oxford, The Clarendon Press, 1958. 217 p.
Bibliography: p. 197-211.

A careful exploration of Mikhailovskii's central intellectual and moral concerns: the "subjective method in sociology," the "struggle for individuality," and the critique of Marxism.

1583. Chambre, Henri.   Le Marxisme en Union Soviétique; idéologie et institutions, leur évolution de 1917 à nos jours. Paris, Éditions du Seuil, 1955. 509 p.
See also entry no. 717.

A close study of Marxist-Leninist theories of law, the state, morality, and economics in the light of (1) the views of Marx and (2) Soviet institutional developments.

1584. Coquart, Armand.   Dmitri Pisarev (1840-1868) et l'idéologie du nihilisme russe. Paris, Institut d'Études Slaves, 1946. 464 p. Bibliography. (Bibliothèque russe de l'Institut d'Études Slaves, v. 21)
See also entry no. 1515.

A detailed account of Pisarev's life and an examination of his thought in its relations to the views of Chernyshevskii and Dobroliubov and the movement of Russian nihilism during the 1860's.

1585. Fetscher, Iring.   Die Freiheit im Lichte des Marxismus-Leninismus. Bonn, Bundeszentrale für Heimatdienst, 1959. 78 p.

A critical analysis of Marxist-Leninist social philosophy (centered on the problem of individual freedom) as seen against the background of Hegel and early Marx.

1586. Fischer, George. Russian Liberalism, from Gentry to Intelligentsia. Cambridge, Harvard University Press, 1958. 240 p.
Bibliography: p. 209-226.
See also entries no. 519 and 629.
An account of the development of liberal ideas and, to some extent, institutions in nineteenth-century Russia; includes such topics as the zemstvo movement and such figures as Petrunkevich, Chicherin, Korolenko, Maklakov, and Miliukov.

1587. Haimson, Leopold H. The Russian Marxists and the Origins of Bolshevism. Cambridge, Harvard University Press, 1955. 246 p.
Bibliography: p. 235-240.
See also entry no. 630.
A study of the development of the Russian revolutionary (Marxist) intelligentsia during the 1890's and early 1900's, focusing upon such issues as Bolshevism *vs.* Menshevism and such figures as Plekhanov and Lenin, Akselrod and Martov.

1588. Hare, Richard. Pioneers of Russian Social Thought; Studies of Non-Marxian Formation in Nineteenth-Century Russia and of Its Partial Revival in the Soviet Union. London, New York, Oxford University Press, 1951. 307 p.
See also entry no. 631.
Essays on the social, political, and historical views of Chaadaev, Belinskii, Khomiakov and the Slavophiles, Hertzen, Chernyshevskii, and Leont'ev.

1589. Hepner, Benoît P. Bakounine et le panslavisme révolutionnaire; cinq essais sur l'histoire des idées en Russie et en Europe. Paris, M. Rivière, 1950. 319 p.
Bibliography: p. 314-319.
A study not only of Bakunin's "revolutionary Panslavism," but also of his early "dialectical nihilism," the French intellectual influence in Russia ca. 1760-1825, and the influence of Schelling and Hegel upon Bakunin and Belinskii during the 1830's and 1840's.

1590. Kindersley, Richard. The First Russian Revisionists; a Study of "Legal Marxism" in Russia. Oxford, Clarendon Press, 1962. 260 p.
Bibliography: p. 244-252.
An examination of turn-of-the-century revisionism in economics, ethics, and theory of knowledge, on the part of such thinkers as Berdiaev, Bulgakov, Potresov, Struve, and Tugan-Baranovskii.

1591.*Kohn, Hans, *ed.* The Mind of Russia; Historical and Political Thought of Russia's Great Age. New Brunswick, N.J., Rutgers University Press, 1955. 298 p. Bibliography.
Brief selections from the writings of such thinkers as Chaadaev,

Belinskii, Hertzen, Pogodin, Khomiakov, I. Aksakov, Chernyshev-skii, Danilevskii, V. Solov'ev, Lenin, Berdiaev, and Fedotov, on such themes as Russian national character, Slavic civilization, and Russia's relation to Western Europe.

1592.* Labedz, Leopold, ed.   Revisionism; Essays on the History of Marxist Ideas. London, Allen and Unwin; New York, Praeger, 1962. 404 p.
See also entry no. 721.

Includes essays by various hands on such Russian Marxists as Plekhanov, Bogdanov, Trotsky, Bukharin, and Deborin.

Most of the papers in this volume were originally published in the quarterly journal *Survey*.

1593. Lange, Max G.   Marxismus, Leninismus, Stalinismus; zur Kritik des dialektischen Materialismus. Stuttgart, E. Klett, 1955. 210 p.
Bibliography: p. 206-210.

A concise survey, with critical analyses of the Leninist and Stalinist versions of philosophical materialism and the "reflection" theory of knowledge.

1594. Malia, Martin E.   Alexander Herzen and the Birth of Russian Socialism, 1812-1855. Cambridge, Harvard University Press, 1961. 486 p.
Bibliography: p. 427-428.
See also entry no. 634.

A thorough exploration of the personal and intellectual influences to which Hertzen responded — including the philosophies of Schiller, Schelling, and Hegel, and the social theories of Saint-Simon, Proudhon, and George Sand.

1595.* Marcuse, Herbert.   Soviet Marxism; a Critical Analysis. New York, Columbia University Press, 1958. 271 p.
See also entry no. 725.

A historical-cultural analysis of Marxist-Leninist ethics and social and political philosophy, with some reference to logic and dialectic. A later edition with a new preface has also been published (New York, Random House, Vintage Russian Library, 1961, 252 p.)

1596. Masaryk, Tomáš G.   The Spirit of Russia; Studies in History, Literature, and Philosophy. Translated from the German original by Eden and Cedar Paul, with additional chapters and bibliographies by Jan Slavik; the former translated and the latter condensed and translated by W. R. and Z. Lee. 2d ed. London, Allen and Unwin; New York, Macmillan, 1955. 2 v.
See also entry no. 269.

Broad synthesis of Russian thought and culture, from Kievan Russia to the beginning of the twentieth century. Separate chapters are devoted to Chaadaev, the Slavophiles, Belinskii, Hertzen, Bakunin, the Nihilists, Lavrov and Mikhailovskii, Solov'ev, and early Russian Marxism. Masaryk's position is politically liberal, philosophically neo-Kantian. A translation of *Russland und Europa; Studien über die geistigen Strömungen in Russland* (Jena, E. Diederichs, 1913, 2 v.), which first appeared in English in 1919 (London, Allen and Unwin; New York, Macmillan, 1919, 2 v.)

1597. Mendel, Arthur P.   Dilemmas of Progress in Tsarist Russia; Legal Marxism and Legal Populism. Cambridge, Harvard University Press, 1961. 310 p.
Bibliography: p. 255-263.
See also entry no. 635.
A study of the opposition — on questions of economics, ethics, and theory of knowledge — between such Populists as Mikhailovskii and such early Russian Marxists as Berdiaev, Bulgakov, Struve, and Tugan-Baranovskii.

1598.* Meyer, Alfred G.   Leninism. Cambridge, Harvard University Press, 1957. 324 p.
See also entry no. 726.
A close critical analysis of Marxist-Leninist social and political philosophy.

1599. Monnerot, Jules.   Sociology and Psychology of Communism. Translated from the French by Jane Degras and Richard Rees. Boston, Beacon Press, 1953. 339 p.
See also entries no. 727 and 1232.
A sustained interpretation of Marxism-Leninism as a form of secularized religion; includes discussion of the relation of dialectical theory to revolutionary practice. Abridged translation of *Sociologie du communisme* (Paris, Gallimard, 1949, 510 p.). London edition (Allen and Unwin) has the title *Sociology of Communism*.

1600. Petrovich, Michael B.   The Emergence of Russian Panslavism, 1856-1870. New York, Columbia University Press, 1956. 312 p.
Bibliography: p. 289-303.
A study of the development of the idea of a political mission and cultural identity common to all the Slavs, in thinkers like Pogodin, Danilevskii, and the Slavophiles.

1601. Plamenatz, John.   German Marxism and Russian Communism. London, New York, Longmans, Green, 1954. 356 p.
The second half of this book includes detailed critical analyses of the social and political philosophies of Lenin, Trotsky, and Stalin.

1602. Plekhanov, Georgii V.   Introduction à l'histoire sociale de la Russie. Translated from the Russian by Eugenia Batault-Plékhanov. Paris, Bossard, 1926. 160 p. (Collection historique de l'Institut d'Études Slaves, no. 3)

General considerations preliminary to a detailed study of Russian social and political thought from the early sixteenth to the late eighteenth century, by a noted Russian Marxist. Includes a critical analysis of the views of Kliuchevskii and S. M. Solov'ev concerning the interrelationship of economic, social, and political factors in Russian history. A translation of volume one, pages 1-130 of *Istoriia russkoi obshchestvennoi mysli* (Moscow, Literaturno-izdatel'skii otdel Narodnogo komissariata po prosveshcheniiu, 1919, 3 v.). A partial English translation of volume two, by Boris M. Bekkar, Eva Abramovitch, and George Rockwell, appeared as *History of Russian Social Thought*, mimeographed edition (New York, New York Board of Education, and Department of Social Sciences, Columbia University, 1938, 224 p.)

1603. Quenet, Charles.   Tchaadaev et les Lettres philosophiques; contribution à l'étude du mouvement des idées en Russie. Paris, Institut d'Études Slaves de l'Université de Paris, 1931. 440 p. (Bibliothèque de l'Institut Français de Léningrad, v. 12)
   A detailed study of Chaadaev's philosophy of history and culture, particularly his view of the relation of Russian to Western European civilization.

1604. Scheibert, Peter.   Von Bakunin zu Lenin; Geschichte der russischen revolutionären Ideologien, 1840-1895. v. 1: Die Formung des radikalen Denkens in der Auseinandersetzung mit deutschem Idealismus und französischem Bürgertum. Leiden, E. J. Brill, 1956. 344 p.
   This first volume in a projected history of revolutionary ideologies in Russia covers the period 1840-1855 and discusses such thinkers as Chaadaev, Stankevich, Belinskii, Hertzen, Ogarev, and Bakunin.

1605. Schultze, Bernhard.   Wissarion Grigorjewitsch Belinskij, Wegbereiter des revolutionären Atheismus in Russland. Munich, A. Pustet, 1958. 219 p.
Bibliography: p. 211-214.
   A study not only of Belinskii's changing attitudes toward traditional religion, but also of his ethics, social philosophy, and philosophy of history.
   For a study which places greater stress on Belinskii's role as literary critic, *see* Herbert E. Bowman, *Vissarion Belinski (1811-1848); a Study in the Origins of Social Criticism in Russia* (Cambridge, Harvard University Press, 1954, 220 p.)

1606. Sowjetideologie heute. Frankfurt am Main, Fischer Bücherei, 1962-1963. 2 v. (v. 1, Dialektischer und historischer Materialismus, by Gustav A. Wetter, 1963, 333 p.; v. 2, Die politischen Lehren, by Wolfgang Leonhard, 1962, 328 p.)
   The first volume contains a concise summary of the main "theses" of dialectical materialism — treated at greater length in Wetter's

Dialectical Materialism (see entries no. 1625 and 1796) — as well as of historical materialism and the Marxist-Leninist critique of capitalism — neither of which is discussed in that work.

1607. Utechin, Sergej V.   Russian Political Thought; a Concise History. New York, Praeger, 1964. 320 p.
Bibliography: p. 279-306.
See also entry no. 640.

  A brief retracing of the main outlines of Russian social and political philosophy, from the ninth to the mid-twentieth century. Includes such topics as Slavophilism, Westernism, Populism, anarchism, religious thought, Marxism, communism, anti-communism.

3. Russian and Soviet Philosophy

1608. Acton, Harry B.   The Illusion of the Epoch; Marxism-Leninism as a Philosophical Creed. London, Cohen and West, 1955; Boston, Beacon Press, 1957. 278 p.

  A concise critical study of dialectical and historical materialism, including Marxist-Leninist ethics and social philosophy.

1609.* Berdiaev, Nikolai A.   The Russian Idea. Translated from the Russian by R. M. French. New York, Macmillan, 1948; London, Geoffrey Bles, 1947. 255 p.
See also entry no. 106.

  A broad survey of the development of Russian thought during the nineteenth and early twentieth centuries — centered on ethics, social philosophy, philosophy of history, and philosophy of religion. Later edition: Ann Arbor, University of Michigan Press, 1962. Translation of *Russkaia ideia; osnovnye problemy russkoi mysli XIX veka i nachala XX veka* (Paris, YMCA Press, 1946, 259 p.)

1610. Blakeley, Thomas J.   Soviet Scholasticism. Dordrecht, D. Reidel, 1961. 176 p.
Bibliography: p. 155-165.

  An interpretive analysis of Marxist-Leninist philosophical method, based on a distinction between specific doctrinal tenets and the more general "meta-dogmata" upon which they rest.

1611. Bocheński, Innocentius M.   Soviet Russian Dialectical Materialism. Translated from the third German edition by Nicolas Sollohub. Dordrecht, D. Reidel, 1963. 174 p.
Bibliography: p. 169-177.

  A compact critical study of contemporary Soviet Marxism-Leninism. The third German edition, published as *Der sowjetrussische dialektische Materialismus (Diamat)* (Bern, Francke, 1960, 180 p.), is substantially revised and enlarged.

1612. Chyzhevs'kyi, Dmytro.   Hegel in Russland. *In* Hegel bei den Sla-

ven. Bad Homburg vor der Hohe, Hermann Gentner Verlag, 1961.
p. 145-396.

A detailed study of the influence of Hegelian philosophy upon
such Russian thinkers as Stankevich, Granovskii, Belinskii, Hertzen,
Bakunin, Chicherin, and Debol'skii. Appeared earlier in *Veröffentlichungen der slavistischen Arbeitsgemeinschaft an der Deutschen
Universität in Prag*, Reihe 1, Heft 9, p. 145-396 (Reichenberg,
Gebrüder Stiepel, 1934). A longer version was published in Russian as *Gegel' v Rossii* (Paris, Dom Knigi, 1939, 357 p.)

1613. Filipov, Aleksandr P. (Alexander Philipov). Logic and Dialectic
in the Soviet Union. Foreword by Ernest Nagel. New York, Research Program on the USSR, 1952. 89 p.

A concise survey of the background and motivation for the
Soviet repudiation of formal logic (as incompatible with "dialec-
tical logic") during the 1920's and 1930's. The author taught in a
Soviet university until the Second World War.

1614. Iakovenko (Jakovenko), Boris V. Filosofi russi; saggio di storia
della filiosofia russa. Florence, La Voce, 1925. 242 p.

Brief critical sketches of the philosophical views of several nineteenth and early twentieth century Russian thinkers. Translation
of *Ocherki russkoi filosofii* (Berlin, Russkoe universal'noe izdatel'-
stvo, 1922, 128 p.)

1615. Joravsky, David. Soviet Marxism and Natural Science, 1917-
1932. New York, Columbia University Press; London, Routledge
and K. Paul, 1961. 433 p.
Bibliography: p. 391-422.
See also entry no. 1780.

A detailed account of the changing relationships between biolo-
gists and physicists on the one hand, and Marxist-Leninists on the
other, during the first 15 years of the Soviet regime; includes a
concise statement of the issues which divided "mechanists" and
"Menshevizing idealists" in the late 1920's.

1616. Kline, George L., *ed. and tr.* Spinoza in Soviet Philosophy; a
Series of Essays, Selected and Translated and with an Introduction
by George L. Kline. London, Routledge and Kegan Paul; New
York, Humanities Press, 1952. 190 p.
Bibliography: p. 177-184.

This brief study of the place and influence of Spinoza (1632-
1677) in pre- and post-Revolutionary Russian thought includes
translations of several essays on Spinoza's philosophy first published in the Soviet Union between 1923 and 1932.

1617. Koyré, Alexandre. La philosophie et le problème national en Russie au début du XIXe siècle. Paris, Champion, 1929. 212 p. (Bibliothèque de l'Institut Français de Léningrad, v. 10)

A meticulous examination of the relationship between German

idealist philosophy and Nicholas I's policy of "official nationalism" (narodnost') in the Russia of the late 1820's and 1830's.

1618. Lieber, Hans J.   Die Philosophie des Bolschewismus in den Grundzügen ihrer Entwicklung. 2d ed. Frankfurt am Main, M. Diesterweg, 1958. 107 p.
Bibliography: p. 103-107.
A historical survey of the development of Marxist-Leninist philosophy, including some account of its origins in pre-Marxist materialism and the Hegelian dialectic.

1619. Losskii (Lossky), Nikolai O.   History of Russian Philosophy. New York, International Universities Press, 1951. 416 p.
Extremely brief sketches of the views of a large number of Russian thinkers, and detailed critical exposition of the thought of a much smaller number — including Vladimir Solov'ev and Sergei Bulgakov. Heavy emphasis upon philosophical theology and philosophy of religion.

1620. Lourié, Ossip.   La philosophie russe contemporaine. Paris, F. Alcan, 1902. 278 p.
Essays in late nineteenth-century Russian philosophy; discussions of the views of Lavrov, Mikhailovskii, Chicherin, Grot, Vladimir Solov'ev, and others, and some reference to trends in psychology and sociology.

1621. Müller-Markus, Siegfried.   Einstein und die Sowjetphilosophie; Krisis einer Lehre. v. 1: Die Grundlagen; die spezielle Relativitätstheorie. Dordrecht, D. Reidel, 1960. 481 p.
A painstaking study of the changing attitude of Soviet Marxist-Leninists toward relativity physics. The present volume, on Einstein's special theory, will be followed by a second, on the general theory.

1622. Russian Philosophy; an Historical Anthology.   Edited by James M. Edie, James P. Scanlan, and Mary-Barbara Zeldin, with the collaboration of George L. Kline. Chicago, Quadrangle Books, 1965. 900 p.
Substantial selections from the philosophical writings of 26 Russian thinkers, ranging from Skovoroda and Radishchev in the eighteenth century to Berdiaev and Losskii in the twentieth. A majority of the selections were translated expressly for this volume.

1623. Soviet Studies in Philosophy. v. 1– 1962– New York. quarterly.
Consists of unabridged English translations of selected articles from such Soviet journals as *Voprosy filosofii* and *Filosofskie nauki.*

1624. Studies in Soviet Thought. v. 1– 1961– Fribourg, Switzerland. quarterly.
Publishes scholarly articles, critical reviews, and brief notes in English, French, and German on current developments in Marxist-

Leninist philosophy in the Soviet Union and in Soviet-bloc countries.

1625.* Wetter, Gustav A.   Dialectical Materialism; a Historical and Systematic Survey of Philosophy in the Soviet Union. Translated from the German by Peter Heath. London, Routledge and Kegan Paul, 1958; New York, Praeger, 1959. 609 p.
See also entry no. 1796.

A comprehensive treatment of Soviet dialectical materialism, seen against its specifically Russian as well as its generally Hegelian-Marxist background — together with Leninist, Stalinist, and post-Stalinist modifications. Translation of *Der dialektische Materialismus; seine Geschichte und sein System in der Sowjetunion* (4th rev. and enl. ed.; Vienna, Herder, 1958, 693 p.). An earlier version was published as *Il materialismo dialettico sovietico* (2d ed.; Turin, G. Einaudi, 1948, 431 p.)

1626. Zen'kovskii (Zenkovsky), Vasilii V.   A History of Russian Philosophy. Translated from the Russian by George L. Kline. London, Routledge and Kegan Paul; New York, Columbia University Press, 1953. 2 v. (947 p.)

A comprehensive historical survey of Russian philosophical thought, both secular and religious, from the eighteenth to the mid-twentieth century. Relatively brief treatment of Russian Marxism; detailed discussion of the views of such philosophers as Vladimir Solov'ev, Shestov, Frank, and Berdiaev, and of such writers as Tolstoi and Dostoevski.

E. RELIGION

1. Christianity

by Georges Florovsky

a. Church history and religious thought

1627. Amburger, Erik.   Geschichte des Protestantismus in Russland. Stuttgart, Evangelisches Verlagswerk, 1961. 210 p.

A short but informative survey of Protestant churches in Russia up to modern times. Good bibliography.

1628. Ammann, Albert M.   Abriss der ostslawischen Kirchengeschichte. Vienna, Thomas Morus Presse, 1950. 748 p.
See also entry no. 473.

The author is Professor for Slavic Church History at the Pontifical Oriental Institute in Rome. The book is a solid and erudite manual, comprehensive and well documented, but it is written from a definite denominational point of view. The author's interpretation in many instances must be critically checked and assessed. It is the only recent book on the subject which covers the whole field in considerable detail. Excellent bibliography. Also published in an Italian edition.

1629. Ammann, Albert M. Untersuchungen zur Geschichte der kirch-
lichen Kultur und des religiösen Lebens bei den Ostslawen. v. 1:
Die ostslawische Kirche im jurisdiktionellen Verband der byzan-
tinischen Grosskirche (988-1459). Würzburg, Augustinus-Verlag,
1955. 288 p.
Bibliography: p. 265-276.
> A companion volume to the author's *Abriss der ostslawischen
> Kirchengeschichte* (*see* entry no. 1628). The author discusses the
> role of the Church in the formation of Russian culture. A second
> part has not yet been published.

1630. Behr-Sigel, E.   Prière et sainteté dans l'Église russe. Paris, Les
Éditions du Cerf, 1950. 180 p. (Russie et chrétienté, no. 5)
> *See also* Iwan von Kologriwof, *Essai sur la sainteté en Russie*
> (Bruges, C. Beyaert, 1953, 447 p.)

1631. Bogolepov, Aleksandr A.   Toward an American Orthodox Church;
the Establishment of an Autocephalous Orthodox Church. New
York, Morehouse-Barlow, 1963. 124 p.
Bibliography: p. 105-108.
> Surveys the canonical position of different Russian Church
> groups in the emigration, especially on the American continent.
> The book is a plea for the formation of an autocephalous Orthodox
> Church in America, on the basis of the old archdiocese of the
> Russian Church. The author discusses the conditions under which
> this goal can be achieved.

1632. Chrysostomus, Johannes.   Die religiösen Kräfte in der russischen
Geschichte. Munich, Verlag Anton Pustet, 1961. 272 p.
> A brief but informative sketch of Russian church history by a
> Roman Catholic writer, intended for the general reader.

1633. Edinaia tserkov'.   One Church. v. 1– 1947– Youngstown, Ohio.
irregular.
> Periodical published by the Exarchate of North and South
> America of the Russian Orthodox Church. Other periodicals deal-
> ing with Eastern Orthodoxy and the churches in East Europe:
> *Kyrios; Vierteljahrsschrift für Kirchen- und Geistesgeschichte
> Osteuropas.* 1936-1943, 1960/61– Königsberg and Berlin.
> *Russian Orthodox Journal.* v. 1– 1927– New York. monthly.
> *Sobornost.* v. 1– 1935– London. 3 no. a year.

1634.*Fedotov, Georgii P.   The Russian Religious Mind. v. 1: Kievan
Christianity. Cambridge, Harvard University Press, 1946. 438 p.
Bibliography: p. 413-424.
See also entries no. 488 and 1373.
> This book is the first volume in a projected series of studies on
> the formation and development of Russian religious character
> which the author was unable to complete because of his death.
> This first volume presents an impressive picture of religious ideas

and practices in the early period, the eleventh and twelfth centuries. It is also a valuable contribution to the study of early Russian literature. The author scrutinizes all extant primary sources in the field with scholarly precision and great literary skill. The weak point of the book is his tendency to exaggerate the originality of Russian spirituality in contrast to the Byzantine.

1635. Fedotov, Georgii P., *ed.*   A Treasury of Russian Spirituality. New York, Sheed and Ward, 1948. 501 p. Bibliography.

See also entries no. 487 and 1380.

The authors of the studies contained in this collection deal basically with the same subject and the same material: inner life and "spirituality" in the Russian Church, in the variety of its expression and in its historical development, with special emphasis on monasticism. All studies are competent, scholarly, well documented, and suggestive. Professor Fedotov's anthology presents an excellent selection of basic texts, hagiographical and instructive, illustrating the whole story from the first times of Christianity in Russia up to the present.

1636. Koch, Hans.   Kleine Schriften zur Kirchen- und Geistesgeschichte Osteuropas. Wiesbaden, Harrassowitz, 1962. 248 p.

Contains collected essays on various topics of East European religious history by one of the foremost German specialists in the field. Dr. Koch, now deceased, was the founder and editor of the valuable periodical *Kyrios.*

1637. Medlin, William K.   Moscow and East Rome; a Political Study of the Relation of Church and State in Muscovite Russia. Geneva, E. Droz, 1952. 252 p. (Études d'histoire économique, politique et sociale, 1)

A competent and critical study. In the opening chapter, the author discusses the Byzantine background and sources of Muscovite political ideology in its relation to the Church. Then he traces the gradual formation of the Muscovite conception, up to its crisis in the time of Peter the Great. Basic findings are ably and suggestively summarized in an epilogue to this piece of thoughtful research.

1638.* Miliukov, Pavel N. (Paul).   Outlines of Russian Culture. Edited by Michael Karpovich. Translated by Valentine Ughet and Eleanor Davis. Philadelphia, University of Pennsylvania Press, 1942. 3 v. Illus.

See also entries no. 472, 1569, and 1815.

A translation of the second volume of the standard work of an eminent Russian historian: *Ocherki po istorii russkoi kul'tury* (St. Petersburg, "Mir Bozhii," 1896-1903, 3 v. in 2). Part one of the English edition is on "Religion and the Church." There are also relevant sections on religious culture in parts two and three, which cover literature and art. The book is written from the point of view of a liberal secular historian. Along with the "Established Church," the author discusses schismatic and sectarian movements at length. The last chapter is on the revolutionary period, brought up to 1930. There is also a brief editor's postscript on later developments, written in 1941. On the whole, it is a fair and stimulating presentation, with a competent command of documentary material.

1639. Pascal, Pierre. Avvakum et les débuts du Raskol; la crise religieuse au XVIIe siècle en Russie. Paris, Istina, 1938. 618 p.
Bibliography: p. 575-598.
See also entry no. 499.
The standard book on the religious history of Russia in the seventeenth century, based on extensive research. Highly imaginative and interpretative, and open to criticism. The author takes sides in the old controversy and claims that the "Church" collapsed in Russia at that time and ceased to exist as an independent body. In this, he goes beyond the evidence.

1640. Russie; pensée religieuse. *In* Dictionnaire de théologie catholique. v. 14/1. Paris, 1939. col. 207-371.
A competent and comprehensive survey of trends and achievements in the field of religious and theological thought in Russia up to the time of publication. Good bibliography.
Part one, up to the establishment of the Holy Synod, is by J. Ledit. Part two, after the establishment of the Holy Synod, by M. Gordillo.

1641. Smolitsch, Igor. Russisches Mönchtum; Entstehung, Entwicklung und Wesen, 988-1917. Würzburg, Augustinus-Verlag, 1953. 559 p. (Das östliche Christentum; Abhandlungen, N.F., Heft 10/11)
Bibliography: p. 9-43.
See also the same author's *Leben und Lehre der Startzen* (Vienna, Thomas-Verlag, 1936, 276 p.)

1642. Stupperich, Robert. Staatsgedanke und Religionspolitik Peters des Grossen. Königsberg, Berlin, Ost-Europaverlag, 1936. 110 p.
A competent study of the subject, although the conclusions are open to criticism. The author takes the side of Peter, and his evaluation of Peter's policy is one-sided. The best essay in the field in a Western language.

1643.* Ware, Timothy. The Orthodox Church. Baltimore, Penguin Books, 1963. 352 p.
The first part of the book is on the history of the Orthodox Church, with several chapters devoted to that of the Russian Church up to the present. Covers the situation of the Church in the Soviet Union and in the emigration. A fair and informative survey, but not without some personal interpretations. The second part deals with faith and worship. In all, the best among recently-published short surveys of the field. Good bibliography.

1644. Winter, Eduard. Russland und das Papsttum. Berlin, Akademie-

Verlag, 1960-1961. 2 v. (376, 649 p.) (Quellen und Studien zur Geschichte Osteuropas, Bd. 6)

> A comprehensive survey based on original research; critical and scholarly, but written from a sharply anti-Roman point of view. Utilizes an enormous amount of factual material, especially in the second volume, in which relations and negotiations between Russia and the Vatican in the eighteenth, nineteenth, and twentieth centuries are discussed. The book is indispensable for any student in the field, in spite of its bias.

1645. Zernov, Nicolas.   Eastern Christendom; a Study of the Origin and Development of the Eastern Orthodox Church. New York, G. P. Putnam's Sons; London, Weidenfeld and Nicolson, 1961. 326 p. Illus., ports., maps.
Bibliography: p. 305-318.

> Contains some sections on the Russian Church. The presentation is elementary, somewhat simplified, and selective. It is a popular book, well written, but without critical analysis of problems and events.

1646. Zernov, Nicolas.   The Russian Religious Renaissance of the Twentieth Century. Darton, England, Longman and Todd, 1963. 410 p.

> The first book in English, or any other language, to give a survey of religious renewal and "conversion" in the ranks of the Russian intelligentsia in this century. The presentation is highly subjective and selective and the book is written in a diffused journalistic style, uncritically and without discrimination. There are numerous factual mistakes, particularly in the erroneous identification of the Russian intelligentsia with the radical and revolutionary groups. The list of writers who, in the opinion of the author, were influenced by the "Religious Renaissance," is inflated, as most of them had not even an indirect relation to it. Well illustrated.

b. Religion (Christian) in the Soviet Union

1647. Anderson, Paul B.   People, Church, and State in Modern Russia. New York, Macmillan, 1944. 240 p.

> A competent and comprehensive analysis of relations between the Soviet State and the Russian Orthodox Church up to the period of the Second World War. It is based on a critical and imaginative perusal of primary sources. In the concluding chapter, the author raises a question about the "Christian Basis for Cooperation with Russia." The book was written during the Second World War, a fact which may account for certain optimistic exaggerations in interpretation and prognosis.

1648. Anglo-Russian Theological Conference, *Moscow, 1956*.   A Report of a Theological Conference Held between Members of a Delegation from the Russian Orthodox Church and a Delegation from the Church of England. Edited by H. M. Waddams. London, The Faith Press, 1957. 120 p.

The larger part of this small volume consists of papers presented by the Orthodox participants in the Conference, covering a wide range of theological topics. Most of them are given in abridged or extract form. "Minutes" and a special résumé of discussions are also included. The book conveys a fair picture of theological attitudes in the present Church of Russia. The papers are of a rather elementary nature.

1649.* Bach, Marcus.   God and the Soviets. New York, Crowell, 1958. 214 p.

Dr. Bach, a professor in the School of Religion, State University of Iowa, has traveled extensively to collect impressions on the state of religion in various parts of the world, spending one month in the Soviet Union in 1957. He skillfully blends his personal observations with the material obtained from outside research.

1650. Baron, J. B., *and* H. M. Waddams, *eds.*   Communism and the Churches; a Documentation. London, SCM Press, 1950. 102 p.

A judicious selection of basic official and representative statements and pronouncements of the authoritative Communist leaders in different countries, including the Soviet Union.

1651. Bissonette, Georges.   Moscow Was My Parish. New York, McGraw-Hill, 1956. 272 p.

The author served as a Roman Catholic chaplain to the American colony in Moscow from 1953 to 1955, when he was ordered to leave the country. He tells his personal story and summarizes his observations. He had an opportunity to travel in Turkestan and other parts of the country.

1652. Cooke, Richard J.   Religion in Russia under the Soviets. New York, Cincinnati, The Abingdon Press, 1924. 311 p.
Bibliography: p. 303-305.

The author, one of the bishops of the Methodist Episcopal Church in the U.S., discusses the basic events in the first years of Soviet rule in Russia.

1653. Curtiss, John S.   Church and State in Russia; the Last Years of the Empire, 1900-1917. New York, Columbia University Press, 1940. 442 p.
Bibliography: p. 411-425.
———. The Russian Church and the Soviet State, 1917-1950. Boston, Little, Brown, 1953. 387 p.
Bibliography: p. 371-378.
See also entry no. 533.
———. Church and State. *In* The Transformation of Russian Society; Aspects of Social Change since 1861. Edited by Cyril E. Black. Cambridge, Harvard University Press, 1961. p. 205-225.

All three studies are well documented. The author's method is to allow the sources to speak for themselves. For the Soviet period, however, the sources available come mainly from Soviet hands. The Church itself is discussed as a "state institution," exclusively on the "official" level, and its inner life is hardly touched upon at all. The perspective of the story is limited. For the study of formal relations between the Church leaders and the Soviet government, however, the works by Dr. Curtiss provide indispensable guidance.

1654. Emhardt, William C.   Religion in Soviet Russia. London, Mow-bray, 1929. 386 p.

The author surveys and discusses the main events in the life of the Russian Church in the first years of the Soviet regime, with special emphasis on the work of Patriarch Tikhon and the attempts of the state to disorganize the Church by favoring the reformist groups within it. The story of the reformist Council of 1923 is told in full, and a special essay on the "Living Church" by Professor S. Troitsky, translated from Russian and edited, is incorporated in the book. A special section deals with attempts of the "Living Church" to take roots in America. Many important documents are given in translation.

1655. Fedotov (Fedotoff), Georgii P.   The Russian Church since the Revolution. New York, Macmillan, 1928. 95 p.

Brief, reliable summary of the first decade after the Revolution, based partly on the author's personal observations. No documentation.

1656. Fletcher, William C., *comp.*   Christianity in the Soviet Union; an Annotated Bibliography and List of Articles; Works in English. Los Angeles, Research Institute on Communist Strategy and Propaganda, University of Southern California, 1963. 95 p.

An extensive bibliography of books and articles in English, containing altogether 588 entries. Included is a list of translations of articles in the Soviet press, prepared under the sponsorship of the National Council of Churches in its series *Religion in Communist Dominated Areas (RCDA)*.

1657. Grunwald, Constantine de.   The Churches and the Soviet Union. New York, Macmillan, 1962. 255 p.

First published in French as *La vie religieuse en URSS* (Paris, Plon, 1961, 246 p.). The author, a native of Russia residing in Paris since 1921, spent the summer of 1960 in the Soviet Union. He tells and interprets his personal impressions in this book. Although his main interest was in the Orthodox Church, he also speaks of Old Believers and "sectarian groups." He discusses at length the problem of antireligious propaganda and religion's chances for survival. The author's estimate of the present Soviet regime is rather optimistic.

1658. Gutsche, Waldemar.   Religion und Evangelium in Sowjetrussland zwischen zwei Weltkriegen, 1917-1944. Kassel, J. G. Oncken, 1959. 156 p.

> Of special interest are sections on the life of Evangelical Christians and Baptists in the Soviet Union. Certain important documents are given in translation.
>
> The author is well acquainted with the previous history of the Russian Evangelical Revival, on which he has written an informative book: *Westliche Quellen des russischen Stundismus* (Kassel, J. G. Oncken, 1956, 144 p.)

1659. Hecker, Julius F.   Religion and Communism. New York, Wiley, 1934. 303 p.

> A considerable part of this book is devoted to an analysis of the historical and philosophical roots of religion and atheism in pre-Revolutionary Russia. More interesting and important is the presentation of the objectives, organization, and achievements of the antireligious movement in the first 15 years of its existence. Some important documents are given in the appendix.
>
> The same author's *Religion under the Soviets* (New York, Vanguard Press, 1927, 207 p.) is an apology for the religious policies of the regime and for the "Living Church" movement, in which the author, an American Methodist, took an active part.

1660. Heyer, Friedrich.   Die Orthodoxe Kirche in der Ukraine von 1917 bis 1945. Cologne-Braunsfeld, R. Müller, 1953. 259 p.
Bibliography: p. 246-248.
See also entry no. 422.

> An important and comprehensive scholarly study, well documented and well presented. The last chapter, describing the Church after the Second World War in areas newly acquired by the Soviets from Poland and Czechoslovakia, is of special interest.

1661. Iaroslavskii, Emel'ian (Y. Yaroslavsky).   Religion in the USSR. New York, International Publishers, 1934. 64 p.

> Mr. Iaroslavskii was the top leader of antireligious propaganda and the head of the Godless League. In this book, he presents the official point of view and discusses the aims and objectives of state policy on the "religious front," as it was called in the 1920's and 1930's.

1662. Institut zur Erforschung der UdSSR.   Religion in the USSR. Edited by Boris I. Ivanov. Munich, Institute for the Study of the USSR, 1960. 236 p. (Research and Materials, Series I, no. 59)

> A collection of essays by émigré authors. Most of the articles deal with the position of the Christian churches, with special emphasis on the situation in the late 1950's. There are also articles on other religious bodies and on the progress of the contemporary antireligious movement. All articles are written from a strictly anticommunist point of view.

1663. Kirche im Osten.   Edited by Robert Stupperich. 1958– Stuttgart. annual.

> Regularly features competent chronicles of events in the churches in Eastern Europe and the Soviet Union.

1664. Kischkowsky, Alexander.   Die sowjetische Religionspolitik und die Russische Orthodoxe Kirche. Munich, Institut zur Erforschung der UdSSR, 1957. 136 p. (Monographien, Serie I, No. 37)

> The author of this monograph is concerned with the variation and development of state and Party policy in relation to the Church, with special emphasis on the shift from persecution to "exploitation." Fairly well documented, with a useful bibliography.

1665. Kolarz, Walter.   Religion in the Soviet Union. New York, St. Martin's Press, 1962. 518 p. Illus.

> The most comprehensive study in the field. In the opening chapter, the author raises the basic question: the extent of the "survival of religion" within the framework of an atheistic state. The author's negative attitude toward the Soviet regime is obvious, but his presentation of facts is fair and well balanced, and is based on a thorough and inclusive use of primary sources. A detailed survey of all existing religious groups and communities is given. The main emphasis is on the contemporary situation, but sufficient information is also supplied on the historical background of each group, beginning with the time of the Revolution. Considerable demographic material is included.

1666. Konferentsiia vsekh tserkvei i religioznykh ob"edinenii v SSSR, posviashchennaia voprosu zashchity mira, *Zagorsk, 1952*. Conference in Defence of Peace of All Churches and Religious Associations in the USSR; Documents and Materials. Moscow, Moscow Patriarchate, 1952. 286 p.

> Material from a conference held in Zagorsk in May 1952. The volume contains a series of statements and allocutions on the problem of world peace, made by the official spokesmen of various religious bodies in the Soviet Union — both Christian and non-Christian — which are formally recognized by the state.

1667. Life in Soviet Russia.   Paris. irregular.

> A set of brief pamphlets prepared by an émigré study group in Paris and edited by Paul B. Anderson. The aim of this publication was to supply a fair selection of informative material from the Soviet press. The most important issues are:
>
> > No. 2/3: Fifteen Years of Religion and Anti-Religion in Soviet Russia. 1933.
> > No.   6: Training for the Godless Ministry. 1934.
> > No.   10: Russia's Religious Future. 1935.

1668. McCullaugh, Francis.   The Bolshevik Persecution of Christianity. New York, Dutton, 1925; London, J. Murray, 1924. 401 p.

The most important part of this book is a detailed eyewitness account and interpretation of the trial of Roman Catholic Archbishop Jan Cieplak, which occupies more than half of the book.

1669. Orthodox Eastern Church, Russian. *Patriarch.* The Russian Orthodox Church: Organization, Situation, Activity. Moscow, Moscow Patriarchate, 1959. 229 p.

The primary value of this official publication of the Moscow Patriarchate lies in its description of the present administrative structure and function of the Russian Orthodox Church. The political aspect of certain activities of the Church is presented guardedly, the reader being left free to interpret them according to his own wisdom.

1670. Soveshchanie glav i predstavitelei avtokefal'nykh pravoslavnykh tserkvei, *Moscow, 1948.* Actes de la Conférence des chefs et des représentants des églises orthodoxes autocéphales. Moscow, Moscow Patriarchate, 1950-1952. 2 v. (447, 479 p.)

Translated and abridged from the original Russian edition, *Deianiia Soveshchaniia glav i predstavitelei avtokefal'nykh pravoslavnykh tserkvei* (Moscow, Moscow Patriarchate, 1949, 2 v.). Contains several reports on various problems and minutes of sessions and discussions. The conference was convened in July 1948 on the occasion of the celebration of the fifth centenary of the autocephalous status of the Russian Church, and was attended by heads and delegates of all Orthodox Churches behind the Iron Curtain, and a few others. Of basic importance are the reports on the Ecumenical movement (by Fr. Gregory Razoumovsky), and on the Roman Church and the policy of the Vatican (by Archbishop Hermogen, Fr. Gabriel Kostelnik, and others). Highly characteristic of the situation in the late 1940's.

1671. Spinka, Matthew. The Church and the Russian Revolution. New York, Macmillan, 1927. 320 p.

——. Christianity Confronts Communism. New York, London, Harper, 1936. 221 p.

——. The Church in Soviet Russia. New York, Oxford University Press, 1956. 179 p.

The author observed developments in the Soviet Union with close attention for many years. His interpretation of events changed during that period, but the informative part of his books is fully reliable. In the beginning he was deeply interested in the conflict between Patriarch Tikhon and the "Living Church." At that time he had some sympathy for the "reformist" tendencies of the latter. Later his attention was focused on the basic tension between the Church and Marxian communism. In his second book, he gives some valuable information on the Protestant sectarian groups. In his last book, he discusses the lives and attitudes of the three patriarchs of the Orthodox Church during the Soviet period: Tikhon, Sergius, and Aleksei. His conclusion is that the church leadership was gradually shifting from open opposition to servile submission to the state. The contemporary situation is discussed exclusively on the level of the foreign policy of the church. Useful bibliographies are included in all three books.

1672. Struve, Nikita.   Les chrétiens en U.R.S.S. Paris, Éditions du Seuil, 1963. 374 p.
The best book on the subject. Both historical and descriptive, with special attention to the situation of the Orthodox Church after the Second World War. The exposition is fair, balanced, and well documented, with accurate references to primary sources. Basic documents are given in French translation in a lengthy appendix. The most important chapters are on the clergy and laity of today, on theological schools and education, and on antireligious propaganda. Reliable information can be found also on the various sectarian bodies, including the new movements. An English edition is in preparation.

1673. Szczesniak, Bolesław, *ed. and tr.*   The Russian Revolution and Religion. Notre Dame, Ind., University of Notre Dame Press, 1959. 289 p.
Bibliography: p. 253-269.
In fact, as the subtitle indicates, this book is "a collection of documents concerning the suppression of religion by the Communists, 1917-1925." The author was primarily interested in the Roman Catholic Church. The documents relate mainly to the very early period, with few of them dating from later than 1923.

1674. Timasheff, Nicholas S.   Religion in Soviet Russia, 1917-1942. New York, Sheed and Ward, 1942. 171 p.
A highly interpretative, but also carefully documented, survey of the main events in the life of the Russian Orthodox Church. The section on the 1930's, for which the source material available is scarce, is of particular value.

1675. U. S. *Joint Publications Research Service.*   The Atheist's Handbook. Washington, 1961. 294 p. (U. S. Joint Publications Research Service. Report no. 8,592)
Important for understanding the aims and methods of atheistic propaganda in the USSR. Translation of portions of *Sputnik ateista* (Moscow, Gospolitizdat, 1959, 544 p.)

2. Islam and Buddhism
by Geoffrey Wheeler

a. Islam

1676. Allen, W. E. D.   The Caucasus. *In* The Baltic and Caucasian States, edited by John Buchan. London, Hodder and Stoughton, 1923. p. 169-259.

A historical and ethnographical account of all the Caucasian peoples, including the Muslims.

1677. Bartol'd, Vasilii V.   Four Studies on the History of Central Asia. Translated from the Russian by V. and T. Minorsky. Leiden, E. J. Brill, 1956-1962. 3 v.

Volume one contains a greatly condensed history of Turkestan from the earliest times to the end of the nineteenth century, but omitting all reference to the Russian conquest, and a history of Semirech'e up to the middle of the eighteenth century. Volume two is a detailed monograph dealing with the life and times of Ulugh Beg, astronomer and statesman (1394-1449). Volume three contains a biography of the poet Mir 'Ali-Shir, and a short history of the Turkman people up to 1884, without detailed reference to the Russian conquest.

1678. Bartol'd, Vasilii V.   Turkestan down to the Mongol Invasion. 2d ed. Translated from the 1900 Russian edition by H. A. R. Gibb and revised and amplified by the author. London, Luzac, 1958. 513 p. (E. J. W. Gibb Memorial Series, n.s., v. 5)

A detailed history of Central Asia from the period of the Muslim invasion down to the appearance of Chingiz Khan. This is a scholarly book based on the work of Arab geographers and historians and includes a geographical survey of Transoxiana. Translation of volume two of *Turkestan v epokhu mongol'skogo nashestviia* (St. Petersburg, 1898-1900, 2 v.)

1679. Bennigsen, Alexandre.   La famille musulmane en Union Soviétique. Cahiers du monde russe et soviétique, v. 1, no. 1, May 1959: 83-108.

A well-documented description of Muslim family life in the USSR before and after the Revolution.

1680. Bennigsen, Alexandre, *and* Chantal Quelquejay.   The Evolution of the Muslim Nationalities of the USSR and Their Linguistic Problems. Translated from the French by Geoffrey Wheeler. London, Central Asian Research Centre, 1961. 57 p.

A concise but scholarly and well-documented account of national groups among the Muslims of the USSR and of their formation into nations under the Soviet regime. Contains valuable information on the status of the various national languages.

Appeared originally in *Cahiers du monde russe et soviétique*, v. 1, no. 3, April–June 1960: 418-465.

1681. Bennigsen, Alexandre, *and* Chantal Quelquejay.   Les mouvements nationaux chez les musulmans de Russie; le "sultangalievisme" au Tatarstan. Paris, Mouton, 1960. 285 p.

A unique description of the movement initiated in 1919 by Sultan Galiyev, a Kazan Tatar, with the object of developing a form of communism attuned to Asian, and particularly to Muslim, requirements. Also contains a history of Tatar nationalist movements.

1682. Carrère d'Encausse, Hélène.   Organisation officielle de l'Islam en U.R.S.S. L'Afrique et l'Asie (Paris), no. 4 (52), 1960: 5-28.

An up-to-date description of Muslim clerical organization in the USSR with some account of the present numbers of clergy and mosques and of the existence of religious literature.

For an English version of this article see the *Central Asian Review*, v. 9, 1961, no. 4: 335-351.

1683. Central Asian Research Centre, *London*.   Islam and Russia; a Detailed Analysis of "An Outline of the History of Islamic Studies in the USSR," by N. A. Smirnov. Introduction by Professor A. K. S. Lambton. London, Central Asian Research Centre, 1956. 87 p.

An abridged version of the original Russian work (*Ocherki istorii izucheniia Islama v SSSR*; Moscow, Izd-vo Akademii nauk SSSR, 1954, 275 p.), this analysis provides a useful summary of the development of Islamic studies in pre- and post-Revolutionary Russia. It also gives an account of the current Soviet attitude towards Islam.

Originally appeared in *Central Asian Review*, v. 2, 1954, no. 4: 282-294; v. 3, 1955, no. 1: 76-88; v. 3, 1955, no. 2: 164-174.

1684. Central Asian Review.   Edited by Geoffrey Wheeler. London, Central Asian Research Centre, in association with St. Antony's College, Oxford. 1953– quarterly.
See also entry no. 241.

This presents an up-to-date and cumulative account of cultural developments in the six Muslim Soviet Socialist Republics of Azerbaijan, Turkmenistan, Uzbekistan, Tajikistan, Kirgiziya, and Kazakhstan. The subjects treated include history, geography, living conditions, demography, the arts, education, irrigation, and communications.

1685. Hayit, Baymirza.   Turkestan im XX. Jahrhundert. Darmstadt, C. W. Leske, 1956. 406 p.
Bibliography: p. 379-385.
See also entry no. 560.

The author is a native of the Uzbek SSR, now living in Germany. After a brief description of conditions prevailing in Turkestan between 1900 and 1917, the book provides a detailed account of the establishment and subsequent development of Soviet power up to 1939.

1686. Kazemzadeh, Firuz.   The Struggle for Transcaucasia, 1917-1921. New York, Philosophical Library, 1951. 356 p.
Bibliography: p. 332-345.
See also entry no. 559.

A history of the national movements among the Armenians,

Georgians, and Azerbaijanis of Transcaucasia between 1917 and 1921, and of the establishment there of the Soviet regime. Also published in London, 1951.

1687. Kolarz, Walter.   Islam. *In his* Religion in the Soviet Union. New York, St. Martin's Press, 1961. p. 400-447.

A detailed account based on Soviet sources of the Soviet attitude and policy towards Islam from the Revolution up to 1960.

1688. Monteil, U.   Les musulmans soviétiques. Paris, Éditions du Seuil, 1957. 189 p.

A popular description of the Muslims of the USSR compiled mainly from the Soviet press.

1689. Pierce, Richard A.   Russian Central Asia, 1867-1917; a Study in Colonial Rule. Berkeley, University of California Press, 1960. 359 p.

A well-documented account of the Russian conquest of Turkestan and of Russian administration of the region up to 1917. Good use is made of both Tsarist and Soviet source material.

1690. Pipes, Richard.   Muslims of Central Asia; Trends and Prospects. Middle East Journal (Washington), v. 9, no. 2-3, Spring–Summer 1955: 147-162, 295-308.

A description of the social and cultural conditions of the Muslims of Soviet Central Asia since the establishment of the Soviet regime, based largely on personal visits to the region and interrogation of Muslim refugees outside the USSR.

1691. Quelquejay, Chantal.   Les sources de documentation sur la religion musulmane en Union Soviétique depuis 1945. Cahiers du monde russe et soviétique, v. 1, 1959-1960, no. 1-2: 184-198, 373-381.

A detailed bibliography of Soviet and non-Soviet source material on Islam in the USSR.

1692. Schuyler, Eugene.   Turkistan. New York, Scribner, Armstrong, 1876. 2 v.

See also entry no. 301.

A very full account of contemporary Muslim life in Russian Turkestan, the Emirate of Bukhara, and northwest Sinkiang. Considerable historical background is provided as well as a description of Russian policy and methods of government. Another edition: London, Sampson, Low, 1876, 2 v.

1693. Skrine, Francis H. B., *and* Edward D. Ross. The Heart of Asia. London, Methuen, 1899. 444 p.

The first half of the book deals with the history of Russian Turkestan from the earliest times until the capture of Tashkent by the Russians in 1865. The second half covers the Russian conquest and the subsequent struggle with the Khanates, and also Turkestan under Russian rule up to 1897. Makes only slight use of Russian source material.

1694.* Wheeler, Geoffrey.   Racial Problems in Soviet Muslim Asia. 2d ed. London, Oxford University Press, 1962. 67 p.

> A concise description of the impact of the Tsarist and Soviet regimes on the Muslims of Russia. Includes demographic details contained in the 1959 census returns.

1695. Zenkovsky, Serge A.   Pan-Turkism and Islam in Russia. Cambridge, Harvard University Press, 1960. 345 p. Illus., maps, index. *See also* entry no. 462.

> A description of the various nationalist movements among the Turkic peoples of Russia and the USSR up to 1921.

b. Buddhism

1696. Kolarz, Walter.   Buddhism. *In his* Religion in the Soviet Union. New York, St. Martin's Press, 1961. p. 448-469.

> This appears to be the only description of Buddhism in Russia and the USSR so far published in any Western language.

3. Judaism

by Moshe Decter

1697. Blake, Patricia.   New Voices in Russian Writing. Encounter, v. 20, no. 4, April 1963: 27-38.

> In the course of an introduction to an anthology of recent writing by the younger generation of Soviet poets and novelists, the author demonstrates the central symbolic and moral role which the Jewish problem plays in the thinking of the liberal intelligentsia.

1698. Braham, Randolph L., *and* Mordecai M. Hauer.   Jews in the Communist World; a Bibliography, 1945-1962. New York, Pro-Arte Publishing Co., 1963. 125 p.

> A selected bibliography of publications in English and other languages. Supplements an earlier compilation by Braham entitled *Jews in the Communist World; a Bibliography, 1945-1960* (New York, Twayne Publishers, 1961, 64 p.), which listed only materials in English.
>
> See also *Pirsumim Yehudiim Bivrit Hamoatzot, 1917-1960* (Jewish Publications in the Soviet Union, 1917-1960; Jerusalem, Israel Historical Society, 1961). Published in Hebrew, this is the most authoritative volume of its kind in any language. It provides a complete bibliography of Hebrew publications, and an exhaustive though not definitive bibliography of Yiddish publications, which were much more numerous in the USSR. Omitted from the latter are "translations into Yiddish from other languages unless they are directly relevant to Jewish problems" and "reprintings of non-Soviet Yiddish literature."

1699. Decter, Moshe.   The Status of the Jews in the Soviet Union. Foreign Affairs, v. 41, no. 2, January 1963: 420-430.
An extensive survey of the problem.

1700. Dubnov (Dubnow), Semen M.   History of the Jews in Russia and Poland from the Earliest Times until the Present Day. Philadelphia, The Jewish Publication Society of America, 1916-1920. 3 v.
Bibliography: v. 3, p. 171-203.
See also entry no. 481.
An authoritative history of pre-Revolutionary Russian Jewry.

1701. Fejtö, François.   Les juifs et l'antisémitisme dans les pays communistes (entre l'intégration et la sécession); suivi de documents et de témoignages. Paris, Plon, 1960. 273 p.
The bulk of this volume consists of documents from the Soviet press and other Soviet publications, with analytical and historical introductions.

1702. Goldberg, Ben Z.   The Jewish Problem in the Soviet Union; Analysis and Solution. New York, Crown, 1961. 374 p.
An analysis, based on firsthand experience, by an American journalist who for many years was close to the leading figures of Soviet Jewish cultural and communal life.

1703. Goldhagen, Erich.   Communism and Anti-Semitism. *In* Abraham Brumberg, *ed.* Russia under Khrushchev. New York, Praeger, 1962. p. 322-338.
An examination of the present situation of Soviet Jews in the light of Soviet political developments since the death of Stalin.

1704. Goldman, Guido G.   Zionism under Soviet Rule, 1917-1928. New York, Herzl Press, 1960. 136 p.
A detailed historical account of the suppression, during the first decade of the Soviet regime, of the Zionist movement, to which large numbers of Soviet Jews had been emotionally devoted.

1705. Hindus, Maurice.   Jew — Russia's Stepson. *In his* House without a Roof; Russia after 43 Years of Revolution. Garden City, N. Y., Doubleday, 1961. p. 297-325.
A detailed account by a long-standing student of Soviet life of the suppression of Jewish culture.

1706. Jews in Eastern Europe.   1960– London. quarterly.
A periodical containing excerpts from the press of the East European countries — particularly the Soviet Union — and from various other sources, dealing with the position of Jews.

1707. Jews in the Soviet Union.   The New Leader (New York), v. 42, no. 33, September 14, 1959.
A special issue of the magazine, devoted entirely to the position of Jews in the Soviet Union.

1708. Kolarz, Walter.   The Secularization of Soviet Jewry. *In his* Religion in the Soviet Union. New York, St. Martin's Press, 1962. p. 372-399.

> Describes the gradual attrition of Judaism in an officially atheist-materialist state.

1709. Leneman, Léon.   La tragédie des juifs en URSS. Paris, Desclée et Brouwer, 1959. 329 p. Illus.

1710. Levy, Hyman.   Jews and the National Question. London, Hillway, 1958. 93 p.

> A valuable monograph written by a leading intellectual in the British Communist Party. The author questions Soviet policy in terms of Soviet and Marxist criteria.

1711. Schechtman, Joseph B.   Star in Eclipse: Russian Jewry Revisited. New York, Yoseloff, 1961. 255 p. Illus.

> An analysis by a historical demographer.

1712. Schwarz, Solomon M.   The Jews in the Soviet Union. Syracuse, Syracuse University Press, 1951. 380 p.
See also entry no. 563.

> A pioneering, basic study. The author analyzes the evolution of Soviet policy toward the Jews and the history of anti-Semitism in the USSR.

1713. Teller, J. L.   The Kremlin, the Jews and the Middle East. New York, Yoseloff, 1957. 202 p.

> The author analyzes Soviet policy toward the Jews in terms of Soviet policy toward other national minorities; he also indicates the role played in this policy by Soviet interests in the Middle East.

F. EDUCATION AND RESEARCH

by Nicholas De Witt

1. Educational System and Practice

1714. Abell, M. A.   Foreign Language Teaching in the USSR. The Modern Language Journal, v. 43, no. 2, February 1959: 72-78.

> A brief but to-the-point review, based on primary sources and personal observations, of the effectiveness and quality of foreign language instruction in the USSR. The emphasis is on the deficiencies of the grammar-translation approach, with a discussion of the difficulties of introducing audio-oral techniques in the Soviet school setting.

1715. Administration of Teaching in Social Sciences in the USSR — Syllabi for Three Required Courses. Ann Arbor, University of Michigan Press, 1960. 136 p.

> A translation of three course syllabi in dialectical and historical materialism, political economy, and the history of the Communist

Party of the Soviet Union, which are required of all students in Soviet higher education as a mandatory political indoctrination component called "social science studies." Each course syllabus has required reading lists.

1716. Alt, Herschel, *and* Edith Alt.   Russia's Children; a First Report on Child Welfare in the Soviet Union. New York, Bookman Associates, 1959. 240 p.
See also entry no. 1216.

Popularly-written essay, summarizing the impressions of a husband-wife team who visited the USSR in the late 1950's, on the realities of child-rearing and educational practices in the Soviet Union. In an attempt to trace the influences of Pavlov and Makarenko on Soviet pedagogy, the conflicts between educational theory and practice, and between professed goals and their actual implementation, are discussed not only in the context of Soviet society but in their relevance to pedagogical theories in the West.

1717. Anweiler, Oskar, *and* K. Meyer, *comps. and eds.*   Die sowjetische Bildungspolitik seit 1917: Dokumente und Texte. Heidelberg, Quelle und Meyer, 1961. 424 p.

A selective compilation in German translation of major Soviet governmental decrees and party pronouncements on education and its administration, policy, and instructional contents during the entire period of the Communist regime from 1917 to 1961. An indispensable source guide to historical research on Soviet educational developments, and especially the role of the Communist Party as a legislative authority over education.

1718. Barghoorn, Frederick C.   The Soviet Image of the United States; a Study in Distortion. New York, Harcourt, Brace, 1950. 297 p.
See also entry no. 872.

A study of the pattern of distortion of facts to fit the ideological and political framework of the propaganda objectives of the Soviet regime. Since many of the distorted messages appear not only in the Soviet press but also in textbooks and instructional materials on various levels of schooling, this book is an indispensable aid to research on the making of the Soviet mind as it was molded during the Stalinist era. The teaching of social sciences and the humanities in the USSR cannot be examined meaningfully without reference to the pattern of distortion discussed in depth in this book.

For a discussion of the use by the Soviet state of cultural exchanges, mass communication media, and education as weapons of psychological warfare against the West, *see* Barghoorn's *The Soviet Cultural Offensive* (Princeton University Press, 1960, 353 p.)

1719. Bauer, Raymond A.   The New Man in Soviet Psychology. Cambridge, Harvard University Press, 1952. 229 p.
See also entries no. 104 and 1229.

A study of Soviet psychology with specific reference to the pedology purge, and a discussion of the radical shift in the mid-

1930's of Soviet experimental psychology to environmental theories of behavior and social conditioning theory. An indispensable tool in the study of Soviet educational theories in the Stalinist period and of the dilemma of the Soviet regime in developing new character for the Soviet man.

See also *Some Views on Soviet Psychology*, edited by Raymond A. Bauer (Washington, American Psychological Association, 1962, 285 p.), a collection of eight essays by prominent American psychologists examining problems of personality development in the Soviet Union.

1720. Bereday, George Z. F., William W. Brickman, *and* Gerald H. Read, *eds.* The Changing Soviet School. Boston, Houghton Mifflin, 1960. 514 p. Illus.

A symposium volume on Soviet educational practice and performance, prepared mainly on the basis of the observations of 70 educators who visited the Soviet Union in the summer of 1958 under the auspices of the Comparative Education Society. Although the bulk of the material presented in the book relates to observations gathered as a result of this field survey, supplemental research on primary and secondary sources was used in order to provide additional factual information. Of particular note are the brief historical survey of educational development in Russia (chapters 2 and 3, by Brickman) and the discussion of the problems of character and moral training under Soviet conditions (chapter 18, by Read). The other topics cover all levels of schooling, with the discussions ranging from adequate factual and analytical studies to haphazard impressionistic statements. Of hundreds of travelogue accounts of Soviet education, this volume is perhaps the best and certainly the most comprehensive attempt not only to report but also to analyze on-the-spot impressions of the qualitative performance of Soviet schools.

1721. Bereday, George Z. F., *and* Jaan Pennar, *eds.* The Politics of Soviet Education. New York, Praeger, 1960. 217 p.

A volume containing 11 essays by different contributors, each of them a student of Soviet affairs. The papers were originally presented at a seminar at the Institute for the Study of the USSR in Munich, Germany, and were subsequently reworked into documented analytical studies. Of particular note are such topics as Party control over Soviet schools by Pennar; antireligious education by Alessio U. Floridi; the teaching of history by William K. Medlin; and, especially, the science education of secondary school teachers by Norton Dodge and the sociological aspects of advanced training by Mark G. Field.

1722. Bowen, James. Soviet Education: Anton Makarenko and the Years of Experiment. Madison, University of Wisconsin Press, 1962. 232 p.

An analysis of the work and writings of Anton Makarenko in their relation to educational theory and practice in the USSR. The educational heritage of pre-Revolutionary Russia and the experimental (progressive) period of the 1920's led to a reassessment of the aims of Soviet education during the period of rapid industrialization in which Makarenko's disciplinary philosophy of upbringing was accepted as a basic tenet. Makarenko's methods, as adopted in penal colonies for youths, and his educational philosophy of subordinating the individual to the will of the collective, are examined in the context of the dilemma of a totalitarian state as it emerged under Stalin. Comparisons are made between the ideal and the real in Soviet education and between the educational philosophies of the authoritarian and democratic types.

1723. Calvert, J. S., R. E. Morgan, *and* C. Sayer.   Physical Education and Sports in the Soviet Union. Leeds, England, 1961. 48 p. (University of Leeds. Institute of Education Research and Studies, Special Reprint Series, no. 21)

    Assessment of the role, objectives, and scope of physical education programs in the USSR in the context of general education and professional sports training programs.

1724. Chauncey, Henry.   Some Comparative Checkpoints between American and Soviet Secondary Education. Comparative Education Review, v. 2, no. 3, February 1959: 18-20.

    Qualitative appraisal of the similarities and differences in the American and Soviet educational effort. The journal cited here, edited by George Z. F. Bereday for the Comparative Education Society, features in most issues articles on various aspects of Soviet education.

1725. Counts, George S.   The Challenge of Soviet Education. New York, McGraw-Hill, 1957. 330 p.

    A discussion of the Soviet educational effort in its multiple relation to the social and political development of Soviet society, with the basic theme that the school in the USSR has become an instrument for attaining the political objectives of a totalitarian state. The book contains a wealth of information and abounds in generous thought-provoking interpretations of Soviet educational objectives, but offers little insight into the actual results of such an effort to mold the "new Soviet man."

    See also *The Country of The Blind*, by George S. Counts and Nucia P. Lodge (Boston, Houghton Mifflin, 1949, 378 p.), which attempts to relate the educational process to the broad ideological and political objectives of the Communist regime during the Stalin era.

1726.* Counts, George S., *ed.*   Khrushchev and the Central Committee Speak on Education. Pittsburgh, University of Pittsburgh Press, 1959. 66 p.

    An English translation of the 1958 educational reform theses of the Central Committee of the Communist Party of the USSR, supplemented by an interpretive comment in which Mr. Counts boldly asserts a tendency towards a return of Soviet educational policy to the more liberal ideal of educating the "whole man" — a fundamental thesis of progressive education — through renewed emphasis upon, and application of, the principle of polytechnism.

See also "*I Want to Be Like Stalin*," translated by George S. Counts and Nucia P. Lodge from the 1946 Russian text of Boris P. Esipov and N. K. Goncharov (New York, John Day, 1947, 150 p.), with interpretive commentary.

1727. Deineko, M. M.   Forty Years of Public Education in the USSR. Moscow, Foreign Languages Publishing House, 1957. 117 p. Illus.

English translation by the Soviet authorities of a propaganda pamphlet, *Sorok let narodnogo obrazovaniia v SSSR* (Moscow, Uchpedgiz, 1957, 275 p.), which glorifies the successes of education in the USSR in the four decades following the October Revolution.

1728. De Witt, Nicholas.   Education and Professional Employment in the USSR. Washington, National Science Foundation, 1961. 856 p. Bibliography: p. 815-836.

A review of the structure, functioning, and contents of education in the USSR on all levels from nursery schools to graduate training and research programs. An assessment of the quantity and quality of education and especially of the results of the Soviet educational effort as they relate to diverse types of manpower, with emphasis upon semiprofessional and professional personnel and patterns of their deployment in the national economy. A 548-page text analyzes qualitative and quantitative trends, and a 265-page appendix presents statistical and other pertinent factual information on enrollments, graduations, and curricula, as well as other materials governing school practices in the USSR.

1729. Engineering Education Exchange Mission to the Soviet Union in November 1958: Final Report.   Journal of Engineering Education, v. 49, no. 9, May 1959: 839-911.

A summary account of the status of and trends in Soviet engineering education, as observed by a group of American engineering educators who visited the USSR in 1958. Extensive compilation of engineering curricula and their evaluation. Discussion of the pattern of Soviet engineering specialization and the quality of education as compared with that in the United States.

1730. Fainsod, Merle.   How Russia Is Ruled. 2d ed. Cambridge, Harvard University Press, 1963. 684 p.
See also entry no. 687.

A classic study among numerous books on the Soviet government and its exercise of power, including control over the schools. Passages dealing with education and its purposes and partisan youth organizations and their functions are required reading for both the student and the layman. Earlier edition: 1953, 575 p.

1731. Feldmesser, Robert A.   Social Status and Access to Higher Education; a Comparison of the United States and the Soviet Union. Harvard Educational Review, v. 27, no. 2, Spring 1957: 92-106.

An analytical article attempting to measure and to compare opportunities for higher education in the two countries.

1732. Field, Mark G.   The Academy of the Social Sciences of the Communist Party of the Soviet Union. The American Journal of Sociology, v. 56, no. 2, September 1950: 137-141.

Review of the functions and activities of this academy of the Central Committee of the Communist Party and the role it plays in the training and research of social scientists in the USSR.

1733. Fisher, Ralph T., Jr.   Pattern for Soviet Youth; a Study of the Congresses of the Komsomol, 1918-1954. New York, Columbia University Press, 1959. 452 p.

See also entry no. 763.

A historical survey of the role of the Young Communist League in the USSR, in society at large, and in the educational effort in particular.

See also *Soviet Youth; Twelve Komsomol Histories* (Munich, Institute for the Study of the USSR, 1959, 256 p.), a collection of essays written by former members of the Young Communist League, with accounts of their personal experiences in the 1920's and 1930's.

1734. Froese, Leonhard, Rudolf Haas, *and* Oskar Anweiler.   Bildungswettlauf zwischen West und Ost. Freiburg im Breisgau, Herder, 1961. 126 p.

A German summary and interpretive view of the issue of educational competition between East (mostly the USSR) and West (mostly the U. S.). The book is a digest of many secondary sources with the sensible reflection: What is the meaning of competition without an adequate definition of the purposes of education?

1735. Hans, Nicholas A.   The Russian Tradition in Education. London, Routledge and Kegan Paul, 1963. 196 p.

Bibliography: p. 180-192.

Substantially revised version of an earlier book by the same author, *History of Russian Educational Policy* (London, P. S. King, 1931, 255 p.), who traces trends in Russian education from the emergence of Western-type schooling under Peter the Great to the Marxist version of populism in the Stalinist era. The thesis is that the "Russian tradition" in education survived the Revolution.

In nine chapters the author attempts to identify this tradition and to cope with the rapidly changing panorama of educational philosophies closely related to intellectual opinions of their times. An image is created of educational movements which evolve in logical sequence from autocracy and traditionalism (from Peter to Alexander the First) to radical revolt, to humanism (N. I. Pirogov), to nationalism (K. G. Uchinskii), to moralism (L. N. Tolstoi), to populism (Chernyshevski-Dobroliubov-Pisarev), to liberalism (of the zemstvo era), to the embodiment of populism in the Soviet version of Marxism. Each leaves a trace of its own, but is it a tradition? This is an account of what the author thinks (based on careful selection) the Russian intelligentsia said in their voluminous writings about what education ought to be, rather than what actually happened in the schools of Russia over three centuries.

1736.*Hechinger, Fred M.   The Big Red Schoolhouse. Garden City, N.Y., Doubleday, 1959. 240 p.

A many-dimensional comparison between Russian and American educational developments and policies, written in popular style. A calm and unbiased interpretation of the Soviet educational drive through its several stages of development, coupled with a penetrating analysis of the American educational posture, it brings unique insight into the controversial topic of the Soviet educational challenge. A revised edition (New York, Dolphin Books, 1962, 200 p.) also discusses Khrushchev's educational reform in the light of the historical forces affecting the Soviet educational scene.

1737. Herzer, Albert.   Bolschewismus und Menschen-Bildung. Hamburg, Gesellschaft der Freunde des Vaterländischen Schul- und Erziehungswesens, 1951. 251 p.

Ideological and political factors affecting the make-up of the "new Soviet man." Among other mass indoctrination weapons, the school is considered to be the principal instrument for molding the individual for citizenship in a collective state.

1738. Informationsdienst zum Bildungswesen in Osteuropa.   Edited by Siegfried Baske. v. 1– 1960– Berlin, Osteuropa Institut an der Freien Universität Berlin. irregular.

Selective though quite extensive and comprehensive bibliographical guide, with some annotations and occasional extensive reviews of books, articles, and source materials on education in the Soviet Union and other Communist countries of Eastern Europe. Listings and reviews deal with source materials on education published in Western Europe and the United States, as well as in Eastern Europe. In addition, this information service presents survey digests on educational developments in individual countries prepared by corresponding or resident German scholars.

1739. Inkeles, Alex.   Public Opinion in Soviet Russia; a Study in Mass Persuasion. Cambridge, Harvard University Press, 1958. 393 p. *See also* entries no. 1013 and 1161.

An examination of mass communication media in the USSR and a study of the techniques of persuasion of Soviet citizens, especially among the young. Indispensable reading in the field of education, for it discusses the instruments used by the Soviet state in molding the opinions of Russian youth outside the formal school structure. Earlier edition: 1950, 379 p.

See also *The Soviet Citizen; Daily Life in a Totalitarian Society* (Cambridge, Harvard University Press, 1959, 533 p.), by Alex Inkeles and Raymond A. Bauer, which sheds light on the operational relationships between education and society in a sociological and political context. Based on interviews of several thousand refugees and defectors from the Soviet Union.

1740. Johnson, William H. E.   Russia's Educational Heritage. Pittsburgh, Carnegie Institute of Technology, 1950. 351 p.
Bibliography: p. 337-343.

Undoubtedly the best and most thorough study to date of the history of educational development, and especially educational ideas, in pre-Revolutionary Russia, with added emphasis on university education. The book discusses educational thought in the context of the political development of the country. It should be not read, but studied.

1741. Kalinin, Mikhail I.   On Communist Education. Moscow, Foreign Languages Publishing House, 1953. 448 p.

An English translation prepared by Soviet authorities from the various writings of this Soviet political leader who was responsible for shaping many educational policies and practices just prior to and particularly during the Stalin era.

1742.* King, Edmund J., *ed.*   Communist Education. London, Methuen; Indianapolis, Bobbs-Merrill, 1963. 309 p.

A collection of 12 essays on education in the USSR (eight essays) and other Communist countries, discussing recent developments from the interpretive and highly subjective point of view of British comparative educators visiting Soviet schools. The topics range from educational psychology and crèches to teacher status and higher education. In part, the essays are travelogues looking at Soviet schools through rose-colored glasses.

1743. Kline, George L., *ed.*   Soviet Education. New York, Columbia University Press; London, Routledge and Paul, 1957. 192 p.

A collection of nine essays by former Soviet citizens describing various aspects of Soviet schooling, primarily from their impressions and experiences in the schools of the 1930's. This insightful view into Soviet school practices serves as an indispensable aid in understanding the Soviet educational process.

1744. Korol, Alexander G.   Soviet Education for Science and Technology. Cambridge, Massachusetts Institute of Technology; New York, Wiley and Sons, 1957. 513 p.
Bibliography: p. 469-480.

A thorough and systematic review of the educational programs, curricula, syllabi, and instructional effectiveness of Soviet educational establishments, particularly in their relation to the quality of scientific training on secondary and higher education levels. On the higher educational level, comparisons of Soviet engineering and science programs are made with those offered in American engineering schools (specifically the Massachusetts Institute of Technology). Professionalization and specialization in Soviet education are explored in detail and related to the economic and political setting in the USSR. The extensive compilation of materials refers to the pre-1955 period.

1745. Krupskaia, Nadezhda K.   On Education. Moscow, Foreign Languages Publishing House, 1957. 254 p.

A Soviet translation into English of some carefully selected and highly censored writings of Lenin's wife, who was very active in education policy-making circles, particularly in the 1920's and early 1930's.

1746. Lazarevich (Lazarevitch), Ida M., *and* Nicolas Lazarevich.   L'école soviétique. Paris, Iles d'or, 1954. 208 p.

A brief, but perhaps the best available, review in French of Soviet education and its institutional and operational features.

1747. Levin, Deana.   Soviet Education Today. New York, De Graff, 1959. 170 p.

An essay on Soviet education written by a British educationist, who — because of her experience as a practicing teacher in foreign schools — specializes in "eyewitness" accounts of schooling in different countries. A honey-sweet account of the Soviet educational system and its alleged faultless and problemless performance, be it under Stalin's rule or under Khrushchev's educational reforms of 1958. Revised edition: New York, Monthly Review Press, 1963, 179 p.

1748. Lindquist, Clarence B., *and* John B. Whitelaw.   Teacher Education in the Soviet Union. *In* U. S. Congress. Joint Economic Committee. Dimensions of Soviet Economic Power. Washington, U. S. Government Printing Office, 1962. p. 305-320.

An assessment of teacher training in the Soviet Union, with information on the supply of teachers and the curricula for teachers of various levels in the educational system.

1749. London, Ivan D.   Evaluation of Some Current Literature about Soviet Education. School and Society, v. 86, no. 2140, November 8, 1958: 9-16.

A review of American assessments of the Soviet educational effort and some critical suggestions for improvement and objectivity in such research.

1750. Makarenko, Anton S.   The Road to Life; an Epic of Education. Moscow, Foreign Languages Publishing House, 1955. 3 v.

See also entry no. 172.

————. Learning To Live.   Moscow, Foreign Languages Publishing House, 1953. 689 p.

————. A Book for Parents.   Moscow, Foreign Languages Publishing House, 1954. 412 p.

Soviet translations into English of the major works of the official Soviet pedagogical theorist, whose views have been embodied in many educational policies and practices of the Soviet regime since the early 1930's. An indispensable aid to those wishing to acquaint themselves with Makarenko's works. Translations of *Putevka v zhizn'*, *Flagi na bashniakh*, and *Kniga dlia roditelei*, respectively.

A German selection of Makarenko's writings was published as *Ausgewählte pädagogische Schriften* (Paderborn, Schöningh, 1962, 290 p.)

Frederic Lilge, an eminent student of the philosophy of education, has appraised Makarenko's life and work critically in his *Anton Semyonovitch Makarenko; an Analysis of His Educational Ideas in the Context of Soviet Society* (Berkeley, University of California Press, 1958, 52 p.)

For a discussion of Soviet pedagogy and Makarenko's role therein from a historical perspective, *see* Lotte Adolphs' *A. S. Makarenko; Erzieher im Dienste der Revolution* (Bad Godesberg, Dürrsche Buchhandlung, 1962, 272 p.)

1751. Medlin, William K., Clarence B. Lindquist, *and* Marshall L. Schmitt. Soviet Education Programs. Washington, U. S. Department of Health, Education and Welfare, Office of Education, 1960. 281 p. (U. S. Office of Education. Bulletin no. 17, 1960)

A comprehensive compilation of curricula for Soviet secondary schools and particularly for higher education institutes training teachers in the USSR, and an analysis of these programs in relation to instructional practice as it can be ascertained not only from published Soviet sources but also through personal observation (the authors visited the USSR). Of particular note are the discussions of current Soviet efforts to introduce polytechnical education and of problems of teacher training as they relate to methodology versus subject-matter content.

See also William K. Medlin's chapter on the USSR in *Comparative Educational Administration*, edited by Theodore L. Reller and Edgar L. Morphet (Englewood Cliffs, N. J., Prentice-Hall, 1962, p. 113-131).

1752. Mikriukov (Mikryukov), M. Students of Moscow University. Moscow, Foreign Languages Publishing House, 1958. 129 p. Illus.

An account of the day-to-day life of Soviet higher education students, dealing with study as well as extracurricular activities in the largest Soviet university.

1753. Olkhovsky, Andrey V. Music under the Soviets; the Agony of an

Art. London, Routledge and Kegan Paul; New York, Praeger, 1955. p. 103-146.

See also entry no. 1853.

The pertinent section deals with the organization and type of musical education offered in the Soviet Union in both general education programs and training programs for professional musicians.

See also A. Lowe and H. S. Pryor, "Music Education in the USSR," *Music Education Journal,* v. 45, June 1959: 28-32, an examination of the role of music education in the context of general school programs on the primary and secondary levels.

1754. Pinkevich (Pinkevitch), Albert P.   The New Education in the Soviet Republic. Translated by Nucia Perlmutter. Edited by George S. Counts. New York, John Day, 1929. 403 p.

Description of the Soviet school in the 1920's by a Soviet educational administrator.

1755. Roggenkamp, Josef G.   Die sowjetische Erziehung. Düsseldorf, Patmos, 1961. 184 p.

General survey of the Soviet system of schooling and its operational features, with some analysis of the current educational reforms.

1756. Rokitiansky, Nicholas J., *and* William K. Medlin, *comps.*   Bibliography of Published Materials on Russian and Soviet Education; a Research and Reference Tool. Washington, U. S. Dept. of Health, Education and Welfare, Office of Education, 1960. 70 p.

A highly useful guide — though incomplete and not well annotated — covering largely Western studies of education in the USSR and also some Russian source material. The former references are frequently selected from obscure journals and give a wide cross section of educationist writings on this topic.

1757. Rosen, Seymour M.   Higher Education in the USSR: Curriculums, Schools and Statistics. Washington, U. S. Department of Health, Education and Welfare, Office of Education, 1963. 195 p. (U. S. Office of Education. Bulletin no. 16, 1963)

Presents descriptive materials on status and trends in higher education in the USSR. Extensive non-analytical compilation of basic information translated from Soviet sources on curricula, admission requirements, specialties, administrative regulations, etc. Gives a roster of institutions of higher learning and presents statistical data on students, faculty, etc.

For an assessment of the planning and supervision of higher education in the Soviet Union, with statistics for various quantitative aspects, *see* the same author's "Higher Education in the USSR," in *Dimensions of Soviet Economic Power,* released by the Joint Economic Committee of the U. S. Congress (Washington, 1962), p. 269-304.

1758. Shore, Maurice J.   Soviet Education: Its Psychology and Philoso-

phy. New York, Philosophical Library, 1947. 346 p.
Bibliography: p. 319-339.

The only study of the fundamental philosophical premises of Soviet education which attempts to relate pedagogical policies and practices in the USSR to the basic assertions concerning the nature of man and his upbringing as these concepts are developed in the major writings of Marx, Engels, Lenin, and Stalin. An indispensable guide to educational concepts of materialist philosophers and Communist ideologists.

1759. Simon, Brian, *and* Joan Simon, *eds.*   Educational Psychology in the USSR. Stanford, Calif., Stanford University Press, 1963. 283 p. *See also* entry no. 1233.

A highly selective collection of 14 essays written by Soviet psychologists. The articles originally appeared in Soviet professional journals and annals, or as chapters in books. They have been carefully edited, however, to give the proper English terminology.

The excellent job of selection makes this book a companion, in a sense, to an earlier volume (*Psychology in the Soviet Union*; Stanford, Calif., Stanford University Press, 1957, 305 p.). All the essays are of recent vintage (1959-1960), and together reflect the trend toward greater experimentation in the area of educational psychology which has taken place in the Soviet Union in recent years. All the articles deal with the processes of learning and the problems of conceptualization and retention. The introduction, prepared by the compilers, discusses the affiliations and careers of the contributors, and research within the Academy of Pedagogical Sciences of the RSFSR.

1760. Soviet Education. 1959– New York, International Arts and Sciences Press. monthly.

Selected articles from Soviet education journals, translated into English.

1761. Timoshenko, Stephen P.   Engineering Education in Russia. New York, McGraw-Hill, 1959. 47 p.

A brief though highly important book by a Russian-born engineering educator who, after nearly 40 years of residence abroad (mostly in America), revisits engineering schools in the Soviet Union and finds that the traditions of engineering inherited from pre-Revolutionary Russia are still very much alive, that his own textbooks are still in use, and that some of his own students carry on research along lines he approves. Soviet professional engineering programs, as offered in higher education institutes, are discussed and evaluated in qualitative terms, with the added insight into instructional problems of an experienced educator. Of particular note is a brief historical survey of engineering education in Russia.

1762. Trace, Arther S.   What Ivan Knows That Johnny Doesn't: a Comparison of Soviet and American School Problems. New York, Random House, 1961. 213 p.

One of the most interesting, and indeed most controversial, interpretive commentaries on Soviet and American education, based on a comparison of the subject matter taught in the two school systems. The book deals largely with what is taught, on the basis of a survey of syllabi and textbooks, with an emphasis on teaching in the humanities and the social sciences.

1763. Ulich, Robert.   The Education of Nations: a Comparison in Historical Perspective. Cambridge, Harvard University Press, 1962. 375 p.

Chapter nine, on the USSR (pages 255-285), in this classic study of comparative education treats the problems of education in Russia from a historical point of view and in the context of current Soviet educational developments in relation to Marxist philosophy. Both topics are developed in global perspective, with the suggestion that perhaps education in Russia is but an example of general educational development in Western civilization.

1764. U. S. *Education Mission to the USSR.* Soviet Commitment to Education. Washington, U. S. Dept. of Health, Education and Welfare, Office of Education, 1959. 135 p. (U. S. Office of Education. Bulletin no. 16, 1959)

A report of the first official U. S. exchange mission to the USSR allowed to visit the Soviet Union under the auspices of the Soviet-American Cultural Exchange Agreement of 1958 and permitted to observe firsthand what the Soviet government wanted it to see. The report is a mixture of travelogue, descriptive fragments of observations from visits to schools of various types, and post-fact evaluations of some of the factual information on instruction programs.

For a simplified, descriptive account of the educational system in the USSR, and its functioning, *see* the U. S. Office of Education's *Education in the USSR* (Washington, 1957, 226 p.)

1765. U. S. *Public Health Mission to the Union of Soviet Socialist Republics.* Report of the United States Public Health Mission to the Union of Soviet Socialist Republics. Washington, U. S. Department of Health, Education and Welfare, 1959. 67 p.
See also entry no. 1226.

Pertinent sections (pages 44-58) of this report on a 1957 tour deal with an evaluation of medical education and research in the USSR from an organizational and qualitative point of view.

Other treatments of Soviet medical education:

Starr, Arnold.   "Medical Education in Soviet Russia." *Journal of Medical Education*, v. 33, no. 12, December 1958: 827-836.

Sigerist, Henry E.   *Medicine and Health in the Soviet Union.* New York, The Citadel Press, 1947. p. 54-79.

Shimkin, Michael B.   "Medical Education in the Soviet Union." *American Review of Soviet Medicine*, v. 1, no. 5, June 1944, p. 465-480.

1766. U. S. *Technical Education Delegation to the Union of Soviet Socialist Republics.* Report of the United States Technical Education Delegation to the Union of Soviet Socialist Republics, May 5-31, 1961. Washington, D. C., American Association of Junior Colleges, 1962. 203 p.

> A detailed survey of the status of semiprofessional education as offered in technicums in the USSR, based on personal observations and supported by factual compilations of information on curricula and syllabi of instruction relating to secondary specialized education.

1767. Vigdorova, F.   Diary of a Russian Schoolteacher. Translated from the Russian by Rose Prokofieva. New York, Grove Press, 1960. 256 p.

> American reprint of an earlier (1954) Soviet translation into English of this fascinating account by a Soviet teacher, who tells about her daily chores in and around an urban school in the USSR.

1768. Volpicelli, Luigi.   L'évolution de la pédagogie soviétique. Neuchâtel, Delachaux et Niestle, 1954. 236 p.

> A survey of Soviet pedagogical theory, rather than the operational aspects of schooling, in historical perspective, though dealing largely with Makarenko and with some treatment of the controversies which preceded his rise to the status of official apostle of Soviet pedagogy. Originally published in Italian as *Storia della scuola sovietica* (Brescia, La Scuola, 1950, 325 p.)

2. Scientific Research

1769. Ashby, Eric.   Scientist in Russia. New York, Penguin Books, 1947. 252 p.

See also entry no. 1193.

> One of the best and most readable essays by a Western observer on the education of Soviet scientists during the mid-1940's, and a thoughtful analysis of the conditions in which Soviet scientists worked under the impact of political dictates, particularly in the area of biological sciences. The personal impressions of an Australian scientist, who, as counsellor of the embassy, was able not only to visit Soviet research institutions and universities but also to assemble extensive factual materials on programs of instruction, syllabi, teaching staffs, etc. The book is a precursor of the crop of post-1945 studies vivisecting Soviet science education and research.

1770. Battelle Memorial Institute.   Directory of Selected Scientific Institutions in the USSR. Columbus, Ohio, Charles E. Merrill, 1963. Unpaginated (approximately 1,000 p.)

> A massive compilation from Soviet sources resulting in an extensive (though still incomplete) institutional directory of 1,135 research establishments in the USSR. Addresses, identifiable senior staff, and a description of main activities are given for each institu-

tion. The directory can be used with ease, for it is accompanied by six different indexes. The introductory section examines the administration of scientific and technological research in the USSR, with emphasis on the 1961 reorganization of institutional control patterns.

1771. Bauer, Raymond A.   The Bolshevik Attitude toward Science. *In* Totalitarianism; Proceedings of a Conference Held at the American Academy of Arts and Sciences, March 1953. Cambridge, Harvard University Press, 1954. p. 141-156.

Appraisal of science as an ideology, in the context of Marxist and Soviet political doctrine.

1772. Buchholz, Arnold.   Ideologie und Forschung in der sowjetischen Naturwissenschaft. Stuttgart, Deutsche Verlags-Anstalt, 1953. 126 p.

Bibliography: p. 105-126.

Systematically arranged survey of various branches of Soviet science, and an examination of research activities under the impact of the ideological and political dictates of the Stalin era. The best available study of the interaction between ideology and science written by a Western authority.

English translation available as *Ideology and Research in Soviet Natural Science* (n.p., 1953, 171 p.)

1773. De Witt, Nicholas.   Education and the Development of Human Resources: Soviet and American Effort. *In* U. S. Congress. Joint Economic Committee. Dimensions of Soviet Economic Power. Washington, U.S. Government Printing Office, 1962. p. 233-268.

An assessment of the aims and structure of the educational systems in the United States and the USSR, with emphasis on the stock of specialized manpower in the two countries.

See also the following writings by the same author:

Soviet Professional Manpower; Its Education, Training and Supply (Washington, National Science Foundation, 1955, 400 p.), a preliminary quantitative and qualitative assessment of Soviet educational efforts on all levels of schooling, with emphasis on specialized professional education.

"Professional and Scientific Personnel in the USSR," *Science*, v. 120, no. 3105, July 2, 1954: 1-4, an initial attempt to piece together fragmentary information on Soviet professional manpower and to interpret its potential.

1774. De Witt, Nicholas.   Reorganization of Science and Research in the USSR. Science, v. 133, no. 3469, June 23, 1961: 1981-1991.

A discussion of the institutional aspects of, and the forces responsible for, the establishment of a new administrative setting and of the planning of scientific and technological research in the USSR.

See also the following articles by the same author:

"The Politics of Soviet Science," *The American Behavioral Scientist*, v. 6, no. 4, December 1962: 7-11, a study of the socio-political factors leading to the reorganization of the scientific research establishment in the USSR.

"Soviet Science: the Institutional Debate," *Bulletin of the Atomic Scientists*, v. 16, no. 6, June 1960: 208-211, an examination of the forces which led to the reform of the scientific organization in the Soviet Union in 1961.

1775. De Witt, Nicholas.   Scholarship in the Natural Sciences. *In* Cyril E. Black, *ed.* The Transformation of Russian Society. Cambridge, Harvard University Press, 1960. p. 385-405.

An examination of the institutional and socio-political factors which affected the development of science in pre-Revolutionary Russia and an assessment of their impact upon Soviet science.

1776. Field, Mark G.   Soviet Science and Some Implications for American Science and Society. Journal of International Affairs, v. 13, no. 1, January 1959: 19-33.

Contrasts science organization in a pluralistic society with the role and institutional framework of Soviet science, which is geared to shifting priorities according to the regime's needs.

1777. Galkin, Konstantin T.   The Training of Scientists in the Soviet Union. Moscow, Foreign Languages Publishing House, 1959. 203 p.

While the book discusses "aspirantura" and advanced degree training programs mainly during the Soviet era, it also puts pre-Revolutionary trends into historical perspective. Deals with the post-higher education training of persons for academic and research careers. The Russian version, *Vysshee obrazovanie i podgotovka nauchnykh kadrov v SSSR* (Moscow, Sovetskaia nauka, 1958, 175 p.), supplies a bibliographical guide to pre-Revolutionary sources and archival materials.

1778. Gorokhoff, Boris I.   Providing U. S. Scientists with Soviet Scientific Information. Rev. ed. Washington, 1962. 46 p.

". . . Seeks to provide detail of a reference nature on the form and extent of Soviet scientific information in the original language and on what is being done to make such data available to American scientists and engineers" in English translation.

1779. Huxley, Julian S.   Soviet Genetics and World Science: Lysenko and the Meaning of Heredity. London, Chatto and Windus, 1949. 244 p.

The first director-general of UNESCO, and an outstanding philosopher and practicing researcher, discusses the Soviet attitude to science in general, as well as the specific controversy between ideology and science in the case of Soviet genetics. The dilemma of totalitarian regimentation of thought in the Soviet case, and the ultimate impact of it upon genetics as a science, are discussed. American edition: *Heredity, East and West* (New York, Henry Schuman, 1949, 246 p.)

1780. Joravsky, David.   Soviet Marxism and Natural Science, 1917–1932. New York, Columbia University Press; London, Routledge and K. Paul, 1961. 433 p.
Bibliography: p. 391-422.
See also entry no. 1615.

A discussion of the development of Soviet Marxist philosophy of natural sciences in its formative years, in the general context of Russia's and the Soviet Union's intellectual history. The conflict between positivism and metaphysics in the Soviet version of Marxism and scientific thought is explored particularly in reference to three levels of power struggle: institutional — between the Communist Academy and the Academy of Sciences; personal — between Deborin's faction and his antagonists; and ideological — between political interpreters of science and actual working scientists. The analysis of this struggle, on the eve of, and during, the first Five-Year Plan reveals the factors which subsequently laid the path for Lysenko's rise to power and Stalinist dictates on Soviet science.

1781. London, Ivan D.   Toward a Realistic Appraisal of Soviet Science. Bulletin of the Atomic Scientists, v. 13, no. 5, May 1957: 169-176.
Critical suggestions for American scholarship in evaluating Soviet theoretical and applied research in the light of the inadequacy of our information concerning the true status and trends in Soviet science.

1782. Osteuropa-Naturwissenschaft.   v. 1– 1957– Stuttgart. semiannual.
A review of the status of science in the Soviet Union and Eastern Europe, published by Deutsche Gesellschaft für Osteuropakunde.

1783. Pipes, Richard, *ed.*   The Russian Intelligentsia. New York, Columbia University Press, 1961. 234 p.
See also entries no. 1188 and 1571.

A "must" in the study of the traditions and trends among the Russian intelligentsia of the nineteenth century. Particularly important as historical background, since the new group called Soviet intelligentsia are "intelligentsia" no more.

1784. Rabinowitch, Eugene.   Soviet Science; a Survey. Problems of Communism, v. 7, no. 2, March–April 1958: 1-9.
A discussion of the status of and trends in Soviet research as they relate to ideological and political factors influencing the scientific effort.

1785. Shumilin, Ivan N.   Soviet Higher Education. Munich, Institute for the Study of the USSR, 1962. 178 p.
A study of the organizational and operational features of higher education programs in historical perspective. Professional education is discussed in various stages: pre-Revolutionary heritage, experimental period of the 1920's, reforms of the 1930's, emerging emphasis on specialization, the Stalinist era, and Khrushchev's poly-

technization drive. The appendix presents a directory of Soviet institutions of higher learning as of 1960.

1786. Strumilin, Stanislav.   The Economics of Education in the USSR. International Social Science Bulletin (UNESCO), v. 14, no. 4, 1962: 633-636.

> A Soviet economist discusses the contribution of education in the USSR to economic development. Calculations are made to show the profitability of education investment and the returns from it. The impact of education, particularly in scientific-technical fields, upon the productivity of labor is stressed.

1787. Turkevich, John.   Science. *In* Harold H. Fisher, *ed.* American Research on Russia. Bloomington, Indiana University Press, 1959. p. 103-112.

> Examines research activities on problems of education and science in the USSR which have been conducted by American universities. In comparison with other disciplines, research on these topics continues to command less attention in the American academic community.

1788. Turkevich, John.   Soviet Men of Science; Academicians and Corresponding Members of the Academy of Sciences of the USSR. Princeton, N.J., Van Nostrand, 1963. 441 p.
See also entry no. 57.

> An extensive collection of the biographies of some 420 Soviet scientists, prominent primarily in physical and biological fields and mainly affiliated with Soviet academies of science and/or universities. The biographical data on each individual were compiled from diverse Soviet official releases, without identification or citation of actual sources. Highly selective criteria of performance were used which excluded a number of prominent researchers in many areas, particularly those active in other than nonsensitive theoretical fields. Each biographical sketch is accompanied by a brief citation of major publications.

1789. Turkevich, John.   Soviet Science in the Post-Stalin Era. The Annals of the American Academy of Political and Social Science, v. 303, January 1956: 139-151.

> Review of the main accomplishments of, and trends in, scientific research in the USSR, and comparison of the scientific manpower potential in the U. S. and the USSR.

1790. U. S. *Atomic Energy Commission.*   Atomic Energy in the Soviet Union. Washington, U. S. Government Printing Office, 1963. 85 p.

> A report on the status of atomic energy research in the USSR by the delegation of American scientists who visited the Soviet Union in May 1963.

1791. U. S. *Congress. House. Committee on Appropriations.*   Comparison of United States and USSR Science Education. Washington, U. S. Government Printing Office, 1960. 74 p.

A brief factual summary comparing the performance of the educational systems in the USSR and the United States in reference to science education and the production of specialized manpower.

See also the following earlier studies:

U. S. Congress. Joint Committee on Atomic Energy. *Engineering and Scientific Manpower in the United States, Western Europe and Soviet Russia.* Washington, U. S. Government Printing Office, 1956. 85 p.

U. S. Congress. Joint Committee on Atomic Energy. *Shortage of Scientific and Engineering Manpower.* Washington, U. S. Government Printing Office, 1956. 487 p. Contains comments of American policymakers on the implications of developments in science and engineering education in the United States and abroad, with particular reference to the Soviet Union.

1792. U. S. *Library of Congress. Aerospace Information Division.* Soviet Russian Scientific and Technical Terms; a Selective List. Washington, U. S. Government Printing Office, 1963. 668 p.

An extensive glossary of terms and abbreviations — including their expansions — for scientific research institutions and educational facilities in the USSR. An indispensable aid to the reader of Soviet technical literature.

1793. U.S. *Library of Congress. Science and Technology Division.* List of Russian Serials Being Translated into English and Other Western Languages. 4th rev. ed. Washington, 1962. 53 l.

A guide to translated material on substantive aspects of scientific research and publications. Index and subject guide are included.

1794. Vucinich, Alexander S.   Science in Russian Culture. v. 1: A History to 1860. Stanford, Calif., Stanford University Press, 1963. 463 p.
Bibliography: p. 421-449.

Examines Russia's scientific thought and institutional development for education (primarily university) and research in the broad context of the intellectual and political development of the nation in the era of autocracy from Peter the Great to the Great Emancipation. Deals with the changing social status of the scientist and his education, and discusses the agencies and instrumentalities of political control in historical perspective. This book, rather than tracing specific developments in each field of science, focuses attention on the broad cultural problem of the emergence of scientism and rationalism in the unique setting of an authoritarian state.

1795. Vucinich, Alexander S.   The Soviet Academy of Sciences. Stanford, Calif., Stanford University Press, 1956. 157 p.
Bibliography: p. 143-150.
See also entry no. 1201.

A study of the institutional and organizational aspects of the Academy of Sciences of the USSR and its branches, largely from the sociological, but partly from historical and political points of view. An excellent account of the interaction of science and ideology, interspliced with an examination of the role of personalities in the institution-building processes and especially their operation as they relate to the power structure of the Soviet regime.

1796.* Wetter, Gustav A.   Dialectical Materialism; a Historical and Systematic Survey of Philosophy in the Soviet Union. Translated from the German by Peter Heath. London, Routledge and Kegan Paul; New York, Praeger, 1959. 609 p.
See also entry no. 1625.

Translation of *Der dialektische Materialismus: seine Geschichte und sein System in der Sowjetunion* (4th rev. and enl. ed.; Vienna, Herder, 1958, 693 p.), which represents the best Western analysis of the philosophy of communism. The sections pertinent to science, scientism, and dialectical methods should be required reading for all students of the interrelationship between Soviet science and ideology.

See also the same author's "Dialectical Materialism and Natural Science," *Survey (Soviet Survey)*, no. 23, January–March 1958: 51-59.

1797. Zirkle, Conway, *ed.*   Death of a Science in Russia. Philadelphia, University of Pennsylvania Press, 1949. 319 p.

A selection of pronouncements of the Lysenko faction of Soviet scientists mounting a political drive against the classical geneticists of the N. I. Vavilov school in the period between 1936 and 1948. The story of Lysenko's rise to power is explored by the editor in the introductory essay. The dilemma of research, caught in the crosscurrents of Russia's intellectual tradition for objectivity and the new political dogmatism, is discussed in terms of the personal tragedy for individuals who had to pay with their lives for upholding scientific truth against the onslaught of Stalinism.

1798. Zirkle, Conway, *and* Howard A. Meyerhoff, *arrangers.*   Soviet Science. A symposium presented on December 27, 1951, at the Philadelphia meeting of the American Association for the Advancement of Science. Washington, D. C., American Association for the Advancement of Science, 1952. 112 p.

An assessment of various fields of science, actual status of accomplishments, and names of leading researchers and schools of thought. In mathematics, biology, physics, and other fields, appraisals are made not only of theoretical and practical advances, but also in the context of the interaction between political and ideological forces, as well as in the context of institutional arrangements for a centrally planned scientific effort.

G. THE FINE ARTS

by Robert V. Allen, in consultation with art historians

Artists of Russian birth whose creative years have largely been spent outside Russia, such as Chagall, Kandinsky, and Gabo, are not included in this bibliography. References to them may be found in general histories of art.

1. Reference Works

1799. Bolotowsky, Ilya.   Russian-English Dictionary of Painting and Sculpture. New York, Telberg Book Corp., 1962. 60 l. Bibliography.

> A useful compilation of art terms which are often not well represented in the general Russian-English dictionaries.

1800. Ettlinger, Amrei, *and* Joan M. Gladstone.   Russian Literature, Theatre and Art; a Bibliography of Works in English, Published 1900-1945. London, New York, Hutchinson, 1947. 96 p. *See also* entry no. 1421.

> Numerous references to Russian arts and artists. Intended to supplement Philip Grierson's *Books on Soviet Russia, 1917-1942* (*see* entry no. 9) by supplying pertinent titles in fields not fully covered by that bibliography.
>
> German-language publications appearing in East Germany in the years since 1945 are listed in *Bibliographie zu Kunst und Kunstgeschichte; Veröffentlichungen im Gebiet der Deutschen Demokratischen Republik* (Leipzig, VEB Verlag für Buch- und Bibliothekswesen, 1956; v. 1, 1945-1953, p. 111-130; v. 2, 1945-1957, p. 146-157). This material includes many translations from Soviet sources.

2. Art History, Surveys, and Collection Guides

1801. Ainalov, Dmitrii V.   Geschichte der russischen Monumentalkunst der vormoskovitischen Zeit. Berlin, Leipzig, W. de Gruyter, 1932. 96 p. 64 plates.

——. Geschichte der russischen Monumentalkunst zur Zeit des Grossfürstentums Moskau. Berlin, Leipzig, W. de Gruyter, 1933. 135 p. 73 plates.

> A comprehensive history of Russian art and architecture to the end of the Renaissance.

1802. Akademiia nauk SSSR.   *Institut istorii iskusstv.* Geschichte der russischen Kunst. Edited by I. E. Grabar', V. N. Lazarev, and V. S. Kemenov. Translated from the Russian by Kurt Küppers. Dresden, Verlag der Kunst, 1957–

> A major scholarly work by an impressive editorial team, including I. E. Grabar', eminent art historian whose *Istoriia russkago*

iskusstva (Moscow, I. Knebel', 1910-1914, 6 v.) is still of great value, and V. N. Lazarev, considered the leading authority on Russian art of the Byzantine period. Splendid illustrations, beautifully produced.

1803. Alpatov, Mikhail V. Russian Impact on Art. Edited with a preface by Martin L. Wolf. New York, Philosophical Library, 1950. 352 p. Illus.

English translation of a general survey written from a dedicated nationalist point of view.

1804. Alpatov, Mikhail V., *and* Nikolai I. Brunov. Geschichte der altrussischen Kunst. Augsburg, B. Filser, 1932. 2 v.

German translation of a scholarly history of medieval Russian art. Volume one contains a history of architecture by Brunov and a history of painting and sculpture by Alpatov. Volume two consists of illustrations.

1805. Bunt, Cyril G. E. Russian Art, from Scyths to Soviets. London, New York, Studio, 1946. 272 p. Plates (part col.)

Bibliography: p. 268.

A popular account covering the period from the seventh century B.C. to the time of writing, in fields of architecture, painting, sculpture, and the applied arts. The twentieth-century period is given slight coverage. Useful photographs of Constructivist architecture of 1920's. Some illustration material and texts reflect Stalinist period.

1806. Ch'en, I-fan (Jack Chen). Soviet Art and Artists. London, Pilot Press, 1944. 106 p. Illus., plates.

An apology for Socialist Realist work.

1807. Descargues, Pierre. The Hermitage Museum, Leningrad. New York, H. N. Abrams, 1961. 320 p. Plates (part col.)

Athough this book is principally concerned with the important collections of West European art in the Hermitage, it provides some information about the operation of the museum and about Russian works in its collections.

The Tretyakov Gallery in Moscow (Gosudarstvennaia Tret'iakovskaia Galereia) is described in *The Tretyakov Gallery; a Short Guide* (Moscow, Foreign Languages Publishing House, 1957, 108 p.)

1808. Fülöp-Miller, René. The Mind and Face of Bolshevism; an Examination of Cultural Life in Soviet Russia. Translated from the German by F. S. Flint and D. F. Tait. New York, London, Knopf, 1928. 433 p. Plates, ports.

Bibliography: p. 411-421.

See also entry no. 1155.

"An examination of the cultural life of Soviet Russia," containing much contemporary material with illustrations and eyewitness descriptions of events. An enthusiastic, non-Russian account of early days of Soviet cultural life, which sometimes is based on not entirely trustworthy materials.

1809. Gibellino Krasceninnicowa, Maria.   Storia dell'arte russa. Rome, P. Maglione, 1935-1937. 2 v. (v. 1: Dal secolo XI al secolo XVII; v. 2: Da Pietro il Grande ai tempi nostri)
Bibliography: v. 1, p. 183-191; v. 2, p. 205-209.

> The text does not deal with any period later than that of the "World of Art." However, the bibliography of volume two includes publications dealing with post-Revolutionary art, and was, at the time of publication, a useful list. The accounts of the work of nineteenth-century artists, in painting, sculpture, and architecture, are of value.
>
> The author's more recent views on modern and contemporary Russian art are to be found in *L'arte russa moderna e contemporanea; pittura e scultura* (Rome, Fratelli Palombi, 1960, 149 p., 48 plates, bibliography). Her views of architecture are set forth in entry no. 1831.

1810. Gray, Camilla.   The Great Experiment: Russian Art, 1863-1922. London, Thames and Hudson; New York, Abrams, 1962. 326 p. Mounted col. illus., plates.
Bibliography: p. 297-306.

> The first attempt in the West to write a history of the period, including abstract schools and early Constructivisim, based mostly on firsthand sources. Detailed bibliography of Russian publications. Extensive illustrative material. Includes typography, theater design, and architecture, as well as painting and sculpture.

1811. Hamilton, George H.   The Art and Architecture of Russia. Baltimore, Penguin Books, 1954. 320 p. Illus., 180 plates, map.
Bibliography: p. 295-299.

> Covers the period from 988 to 1917 in architecture, painting, and sculpture. Contains useful information and illustrative material.

1812. Lehmann-Haupt, Hellmut.   Art under a Dictatorship. New York, Oxford University Press, 1954. 277 p. Illus., ports.

> A study discussing the impact of the promulgation of Socialist Realism on Soviet art and artists.

1813. Lo Gatto, Ettore.   Gli artisti italiani in Russia. Rome, La Libreria dello Stato, 1934-1943. 3 v.

> Limited to Italian artists working in Russia from the sixteenth to the nineteenth century. Contains material not previously used.

1814. London, Kurt.   The Seven Soviet Arts. Translated by Eric S. Bensinger. London, Faber and Faber, 1937. 381 p. Illus., plates, ports., diagr.

> Lively and well-documented treatment of cultural developments in Russia and the Soviet republics in the fields of music, literature, theater, ballet, painting, plastic arts, architecture, film, radio and phonograph, artists' organizations, systems of artistic training, and

cultural principles. Offers interesting accounts of discussions among painters and bureaucrats on "Socialist Realism" in the early 1930's, as well as a useful description of administration in the art field.

1815.* Miliukov, Pavel N. (Paul).   Outlines of Russian Culture. Edited by Michael Karpovich. Translated by Valentine Ughet and Eleanor Davis. v. 3: Architecture, Painting and Music. Philadelphia, University of Pennsylvania Press, 1942. 159 p.
See also entries no. 472, 1569, and 1638.
Contains a critical and philosophical study of these arts. Unillustrated.

1816. Réau, Louis.   L'art russe des origines à Pierre le Grand. Paris, H. Laurens, 1921. 387 p. Illus. (maps), plates.
Bibliography: p. 365-371.
————. L'art russe de Pierre le Grand à nos jours. Paris, H. Laurens, 1922. 291 p. Plates, ports.
Bibliography: p. 271-277.
Reliable pioneer history of the subject, covering a wide field of painting, architecture, sculpture, and the applied arts. Provides particularly useful descriptions of the "Wanderers" and "World of Art" movements. Post-Revolutionary movements are not treated. The author looks to the formation of a "national but not nationalistic" school of art, a balance between the various "extravagances" which he has described.

1817. Rice, Tamara T.   A Concise History of Russian Art. New York, Praeger, 1963. 288 p. Illus. (part col.), ports., map, plans.
Bibliography: p. 272-273.
Covers the period from the conversion of Russia to Christianity in 988 to the Revolution in 1917. Profusely illustrated, concise account.
Uses some of the material presented in the author's earlier *Russian Art* (West Drayton, Middlesex, Penguin Books, 1949, 276 p.)

1818. Umanskij, Konstantin.   Neue Kunst in Russland, 1914-1919. Preface by Leopold Zahn. Potsdam, G. Kiepenhauer, 1920. 72 p.
The first study in German of Russian modern art (especially Suprematism and Constructivism). Contains tables of exhibitions which are still useful.

1819. Voyce, Arthur.   The Moscow Kremlin; Its History, Architecture, and Art Treasures. Berkeley, University of California Press, 1954. 147 p. Illus.
Bibliography: p. 139-142.
A condensed treatment of the subject with emphasis on its historical development.
Striking color illustrations of the Kremlin, its buildings, and the treasures of its museum are to be found in David Douglas Duncan's *The Kremlin* (Greenwich, Conn., New York Graphic Society,

1960, 170 p.), while other photographs, by Karel Neubert, are provided by *Treasures in the Kremlin,* edited by B. A. Rybakov (London, Peter Nevill, 1963, 120 plates).

1820. Wulff, Oskar K. Die neurussische Kunst im Rahmen der Kulturentwicklung Russlands von Peter dem Grossen bis zur Revolution. Augsburg, B. Filser, 1932. 2 v.

Comprehensive study of Russian art of the eighteenth and nineteenth centuries in terms of the historical evolution of the Russian people.

3. Painting

1821. Benois, Alexandre (Aleksandr Benua). The Russian School of Painting. Translated from the Russian by Abraham Yarmolinsky. Introduction by Christian Brinton. London, T. Werner Laurie, 1916. 199 p. Illus.

A pioneer work in the field of art history in Russia which remains an authoritative and basic exposition of the subject. The author, a painter and highly influential art critic of his day, created the important "World of Art" group in the 1890's. His account begins with the period of Peter the Great and ends with the Symbolists. A personal, lively, and scholarly history.

1822. Fiala, Vladimir. Russian Painting of the 18th and 19th Centuries. Translated by Jean Layton. Prague, Artia, 1956. 14 p., 178 col. plates.

Detailed biographical notes on the 59 artists whose work is illustrated in the publication make up the bulk of the text. The plates are of good quality and offer a judicious illustration of the best in eighteenth and nineteenth century Russian art. A short introductory essay discusses the theme in Marxist terms.

1823. Kondakov, Nikodim P. L'icone russe. Prague, Seminarium Kondakovianum, 1928-1933. 4 v. Col. fronts. (v. 3-4), illus., plates (part col. mounted)

Volumes one and two consist of 65 plates in color and of 136 gravure plates, respectively. The third and fourth volumes contain a Russian-language text, with summaries in French, referring to the plates.

An abridged translation of this text was made by Ellis H. Minns and appeared as *The Russian Icon* (Oxford, Clarendon Press, 1927, 226 p.)

There are numerous other works on Russian icons, including Tamara Talbot Rice's *Icons* (London, Batchworth Press, 1959, 192 p., 65 col. plates), and Konrad Onasch's *Ikonen* (Gütersloh, Gütersloher Verlagshaus, 1961, 431 p., 28 mounted illustrations, 151 col. plates, bibliography). An English translation of the latter work appeared as *Icons* (London, Faber and Faber, 1963, 423 p.)

1824. Ouspensky, Léonide, *and* Vladimir Lossky. The Meaning of Icons. Boston, Book and Art Shop, 1956. 222 p. Illus., 59 plates.

The religious and cultural significance of religious painting, with special reference to Orthodox usage. A translation of *Der Sinn der Ikonen* (Bern, U. Graf, 1952, 222 p.)

1825. Schweinfurth, Philipp.   Geschichte der russischen Malerei im Mittelalter. The Hague, M. Nijhoff, 1930. 506 p. Illus., plates.

A general history, supported by significant research, of medieval Russian painting.

1826. Soviet Painting; 32 Reproductions of Paintings by Soviet Masters. Moscow, Leningrad, State Art Publishers, 1939. 11 p., 32 mounted col. plates.

An album of colored reproductions, each of which is accompanied by a short note providing brief descriptive material and biographical data on the artist. The best of the Socialist Realist school is represented.

1827. United Nations Educational, Scientific, and Cultural Organization. USSR Early Russian Icons. Preface by Igor Grabar', with texts by Viktor Lasareff and Otto Demus. Greenwich, Conn., New York Graphic Society by arrangement with UNESCO, 1958. 28 p. Illus., 32 col. plates. (UNESCO World Art Series, 9)

Exceptionally good reproductions accompanied by studies by outstanding Soviet and German scholars.

4. Folk and Decorative Art

1828. Il'in, Mikhail A.   Russian Decorative Folk Art. Translated from the Russian by A. Shkarovsky. Edited by J. Katzer. Moscow, Foreign Languages Publishing House, 1959. 134 p. Illus.

A popular essay which dwells chiefly on the nineteenth and twentieth centuries, emphasizing work being produced at the time of writing. This emphasis is reflected in the illustrations. Informative within these limits.

Russian peasant arts and crafts on the eve of the First World War are discussed in the following works: *Peasant Art in Russia*, edited by Charles Holme (London and New York, The Studio, 1912, 52 p., 86 plates [12 col.]); and *Russkoe narodnoe iskusstvo na vtoroi Vserossiiskoi kustarnoi vystavkie v Petrogradie v 1913 g.* (Russian Folk Art at the Second All-Russian Handicrafts Exhibition in Petrograd in 1913). Petrograd, 1914. 130 p., 88 plates. Contains captions and an abridged text in French.

A French student of the "images d'Épinal," Pierre L. Duchartre, has written a study of the Russian equivalent, the "lubki" or popular prints, and of Russian engraved chapbooks, in *L'imagerie populaire russe et les livrets gravés, 1629-1885* (Paris, Gründ, 1961, 187 p.), which contains many illustrations and, on pages 186-187, a short bibliography.

1829. Makovskii, Sergei K.   Talachkino. L'art décoratif des ateliers de

la princesse Ténichef. St. Petersburg, Édition "Sodrougestvo," 1906.
75 p. Illus., 126 plates.

Accounts of an attempt to revive folk art traditions of the pre-Petrine era. Contains two essays, one by Makovskii and another by the painter Nikolai K. Roerich, concerning the art colony at Talashkino (Talachkino) sponsored by Mariia K. Tenisheva in the early years of the twentieth century.

The quite different decorative art of the Russian Court jeweller Karl Gustavovich Fabergé (Carl Fabergé) is discussed in Abraham K. Snowman, *The Art of Carl Fabergé* (2d ed.; Boston, Boston Book and Art Shop, 1962, 186 p., plates, bibliography), which is illustrated with many evidences of the level of taste in the declining years of the Empire.

5. Architecture and Sculpture

1830. Buxton, David R.   Russian Mediaeval Architecture, with an Account of the Transcaucasian Styles and Their Influence in the West. Cambridge, England, Cambridge University Press, 1934. 112 p. Illus., 108 plates.
Bibliography: p. 105-107.

The most important study in English of Armenian sources for Russian masonry and wooden architecture in the Middle Ages. With many illustrations from the author's photographs.

1831. Gibellino Krasceninnicowa, Maria.   L'architettura russa nel passato e nel presente. Rome, Fratelli Palombi, 1963. 228 p. Illus., plates.
Bibliography: p. 205-211.

Primary attention is given to Russian architecture in the years prior to the nineteenth century, and the Soviet period is discussed in three short chapters.

1832. Halle, Fannina W.   Die Bauplastik von Vladimir-Ssusdal, russische Romanik. Berlin, E. Wasmuth, 1929. 84 p., 69 plates.
Outstanding study of early medieval sculpture.

1833. Hautecoeur, Louis.   L'architecture classique à Saint-Pétersbourg à la fin du XVIIIe siècle. Paris, H. Champion, 1912. 115 p., 14 plates. (Bibliothèque de l'Institut français de Saint-Pétersbourg, t. 2)
Bibliography: p. 103-108.

The first important study of the characteristic Russian classicism of the eighteenth and early nineteenth centuries.

The art and architecture of St. Petersburg are also discussed in Louis Réau, *Saint Pétersbourg* (Paris, H. Laurens, 1913, 198 p.)

1834. Lisitskii, Lazar' M. (El Lissitzky).   Russland; die Rekonstruktion der Architektur in der Sowjetunion. Vienna, A. Schroll, 1930. 103 p. Illus., plates, plans. (Neues Bauen in der Welt, Bd. 1)
Authoritative and detailed account of modern Russian architec-

ture by a prominent Constructivist typographer and architect. Valuable photographs of major buildings and projects.

For Lisitskii's own work, *see* Horst Richter's *El Lissitzky* (Cologne, Galerie Christoph Czwiklitzer, 1958, 86 p., plates), which provides a long and well-documented essay on Constructivism, with useful notes and bibliography. The illustrations comprise the artist's folio of lithograph designs for the futurist opera "Victory Over the Sun."

1835. Lukomskii, Georgii K.   Charles Cameron (1740-1812); an Illustrated Monograph on His Life and Work in Russia, Particularly at Tsarskoe Selo and Pavlovsk. . . London, Nicholson and Watson, 1943. 102 p.

The only available study of the Scottish architect whose neoclassic work, influenced by that of Robert Adam, determined the character of late eighteenth-century Russian classicism.

1836. Mikhailov, B. P.   Architektur der Völker der Sowjetunion. Berlin, Henschelverlag, 1953. 100 p. Illus.

Selections of articles from the Large Soviet Encyclopedia on the architecture of the constituent republics of the USSR.

1837. Voyce, Arthur.   Russian Architecture; Trends in Nationalism and Modernism. New York, Philosophical Library, 1948. 282 p. Illus., maps.

Critical survey covering Soviet architectural work, with most space given to Socialist Realist construction.

1838. Weidhaas, Hermann.   Formenwandlungen in der russischen Baukunst. Halle, Akademischer Verlag, 1935. 108 p., 43 plates.

A pioneering study of the problems of formal influence and metamorphosis in Russian medieval architecture.

H. MUSIC

by Boris Schwarz

1. Reference Aids

1839. Belza (Boelza), Igor' F.   Handbook of Soviet Composers. Edited by Alan Bush. London, Pilot Press, 1944. 101 p.

Brief sketches of 40 composers, arranged alphabetically. The author, a well-known Soviet critic, offers mainly facts, not evaluations. Some "Stalinist" criteria are in evidence (see "Shostakovich"). Mr. Bush, a British composer, provides a warmly sympathetic foreword.

See also Alexandra Vodarsky-Shiraeff, *Russian Composers and Musicians* (New York, H. W. Wilson, 1940, 158 p.)

See also the pertinent parts on Russian music and musicians in the following general reference works:

Baker, Theodore.   *Biographical Dictionary of Musicians*. 5th ed., completely revised by Nicolas Slonimsky. New York, G. Schirmer, 1958. 1,855 p.

Cobbett, Walter W., *ed.* *Cobbett's Cyclopedic Survey of Chamber Music.* London, Oxford University Press, 1929. 2 v. Reprinted 1963, with an additional third volume.

Grove, *Sir* George. *Dictionary of Music and Musicians.* 5th ed., edited by Eric Blom. London, Macmillan; New York, St. Martin's Press, 1954. 9 v. Supplementary volume, 1961.

Die Musik in Geschichte und Gegenwart; allgemeine Enzyklopädie der Musik. Edited by Friedrich Blume. Kassel, Basel, Bärenreiter, 1949– (11 v., A-Schn, published to date).

Thompson, Oscar, *ed.* *The International Cyclopedia of Music and Musicians.* 7th ed., edited by Nicolas Slonimsky. New York, Dodd, Mead, 1956. 2,394 p.

Slonimsky, Nicolas. *Music since 1900.* 3d rev. and enl. ed. New York, Coleman-Ross, 1949. 759 p.

2. History and Criticism

1840. Abraham, Gerald E. H.   On Russian Music. London, Reeves, 1939. 279 p.

——. Studies in Russian Music. London, Reeves, 1935. 355 p.

Two collections of valuable essays on nineteenth-century Russian music (mainly opera), each discussing either a single work or a certain aspect of a composer. Some broader topics, such as "The Whole Tone Scale in Russian Music" and "The Evolution of Russian Harmony," are included.

1841. Asaf'ev, Boris V. (Igor' Glebov).   Russian Music from the Beginning of the Nineteenth Century. Translation and introduction by Alfred J. Swan. Ann Arbor, Mich., J. W. Edwards, 1953. 329 p. (American Council of Learned Societies. Russian Translation Project, Series 22)

A survey of Russian music from Glinka's predecessors to Stravinsky and Prokofiev. The material is organized by genres, i.e. chapters on opera, song, instrumental music, etc. Despite occasional sketchiness, the topical treatment is brilliant. In this translation of *Russkaia muzyka ot nachala XIX stoletiia* (Moscow, 1930), a 9-page preface and a 12-page appendix on chamber music are missing. Asaf'ev's footnotes, with numerous additions by the translator, are collected on pages 277-324. An index is sorely lacking.

See also Asaf'ev's *Tschaikovskys Eugen Onegin; Versuch einer Analyse des Stils und der musikalischen Dramaturgie* (Potsdam, Athenaion, 1949, 150 p.); and Vladimir Fédorov, "B. V. Asaf'ev et la musicologie russe avant et après 1917," *Revue de musicologie* (Paris), v. 41, July 1958: 102-106.

1842. Buketoff, Igor.   Russian Chant. *In* Reese, Gustave. Music in the Middle Ages. New York, Norton, 1940. p. 95-104.

A comprehensive summary incorporating recent scholarly research. Note the useful bibliography on page 435.

See also Alfred J. Swan, "The Znamennyi Chant of the Russian Church," *The Musical Quarterly* (New York), v. 26, April, July, and October 1940; Victor Belaev, "Early Russian Polyphony," *Studia Memoriae Belae Bartók Sacra* (Budapest, 1956), p. 307-325; and Jacques Handschin, "Le chant ecclésiastique russe," *Acta Musicologica* (Basel), v. 24, 1952: 3-32. *See also* entry no. 1855.

1843. Calvocoressi, Michel D.   A Survey of Russian Music. Harmondsworth, England, New York, Penguin Books, 1944. 142 p.

A masterful condensation, written in a personal and fluent style. There are frequent quotations from other experts. Three chapters are devoted to music in the USSR, and a final chapter deals with Russian composers in other countries.

1844. Cui, César.   La musique en Russie. Paris, Fischbacher, 1880. 174 p.

Written in French by a member of the "Five," this book represents (in the words of Rosa Newmarch) an "interesting, but in many respects misleading" point of view. The publication has a certain documentary value, particularly in the discussion of three operas of the 1870's: Rimski's *Pskovitianka*, Musorgski's *Boris*, and Dargomyzhski's *Stone Guest. A Note on Cui*, initialed C. B. (Bannelier), is appended (p. 163-172).

1845. Handschin, Jacques.   Gedenkschrift; Aufsätze und Bibliographie. Bern, Stuttgart, Paul Haupt, 1957. 397 p.
Bibliography: p. 9-20.

This posthumous collection of articles by the noted Russo-Swiss musicologist contains 12 (mostly brief) essays on various aspects of Russian music. They range from Church Chant to Stravinsky and are written with keen insight.

1846. Jarustovskii, B. M. (Boris Jarustowski).   Die Dramaturgie der klassischen russischen Oper. Translated from the Russian by Ruth E. Riedt. Berlin, Henschelverlag, 1957. 664 p. Illus.

In Soviet musical terminology, "classical" spans the period from Glinka to Rimski-Korsakov. The author analyzes the Russian opera as musical theatre: subject, scenario, libretto, musical characterization, etc., are investigated as components of the operatic masterpieces of nineteenth-century Russian repertoire. The final chapter (pages 610-663) surveys the Soviet opera. Translation of *Dramaturgiia russkoi opernoi klassiki* (Moscow, 1952, 376 p.)

1847. Keldysh, Iurii V. (Juri Keldysch).   Geschichte der russischen Musik. Translated from the Russian by Dieter Lehmann. v. 1, pt. 1. Leipzig, Breitkopf und Härtel, 1956. 148 p.

A translation of the initial section of the first volume of Keldysh's three-volume history, *Istoriia russkoi muzyki* (Moscow, Gos. muzykal'noe izd-vo, 1947). This excerpt spans the period from the earliest times through the seventeenth century; no further installments are planned. Though a torso, the publication is scholarly and informative. Good musical examples, but no bibliography or index.

By the same author: "La musique russe au XIXe siècle," in *Contributions à l'histoire russe* (Neûchatel, Éditions de la Baconnière, 1958), p. 267-295.

1848. Laux, Karl. Die Musik in Russland und in der Sowjetunion. Berlin, Henschelverlag, 1958. 463 p., 165 musical examples, 98 illus.

The author, who is active in East Germany, has written a decidedly Slavophile history, incorporating much of the latest Soviet research. Particularly informative, though at times too laudatory, is his presentation of Soviet music and musical life. The book was subjected to Soviet criticism for alleged errors. Nevertheless it is highly useful because of its abundant documentation, its clear textbook-like organization, and many firsthand reports of the Soviet scene. Each chapter is followed by a bibliography.

1849. Leonard, Richard A. A History of Russian Music. New York, Macmillan, 1957. 395 p. Ports.
Bibliography: p. 373-376.

This is the most recent English-language history of Russian music. It appears to be based entirely on non-Russian sources and incorporates little, if any, of the latest Soviet research. Pages 284-372 are devoted to music in the Communist state. The bibliography is limited to materials in the English language. In spite of a certain lack of original thinking and perceptiveness, it is a useful, up-to-date survey — particularly in view of the venerable age of most histories of Russian music in English.

1850. Livanova, Tamara N. Die Kritikertätigkeit der russischen klassischen Komponisten. Translated from the Russian by Günter Comte. Halle (Saale), Mitteldeutscher Verlag, 1953. 80 p.

Many of the Russian composers of the nineteenth century (the "classics") were active as critics or commentators on musical topics — some occasionally, others regularly. Their ideas and opinions, especially those coinciding with current Soviet esthetic views, are now highly esteemed in the USSR. A translation of *Kriticheskaia deiatel'nost' russkikh kompozitorov-klassikov* (Moscow, 1950, 100 p.)

1851. Mooser, Robert A. Annales de la musique et des musiciens en Russie au XVIIIe siècle. Geneva, Édition Mont-Blanc, 1948-1951. 3 v. (1,462 p.) 223 illus.

A monumental work with a wealth of data on diverse aspects of musical activities in Russia during the eighteenth century. However, foreign musicians seem to prevail.

For insight into indigenous Russian musical culture, Tamara Livanova's *Russkaia muzykal'naia kul-tura 18-ogo veka* (untranslated; Moscow, 1952-1953) is still indispensable. Mooser gives Livanova credit in his *Opéras, intermezzos, ballets, cantates, ora-*

torios joués en Russie durant le XVIIIe siècle (2d ed.; Geneva, Monaco, 1955).

Related in topic is Mooser's *L'opéra comique français en Russie au XVIIIe siècle* (2d ed.; Geneva, Monaco, 1954).

1852. Newmarch, Rosa H.   The Russian Opera. New York, Dutton, 1914. 403 p.

When this book appeared it was a pioneering effort. Now clearly dated, it retains a certain usefulness, though too much space is given to operatic plots.

An informative, concise survey is *Russian Opera* by Martin Cooper (London, Parrish, 1951, 65 p.), but the final chapter on Soviet realism is already out of date.

Donald J. Grout discusses Russian opera in *A Short History of Opera* (New York, 1947, p. 463-479, 518-521), a new edition of which is in preparation.

See also Dieter Lehmann, *Russlands Oper und Singspiel in der 2. Hälfte des 18. Jahrhunderts* (Leipzig, 1958).

1853. Olkhovsky, Andrey V.   Music under the Soviets; the Agony of an Art. London, Routledge and Kegan Paul; New York, Praeger, 1955. 427 p.

Bibliography: p. 315-398.

See also entry no. 1753.

The author, for 16 years a music professor at the conservatories of Leningrad, Kharkov, and Kiev, left the Soviet Union in 1942. His book is less a history than a description of musical conditions under the Soviet regime, mainly prior to the Second World War. While it displays considerable anti-Soviet feeling, it contains much information not easily obtainable elsewhere. The author supports his firsthand observations with many quotations from Soviet sources and from writings of his teacher Asaf'ev. Appendixes "A" through "D" contain documents and quotes (pages 278-314). The extensive bibliography lists mostly Russian materials.

1854. Poliakova, Liudmila V.   Soviet Music. Translated from the Russian by Xenia Danko. Moscow, Foreign Languages Publishing House, 1961. 183 p. Illus.

Designed to give the foreign reader a panoramic view of music composed in the Soviet Union during the past 40-odd years. The multi-national cultural approach of the USSR is stressed, though composers of Russian nationality emerge as the most important. The material is arranged by genres (e.g. symphonies, oratorios, operas, etc.); the presentation is non-technical and non-critical. Excellent illustrations. This is one in a series of useful music books in English prepared and published in Moscow (*see also* entries no. 1869, 1875, and 1879).

1855. Riesemann, Oskar von.   Die Notationen des alt-russischen Kirchengesanges. Leipzig, Breitkopf und Härtel, 1909. 108 p. Facsims.

A valuable summary of the state of scholarly knowledge at the time, using hitherto untranslated Russian sources, with fine illustrations.

By the same author: "Der russische Kirchengesang," in *Handbuch der Musikgeschichte*, edited by Guido Adler (Frankfurt am Main, 1924), p. 115-121.

See also Peter Panóff, "Die altslavische Volks- und Kirchenmusik," in *Handbuch der Musikwissenschaft*, edited by Ernst Buecken (Potsdam, 1930), p. 13-31, with good illustrations, *and* entry no. 1842.

1856. Slonimsky, Nicolas. The Changing Styles of Soviet Music. Journal of the American Musicological Society, v. 3, Fall 1950: 236-255.

The author divides Soviet music into three phases — 1917 to 1927, 1927 to 1936, and 1936 to 1950 — and proceeds to analyze each of them. He supports his findings with ample quotations and musical examples.

Less technical, but equally informative, is his article "Soviet Music and Musicians" in the *Slavonic and East European Review*, v. 22, December 1944: 1-18.

See also Slonimsky's contribution "Music and Composers" in *U.S.S.R.: a Concise Handbook* (New York, 1947).

1857. Souvtchinsky, Pierre, *ed*. Musique russe; études réunies. Paris, Presses universitaires de France, 1953. 2 v. (405 p.) Music.

A collection of stimulating essays by French and Russo-French authors and musicians. The topics range from discussions of twentieth-century composers (Skriabin, Prokofiev, Stravinsky, Shostakovich) to broad subjects such as "Debussy et ses rapports avec la musique russe" by André Schaeffner. Among the contributors are Boulez, Poulenc, Koechlin, and Barraud. Vladimir Fédorov's "Rossica" (p. 397-405) is a good critical bibliography for the years 1941 through 1950.

See also Souvtchinsky's essay "Génie de la musique russe" in the journal *Contrepoints* (Paris), 1950, no. 6.

1858. Die sowjetische Musik im Aufstieg; eine Sammlung von Aufsätzen. Translated from the Russian and edited by Wolfram Sterz and others. Halle (Saale), Mitteldeutscher Verlag, 1952. 405 p. Music.

Nine essays by noted Soviet critics on recent developments in Soviet opera, ballet, chamber music, concertos, etc. The obvious purpose of this publication was to prove that Soviet musical productivity was actually stimulated by the musico-political feud of 1948, not throttled as Western critics had predicted. Under discussion is the music composed soon after the events of 1948. Translation of *Sovetskaia muzyka na pod"eme* (Moscow, 1950, 276 p.)

1859. Stasov, Vladimir V. 25 Jahre russischer Kunst: Unsere Musik. Edited by A. Lebedev and P. Stchipunov. Dresden, VEB Verlag der Kunst, 1953. 74 p.

This essay, written in 1882-1883, is a historic document. Stasov's discussion ranges from Glinka to Liadov and Glazunov, with particular attention to the "Five." Tchaikovsky and A. Rubinstein are treated with some condescension. Such "errors" are corrected by the Soviet editors, who also provide a good introduction and useful notes. Pending an English translation (in preparation), this small publication fills a need. A partial translation from volume two of his *Izbrannye sochineniia* (Moscow, 1952).

3. Biographies, Autobiographies, Memoirs

a. Collections

1860. Calvocoressi, Michel D., *and* Gerald Abraham.   Masters of Russian Music. London, Duckworth; New York, Knopf, 1936. 511 p.
    Fourteen biographical essays by two of the foremost scholars in the field. Calvocoressi writes on Balakirev, Borodin, Cui, Dargomyzhski, Glazunov, Liadov, and Liapunov; Abraham on Glinka, Musorgski, Rimski-Korsakov, Skriabin, Serov, Taneev, and Tchaikovsky. The essays vary in length from two pages for Liapunov to 88 pages for Rimski-Korsakov; in fact, Abraham's essays on Tchaikovsky and Rimski have appeared as separate books (London, 1949). The collection stresses the "lives" rather than the "works," although each composer's musical characteristics are well defined. There are no lists of works; the bibliography (pages 501-502) indicates that Soviet materials published in the 1920's and early 1930's have received attention.

1861. Moisenco, Rena.   Realist Music; 25 Soviet Composers. London, Meridian Books, 1949. 277 p. Plates, ports., music. Supplement: London, Fore Publishers, 1950. 32 p.
Bibliography: p. 253-256.
    A "Theory of Socialist Music" (p. 17-37) precedes the main biographical part. The information is drawn from Soviet sources. The evaluations represent the Stalin-Zhdanov viewpoint and should be accepted with reservation.
    Dealing with a similar topic and offering better-balanced judgments is Gerald Abraham, *Eight Soviet Composers* (London, Oxford University Press, 1943, 102 p.); included are Shostakovich, Prokofiev, Khachaturian, Knipper, Shebalin, Kabalevsky, Dzerzhinsky, and Shaporin.

1862. Riesemann, Oskar von.   Monographien zur russischen Musik. Munich, Drei Masken Verlag, 1923-1926. 2 v.
    Volume one (1923): Die Musik in Russland vor Glinka; M. I. Glinka; A. S. Dargomyschski; A. N. Sseroff. 463 p. text, 28 p. music. Volume two (1926): Modest Petrowitsch Mussorgski, 526 p. text, 28 p. music.
    The author's Russo-German background uniquely qualifies him for his task. His views represent pre-Soviet musicography. Biography rather than musical evaluation is stressed. Some of the con-

clusions are dated because of more recent Soviet research, particularly in the pre-Glinka period and on Musorgski. Volume two appeared in an English translation by Paul England as *Moussorgsky* (New York, Knopf, 412 p., no music).

1863. Sabaneev, Leonid L.   Modern Russian Composers. Translated from the Russian by Judah A. Joffe. New York, International Publishers, 1927. 253 p.

The "modern" composers under discussion belong to the 1910's and 1920's. Though dated, the book contains usable information because of the author's personal contact with most of the composers mentioned; the non-technical presentation is intended for the "foreign" reader. Note the brief essay on Roslavets, a Russian twelve-tone pioneer now ignored in the USSR. Sabaneev left the Soviet Union in 1926; until then he was known as an influential critic and early adherent of Skriabin.

See also Lazare Saminsky, *Music of Our Day* (New York, 1932), which refers to Sabaneev and discusses some of the same composers ("New Russians and Their Alma Mater," p. 167-256).

1864. Seroff, Victor I.   The Mighty Five; the Cradle of Russian National Music. New York, Allen, Towne and Heath, 1948. 280 p. Ports.
Bibliography: p. 256-267.

Zetlin, Mikhail O.   The Five; the Evolution of the Russian School of Music. Translated and edited by George Panin. New York, International Universities Press, 1959. 344 p. Illus.

The "Five" are, of course, Balakirev, Borodin, Cui, Musorgski, and Rimski-Korsakov. Seroff writes their "story," rather than a musical evaluation. The numerous quotes from letters, diaries, and conversations remain unidentified as to source; however, there is a bibliography of (mostly Russian) materials "consulted" (pages 256-267). Zetlin penetrates somewhat more deeply into the intellectual background of the "Five" without coming to grips with the musical problems. His presentation is scholarly, but lacks all scholarly apparatus such as footnotes, references, bibliography, or work catalogues.

b. Monographs, autobiographies, memoirs [6]

Hector Berlioz

1865. Berlioz, Hector.   Memoirs. Annotated and edited by Ernest Newman. New York, A. Knopf, 1932. 533 p.

Two chapters (pages 422-444) deal with his successful Russian journey in 1847.

Among other Western musicians who have left reminiscences concerning their experiences in Russia are Louis Spohr, Clara Schumann, Richard Wagner, Hans von Bülow, Franz Liszt, and Leopold Auer. Their memoirs, letters, and diaries are an interesting source of information.

[6] Arrangement is alphabetical by name of the subject.

Aleksandr P. Borodin

1866. Dianin, Sergei A. (Serge).   Borodin. Translated from the Russian by Robert Lord. London, New York, Oxford University Press, 1963. 356 p. Illus., ports., music.

An authoritative monograph by a scholar who has worked on Borodin materials since the 1920's. Evenly divided between "life" and "works," both sections provide new facts and conclusions. There is a detailed list of Borodin's compositions, but no bibliography. Numerous musical examples and illustrations clarify and enliven the text. Translation of *Borodin; zhizneopisanie, materialy i dokumenty* (Moscow, 1955, 372 p.)

For an important period in the composer's life, *see* "Borodin in Heidelberg" by David Lloyd-Jones, in *The Musical Quarterly* (New York), October 1960: 500-508.

Gerald Abraham's *Borodin* (London, 1927) is still useful for its survey of the best-known works.

1867. Habets, Alfred.   Borodin and Liszt. Translated from the French by Rosa Newmarch. London, Digby, Long, 1895. 199 p. Illus. (music)

Habets, a Belgian, visited Russia in 1885 and knew Borodin personally; his reminiscences are warm and sympathetic. Informative are the descriptions of Liszt, drawn from Borodin's letters to his wife and to César Cui (the meetings between Liszt and Borodin took place in 1877 and 1881). However, the biographical part of the book (based on Stasov's *Borodin*) is rather dated, as is the translator's lengthy preface on Russian music.

Mikhail I. Glinka

1868. Glinka, Mikhail I.   Memoirs. Translated from the Russian by Richard B. Mudge. Norman, University of Oklahoma Press, 1963. 264 p. Illus., ports., music.

These "Notes" are an important personal document. They were completed in 1856, one year before the composer's death, but were not published until 1870. The English edition, competently translated, would have profited by a scholarly preface in place of the perfunctory translator's note. The footnotes are obviously based on the annotations of the Russian edition. The appendixes (pages 245-252) are meager and there is no bibliography nor a catalogue of compositions. Translation of *Zapiski*, new edition, edited by V. Bogdanov-Berezovskii and A. Orlova (Leningrad, 1953).

Aram I. Khachaturian

1869. Shneerson, Grigorii M.   Aram Khachaturian. Translated from the Russian by Xenia Danko. Moscow, Foreign Languages Publishing House, 1959. 103 p.

Khachaturian, born an Armenian and educated in Moscow, represents the multi-national cultural feature of the USSR. Shneerson intermingles biography with a survey of the works in an attractive manner. No critique is attempted, nor is the musico-political feud of 1948 mentioned, though Khachaturian was involved. Excellent illustrations, selective works list, no bibliography.

Nikolai Miaskovskii

1870. Ikonnikov, Aleksei A.   Myaskovsky: His Life and Work. Translated from the Russian. New York, Philosophical Library, 1946. 162 p. Ports., facsims., music.

Miaskovskii, one of Russia's eminent composers, died in 1950. This book is a translation of *N. Miaskovskii* (Moscow, 1944, 44 p.), a monograph which was completed in 1941; an appendix was added in 1943, but the last and creatively important years are not included. The biographical part (pages 1-24) is brief; works and style are discussed in some detail. A catalogue of compositions up to 1943 is appended.

Modest P. Musorgski

1871.* Calvocoressi, Michel D.   Modest Mussorgsky; His Life and Works. London, Rockliff; Fair Lawn, N. J., Essential Books, 1956. 322 p.

This is Calvocoressi's definitive book on Musorgski, incorporating his conclusions after a study of the original versions of the compositions, made available in P. Lamm's "academic edition." It supersedes the earlier *Mussorgsky, the Russian Musical Nationalist* (London, 1919), an imperfect translation from the French (Paris, 1908), as well as *Mussorgsky* in the series "The Master Musicians" (London, New York, 1946). The latter was left unfinished at the time of Calvocoressi's death in 1944 and was completed by Gerald Abraham.

1872. Godet, Robert.   En marge de Boris Godounof. Paris, Alcan; London, Chester, 1926. 2 v. (550 p.) Illus. (music)

Transcending its modest title, this is a perceptive study of various aspects of Musorgski's life and work. The author, a French man of letters who assisted in the publication of the original version of *Boris* (Chester, London, 1925), pleads for the acceptance of the composer's "true" Boris, as opposed to the "false" Boris in Rimski-Korsakov's edition.

See also Victor Belaev, *Musorgsky's Boris Godunov: Its New Version*, translated from the Russian by S. W. Pring (London, Oxford University Press, 1928, 60 p.)

1873. Leyda, Jay, *and* Sergei Bertensson, *eds. and trs.*   The Musorgsky Reader; a Life of Modeste Petrovich Musorgsky in Letters and Documents. New York, Norton, 1947. 474 p. Illus., ports., music.

An indispensable collection of source materials, skillfully translated and copiously annotated by the well-informed editors. Arranged in chronological order are letters and documents of, to, and about Musorgski. The appendix (pages 423-462) includes a listing of his works (according to the "academic edition" of Pavel Lamm, Moscow, London, 1928-1939) and a bibliography of (mostly Russian) sources (pages 459-462). Translated from *Musorgskii; pis'ma i dokumenty* (Moscow, 1932, 576 p.), and *Pis'ma k A. Golenishchevu-Kutuzovu* (Moscow, 1939, 116 p.)

Sergei S. Prokofiev

1874. Nest'ev, Izrail' V. (Israel V. Nestyev).   Prokofiev. Translated from the Russian by Florence Jonas. Foreword by Nicolas Slonimsky. Stanford, Calif., Stanford University Press, 1960. 528 p. Illus., ports., facsim., music.

A fine translation of *Prokof'ev* (Moscow, 1957, 527 p.), this is the most detailed biography of Prokofiev in any language. It supersedes the same author's *Sergei Prokofiev: His Musical Life* (New York, A. Knopf, 1946). Nest'ev's scholarship is evident and his analyses are often perceptive; however, they do not yet fully reflect the recent liberalized Soviet attitude toward Prokofiev's "foreign" period.

For detailed critiques of the book, see *The Musical Quarterly*, April 1961, p. 263-270 (by Boris Schwarz) and *Journal of the American Musicological Society*, Spring 1963, p. 100-108 (by Malcolm Brown).

1875. Prokof'ev, Sergei S.   Autobiography, Articles, Reminiscences. Compiled and edited, with notes, by S. Shlifstein. Translated from the Russian by Rose Prokofieva. Moscow, Foreign Languages Publishing House, n.d. 334 p.

The "Autobiography" (p. 15-89) extends to 1936. It is followed by "Articles and Notes," usually terse and revealing, written by Prokofiev for various journals (p. 93-137). The "Reminiscences" by colleagues and friends, and a classified, chronological catalogue of compositions complete the volume. Despite a regrettable abridgment, this translation of *S. S. Prokof'ev; materialy, dokumenty, vospominaniia* (Moscow, 1956, 467 p.) contains valuable source material. An enlarged second edition in Russian was published in Moscow in 1961 (707 p.)

Sergei V. Rachmaninoff

1876. Culshaw, John.   Sergei Rachmaninov. London, Dennis Dobson, 1949. 174 p. Ports., music.

Alone among Rachmaninov's biographers, Culshaw attempts a critical evaluation of his compositions, offering balanced judgments.

Sergei Rachmaninoff; a Liftetime in Music, by Sergei Bertensson and Jay Leyda (New York, New York University Press, 1956, 464 p.), is warmly written, and its factual accuracy is enhanced by the help the authors received from Sophia Satin, the composer's sister-in-law.

Much criticized were *Rachmaninov's Recollections* (New York, 1934), actually a book by O. von Riesemann, based on some private conversations with the composer.

See also the belletristic biography *Rachmaninoff* by V. I. Seroff (New York, 1950).

Nikolai A. Rimski-Korsakov

1877. Rimskii-Korsakov, Nikolai A.   My Musical Life. Translated from the fifth revised Russian edition by Judah A. Joffe. Edited by Carl Van Vechten. New York, Knopf, 1942. 480 p. Illus., facsim., ports.

> This is the best edition in English; an earlier translation using the second Russian edition (New York, 1923) is less satisfactory. Rimski's autobiography, while not entirely reliable in matters of chronology, offers an authentic picture of musical life in Russia during the later nineteenth century, and his observations on his fellow musicians are invaluable. Translation of *Letopis' moei muzykal'noi zhizni* (Moscow, 1935, 396 p.)

Anton and Nikolai Rubinstein

1878. Bowen, Catherine D.   Free Artist: the Story of Anton and Nicholas Rubinstein. New York, Random House, 1939; Boston, Little, Brown, 1961. 412 p.

> Despite its novelistic style, this book contains much information concerning musical conditions in nineteenth-century Russia and the role of the brothers Rubinstein in establishing the conservatories of St. Petersburg and Moscow. The appendix (pages 375-402) has a catalogue of Anton Rubinstein's compositions, compiled by Otto E. Albrecht, and a good bibliography.

> *See also* A. Rubinstein's *Autobiography*, translated from the Russian by A. Delano (Boston, 1892).

Dmitrii D. Shostakovich

1879. Rabinovich, David A.   Dmitry Shostakovich, Composer. Translated from the Russian by George Hanna. Moscow, Foreign Languages Publishing House, 1959. 165 p. Illus.

> Designed for foreign readers, this monograph limits the biography to a minimum and stresses the creative path, ending with the Eleventh Symphony. The author represents the "official" Soviet viewpoint when he speaks of the composer's "former infatuation for modernism" or when he discusses the musico-political crises of 1936 and 1948. Excellent illustrations, but no work list or bibliography.

> Ivan Martynov's *D. Shostakovich; the Man and His Work* (New York, 1947) is written warmly and perceptively, though by now somewhat out of date.

> For an intimate view of the composer's family background, *see* Victor I. Seroff, *D. Shostakovich* (New York, Knopf, 1943), written in collaboration with Nadejda Galli-Shohat, the composer's aunt.

Aleksandr Skriabin

1880. Hull, Arthur E.   A Great Russian Tone-Poet: Scriabin. London, K. Paul, Trench, Trubner; New York, Dutton, 1918. 304 p. Illus.

> In the absence of an up-to-date evaluation of Skriabin, this book

(though termed "not completely reliable" by Percy Scholes) is a serviceable guide to his works. The life is treated briefly, the compositions are analyzed in considerable detail (pages 82-274, with 165 musical examples). A special critical catalogue of the piano works is appended.

See also A. J. Swan, *Scriabin* (London, 1923), which is a shorter, more generalized monograph. Of professional interest is the article by Zofia Lissa, "Geschichtliche Vorform der 12-Ton Technik" in *Acta Musicologica*, v. 7 (1935), p. 15-21.

A Soviet viewpoint is offered in L. Danilevich, *A. Skrjabin* (translated into German; Leipzig, 1954).

Igor F. Stravinsky

1881.*Stravinskii (Stravinsky), Igor' F.   An Autobiography. New York, Norton, 1962. 176 p.

Originally published in French as *Chroniques de ma vie* (Paris, 1935, 2 v.), the chronicle is factual and restrained.

Much autobiographical material is also contained in the four volumes written with Robert Craft: *Conversations*, 1959; *Memories and Commentaries*, 1960; *Expositions and Developments*, 1962; *Dialogues and a Diary*, 1963 (all New York, Doubleday). The last-named contains Craft's interesting report on Stravinsky's Russian journey in 1962, first published in *Encounter* (London), June 1963.

See also Stravinsky's *Poetics of Music*, six lectures delivered at Harvard in 1939-1940 and reprinted New York, Vintage, 1956; particularly chapter 5, "The Avatars of Russian Music."

1882. Vlad, Roman.   Stravinsky. Translated from the Italian by Frederick and Ann Fuller. London, New York, Oxford University Press, 1960. 232 p. Port., music.
Bibliography: p. 225-226.

In the mass of Stravinsky materials, this book stands out as the most up-to-date analytical study of his works, with special attention to his late "serial" period. The biographical background is merely sketched.

For a more personal view, *see* Alexandre Tansman, *Stravinsky: the Man and his Music* (New York, 1949), though the work analyses end with the Symphony in Three Movements (1945).

A thought-provoking collection of essays is Paul H. Lang, *ed.*, *Stravinsky: a New Appraisal of his Work* (New York, Norton, 1963; reprint of *The Musical Quarterly*, July 1962, with work list added). Next to Lang's challenging reappraisal are analyses by Edward Cone, Wilfrid Mellers, Lawrence Morton, and Robert Nelson, and "Stravinsky in Soviet Russian Criticism" by Boris Schwarz. Excellent bibliography by C. D. Wade.

Petr I. Tchaikovsky

1883. Abraham, Gerald E. H., *ed.*   The Music of Tchaikovsky. New York, Norton, 1946. 277 p., 124 musical examples.

Shostakovich, Dmitrii, *and others.*   Russian Symphony; Thoughts about Tchaikovsky. New York, Philosophical Library, 1947. 271 p.

Two symposia on Tchaikovsky's music arranged by genres, one mainly by British, the other by Soviet experts. The English approach is more specific and analytical, the Russian more general and literary; both are useful and informative. The Soviet collection lacks a section on the songs but has a chapter on "The Archives of the Tchaikovsky Museum" at Klin.

1884. Tchaikovsky (Chaikovskii), Modeste. The Life and Letters of Peter Ilich Tchaikovsky. Edited from the Russian with an introduction by Rosa Newmarch. London, John Lane, 1906. 782 p.

This edition is considerably abridged; the German translation by Paul Juon (Leipzig, 1901-1902, 2 v.) is closer to the original, *Zhizn' Petra Il'icha Chaikovskogo* (Moscow, 1900-1902, 3 v.). Modeste's biography of his famous brother retains certain basic values though it is marred by some factual errors and omissions.

See also Catherine Drinker Bowen *and* Barbara von Meck, *Beloved Friend: the Story of Tchaikovsky and Nadejda von Meck* (New York, Random House, 1937, 484 p.), containing a partial translation of *Chaikovskii: perepiska s N.F. fon-Mekk* (Moscow, 1934-1936, 3 v.); some of the original letters are paraphrased, however, and the "story" element is overstressed.

1885. Tchaikovsky (Chaikovskii), Petr I. The Diaries of Tchaikovsky. Translated from the Russian, with notes, by Wladimir Lakond. New York, Norton, 1945. 365 p. Illus., music, ports.

These diaries, numbered one through eleven (number two is lost), span the years 1884-1891; the first dates back to 1873. The entries range from brief jottings to extended esthetic thoughts on Beethoven, Mozart, Glinka, and others. Diary number eleven (April–May 1891; pages 299-336) describes the American journey. The editor's notes are copious and helpful. Translation of *Dnevniki Chaikovskogo* (Moscow, Gosizdat, 1923).

1886. Weinstock, Herbert. Tchaikovsky. New York, Knopf, 1943. 386 p. Illus., plates, ports.
Bibliography: p. 383-386.

The author makes use of the extensive Soviet research of the 1920's and 1930's and tries to correct some alleged misconceptions of previous biographers. The result is a factually accurate book free of the usual adulation, but it seems to lack warmth toward its subject. The stress is on biography rather than musical analysis. The selective bibliography is limited to Russian and English materials.

For a brief orientation, Edwin Evans' *Tchaikovsky* (in "The Master Musicians") is still usable, though the original dates back to 1906 [revised in 1935 and newly revised by Gerald Abraham in 1963 (New York, Collier, 192 p.)]

4. Serials

1887. Musik des Ostens; Sammelbände für historische und vergleichende Forschung. v. 1– 1962– Kassel, Basel, Bärenreiter.

A new journal published by the Johann-Gottfried-Herder-For-schungstelle für Musikgeschichte. Volume one has two contributions by Elmar Arro, "Hauptprobleme der Osteuropäischen Musikge-schichte" (p. 9-48) and "Über einige neuere deutsche Publika-tionen zur russischen Musikgeschichte" (p. 122-140).

1888. Musik und Gesellschaft.   1952– Berlin (East). monthly.
    Organ of the (East) German Union of Composers and Musicolo-gists, this journal is an important source of information concerning music in Eastern Europe, particularly the Soviet Union.

1889. Russland; Sonderheft des *Anbruch*.   Vienna, Universal-Edition, March 1925. 187 p.
    An outstanding special issue of the Austrian music journal *Musik-blätter des Anbruch*, with contributions from prominent Soviet and Western critics — Glebov, Ivanov-Boretzki, Belaev, Sabaneev, Wel-lesz, Adolf Weissmann, and others. The three sections are entitled "The New Times," "The New Style," and "The New Men."

5. Music and Politics; Soviet Music Education; Other Aspects of Music

1890. Bowers, Faubion.   Broadway, U.S.S.R.; Ballet, Theatre and Enter-tainment in Russia Today. New York, Thomas Nelson, 1959. 227 p. Illus.
    See also entry no. 1915.
    The author, a perceptive observer, describes his impressions dur-ing a study trip to the Soviet Union. Music is discussed on pages 200-214, operetta on pages 178-182, ballet on pages 13-59.
    See also Yuri Slonimsky's symposium *The Soviet Ballet* (New York, Philosophical Library, 1947, 285 p.), particularly Vera Va-sina's contribution, "Music of the Soviet Ballet" (p. 27-34).

1891. Iarustovskii (Yarustovsky), Boris.   The Young Composers. Trans-lated by Nicolas Slonimsky. The Atlantic Monthly, June 1960: 96-100. (Special issue: The Arts in the Soviet Union)
    The author, a Soviet musicologist who visited the U.S. in 1959, discusses some of the younger Soviet composers and the principles governing their work.
    See also Grigorii Shneerson, "The Composer in the Soviet Un-ion" in *The Concert-Goer's Annual No. 2*, edited by Evan Senior (New York, Doubleday, 1958), p. 122-131, for a Soviet description of creative work in the USSR.
    A recent view of music in the USSR is given in Boris Schwarz, "Soviet Music since World War II," *The Musical Quarterly*, v. 51, January 1965.

1892. Jelagin, Juri.   Taming of the Arts. Translated from the Russian by Nicholas Wreden. New York, Dutton, 1951. 333 p.
    See also entry no. 1910.
    Interesting personal experiences of a violinist in Moscow dur-

ing the decade 1930-1940. There are some unvarnished revelations about young Khrennikov and other musicians who have become prominent since then. The anti-Soviet bias of the author seems to color some of his judgments. Part one deals with the theater, part two with music. Translation of *Ukroshchenie iskusstv* (New York, Izd-vo im. Chekhova, 1952, 434 p.)

1893. Khrushchev, Nikita S.   Khrushchev on Culture. Edited by Walter Z. Laqueur, Victor S. Frank, and others. London, 1963. 48 p. (Encounter Pamphlet no. 9)

Chairman Khrushchev's speech on March 8, 1963, dealt at length with Soviet cultural life, including literature, painting, cinema, and music. Many Western observers interpreted it as a halt in the trend toward liberalization of the arts. This pamphlet, published by the British monthly journal *Encounter*, reprints the, by now, historic speech and discusses its implications. Also appeared in *Current Digest of the Soviet Press*, v. 15, no. 10, April 3, 1963: 7-13; v. 15, no. 11, April 10, 1963: 6-12.

Related articles are: Fred K. Prieberg, "The Sound of New Music" in *Survey* (London), January 1963, and "Music," *ibid.*, July 1963. Also "Soviet Music since Stalin" in *Saturday Review*, March 30, 1963, by Boris Schwarz.

1894. Krebs, Stanley D.   Soviet Music Instruction; Service to the State. Journal of Research in Music Education, v. 9, no. 2, Fall 1961: 83-107.

The author, an American composer who studied at the Moscow Conservatory, gives an informative summary of Soviet higher education in music.

See also Alexander Nikolayev (Dean of the Moscow Conservatory), "Musical Education in the USSR," in the *Canadian Music Journal*, v. 3, no. 1, Autumn 1958: 4-11.

1895. Schwarz, Boris.   Beethoveniana in Soviet Russia. The Musical Quarterly (New York), v. 47, January 1961: 4-21; More Beethoveniana in Soviet Russia. *ibid.*, v. 50, April 1963: 143-149.

A survey of Beethoven materials (letters, sketches, and musical manuscripts) in Soviet libraries, museums, and archives.

1896. Verzeichnis der in Deutschland seit 1868 erschienenen Werke russischer Komponisten.   Leipzig, Friedrich Hofmeister (Unter Lizenz der Sowjetischen Militäradministration in Deutschland), n.d. 253 p.

Because Russia did not adhere to international copyright agreements, many Russian composers had their works published in Germany in order to enjoy copyright protection. This catalogue lists all such compositions published in Germany from 1868 to the date of its appearance (in the 1950's).

For a related topic, *see also* Cecil Hopkinson, *Notes on Russian Music Publishers*, Bath (England), printed privately, 1959, 10 p.

1897. Werth, Alexander. Musical Uproar in Moscow. London, Turnstile Press, 1949. 103 p.

A well-documented, highly readable account of the musico-political events which led to the party decree of February 10, 1948, and to the official criticism of prominent musicians such as Shostakovich, Prokofiev, and others. Excerpts from speeches and transcripts of verbal exchanges are interwoven with the perceptive personal observations of the author, a British correspondent interested in Soviet affairs.

It should be remembered that the 1948 decree was superseded by the decree of May 28, 1958. *See* Alexander Werth, *Russia under Khrushchev* (New York, Crest, 1962), p. 262-271.

I. THEATER AND CINEMA

1. Theater

by François de Liencourt

a. General reference works and bibliographies

1898. Dana, Henry W. L. Handbook on Soviet Drama; Lists of Theatres, Plays, Operas, Ballets, Films and Books about Them. New York, American-Russian Institute, 1938. 158 p.

A very useful bibliographical guide, containing lists of the theaters in the Soviet Union and lists of plays in the Soviet Union, and indicating the main English translations of Soviet plays.

1899. Enciclopedia dello spettacolo. v. 9. Rome, Casa Editrice Le Maschere, 1962. 2172 cols. Illus.

Articles: URSS, col. 1306-1358: Theater, opera, and ballet.
1. Teatro drammatico, col. 1306-1322, by Ettore Lo Gatto and Angelo Mario Ripellino, with excellent illustrations.
2. Teatro musicale, col. 1322-1330.
3. Balletto, col. 1330-1333, by Nathalie René Roslavleva.
Transcaucasia, col. 1067-1091, by Glauco Viazzi.
Ucraina, col. 1210-1211, by Angelo Mario Ripellino.

See also Blanch M. Baker, *Theatre and Allied Arts; a Guide to Books Dealing with the History, Criticism, and Technic of the Drama and Theatre, and Related Arts and Crafts* (New York, Wilson, 1952, 536 p.), with a section on Russia and Eastern Europe on pages 145-155.

For a bibliography of Russian authors in English translation, *see* Frank W. Chandler's *Modern Continental Playwrights* (New York and London, Harper, 1931, 711 p.)

b. Surveys and histories of the theater

(1) General

1900. Gorchakov, Nikolai A. The Theater in Soviet Russia. Translated

by Edgar E. Lehrman. Edited by Ernest J. Simmons. New York, Columbia University Press, 1957. 480 p. Illus.
Bibliography: p. 455-459.

The author is a former Soviet actor who worked as a directorial assistant of Meyerhold and Tairov. The American edition is well documented on the pre-1939 history of the Soviet theater and contains a bibliography of Russian works. Translation of *Istoriia sovetskogo teatra* (New York, Izd-vo im. Chekhova, 1956, 414 p.)

1901. Gregor, Joseph, *and* René Fülöp-Miller. The Russian Theater; Its Character and History, with Especial Reference to the Revolutionary Period. Translated by Paul England. Philadelphia, Lippincott, 1929; London, Harrap, 1930. 129 p. Illus.

First published in German. The first part, by Fülöp-Miller, discusses the social background of the Russian theater; the second, by Gregor, is exclusively devoted to "an analysis of the methods of artistic representation." Large and unique collection of photographs.

1902. Lo Gatto, Ettore. Storia del teatro russo. Florence, Sansoni, 1952. 2 v. (v. 1, 628 p.; v. 2, 645 p.) Illus.

This is a basic work on the subject by an established scholar. It covers in detail the history of the Russian theater up to the time of writing, also opera and ballet. Numerous illustrations and very good bibliography.

1903.* Slonim, Mark L. Russian Theater from the Empire to the Soviets. Cleveland, World Publishing Co., 1961. 345 p. Illus.

A book for the general reader, starting with the early beginnings of the Russian theater and ending with today's Soviet drama. The best documented chapters concern the Moscow Art Theater, Meyerhold, and the directors of the early twenties.

(2) Pre-1917

1904. Coleman, Arthur P. Humor in the Russian Comedy from Catherine to Gogol. New York, Columbia University Press, 1925. 94 p.

An analysis of Russian humor in the chief comedies of Fonvizin, Griboedov, and Gogol', with references to the plays of Catherine II and other minor playwrights.

1905. Evreinov, Nikolai N. (Nicolas Evreinoff). Histoire du théâtre russe. Introduction and French adaptation by G. Walter. Paris, Éditions du Chêne, 1947. 453 p.

A survey of the history of the Russian theater until the Revolution, by the famous Russian playwright and stage manager. The author states his views without attempting to give bibliographical references.

1906. Patouillet, Jules. Ostrovski et son théâtre de moeurs russes. Paris, Plon-Nourrit, 1912. 481 p.
See also entry no. 1513.

The author gives a detailed description of Ostrovskii's works and of their social and historical background.

1907. Patouillet, Jules. Le théâtre de moeurs russes des origines à Ostrovski, 1672-1850. Paris, Champion, 1912. 154 p. (Bibliothèque de l'Institut français de Saint-Petersbourg, t. 1)

A useful book on the early history of Russian drama with footnotes and a bibliography.

1908. Varneke, Boris V. History of the Russian Theatre, Seventeenth through Nineteenth Century. Original translation by B. Brasol. Revised and edited by Belle Martin. New York, Macmillan, 1951. 459 p. (American Council of Learned Societies. Russian Translation Project, Series 8)

A useful and detailed account of the period indicated in the title. The 1939 Russian edition from which the translation was made, *Istoriia russkogo teatra XVII-XIX vekov*, was a revised form of a classic textbook.

(3) Soviet period

1909. Bradshaw, Martha, *ed.* Soviet Theaters, 1917-1941; a Collection of Articles. New York, Research Program on the U.S.S.R., 1954. 371 p. (Studies on the U.S.S.R., no. 7)

Contents: Urlovski, Serge. Moscow Theaters 1917-1941.

Volkov, Boris. The Red Army Central Theater in Moscow.

Yershov, Peter. Training Actors for the Moldavian and Bulgarian Theaters, 1934-1938.

Ramensky, Gabriel. The Theater in Soviet Concentration Camps.

Hirniak, Yosip. Birth and Death of the Modern Ukrainian Theater.

A series of interesting articles by former Soviet theater people, with good bibliographical material.

1910. Jelagin, Juri. Taming of the Arts. Translated from the Russian by Nicholas Wreden. New York, Dutton, 1951. 333 p.
See also entry no. 1892.

The author, a musician who worked with the Soviet theaters, gives interesting information on the policy of the Party toward the theater, especially concerning Meyerhold.

1911. Liencourt, François de. Le théâtre, le pouvoir et le spectateur soviétiques. Cahiers du monde russe et soviétique, v. 2, no. 2, April–June 1961: 166-212; v. 2, no. 3, July–September 1961: 277-299.

The first article deals with the policy of the Soviet authorities in the field of the theater, the second with the attitude of the theatergoers towards the repertoire. Both contain many references to books and articles in the Soviet press, mainly from 1953 to 1960.

1912. Rühle, Jürgen.   Das gefesselte Theater; vom Revolutionstheater zum Sozialistischen Realismus. Cologne, Berlin, Kiepenheuer und Witsch, 1957. 456 p. Illus.
Bibliography: p. 443-448.

> The first part (pages 11-132) is on the Soviet theater before the Second World War (Gorky, Stanislavsky, Meyerhold, Tairov, Vakhtangev). The third part is on problems of the Communist theater, with interesting observations on the theater policy of the Soviet Union after the war.

1913. Sayler, Oliver M.   The Russian Theatre. 2d rev. and enl. ed. Introduction by Norman Hapgood. New York, Brentano, 1922. 346 p. Illus.

> A first edition was published under the title *Russian Theatre under the Revolution* (Boston, Little, Brown, 1920, 273 p., illus.)

1914. Zamiatin, Evgenii I. (Eugène Zamiatine).   Le théâtre russe contemporain. Mercure de France, November 15, 1932: 50-71.

> A brilliant survey of the problems of the Soviet theater at a time when "proletarian art" was on the wane and before the heyday of Stalin's interference.

c. Eyewitness accounts

1915. Bowers, Faubion.   Broadway, U.S.S.R.; Ballet, Theatre and Entertainment in Russia Today. New York, Thomas Nelson, 1959. 227 p. Illus.
See also entry no. 1890.

> For the general reader. A lively account of a visit to Russia in 1958 by an American theater critic, with interesting photographs of recent Soviet performances. Also available in a British edition.

1916. Carter, Huntly.   The New Spirit in the Russian Theatre, 1917-28. London, New York, Brentano, 1929. 348 p. Bibliography, illus.

> A study of new tendencies in the theater in Russia, with a good bibliographical list of plays produced each season and interesting illustrations. A rewritten version of his earlier book, *The New Theatre and Cinema of Soviet Russia* (London, Chapman and Dodd, 1924, 277 p.)

1917.* Houghton, Norris.   Moscow Rehearsals: the Golden Age of the Soviet Theatre. New York, Grove Press, 1962. 291 p. Illus.

> A description of theater staging, performing, training, and teaching in Moscow, mainly from the viewpoint of "a theatre craftsman," but also valuable in the fields of drama repertoire and aesthetics. First published in 1936 (New York, Harcourt, Brace, 291 p.)

1918. Houghton, Norris.   Return Engagement; a Postscript to "Moscow Rehearsals." New York, Holt, Rinehart and Winston; London, Putnam, 1962. 214 p. Illus.

Very interesting both for the general reader and the specialist (in spite of the lack of bibliography). Mr. Houghton, who spent three months in Moscow during the fall of 1960, gives a lively account of Soviet theater staging and teaching and of the life of the actors. He compares the state of the Moscow theater today with what he observed 25 years earlier and summed up in *Moscow Rehearsals* (*see* entry no. 1917).

1919. Van Gyseghem, André.   Theatre in Soviet Russia. London, Faber and Faber, 1943. 220 p. Illus.

The author, who worked at the Realistic Theater in Moscow during 1935, gives an account of the Soviet theaters and of the work of their directors, playwrights, and companies since the Revolution. The book includes a repertoire of the leading Moscow theaters in 1935-1936.

d. Special aspects of the theater

1920. Ayvasian, Kourken.   The Theater in Soviet Azerbaidzhan. New York, Research Program on the U.S.S.R., 1955. 29 p. (East European Fund. Mimeographed Series, no. 74)

A study by a former lecturer at the Baku State University who served as consultant to the Armenian, Azerbaijani, and Russian theaters in Baku.

1921. Kommissarzhevskii, Fedor F. (Theodore Komisarjevsky).   Myself and the Theatre. London, Heinemann, 1929, 203 p.; New York, Dutton, 1930, 205 p. Illus.

An account of the author's experiences in the Russian theater until he emigrated in 1919. Most of the book concerns pre-Revolutionary theater, with a vivid study of the work of Vera Kommissarzhevskaia, the author's sister.

1922.* Magarshack, David.   Chekhov, the Dramatist. London, Lehmann; New York, Auvergne, 1952. 301 p. Illus.

See also entry no. 1484.

An analysis of the development of Chekhov's art as a dramatist. Contains much interesting information on each of Chekhov's plays and many photographs of their staging by the Moscow Art Theater.

1923. Meierkhol'd (Meyerhold), Vsevolod E.   Le théâtre théâtral. Translated with an introduction by Nina Gourfinkel. Paris, Gallimard, 1963. 318 p. Illus.

A good selection of texts by Meyerhold and of reminiscences or articles about him and the plays he staged.

1924. Ripellino, Angelo M.   Majakovskij e il teatro d'avanguardio. Turin, Giulio Einaudi, 1959. 286 p.

A well-documented study on the Soviet modern theater of the twenties by a competent specialist.

1925. Seduro, Vladimir.   The Byelorussian Theater and Drama. Edited by Edgar H. Lehrman. Foreword by Ernest J. Simmons. New York, Research Program on the U.S.S.R., 1955. 517 p. (Studies on the U.S.S.R., no. 10)
Bibliography: p. 428-480.
    A study of the Byelorussian theater under Soviet rule by a former Soviet citizen who worked in that field.

1926.*Sosin, Gene.   The Children's Theater and Drama in Soviet Education. *In* Simmons, Ernest J., *ed.* Through the Glass of Soviet Literature. New York, Columbia University Press, 1953. p. 159-200.
    A good study of the children's theaters in the Soviet Union and of their repertoire from 1918 to 1950. Based on Soviet documentation and interviews with Russian displaced persons.

1927.*Stanislavskii, Konstantin S.   Stanislavsky on the Art of Stage. Translated with an introductory essay on Stanislavsky's system by David Magarshack. New York, Hill and Wang, 1961. 311 p. Illus.
    A useful selection of essays and articles by the founder of the Moscow Art Theater. Translation of *Besedy v studii Bol'shogo teatra v 1918-1922 gg.*
    For a biography of Stanislavsky, *see* David Magarshack's *Stanislavsky, a Life* (New York, Chanticleer Press, 1951, 414 p.)

1928. Tairov, Aleksandr Ia. (Alexander Tairoff).   Das entfesselte Theater; Aufzeichnungen eines Regisseurs. 2d ed. Potsdam, Gustav Kiepenheuer, 1927. 112 p. Illus.
    An important book in which the famous stage manager develops his theory of a synthetic theater, free from naturalism, but different from Meyerhold's conventional theater. Translation of *Zapiski rezhissera* (Moscow, 1921, 189 p.)

1929. W. Meierhold; Auslandstournée 1930.   Berlin, Energiadruck, 1930. 46 p. Illus.
    A program published on the occasion of Meyerhold's tour of Germany, with short descriptions of the main actors and illustrated notices on the staging of "The Revizor," "The Magnificent Cuckold," etc.

1930. Yershov, Peter.   Comedy in the Soviet Theater. Published for the Research Program on the U.S.S.R. New York, Praeger, 1956. 280 p.
    A useful survey of the different genres of comedy in the Soviet Union from 1917 to the death of Stalin. The author was before the war a teacher of literature at the theatrical school in Odessa.

e. Ballet

1931. Benois, Alexandre.   Reminiscences of the Russian Ballet. Translated by Mary Britnieva. London, Putnam, 1941. 414 p. Illus.

A central personality in the story of the Russian ballet and a pioneer art critic, the author covers the period from the mid-nineteenth century up to 1914. His book relates ballet to the contemporary art world and is a firsthand description of the beginnings of the Diaghilev Ballet, which owed much of its inspiration to Benois.

1932. Dictionary of Modern Ballet.   General editors: Francis Gaden and Robert Maillard. London, Methuen; New York, Tudor Publishing Co., 1959. 360 p. Illus.

Authoritative writers give a very full and good coverage of Russian works. A translation of the French *Dictionnaire du ballet moderne* (Paris, F. Hazan, 1957, 359 p.)

1933.* Grigoriev, Sergey L.   The Diaghilev Ballet, 1909-1929. Translated and edited by Vera Bowen. London, Constable, 1953. 289 p. Illus.

A detailed narrative by an important firsthand witness who was Diaghilev's managing director from the inception of his ballet company. It is the most authoritative and reliable account of the subject to date. Complete annotated list in the appendix.

1934.* Karsavina, Tamara.   Theatre Street; the Reminiscences of Tamara Karsavina. Rev. and enl. ed. London, Constable, 1948. 302 p. Illus.

Contains a valuable account of the dancer's education in the Imperial Ballet School in St. Petersburg at the beginning of the twentieth century. The author, one of the greatest Russian dancers, came from a dancer's family already established and familiar with the theater.

1935. Lifar, Serge.   A History of Russian Ballet from Its Origins to the Present Day. Translated by A. Haskell. London, Hutchinson; New York, Roy, 1954. 328 p. Illus.

As a prominent member of Diaghilev's company, Mr. Lifar gives pride of place to the description of this period, on an intimate and personal level. Little space and small consideration is given to the Soviet period. This, however, is the only history of Russian ballet in English to deal with the subject as a whole. Translation of *Histoire du ballet russe* (Paris, Nagel, 1950, 322 p.)

1936. Slonimskii, Iurii I. (Yury Slonimsky).   The Bolshoi Theatre Ballet; Notes. Translated from Russian. Moscow, Foreign Languages Publishing House, 1956. 121 p. Illus.

Primarily a picture book. The text is a popular and brief account of the history of the Bolshoi Ballet Company and School since its inception in 1773. The early period is rapidly covered and three-quarters of the book is devoted to the Soviet period.

2. Cinema
by John Minchinton

a. History of the cinema

1937. Arosev, Aleksandr Ia., *ed.*   Soviet Cinema. Moscow, VOKS, 1935. 312 p.

> A survey of all fields of contemporary Soviet cinema, with contributions from numerous film makers and observations by foreigners and others outside the industry. Includes a translation — and a copy of the original — of the decree signed by Lenin in 1919 nationalizing the film industry. Profusely illustrated, with some rare production photographs, and brief, illustrated biographies of 19 directors.

1938. Babitsky, Paul, *and* John Rimberg.   The Soviet Film Industry. New York, Praeger, 1955. 377 p. Index. (Studies of the Research Program on the U.S.S.R., no. 12)

> An annotated account of Soviet production methods, administration, and ideology by Babitsky, once a scenarist at Kiev and Moscow, and an analysis of social characteristics of heroes and villains by Rimberg. Appendixes give texts of Soviet decrees and directives pertaining to the film industry and biographical data on 32 directors.

1939. Bryher, Winifred.   Film Problems of Soviet Russia. Territet, Switzerland, Pool, 1929. 140 p., 42 plates, index.

> A personal estimation of contemporary Soviet cinema; chapters on Kuleshov, Eisenstein, Pudovkin, Room, and various aspects such as sociological film.

1940. Carter, Huntly.   The New Theatre and Cinema of Soviet Russia. London, Chapman and Dodd, 1924. 277 p., 2 plates. Illus.

> One chapter in this book is devoted to the cinema (pages 232-254), and discusses "Gos-Kino," "Prolet-Kino," "The Revolutionary Kino," and "Bourgeois or Commercial Kino." This important study was the first book on the cinema to be published in English and pre-dates the revolutionary period stimulated by Eisenstein, Pudovkin, etc.

1941. Dickinson, Thorold, *and* Catherine de la Roche.   Soviet Cinema. London, The Falcon Press, 1948. 136 p., 48 plates.

> A survey of Russian and Soviet film production. The first section, by Dickinson, is titled "The Silent Film in Russia," but is essentially about Soviet cinema until the transition to sound at the end of the twenties. The second section, by De la Roche, is titled "The Soviet Sound Film," and takes its subject to 1947. There are two appendixes: synopses of Eisenstein's *October* and *Old and New* (*The General Line*).

1942. Eisenstein, Sergei M.   Notes of a Film Director. Compiled and edited by R. Yurenev. Translated by X. Danko. London, Lawrence and Wishart, 1959. 208 p., 25 plates. Illus. (26 pages of drawings)

A collection of more "popular" essays, with a foreword by the author dated August 1946. Subjects include the author's films, color, stereoscopy, Gorky, Tisse, Prokofiev, and Chaplin. Some of these essays appear in other collections.

The only full script by Eisenstein presently available is *Ivan the Terrible; a Screenplay*, edited by Ivor Montagu and translated by Ivor Montagu and Herbert Marshall (New York, Simon and Schuster, 1962; London, Secker and Warburg, 1963, 320 p.), which is illustrated throughout with photographs from the film and drawings by Eisenstein. Includes a note, "My Drawings," which is an introduction by the author to a collection of sketches, and notes by V. Nikolskaya on Eisenstein's annotations to the scenario, as well as a select bibliography of writings on the film by Eisenstein and others. A translation of *Ivan Groznyi; kinostsenarii* (Moscow, Goskinoizdat, 1944, 188 p.)

1943. Idestam-Almquist, Bengt.   Rysk Film; en konstart blir till. Stockholm, Wahlström and Widstrand, 1962. 222 p. Illus., index.

One of the most recent histories of Russian and Soviet silent cinema, this book comments on various political and artistic influences, both national and foreign.

1944. Karmen, Roman.   Soviet Documentary. Translated by Catherine de la Roche. *In* Manvell, Roger, *ed.* Experiment in the Film. London, The Gray Walls Press, 1949. p. 171-188.

A chapter considering the experimental qualities of Soviet documentary films; in fact, a short history of Soviet documentary and its leading exponents, such as Dziga Vertov and Esvir Schub.

1945. Kerr, Alfred.   Russische Filmkunst. Berlin, Ernst Pollak, 1927. 28 p., 144 plates.

A collection of finely reproduced, and mostly rare, still photographs from Soviet silent films.

1946. Lavrenev (Lawrenjew), Boris A.   Der russische Revolutionsfilm. Zürich, Verlag Sanssouci, 1960. 36 p., 24 plates.

A small mosaic of fact and comment on Soviet cinema, culled from Lenin, Pudovkin, Dovzhenko, Stalin, Eisenstein, Khatchaturian, Gide, Mayakovsky, Lunacharsky, and Kerr, with an introductory essay by the author.

1947. Lebedev, Nikolai A.   Il cinema muto sovietico. Translated from the Russian by Vera Dridso. Introduction by Guido Aristarco. Turin, Giulio Einaudi, 1962. 624 p., 48 plates. Index.

An invaluable survey of Russian and Soviet silent cinema, with chapters on general history and the work of individual film makers. The filmography (184 pages), listing under year of production the major films between 1907 and 1931, is particularly useful, giving reelage, metrage, and basic credits. Translation of *Ocherk is-torii kino SSSR*. v. 1: *Nemoe kino* (Moscow, Goskinoizdat, 1947).

1948. Leyda, Jay.   Kino; a History of the Russian and Soviet Film. New York, Macmillan; London, Allen and Unwin, 1960. 493 p., 32 plates. Index.

A standard reference work covering the period 1896-1947, with a postscript for 1948-1958. With appendixes, including a select list of films from 1908-1958, and annotation of sources listed under chapter headings.

1949. London, Kurt.   Films. *In his* The Seven Soviet Arts. Translated by Eric S. Bensinger. London, Faber and Faber, 1937. p. 269-296.

A chapter in a book on the Soviet arts, based on the author's travels in the USSR. A brief but useful survey of, and observations on, the contemporary scene.

1950. Marchand, René, *and* Pierre Weinstein.   Le cinéma. Paris, Rieder, 1927. 174 p., 20 plates. (L'art dans la Russie nouvelle, 1)

More detailed than Moussinac's *Le cinéma soviétique* (*see* entry no. 1951), but equally important in its reflection of the intense foreign interest in Soviet silent cinema, this survey includes chapters on exhibition, newsreel, film school, etc. Includes an "index" of the most important films produced between October 1917 and the end of 1925, listed under production group headings; entries note number of reels, scenarist, and director, and give brief descriptions.

1951. Moussinac, Léon.   Le cinéma soviétique. Paris, Gallimard, 1928. 221 p., 16 plates. Ports.

A survey of contemporary Soviet cinema by a leading French critic, setting out its organization and theories and discussing its leading directors. This book is a significant reflection of the impact of Soviet silent cinema on Western intellectuals.

1952. Pudovkin, Vsevolod I., G. Alexandrov, *and* I. Piryev.   Soviet Film; Principal Stages of Development. Bombay, People's Publishing House, 1951. 58 p., 9 plates.

Three essays which reflect the rationale of the period. The first, by Pudovkin, is entitled *Principal Stages of Development*, and is a speech given at a meeting of the Cine-Technicians' Association, Calcutta, 1951. The other essays, *Soviet Films on Foreign Screens* by Alexandrov, and *Our People's Art* by Piryev, first appeared in *Tridtsat' let sovetskoi kinematografii* (Thirty Years of Soviet Cinematography; Moscow, Goskinoizdat, 1950, 411 p.)

1953. Roshal, Grigorii.   Soviet Film. Translated by Catherine de la Roche. *In* Manvell, Roger, *ed.* Experiment in the Film. London, The Gray Walls Press, 1949. p. 153-170.

A chapter considering the experimental qualities of Soviet feature films.

1954. The Soviet Cinematography.   Bombay, People's Publishing House, 1950. 244 p., 20 plates.

> The publishers state that the material in the book is drawn from Soviet sources. It is a quite comprehensive survey of Soviet film production — feature, documentary, scientific, and educational — and exhibition at the time of publication. In addition, there are articles on subjects such as the portrayal in Soviet cinema of Stalin, Soviet woman, the Soviet worker, and the Soviet collective farmer, which also reflect the period.

1955. Soviet Films, 1938-1939.   Moscow, State Publishing House for Cinema Literature, 1939. 124 p.

> Essentially a photographic survey of contemporary production, illustrating a number of now classic films and their makers. Ten pages are devoted to the All-Union State Cinema Institute film school and its students and professors.

b. Film theory

1956.* Eisenstein, Sergei M.   Film Form, and The Film Sense. Edited and translated by Jay Leyda. New York, Meridian Books, 1957. 279, 282 p.

> *Film Form*, subtitled *Essays in Film Theory*, was published separately in American (New York, Harcourt, Brace, 1949) and British (London, Dobson Books, 1951) editions. The compilation of this book of essays, dating from 1928 to 1944, was one of the author's last works. Particular emphasis is placed on analysis of the sound film medium. Sources are annotated.
>
> *The Film Sense* is Eisenstein's *book* of film theory, written by a film maker for film makers. The first edition was published in 1942, and also issued separately in American (New York, Harcourt, Brace, 1942) and British (London, Faber and Faber, 1943, 1948) editions. Appendixes include "The Work of Eisenstein" (1920-1947), sequences from *Strike*, and the projected *An American Tragedy, Sutter's Gold, Qué Viva México!*, and *Ferghana Canal*. Bibliography of Eisenstein's writings then available in English. Sources are annotated.

1957. Nizhnii, Vladimir B.   Lessons with Eisenstein. Edited and translated by Ivor Montagu and Jay Leyda. London, Allen and Unwin, 1962; New York, Hill and Wang, 1963. 182 p., 4 plates. Illus., index.

> The author, a former pupil and later lecturer at the State Cinema Institute film school in Moscow, dramatically recreates some of Eisenstein's lectures, making use of his recollections and the lecture stenograms preserved in the archives. The English edition is adapted from two Soviet editions: one for the use of the Institute (1957), and a larger, public edition (1958). Appended is Eisenstein's "Programme for Teaching the Theory and Practice of Film Direction," first published in Russia in 1936. Chapters are annotated.
>
> Translation of *Na urokakh rezhissury S. Eizenshteina*.

c. Personalities

1958. Cherkasov, Nikolai K.   Notes of a Soviet Actor. Moscow, Foreign Languages Publishing House, 1957. 228 p., 44 plates.

Cherkasov, an outstanding theater and film actor, gives *inter
alia* observations on working methods in Soviet film making and on
several important directors with whom he has worked: Eisenstein,
Alexandrov, Petrov, Zarkhi, Heifits, and Roshal. Translation of
Zapiski sovetskogo aktera (Moscow, Isskustvo, 1953, 389 p.)

1959. Seton, Marie.   Sergei M. Eisenstein, a Biography. London, Bodley Head; New York, Wyn, 1952. 533 p., 65 plates. Illus., index.

"This biography is a personal portrait of Eisenstein. It relates
the man to his work and attempts to answer the many questions
asked about him" (from the author's introduction). An immensely
detailed, intimate, and, in parts, controversial book. Appendixes
include an autobiographical note by Eisenstein, published in 1933;
notes on his lectures in London and Moscow; and his introduction
to the scenario of *Qué Viva México!* Later edition: New York,
Grove Press, 1960.

Other noteworthy biographies of Eisenstein:

Idestam-Almquist, Bengt. *Eisenstein, ett konstnärsode i Sovjet.*
Stockholm, KF:s Bokförlag, 1951. 269 p. Index. The first significant
biography to be published after Eisenstein's death. Chapters on his
work alternate with chapters considering the influence of Hegel,
Marx, Japanese theater, Freud, and socialist realism.

Amengual, Barthelemy.   "S. M. Eisenstein." *Premier plan* (Lyon),
no. 25, 1962. 111 p. Plates. A thorough and workmanlike, though
provocative, examination of Eisenstein's work and influence, and
of the influences which worked upon him. Published by Société
d'Études de Recherches et de Documentation Cinématographiques.

1960.* Pudovkin, Vsevolod I.   Film Technique, and Film Acting. Translated from the Russian by Ivor Montagu. London, Vision, 1958.
388 p. Filmography, illus.

First published separately in English in 1929 and 1935. *Film
Technique* is a collection of Pudovkin's writings and lectures, dating
from 1926, which sets out his theories on the subject, including
reference to his first sound film. *Film Acting* is a course of lectures
delivered at the State Institute of Cinematography film school in
Moscow. Together, in a memorial edition, these works argue Pudovkin's theories of film art.

An earlier edition: London, Vision, 1954, 204 and 153 p. Another edition: New York, Grove Press, 1960, 388 p.

index

Includes names of authors, compilers, editors, translators, and sponsoring organizations; titles of publications; and principal subject headings. Titles of books are italicized, and titles of articles and parts of books are in quotation marks. Numbers refer to entries, not pages. The lower case letter "a" following an entry number indicates that the title is to be found in the annotation to that entry.

A. P. Chekhov, 1497
A. S. Makarenko; Erzieher im Dienste der Revolution, 1750a
A. Skrjabin, 1880a
Abbe, James E., 78
Abell, M. A., 1714
Abercrombie, Lascelles, 1511
Aboriginal Siberia, 307
Abraham, Gerald, 1840, 1860, 1861, 1866, 1871, 1883
Abramovitch, Eva, 1602
Abriss der ostslawischen Kirchengeschichte, 473, 1628, 1629a
Abstracts, *see* Translations, abstracts, and indexes
Academy of International Law, 858
"The Academy of Social Sciences of the Communist Party of the Soviet Union," 1732
Accounting in Soviet Planning and Management, 1058
The Accused, 823
Acoustic Theory of Speech Production, 1268
Acta Baltica, 426a
Actes de la Conférence des chefs et des représentants des églises orthodoxes autocéphales, 1670
Actes magiques, rites et croyances en Russie subcarpathique, 1540
Acton, Harry B., 1608

The Acts and Miracles of our Dear and Holy Father, Sergius, 1400a
Adams, Arthur E., 386, 402, 869
Adler, Guido, 1855
Administration of Teaching in Social Sciences in the USSR — Syllabi for Three Required Courses, 1715
Adolphs, Lotte, 1750
Afinogenov, A. N., 1470
Africa and the Communist World, 907
Afterthoughts, a Sequel to "Return from the USSR," 161
Agabekov, Grigorii S., 808
Against Aggression, 890
The Agrarian Foes of Bolshevism, 638
Das Agrarsystem der Sowjetunion, 1092
The Agricultural Labor Force and Population of the USSR, 1926-41, 346
Agricultural Russia and the Wheat Problem, 1093
Agricultural Russia on the Eve of the Revolution, 1090
Agriculture, 1084-1094
"Aims and Methods of Soviet Terrorism," 815a
Ainalov, Dmitrii V., 1801
"The Ainu Problem," 319a
Air and rocket forces, 995-999
Akademiia nauk SSSR. Institut gosudarstva i prava, 568, 612

407